In the uncertain hour before the morning
Near the ending of interminable night
At the recurrent end of the unending
After the dark dove with the flickering tongue
Had passed below the horizon of his homing ...

We shall not cease from exploration
And the end of all our exploring
Will be to arrive where we started
And know the place for the first time.

T.S. Eliot
Four Quartets
Little Gidding

To Joyce, Winston, Maria, Newton and Mouton, whose tolerance, support and inspiration enabled us to proceed with this work.

Prescribing information and registration status for the different
products mentioned might differ between countries.
Please consult prescribing information for these products in your respective country.

Irvin M. Modlin, M.D., Ph.D., FRCS (Ed), FRCS (Eng), FCS (SA), FACS
Professor of Surgery
Dir., Gastric Surgical Pathobiology Research Group
Yale University School of Medicine
Department of Surgery
P.O. Box 208062
New Haven, Connecticut 06520-8062
USA

George Sachs, M.B., Ch.B., D.Sc.
Professor of Physiology and Medicine, UCLA
Wilshire Chair in Medicine, UCLA
Senior Medical Investigator, US Veterans Administration
Veterans Administration Medical Center
11301 Wilshire Blvd.
Los Angeles, California 90073
USA

Editorial Directors: Prof. Irvin M. Modlin, Prof. George Sachs
Art direction and design: Sudler&Hennessey, Milano
Editing and coordination: Cicero, Milano
Illustrations: Biodesign Communications, CA, George Sachs and Irvin M. Modlin
Typesetting and layout: Design in Progress, Milano
Separations and lithography: Fotolito Farini, Milano
Printed by Druckerei Konstanz GmbH, Konstanz

© 1998 Schnetztor-Verlag GmbH Konstanz

ISBN 3-87018-144-3

Irvin M. Modlin M.D., Ph. D., FRCS (Eng), FRCS (Ed), FCS (SA), FACS
Professor of Surgery
Dir., Gastric Surgical Pathobiology Research Group
Yale University School of Medicine
Department of Surgery

George Sachs M.B., Ch.B., D.Sc.
Professor of Physiology and Medicine, UCLA
Wilshire Chair in Medicine, UCLA
Senior Medical Investigator, US Veterans Administration
Veterans Administration Medical Center

ACID RELATED DISEASES

BIOLOGY AND TREATMENT

Schnetztor–Verlag GmbH D-Konstanz

Acknowledgements

We are both indebted to Byk Gulden and Ulrich Sorger, without whose support this work would never have seen the light of day. Considerable encouragement was provided by John Littlefield, who provided balance and perspective when needed. Florence Manger and Dr. Clive Cain as well as Michael Gimbol supported the endeavour despite constant other demands on their time. The generous support provided by both Byk Gulden and Wyeth Ayerst facilitated the consummation of this endeavor. A particular debt of gratitude is due to the precise perspectives in regard to the subject of proton pump inhibition provided by Dr. Alex Simon and to Dr. Klaus Melcher for the discussions on *Helicobacter pylori*. George Sachs would like to thank Prof. Heinz Radtke for his generous support for some of the research presented in this book.

Both Michele Buzzi and Bruno Stucchi deserve the highest commendation for applying their rigorous standards, and extraordinary attention to both textual detail and creative design. Tiziana Paglia was responsible for resolving a tangled melange of history biochemistry and clinical science into an orderly construct. Much of the illustrative work was undertaken by Steve Lustig, who labored mightily under the tribulations afflicted upon him by two individuals who believed that only they were capable of envisioning the appropriate visual quantification of scientific information.

Numerous institutions and individuals have generously provided us with access to material and allowed its usage. These include the Yale University School of Medicine Library, the Yale Journal of Biology and Medicine; the Huntarian Museum and Library of the Royal College of Surgeons of England; the Royal Society of Medicine; the Royal College of Physicians of England; and the Welcome Institute for the History of Medicine. A number of individuals including Herbert Helander, Nils Lambrecht, David Scott, Nicholas Wright, Robert Genta, Neal Seymour, Nat Soper, Laura Tang, Mark Kidd and Joe Pisegna contributed either personal material, scientific information or their valuable time. Innumerable colleagues, scientific collaborators and friends have generously provided us with the benefit of their years of experience in the discussion of information emanating from their research efforts; *Ars Gratia Artis*.

We are both entirely responsible for any errors, oversights, and misinterpretations of either the history or scientific data expressed in this text, although Dr. Sachs believes that any such possibility to be so remote as to hardly warrant consideration. At a personal level I wish to acknowledge William Prout, whose original work in Edinburgh engendered in me so monstrous a curiosity regarding the subject of acidophiles. His initially extraordinary observation that the atomic weights of all elements would be exact multiples of hydrogen stimulated more investigation than almost any other generalization that has ever been made in the field of chemistry; his subsequent identification of the presence of free hydrochloric acid in the stomach in 1823 remains one of the classics of physiology. The subsequent extraordinary contributions by Peter Mitchell on the subject of chemiosmotic proton circuits in biological membranes provided the intellectual impetus to not only resolve the membrane biology of the proton pump, but to develop therapeutic applications of considerable relevance to clinical medicine.

The credo of the application of the scientific method to the resolution of clinically relevant problems embraces the progress made in the resolution of acid peptic disease – a worldwide disease entity of major proportions. Thus the conceptual expansion of the initial early 19th century experiments of Prout have culminated in the elucidation of the Proton Pump not only as a biochemical entity, but as a therapeutic target of considerable relevance. Such events are best summarized in the words of Peter Mitchell: "*When seen retrospectively, the evolution of ideas and knowledge, like organic evolution, tends to take on a deceptively logical and inevitable appearance. But, as it actually happens, the quest for truth through the test of imaginary concepts against reality is bound to be an uncertain and hazardous adventure entailing disappointments as well as pleasant surprises.*" We hope that the contents of this book will afford the reader not only pleasure and information, but the opportunity to reflect on the application of science to the resolution of acid peptic disease.

Contents

The Production of Acid in the Stomach 1

The Discovery of Acid 3
   From antiquity to the 18th century 3
   The nature of digestive agents 5
   The discovery of hydrochloric acid 7

The Discovery of Ion Pumps 9
   Bioenergetics and chemi-osmosis 10
   P ATPases 11

Ion Motive ATPases 13
   Multimeric pumps 13
   Oligomeric pumps 15

The Gastric Acid Pump 18
   Reaction pathway of the H,K ATPase .18
   Kinetics of the H,K ATPase 19
   Membrane potential and the H,K ATPase 21
   2D structure of the gastric H,K ATPase 21
   3D structure of P type ATPases 30
   A structure function model of the H,K ATPase 32

   References 34

The Regulation of Gastric Acid Secretion 37

Progress Towards the Physiology of the Stomach 39
   Gastric fistulae: a unique opportunity .39
   "Le Milieu Intérieur" 41
   Defining gastric secretion 42
   Concepts of digestion 44
   Vagal physiology and gastric function 44
   Ulcer models and EGF 47
   The role of histamine 48
   The discovery of hormones 53

Gastric Acid Secretion 61
   Central regulation 62
   Neural regulation of acid secretion 64
   Paracrine regulation 68
   Endocrine regulation 68
   Control of gastric acidity 69
   Cellular regulation 70
   G cell 86
   D cells 90

The Parietal Cell 92

Development of the parietal cell 93

Morphology 93

Receptors 94

Intracellular signals 98

Activation of the H,K ATPase 103

Assembly and trafficking of the H,K ATPase 104

Synthesis and turnover of the H,K ATPase 105

Parietal cell homeostasis 106

References 110

Pharmacology of Acid Secretion 113

History of Therapeutic Approaches to Acid Related Diseases 115

The evolution of therapy 115

Diet 115

Surgery 116

Antacids-surfactants 116

Protective agents 117

Gastric receptors 117

The atropine family 117

Prostaglandins 117

The H2 receptor antagonists 118

Gastrin antagonists 119

Proton pump inhibitors (PPI's) 119

Acid pump antagonists 120

Inhibition of the Histamine 2 Receptor 121

Histamine antagonists 121

The Histamine 2 receptor 122

Pharmacology of H2 receptor antagonism 123

Inhibition of the Gastric Acid Pump 126

The ATPases as targets for drugs 126

The target amino acids in the gastric H,K ATPase 127

Digoxin target in the Na,K ATPase 127

Target region of the H,K ATPase 128

The substituted pyridyl methylsulfinyl benzimidazoles 128

K competitive inhibitors 138

In vivo inhibition by proton pump inhibitors 139

In vivo inhibition by acid pump antagonists 141

References 142

The Biology of Acid Related Disease 147

The Barriers of the Upper Gastro-Intestinal Tract 149

Introduction 149

Historical aspects 149

The esophageal epithelium 151

Esophageal handling of acid and pepsin 152

Rationale for treatment of GERD with PPI's 153

The gastric epithelium 154

Duodenal barrier 160

Intragastric pH 161

Hypochlorhydria and achlorhydria 161

Quantification of gastric acid secretion 162

Factors effecting gastric acid secretion 163

Low acid states 164

Clinical relevance of gastrin levels and PPI therapy 168

Pepsin 169

History of pepsinogen 169

Properties of pepsinogen 172

Pepsinogen 173

Regulation of secretion 174

Significance of pepsinogen 177

Intrinsic Factor 179

Historical issues 179

Cobalamin 179

Intrinsic factor 180

Cobalamin absorption 182

Regulation of Growth of Gastric Epithelium 184

Introduction 184

Cell growth in the stomach 184

Growth receptors in gastric mucosa 185

Epithelial restitution 187

Mucosal healing and trefoil peptides .187

Interference with gastric healing 192

References 194

Gastric and Duodenal Ulcer Disease 197

History 199

Introduction 199

Early management of peptic ulcer disease 201

Gastric surgery 204

Surgery of the vagus 208

Peptic Ulcer Disease 217

General 217

Pathogenesis 219

pH and disease 220

Diagnosis 221
Medical management 222
Complications of peptic ulcer disease 230
Hypergastrinemia 236

Gastrin Carcinoid 242
Histology 242
Development 243
Experimental model Mastomys natalensis 245
Clinical considerations 246

Dyspepsia 253
Non-ulcer dyspepsia 253
Dyspepsia and heartburn 255

Intravenous Use of Acid Suppressants 257
H2 receptor antagonists and proton pump inhibitors 257
Acute medical indications 257
for intravenous use of acid suppressants
Surgical indications for intravenous use of acid suppressants 259

References 260

Gastro-Esophageal Reflux Disease 263
the Problem of the Next Millennium

Evolution of the Disease 265
Etiology 268

Biology 272
The esophageal epithelium 272
Esophageal anatomy and physiology 273
Gastroesophageal junction 273
The lower esophageal sphincter 274

Physiology and Functional Studies 276
Esophageal function testing 276
Pathophysiology 281

Management 284
Lower esophageal sphincter function in GERD 284
Therapeutic targets 285
Gastric acidity 288
Gastroesophageal reflux disease and esophageal pH 289
Helicobacter pylori 291
Determination of GERD and management 292
Economics 300

Barrett's 302
Malignant transformation of the esophageal epithelium 302

Consensus 308
    Management consensus 308

References 312

Helicobacter Pylori 315

History 317
    Introduction 317
    Early bacteriology 317
    Early data on gastric bacteriology 318
    Twentieth century 321
    Ammonia and gastric urease 325
    Discovery of H. pylori *and its etiological role in peptic ulcer* 326

Biological Basis of Gastric Colonization by *Helicobacter* 328
    Introduction 328
    Bacterial bioenergetics 328
    Structure of H. pylori 330
    The bacterial genome 331
    Survival and growth characteristics of H. pylori 331
    Bioenergetic profile of H. pylori 332
    Cytoplasmic pH 332
    Membrane potential 333
    Acid adaptation by H. pylori *by activation of urease* 335
    Urease activation and growth 339
    Surface urease activity 340
    Urease is essential for H. pylori 341

Pathogenicity 342
    Adhesion 343
    Immunogenic effects 344

Infection and its Consequences 345
    Gastric acid secretion after infection 345
    H. pylori *and its gastric environment* 347
    The role of urease and NH_3 *in ulcer etiology* 350
    Mucosa Associated Lymphoid Tissue (MALT) lymphoma 351
    Diagnosis 355
    Relevance as a disease entity 356
    Epidemiology 357
    Treatment 358
    Economics and data analysis 359

References 364

The 21ˢᵗ Century 367

PREFACE

William Prout (1785-1850), in 1823 identified muriatic (hydrocloric) acid in the gastric juice of animals and humans.

John Sydney Edkins (1863-1910), described in 1905 a chemical agent in the antrum which stimulated gastric acid secretion. He proposed that it be known as gastrin.

The acid related diseases, duodenal and gastric ulcer and reflux esophagitis have plagued man and animals throughout recorded history. It is a tribute to the scientific advances of the twentieth century that whereas gastrectomy was introduced at the end of the nineteenth century and at the beginning of the twentieth, the statement "no acid, no ulcer" had just been enunciated. Now, at the end of the second millennium, we are able to control acid secretion at will and to cure duodenal and gastric ulcers of non-iatrogenic origin by treating a gastric infection.

Sustenance of life on this planet requires food, be it molecules or organisms. With the development of multicellular creatures came specialized organs for digestion and absorption. Acid was used very early as a means of preparing food for absorption and the development of tubes entering and leaving the acid-producing organ was also an early evolutionary happening.

The modern esophagus, stomach and duodenum have specialized epithelial cells, specialized musculature and specialized innervation, each to enable effective and trouble free digestion and passage of food for further digestion and absorption by the small intestine. Although we have come a long way in our understanding of the processes available to these organs in day to day existence, there is at least as much to learn in front of us as there was behind.

It is always surprising that it took civilized man so long to learn the fundamentals of mammalian biology exemplified by events such as William Harvey's description of the route of circulation or William Prout's proof that the stomach produces hydrochloric acid. Replacement of superstition with scientific method had to wait in the Western world until the passing of the Middle Ages with the fall of Constantinople in 1453.

The digestive tract before Leonardo and Vesalius remained simply an object of ill understood function as suggested by the terminology employed by Shakespeare and dramatists of his time. Thus in keeping with Greek and Roman usage, the stomach (*ventriculus*) was equated with the belly (*venter*) as noted in the parable about "the belly and the members" in Coriolanus or the episodes of Falstaff and Justice Greedy (Massinger). Indeed, the stomach was most often characterized as involved with gluttony or drinking by the Elizabethans whereas the Persian poets such as Saadi noted that an empty belly supported mental and spiritual activity. Later thoughts on the stomach suggested that the entire gastrointestinal tract was associated with pluck and courage ("guts").
The identification of gastric acidity as an internally generated event and its relationship to digestion was a phenomenon of the early nineteenth century. Studies of gastric function in those days are exemplified by the studies of Beaumont on a gastric fistula patient.

Ismar Boas (1858-1938), the founder of gastroenterology as a speciality and the editor of the first medical journal for digestive diseases.

Theodor Billroth (1829-1894), an accomplished musician, poet, scholar and medical teacher. His surgical skills enabled the first successful gastrectomy in 1881.

Sir Henry Hallett Dale (1875-1968), a pioneer in the isolation of histamine and the determination of its function.

Sir James Black (c. 1990), awarded the Nobel Prize in 1988 for developing the concept of H2 receptor antagonists and their therapeutic utility.

The central regulation of gastric digestive activity was initially delineated by I. Pavlov with his trained dogs. The discovery by W. Bayliss and E. Starling in 1902 of the hormone secretin and its stimulatory effect on pancreatic secretion established the basis for hormonal regulation of gastric secretion. Edkins was a man before his time in his discovery of gastrin.

The recognition in this first part of the century that the mucosal damage was caused by acid and that this acid could be decreased by luminal neutralization resulted in a wave of enthusiasm for antacid preparations, bland diets and milk infusion as therapeutic options. Surgery was probably the most effective means of treating recurrent peptic ulcer until the development of specific pharmacological agents. By 1881 Billroth, Péan and Rydiger had resected the stomach and Wölfler had successfully developed the procedure of gastroenterostomy. By the turn of this century, Moynihan of Leeds had transformed the treatment of peptic ulcer disease into a unique surgical discipline. With expanding understanding of the regulation of acid secretion, gastrectomy was successively replaced by vagotomy pioneered by Dragstedt, then selective vagotomy by Griffith and Harkins in 1957 and finally, in 1967, Holle and Hart introduced highly selective vagotomy.

One decade later, the introduction of drugs capable of blocking acid secretion by H2 receptor antagonism revolutionized the management of the disease process and almost obliterated surgery as a therapeutic option for peptic ulcer except in cases of emergency. GERD however may still be treated even today by laparoscopic fundoplication, given that pharmaceutical normalization of the lower esophageal sphincter has not been achieved.
The identification of the molecular basis of acid secretion – the proton pump – resulted in development of a new class of therapeutic agents – the proton pump inhibitors. By identifying the pump as a target, an almost complete inhibition of acid secretion with predictable therapeutic efficacy has been achieved.

Most recently, the description of *H. pylori* in the gastric mucosa and its correlation with ulcer disease has suddenly and unexpectedly led to the curing of peptic ulcer disease. We still await a simple therapeutic regimen for eradication of this organism but this will undoubtedly happen.
Even though acid related diseases are now being effectively treated, problems that derive from abnormalities of esophageal and gastric biology, such as cancer of these organs, are still virtually untreatable. The advances made and being made in genomic biology hold much promise in these areas in the XXI century. This book is focused on gastric biology. It takes a historical path to introduce present day discoveries and concepts and uses these concepts to explain modern day treatment of acid related disease.

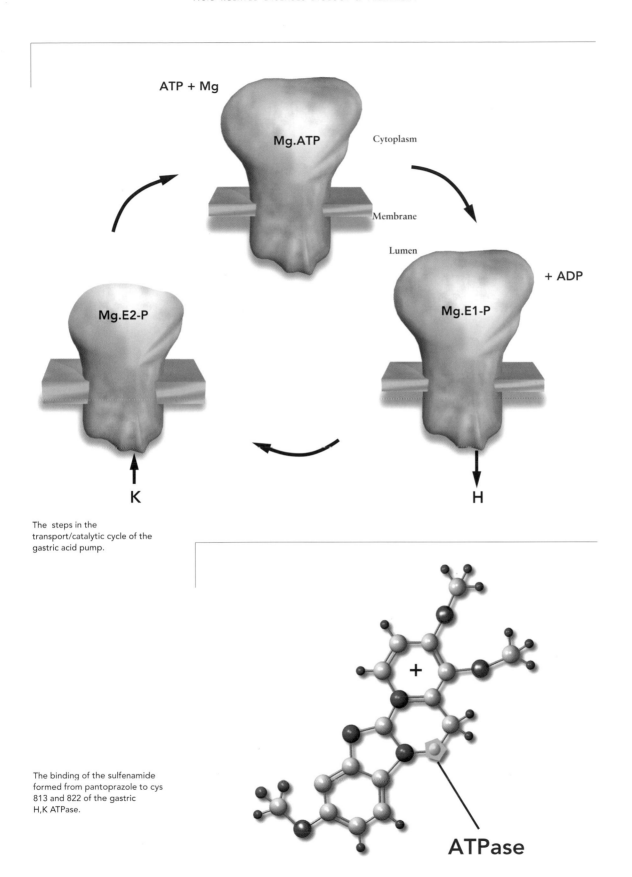

ATP + Mg

Mg.ATP

Cytoplasm

Membrane

Lumen

Mg.E2-P

Mg.E1-P

+ ADP

K

H

The steps in the
transport/catalytic cycle of the
gastric acid pump.

The binding of the sulfenamide
formed from pantoprazole to cys
813 and 822 of the gastric
H,K ATPase.

ATPase

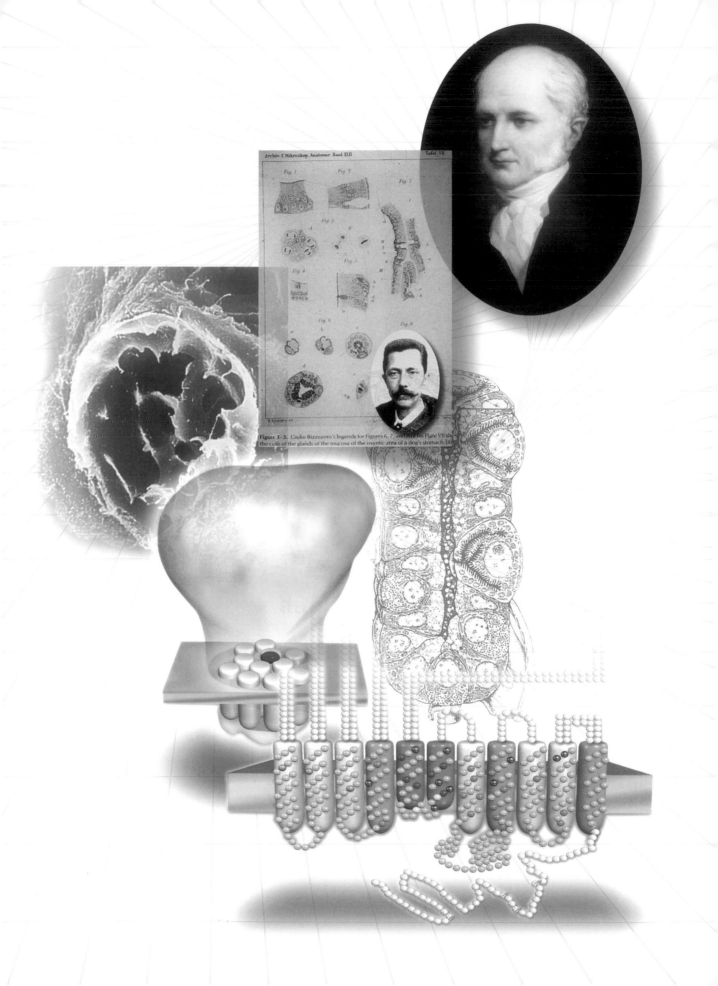

Archiv. f. Mikroskop. Anatomie. Band XLII   Tafel. VII

Figure 3-3. Giulio Bizzozero's legends for Figures 6, 7, and 8 of his Plate VII show the cells of the glands of the mucosa of the oxyntic area of a dog's stomach. [Fr...

THE PRODUCTION OF ACID IN THE STOMACH

CHAPTER 1
The Discovery of Acid

CHAPTER 2
The Discovery of Ion Pumps

CHAPTER 3
Ion Motive ATPases

CHAPTER 4
The Gastric Acid Pump

CHAPTER 1
THE DISCOVERY OF ACID

Hippocrates (460-370 B.C.) provided Greek medicine with its scientific spirit and ethical ideals. He practiced on the island of Kos where he developed a school of medicine which crystallized the loose knowledge of the Coan and Cinidian schools into systematic science. His philosophies permeated society and formed the basis of rational medical thought for centuries thereafter.
In early Greek pathology the efforts of the body to bring the humors from a raw, fermented status *(apepsia)* to a normal *(pepsis)* were associated with the idea of cookery or coction, a view of the digestive process which survived until the 17th century.

Diocles of Carystos (c. 350 B.C.) entertained some of the earliest ideas of therapeutic intervention in dyspepsia.

Paracelsus (1493-1541) underwent medical training in Ferrara (1515) and subsequently taught at Freiburg and Strasbourg (1525). He was appointed Professor of Medicine in Basel in 1527 and publicly burned the books of Galen and Avicenna. He rejected the old notion of the four elements – earth, air, fire and water. Instead, he proposed that the forces of energy that governed the universe were the archei and maintained that physiologic processes, diseases and drugs were chemical changes governed by the chief *archeus*.

In the earliest times, physicians believed that the various organs were the seat of separate spiritual agencies that, in a divine manner, controlled bodily function. The ancient Greeks proposed that digestion was a process of concoction or heating and, in this evolution, food was converted initially to chyle and then to the four humors (blood, phlegm, yellow and black bile) prior to use by the mortal body. Hippocrates had, in fact, called the process of digestion *pepsis* and proposed that it was not dissimilar to the preparation of food by cooking. Galenic physiology proposed that successive cooking processes occurred sequentially in the stomach, intestine and liver, until food was finally converted into blood.

The question of acid in the stomach

The early Greeks were not aware of acids in the modern sense of chemistry, but identified them only as bitter-sour liquids. Diocles of Carystos (circa 350 B.C.) specified sour eruptions, watery spitting, gas, heartburn and epigastric hunger pains radiating to the back (with occasional splashing noises and vomiting) as symptoms of illness originating in the stomach. 300 years later, Celsus (30 B.C.-25 A.D.) recognized that certain foods were acidic and recommended that *"if the stomach is infested with an ulcer…, light and gelatinous food must be used… and everything acrid and acid is to be avoided"*.

There appears to have been little further development in understanding the function of the stomach and the nature of digestive processes until the 16th century. Philippus Aureolus Theophrastus Bombastus von Hohenheim (Paracelsus) was born in Ensiedeln near Zürich in 1493. He was an alchemist-physician and a proponent of chemical pharmacology and therapeutics who had enormous influence on the medical thinking of his day.

Paracelsus believed there to be acid in the stomach and that it was necessary

for digestion. His belief that gastric acid was of extracorporeal origin was of course wrong. Nevertheless he recognized the importance of chemistry and its relation to disease, rejecting Galenism and the mysticism of humors and health.

Jean Baptiste van Helmont (1577-1644) founded the Iatrochemical School. This maintained that the principal *archeus*, Blas, was controlled by the sensitive and motive soul, *anima sensitiva motivaque*, in the "pit of the stomach" (solar plexus). From this site, all chemical physiologic processes were regulated.

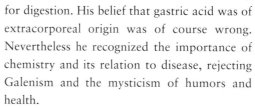

Jean Baptiste van Helmont (1577-1644), founder of the Iatrochemical School proposed that acid might be a mineral acid, such as nitric or hydrochloric acid. He produced *spiritus salis marini* - spirits of sea salt (hydrochloric acid) by distillation of salt and clay and noted that it could dissolve human kidney stones (*duelech*) in much the same manner as juice from the stomach of a bird.

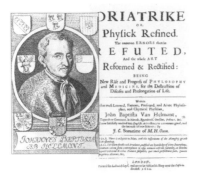

He believed that digestion began in the stomach by the intermittent fermentation of acid and that, thereafter, a number of other fermentation processes took place, including that of bile in the duodenum.

In further observations, he recognized that acid alone did not decompose food *in vitro*, and he postulated the existence of another agent typified as a ferment.

The Iatromathematical School

The chemical views propounded by Paracelsus, van Helmont and others were strongly opposed by the Iatromathematical School, which maintained that all physiologic happenings should be treated as fixed consequences of the laws of physics. This group included such individuals as Descartes, Borelli, Sanctorius, Pitcairn and Boerhaave.

Thus, Borelli (1608-1679) and his disciples favored the view that the stomach was but a mechanical mill, grinding up its contents into chyme. Mobius denied the existence of gastric acid, and Archibald Pitcairn interpreted all function in terms of mechanical activity.

The members of the Iatromathematical School cared little for the new science of chemistry, and their postulates faded into such sterile eccentricities as the proposal by Pitcairn to base the whole of medical practice on mechanical principles. Thus, in 1727, Pitcairn questioned the Iatrochemical group:

Iatromechanical representation of the *"hand that feeds"*. This representation of mechanical devices as the components of the human organism was applied in the most extreme fashion by the Neapolitan mathematician, Giovanni Alfonso Borelli (1608-1679). In his view, locomotion, respiration and digestion (the grinding and crushing action of the stomach), were purely mechanical processes.
This mechanical allegory was expanded to an extreme form by G. Baglivi who proposed that the body was a machine which could be regarded as being composed of numerous smaller machines. Thus the teeth were scissors, the chest a bellows, the stomach a flask, the viscera and glands - sieves and the heart and vessels a system of waterworks.

"...*Why upon the digestion of food upon the stomach, which is easily [as] digestible as the food, yet the stomach itself should not be dissolved*".

Almost 250 years were to pass for an explanation based on the "gastric barrier".

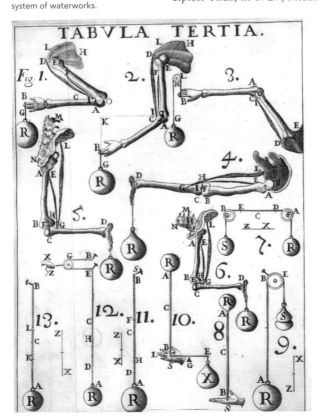

G.A. Borelli (1608-1679), a pupil of Galileo and a close associate of Malpighi, applied the mechanical view to the human organism in a extreme fashion. He wrote *De motu animalium* which probably reflects the influence of William Harvey (1578-1657).

The nature of digestive agents

Phases of discovery

1. Appreciation that gastric contents were acid

2. Acid - a product of secretion or fermentation

3. Nature of the acid

4. Quantification

5. Mechanism of secretion

6. Regulation of secretion

The phases of discovery which enabled comprehension of the mechanism and regulation of gastric acid secretion and facilitated the development of therapeutic intervention.

René Antoine Ferchault de Réaumur (1683-1757). Born at la Rochelle, the son of a prominent local judge, he was regarded as a prodigious intellect even as a child. By the age of 25 years, he was elected to the Académie des Sciences and was closely involved in the court of Louis XIV. He studied metallurgy and contributed notably to the process whereby wrought iron could be converted into steel. This not inconsequential contribution to a kingdom with major armies and territorial imperatives won him the grace and favor of the king and an annual pension of 12,000 francs for life. His acceptance of this reward was conditional upon its reversion to the Académie after his death.

Attempts to define the nature of digestive agents were aided first by the ingenuity of investigators in developing methods of obtaining gastric juice, and secondly by the development and recognition of indicator dyes.

These vegetable-derived substances changed color when exposed to appropriate acids or alkalis and allowed identification of the nature of the material being tested. In particular, controversy centered around the chemical nature of the acid in the stomach and the debate as to whether it was primarily secreted by the stomach or derived in some way from ingested food.

Methods of obtaining gastric secretion

Necropsy of animals

In 1692, Viridet experimented with dogs, cats, squirrels, hares, pigs and eagles. The animals were killed either after a meal or fasting, and the gastric contents were collected by opening the abdomen. Viridet noted that *solutio heliotropii* (tincture of heliotrope) could, by turning red, indicate the presence of acid. In a classic study, he killed a specially fattened pig and poured tincture of heliotrope down its throat.

The blue color was noted to be preserved even to the entrance of the stomach; in the stomach, however, an intense red solution was evident. Viridet noted that the stomach smelled of acid and that this resembled the odor of fermentation. He also noted that, in humans, acid could be recognized in the esophagus, but this was because of regurgitation of the contents of the stomach.

"*We experience it by an acid in the mouth*", he wrote. "*The condition was not a natural one*".

The use of sponges

In 1752, Réaumur, the French naturalist, noted that birds of prey vomited indigestible objects, such as feathers and bones. Therefore, he experimented with a tame buzzard by feeding it small, hollow metal tubes containing a variety of food. When the tubes were recovered, it was apparent that the food had dissolved without putrefaction, leaving a bitter yellow fluid. To study the nature of this fluid, Réaumur placed sponges in the small metal tubes and, on recovery, squeezed these to obtain the gastric juice. The latter was a sour fluid that turned blue [litmus] paper red. Réaumur attempted to study in vitro digestion by incubating the gastric juice with meat. The meat, however, failed to digest completely, although he noted that the gastric juice had prevented the onset of "corruption." He interpreted the failure of this study to indicate that either digestion required a high temperature or that the gastric juice required constant renewal. Alternatively, it was possible that, in the *in vitro* situation, the evaporation of a volatile acid had taken place. At this stage, the pet buzzard died and Réaumur ceased his studies with birds.

Self-induced-emesis

In 1760, Reuss found that, even with preliminary alkalization of the stomach, the ingestion of a meal of meat and vegetables resulted in secretion of acid.

The vomit had an acid taste and turned an infusion of "*campanules a feuilles*

In 1777 Edward Stevens presented his inaugural thesis *De Alimentorum Concoctione,* to the University of Edinburgh. He may have been the illegitimate half-brother of Alexander Hamilton (1755-1804) and had been born on the island of St. Croix in the Leeward Islands. After graduating from Kings College in New York (now Columbia University) in 1774 he pursued his further medical studies in Scotland from 1775. His thesis was dedicated to Alexander *tertius* Monro. During the time he studied at Edinburgh, he became the president of the medical student society. He subsequently returned to become a Professor of Medicine at Columbia in New York and thereafter Consul General in Santo Domingo. He failed to further pursue investigative studies of the stomach.

rondes" red. Gosse, in 1783, repeated the studies more elegantly. He had, as a child, developed the faculty of aerophagy and self-induced emesis, whereas Reuss required taking an emetic. By inducing emesis at specific times after eating, Gosse was able to demonstrate that digestion began within 30 minutes of eating and was concluded by approximately two hours. Gosse, however, was not able to find acid or alkaline gastric juice. He suggested that secretion occurred by a mechanical process whereby food stretched the internal lining of the stomach but was, however, able to report that some food was partially digestible, while other food was completely digestible.

An experiment of in vitro digestion

Edward Stevens was the first to perform an experiment of in vitro digestion successfully. He thus proved that the gastric juice itself contained the active principle necessary for the assimilation of food. Stevens obtained the services of a Hungarian Hussar, who was visiting Edinburgh and whose means of livelihood was to entertain the populace by swallowing stones and then regurgitating them. Using perforated silver spheres so constructed as to hold meats, vegetables, worms and leeches, Stevens observed that all were digested when passed through the rectum. He did not use a sponge and, thus, did not attempt to extract gastric juice and evaluate the presence of acid.

Lazzaro Spallanzani (1729-1799) discovered the digestive power of saliva and confirmed the solvent properties of gastric juice. He noted that ingestion of large quantities of strawberries and wine interfered with sleep by producing severe eructation from the stomach to the mouth, accompanied by a sharp, acidic taste. He interpreted this as acidity but regarded it as an abnormal phenomenon. In 1784 he collaborated with Scopoli, a professor of chemistry in Pavia. The latter reported that the gastric juice from the crows that Spallanzani was studying contained *"pure water, some soapy and gelatinous animal substances, sal ammoniam and earthy matter similar to that found in all animal liquids".* Spallanzani and Hunter disagreed regarding the presence of acid in the stomach and its function if any. They corresponded vigorously on this issue.

Digestion is a chemical process

In 1780, Lazzaro Spallanzani, who was the professor of Natural History in Pavia, published his extensive observations in this area. He had used the methods of Réaumur upon fish, frogs, snakes, cattle, horses, cats, dogs and himself. In 1783, he finally proved that digestion in vitro as well as in vivo was a chemical process, but he asserted that gastric juice was neutral.

The results of Spallanzani bear comment, because the studies were performed in great detail and with considerable care. He initially swallowed linen bags containing food and bread and collected them for examination after they had been passed through the rectum. Later, he substituted small metal tubes to avoid any possibility of trituration. In both instances, he could find no trace of remaining food. At this time, it was believed that three types of fermentation existed: vinous, acid and putrid. Because he could find no evidence of fermentation, he postulated that digestion was by an acid or a putrefactive principle. The latter he disregarded, because gastric juice prevented putrefaction and, according to the results of his experiments, there had been no evidence of putrefaction.

[447]

Received May 18, 1772.

XXXI. *On the Digestion of the Stomach after Death,* by John Hunter, F. R. S. and Surgeon to St. George's Hospital.

"The stomach of a boy (Master Stevens) with the whole cardiac extremity destroyed after death by the action of the gastric juice". (Specimen 592, Hunterian Museum).

Albert von Haller (1708-1777). He was a pupil of Boerhaave and the professor of anatomy, medicine and botany in Gottingen from 1736 to 1753. In his 17 years in Gottingen he wrote approximately 13,000 scientific papers and ultimately produced his masterpiece *Elementa Physiologicae Corporis Humanae* (1759-1766) which confirmed his reputation as the physiologist of his age. Von Haller recognized the use of bile in the digestion of fat, but declared that gastric juice was not acid, alkaline or a ferment, and believed that any acid found in the gastric juice was from the degeneration of food.

Spallanzani, however, was uncertain about his findings regarding the acidity of gastric juice. He corresponded and worked with a number of colleagues to resolve this question. In 1785, Spallanzani collaborated with Carminati, who was the professor of medicine at Pavia. Carminati was the first to detect the acidity of the contents of a meal. He said:

"It is clear that the human gastric juice is neutral as the physiologists, such as von Haller and Spallanzani, have taught; that this is true in crows, in dogs, and in cats which eat and digest with equal facility both animal and vegetable substances; and that in fact this humor consists of a water, a small amount of marine salt, and an animal substance... I had already recognized in 20 crows that the gastric juice was neutral when I obtained in July two crows who's gastric juice distinctly turned tincture of heliotrope red, produced immediate and complete curdling of milk, and, in every way, proved similar to that of carnivorous animals. The novelty of this led me to enquire into its cause and I found that the birds for many days past had been fed exclusively on meat... The same happened in dogs and cats fed entirely on meat for ten or more days as in the crows. Their gastric juice had all the properties of that of crows on a meat diet".

Spallanzani was advised to test birds on a meat-free diet; he also found marine acid in the juice squeezed from sponges fed to five ravens that were fed on vegetables for 15 days. Later, Brugnatelli, in 1786, and Werner, in 1800, found the contents of the stomachs of sheep, cats, fish and birds to be acid. Despite the relatively clear evidence produced by Spallanzani and his colleagues that there was acid in the stomach and that it was hydrochloric acid, considerable controversy persisted. Indeed, many of the investigators of this area reversed their thoughts a number of times during the study of the subject.

Thus, even among the minds of the most eminent physicians of the day, confusion reigned, not only as to the presence of acid, but as to the exact nature of the substance.

The discovery of hydrochloric acid

The final resolution to the question of the exact nature of acid produced by the stomach was provided in 1823 by William Prout, a brilliant physician with diverse interests outside of medicine.

Prout was productive in the fields of chemistry, meteorology, physiology and clinical medicine. In addition, he was one of the first scientists to apply chemical analysis to biological materials. He was, thus, able to demonstrate circadian rhythms in his own expired carbon dioxide and he proposed that the destruction of tissues produced excretory materials, such as uric acid, urea and carbonic acid. In 1827, he developed a classification of foods into subgroups: saccharinous (carbohydrates), oleaginous (fats) and albuminous (proteins).

Of particular interest, however, was Prout's investigation of the nature of acid

	No.1	No.2	No.3
gr.	gr.	gr.
Muriatic acid in union with a *fixed alkali*†	·72	·95	1.72
——————— with ammonia	1·36	·76	·40
——————— in a *free or unsaturated state*	1·59	2·22	0·72
Total	3·67	3·93	2·83

Prout's original calculations confirming the presence of muriatic acid in the stomach.

III. *On the nature of the acid and saline matters usually existing in the stomachs of animals.* By WILLIAM PROUT, M. D. F. R. S.

Read December 11, 1823.

THAT a free, or at least an unsaturated aci[d]... in the stomachs of animals, and is in some m[anner]... with the important process of digestion, se[ems]... the general opinion of physiologists till the [time of SPALLAN]ZANI. This illustrious philosopher concluded [from nume]rous experiments, that the gastric fluids, wh[en in their] natural state, are neither acid nor alkaline. [SPALLAN]ZANI, however, admitted that the contents of the [stomach are] very generally acid ; and this accords not only wi[th my own] observation, but with that, I believe, of almost every [indivi]dual who has made any experiments on the subject.

With respect to the nature of this acid, very various opinions have been entertained. Some of the older chemists seem to have considered it as an acid, *sui generis* ; by others it was supposed to be the phosphoric, the acetic, the lactic acid,† &c. No less various have been the opinions respecting

Frontispiece of Prout's original manuscript presented at the Royal Society (London, 1823). This piece of work irrefutably demonstrated that gastric acid in humans and other animals was hydrochloric acid. Tha gastric juice was provided by the surgeon Sir Astley Cooper of Guy's Hospital.

secretion. At an earlier stage of his studies, he supported phosphoric acid as the acid agent of the stomach. On December 11, 1823, at the Royal Society of London, Prout presented his landmark paper, *On the Nature of Acid and Saline Matters Usually Existing in the Stomach of Animals*.

This presentation was unique in two ways. First, Prout had specifically identified hydrochloric acid in the gastric juice of many species (man, dog, rabbit, horse, calf and hare), and second, he was able to quantify the free and total hydrochloric acid and chloride present. The acid was measured by neutralization with a potash solution of known strength and the chloride by titration with silver nitrate.

So advanced were his ideas that he proposed that chloride may be secreted from blood to lumen by electrical means and that, when gastric acid was secreted, the blood would become alkaline (now recognized as the postprandial alkaline tide). More than 100 years were to elapse before his subsequent proposal was confirmed.

The timing of some of the observations relating to the elucidation of elements of gastric physiology with reference to individuals involved in the studies.

History of gastric acid		
1622	van Helmont	Acid ferment - digestion
1752	Réaumur	Buzzards - solvent effect
1762	Reuss	Self emesis - Harebells - red
1777	Spallanzani	Chemical theory of digestion
	Scopolli	Crow - marine acid (luna cornea)
1803	Young	? Phosphoric acid
1823	Prout	Hydrochloric acid
1826	Tiedman	Hydrochloric acid
	Gmelin	Hydrochloric acid
1826	Leuret	Lactic acid
	Lassaigne	Lactic acid
1833	Beaumont	Gastric physiology + HCl
1835	Schwann	Pepsin

CHAPTER 2
THE DISCOVERY OF ION PUMPS

Cell membranes are made up of phospholipid bilayers such that the charged head groups face outward towards the water phase and the fatty acids are internal making a hydrophobic core. For charged or hydrophilic molecules to cross the bilayer, pathways must be established to allow these molecules to move across the membrane without encountering the hydrophobic barrier. Transport proteins allow such molecules to move across the part of the protein that is placed across the hydrophobic core of the membrane, the membrane domain of the protein without contacting the hydrocarbon phase of the cell membranes. The ion or hydrophilic substance must be enclosed by the membrane domain of the protein therefore there are several chains of amino acids that surround the transported species. Transport proteins therefore are often rather large proteins with several amphipathic sequences of about 21 amino acids that are threaded in and out through the membrane forming a polytopic integral membrane protein. Some of these membrane sequences are structural scaffolds and some are responsible for the movement of molecules across the membrane.

Some transporters allow molecules to diffuse down their concentration gradient resulting in passive transport; some couple diffusion in one direction to another molecule (usually an ion) diffusing in the opposite direction resulting in countertransport; some couple diffusion in one direction to another molecule moving downhill in the same direction to give cotransport. Some, like the gastric acid pump, couple energy yielding reactions such as the breakdown of ATP directly to transport to produce primary active transport.

Interaction of Alpha and Beta Subunits of H,K ATPase

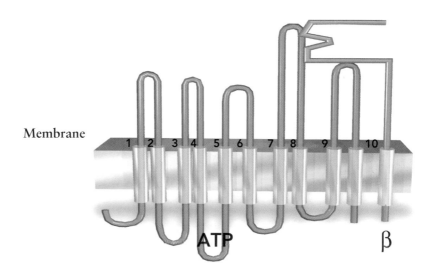

Membrane

A 2 dimensional model of the gastric acid pump showing the 10 transmembrane segments of the catalytic (alpha) subunit and the single transmembrane domain of the beta subunit. The illustration also shows the association in the 7-8 loop of the alpha subunit with two regions of the beta subunit.

Acid secretion by the stomach was long recognized as an active transport process since the concentration of hydrogen ions in the gastric juice is about 106 times higher than in the blood. In the 1920's, the colored cytochrome oxido-reductases were discovered by Keilin and Hartree. They postulated the presence of a cytochrome chain such that electrons were transferred from a substrate such as succinic acid step wise down the respiratory chain consisting of cytochrome b then c and then a_3 eventually reaching oxygen. This chain of oxido-reductases accounted for mitochondrial oxidation of substrates. Plant physiologists then suggested that oriented oxido-reductases across a membrane could separate H^+ and electrons.

This concept was then applied to acid secretion by the stomach and was known as the redox hypothesis of acid secretion. Inherent in the redox hypothesis is development of a current across the membrane providing an electrogenic mechanism for acid secretion across the membrane containing the pump. This electrogenic mechanism for acid secretion dominated thinking in the 1950s and early 1960s largely due to the contributions of electrophysiologists such as Warren Rehm first in Louisville and then in Birmingham.

A strong proponent of this idea was E.J. Conway in Dublin who had participated in a classical series of experiments just before WWII in Cambridge proving active transport of Na and K across cell membranes. Coincidentally, he was later responsible for developing an assay for urease and showed the presence of urease in the stomach. This urease was not recognized as the property of an infective organism, *H. pylori*, for another 40 years!

Bioenergetics and chemi-osmosis

A gastric ulcer contracted by a scientist working in transport prior to effective therapy resulted in one of the major conceptual revolutions in biology. ATP had been discovered by Engelhardt in Russia in 1939 as the major chemical energy store in biology. It was soon recognized that there were two major sources of ATP, glycolysis (substrate level phosphorylation described by Ephraim Racker in 1949) and oxidative phosphorylation in mitochondria. An enormous amount of effort was spent trying to specify the mitochondrial "substrate" that transferred high energy phosphate to ADP to account for oxidative phosphorylation. However, in 1961, Ephraim Racker isolated the mitochondrial ATPase and showed that it was composed of 2 sectors, a membrane sector, F_0 and a mitochondrial matrix sector, F_1. This ATPase is involved in bioenergetic conservation.

Peter Mitchell and his publication, which explained the synthesis of ATP by living organisms.

In 1957, Peter Mitchell, whose work had focused on transport in bacteria, acquired a severe gastric ulcer (due to the excessive consumption of haggis?) while Reader in Zoology at Edinburgh University. He postulated to his students that acid secretion by the stomach was due to the splitting of water by a vectorial ATPase, so that H^+ was extruded and OH^- was retained in the cell. In reading about the redox hypothesis of acid secretion, he realized that if redox pumps of mitochondria were oriented across the membrane, they would generate a gradient of H^+ or an electrical potential able to move H^+ inward across the mitochondrial membrane across a variety of proteins. With his vectorial ATPase running in reverse, an inward flow of H^+ would result in the synthesis of ATP.

This simple idea changed the concept of "substrate level" oxidative phospho-rylation into a H^+ electrochemical gradient mechanism for ATP synthesis by mitochondria, chloroplasts and aerobic bacteria using the F_1F_0 ATPase running as an ATP synthase driven by the inwardly directed (outward in the case of chloroplasts) electrochemical gradient of H^+.

This chemi-osmotic hypothesis was elegantly proven twelve years later by mixing a light driven proton pump, bacterial rhodopsin, with the mitochondr-ial F_1F_0 ATPase in liposome membranes. Shining light on these vesicles in the presence of ADP and inorganic phosphate resulted in the synthesis of ATP. ATP synthesis in this reconstituted system had to be due to the gradient of H^+ gener-ated by the rhodopsin oriented inside out in these vesicles moving across the inside-out ATPase. This experiment was also performed in Ephraim Racker's laboratory.

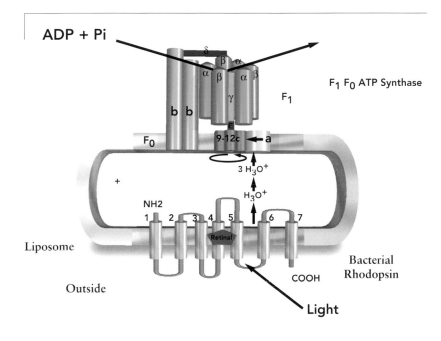

One of the classical experiments in biology ranking in significance with experiments discovering the genetic code. Two integral membrane proteins are re-consti-tuted together in liposomes. One is a light driven proton pump, bacterial rhodopsin (below), the other is the complex F_1F_0 ATPase, the ATP synthase (above).

It is interesting that Peter Mitchell also conceived of the correct model for bacterial flagellar motion as being driven by a rotating proton motor, a concept later applied to the mechanism of the F_1F_0 ATPase.

P ATPases

The sodium pump, the Na,K ATPase, was discovered by Jens Skou in 1957. It was recognized as the mechanism for maintaining Na and K gradients across cell membranes because of stimulation of ATP hydrolysis by the simultaneous presence of Na and K and by its inhibition with a cardiac glycoside, strophan-thidin, a specific inhibitor of formation of Na and K gradients. These cardiac glycosides have been in use since the 18th century for treatment of congestive heart failure, with "dropsy" as a presenting sign. Seminal work by Robin Post established the mechanism of the sodium pump as being via phosphorylation (energization)-dephosphorylation (de-energisation) of the enzyme and exchang-ing 3 Na^+ for 2 K^+. This pump is therefore electrogenic.

The positive inotropic effect of digitalis on the heart is now recognized to be somewhat indirect. When the Na pump in the heart is inhibited, cell Na increases and K decreases. The cell potential is maintained by the $[K]_i /[K]_0$ ratio and therefore starts to fall. The $3Na^+/Ca^{2+}$ exchanger, which moves Ca out of heart cells, slows both because of the fall of the inward Na gradient and the decrease in membrane potential. The increase in $[Ca]_i$ increases the force of contraction of the myocyte. In the normal heart, there is always risk of induction of arrhythmia due to the depolarization and inappropriate activation of voltage dependent membrane channels. In the failing heart there is danger of calcium overload. Nevertheless digoxin is still in wide use today to treat left sided heart failure as a specific inhibitor of the Na,K ATPase.

This discovery was followed by the description of the Ca ATPases, found in both intracellular membranes such as the sarcoplasmic reticulum (SERCA ATPases) and on the plasma membrane (PM Ca ATPases). These are also considered to be electrogenic exchanging Ca for H. The PM Ca ATPases are uniquely regulated by the binding of calmodulin to the C terminal region of this single subunit enzyme.

Work on acid secretion by isolated frog mucosae in the 1960's had started to point towards an ATP rather than a redox based mechanism. In the early 1970s, a K^+ stimulated ATPase was found in frog stomach. A K^+ dependent acid transport was found in isolated gastric vesicles. Then it was shown that the mechanism of this ATPase was similar to that of the Na pump but was an electroneutral ATP driven H^+ for K^+ exchange. Permeabilized gastric parietal cells in rabbit gastric glands were able to secrete acid when ATP was added to the bathing solution in the presence of high concentrations of K^+. The ATP dependence and involvement of the H,K ATPase in acid secretion by the parietal cell was finally established.

Recognition of the mechanism of acid secretion then led to the development of a new class of anti-ulcer drugs, the substituted pyridyl methyl-sulfinyl benzimidazoles. These are now the mainstay for treatment of most acid related diseases. Both the sodium pump and the acid pump are specific drug targets. A general model for this type of pump is shown in the figure.

A general model of the sodium and gastric acid pumps identifying their domains and their two subunits. The cytoplasmic domain binds ATP, becomes phosphorylated and releases ADP and Pi. The stalk transduces the conformational change due to phosphorylation/dephosphorylation to the membrane domain which contains the ion transport pathway, binding Na or H with high affinity (ion "in") in one conformational state, and with low affinity in a second conformational state (ion "out"). Conversely, K is bound with high affinity in the ion "out" conformation and with low affinity in the ion "in" conformation (see chapter 3).

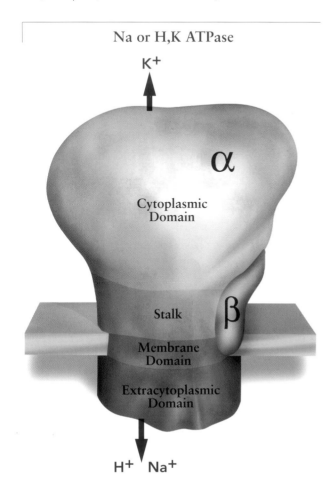

Na or H,K ATPase

CHAPTER 3
ION MOTIVE ATPASES

Various ATPases have been described that drive the transport of cations across biological membranes. The classes of ion motive ATPases thus far described are listed in the following table and can be classified into multi-subunit and single or two subunit types, the F_1F_0 and V ATPases representing the former and the P type the latter. The class of ATPases represented by the P glycoproteins or ABC transporters will not be discussed here.

They have cytoplasmic domains that bind ATP and that transduce the energy from ATP hydrolysis into conformational changes, enabling binding of the ion from the cytoplasmic face of the membrane and release of the ion from the extracytoplasmic face of the membrane. The cytoplasmic domain of the P type ATPases or the cytoplasmic or intra-mitochondrial subunits of the V or F_1F_0 ATPases contain the energy transduction sequences that transmit the ATP induced conformational changes via a stalk region to the membrane domain. Their sequence or that of one or more of their subunits contains several relatively hydrophobic amino acid clusters of about 21 amino acids that are membrane inserted. These membrane segments form the transmembrane domain of these pumps and contain the ion pathway across the membrane. These segments are arranged as a compact cluster of membrane inserted segments with varying degrees of tilt. Alterations in tilt are related to the ion transport mechanism across the pump membrane.

A classification of the various ion motive ATPases.

Classes of Ion Motive ATPases			
F_1F_0	V type	P type	
Mitochondria	Brain	**Small cation**	**Transition Metals**
Chloroplasts	Renal	Na, K, H	Cu, Co, Zn
Bacteria		Ca, Mg	Ni

Multimeric pumps

F_1F_0 type of ATPases/ATP synthases

These are found in the inner bacterial, chloroplast and mitochondrial membranes and catalyze the synthesis of ATP from ADP + Pi by dissipation of the electrochemical gradient of H^+ generated across these membranes by oriented redox pumps. Working in reverse, they are able to pump H^+.

These are multi-subunit pumps with a cytoplasmic domain consisting of a trimer of two subunits (α and β) as well as 3 other peptides (γ, δ, ε) connected to a 3 subunit membrane domain (a, b_2, c_{9-12}) as shown in the following figure. The γ subunit connects the F_0 to the center of the alpha-beta trimer. The remarkable rotary mechanism of this ATP synthase has been deduced by kinetic analysis, cross-linking studies and high resolution crystals of the alpha-beta trimer. It is thought that H_3O^+ traverses part of the membrane domain of the a subunit of F_0 driven by the electrochemical gradient for H^+. Three or four H^+ are then donated to the c subunit (assembled as a nonamer or dodecamer) initiating a single step ratchet like rotation of the c complex. This forces a rotation of the γ subunit altering the conformation successively of each dimer of the F_1 alpha-beta trimeric complex. After this step rotation, the H_3O^+ is dispersed into the inner mitochondrial space. The two b subunits are attached to the δ subunit that sits on top of the alpha-beta trimer. Hence the alpha-beta trimer is fixed. The c and the ε subunit are attached to the γ subunit. The c complex (c, γ, ε) is mobile. The γ subunit rotation results in a relative change in affinity for the binding of ADP and Pi relative to ATP by decreasing the binding of the latter allowing release of ATP from the alpha-beta monomer. Hence the driving force for ATP synthesis is cyclic changes in the relative affinities of the various substrates, ATP, ADP and Pi. Operating in reverse, the synthase acts as an electrogenic proton pump. This is the only cation pump that appears to function physiologically in a reversible manner.

F_1F_0 ATPase/synthase

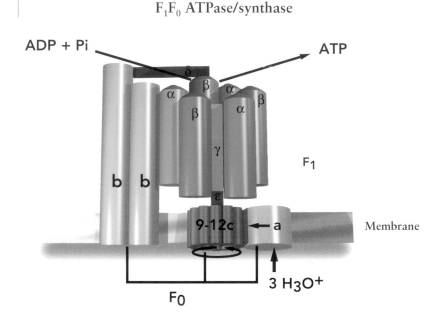

A model of the F_1F_0 ATPase showing that the F_0 subunit is composed of 3 gene products. The a subunit transmits H^+ or hydronium ion, H_3O^+, to the c subunit, which is usually represented as a nonamer or dodecamer. As a result of this transmission, the c complex rotates along with the γ, ε complex, the former distributing energy successively to each alpha-beta dimer of the trimeric F_1 sector. The 2 copies of the b subunit of the F_0 ATPase fix the relationship between the F_1 and F_0 subunits by binding to the δ subunit and to the mitochondrial membrane. This is the ATP synthase direction. Reversal of direction results in proton pumping.

V type ATPases

This rotational paradigm probably extends to the V type ATPases which are also multi-subunit pumps. These are electrogenic proton transport multi-subunit ATPases present in a variety of membranes and are responsible for acid secretion into intracellular compartments (lysosomes, Golgi, neurosecretory granules) or into the lumen of the renal collecting duct or across the ruffled border of the osteoclast. In contrast to the F_1F_0 ATPases, they are unable to synthesize ATP hence operate only in the proton pumping direction.

The minimal pH of the compartment that these pumps are able to generate is about 4.0. There are two major subtypes in mammals, the renal and the brain isoforms, but more subtypes may be discovered. The V ATPase contains seven to ten subunits organized into two distinct domains. The cytoplasmic domain contains five different subunits with molecular weights between 72 and 26 kDa, and the membrane domain contains two different subunits with molecular masses of about 20 and 16 kDa. The A cytoplasmic subunit (molecular mass of

72 kDa) in cooperation with the B cytoplasmic subunit (molecular mass of 57 kDa) contains the catalytic site and the membrane subunits a and c conduct protons across the membrane. Recently three variants of a 116 kDa subunit have been cloned suggesting a larger family of V type ATPases.

Oligomeric pumps

P type ATPases

The enzyme class to which the gastric H,K ATPase belongs is called the P type ATPase family. These enzymes are phosphorylated and dephosphorylated during their enzyme cycle. Enzymes of this family, with similar functions namely transport or counter transport of small cations or transition metals across membranes, often use similar amino acid sequences in regions that perform the same function, such as the binding of ATP or the sequence that is phosphorylated during the transport cycle. These are signature sequences. Often the arrangement of their transmembrane segments is retained to give a similar placement of relatively hydrophobic regions, producing recognizable transmembrane footprints. There are three subfamilies within the family of P type ATPases. The Kdp ATPase of *E. coli* is composed of three subunits, one of which is phosphorylated. Another type transports small cations such as Na, K, H, Ca and Mg, the third type transports transition metals such as Cu, Cd, Zn or Co. The latter group has 8 transmembrane segments as compared to the 10 transmembrane segments in the former. They do however share the phosphorylation and ATP binding signature sequences which has enabled their identification by library screening. They have a similar mechanism of transport. They bind the extruded ion at high affinity along with Mg ATP. Phosphorylation of the enzyme by ATP follows. A conformational change results, with the outwardly transported ion moving into the membrane domain and then appearing at the outside face bound with low affinity. The outwardly transported ion is then released. In the countertransport pumps there is binding of the inwardly transported cation with high affinity and this cation then moves into the cell across the membrane domain as the pump de-phosphorylates and the inward bound cation is released from a lower affinity state upon rebinding of ATP as illustrated for the H,K ATPase.

Catalytic Subunit of Gastric Acid Pump

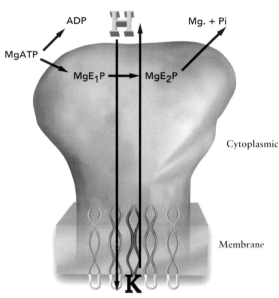

A model of the transport catalyzed by the gastric acid pump, the H,K ATPase. As a function of the binding of ATP and Mg, the enzyme is phosphorylated and binds H$^+$ from the cytoplasmic surface in the E$_1$-P state. This converts spontaneously to the E$_2$-P state, releasing protons to the outside and binding potassium also from the outside. As E$_2$-P breaks down, K$^+$ is transported inward, resulting in H$^+$ for K$^+$ exchange.

Transition metal P type ATPases

There are many transition metals that are toxic to bacteria, thus various P type ATPases have been generated to aid in export of toxic cations such as Cd^{2+}. Also some transition metals are essential to life and pumps have appeared that import Cu^{2+}. At high concentrations, Cu^{2+} is also toxic and Cu^{2+} export pumps are present in bacteria and even in man, such as the product of the Menckes gene.

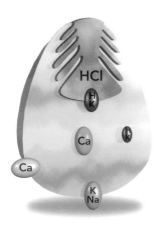

The pumps of the parietal cell. The gastric H,K ATPase is either in cytoplasmic membranes or in the canalicular membrane (red). There are two Ca ATPases, the plasma membrane Ca ATPase and the endoplasmic reticulum ATPase, responsible for Ca homeostasis, and finally the Na,K ATPase maintaining cationic homeostasis and supplying K for acid secretion.

Mutation in this gene produces Wilson's disease with retinal discoloration and dysfunction. These enzymes have 8 transmembrane segments. 3 of these transition metal pumps are present in *H. pylori* genome and they have all been cloned. One appears to be able to function as a copper export ATPase; the function of the others is not known. The phosphorylation consensus sequence and ATP binding domains are present in the cytoplasmic loop between the 5th and 6th transmembrane domains. These pumps in *H. pylori* might become targets of drugs designed to eradicate this organism by monotherapy.

Alkali cation ATPases

There are several mammalian members of this family, the fungal H ATPases, the Na,K ATPases, the H,K ATPases, the SERCA (sarcoplasmic and endoplasmic reticulum), Ca transport ATPases and the PM (plasma membrane) Ca ATPase. Characteristically the mammalian enzymes all perform countertransport, exchange of a cellular cation with an extracellular cation. The fungal enzymes transport only H$^+$ outward. The parietal cell possesses a variety of these small alkali cation ATPases as shown, each subserving a different function.

SERCA ATPases

These are thought to be Ca/H exchange pumps that are found in sarcoplasmic and endoplasmic reticulum and are responsible in part for calcium homeostasis in cell cytoplasm by sequestration of Ca in the intracellular stores of the endoplasmic reticulum and for removal of Ca into the sarcoplasmic reticulum after a contraction. As with the other P type ATPases there are various isoforms of the SR ATPase, differing in their expression in fast and slow twitch skeletal muscle (SERCA 1 and SERCA 2). The endoplasmic reticulum Ca ATPase has the usual 10 transmembrane segments, plus an additional transmembrane segment at the C terminal end. This latter segment is probably used as a retention signal keeping the pump in the endoplasmic reticulum. It does not seem that they require association with any other protein for stable expression in intracellular membranes. Their homology with the Na,K or H,K ATPases is about 25%, although their topographical profile is quite similar.

Plasma membrane Ca ATPases

There are four genes encoding isoforms of the PM Ca ATPase and alternative splicing generates other isoforms of this single subunit plasma membrane transport ATPase. These Ca transport ATPases are regulated by calmodulin and a variety of kinases and afford cells the ability to regulate cytoplasmic calcium by extrusion of the cation across the plasma membrane. They have again about 20% homology with the Na,K and H,K ATPase alpha subunits.

Na,K ATPases

There are 3 isoforms of these ATPases that all extrude Na and reabsorb K, with a 3 for 2 stoichiometry. This unequal stoichiometry generates a potential across the cell membrane, inside negative. They consist of two tightly associated subunits, the alpha subunit composed of about 1000 amino acids and the beta subunit composed of about 300 amino acids that is N glycosylated at 3 or more sites in the extra-cytoplasmic region. All of these sodium pumps generate a transmembrane current and membrane potential. Since many cell processes depend on inward electrogenic co-transport of Na^+ with nutrients such as amino acids or glucose, the generation of a transmembrane potential, inside negative, is of physiological importance not only for maintenance of a transmembrane potential due to the outward K^+ gradient, but also for nutrition of the cell and regulation of $[Ca]_i$ by calcium channels or Ca/H exchange in the case of the heart.

There are three isoforms of the alpha subunit, alpha 1, alpha 2 and alpha 3. The alpha subunit contains ten transmembrane segments. The N terminal and C terminal segments are cytoplasmic and the loop between the 4th and 5th segments contains about 400 amino acids with the phosphorylation consensus site and ATP binding domain present in this region. The alpha subunit is therefore the catalytic domain of the sodium pump similar to the gastric H,K ATPase.

There are also three isoforms of the beta subunit, beta 1, beta 2 and beta 3. Presumably each isoform is expressed along with its alpha partner and assembled in the endoplasmic reticulum as an alpha-beta heterodimer. The beta subunit has a single transmembrane segment and is a type II membrane protein with the N terminal cytoplasmic and the C terminal sequence extracytoplasmic. There are several N linked glycosylation consensus sequences (NXT or NXS) and 3 disulfide bonds in the extracytoplasmic domain. The function of the beta subunit of this ATPase is not very clear. Alteration of its structure by disulfide reduction inhibits ATPase activity. In its absence, the alpha subunit is unstable and does not reach the plasma membrane so it is required for structural stability. Why the alpha subunit is unstable in the absence of the beta subunit is not obvious, since the plasma membrane Ca ATPase has similar topology but does not require a beta subunit for stable plasma membrane expression.

The three isoforms of the Na pump are differentially expressed in different tissues, with therefore specialized functions. The alpha1-beta1 isoform is the most common form and is regarded as the housekeeper for maintenance of Na^+ gradients. The other isoforms vary in their affinity for ions and cardiac glycosides. The alpha2-beta2 isoform may be the target for cardiac glycosides in the heart.

The H,K ATPases

There are two isoforms of these that are known. Both are alpha-beta heterodimers. The H,K alpha1-beta1 is the gastric H,K ATPase. The alpha subunit contains the phosphorylation consensus sequence and ATP binding domain. The beta subunit has 7 N-linked glycosylation consensus sequences that are glycosylated and again is also required for stability of the gastric pump. The alpha subunit is about 75% homologous to the alpha subunit of Na pump and the beta subunit is about 40% homologous to the beta2 subunit of the Na pump. The H,K alpha2-beta2 ATPase has a similar homology to the gastric and Na pumps and although called a H,K ATPase, probably transports K but not H. The H,K alpha2-beta2 is found in colon and kidney. This enzyme may be misnamed, since, although it has been shown that it is upregulated in the kidney with K depletion, there is no evidence that proton transport is catalyzed by this pump. The beta subunit utilized by this isoform appears to be unique and has recently been cloned from the colon.

CHAPTER 4
THE GASTRIC ACID PUMP

The gastric H,K ATPase exchanges H for K at equal stoichiometry. Even though the outward and inward parts of the transport cycle are electrogenic, pump transport is electroneutral and does not generate a transmembrane potential.

The general transport process that the alpha subunit of this pump catalyzes is shown in the following figure.

Parietal Cell Cytoplasm
Mechanism of Acid Secretion

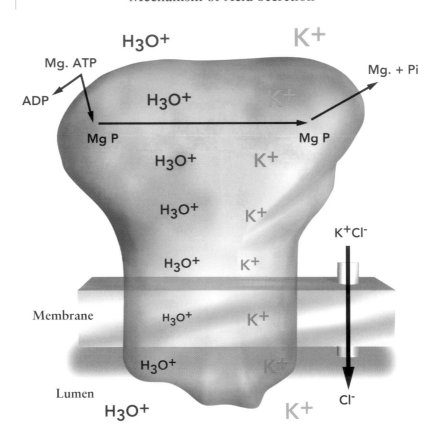

This diagram illustrates the general mechanism of acid secretion catalyzed by the H,K ATPase. It secretes acid only when present in the canalicular membrane. There is activation of a K$^+$/Cl$^-$ pathway that enables efflux of KCl and H$_2$0 from the cytoplasm of the parietal cell. The K now present in the lumen of the secretory canaliculus of the parietal cell is transported inward in exchange for H$_3$O$^+$ by the cycle of phosphorylation/ dephosphorylation on the catalytic subunit of the H,K ATPase leaving HCl in the canalicular lumen.

Reaction pathway of the H,K ATPase

The Na,K ATPase exchanges intracellular sodium ions for extracellular potassium ions, the gastric ATPase H$_3$O$^+$ for extracellular potassium and the sarcoplasmic or endoplasmic reticular Ca pump cytoplasmic Ca for H$^+$ in the sarcoplasmic reticulum. In the outward reaction transporting either Na or H$^+$ or Ca^{2+}, the catalytic subunit is phosphorylated by ATP and in the inward reaction the phospho-enzyme is dephosphorylated by K$^+$ or H$^+$ (in the case of the sarcoplasmic reticulum Ca ATPase). In order to achieve uphill transport at a significant rate, there has to be a decrease in binding site affinity on the side of the membrane from which the ion is transported and re-orientation of this site towards the side to which the ion is transported.

A conceptual model for this, that has experimental foundation, is that the transported ion enters the membrane domain from one side and binds to a site with relatively high affinity upon phosphorylation, to provide the transporting conformation. Then the membrane domain closes to occlude the ion to provide the occluded conformation. Another conformational change then opens the membrane domain to allow the ion being removed from the cytoplasm to escape from the other side of the membrane from a lower affinity state of the ion binding site. Binding of the counter-transported ion induces the converse changes in affinity and conformation, the ion binding with relatively high affinity to the outside face, occluding and releasing from the low affinity state to the cytoplasm.

The experiment on the Na pump that established occlusion took advantage of the fact that this enzyme forms a phosphorylated intermediate. In the presence of 100 mM Na and ATP phospho-enzyme is formed at a constant rate. Various other cations can substitute for K^+ in the dephosphorylation reaction, such as Rb^+, Cs^+ or NH_4^+. These are K^+ surrogates. If the concentration of these cations is set to give equal rates of dephosphorylation but the enzyme turns over at a different rate, the rate limiting step must be subsequent to dephosphorylation and before rephosphorylation. It was postulated that this step was the unbinding of the occluded cation present in the membrane domain of the dephosphorylated enzyme.

This was then shown to be correct by demonstrating the binding of $^{86}Rb^+$ to the pump in the presence of ouabain and showing that the addition of ATP resulted in de-occlusion. Similar binding of cation has also been demonstrated for the sarcoplasmic reticulum Ca ATPase and the gastric H,K ATPase establishing the mechanistic similarity of these enzymes.

The scheme of their reaction is shown in the figure in the following page. This shows that the enzyme exists in three major conformations, with ion binding sites facing inward the "in" conformation, ion binding sites facing outward the "out" conformation and ion sites occluded the "occ" conformation. The transition between these conformations is driven by ATP binding, trans-phosphorylation and dephosphorylation.

Kinetics of the H,K ATPase

Kinetic studies on the H,K ATPase have defined the reaction steps shown in the following figure. Understanding of the overall catalytic cycle of this ion pump has facilitated a mechanistic description of the process of acid secretion by the stomach. From this derives our understanding of stimulation of acid secretion and the processes inhibited by the proton pump inhibitors.

The key structural change in the ion binding site apart from sidedness is the size of the ion it can accomodate. In the "in" conformation, the smaller hydronium ion, H_3O^+, is accomodated. In the "out" conformation the smaller ion is weakly bound as compared to the larger partially hydrated K^+. Experimental evidence for the reaction cycle described above has been obtained using rapid kinetic analysis of the rate of formation and destruction of phospho-enzyme generated from ^{32}P-ATP at different pH and potassium concentrations.

Parietal Cell Cytoplasm
Mechanism of Acid Secretion

This illustrates the reaction cycle for the gastric H,K ATPase. Similar cycles have been postulated for the other mammalian small cation P type ATPases.

With binding of hydronium and Mg ATP to the enzyme in the ion site "in" conformer E_1, the phosphorylated form MgE_1-$P.H_3O^+$ is generated. This spontaneously moves into the occluded conformer and thence to the ion site "out" form, E_2.

The hydronium ion binding has reduced affinity when the enzyme is in the E_2 state. K is bound with relatively high affinity to this phosphorylated E_2 form.

The enzyme is dephosphorylated as the occluded E_2. K^+ conformer is generated which then decays spontaneously to the $E_1.K^+$ form and K^+ release is stimulated by the rebinding of Mg ATP.

The rate of formation of the phospho-enzyme and the K^+-dependent rate of breakdown are sufficiently fast to allow the phospho-enzyme to be an intermediate in the overall ATPase reaction. The initial step is the reversible binding of ATP to the enzyme in the absence of added K^+ ion, followed by a Mg^{2+} (and proton) dependent transfer of the terminal phosphate of ATP to the catalytic subunit (E_1-$P•H^+$). The Mg^{2+} remains occluded until dephosphorylation. Increasing hydrogen ion concentration on the ATP-binding face of the vesicles accelerated phosphorylation, whereas increasing potassium ion concentration inhibited phosphorylation. Increasing hydrogen ion concentration reduced K^+ inhibition of the phosphorylation rate. Decreasing hydrogen ion concentration accelerated dephosphorylation in the absence of K^+ and K^+ on the luminal surface accelerated dephosphorylation. Increasing K^+ concentrations at constant ATP decreased the rate of phosphorylation and increasing ATP concentrations at constant K^+ concentration accelerated ATPase activity and increased the steady state phospho-enzyme level. Therefore, inhibition by the alkali cations is due to cation stabilization of a dephospho E_1 form at a cytosolically accessible cation-binding site. Occlusion was demonstrated directly by showing ^{86}Rb binding to the enzyme at low temperature that was released by the addition of ATP.

The addition of K^+ to the enzyme-bound acyl-phosphate results in a two-step dephosphorylation. The faster initial step is dependent on the concentration of K^+. The second phase of EP breakdown is accelerated in the presence of K^+ but, at K^+ concentration exceeding 500 uM, the rate becomes independent of K^+ concentration. This shows that two forms of EP exist. The first form, E_1P, is K^+ insensitive and converts spontaneously to E_2P, the K^+ sensitive form. ATP binding to the H,K ATPase occurs in both the E_1 and the E_2 state, but with a lower affinity in E_2 state. As for the Na pump, various cations such as Rb^+, Cs^+, NH_4^+ and Tl^+ can act as K^+ substitutes or surrogates. As will be seen later, design of K^+ competitive inhibitors of the H,K ATPase take advantage of the surrogate properties of NH_4^+.

Membrane potential and the H,K ATPase

The gastric H,K ATPase is electro-neutral, in contrast to the Na,K ATPase, since the same number of H ions is exported compared to the number of K ions imported. However, each half of the reaction cycle generates an equal but opposite membrane potential as the ion traverses the membrane domain.

The H^+ for K^+ stoichiometry of the H,K ATPase was reported to be one or two per ATP hydrolyzed. The H^+/ATP ratio was independent of external KCl and ATP concentration. If care is taken to measure initial rates in tight vesicles, the ratio is 1ATP:2H:2K. Since at full pH gradient the stoichiometry must fall to 1ATP:1H:1K, this pump displays a variable stoichiometry.

2D structure of the gastric H,K ATPase

Eventually a complete description of the mechanism of the H,K ATPase will include a detailed 3D structure of the enzyme with the changes seen upon binding ATP, phosphorylation and ion binding and transport. However, the 3D structure is elusive, so methods have been developed to understand enzyme structure as it is related to transport at lower resolution, but nevertheless useful in structure-function analysis. 2D crystals of the Neurospora proton pump and of the sarcoplasmic reticulum Ca pump show that there are 10 membrane inserted segments in these single subunit pumps with a stalk connecting these to a large cytoplasmic domain and a small extracytoplasmic domain.

The catalytic subunit is similar in general structure to that of other mammalian small cation P type ATPases. Composed of 1034 or 1035 amino acids, it has a large cytoplasmic domain, a connecting stalk or energy transduction domain, a transmembrane domain and a small extracytoplasmic domain. The beta subunit has a N terminal cytoplasmic sequence of about 60 amino acids, a transmembrane domain of about 30 amino acids and a C terminal domain containing about 200 amino acids with 7 N-linked glycosylation sites. Although the function of the pumps that have been sequenced is usually known, it is not possible by inspection of the sequence to predict which ion is transported by which sequence. In the 1980s, when cDNA and hence amino acid sequences became available, there was hope that linear sequence would provide mechanistic clues as to protein function. Amino acid sequencing has enabled enormous advances in the fields of phenotyping cells, analyzing families of proteins, defining interacting proteins and signature sequences but has not fully enabled functional or mechanistic analysis. Biochemical, molecular and structural features are necessary in addition to be able to call the function of a protein sequence.

The catalytic subunit amino acid sequence

The primary sequences of the a subunits deduced from cDNA have been reported for several species such as pig rat, rabbit and human. The hog gastric H,K ATPase α subunit sequence deduced from its cDNA consists of 1034 amino acids and has a MWt of 114,285. The sequence based on the known N-terminal amino acid sequence is one less than the cDNA derived sequence and begins with glycine. The degree of conservation among the a subunits is extremely high (over 97% identity). The human gastric H,K ATPase gene has 22 exons and encodes a protein of 1035 residues including the initiator methionine residue (MWt=114,047). These H,K ATPase a subunits show high homology (~60 % identity) with the Na,K ATPase catalytic a subunit. The distal colon K ATPase α subunit has also been sequenced and shares 75% homology with both the H,K and Na,K ATPases.

The amino acid sequence derived from the cDNA for the hog enzyme is shown in the figure on page 30, compared to the sequence for the alpha1 subunit of the Na,K ATPase from the same species. This shows that the sequences are 75% homologous. Regions of identity are the phosphorylation consensus sequence and the ATP binding domain and many of the cytoplasmic regions have high homology as compared to the transmembrane regions. It is remarkable that, even with the detailed knowledge of the amino acid sequence, the function of the protein must be measured experimentally and cannot be predicted.

The reactive sites of the catalytic subunit

The gastric α subunit has conserved sequences along with the other P type ATPases for the ATP binding site, the phosphorylation site, the pyridoxal 5'-phosphate binding site and the fluorescein isothiocyanate binding site. These sites are in the ATP binding domain in the large cytoplasmic loop between membrane spanning segments 4 and 5.

In the case of the hog gastric H,K ATPase, pyridoxal 5'-phosphate bound at lys^{497} of the α subunit in the absence but not the presence of ATP, suggesting that lys^{497} is present in the ATP binding site or in its vicinity. The phosphorylation site was observed to be at asp^{386}. Fluorescein isothiocyanate (FITC) covalently labels the Na,K and the gastric H,K ATPases in the absence of ATP. The binding site of FITC was at lys^{518}. However, several additional lysines such as those at positions 497 and 783, were shown to react with FITC during the inactivation of the Na,K ATPase and to be protected from reaction with FITC when ATP was present in the incubation. Based on these data, similar lysines of the H,K ATPase could be near or in the ATP binding site which is therefore formed by several non-adjacent stretches of the cytoplasmic amino acid sequence.

The membrane domain of the catalytic subunit

The hydropathy plot of the H,K ATPase is shown in the following figure and is similar in the P type ATPases that transport the small cations, H, Na, K, Ca and Mg. This plot defines the potential transmembrane or membrane inserted segments and the methods that have been used to define these segments of the acid pump are also illustrated in this figure.

The methods used to determine the number and position of trans-membrane segments shaded and numbered in the hydropathy plot. The lower set of arrows denotes sites determined to be tryptic cleavage sites by amino acid sequencing of the digested, separated fragments, the darker, shorter arrows indicate those cysteines derivatized by one or other of the PPI's. These methods showed the first 8 segments. TM9 and 10 were detected by *in vitro* transcription/translation.

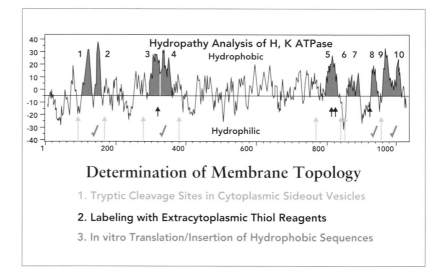

The membrane domain of the enzyme contains the ion transport pathways. There must be a hydrophilic pathway in the membrane domain that the ions can traverse as the cytoplasmic domain changes conformation as a function of phosphorylation and dephosphorylation.

It can be seen that there are 5 regions of hydrophobicity suggesting the possible presence of ten membrane segments. These have been established experimentally by determining the residual membrane domains after removal of the cytoplasmic sectors by tryptic digestion of cytoplasmic side out vesicles, by in vitro translation scanning and by sites of labeling with extracytoplasmic inhibitors of the enzyme such as the proton pump inhibitors or the acid pump antagonists.

Transport region of the membrane domain

To establish the regions of the membrane domain transporting H_3O^+ outward and K^+ inward, a variety of sites have been mutated in this pump but more extensively in the sarcoplasmic reticulum Ca pump and the Na,K ATPase. Measurements have been made of enzyme activity, cation binding (occlusion) and transport in these mutants. In the membrane domain, mutations of especially carboxylic and hydrophilic amino acids in the region of M 4,5,6 and 8 affect ion binding and transport. It is therefore considered that these trans-membrane sequences enclose the ion pathway across the membrane.

The carboxylic and other hydrophilic side chains of the amino acids provide binding sites for the cations. When the amino acid sequences of the Na,K, H,K and sarcoplasmic reticulum Ca ATPases are compared, there is conservation of several of these carboxylic or hydrophilic amino acids in certain transmembrane segments.

The carboxylic acids in TM4, 5, 6 and 8 are conserved as well as the motifs surrounding these amino acids suggesting a commonality of functions such as ion binding. The amino acid sequences thought to be within the membrane domain and on the outside face of the pump are illustrated in the figure on page 24.

H,K and NaK alpha alignment & Phosphorylation site & Membrane Sequences & Alpha-Beta Interaction

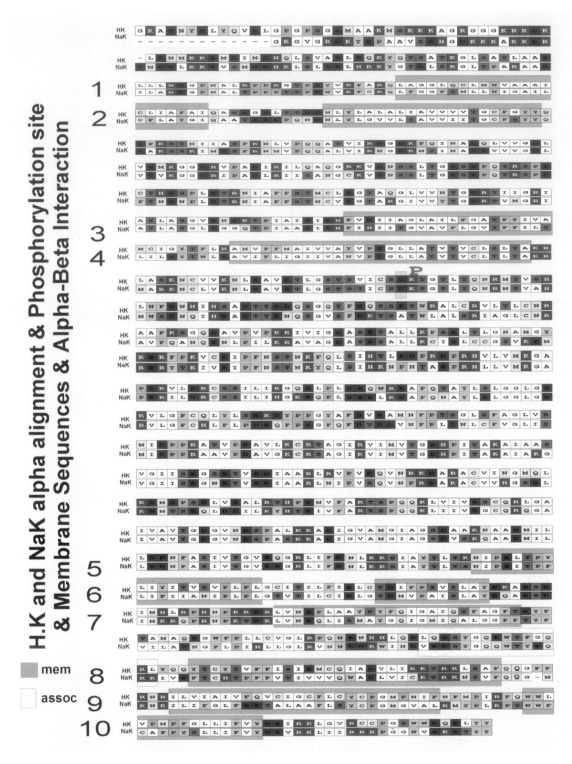

A comparison of the amino acid sequences of the gastric H,K ATPase and the alpha1 isoform of the Na,K ATPase. Highlighted are the aspartyl group that is phosphorylated, the regions of high identity in the ATP binding domain along with the lysine that reacts with FITC, the lysine that reacts with pyridoxal phosphate and the region of the large extracytoplasmic loop between TM7 and TM8 that interacts with the beta subunit. It can be seen that there is overall similarity but also large differences.

H,K & Na,K beta alignment showing membrane segment disulfide cysteines & glycos'n & alpha assoc'n regions

The alignment of beta sequences of proton and sodium pump showing conservation of the extracytoplasmic cysteines and the single transmembrane domain.

Schematic diagram of the membrane segments of the alpha and beta subunits of the gastric H,K ATPase illustrating the amino acids in the membrane domain of each subunit.

Highlighted are the transport segments in TM4, M5,M6 and TM8, the hydrophilic and charged amino acids in the membrane domain.

The M5 and M6 segments are presented here as membrane inserted but not transmembrane and this structure may reflect mobility of this segment of the pump, which is crucial for ion transport.

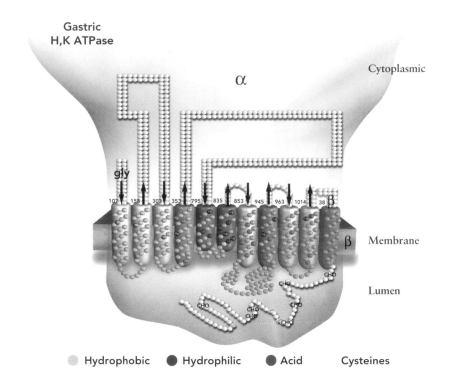

Structural changes and transport

The relationship between the cytoplasmic domain and the transmembrane domain changes as a function of the transport conformation. This statement is based on the findings with fluorescent probes that change their quantum yield as a function of the hydrophobicity of their environment. When the H,K ATPase is in the ion binding site "in" conformation, the distance between the inner boundary of the cytoplasmic domain and the inner boundary of the membrane domain is small. With the ion binding site in the "out" conformation, this distance increases as measured by the K dependent quenching of fluorescence of FITC bound to lys [516] of the amino acid sequence. Conversely the distance between the outer edge of the membrane domain and the inner surface is larger with the ion site "in" conformation and smaller with the ion site "out" conformation. The enzyme therefore contracts its cytoplasmic domain as the ion is transported outward and associated with this is a degree of extrusion of the membrane domain. As the counter-transported ion binds to the outside surface the outside binding site moves towards the cytoplasm.

There is evidence that the more mobile part of the membrane domain is the 5th and 6th transmembrane segment pair and its connecting loop. For example, tryptic cleavage of cytoplasmic side out vesicles cut the cytoplasmic chain prior to M5 at different places depending on either the length of digestion or the absence or presence of K[+]. The first N terminal cutting site is at position 776 and then at 784 and finally at 792 after longer digestion or in the presence of K, whereas the C terminal cutting site does not change. After digestion in the presence of K when the residual membrane domain is treated at pH 10, of the 5 transmembrane segment pairs, first the M5/M6 are removed and then

TM7/loop/TM8. *In vitro* translation of TM5/TM6 also shows that these relatively hydrophilic membrane segments probably do not interact fully with the hydrophobic lipid phase but more with the protein surface of other transmembrane segments. TM7 also does not act as a membrane insertion sequence in *in vitro* translation. The cluster of M5/M6 and TM7/TM8 may provide the flexibility within the membrane domain that is necessary for transport competence.

The β subunit

The primary sequences of the β subunits have been reported for rabbit, hog, rat, mouse and human enzymes and contain about 290 amino acids. The hydropathy profile of the β subunit appears less ambiguous than the α subunit. There is one membrane spanning region predicted by the hydropathy analysis, which is located at the region between positions 38 and 63 near the N-terminus. Tryptic digestion of the intact gastric H,K ATPase produces only one small cleavage of the N terminal segment of the β subunit on SDS gels. Wheat germ agglutinin (WGA) binding of the β subunit is retained. These data indicate that most of the β subunit is extra-cytoplasmic and glycosylated. When lyophilized hog vesicles are cleaved by trypsin followed by reduction, a small, non-glycosylated peptide fragment is seen on SDS gels with the N terminal sequence AQPHYS which represents C-terminal region beginning at position 236 in the pig sequence. This small fragment is not found either after trypsinolysis of intact vesicles nor in the absence of reducing agents. A disulfide bridge must therefore connect this cleaved fragment to the β subunit containing the carbohydrates. The C-terminal end of the disulfide is at position 262. This leaves little room for an additional membrane spanning α helix. Hence the β subunit has only one membrane spanning segment. The comparison between the beta sequence of the rat gastric H,K ATPase and the beta 2 sequence of the rat Na,K ATPase is shown in the figure on page 25.

Region of association of the α and β subunits

The β subunit of both the Na,K and H,K ATPase is necessary for targeting the complex from the endoplasmic reticulum to the plasma membrane. It also stabilizes a functional form of both the gastric H,K and Na,K ATPases.

The region of association of the two subunits helps explain this functional association.

In the case of the Na,K ATPase, the last 161 amino acids of the α subunit are essential for effective association with the β subunit. Further, the last 4 or 5 C terminal hydrophobic amino acids of the Na+ pump β subunit are essential for interaction with the α subunit whereas the last few hydrophilic amino acids are not. Expression of sodium pump α subunit along with the β subunit of either sodium or proton pump in Xenopus oocytes has shown that the β subunit of the gastric proton pump can act as a surrogate for the β subunit of the sodium pump for membrane targeting and ^{86}Rb+ uptake. This implies homology in the associative domains of the β subunits of the two pumps. The H,K ATPase α subunit requires its β subunit for efficient cell-surface expression. Expression of chimers of the alpha subunits of the Na,K and Ca ATPases showed that the C-terminal half of the α subunit assembled with the β subunit.

In order to specify the region of the α subunit associated with the β subunit, the tryptic digest was solubilized using non-ionic detergents such as NP-40 or $C_{12}E_8$. These detergents allow the holoenzyme to retain ATPase activity. The tryptic fragments were then adsorbed to a WGA affinity column. Following elution of the peptides not associated with the β subunit binding to the WGA column, elution of the β subunit with 0.1 N acetic acid eluted almost quantitatively the M7/loop/M8 sector of the α subunit. These data show that this region of the α subunit is tightly associated with the β subunit such that non-ionic detergents are unable to dissociate it from the β subunit.

If tryptic digestion is carried out in the presence of K^+, a fragment of 19-21 kDa is produced which contains the M7 segment and continues to the C terminal region of the enzyme. When this digest is solubilized and passed over the WGA column as outlined above, in addition to the 19-21 kDa fragment, a fragment representing the M5/loop/M6 sector is now also retained by the β subunit. Hence provided there is no hydrolysis between M8 and M9, an additional interaction is present between the α and β subunits or between the M5, 6 and M9, 10 regions of the α subunit. The antibody mAb 146-14 also recognizes the region of the α subunit at the extra-cytoplasmic face of the M7 segment as well as a region of the β subunit enclosed by the second disulfide bridge. These data suggest interaction between these regions such that this assembled region is presented during generation of antibody, a finding consistent with the association found by WGA column chromatography.

If the tryptic digestion is carried out on solubilized enzyme, WGA fractionation of FMI-labeled tryptic fragments of detergent-solubilized H,K ATPase showed that a fragment Leu 854 to Arg 922 of the alpha subunit was bound to the beta subunit.

Analysis by the yeast two-hybrid system showed that only the region containing a part of TM7, the loop and part of TM8 was capable of giving positive interaction signals with the ectodomain of the beta subunit, in agreement with the data from digestion. This method uses a split nuclear transcription factor (β-galactosidase) to determine interactions between different proteins or different fragments. The binding domain and activating domain of the factor are expressed on separate vectors and different fragments of the cDNA sequence are ligated onto one or other vector. When there is interaction, the β-galactosidase gene is expressed and can be assayed either by the development of a blue color or by a direct luminescent enzyme assay.

The sequence in the extracytoplasmic loop close to TM8, namely Arg 897 to Thr 928, was identified as being the site of interaction using this method. Hence we deduced that there is strong interaction within the sequence Arg 897 to Arg 922 in the alpha subunit and the extracytoplasmic domain of the beta subunit. Using yeast two hybrid analysis, two different sequences in the beta subunit, Gln 64 to Val 126 and Ala 156 to Arg 188, were identified as containing association domains in the extracytoplasmic sequence of the beta subunit. The results using the assay vectors are shown in the table on the following page.

This table demonstrates the results found for yeast two hybrid analysis of regions of the alpha and beta sequences that show interaction as illustrated in the sequence alignments. The amino acids are numbered in terms of their linear sequence where these inserts gave a signal (blue or luminescence) indicating transcription of beta-galactosidase. The alpha sequences #869-933 and 898-928 (near TM8) in the binding vector interact with the activating domain vector containing the whole extracytoplasmic domain of beta, or two regions between #64-130 and #156-188 showing that two regions of beta associate with this region of alpha.

Vectors	Lift assay	Luminescence	
pASα869-933 [TM7-8]	pACβ64-291	blue after 3 h	179.35 ± 27.38
pASα898-928 [TM7-8]	pACβ64-291	blue after 3 h	159.95 ± 20.08
pASα869-933 [TM7-8]	pACβ64-130	blue after 3 h	50.10 ± 1.93
pASα898-928 [TM7-8]	pACβ64-130	blue after 3 h	66.04 ± 10.69
pASα869-933 [TM7-8]	pACβ156-188	blue after 3 h	54.42 ± 3.65
pASα898-928 [TM7-8]	pACβ156-188	blue after 3 h	59.95 ± 10.04

M5/M6 domain, a transport region of the catalytic subunit

As discussed above, this region of the membrane domain of the enzyme is thought to be intimately involved with the ion transport pathway. This is based on studies of site directed mutagenesis, extractability from digested membranes and conformationally sensitive cutting sites at the N terminal end of this region. It is also the binding site for the covalent inhibitors, the substituted pyridyl methylsulfinyl benzimidazoles, the proton pump inhibitor (PPI) class of drug. These are thiophilic reagents and therefore can bind covalently to the –SH group of cysteines. There are two cysteines in the M5/M6 domain, at position 813 and 822. When radioactive omeprazole is used to define which of these cysteines is involved, it is found at position 813.

However, removal of this cysteine by mutagenesis does not appear to prevent inhibition by PPI's such as omeprazole or rabeprazole. Mutation of cys 822 to gly prevented omeprazole and rabeprazole inhibition. These data might suggest that binding at cys 822 is required for labeling of cys 813. In the absence of cys 813, there could be reaction at cys 822 or perhaps binding is sufficient for inhibition. What these data imply is that both cys 813 and cys 822 are accessible by a bulky cation, either the protonated form of omeprazole or its sulfenamide derivative.

Transmembrane insertion of the native M5 sequence does not occur. However, in the Na,K ATPase mutation of either proline in the sequence PLPL or the asparagine preceding this sequence permitted full membrane insertion. This would suggest that the actual structure of M5-M6 is not a hairpin with two transmembrane segments as illustrated by the standard model, but that M5 and M6 are membrane inserted but not transmembrane as suggested by the model shown in the following figure. This structure is similar to the structure proposed for the S4 segment of the shaker K channel which is mobile in its membrane setting allowing gating of the K channel.

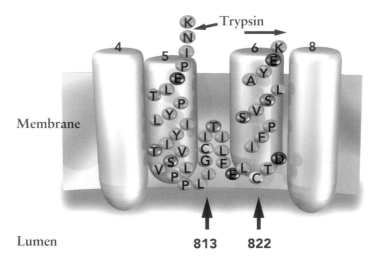

Transport Region of Acid Pump

A tentative model of the M5 M6 region of the H,K ATPase with only partial membrane insertion of these sequences enabling access of the PPI's to both cys 813 and 822.

3D structure of P type ATPases

Crystal structure

The only ion pump for which a detailed structure is available is bacteriorhodopsin. 2 dimensional crystals of this molecule have been diffracted to a resolution of 2.8 Å. There are 7 transmembrane helices with topological similarity to the G7 receptor proteins. The crucial all trans retinal group that isomerizes to 13 cis retinal with light is bound to lys[216] in the middle of the membrane as a Schiff base (R2.C=NR'). Asp[85] and glu[96] are on the cytoplasmic and extra-cytoplasmic side of the retinal group. Isomerization of the retinal alters the directionality and pKa of the lysine[216] Schiff base allowing sided deprotonation towards the outside surface with donation to glu[96]. The Schiff base is then reprotonated from asp[85]. There appears to be tilting of the transmembrane helices which form a narrow channel on the cytoplasmic side and a broader channel on the extra-cytoplasmic side of the retinal moiety. All the helices participate in forming the ion pathway on one side or the other of the membrane. Protonation from the cytoplasmic side and deprotonation of the Schiff base to the extra-cytoplasmic face depends on the change in orientation of the Schiff base and a change in the peptide conformation on either side of this base.

Ion pumping by bacterial rhodopsin involves a change of conformation in the central part of the membrane domain which acts like a switch sending energized protons from one side of the membrane to the other. This change in conformation is driven by the isomerization of a bound retinal photo-absorptive pigment. Changes in binding energy are driven by the change in tilt of a significant number of transmembrane helices (Henderson). The active outward transport of protons is driven by changes in tilt of some of the transmembrane segments.

EP type pumps lack photo-absorptive pigments but here the cycle of phosphorylation and dephosphorylation determines both the switching and the conformational change in these pumps and is transmitted from the cytoplasmic to the membrane domain.

The cytoplasmic domains of P type ATPases are much larger than those of bacterial rhodopsin, reflecting the fact that ATP, not light, is used as an energy source for vectorial ion transport and that its energizing site for ion transport cannot be within the membrane.

The analysis of crystals of this type of pump is most advanced for the sarcoplasmic reticulum Ca ATPase and for the H pump of Neurospora. Given that the transmembrane topology of these pumps is similar, it is likely that the analysis carried out on these pumps will apply in general to all P type ATPases.

Reconstruction of 2 dimensional crystals of the Ca^{2+} ATPase showed that this P type enzyme consisted of three distinct segments fitting into a box of 120Å (height) x 50Å (perpendicular to the dimer ribbons) x 85Å (along the dimer ribbons). The enzyme has a highly asymmetric mass distribution across the lipid bilayer. The cytoplasmic region comprises ~70% of the total mass, whereas the luminal region has only ~5%.

The cytoplasmic domain was shown to have a complex structure similar to the shape of the head and neck of a bird. The "head" is responsible for forming dimer ribbons and contains the ATP binding domain. The "neck" represents the stalk domain about 25Å long consisting of four segments. The transmembrane part consists of three segments defined as A, B and C segments: the largest segment (A segment) consists of two parts, one vertical (A2) and the other inclined (A1); the B segment is also tilted and connected to A2 and a third membrane segment (C segment).

The interpretation of this structure was that there is a 6 transmembrane segment core and two transmembrane pairs are associated with the external surface of this core. The resolution was 8A, still insufficient to assign amino acid sequences to the transmembrane helices.

The two dimensional structure crystals of the H,K ATPase formed in an imidazole buffer containing HVO_4^- and Mg^{2+} ions was resolved at about 25Å. The average cell edge of the H,K ATPase was 115Å, containing four asymmetric protein units of 50Å x 30Å, whereas the unit cell dimension of the $Co(NH_3)_4$ ATP-induced crystals of Na,K ATPase was 141Å. This suggests a more compact packing of the H,K ATPase than the Ca ATPase or the Na,K ATPase. Recently, two-dimensional crystals of the Na,K ATPase were reported to be best formed at pH 4.8 in sodium citrate buffer and to represent an unique lattice (a = 108.7, b = 66.2, r = 104.2) by electron cryo-microscopy. There are two high contrast parts in one unit cell.

The trypsinized Na,K-ATPase membranes were analyzed by electron microscopy. Both surface particles observed by negative staining and the protruding cytoplasmic portion of the α subunit were removed but general membrane structure was preserved. Intramembranal particles defined by freeze-fracture were preserved after trypsinolysis, showing that the remaining membrane protein fragments retained their native structure within the lipid bilayer after proteolysis. The figure shows the hypothetical arrangement of the protein of the H,K ATPase providing a more refined model of the structure shown at the beginning of this section.

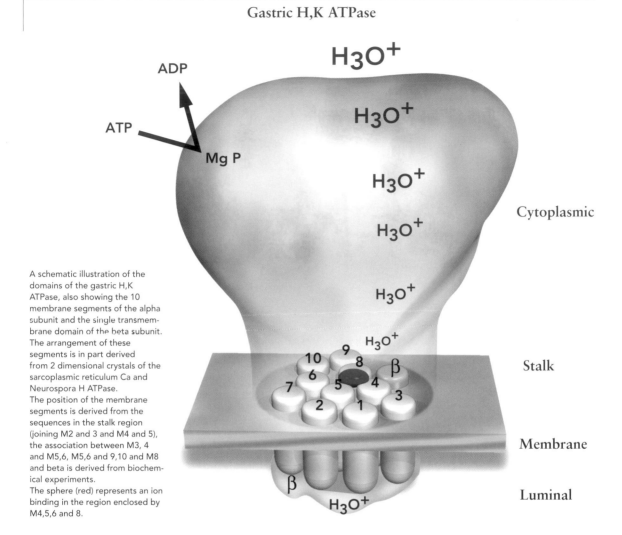

Gastric H,K ATPase

A schematic illustration of the domains of the gastric H,K ATPase, also showing the 10 membrane segments of the alpha subunit and the single transmembrane domain of the beta subunit. The arrangement of these segments is in part derived from 2 dimensional crystals of the sarcoplasmic reticulum Ca and Neurospora H ATPase.
The position of the membrane segments is derived from the sequences in the stalk region (joining M2 and 3 and M4 and 5), the association between M3, 4 and M5,6, M5,6 and 9,10 and M8 and beta is derived from biochemical experiments.
The sphere (red) represents an ion binding in the region enclosed by M4,5,6 and 8.

A structure function model of the H,K ATPase

The above data prove the presence of 10 membrane spanning or inserted segments of the catalytic subunit of the H,K ATPase. The boundary amino acids of these transmembrane segments are defined by a combination of these techniques along with alignment with other P type ATPases and molecular modeling. The membrane domain is a compact structure as anticipated from the transport of small cations and demonstrated by the difficulty of cross linking membrane segments by hydrophobic cross linking reagents. Crystal analysis of the sarcoplasmic reticulum Ca ATPase shows the presence of a core structure with 4 segments external to the core.

The 4th, 5th, 6th and 8th membrane segments of the α subunit are shown with TM9 at the back. Illustrated in this model is the putative transport pathway contained within these membrane segments. A series of site directed mutagenesis studies in the Na,K and sarcoplasmic reticulum Ca ATPases have defined these regions (4,5,6 and 8) as important for transport and occlusion. The ion "in" conformation is shown with ion binding in the region of these membrane segments close to the interface of the membrane domain and the stalk of the figure. A change of tilt in these segments moves the ion binding site to the outside face of the pump.

This P type ATPase is the enzyme that is inhibited by the PPI's. Their target is found in the transport segment of the pump and their mechanism will be discussed in a subsequent section of this book.

Ion "In" Conformation   Ion "Out" Conformation

Membrane

A magnification of the transport region of the H,K ATPase that includes TM4, M5,M6 and TM8. The binding of the ion (H_3O^+) in the "in" configuration allows ATP binding and protein phosphorylation. This changes the protein to the ion "out" conformation by altering the tilt of the four helices.

From this form, H_3O^+ can be released but the binding of K is necessary to reverse the position of the ion binding sites. The M5/M6 membrane sequences are membrane inserted but not transmembrane segments, whereas TM4 and TM8 are transmembrane.

REFERENCES

Ahn, K.Y., Kone, B.C. *Expression and cellular localization of mRNA encoding the "gastric" isoform of H,K-ATPase alpha-subunit in rat kidney.* Am. J. Physiol. 268, F99-F109 (1995).

Andersen, J., Vilsen, B. *Structure-function relationships of cation translocation by Ca^{2+} and Na,K-ATPases studied by site directed mutagenesis.* FEBS Letters 359, 101-106 (1995).

Auer, M., Scarbrough, G.A., Kuhlbrandt, W. *Three dimensional map of the plasma membrane H+ ATPase in the open conformation.* Nature 392, 840-843 (1998).

Bamberg, K., Sachs, G. *Topological analysis of the H,K ATPase using in vitro translation.* J. Biol. Chem. 269, 16909-16919 (1994).

Bayle, D., Weeks, D., Sachs, G. *The membrane topology of the rat sarcoplasmic and endoplasmic reticulum calcium ATPases by in vitro translation scanning.* J. Biol. Chem. 270, 25678-25684 (1995).

Berglindh, T., Helander, H.F., Obrink, K.J. *Effects of secretagogues on oxygen consumption, aminopyrine accumulation and morphology in isolated gastric glands.* Acta Physiol. Scand. 97, 401 (1976).

Besancon, M., Shin, J.M., Mercier, F., Munson, K., Miller, M., Hersey, S., Sachs, G. *Membrane topology and omeprazole labeling of the gastric H,K-adenosinetriphosphatase.* Biochemistry, 32, 2345-2355 (1993).

Clarke, D.M., Loo, T.W., Maclennan, D.M. *Functional consequences of aterations to polar amino acids located in the transmembrane domain of the Ca-ATPase of the Sarcoplasmic reticulum.* J. Biol. Chem. 265, 6262-6267 (1990).

Claros, M.G., von Heijne, G. *TopPred II, an improved software for membrane protein structure predictions.* Comput. Appl. Biosci. 10, 685-686 (1994).

Celsus, A.C. *Of the disorders of the stomach and their cures.* In: *De Medicina.* Translated by J Griene. Book IV, London.: Wilson and Durham, 1756, p. 196-201.

Cyrklaff, M., Auer, M., Kuhlbrandt, W., Scarborough G.A. *2-D structure of the Neurospora crassa plasma membrane ATPase as determined by electron cryomicroscopy.* EMBO J. 14, 1854-7 (1995).

Davies, R.E. *The mechanism of hydrochloric acid production by the stomach.* Biol. Revs. 26, 87 (1951).

Dibona, D.R., Ito, S., Berglindh, T., Sachs, G. *Cellular site of gastric acid secretion.* Proc. Natl. Acad. Sci. U.S.A. 76, 6689 (1979).

Feng, J., Lingrel, J.B. *Analysis of amino acid residues in the H5-H6 transmembrane and extracellular domains of Na,K-ATPase alpha subunit identifies threonine 797 as a determinant of ouabain sensitivity.* Biochemistry 33, 4218-24 (1994).

Forte, J.G., Ganser, A., Beesley, R., Forte, T. M. *Unique enzymes of purified microsomes from pig fundic mucosa.* Gastroenterology 69, 175-189 (1975).

Forte, J.G., Soll, A. *Cell biology of hydrochloric acid secretion.* In: *Handbook of Physiology. The Gastrointestinal System III.* Edited by J. G. Forte and S. G. Schultz. Bethesda, Maryland: American Physiological Society, 1989, p. 207-228.

Forte, T. M., Machen, T. E., Forte, J.G. *Ultrastructural changes in oxyntic cells associated with secretory function. A membrane recycling hypothesis.* Gastroenterology 73, 941 (1977).

Foster, M. *Van Helmont and the rise of the chemical physiology.* In: *Lectures on the History of Physiology.* Boston: Cambridge University Press, 1924, p. 120-143.

Fulton, J.F. *René Antoine Ferchault de Réaumur.* In: *Selected Readings in the History of Physiology.* Springfield, IL: Charles C. Thomas, 1966; p. 68-170.

Garrison, F.H. *The seventeenth century.* In: *The History of Medicine.* Philadelphia: W.B.Saunders Co., 1963, p. 257-258.

Gibert, A.J., Hersey, S.J. *Morphometric analysis of parietal cell membrane transformations in isolated gastric glands.* J. Membrane Biol. 67, 113 (1982).

Glynn, I.M., Karlish, S.J. *Occluded ions in active transport.* Ann. Rev. Biochem. 59, 171 (1990).

Golgi, C. *Sur la fine organisation des glandes peptiques des mammiferes.* Arch. Ital. Biol. 19, 448 (1893).

Helander, H.F. *The cells of the gastric mucosa.* Internat. Rev. Cytol. 70, 217 (1981).

Helander, H.F., Hirschowitz, B.I. *Quantitative ultrastructural studies on gastric parietal cells.* Gastroenterology 63, 951 (1972).

Henderson, R., Baldwin, J.M., Ceska, T.A., Zemlin, F., Beckmann, E., Downing, K.H. *Model for the structure of bacteriorhodopsin based on high-resolution electron-cryomicroscopy.* J. Mol. Biol. 213, 899-929 (1990).

Hersey, S.J., Perez, A., Matheravidathu, S., Sachs, G. *Gastric H^+K^+-ATPase in situ, evidence for compartmentalization.* Am. J. Physiol. 257, G539 (1989).

Hippocrates. *The Genuine Works of Hippocrates.* Translated by F. Adams. London: Syderham Soc., 1899; p. 155-161.

Ito, S. *Functional gastric morphology.* In: Johnson, L. R. (ed), *Physiology of the Gastrointestinal Tract.* Vol 1, 2nd edition, New York, Raven Press, 1987, p. 817.

Ito S., Schofield, G.C. *Studies on the depletion and accumulation of microvilli and changes in the tubulovesicular compartment of mouse parietal cells in relation to gastric acid secretion.* J. Cell Biol. 63, 364 (1974).

Jewell, E.A., Lingrel, J.B. *Site directed mutagenesis of the Na,K ATPase. Consequences of the substitutions of negatively charged amino acids localized in the transmembrane domains.* Biochem. 32, 13523-13530 (1993).

Lee, J., Simpson, G., Scholes, P. *An ATPase from dog gastric mucosa: changes of outer pH in suspensions of dog membrane vesicles accompanying ATP hydrolysis.* Biochem. Biophys. Res. Commun. 60, 825-832 (1974).

Lundegardh, H. *Investigations as to the absorption and accumulation of inorganic ions.* Ann. Agric. Coll. Sweden 8, 233 (1940).

MacLennan, D.H., Brandl, C.J., Koreczak, B., Green, N.M. *Amino acid sequence of the Ca^{2+} Mg^{2+} dependent ATPase from rabbit muscle sarcoplasmic reticulum, deduced from its complementary DNA sequence.* Nature 316, 696-700 (1985).

Maeda, M., Ishizaki, J., Futai, M. *cDNA cloning and sequence determination of pig gastric (H+ + K+)-ATPase.* Biochem. Biophys. Res. Commun. 157, 203-209 (1988).

Melchers, K., Weitzenegger, T., Buhmann, A., Steinhilber, W., Sachs, G., Schafer, K.P. *Cloning and membrane topology of a P type ATPase from Helicobacter pylori.* J Biol Chem 271, 446-457 (1996).

Mercier, F., Bayle, D., Besancon, M., Joys, T., Shin, J.M., Lewin, M.J.M., Prinz, C., Reuben, A.M., Soumarmon, A., Wong, H., Walsh, J.H., Sachs, G. *Antibody epitope mapping of the gastric H,K-ATPase.* Biochim. Biophys. Acta, 1149, 151-165 (1993).

Mitchell, P. *Chemiosmotic coupling in oxidative and photosynthetic phosphorylation.* Biol. Rev. 41, 445-502 (1966).

Modlin, I.M. From Prout to the Proton Pump - *A history of the Science of Gastric Acid Secretion and the Surgery of Peptic Ulcer.* SG&O 170, 81-96 (1990).

Pitcairn, A. *A dissertation upon the motion which reduces the aliment in the stomach to a form proper for the supply of blood.* In: *The Whole Works.* Translated by G. Sewell and J. T. Desaguliers. London: J. Pemberton, 1727, p. 106-138.

Post, R.L. *A reminiscence about sodium, potassium-ATPase.* Ann NY Acad. Sci. 242, 6-11 (1974).

Prout, W. *On the nature of the acid and saline matters usually existing in the stomach of animals.* Philos. Trans. 114, 45 (1824).

Rabon, E. C. and M. A. Reuben. The mechanism and structure of the gastric H,K-ATPase. Annu. Rev. Physiol. 52, 321-344 (1990).

Rabon, E.C., Smillie, K., Seru, V., Rabon, R. *Rubidium occlusion within tryptic peptides of the H,K-ATPase.* J. Biol. Chem. 268, 8012-8018 (1993).

Racker, E. *Resolution and reconstitution of biological pathways from 1919 to 1984.* Fed. Proc. 42, 2899-909 (1983).

Reaumur, René, A.F. de. *Sur la digestion des oiseaux.* Mem. Acad. Roy. d. Sc. Paris, 1752, pp. 266.

Rehm, W.S., Sanders, S.S. *Electrical events during activation and inhibition of gastric HCl secretion.* Gastroenterology 73, 959-969 (1977).

Reti, L. *How old is hydrochloric acid?* Chymia 10, 11-23 (1965).

Reuben, M.A., Lasater, L. S., Sachs, G. *Characterization of a beta subunit of the gastric H+/K(+)-transporting ATPase.* Proc. Natl. Acad. Sci. U.S.A. 87, 6767-6771 (1990).

Sachs, G., Chang, H.H., Rabon, E., Schackman, R., Lewin, M., Saccomani, G. *A nonelectrogenic H+ pump in plasma membranes of hog stomach.* J. Biol. Chem. 251, 7690-7698, 1976.

Schertler, G.F.X, Villa, C., Henderson, R. *Projection structure of rhodopsin.* Nature 362, 770-2 (1993).

Scott, D.R., Helander, H.F., Hersey, S.J., Sachs, G. *The site of acid secretion in the mammalian parietal cell.* Biochim. Biophys. Acta 1146, 73 (1993).

Shin, J.M., Kajimura, M., Arguello, J.M., Kaplan, J.H., Sachs, G. *Biochemical identification of transmembrane segments of the Ca2+-ATPase of sarcoplasmic reticulum.* J. Biol. Chem. 269, 22533-22537 (1993).

Shull, G.E. *cDNA cloning of the beta-subunit of the rat gastric H,K-ATPase.* J. Biol. Chem. 265, 12123-12126 (1990).

Shull, G.E., Lingrel, J.B. *Molecular cloning of the rat stomach (H+ + K+)-ATPase.* J. Biol. Chem. 261, 16788-16791 (1986).

Skou, J.C. *The influence of some cations on an adenosine triphosphatase from peripheral nerves.* Biochim. Biophys. Acta 23, 394-401 (1957).

Smith, D.L., Tao,T., Maguire, M.E. *Membrane topology of a P-type ATPase. The MgtB magnesium transport protein of Salmonella typhimurium.* J. Biol. Chem. 268, 22469-79 (1993).

Smolka, A., Helander, H.F., Sachs, G. *Monoclonal antibodies against gastric H+,K+ ATPase.* Am. J. Physiol. 245, G589 (1983).

Spallanzani, A.L. *Della digestione degli animali.* In: *Fisica animale,* Venice, 1782.

Spallanzani, A.L. *Dissertazioni de Fisica Animale e Vegetabile.* Modena: Società Tipografica, 1780.

Stewart, B., Wallmark, B., Sachs, G. *The interaction of H+ and K+ with the partial reactions of gastric H,K-ATPase.* J. Biol. Chem. 256, 2682-2690 (1981).

Swarts, H.G., Klaassen, C.H., de Boer, M., Fransen, J.A., De Pont, J.J. *Role of negatively charged residues in the fifth and sixth transmembrane domains of the catalytic subunit of gastric H+,K+-ATPase.* J. Biol. Chem. 271, 29764-29772 (1996).

Toh, B.H., Gleeson, P.A., Simpson, R.J., Moritz, R.L., Callaghan, J.M., Goldkorn, I., Jones, C.M., Martinelli, T.M., Mu, F.T., Humphris, D.C. et al. *The 60- to 90-kDa parietal cell autoantigen associated with autoimmune gastritis is a beta subunit of the gastric H+/K+-ATPase (proton pump).* Proc. Natl. Acad. Sci. U. S. A. 87, 6418-6422 (1990).

Toyoshima, C., Sasabe, H., Stokes, D.L. *Three-dimensional cryo-electron microscopy of the calcium ion pump in the sarcoplasmic reticulum membrane* [published erratum appears in Nature 1993 May 20; 363 (6426), 286] Nature 362, 467-71.(1993).

Walderhaug, M.O., Post, R.L., Saccomani, G., Leonard, R. T., Briskin, D.P. *Structural relatedness of three ion-transport adenosine triphosphatases around their active sites of phosphorylation.* J. Biol. Chem. 260, 3852-3859 (1985).

Wang, S.G., Eakle, K.A., Levenson, R., Farley, R.A. *Na+-K+-ATPase alpha-subunit containing Q905-V930 of gastric H+-K+-ATPase alpha preferentially assembles with H+-K+-ATPase beta.* Am. J. Physiol. 272, pC923-30 (1997).

Wolosin, J.M., Forte, J.G. *Stimulation of oxyntic cell triggers K+ and Cl- conductances in apical H+-K+-ATPase membrane.* Am. J. Physiol. 246, C537-C545 (1984).

Yao, X., Thibodeau, A., Forte, J.G. *Ezrin-calpain 1 interactions in gastric parietal cells.* Am. J. Physiol. 265, C36 (1993).

Zhang, P., Toyoshima, C., Yonekra, K., Green, N.M., Stokes, D.L. *Structure of the calcium pump from sarcoplasmic reticulum at 8A resolution.* Nature 992, 835-839 (1998).

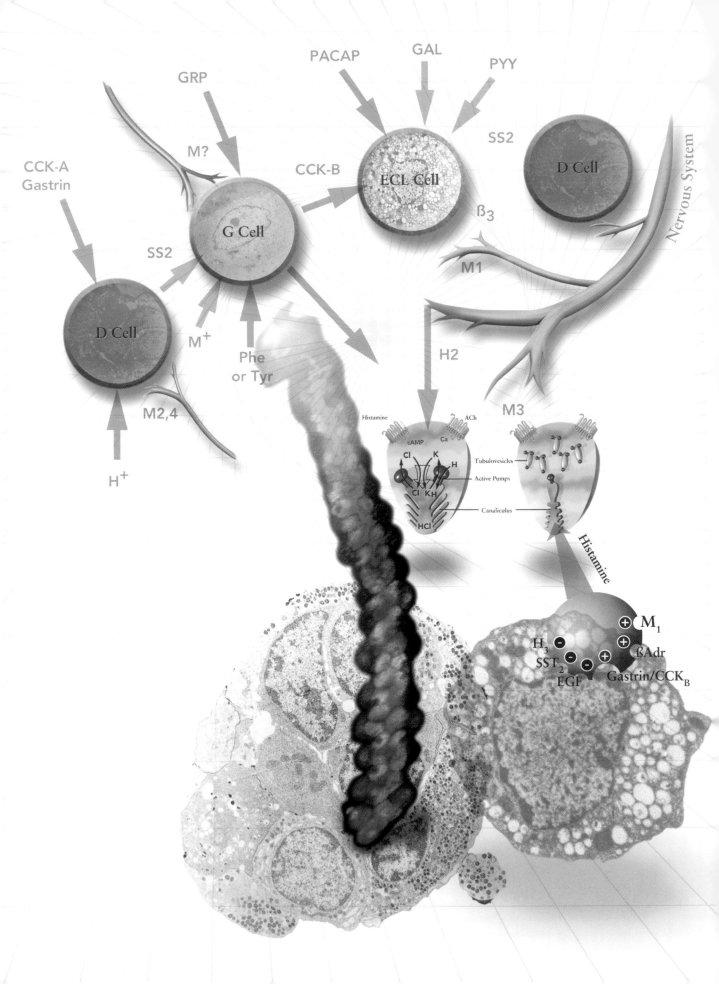

THE
REGULATION
OF
GASTRIC ACID
SECRETION

CHAPTER 1

**Progress Towards the
Physiology of the Stomach**

CHAPTER 2

Gastric Acid Secretion

CHAPTER 3

The Parietal Cell

CHAPTER 1
PROGRESS TOWARDS THE PHYSIOLOGY OF THE STOMACH

Gastric fistulae: a unique opportunity

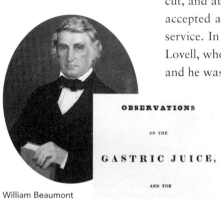

OBSERVATIONS

ON THE

GASTRIC JUICE,

AND THE

PHYSIOLOGY OF DIGESTION.

BY WILLIAM BEAUMONT, M. D.
Surgeon in the U.S. Army.

William Beaumont (1785-1853). His contributions are best summarized by William Osler in the preface of Jesse Meyer's book, *Life and Letters of Dr. William Beaumont.* "The man was greater than his work... The pioneer physiologist of the United States and the first to make a contribution of enduring value, his work remains a model of patient, persevering research. The highest praise that we can give is to say that his life fulfilled the ideal with which he set out, and which he so well expressed in the sentence: 'Truth, like beauty, is when unadorned adorned the most, and in prosecuting these experiments and enquiries I believe I have been guided by its light'".

William Beaumont and the case of Alexis St. Martin

William Beaumont was born on November 25, 1785 in Lebanon, Connecticut, and at the age of 22, began his study of medicine. In the War of 1812, he accepted a position in the Army as an acting surgeon's mate and saw active service. In 1819, after a brief spell in practice, his former colleague, Joseph Lovell, who had now become surgeon general, offered Beaumont a commission, and he was assigned to Fort Mackinac.

Fort Mackinac was located on the island of Michel Mackinac at the junction of Lakes Huron and Michigan. Beaumont was the only physician within 300 miles and was often busy because of frequent brawls among Indians and fur traders. On the morning of June 6, 1822, a 19 year old voyageur, Alexis St. Martin, was accidently shot in the left upper abdomen and chest. Beaumont was called to see the victim and noted a disastrous wound. He thought the chances of survival to be slim and remarked *"The man cannot live 36 hours; I will come and see him by and by"*.

Surprisingly, St. Martin survived, and after about ten months, his wound was largely healed, but a gastric fistula remained. During this time, Beaumont had been actively involved in the care of St. Martin. By this stage, St. Martin had become penniless; the county authorities, refusing further support, proposed transporting him 1,500 miles back to his birthplace in Cana-

A reproduction of Beaumont and his patient St. Martin (c. 1822) in the room of his home at Fort Mackinac.

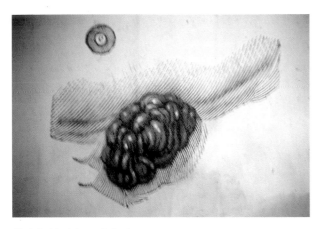

Alexis St. Martin's gastric fistula. Through this "window in the stomach" Beaumont was able to elucidate the principles of gastric digestion.

da. Beaumont opposed the proposal, fearing for the safety of his patient and wishing to study his condition further. In April 1823, Beaumont moved his patient into his own home, where he remained for almost two years under constant care and attention. In 1824, Beaumont had sent his commanding officer (Surgeon General Lovell) a manuscript concerning this patient. It was published in the Medical Recorder as *A Case of Wounded Stomach by Joseph Lovell, Surgeon General, U.S.A.* The oversight of his omission as an author was soon remedied and Beaumont was instated as a co-author.

At this stage, Beaumont recognized the unique opportunity that St. Martin's gastric fistula presented, and began his epic investigation into gastric function and digestion. In 1826, his first paper was published but, unfortunately, further studies were curtailed by his military transfer to Fort Niagara and the disappearance of St. Martin into Canada. It took Beaumont until 1829 to locate St. Martin and arrange a job for him with the American Fur Company. Under the auspices of the company, St. Martin was sent to Fort Crawford on the Upper Mississippi River, where Beaumont was then stationed. During the next two years, many experiments were performed, but thereafter, St. Martin and his family became so homesick and discontented that they returned to Canada.

Studying St. Martin had by now become an obsession for Beaumont, and he attempted to travel to Europe with him for further scientific investigation. Although this proposed trip failed, he was, with the help of Lovell, able to enlist St. Martin in the United States Army to forestall any further episodes of abscondment, which would hence be regarded as desertion. Thereafter, Beaumont entered into a formal written agreement with St. Martin as his "human guinea pig". In return for allowing the study of his stomach and digestion, St. Martin was to receive board, lodging and a certain sum of money for the year.

A. St. Martin at the age of 67. Beaumont arranged a contract whereby St. Martin was employed by the U.S. Army and paid as an experimental subject.

Despite being an unpleasant and dissolute person to work with, St. Martin was studied by Beaumont without further interruption until November 1, 1833. At this stage, he again disappeared into Canada and Beaumont was never able again to work with him. St. Martin died at the age of 83 and, in fact, outlived his physician, Beaumont, by several years.

Beaumont studied the physiologic manifestation of digestion and produced a classic text on the subject in 1833. Despite his lack of training as a physiologist and his relatively unsophisticated medical background, Beaumont's work remained a model on the subject.

In essence by 1833 Beaumont had been able to outline the basic principles of digestion in a human and establish the presence of hydrochloric acid in gastric juice.

Jacob Helm, Vienna. The frontispiece of the *Gesundheits - taschenbuch* of 1803 documenting Helm's experience with his patient T. Petz. She died in 1802 after having been studied for 5 years. Helm's report documented digestion and to a large extent, repeated the observations which had previously been detailed by Spallanzani and Gosse.

The gastric fistula of Madeline Gore. At the age of 20 yrs. she fell down stone stairs and thereafter always walked bent over to the left. Eighteen years later, she developed a lump over her stomach which broke down and became a fistula through which food passed.

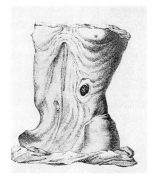

Although the studies of a patient with gastric fistula were unique for North America in the 19th century, in Europe, similar observations had been made previously. In 1797, Jacob Anton Helm of Vienna studied a 58 year old woman, Theresia Petz of Breitenwaida, who had a spontaneous gastric fistula. Using a hired person, Zyriak Sieddeler, and himself, with his own brother as a control, Helm performed meticulous studies of digestion, intragastric temperature and salivary function. Helm had no skills in chemistry and he did not measure acid, nor was he able to demonstrate a change in the color of dye to indicate the presence of acid.

Similarly, in 1801, Rouilly transferred to the care of Dupuytren and Bichat in Paris a patient, Madeline Gore, with a gastric fistula. Gore's gastric juice was analyzed by Clarion, a professor of chemistry, who performed the first quantitative assessment of gastric juice. Clarion found neither acid nor alkali and concluded that gastric juice was identical with saliva. This conclusion remained dogma in the French medical profession so that, even in 1812, when Montegre reported acid in fasting and meal-stimulated gastric juice, he attributed this acid to the digestion of food and saliva.

"Le Milieu Intérieur"

By the sixteenth century, there still existed considerable controversy as to the events that occurred in the lumen of the stomach. A number of reactionary and thoughtful individuals including Paracelsus, Van Helmont and Spallanzani had written effectively about their individual concepts of gastric function. Their ideas ranged from chemical principles of an undefined nature, to *archei* (spirits), to the presence of acid as proposed by Spallanzani. Many investigators in numerous countries considered the fundamental problem of digestion at many different levels. Of particular interest was the philosophical approach utilized by individuals who, though learned, had no formal training in science. Most interesting amongst these was the gourmand Brillat-Savarin.

Jean Anthelme Brillat-Savarin (1755-1826)

The preoccupation of the French with food was never better exemplified than in the life and writings of the gourmet Brillat-Savarin. Indeed his philosophical observation antedated by many years the concept of the central modulation of gastric secretion.

He worked in Paris for years on a book called *The Physiology of Taste* which was finally published in 1825. It consisted of a series of thoughtful essays which detailed his ideas regarding the preparation of food, its role in philosophy and life, and the role of digestion and different foods in behavior. Chapters include discussions of osmazomes, the erotic power of truffles, the nature of digestion and the dangers of acids. Much of the content of this work reflects Savarin's interactions with philosophers and physicians of his time. Indeed guests at his table included Napoleon's physician Corvisart, the surgeon Dupuytren, the pathologist Cruveilhier and other great literary and scientific minds of his time. Conversations amongst these individuals would no doubt have provided Savarin with considerable information regarding the chemistry of food and its relationship to the physiology of digestion.

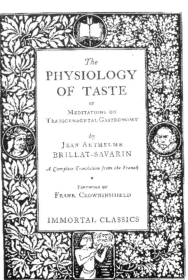

Jean Anthelme Brillat-Savarin (1755-1826).
He spent two years in America, initially in New York where he taught language and played violin in an orchestra at the John Street theater. Since New York did not satisfy his intellectual and culinary tastes, he subsequently moved to Hartford, Connecticut where he spent almost two years becoming familiar with American culture and food before returning to France.
He believed that the chemical nature of food profoundly influenced human physiology and emotional behavior.

Defining gastric secretion

The question of acid in the stomach had been a vexatious one for many years. Opinions had ranged from there being no acid in the stomach at all, to its originating from the pancreas. Physicians of the 15th and 16th centuries felt that any acid present in the stomach was the result of putrefaction or fermentation and did not in any way reflect an active secretory process of the body or the stomach itself. It was, however, the general opinion of physiologists up to the time of Spallanzani, that a free or at least unsaturated acid, usually existed in the stomach and was necessary for digestion. Indeed the studies of Edward Stevens in Edinburgh and Lazzaro Spallanzani in Pavia had concluded that the antiseptic powers of gastric juices invalidated the possibility of fermentation as a means of gastric digestion.

A second controversial issue surrounded to what the exact nature of the acid might be. Johann Tholde had first described the acid known as hydrochloric acid, although it had also been called muriatic acid for many years. The detection of this substance in the stomach was first reported by William Prout in

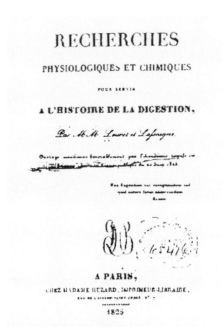

The publication of Leuret and Lassaigne's work in 1825 defined their contribution to gastrointestinal physiology. They presciently noted that duodenal acid stimulated pancreatic secretion but concluded erroneously that the stomach secreted lactic acid.

№ 81.

О ВЛІЯНІИ КИСЛОТЪ

In 1894 Dolinsky, a student of Pavlov, published his thesis detailing the ability of acid in the duodenum to stimulate pancreatic secretion.

1823. At a meeting of the Royal Society in London on December 11, 1823, in a lucid and elegant discourse, he provided incontrovertible evidence that gastric juice of many different animals (hares, dogs, horses, cats) contained hydrochloric (muriatic) acid. In addition, Prout demonstrated that the same acid was present in dyspeptic patients, and that the amount of this acid appeared to be related to the degree of dyspepsia. Thus, the subject of the exact nature of the acid in gastric juice appeared to be resolved. Unfortunately, however, this was not to be the case since physiologists as eminent as Claude Bernard were of the opinion that lactic acid (a product of fermentation) was present in gastric contents. Indeed, as late as 1885, Ewald and Boas reported that all acid present in the stomach at the beginning of a meal was lactic. It was their theory that hydrochloric acid gradually replaced the lactic acid during eating, with the result that, by the end of a meal, only hydrochloric acid was evident.

The French Académie des Sciences was interested in the exact nature of acid in the stomach and established an essay contest for which they offered a prize of 3,000 francs for the answer to this question. A panel of distinguished judges was selected to evaluate the essays. One year later, the prize was awarded jointly to Leuret and Lassaigne of Paris, and Tiedemann and Gmelin of Heidelberg. Leuret and Lassaigne declared that the acid in gastric juice was lactic, whilst Tiedemann and Gmelin confirmed Prout's earlier observations that it was hydrochloric acid. When asked to share the prize, the Germans declined and withdrew, having been offended by the contradiction provided by the judges. At this time, Berzelius was regarded as the ranking authority on chemistry in Europe. As a result, his comments on the literature were anxiously scanned by authors in an attempt to gauge the level of acceptance of their thoughts. Thus Wöhler, in a letter of May 17, 1828, told Berzelius how pleased Tiedemann and Leopold Gmelin were to have noted in the Årsberättelser 7, 297, the deprecatory comments of Berzelius about the "*unbedeutende Arbeit*" of Leuret and Lassaigne.

The work of Leuret and Lassaigne was not inconsequential. Their experimental studies on dogs demonstrated for the first time that acid introduced into the duodenum elicited the secretion of pancreatic juice and bile.

Seventy years later, in 1894, a student of Pavlov, Ivan Leukich Dolinsky, rediscovered this effect and noted that acid in the duodenum of the dog stimulated pancreatic secretion. It was on the basis of the earlier French observations that William Bayliss and his brother-in-law Ernest Starling, on the afternoon of January 16, 1901, tested Dolinsky's thesis and proved the existence of chemical messengers (hormones) which regulated secretion.

Concepts of digestion

Claude Bernard (1813-1878) was born of a modest family in the town of Saint Julien in the Rhône; he attended a Jesuit college at Villefranche and then became a pharmacist's assistant in Lyons. Bernard is best known for his book on experimental physiology in which he outlined a number of the major concepts which he felt were critical to the pursuit of physiological science. In particular, his delineation of the "*miliéu intérieur*" has remained one of the critical physiological observations ever made.

On December 7, 1843 Claude Bernard presented his thesis *The Gastric Juice and its Role in Nutrition* for the doctorate in Medicine to the Faculty of Medicine in Paris. The thesis was considered to be of modest quality and failed to recognize the presence of pepsin in the gastric juice.

Apart from his numerous contributions, which included the identification of the glycogenic function of the liver and the delineation of the vasomotor mechanism, Bernard was noted for his contributions to the study of digestion. Prior to his work it had been held that gastric digestion itself encompassed all digestive physiology. Bernard however demonstrated that "*gastric digestion is only a preparatory act*" and in particular delineated the enzymatic role of the pancreas. He demonstrated that pancreatic juice emulsified fat, converted starch into sugar and was a solvent for proteins undigested by the stomach. Bernard was a creative investigator and had adopted Nicholas Blondlot's canine model of the gastric fistula for the study of gastric secretion. In 1840, Blondlot of Nancy, a surgeon, had utilized Bernard's innovative experimental model to determine that there was no acid or chloride in the stomach and concluded that the active principle was 1% calcium phosphate. Blondlot had been inspired to devise his canine model after reading of Beaumont's studies of Alexis St. Martin. His innovative work in this area was later taken up by Pavlov who constructed a series of vagally innervated and denervated pouches to evaluate the effects of neural regulation on gastric secretion. This was the so-called "Pavlov pouch" which formed the basis of many of the subsequent experimental models utilized by the great physiologist and his pupils.

Vagal physiology and gastric function

Investigations on the vagus nerve began two thousand years ago. Marinus, in the first century A.D., studied the anatomy of the vagi and was the first to assign to the cranial nerves a numeric sequence. Although none of the original work by Marinus survives today, Galen cited his studies in the second century anatomy text, *On the Usefulness of the Parts of the Body*.

Galen, who was born in Pergamon Mysia, which is now part of Turkey, in 130 A.D., expanded on the work of Marinus by speculating on the possible function of the nerves to the stomach.

> "*The stomach must have very accurate perception of the need for food and drink. Hence, most of these nerves seem to be distributed to its so-called [cardiac] orifice and afterwards to all the other portions of it as far as its lower end*".

The anatomy of the vagus, undoubtedly, contributed to the name applied to it. The term *vagus*, or *per vagum*, means "wandering part". A more anatomically correct name was given to the nerve in the early 19th century when the

The Vesalian (1543) concept of the distribution of the vagus nerve to the viscera was contained in *De Humani Corporis Fabrica Libri* (1543). The book was dedicated to the Holy Roman Emperor, Charles V, and was printed by Johannes Oporinus of Basel, the blocks having been carried by mule over the Alps from Padua. They survived intact in the library of Munich until July 16, 1944, when it was destroyed by an Allied air raid. This unique treatise provided the basis for a completely novel understanding of human anatomy. The illustrations were undertaken by Jan Stephan van Calcar, a fellow Belgian and one time pupil of Titian. Vesalius was unique in that he filled all three traditional roles as the surgeon, the demonstrator and the lecturer and is here shown as demonstrating the anatomy (Copyright J.Norman & Co Inc.)

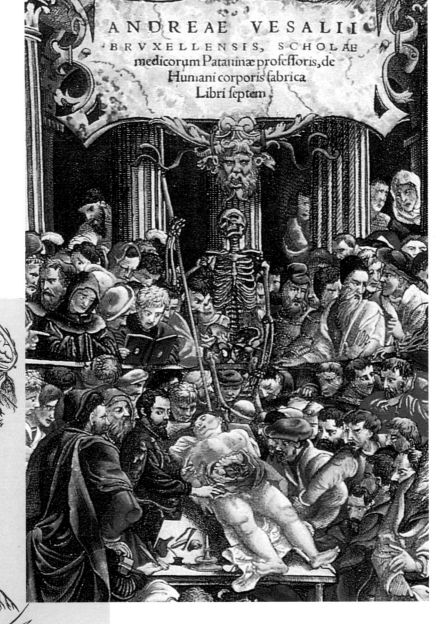

term pneumogastric appeared in the French and Italian literature. It then became a frequent term in the English and American literature. In Germany, however, the nerve was always referred to as the vagus. Thus, by the end of the 19th century, when German scientific research attained prominence, the term pneumogastric fell from common usage in the surgical community.

Once its anatomy became better defined, studies into vagal function were initiated. In 1814, Brodie published some of the first known experiments on vagal physiology and gastric function. In the report of his findings to the

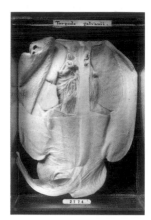

A specimen of a Torpedo fish (c. 1810) from John Hunter's original collection at the Royal College of Surgeons of England. It was used to study the concept of the "electrical activity" which resided in nerves.

Royal Society of London, he noted that his work was inspired by Edward Home's report of "*some facts which render it probable that the various animal secretions are dependent on the influence of the nervous system*". Home, in fact, studied secretion in the electric eel:

> "*Since in these fish the abundance of nerves connected with the electrical organs proves that this power resides in them, and since the arrangement of many nerves in animal bodies has evidently no connexion with sensation, it seems not improbable that these may answer the purpose of supplying and regulating the organs of secretion*".

Thus, the observation by Home on the electric eel inspired Brodie to be the first to perform the surgical procedure that is now accepted as a vagotomy. The pioneering work of Brodie, however, was not on humans, but on a total of four dogs. His first experiment was a bilateral cervical vagotomy.

He noted that this operation prevented arsenic-stimulated gastric secretion, but was complicated by the development of severe respiratory compromise. To remedy the subsequent respiratory embarrassment, he modified his procedure to that of a subdiaphragmatic vagotomy. With the latter operation, the animals no longer experienced the "laborious breathing" and circulatory arrest observed during cervical vagotomy.

The earlier findings of "no watery or mucous fluid in the stomach or small intestines" seen with the cervical vagotomy were confirmed in the animals that underwent abdominal vagotomy. Brodie concluded "*that the suppression of secretion in all of them was to be attributed solely to the division of the nerves: and all of the facts which have been stated sufficiently demonstrate, that the secretions of the stomach are very much under the control of the nervous system*".

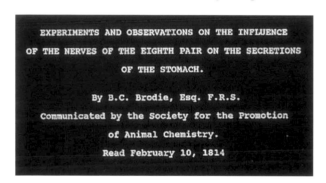

EXPERIMENTS AND OBSERVATIONS ON THE INFLUENCE OF THE NERVES OF THE EIGHTH PAIR ON THE SECRETIONS OF THE STOMACH.

By B.C. Brodie, Esq. F.R.S.

Communicated by the Society for the Promotion of Animal Chemistry.

Read February 10, 1814

Frontispiece of Brodie's description of the effects of the VIII nerve. Since not all the cranial nerves had been recognized, the vagus was referred to as the VIII nerve.

This observation was a watershed in the history of gastrointestinal physiology, as the concept of nervous control of gastrointestinal secretion had not been previously demonstrated.

Pavlov's delineation of vagal function

Later in the 19th century, Rokitansky and Bernard confirmed the findings of Brodie when they observed decreased gastric secretion and motility after vagotomy. Despite the contributions of these eminent physiologists, the modern era of the study of vagal physiology was initiated and dominated by Ivan P. Pavlov. Although he achieved principal recognition for his investigation of conditioned reflexes, his methods and the results of his observations on vagal function laid the foundation for the subsequent study of the nervous control of gastrointestinal function.

Pavlov was a graduate of the Medico-Chirurgical Academy in St. Petersburg, Russia, in the late

Ivan Pavlov as a youth. Born in 1849, the first son of an impoverished priest in Ryazan, he was awarded a Nobel Prize in 1904 for research on the activity of the digestive glands. Pavlov regarded the physiologist Elie Tsyon as his inspiration and his studies with Heidenhain of Breslau and Ludwig of Leipzig as having been critical to his success.
His work was aided by his brilliant ambidextrous surgical skill in devising experimental models.

A vagally innervated Pavlov pouch. These studies were undertaken by P.P. Khigine in collaboration with Pavlov. Confusion arose as to the authorship since the work was performed by P.P. Khizhin but when it was published, Pavlov's name was omitted and the student's name translated into the French form, Khigine. The dogs utilised for studies were also a source of research income for the laboratory, since their gastric juice was sold as a rejuvenant medication for elderly men.

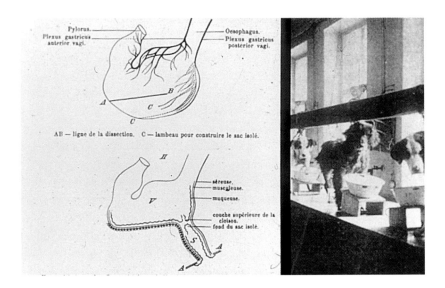

19th century. His scientific philosophy was greatly influenced by the work of Lister and Pasteur.

Pavlov's theory of "nervism" was a momentous postulate for the times in which he lived. He explained it as "*a physiological theory which tries to prove that the nervous system controls the greatest possible number of bodily activities*". It was from the hypothesis of nervism that Pavlov investigated the effects of vagal stimuli on gastric secretion.

Initially, he examined the work of his predecessors and recognized that most of their experiments used cervical separation of the vagi. With this protocol, Pavlov observed that most of the body functions of the animals "came to a standstill".

The first studies performed in his newly created modern operating rooms generated canine surgical models with diverted cervical esophagi.

Thus, Pavlov devised a simple method for studying the cephalic phase of gastric function. The dogs were then fed and their gastric output measured. It was evident that up to 700 milliliters of the "purest gastric juice" was secreted by the stomachs of the dogs after the sham feeding. After cervical esophageal diversion, subdiaphragmatic vagotomy was undertaken and it was evident that secretion of gastric juice was dramatically reduced after sham feeding.

"*It is obvious*", Pavlov concluded, "*that the effect of feeding was transmitted by nervous channels to the gastric glands*". Final confirmation of this finding was obtained by excitation of the vagi of the dogs with electrical impulses and the observation of increased gastric secretion.

Ulcer models and EGF

In 1940 the genesis of the ulcer disease was still unknown. Controversy continued regarding the role of the vagus or of chemical regulators in generating increased acid secretion. Without a defined regulatory system for acid secretion, no rational understanding of ulcer biology could be derived.

Experimental models of ulcers had been produced under a number of circumstances. Anton Wölfer, who had performed the first gastrojejunostomy as treat-

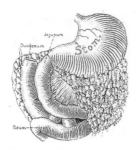

Williamson and Mann's initial report of the experimental preparation needed to generate peptic ulcer.

The Mann-Williamson Model provided the experimental surgical basis for the evaluation of the cause of ulcer disease.

ment for peptic ulcer in Theodor Billroth's Vienna clinic in 1881, noted that an ulcer at the stoma followed in up to 34% of his patients.

Subsequently Frank Mann of the Mayo Clinic noted that the neostomal ulcers resulting from gastrojejunostomy reflected a critical relevance of the anatomic and physiologic location of the lesion. He devised the Mann-Williamson experimental operation which was used for the next thirty years as the basic test for a new procedure to prevent or cure a peptic ulcer.

The procedure was constructed to enable the duodenum to drain its secretions and those of the pancreas and liver at a distance from the pylorus. Ten of the first fourteen of Mann and Williamson's dogs had chronic ulcers at the point where the gastric contents impinged upon the jejunal mucosa. At this stage the beneficial effects of urogastrone which had been identified by David J. Sandweiss, a gastroenterologist at the Harper Hospital in Detroit were studied. He had noted that out of 70,310 gravid women admitted to the hospital, only one exhibited a peptic ulcer and proposed that a substance secreted in the urine of pregnant women might be utilized in the treatment of peptic ulcer disease. Sandweiss and his colleagues were able to demonstrate some signs of fibroblastic proliferation and healing of ulcers in dogs, and some amelioration of symptoms in humans.

By 1940, Gray had prepared a pyrogen free inhibitor from the urine and named it urogastrone. In 1967 Harry Gregory of Imperial Chemical Industries in a preliminary report stated that he had prepared a pure urogastrone which consisted of 28 amino acids. In 1975, however, he published a composition of urogastrone which had a sequence of 53 amino acids and was similar to epidermal growth factor. In this paper, Gregory commented that over 30 years previously, Sandweiss had observed that urogastrone *"produced a beneficial effect on experimental ulcers by promoting fibroblastic proliferation and epithelialization of the mucosa"*.

The role of histamine

The first experiments with histamine

The regulation of acid secretion, however, was to require a completely different route to establish a therapeutic basis for management. The unwitting initiator of the research which would lead finally to the development of the H2 receptor antagonists was Henry Dale.

Henry Dale (c. 1915). At the age of 29, Dale accepted a research position at the Welcome Physiological laboratory in order to obtain finance to marry. Henry Williams asked him *"that when Dale could find the opportunity for it without interfering with plans of his own, it would give him special satisfaction if he (Dale) would make an attempt to clear up the problem of ergot..."*. In 1936 Dale was awarded the Nobel Prize for his contribution with Otto Loewi to the chemical transmission of nerve impulses (acetylcholine).

"Beta-1, as we called it, is, of course, the now almost too familiar histamine; and this was always the obvious name for it. Somebody, however, had objected to its use, as infringing his trademark rights in a name to which its resemblance was, in fact, only distant. Later somebody called it histamine and then the road was clear".

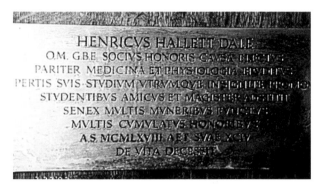

Epitaph: Trinity Chapel,
Cambridge. Sir Henry Hallett Dale
O.M., G.B.E., Honorary Fellow.
Equally learned in medicine and in
physiology, he signally advanced
both disciplines by his discoveries.
He stood by his students as friend
and teacher. After a long life with
many responsibilities he died in
1968 at the age of ninety-three.

Working with the chemist George Barger, Dale applied Kutscher's silver method to a specimen of ergot dialysatum and *"isolated a few centigrams of the picrate of an intensively active base, which produced a characteristic action on the cat's non-pregnant uterus in a minute dose"*. Barger and Dale identified the base as beta-imidazolylethylamine, and compared it with an authentic sample which had been obtained by the putrefaction of histidine.

The supplement of the Oxford English dictionary attributes the first use of the term "histamine" to the Journal of Chemistry, civ, 1913. Dale worked extensively in the area of the pharmacological and physiological actions of histamine between 1910 and 1927 but failed to detect his role in promoting acid secretion by the glands of the stomach.

It remained for Leon Popielski, a student of Pavlov's, to identify the acid secretory effects of histamine. After leaving Pavlov's laboratory in 1901, Popielski had been placed in charge of the military bacteriological laboratory in Moscow. His initial work was on the mechanism of the intravenous injection of Witte's peptone (a peptic digest of fibrin) in causing a fall of blood pressure. This research continued after he had become the Professor of Pharmacology at the University of Lemberg, and Popielski believed that he had identified a substance, "vaso dilantine", as a component of Witte's peptone distinct from histamine or choline. On October 28, 1916 in the course of experiments on the effect of the injection of an extract of the pituitary gland upon gastric secretion, Popielski injected 32 mg of beta-imidazolylethylamine hydrochloride subcutaneously into a dog with a gastric fistula. Over the next 5.75 hours, the dog secreted 937.5 ml of gastric juice having a maximum acidity of 0.166 N. Because similarly stimulated secretion was unaffected by section of the vagus or by atropine, Popielski concluded that beta-imidazolylethylamine acts directly on the gastric glands.

Due to the first World War, Popielski's paper describing these results was unfortunately not published until 1920.

Clinical relevance of histamine in gastric secretion

The key protagonist in the elucidation of the role of histamine and its clinical relevance in gastric secretion was Charlie Code. Code had grown up in Winnipeg and received an M.D. degree from the University of Manitoba in 1933. He worked at the Mayo Clinic with Frank Mann, then obtained support to study in London, where he first worked with Charles Lovatt Evans at the University College of London. In his further studies with Sir Henry Dale at the National Institutes for Medical Research, Code demonstrated that 70-100% of histamine in unclotted blood is in the white cell layer and that clotting liberates 60-90% of this into the serum.

Code continued to be fascinated by the effect of histamine and its bioactivity. Since its rapid disappearance from the blood made it difficult to study, he developed the technique of suspending histamine in beeswax which was then

Charles Code (c.1978).
Utilizing a unique blend of perceptive enquiry, rigorous investigative methodology and shrewd common sense. Code carefully defined the role of histamine as a principal physiological regulator of parietal cell secretion. In addition, his work on mucosal injury provided the basis for defining the pathogenesis of the ulcer lesion.

injected subcutaneously. The biological test for the effectiveness of histamine liberation was to measure the acid secretion of the animal. In these studies of histamine stimulated acid secretion from the Heidenhain pouches of dogs, Code was assisted by the surgeons Owen Wangensteen and Richard Varco. It became apparent that with increasing doses of histamine and increasing acid secretion, duodenal ulcers could be initiated not only in dogs but in a number of other animal species including chickens, woodchucks, calves, monkeys, and rabbits. Code concluded that the experiments incriminated gastric juice as the factor in the production of peptic ulcer and noted the relationship of histamine to this event.

Parietal cell mass, acid secretion and histamine

The precise relationship of histamine to acid secretion was firmly established by Andrew Kay of Glasgow who had developed the augmented histamine test. Mepyramine maleate was utilized to block the systemic effects of histamine. The ability of histamine to stimulate acid secretion was measured at a dose of 0.1 mg/10 kg of body weight and maximal acid secretion determined in different groups of patients. The dose response curves for acid secretion in human subjects in response to intravenous infusion of histamine were subsequently determined by Wilfred Card of the Western General Hospital in Edinburgh in conjunction with I.N. Marks.

Marks and Card then applied their method of estimating parietal cell mass to 17 patients with duodenal ulceration, chronic gastric ulceration or carcinoma of the stomach, whose stomachs had been removed at surgery. They were able to establish that the maximal acid output correlated with the parietal cell mass utilizing quadratic equation analysis. Thereafter, Marks working with Simon Komarov and Harry Shay at the Fels Research Institute of the Temple University of Philadelphia, was able to correlate the maximal secretory response of dogs to the estimated total parietal cell mass of each stomach.

The identification of effective antihistaminic agents

In parallel with the evaluation of the pathogenesis of peptic ulcer disease and the pharmacology of histamine, a strong interest developed in identifying agents which might prevent the action of histamine.

By 1957 a long list of antihistaminic agents had been proposed and studied by Keir and his colleagues without identification of an agent effective in the inhibition of acid secretion.

In 1966, A.S.F. Ash and H.O. Schild of the University College London stated:

> "At present, no specific antagonist is known for the secretory stimulant action of histamine in the stomach".

Wilfred Card (left) of Edinburgh and his young colleague I.N. Marks provided the basis for relating parietal cell mass to acid secretion. I.N. Marks a peripatetic and perspicacious scholar of gastric science defined the unique relationship between parietal cell mass, acid secretion and the likelihood of ulceration. His cautious approach to novel therapeutic strategies was characterized by the adage *"Mundus vult decipe, ergo decipiatur"*.

Clin. Sci., 1960, 19, 147.

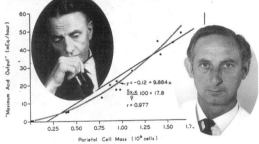

THE RELATIONSHIP BETWEEN THE ACID OUTPUT OF THE STOMACH FOLLOWING "MAXIMAL" HISTAMINE STIMULATION AND THE PARIETAL CELL MASS
By W. I. CARD and I. N. MARKS*
(From the Gastro-Intestinal Unit, Western General Hospital, Edinburgh, Scotland, and the Department of Medicine, University of Edinburgh, Scotland)

The structure of histamine and the modifications undertaken to produce cimetidine a clinically effective H₂ receptor blocking agent without the serious side effects of the earlier compounds.

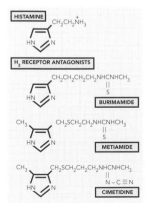

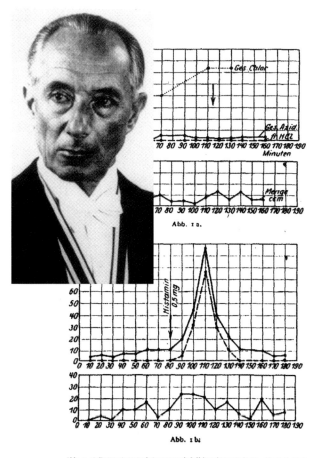

Abb. 1 a.

Abb. 1 b.

Abb. 1. a) Fraktionierte Ausheberung nach Coffeïnprobetrunk; b) Derselbe Patient bei fraktionierter Ausheberung nach Histamininjektion. Zeichenerklärung dieser und der folgenden Abbildungen: oberes Koordinatensystem Phenolphthaleinwerte·—·; ·—·—·; Dimethylamidoasobenzol; ●····● Gesamtchloride; ↓ Entleerung der Reizlösung beendet; ⡁ Histamininjektion; unteres Koordinatensystem ·—·; Menge Magensaft in Kubikzentimeter. Abszisse in beiden Systemen: Zeit in Minuten.

Gerhard Katsch of Greifswald (1887-1961). Katsch introduced quantitative gastric function tests (1925) with caffeine or histamine ("*kinetic method*") to evaluate gastric secretory capacity.

Ash and Schild suggested the symbol H1 for receptors that are specifically antagonized by low concentrations of antihistaminic drugs, implying that there is another class of histamine receptors, that mediates the acid secretory action of histamine.

At this stage, James Black a pharmacologist working for Smith Kline and French in Welwyn Garden City, England provided an observation of considerable significance. After synthesizing and testing "about 700 compounds" his group in 1972 announced that a compound (burimamide) which possessed an imidazole ring but with a side chain much bulkier than that of histamine antagonized the responses to histamine that were not antagonized by drugs acting on the H1 receptor.

Included in these responses were the inhibition of the secretion of acid. Black therefore proposed that there existed a homogenous population of non-H1 receptors that he chose to term "H2" receptors.

It was evident that burimamide inhibited pentagastrin stimulated as well as histamine stimulated acid secretion and Black suggested that H2 blockade might resolve the long debated question of whether histamine was the final common mediator of acid secretion.

The presence of histamine in the gastric mucosa

Thus, the wheel had turned the full circle from Pavlovian nervism to the moment of the chemical mediator. It was now clear that there was a chemical phase of the stimulation of gastric secretion in addition to the nervous phase which Pavlov had done so much to establish.

At a Ciba Foundation symposium held in honor of Sir Henry Dale in London on April 6 and 7, 1955, Charlie Code began his contribution by saying:

> "*An overwhelming mass of decisive evidence is now available showing that stimulation of gastric secretion is a physiological function of histamine*".

The evidence for histamine being present in the gastric mucosa had initially been presented by John Jacob Abel on April 25, 1919. Abel was convinced that all the "*motilines, peristaltic hormones, vaso dilantins and histamine-like substances in tissues were one and the same substance - histamine.*"

He succeeded in isolating and identifying histamine as the pictrate in extracts of the pituitary gland and stated that "*histamine is the essential therapeutically active constituent of the hypophysis*". Subsequently, Code demonstrated significantly more histamine in the oxyntic mucosa than in the antrum. Wilhelm

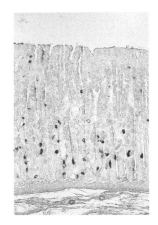

Histamine staining of the ente-rochromaffin like (ECL) cells in rat gastric mucosa.

Feldberg and Jeffrey Harris then sought the cellular locus of histamine in the gastric mucosa. The highest concentration was identified as near the lumen, where the parietal cells are at their greatest density, and in the region of the muscularis mucosa. In 1959, A. N. Smith, a Glasgow surgeon, found a similar distribution of histamine in the human gastric mucosa and noted that histamine had no higher concentration in tissues from patients with duodenal ulcer and high rates of acid secretion than in those from patients with gastric cancer and low rates of acid secretion.

R. Thunberg of Lund used a fluorescent method for detecting histamine in the mucosa and noted a high concentration in the region of the parietal cells and a low concentration in the submucosa. He noted that the cells in the submucosa were definitely mast cells but those lying close to the parietal cells did not stain like mast cells.

Eugen Werle had demonstrated in 1936 that an enzyme present in guinea pig tissues converts histidine to histamine by decarboxylating the substrate. The activity of this enzyme was characterized as the "histamine forming capacity" and it was believed that histamine formation and histamine storage occurred in the same cells. In 1965 R. S. Levine of Yale demonstrated that when histidine decarboxylase was blocked with a hydrazino analog of histidine, the histamine concentration within the gastric mucosa of the rat was reduced. Kahlson was convinced that histamine was essential for exciting gastric secretion and demonstrated that histamine forming capacity is labile. He demonstrated that the histamine content of the mucosa falls slightly when the rat is fed, and reaches its nadir when the histamine forming capacity is at its maximum.

Charles Best, who was later to achieve fame for his work in the area of insulin, had noted that histamine in fresh ox or horse lung rapidly disappears when the tissues autolyze at 37 °C. Best demonstrated that the disappearance of histamine is inhibited by cyanide and concluded that an oxidated process ruptures the imidazole ring. He called the enzyme histaminase but it was subsequently renamed diamine oxidase after it was noted to inactivate histamine by oxidative deamination. Code asserted that histaminase was absent from the gastric mucosa and that histamine brought by the blood or released within the mucosa is in a preferred position:

"a most propitious and essential circumstance if minute amounts of histamine are to have their full effects on the secretory cells".

THE INACTIVATION OF HISTAMINE.

BY C. H. BEST AND E. W. McHENRY

(From the Department of Physiological Hygiene, University of Toronto.)

THE transient effects produced . . . ravenous or subcutaneous injection of small or moderate . . . ine suggest that the body may possess an efficient . . . n or inactivation of this substance. When histami . . . intravenously, relatively large amounts can be adm . . . appearance of the characteristic signs which the . . . f small quantities to the same animal produce. It . . . t very little histamine is found in the urine even aft . . . injection of large doses of the substance [Oehme, 191 . . . ty that the amine may be eliminated by passage from th . . . to the intestine has not been investigated.

Charles Best (c.1928). Subsequent to his discovery in 1922 of insulin with Frederick G. Banting, he worked extensively in the area of histamine and described the enzyme, histaminase.

Studying histamine in the gastric juice of dogs and cats, Nils Emmelin and Georg Kahlson noted that it was present in the juice whether spontaneously secreted or in response to stimulation of the vagus, injection of acetylcholine or during the cephalic phase of digestion. They therefore concluded that the parietal cell activity no matter how stimulated, involved liberation of histamine into gastric juice and that histamine was the final common mediator.

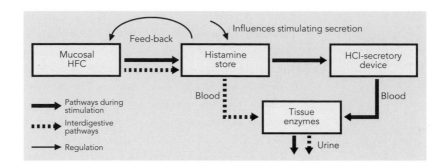

G. Kahlson's 1964 model of histamine synthesis and mobilization in the gastric mucosa.
He postulated a feedback control of the histamine forming capacity (HFC) of the mucosa by the histamine content of the mucosa itself. Some thirty years later the validity of this prescient suggestion appears confirmed by the identification of different histamine receptor subtypes on the ECL cell and their ability to regulate histamine secretion.

The discovery of hormones

Ernest Henry Starling (1866-1927) was a scientific pluralist of astounding intellectual vigour. His studies resolved the regulation of pancreatic function, lymph formation and peristalsis. In addition, he was the first to enunciate "the law of the heart". The novel observations of the existence of a chemical messenger system in his *Croonian Lectures* (1905) laid the foundation for the discipline of endocrinology. It is of interest that Starling stated "chemical means" could control not only "activity" but also "growth". It required almost a century for scientists to grasp the potential significance of growth factors as the new discipline of "cellular messengers".

Sir. William Maddock Bayliss (c. 1910) in the physiological laboratory of University College, London. He was the scientific partner of Starling for 30 years.

In 1902, Bayliss and Starling opened a new era in physiologic thought by demonstrating that there existed, besides the nervous system, a hormonal system for the integration of organ function. Prior to this proposal, it had been assumed that the physiologic regulation of function was entirely of neural origin. Three years later, Starling, in the delivery of his famous Croonian lectures to the Royal College of Physicians of London on "*The Chemical Correlations of the Functions of the Body*", was able to instance the discovery of gastrin as the second example, after secretin, of a hormone. In 1825, Francois Leuret and Jean Louis Lassaigne had demonstrated that after applying vinegar to the first part of the small intestine, biliary and pancreatic juice secretion was rapidly initiated. They postulated:

> "*If an acid stimulates duodenal secretions and dilates the ducts of the liver and pancreas, chyme ought to do the same thing for it is always acid*".

Some 70 years later, the fact that acid in the duodenum stimulates pancreatic secretion was rediscovered in Pavlov's St. Petersburg laboratory by his student, Ivan Leukich Dolinsky.

Secretin and gastrin

On the afternoon of January 16, 1901, William Bayliss and his brother-in-law Ernest Starling repeated Dolinsky's original experiments.

> "*In an anaesthetized dog, a loop of jejunum was tied at both ends and the nerve supplying it dissected out and divided so that it was connected with the rest of the body only by its blood vessels. On the introduction of some weakened HCl into the duodenum, secretion from the pancreas occurred and continued for some minutes. After this had subsided a few cubic centimeters of acid were introduced into the enervated loop of jejunum. To our surprise a similarly marked secretion was produced. I remember Starling saying: 'Then it must be a chemical reflex'. Rapidly cutting off a further piece of jejunum he rubbed its mucous membrane with sand in weak HCl, filtered, and injected it into the jugular vein of the animal. After a few moments the pancreas responded by a much greater secretion than had occurred before. It was a great afternoon*".

William Bate Hardy (1864-1934).
He first suggested the use of the word "hormone" - derived from the Greek "hormàein" - to set in motion, excite or stimulate. Starling adopted it as a descriptive term for his proposal of a class of chemical messengers.

Bayliss and Starling's conclusions were that acid liberated a chemical messenger from cells of the duodenal and jejunal mucosa and that the messenger travelling through the blood excited the pancreas to secrete.

They named this substance secretin and some years later at the suggestion of William Hardy utilized the word "hormone" to characterize a chemical messenger of this type.

In subsequent studies they demonstrated that extracts from the mucosa of the small intestine of dogs, cats, rabbits, oxen, monkeys, frogs and men stimulated the secretion of normal pancreatic juice whereas extracts of the ileum did not. In addition, they noted that secretin did not stimulate secretion of gastric juice or of succus entericus but that it probably stimulated secretion of bile.

These observations stimulated John Sidney Edkins, a teacher of physiology at St. Bartholomew's Hospital Medical School in London, to evaluate the control of gastric secretion.

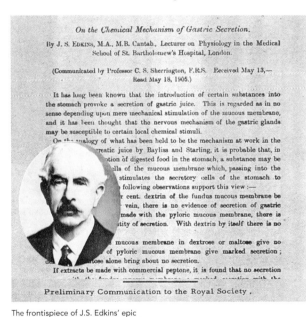

The frontispiece of J.S. Edkins' epic communication which documented the existence of a novel antral stimulant of acid secretion – gastrin (1905). Edkins entered Cambridge University as a scholar of Caius College in 1881. Such was his ability that he was awarded two scholarships; one in mathematics and the other in natural sciences. After Cambridge he worked with C.S. Sherrington in Liverpool (later to attain a Nobel Prize in Neurophysiology). Edkins taught with great distinction at St. Bartholomew's in London and subsequently became Chairman of Physiology at Bedford College for Women in 1914. In this capacity he was responsible for training the majority of women physiologists in England between 1914 and 1930. Apart from his fundamental observations in regard to gastrin he worked with Langley on pepsin. It is of particular note that he was not only a great oarsman but also a superb croquet player and President of the British croquet association from 1935-1937. The last subject that Edkins investigated was the presence of bacteria in the gastric mucosa and the changes they undergo during digestion.

Even prior to the studies of Bayliss and Starling and their description of secretin, Edkins had sensed that absorbed peptones might liberate a chemical messenger. His ruminations in this area led him to conclude that there might well be a "gastric secretin". On May 18, 1905 he obtained sufficient evidence to make a preliminary communication to the Royal Society on this matter. His recognition that there might be in the gastric mucosa, a pre-formed substance that is absorbed into the portal stream and returned to the circulation to stimulate the fundic oxyntic glands was a critical hypothesis. In a modest paper titled *On the Chemical Mechanisms of Gastric Secretion*, he described how various extracts of antral mucosa potently stimulated gastric secretion in anesthetized cats.

It was unfortunate for Edkins that a large number of distinguished investigators provided substantial and "apparently incontrovertible" evidence in support of the theory that the active principal in his extract was histamine.

More than a quarter of a century was to elapse before Simon Komarov in 1938 recognized the sad trick that nature had played on Edkins. In antral mucosa there is both histamine and a protein-like substance with a bioactivity that mimics the action of histamine on gastric acid secretion. Komarov precipitated with trichloroacetic acid, a diluted acid extract of antral mucosa and obtained a protein free fraction that was histamine free yet strongly stimulated gastric acid secretion. He thus rediscovered the antral hormone originally noted by Edkins.

Nevertheless, the concept of a hormonally mediated regulatory system in the gastrointestinal tract remained a considerable issue for Pavlov and the supporters of the nervism doctrine. In his biography of Pavlov, Babkin noted the turbulence generated by the observations of Bayliss and Starling as well as Edkins.

"I think it was in the fall of 1902 that Pavlov asked V. V. Savich to repeat the secretin experiments of Bayliss and Starling. The effect was self evident. Then, without a word, Pavlov disappeared into his study. He returned half an hour later and said: 'Of course, they are right. It is clear that we did not take out an exclusive patent for the discovery of truth' ".

Subsequent to this admission, a series of experiments were undertaken utilizing a unique dog model that Pavlov himself had constructed. In three successive operations, a Pavlov pouch, then a gastric fistula and a duodenal fistula were produced. In the third operation, Pavlov sectioned the pylorus between two clamps closing both the pyloric and duodenal stumps. Since the stomach was now separated from the small intestine, continuity was established by connecting the gastric and duodenal fistulas with a glass and rubber cannula.

The experiments demonstrated that food substances and (in particular meat extracts) in the stomach stimulated acid secretion by the Pavlov pouch. This led to the conclusion that the stomach might not be a single organ but represents a body component with one function and a pyloric unit with a separate biologic responsibility. Thereafter the *pars pylorica* was resected and confirmed histologically to have been completely removed. In a subsequent set of experiments when meat extract was put into the antrectomized stomach, the Pavlov pouch

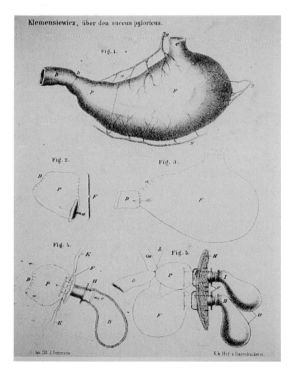

Klemensiewicz pouch (1875). Since it was difficult to study gastric juice without contamination by saliva, food or duodenal content. Rudolf Klemensiewicz of Graz constructed an isolated antral pouch and noted succus pyloricus to be alkaline and viscous.
Rudolf Heidenhain in 1879 was so impressed by this technique that he subsequently constructed a pouch from the acid-secreting segment of a canine stomach and noted the juice to be acid and contain pepsin.

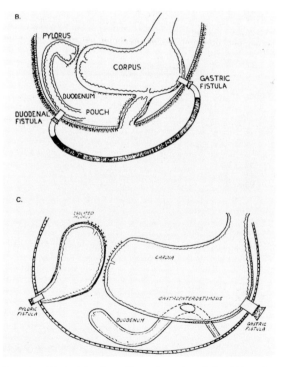

Examples of Pavlov's intellectual ingenuity and surgical ambidexterity (1906). B) In three successive operations a Pavlov pouch and gastric fistula were constructed followed by a duodenal fistula and then separation of the pyloric area from the corpus. In (C) a similar technique was utilized to produce an entirely separate pyloric pouch. Pavlov noted that meat extract in this "antral" pouch caused increased gastric secretion from the fundic pouch. This observation was consistent with Edkins' "gastrin" hypothesis but Pavlov did not pursue the issue of the nature of the chemical link, being of the persuasion that "nervism"was the only issue.

failed to secrete. It was then concluded that chemical stimuli act on the mucosa of the pylorus and not on that of the body of the stomach.

In a subsequent series of experiments, Pavlov made a pouch of the pyloric antrum in a dog that also had a gastric fistula and a gastroenterostomy.

He noted that introduction of chemical substances such as meat extract into an isolated and either innervated or denervated pyloric pouch resulted in a flow of gastric juice from the fundus. Sadly neither Pavlov nor any of his immediate students sought to identify the nature of the chemical messenger which linked the pyloric mucosa and the oxyntic cells.

The chemical identification of gastrin: Komarov

Simon Komarov had spent three years (1910-1913) in Pavlov's St. Petersburg laboratory. During this time he had met with Babkin who had come from the United States to work with Pavlov. When Babkin became the Professor of Physiology at McGill in 1930, he hired Komarov as his research assistant to work on the organic constituents of gastric secretion particularly mucus. It was at Babkin's initiation and with his support that Komarov undertook the series of studies which allowed him to finally identify and isolate the active extract of the antrum as gastrin. Komarov was a meticulous chemist and at crucial stages in his extraction procedure, he assayed the product by injecting it intravenously into anesthetized cats. He utilized boiled, minced hog antral mucosa extracted in 0.15 N HCl and after filtering the extract, precipitated the active component with trichloro-acetic acid. The acid was removed with organic solvents and the active components were re-dissolved in saline solution and once more precipitated by salting out with sodium chloride.

After numerous tedious repetitions of precipitation, extraction, salting out and further extraction, a powder that was a protein in nature was obtained. Komarov said it was free of choline and "organic crystalloids", but could say nothing further about its chemical nature. The product did not lower the blood pressure of anesthetized cats when injected intravenously and therefore did not contain histamine. Komarov believed that he was justified in calling it gastrin for this reason:

"In all cases without exception the pyloric preparation, injected in quantities equal to 5 gm of mucosa, elicited a copious secretion of gastric juice, which was characterized by high acidity and low peptic power and which was not affected by atropine even in large doses".

Komarov, in addition, identified a small amount of gastrin in the duodenal mucosa but none in the jejunal mucosa. These facts were long used to explain the intestinal phase of gastric secretion. He also noted that there was no gastrin evident in the oxyntic mucosa but a small amount present in the mucosa of the cardia. Once his manuscript had been published in 1938, it was evident that all parties except Ivy accepted the reality of gastrin as a chemical and physiological entity.

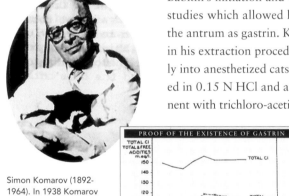

Simon Komarov (1892-1964). In 1938 Komarov successfully documented that gastrin existed as a chemical entity separate from histamine. It is reported that Edkins' widow attended a subsequent presentation of this work and expressed gratitude at the vindication of her husband's original observations. A graph from the original publication of S.A. Komarov in 1942 (Rev. Can. Biol.) demonstrating the acid response of an anesthetized cat to an intravenous injection of "gastrin" (histamine free antral mucosal extract) and the effect of atropine on the response.

The isolation and characterization of gastrin

Thereafter the further thrust of investigation in the area of gastrin related to attempts to isolate and purify the substance. Gregory and Tracy were the first to devise a method of extracting gastrin using trichloro-acetic acid in acetone. This produced a histamine free preparation and by using adsorption on a column of calcium phosphate gel and displacement by a gradient of phosphate, they obtained a product sufficiently pure to be tested on human subjects. Unfortunately, although the substance was more potent than histamine on a weight basis, it was apparent on paper electrophoresis that it was inhomogeneous. Thereafter they extracted a gastrin-like substance from a small pancreatic tumor of a patient with Zollinger-Ellison syndrome. Gregory demonstrated this work on April 26, 1962 at a meeting in New York at which Simon Komarov was the chairman.

The data on the amino acid composition and molecular weight indicated to Gregory that gastrin was a heptadecapeptide of about 2114 daltons.. On Christmas Day 1962, Gregory and Tracy noted that they had identified two gastrins instead of one. These were called gastrin I and gastrin II. With the help of Kenner they published the structure of the two gastrins in the December 5, 1964 issue of "*Nature*" and noted that the difference was that the tyrosine on gastrin II was sulfated.

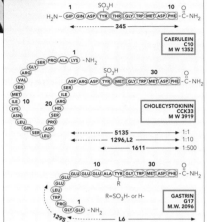

Rod Gregory (c. 1975) of London obtained a Rocke-feller Travelling Scholarship (1939-40) to work with A. C. Ivy in Chicago. Since he had been working in cardiac physiology, he translated the 1928 edition of Babkin's *Die äussere Sekretion der Verdau-ungsdrüsen* in order to increase his knowledge of gastrointestinal physiology. Prior to his work on gastrin he also investigated histamine with Code at the Mayo Clinic.
The diagram on the right shows the structure and sequence of gastrin. To facilitate communication the peptide sequences are numbered from the N terminal amino acid. Big gastrin, CCK and caerulein share many physiological properties since they possess the same C-terminal tetrapeptide.

Gastrin RIA could differentiate normal plasma levels from hyper-gastrinemia and by use of a secretin i.v. bolus identify a neoplastic source of gastrin arising from gastrinoma tumors.

Clinical and biological relevance of gastrin

It now remained to determine the clinical and biological relevance of gastrin. In 1958, Solomon Berson and Rosalyn Yalow published their manuscript documenting the use of radio immunoassay to measure plasma insulin.

In 1967, James McGuigan utilized the principle of this methodology to devise a radio immunoassay for gastrin. He refined the methodology further by developing a double antibody technique and was able to measure gastrin in human serum. Similar studies were undertaken by Hansky and Cain and it was apparent that different gastrin levels were evident in fasting versus fed patients or individuals with the Zollinger-Ellison syndrome.

The technique of the gastrin radio immunoassay was further modified by Yalow and Berson and it became apparent that plasma levels could differentiate between patients with various disease states.

In addition it was evident that hypergastrinemia associated with achlorhydria could be inhibited by oral administration of 300 ml of 0.1 N HCl by straw or by stomach tube.

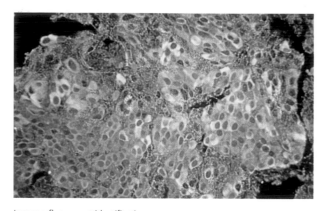

Immuno-fluorescent identification of gastrin cells. The use of immuno-fluorescent labeled antibodies to a specific peptide allowed a more precise identification of the secretory granules of a particular endocrine cell.

This confirmed the role of luminal pH in the regulation of antral gastrin secretion and of a class of HCl to antral glands.

The cellular site of gastrin secretion

Little, however, was known of the precise cellular site of gastrin secretion until 1967, when Enrico Solcia of the University of Pavia described a cell (the G cell) in the antral mucosa which he proposed as the site of gastrin secretion. He noted that the G cell had a distribution corresponding to that of gastrin being most numerous in the mid part of the pyloric glands. It was bottle shaped, with a narrow neck extending to the lumen of the glands between mucous secreting cells and its luminal surface was covered with a fringe of micro villi. Specific secretory granules, protein in nature, were present in the basal part of the cells which exhibited a well developed Golgi complex.

Using direct immuno-fluorescence methodology McGuigan was able to demonstrate that these cells contained gastrin. He noted that the immuno-fluorescence in the granules of the cytoplasm of the cells in the pyloric glands exhibited a distribution which corresponded to that of the G cells.

Subsequently both A.G.E. Pearse and W. Creutzfeldt conclusively demonstrated that the cells showing immuno-fluorescence when treated with a gastrin antibody were the argyrophil G cells.

Following the morphological and immuno-cytochemical localization of these G cells, numerous investigators attempted to relate alteration of the numbers of these cells to various disease processes. The condition of G cell hyperplasia was initially thought to represent a cause of peptic ulcer disease; whilst in conditions of achlorhydria significant hyperplasia of the G cells was felt to be related to the hypergastrinemia which accompanied pernicious anemia and atrophic gastritis.

Linkage between gastrin and histamine: the ECL cell as the source of histamine

Although the discovery of secretin by William Bayliss and Ernest Starling of London in 1902, provided the first scientific evidence that the gut was an endocrine organ, some of the histological and pathological aspects had been described prior to Starling's proposal. In 1867, Paul Langerhans of Berlin noted clumps of cells in the pancreas that were separate from the acini. These were later named the "islands" or "islets of Langerhans". The next year Rudolf Heidenhain of Breslau, Prussia found chromaffin cells (EC) in the gastric mucosa and in 1897 Nikolai Kulchitsky in Russia noted similar cells in the crypts of Lieberkuhn in the intestinal mucosa. The early literature thus abounds with complex descriptions of Heidenhain cells, Nicolas cells, Kulchitsky cells, Nussbaum cells, Ciaccio cells, Schmidt cells, Feyrter cells and Plenk cells. Broadly these cells were codified according to their staining properties (enterochromaffin, argentaffin, argyrophil, pale or yellow cells) and recognized

Neck of a gland from a human stomach (R.R. Bensley, 1928):
m = neck chief cells;
z = body chief cells;
p = parietal cells.

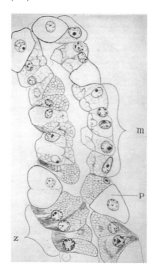

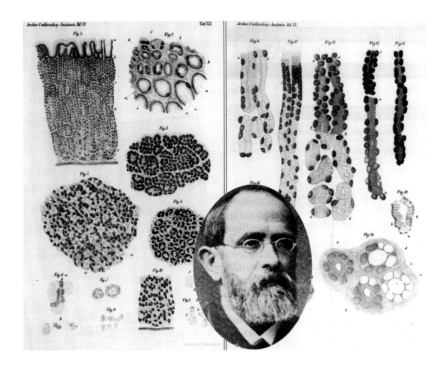

Rudolf Peter Heidenhain (1834-1897). An eminent physiologist and histologist, he described the secretory cycle of the chief cells and their production of pepsin as well as documenting acid production from the parietal cells.
Of particular interest was his identification of a third type of small, granulated, yellow staining cell on the surface of the gastric glands – almost certainly the ECL cell of today.

simply as being morphologically different to other intestinal mucosal epithelial cells. Later in 1914, Pierre Masson of Montreal found them to be argentaffin and suggested they formed "a diffuse endocrine gland" in the intestines. Unfortunately, fourteen years later he proposed that these cells were neuracrine and that they originated in the intestinal mucosa and subsequently migrated into the nerves. In the 1930's Friedrich Feyrter of Gdansk, Poland also described a diffuse endocrine organ which included the gastro-enteropancreatic (GEP) argentaffin cells and also many argyrophil cells. To these he attributed a paracrine function. Much later, Everson Pearse of London incorporated all of these different cell types into a group collaquation identified as the amine precursor uptake decarboxylation (APUD) series.

A careful perusal of the early writings and drawings of Heidenhain suggests that in 1870, he had first noticed the existence of the enterochromaffin-like (ECL) cell although was not able to define its role. Heidenhain's classic research on the structure of the gastric gland had noted that the "Labzellen" (rennin cells) were separate to a second type of cells which he termed "Hauptzellen" which formed the complete lining to the gland. Since he felt the "Labzellen" were more peripheral, he therefore renamed them as "Belegzellen". These two types of cells identified by R. Heidenhain and independently by Rollett, are now known as the parietal cell (Belegzelle) and the chief cell (Hauptzelle) respectively. It is, however, of particular interest to note that in addition to these cell types Heidenhain identified a *third type of cell in the form of minute oval elements found adhering to the external surface of the epithelial tube (gastric gland) and particularly conspicuous in preparations made with bichromate solutions in which they stained a deep yellow color*". These cells were noted to occupy a parietal position on the surface of the glands in both the rabbits and numerous other animals studied by Heidenhain and were particularly notable by the deep yellow stain which they took on with bichromate solutions. Similar observations were noted by Nicolas (1891), Kull (1924) and others in various portions of the alimentary tract and studied by Kull under the name of "the cells of Nicolas". Harvey and Bentley found that in fresh preparations these cells closely studded with minute granules which stained crimson in neutral red, or blue in the various Nile blues employed by them as indicators. They possessed a centrally located nucleus similar to that of other epithelial cells and were in all probability the same cells described by Twort (1924) under the title *The Demonstration of a Hitherto Undescribed Type of Cell in the Glands of the Stomach.*

Similar cells but in a somewhat different position in the gastric gland were identified by Nussbaum and Stohr and presumably may have represented other endocrine cell types of the fundus of the stomach.

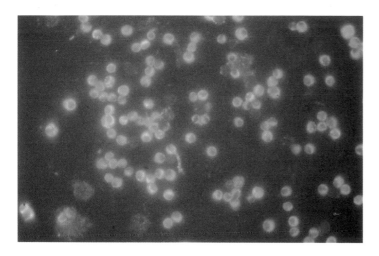

A pure preparation of isolated ECL cells, identified with fluorescent labeled histamine antibody. The novel ability to produce a pure isolated ECL cell preparation has facilitated the evolution of the investigation of the role of this cell in the regulation of parietal cell secretion. Since it contains substances other than histamine it may have as yet unanticipated functions in fundic mucosa.

By 1969, Forssmann was able to recognize at least five different types of endocrine cells both by ultrastructures and immunohistology (serotonin, glucagon, catecholamine, gastrin, and secretin containing cells). This observation contradicted the previous prevailing opinion that the enterochromaffin cell was the only endocrine cell type to be found in the gastric mucosa and that its sole product was serotonin. Indeed, within two years Hakanson and Capella independently identified the existence of histamine storing argyrophil cells in the murine stomach and noted their equivalent in other mammals and fish. The description in 1971 of the enterochromaffin-like histamine containing cell of the fundus of the stomach constitutes the first precise recognition of the cell in this era.

The histamine 2 receptor

The synthesis of H1 histamine antagonists had inaugurated the era of novel chemicals acting as agonists or antagonists of small molecule ligands that were useful clinically. The recognition that adrenergic receptors were divided into α and β subtypes led Black to the synthesis of the first β adrenergic antagonist, propranolol. It had been recognised that H1 antagonists were relatively inactive against gastric acid secretion and Keir postulated the presence of a H2 receptor subtype in the gastric mucosa. Black and his colleagues after 8 years synthesized the first H2 receptor antagonist, burimamide. The chemical difference between H1 and H2 antagonists is that the former contain major modifications of the imidazole ring, the latter modifications of the ethylamine side chain. The first successful H2 antagonist, cimetidine was launched in 1977.

CHAPTER 2
GASTRIC ACID SECRETION

One of the unique properties of the mammalian stomach is its ability to secrete large quantities of 0.16 N hydrochloric acid. This secretory process represents one element in an elaborate system that allows higher organisms to regulate their food intake. Gastric acid secretion represents the outcome of several regulatory signals. Secretion can be initiated by a wide variety of factors related to the ingestion of food and the caloric status of the individual. In most current texts of physiology the regulation of acid secretion is considered as occurring in "phases", which were previously termed the cephalic, gastric, and intestinal phases and believed to function in an overlapping manner in the regulation of acid secretion.

The terms implied that individual regulatory mechanisms originated in the central nervous system (cephalic phase) or in the periphery (gastric and intestinal phases). Since our current understanding of such mechanisms recognizes that both the central and peripheral components function as parts of an overlapping and integrated process, the use of the term phase has become inaccurate. The central regulation of acid secretion involves the cortical and spinal cord structures, peripheral regulation is defined as neural, endocrine and paracrine pathways. In this section we initially discuss the general principles of regulation of gastric acid

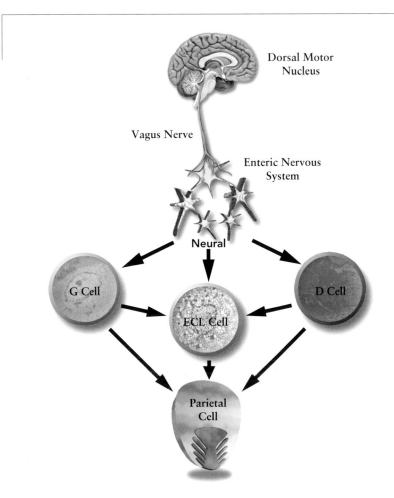

An illustration of the regions of regulation of gastric acid secretion, divided into central Dorsal Motor Nucleus (DMN), Enteric Nervous system (ENS), neural, endocrine and paracrine.

secretion by the brain, nerves and endocrine or paracrine cells. Thereafter we detail the transmitters and their effects on individual cells. Finally we outline regulation at the level of the parietal cell.

The complexity of neural, endocrine and paracrine regulation is illustrated in the following table, which displays ligands that have been shown to affect gastric acid secretion by direct action on gastric mucosal cells as well as their probable cellular site of action.

There is therefore a remarkable number of ligands used to control acid secretion in the gastric mucosa, showing that the process of digestion of food has been refined over the time course of evolution to a remarkably exact system.

The various ligands that have been shown to affect functions of isolated gastric cells. All of these also affect acid secretion in vivo, but understanding of their pathways has required studies on isolated cell, gland and organ.

Receptor	Cell Type				
	ECL	G	D	Parietal	Chief
CCK-A	No	No	Yes	No	Yes
CCK-B	Yes	Yes	Yes	Yes	No
PACAP	Yes	?	VIP	?	Yes
M1, 3, 5	Yes	Yes	No	Yes	Yes
M2, 4	No	No	Yes	No	No
GRP	No	Yes	Some	?	?
SST	Yes	Yes	Yes	Yes	Yes
Ca	?	Yes	?	?	?
Y1	Yes	?	?	?	?
GAL	Yes	?	?	?	?
Histamine	H3/H1	No	H3	H2	Species
CGRP	No	No	Perhaps	No	No
Aminoacids	No	Perhaps	No	No	No
pH	No	Perhaps	Perhaps	No	No

Central regulation

The central nervous system (CNS) particularly via the vagus is responsible for the initiation of acid secretion. Although it is well recognized that the sight, smell, taste, or thought of food can stimulate acid secretion, it is less appreciated that hypoglycemia itself comprises virtually the strongest central stimulus for acid secretion. Thus insulin is a powerful stimulant and its effect is mimicked by 2 deoxy-glucose which, by forming 2 deoxy-glucose 6 phosphate, effectively acts to inhibit glucose metabolism in the regulatory centers of the CNS.

There are two crucial events necessary for stimulation of acid secretion, activation of the parietal cell and increased blood flow. The stimulation of blood flow depends on the release of nitric oxide (NO) from the endothelial cells in the gastric vasculature and this may be due to stimulation by calcitorin gene related peptide (CGRP) or by histamine acting at a H2 receptor. Activation of the parietal cell depends on vagal stimulation of the enteric nervous system (ENS). All the interneuronal connections in the ENS are muscarinic since adequate doses of atropine ablate acid secretion induced by sham feeding or even thyroid releasing hormone (TRH) central injection. H2 antagonists in the rat can only block 60% of acid secretion due to sham feeding, therefore pathways other than those impinging on the ECL cell account for 40% of central stimulation of acid secretion.

There are several regions within the CNS responsible for detecting and transmitting central stimuli. The dorso-motor nucleus of the vagus (DMNV), the hypothalamus, and the nucleus tractus solitarius (NTS) have been identified as central structures that are key participants in the regulatory process. The final integration of central stimuli appears to occur in the DMNV, which supplies stimulatory efferent fibers to the stomach via the vagus nerve. Its destruction eliminates central stimulation of acid secretion, whereas electrical stimulation results in a strong secretory response. The DMNV appears to function as a central integrator of function and does not appear to initiate stimulation itself but rather to integrate central sensory input which arises primarily from the hypothalamus or as visceral sensory input from the NTS. Vagal efferents to the stomach arise also from the nucleus ambiguus (NA), but these appear to be primarily involved in regulating motility rather than secretion.

In the hypothalamus, several sites have been identified as exerting stimulatory and inhibitory influences on acid secretion. The ventro-medial hypothalamus (VMH) appears to exert a tonic inhibitory influence, since its ablation enhances secretion, while electrical stimulation suppresses secretion. The VMH appears to function by inhibiting the stimulatory signals arising from the lateral hypothalamus (LH) and adjacent medial forebrain bundle (MFB). The latter two structures mediate the response to the hypoglycemic stimulation of acid secretion. Both direct and indirect connections from LH and MFB to DMNV have been identified.

The NTS also responds directly to glucose deprivation and initiates stimulation of acid secretion mediated via the DMNV. In addition to the glucose deprivation response, the NTS also receives major other neural inputs which include taste fibers and visceral afferents which presumably participate in the modulation of the secretory process. The former probably initiate acid secretion related to taste. Visceral afferent input to the NTS arises primarily from synapses in the inferior ganglion of the vague. Greater than 95% vagal neural fibres are afferent rather than efferent. This means that visceral sensory input to the CNS plays an important part in the continuous central modulation of gastric function and is necessary to assure integration of CNS and peripheral mechanisms.

Sensory information from the stomach is relayed to the CNS by both vagal afferent fibers and sympathetic afferent fibers. The sensory receptors of the stomach consist primarily of unmyelinated nerve endings that detect mechanical (distension and touch), chemical, and thermal stimuli. Receptive fields for the sympathetic afferents appear to lie mainly within the smooth muscle layers and surrounding blood vessels. Despite this location, the sensory fibers are more sensitive to chemical (e.g., bradykinin) than to mechanical stimulation. The recognition that bradykinin is a mediator of inflammatory responses suggests that these sympathetic afferents encode painful sensations associated with gastritis and ulcers. This concept was initially recognized by Wolf and Wolff, in their observations of Tom, a patient with a permanent gastric fistula. Except for major distension, the normal stomach is relatively insensitive to mechanical and chemical stimuli at least in terms of pain. On the other hand, inflamed regions of the mucosa are quite sensitive to application of chemicals and even light touch. It is thus likely that the pain associated with gastritis may arise from the release of inflammatory mediators or the sensitization of sympathetic sensory fibers. In this respect the observation that the sympathetic receptors which respond to bradykinin also respond to capsaicin , the irritant component of cayenne pepper, may be of relevance. Capsaicin is a sensory neurotoxin which exerts its effects by opening calcium channels in the plasma membrane of sensory nerve endings. This first results in stimulation of the nerve but prolonged application leads to degeneration of the nerve fiber and loss of sensation.

Vagal afferent fibers are found in the smooth muscle layers and the mucosa of the stomach. The receptors in the muscle layers are primarily tension or stretch receptors capable of detecting motility changes. Although these receptors detect and regulate motility of the muscle layers, they also are involved in the vagovagal reflexes (so called long reflexes) associated with distension dependent secretory activity, an important element in the peripheral regulation of acid secretion.

Neural regulation of acid secretion

The primary function of the peripheral neural regulatory mechanisms is to modulate and integrate the stimuli (histamine and gastrin) which act directly on the parietal cell itself. This section therefore addresses the known neuronal factors involved in regulation of the parietal cell, directly or indirectly.

Cholinergic

The efferent fibers of the vagus nerve do not innervate the parietal cells directly but synapse with ganglion cells of the enteric nervous system (ENS). It is thus likely that the CNS serves to modulate the ENS regulatory mechanisms since there exists a great numerical disparity between efferent vagal fibers and ganglia of the ENS. Approximately 2,000 vagal fibers synapse with an estimated 10 million ganglia, suggesting that rather than exert any direct control of parietal cell function an intermediate class of modulators exists.

The majority of the cell bodies of enteric neurons are found in the two plexuses, the myenteric (Auerbach's plexus) and the submucosal (Meissner's plexus). Since the enteric plexuses of the stomach have not been studied in as much detail as those of the small and large intestine, a description of the organization and function of the gastric enteric neurons relies often on information gleaned from other segments of the gastrointestinal tract.

The myenteric plexus lies between the circular and longitudinal layers of smooth muscle and is primarily associated with coordination of motility. The sub-mucosal neurons supply nerve fibers directly to the mucosal cells as well as to the loosely arranged smooth muscle cells contained within the sub-mucosal layer. The sub-mucosal ganglia receive a variety of synaptic inputs which include projections from the myenteric plexus as well as extrinsic nerve fibers which consist primarily of post-ganglionic sympathetic fibers.

An important feature of the ENS, as with other components of the autonomic nervous system, is that the post-ganglionic nerve fibers are polymodal releasing two or more neurotransmitters. Individual nerve fibers may thus contain both a conventional neurotransmitter, e.g., acetylcholine (ACh) or norepinephrine, and one or more neuropeptides such as pituitary adenyl cyclase activating peptide (PACAP), galanin or calcitonin gene releasing peptide (CGRP). Whether both types of transmitter are released simultaneously or differentially is unclear, but this configuration provides opportunity for a single nerve fiber to engender a number of diverse responses. Another feature of many post-ganglionic nerve fibers of the ENS is that transmitter release can occur along an extended length of the nerve axon. This reflects the existence of periodic swellings or varicosities along the axon that are assumed to be the sites for transmitter release. Post-ganglionic nerve fibers and epithelial cells of the stomach do not exhibit conventional synapses, usually evident at the neuromuscular junction, although some nerve fibers terminate near the mucosal cells. This spatial organization suggests that transmitters are released into the extracellular space and diffuse to nearby cells where they may act if appropriate cellular receptors are present. The advantage of regional rather than conventional synapses is activation of several cells but possibly a number of divergent cell types as well as obviating the formation of new synapses as the epithelial or endocrine cells are replaced.

ACh exhibits a number of different actions when it is released from post-ganglionic nerve fibers in the fundic mucosa. Regional release of ACh activates parietal cells directly by binding to an M3 subtype muscarinic receptor. ACh stimulates some (10-20%) of the fundic enterochromaffin like (ECL) cells via an M1 receptor to release histamine, which in turn stimulates the parietal cell by binding to an H2 histamine receptor. In the gastric antrum, ACh is able to stimulate all the G cells to secrete gastrin. This hormone is conveyed via the systemic circulation to the fundus. At this site, gastrin activates the ECL cell via a gastrin/CCKB receptor to release histamine. In the antrum, ACh also inhibits the release of somatostatin from D cells, which removes a tonic inhibition of gastrin release and thus indirectly augments acid secretion by elevation of gastrin.

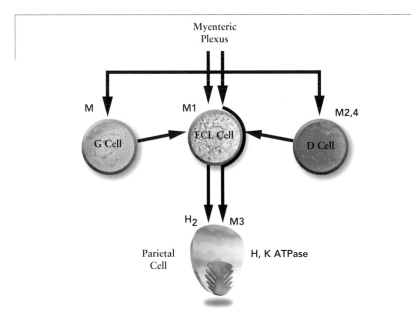

The actions of acetylcholine on the regulatory mechanisms of acid secretion. Atropine ablates acid secretion emphasizing the importance of muscarinic receptors. Pirenzepine and telenzepine are M1 antagonists also effective on acid secretion suggesting that the transmission in the myenteric plexus is via a M1 receptor.

Adrenergic

There is some evidence that the sympathetic fibres in the gastric mucosa are involved in regulation of blood flow and perhaps also are able to stimulate ECL cell release of histamine. In general, sympathetic innervation appears to play a minor role in regulation of gastric function.

Peptidergic pathways

A variety of neuro-peptides have been shown to affect acid secretion, such as gastrin releasing peptide (GRP), calcitonin gene related peptide (CGRP), galanin and pituitary adenylate cyclase activating peptide (PACAP). Some of these are targeted to one or other of the gastric endocrine cells. A problem that has arisen in interpretation of *in vivo* data is that both activating and inhibitory peptides can be released at the same time, thus confounding analysis of possible physiological consequences of their release.

Gastrin releasing peptide (GRP)

This is a member of the subfamily of peptides that terminate Leu-Met-NH$_2$ and is 27 amino acids in length. Immunoreactivity is found in nerves but not in endocrine cells in the intestine but it is also found in endocrine cells in the stomach. Vagal stimulation increases GRP in the venous outflow of the stomach and GRP antibodies or antagonists reduce gastrin release whether caused by vagal stimulation or peptone meals. There is therefore good evidence that GRP is an important non-cholinergic neural mediator of gastrin secretion. The release of somatostatin that is observed following GRP administration may be indirect, perhaps due to the effect of the elevated gastrin on the fundic D cell. Hence it is not surprising that the maximal effect of GRP on acid secretion is found in the lower regions of the dose response curve since at higher levels somatostatin release probably predominates. GRP stimulates Ca^{2+} signaling in an isolated G cell preparation. It might be expected that GRP would stimulate fundic but not antral D cells.

Calcitonin gene related peptide (CGRP)

This is a 37-residue peptide with a disulfide bridge and a C-terminal amide. CGRP immuno-reactive afferent nerve fibres are found in the gastric myenteric plexus, muscle, submucosal blood vessels and mucosa. The peptide inhibits gastric acid secretion whether given centrally or peripherally. The latter is probably due to stimulation of somatostatin release and no effect has been found in isolated rat ECL cells. Inhibition of acid secretion by injected CGRP must be due to effects on either antral or fundic D cells or both.

Galanin

This is a 29 amino acid peptide found in nerve endings in the gastric mucosa that inhibits basal and pentagastrin stimulated acid secretion.

There are three isoforms of the galanin receptor, one of which inhibits and the other apparently stimulates calcium signaling. Galanin inhibits gastrin release but also inhibits gastrin stimulated acid secretion. It does not inhibit bethanechol or histamine stimulated acid secretion. It therefore has an additional site of action distal to the G cell. Galanin interferes with stimulation of the ECL cell by a pertussis toxin sensitive pathway. This peptide has dual sites of inhibitory effect, both the G and ECL cell.

PACAP

The pituitary adenylate cyclase activating peptide is the newest member of the VIP/glucagon/secretin family. It is released from nerves although their location in the GI tract is not known. The PACAP receptor exists as several splice variants and PACAP stimulates Ca^{2+} signaling in pancreatic acinar cells showing that this receptor is coupled to both adenylate cyclase and phospholipase C. PACAP stimulates calcium signals and histamine release from the ECL cell. Several variants of this receptor have been shown to be present by RT/PCR of an ECL cell cDNA library.

Whereas injection of PACAP inhibits acid secretion, when this is done in the presence of anti-somatostatin antibody, stimulation of acid secretion results. D cells have VIP receptors, hence injection of PACAP will non-selectively release somatostatin. Local neural release will result in ECL cell stimulation and acid secretion. VIP nerves are presumably those that stimulate the D cell. PACAP also stimulates ECL cell growth as effectively as gastrin. Presumably its release is acute, that of gastrin chronic.

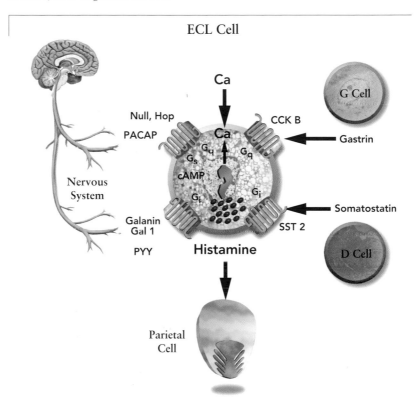

Major neural and endocrine regulation of ECL cell histamine release showing PACAP and galanin/PYY as the neural and gastrin and somatostatin as the endocrine mediators

The CCK-B and the PACAP receptor appear to be functionally the most important in terms of stimulation of histamine release from the ECL cell, the former endocrine the latter neural.

Vasopressin

This peptide also inhibits gastric acid secretion but only in the intact animal. Its action is exerted on gastric mucosal blood flow. Upon stimulation, there is a large increase in mucosal perfusion and this is essential for normal acid secretion. If blood flow is impeded with consequent relative hypoxia of the parietal cell, acid secretion is also inhibited.

Paracrine regulation

Histamine

Initially it was proposed that histamine is released from mucosal mast cells but more recent studies indicate that gastric histamine is released from a specialized endocrine cell of the stomach, the ECL cell. The release of histamine from the ECL cell is regulated by various factors involving neural, endocrine, paracrine, and autocrine pathways such as PACAP, galanin.

Somatostatin

The peptide is released from both fundic and antral D cells. The latter are more numerous. Somatostatin release is used almost universally as a down regulator of cellular function and therefore, although a peptide, must have a short half life to ensure organ specificity. This allows classification of this inhibitor as being a paracrine mediator of acid secretion.

Endocrine regulation

Gastrin

This is the major stimulatory peptide for histamine release from the ECL cell. It is present in the G cells of the antral gland, in about the mid-region in the human stomach. It is released from the G cell in response to aromatic amino acids or amines in the gastric lumen and in response to cholinergic stimulation or GRP released from post-ganglionic fibres of the vagus nerve. Acidification of the gastric lumen inhibits gastrin release. Although its effect on gastric acid secretion has been relegated to a secondary effect by stimulation of histamine release from the ECL cell, gastrin remains the major endocrine regulator of gastric acid secretion. Changes in circulating gastrin account for most of the gastric response to feeding.

Cholecystokinin (CCK)

This peptide is present in both the pancreas and duodenum and has a broad spectrum of activities. Of particular interest in terms of gastric physiology is its ability to stimulate the D cell and the chief cell of the gastric mucosa at high affinity on a CCK-A receptor. It is about equally effective as gastrin in stimulation of ECL cell Ca signaling and histamine release but the CCK-A octapeptide (non-sulfated) does not result in growth stimulation of the ECL cell *in vitro*.

Peptide YY (PYY)

This peptide was first isolated from the intestine. PYY and neural peptide (NPY) interact with three receptor subtypes, Y1, Y2 and Y3. PYY is released by meals and relatively large doses have been shown to inhibit gastrin stimulated acid secretion. This peptide may be a component of enterogastrone, a complex group of factors released during the intestinal phase of digestion resulting in inhibition of gastric acid secretion. The ECL contains the Y1 receptor subtype and histamine release and calcium signaling are inhibited by PYY.

Enterogastrone

Gastric inhibitory peptide (GIP) and glucagon like peptide (GLP) are thought to be components of the factors released during the intestinal phase of digestion that inhibit acid secretion. Relatively high doses of GIP and GLP inhibited gastrin induced signaling and histamine release from ECL cells.

Secretin

A complex feed back mechanism exists communicating to the stomach from the intestine. Secretin inhibits gastric acid secretion presumably in part by stimulation of the D cell. However it also inhibits, at least in some species, histamine stimulated acid secretion, indicating a direct action on the parietal cell.

Control of gastric acidity

The interaction of the triumvirate of the ECL cell, G cell, and D cell serves to regulate the release of histamine as illustrated in the simplified model of the figure.

A schematic model illustrating the regulation of acid secretion by interactions of the ECL, G and D cells with each other and with the parietal cell.

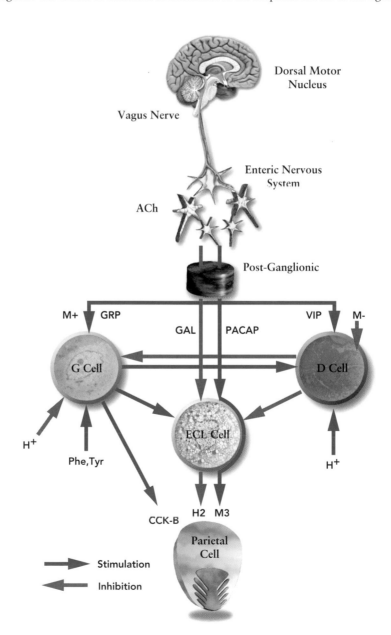

Since histamine together with ACh, and possibly gastrin, are responsible for the activation of the parietal cell and somatostatin, epidermal growth factor (EGF), galanin and secretin inhibit the parietal cell, the secretion of acid represents an example of neural, endocrine and paracrine positive and negative interactions. The overall goal of these processes is to regulate the acidity of the gastric contents. The regulatory mechanisms must be able to detect the intra-gastric pH and respond with celerity and accuracy.

The only known mechanism which at this time corresponds to such requirement is the suppression of gastrin release by pH <3.0. The low pH may in fact be detected by the antral D cell, and release of somatostatin resulting in the suppression of gastrin secretion. This relatively simple feedback loop between acid secretion and gastrin release appears to function *in vivo* as indicated by the observation that disruption of the loop by anti-secretory agents such as H2 receptor antagonists or pump inhibitors, culminates in hypergastrinemia. While the pH dependence of gastrin secretion represents the major known mechanism for control of gastric acidity, it is unlikely that so simple a feedback loop can account fully for the maintenance of gastric pH. Other mechanisms must be present if only to regulate those types of acid secretion which are independent of gastrin, e.g., due to direct ACh stimulation of the parietal cell.

Cellular regulation

The interplay between the different regulatory cells of the stomach has been largely elucidated by studies of responses to injection of substances *in vivo* and by studies of responses of isolated cells either in terms of calcium signaling or release of ligand. The figure summarizes many of the observations to be discussed.

Receptors of Gastric Endocrine Cells

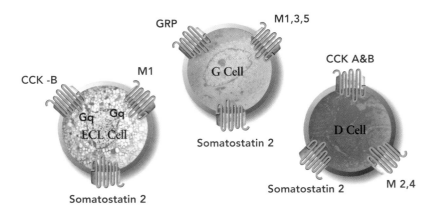

A few of the receptors defined on the gastric endocrine/paracrine system. The ECL and G cell upregulate acid secretion and the D cell.

Endocrine cells

The gastric mucosa is endowed with a rich array of endocrine cell types. At least seven distinct endocrine cells have been identified based on ultra-structural features: the enterochromaffin (EC) cell, the ECL cell, the D cell, the A cell, the P cell, the gastrin (G) cell and the X cell. As a group they represent approximately 2% of the cells in the fundic mucosa of the rat whereas in man they are somewhat less numerous (0.5-1%). In total, they constitute an

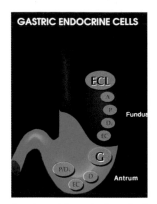

A cartoon of the endocrine cells of the antrum and fundus.
The critical relationship between the antral G cell and the fundic ECL cell is pivotal in the modulation of acid secretion.

endocrine organ approximately equal in size to that of the endocrine pancreas.

In humans, EC cells are found in the antrum and oxyntic mucosa. Their main secretory product is 5-hydroxytryptamine (5-HT). It is this monoamine which reduces silver and chromium, constituting the argentaffin and chromaffin reactions respectively. D cells secrete somatostatin and are distributed throughout the antral and oxyntic mucosa but are more numerous in the antrum. They display argyrophilic staining (i.e., they accumulate silver precipitates from a silver nitrate solution when treated with an exogenous reducing agent) and may be labeled immuno-histochemically using anti-somatostatin antibodies. Gastrin producing G cells are located in the antrum. They are argyrophilic and may be labeled using antibodies against gastrin. The X cells, the function of which remains unknown, are found almost exclusively in the oxyntic gastric mucosa. They are stained with amylin antisera and the Grimelius silver stain. D1 cells are so named because upon electron microscopy they display granules resembling those found in D cells. Similarly, P cells have granules which resemble those of pulmonary endocrine cells. Both of these cell types are found in the antral and oxyntic mucosa in man, and their biological function remain to be delineated.

Definitive study of the regulation of these cells has been difficult due to the fact that each group comprises less than 1% of the total mucosal fraction and they cross talk. It has been difficult to obtain pure preparations, except in the case of the ECL cell. A number of strategies have been utilized to produce enriched endocrine cell populations. Highly purified endocrine cells are necessary in order to prevent cross talk between cells when studying effects of ligands on release of transmitters. Single cell video imaging under superfusion conditions allows measurement of signaling in the absence of cross talk even in relatively impure preparations provided the cells being studied can be definitely identified. A means of purification or enrichment of different gastric endocrine cells is presented in the figure below. This strategy has been applied most

Method for Endocrine Cell Isolation and Evaluation

Methods for purification or enrichment of endocrine cells of the gastric epithelium, involving digestion, elutriation and either density gradient fractionation or fluorescent automated cell sorting (FACS) followed by short term culture to improve cell responsiveness. The cells are studied either for calcium signaling or for release of contents.

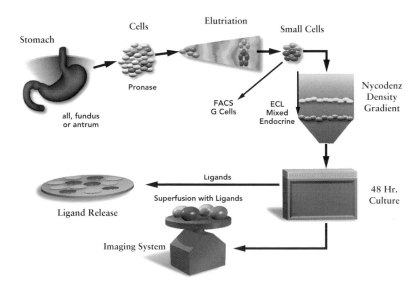

successfully to the ECL cell of rat mucosa producing a preparation containing up to 90% ECL cells. Since this cell plays a central role in stimulation of acid secretion, it forms the major focus of our analysis of gastric endocrine cells.

The ECL Cell

General characteristics

The enterochromaffin-like cell is the critical interface between the peripheral and central regulation of acid secretion. Its pivotal role is achieved by the secretion of histamine which appears to be predominantly activated by gastrin

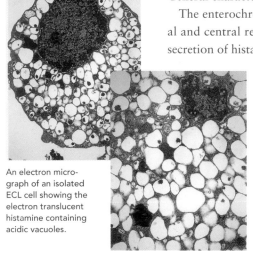

An electron micrograph of an isolated ECL cell showing the electron translucent histamine containing acidic vacuoles.

though influenced by PACAP and many other factors. There is evidence for at least 4 activating receptors in the ECL cell population isolated from rat gastric mucosa. The CCK-B and PACAP receptors are likely to be dominant in positive regulation of ECL function and therefore histamine dependent acid secretion as shown in the figure. Much of cholinergic mediation of acid secretion may be due to the direct effects of acetylcholine on the parietal cell itself as discussed later.

Somatostatin and galanin are major local inhibitors, with secretin and PYY playing a putative role.

Receptors for activation and inhibition of the ECL cell showing the refinement of regulation of one of the paracrine cells involved in regulation of acid secretion. It remains difficult to determine which of these regulators is functioning at any stage of gastric digestion.

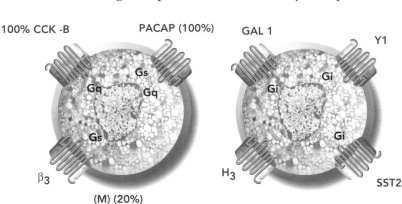

The ECL cells comprise about one third of the endocrine cells in the oxyntic (acid secreting) mucosa of most vertebrates. They are small, 8-10 μ diameter cells which contain numerous electron translucent cytoplasmic vesicles, many of which have an electron dense core. ECL cells store histamine and contain histidine decarboxylase, the enzyme required for histamine synthesis. The obvious role of the ECL cells is to release histamine, which acts as a paracrine agent to stimulate the parietal cells. It has been demonstrated that the vesicles contain other regulatory compounds such as chromogranin and pancreastatin but neither the specific compounds nor their functional significance have been defined.

The ECL cells are sub-epithelial and are not in direct contact with the lumen of the stomach. They are therefore not affected directly by gastric contents. The other cell type of the oxyntic mucosa that contains histamine is the mast cell that in different forms is found throughout the gastrointestinal tract. It was initially thought that a specialized type of mast cell was responsible for releasing the histamine associated with acid secretion since the mast cells were regarded as traditional source of histamine released in response to inflammatory processes. This mistaken assumption was refuted by the recent development of preparations of isolated purified ECL cells which allowed conclusive identification of the ECL cell as the source of the gastric histamine responsible for acid secretion. Although the role of the mast cell in acid secretion has been repudiated, it remains the cellular source of the histamine released during gastric inflammatory events.

ECL cells can be identified by silver staining techniques and more specifically by immunocytochemistry utilizing antibodies against histamine or histidine decarboxylase (HDC). In mammals, the ECL cells are only found in the acid secreting fundic mucosa, where they are most evident in the basal third of the mucosa. Their location is peripheral in the gastric gland and while they are found in proximity to parietal cells they appear to be particularly associated with chief cell rich areas. They were initially defined in 1967, by Hakanson and Owman who coined

A Northern blot of gastric fundus and parietal ECL cells demonstrating the large amount of HDC in the ECL cells.

the term *Enterochromaffin-like cell*. ECL cells constitute the major endocrine cell type in normal human gastric oxyntic mucosa, constituting $30 \pm 9\%$ of the endocrine cell mass of this region. ECL cells display immunoreactivity for antibodies against a wide array of markers including chromogranin A, neuron-specific enolase, calbindin and the α subunit of human chorionic gonadotrophin.

ECL cells take up and decarboxylate a variety of aromatic amino acids, e.g. exogenous 5-HT, L-3,4-dihydroxyphenylalanine (L-DOPA), and store the respective amine formed. This ability categorizes ECL cells as belonging to the amine precursor uptake and decarboxylation (APUD) family of endocrine cells. The histamine forming enzyme, histidine decarboxylase, can be detected together with histamine in ECL cells.

ECL cells exhibit a unique and characteristic structure. They are irregular in shape with numerous and prominent cytoplasmic extensions. There is a large eccentrically located nucleus surrounded by numerous electron translucent vesicles with eccentric granules. Additionally electron dense granules are present. The distinction between these two cytoplasmic inclusions may either reflect stages in the processing of one product or the packaging of different products to different organelles. The transparent vesicle generates an internal acidity and accumulates histamine driven by the acid gradient.

ECL Cell function

The response of the ECL cell to a variety of agents can be divided into 3 phases, acute, intermediate and chronic relating to release of histamine, histamine homeostasis and cellular response to histamine demand as shown in the next figure.

Not only is the ECL cell the central player on the stage of acid secretion, it has also stolen much of the limelight from other regulatory cells due to now outdated questions as to the safety of proton pump inhibitors.

Major Activating and Inhibitory G7 Receptors on Rat ECL Cells and Time Course of Gastrin Effects

Gastrin   ACh   PACAP

ECL Cell

Galanin   Y1   Somatostatin

Gastrin

Seconds	Minutes	Hours
Histamine Release	Histidine Decarboxylase	Growth

The major receptors on the rat ECL cell and the different phases of ECL cell responses to gastrin (and PACAP). Histamine release is virtually instantaneous, histidine decarboxylase is rapidly up-regulated and after some hours ECL cell DNA synthesis is stimulated following gastrin administration.

Histamine

Of all the agents identified in or secreted by the ECL cell, histamine is of the most physiologically relevant. The principal regulator of histamine secretion is gastrin. In the isolated ECL cell preparation stimulation of histamine release by the addition of gastrin is detectable within 5 minutes. An initial peak at 5 minutes is evident and thereafter release is linear for at least 60 minutes. An overall 3-5 fold increase of histamine over baseline is detectable. The EC_{50} for gastrin stimulation of histamine release is 3×10^{-10} M and cholecystokinin (CCK) is equipotent in stimulation of histamine release. Histamine release can be blocked by a variety of CCK-B antagonists (L365,260, $IC_{50}=5\times10^{-8}$ M) but very high concentrations of CCK-A antagonists (L364,718) are required for blockade of histamine secretion consistent with the presence of a CCK-B receptor rather than a CCK-A receptor on the ECL cell membrane. The general tyrosine kinase inhibitor, genistein (10^{-4} M), had no effect on gastrin stimulated histamine secretion although it blocked gastrin induced proliferation.

The accumulation of histamine within the granules of the ECL cell depends upon an acid gradient generated by a V-type ATPase driving histamine uptake across an amine transporter. The vesicular monoamine transporter VMAT2 subtype but not the VMAT1 subtype is expressed in the fundic epithelium perhaps because of some preference for diamines such as histamine. The expression of VMAT2 is upregulated in low acid states, probably by a mechanism secondary to hypergastrinemia. Current information is consistent with an ECL cell localization of this VMAT2 subtype in the rat gastric corpus.

The ECL cell possesses the enzyme histidine decarboxylase which is the only enzyme involved in histamine biosynthesis. The enzyme is stimulated *in vivo* by a gastrin induced increase in gene transcription. It has been proposed that the rapid elevation induced by gastrin *in vitro* suggests that, besides an increase in gene transcription, there may also be activation of pre-existing enzyme as has been described in the regulation of other decarboxylases.

ECL Cell

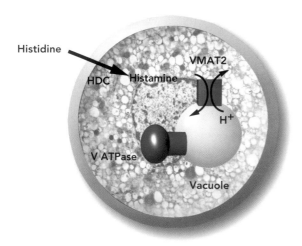

Histidine   VMAT2   HDC   Histamine H^+ V ATPase   Vacuole

Histamine biosynthesis and accumulation in the secretory vacuoles of the ECL cell. Histidine is taken up and decarboxylated to histamine by HDC. The histamine is accumulated in the vacuole due to the H^+ gradient formed by a V type ATPase and the presence of a histamine countertransport protein in the vacuolar membrane.

Stimulation of histamine release

Histamine is released by a direct action of gastrin at physiological concentrations. The gastrin receptor associated with histamine release has been characterized pharmacologically as being of the CCK-B subtype. The CCK-B subtype receptor recently has been cloned from canine parietal cells and rat brain as well as rodent ECL cells and shows typical signature sequences for a guanine nucleotide binding protein (G protein) coupled receptor as does the CCK-A subtype receptor. Typically, trimeric G protein coupled receptors are linked to alterations of intracellular cAMP or calcium. Gastrin stimulation of the ECL cells was shown to be associated with an elevation of intracellular calcium.

Histamine release from isolated ECL cells is also stimulated by PACAP as effectively as gastrin. This neuropeptide elevates intracellular Ca to a level similar to that of gastrin with essentially the same time course as shown in the figure.

The regulation of [Ca], by PACAP and gastrin in the ECL cell, showing the characteristic biphasic response. The initial transient is due to release of calcium from intracellular stores, the steady state is due to enhanced Ca entry from the medium.

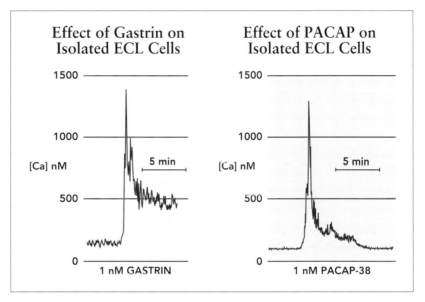

Given that at best ACh is a weak stimulant of a population of ECL cells, PACAP may be the significant neural mediator of histamine release by the ECL cell.

Forskolin, a stimulant of cAMP production, is also effective in releasing histamine and the action of PACAP may combine both cAMP and Ca elevation. Although injection of PACAP appears to inhibit acid secretion, simultaneous administration of somatostatin neutralizing antibody turns this inhibition into stimulation. Hence injected PACAP may stimulate both the D cell and ECL cell, a finding also found in *in vitro* models. This D cell stimulation is presumably at a VIP receptor, whereas the stimulation of the ECL cell is at a PACAP receptor.

The physiological significance of ECL cell stimulation by β adrenergic agonists is unclear, but may indicate multiple neural factors for regulation of the function of this cell. There is some evidence that the β-receptor on the ECL cell is of the β3 subtype.

The amount of histamine released from a single ECL cell is extremely small. The total histamine content of an ECL cell is estimated to be on the order of 30 fmol and ~3% of the content, or 1 fmol, is released per hour under constant stimulation *in vitro*. It is not surprising, therefore, that it has been difficult to detect histamine in the blood during acid secretion or that the histamine release from ECL cells does not result in any systemic effects. The local concentration of histamine required to maximally stimulate the parietal cells is on the order of 1 pM. After ECL cell stimulation, this concentration must be achieved within a few minutes, suggesting that the volume of extracellular fluid supplied by a single ECL cell must be exceedingly small (1 nl or less). Thus the distance over which a single ECL cell regulates acid secretion may be very limited, perhaps only a few microns. Because the ECL cells are distributed primarily in the lower portion of oxyntic glands, it is possible that activation of more distant parietal cells may be achieved either by the cells having long dendritic processes or by transport of histamine in the microcirculation. At present there is little evidence to support either postulate.

Interleukin 1-β, an inflammatory lymphokine involved in gastritis, induces histamine secretion from ECL cells. It is proposed that interleukin 1-β, may be responsible for modulating peripheral acid secretion during *H. pylori* infection.

Inhibition of histamine release

Somatostatin at physiological concentrations inhibits gastrin stimulation of histamine release from ECL cells. Natural somatostatin, somatostatin-14, and a synthetic agonist, selective for the subtype 2 somatostatin receptor, were effective in inhibiting histamine release and the steady state rise of $[Ca]_i$ due to stimulation by gastrin. This result indicates that somatostatin acts through a subtype 2 receptor to block gastrin induced calcium entry into the ECL cell. Somatostatin is known to be a physiological inhibitor of acid secretion and its inhibition of histamine release would account for this inhibitory action. Pertussis toxin preincubation blocks the action of somatostatin showing that the G7 receptor binding somatostatin is G_i coupled.

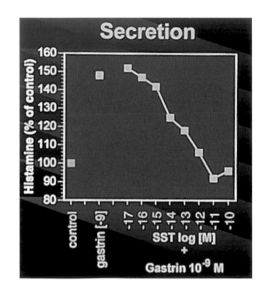

Somatostatin inhibits acid secretion *in vivo* also by blocking gastrin release from antral G cells. Somatostatin inhibits histamine stimulated acid secretion *in vitro* in isolated gastric glands and parietal cells where the release of gastrin is not involved. It has been suggested that somatostatin acts directly on the parietal cells, but part of the inhibitory action could result from somatostatin modulation of ECL cell activity.

The exact source of somatostatin acting on the oxyntic mucosa has been matter of some debate since cells containing somatostatin, D cells, are present both in the antrum and the oxyntic mucosa. Additionally, postganglionic nerve fibers in the submucosa contain somatostatin which may act as a neural transmitter. Since mucosal D cells, both in the antrum and fundus, possess elongated basal processes, somatostatin released locally may function as a paracrine regulator.

The inhibition of gastrin stimulated histamine secretion from ECL cells by somatostatin.

In addition to somatostatin, the release of histamine from ECL cells is inhibited by histamine itself. The histamine H3 receptor agonist, α-methylhistamine, inhibited while the H3 receptor antagonist thioperamide potentiated gastrin stimulated histamine release. This suggests an autocrine feedback regulation of ECL function but this has not been shown to occur physiologically.

The neuropeptide galanin is found in gastric neurons and gastric nerves. It potently inhibits histamine release from ECL cells and may be the important neural mediator for shut down of ECL cell function at the end of gastric digestion. The figure illustrates the inhibition of histamine release found when galanin is added to a purified rat ECL cell preparation. Tolerance is also evident.

The effect of galanin and galanin fragments on histamine release from ECL cells, showing that galanin is an effective neuropeptide inhibitor of ECL cell function and that the receptor is a Gal 1 receptor based on a lack of response to gal 9-29.

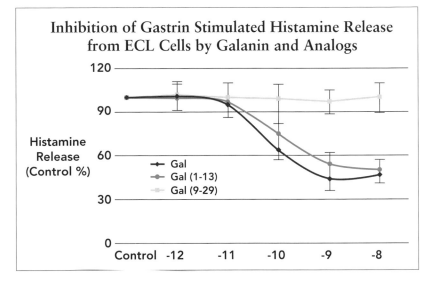

Inhibition of Gastrin Stimulated Histamine Release from ECL Cells by Galanin and Analogs

Histamine Release (Control %)

- Gal
- Gal (1-13)
- Gal (9-29)

Control -12   -11   -10   -9   -8

Human gastric mucosa expressses galanin receptor mRNA and this peptide may be important in neurally mediated inhibition of acid secretion. In order to determine whether galanin affects the ECL cell directly, the effect of the peptide was measured on calcium signaling and histamine release. Galanin dose dependently inhibited gastrin stimulated histamine release with an IC_{50} of 10^{-10} M as did the N-terminal (1-13) fragment of galanin with tenfold lower affinity. Pertussis toxin (PTX) partially blocked this inhibitory effect as did one galanin inhibitor, galantide, but not other galanin inhibitors such as galanin spantide I or galanin (1-13)-pro-pro-(ala-leu)2-ala. Both Ca^{2+} release and elevation of Ca^{2+} entry due to gastrin stimulation of the CCK-B receptor were blocked by equimolar concentrations of galanin. Inhibition of gastrin stimulated histamine release from the ECL cell is the likely mechanism of acid secretory inhibition by galanin *in vivo*. The pharmacology of this galanin receptor on the ECL cell distinguishes it from the brain receptor.

PYY is a peptide released from intestinal endocrine cells and has been found to be an effective inhibitor of calcium signaling and histamine release in isolated rat ECL cell preparations. Gastrin stimulated histamine release was inhibited with an IC_{50} of 2×10^{-9} M. The finding of inhibition of histamine release and of calcium entry by PYY and [Pro34]-PYY and no effect of PYY (3-36) identified the presence of an inhibitory Y1 receptor subtype. RT-PCR of ECL cell RNA showed that the receptor was the non-truncated Y1 isoform. The inhibitory action of PYY and related peptides on gastrin stimulated histamine release and calcium signalling was abolished by pretreatment with pertussis toxin (PTX) at 200 ng/ml. Additive, but not synergistic, inhibitory effects of PYY and somatostatin on gastrin-stimulated histamine release were observed. Therefore activation of a Y1 inhibitory receptor subtype present on the gastric ECL cell that inhibits gastrin induced ECL cell histamine release and Ca^{2+} entry by activation of a Gi or Go class of protein, may account for inhibition of gastric acid secretion by PYY released from the small intestine (enterogastrone).

The insulin receptor-related receptor (IRR) is a member of the insulin receptor family and has a primary structure similar to the insulin receptor (IR) and the insulin-like growth factor-1 receptor (IGF-1R). In contrast to the widespread expression of IR and IGF-1R, the expression of IRR mRNA is highly restricted to the kidney (cortical renal tubules) and stomach (oxyntic gland area). Utilizing *in situ* hybridization, IRR mRNA has been localized to the basal third of oxyntic fundic glands, where it was co-localized with mRNA for histidine decarboxylase, a marker for ECL cells. Although the function of IRR is not known, the localization of the IRR to the ECL cell suggests that it may play an important role in these cells.

The following table summarizes some of the properties of the major inhibitors of ECL cell function that have been described.

The inhibitory ligands for the ECL cell showing the subtype expressed and their effects on calcium and histamine, as well as their pertussis toxin sensitivity (G_i coupling).

Ligands	Inhibitors of ECL Cells			
	Gal	PYY	SS	His3
R Subtype	Gal 1	Y_1	$SSTR_2$	H3
Ca/Release	Yes	No	Yes	Yes
Ca/Entry	Yes	Yes	Yes	Yes
Histamine/Basal	Yes	No	Yes	?
Histamine/Stimulated	Partial	Partial	Complete	Complete
PTX sensitive	Partial	Complete	Complete	?

Signal transduction

The cascade of the second messenger system for histamine release in the ECL cell has not been characterized. Isolated ECL cells studied in a perfusion chamber exhibit a biphasic increase in intracellular calcium when exposed to gastrin or PACAP. An early transient presumably due to the release of calcium from intracellular stores is followed by a steady state increment due to calcium entry. Blockade of calcium entry by La^{3+} blocks histamine release. It is likely that the increase in cell calcium causes the activation of a variety of calcium dependent signalling pathways including protein kinase C. The C kinase activator, the phorbol ester, tetradecanoyl-13-phorbol acetate (TPA) stimulates histamine release, supporting the proposal that this protein kinase is a component of the calcium dependent histamine stimulation pathway. Since forskolin (an intracellular stimulant of adenylate cyclase) is also a potent agonist of histamine release, a role for cAMP in histamine secretion is likely. This proposal is supported by increased cAMP levels in forskolin stimulated ECL cells

Stimulation of ECL cells by gastrin results in granule exocytosis. The granule membrane contains a V-type ATPase which generates an electrochemical gradient of protons at the expense of ATP. The identification of red fluorescent acridine orange-loaded granules dependent on this acid gradient may be used to assess ECL cell enrichment during the preparation of isolated ECL cells from the gastric fundic mucosa. This pump is electrogenic and therefore requires an ion conductance in parallel to generate an acid gradient. Since the histamine granule is acidic it is likely that this is due to either a K^+ or Cl^- conductance in its membrane. It is probable that the chloride ion serves as the co-ion for the H^+ transported by the V-ATPase in the membrane of the secretory granule since the cytoplasm of the cell has a high K^+ concentration and a K^+ gradient would be in the incorrect direction for it to function as an effective co-ion. During exocytosis the granule membrane fuses with the ECL cell plasma membrane and in doing so acquires a Cl^- conductance. Whole cell current analysis of the ECL cell has shown a resting potential of ~ -50 mV in contrast to the mast cell which has a potential close to zero. This potential is due largely to the activity of a depolarization activated K^+ current which also maintains the potential difference after stimulation of exocytosis. Gastrin, CCK-8 and TPA, which all increase histamine secretion presumably by stimulation of exocytosis, activate a Cl^- current which is thought to represent the fusion of the histamine vesicle with the plasma membrane. Increased medium $[K^+]$ has been noted to result in stimulation of histamine release.

The formation of histamine containing vesicles involves accumulation of histamine via the H^+/histamine antiporter which results in accumulation of active osmolytes. The vesicles grow in size during the process of fluid accumulation consistent with their accumulation of histamine. When the ECL cells are activated by acute gastrin stimulation, both histamine and pancreastatin in the vesicles are released via exocytosis.

Histidine decarboxylase regulation

A role for histamine regulated HDC activity in histamine secretion was initially postulated by Kahlson in 1964. Histamine secretion and synthesis are intimately coupled, and store depletion is often the signal for enzyme synthesis. HDC activation may be initiated by such an event. A second possibility is that the secretory signal cascade initiated by ligand binding results in enzyme activation. The initial histamine secretory response (exocytosis) is followed by a linear HDC activation, suggesting that HDC activity is responsive to histamine secretion. However, the synthesis of newly transcribed HDC mRNA, may also occur in an *in vitro* setting and thus play a role in the synthesis of histamine.

Gastrin appears to play a significant role in the regulation of HDC. Histidine decarboxylase is a homodimeric pyridoxal phosphate dependent enzyme that produces the physiological 1,4-diamine, histamine. Mammalian HDC's exhibit extensive homology with the aromatic amino acid decarboxylase which produces serotonin and tryptamine. These enzymes share common catalytic properties. However, there is little sequence homology between these enzymes and the putrescine producing ornithine decarboxylase (ODC). Both HDC and ODC have short half lives, and there is in both a PEST (proline-glutamyl-serine-threonine) region which confers constitutive degradation and polyamine responsiveness in both proteins. Histamine indeed, is known to behave like a polyamine analogue and is able to regulate ODC, intracellular polyamine levels, and cell growth *in vivo* and *in vitro*.

In vivo studies indicate that ECL cell HDC activity and histamine concentration are directly dependent on circulating gastrin levels. Gastrin induced activation of HDC is associated with a progressive increase in the level of HDC mRNA *in vivo*. This gastrin evoked increase in HDC mRNA was slower and less marked than the increase in HDC activity. Fasting reduced HDC message by 3- to 4-fold after 48 hours while re-feeding induced a rapid increase in message that was detectable within 30 minutes by RT-PCR. HDC enzymatic activity and mRNA abundance varied in parallel, suggesting that HDC mRNA was important in the overall regulation of gastric mucosal HDC activity.

In an isolated culture of ECL cells a linear increase in gastrin stimulated HDC activity was noted over 60 minutes. HDC levels were elevated up to 3-fold during this time. In a similar system of acutely isolated ECL cells it has been noted that gastrin stimulated HDC activity with an EC_{50} of 10^{-10} M and an EC_{max} of 10^{-8} M. Maximal stimulation resulted in a time-dependent increase of HDC activity with linear kinetics up to 30 min, and no further increase between 30 and 60 min. In basophil leukemia cells, phorbol esters have been noted to increase HDC gene expression after 2-4 hours of incubation by 50% due to increased protein synthesis. The accelerated time course and amplified levels of HDC noted in ECL cells suggest that a second factor such as post-translational activation of HDC might be involved rather than only stimulation of HDC synthesis.

ECL cell ontogeny

Studies using an o-pthalaldehyde method (low sensitivity and specificity for histamine detection) failed to detect developing ECL cells in embryonic gastric mucosa. Detectable ECL cells only appeared at the end of the first postnatal week. After birth, an accelerated production of ECL cells was evident until postnatal day 21 (P21) by which time levels and distribution were similar to those noted in adult animals. During this period of expansion, ECL cells undergo a number of developmental and structural changes. By P3, mucosal ECL cells display long, thin processes traversing the length of gastric glands, making contact with glandular cells. By P7 an increase in the overall proportion of ECL cells possessing "paracrine-processes" was evident, and by P14 almost no histamine or histidine decarboxylase immuno-reactive cells were detectable in the upper third of gastric glands. These now displayed a morphology similar to that of adult rats. By P14 the majority of ECL cells had formed aggregates in the basal parts of the glands.

Regulation of ECL cell proliferation

The biological relevance of ECL cell hyperplasia or carcinoids had been recognised for many years in the context of the massive hypergastrinemia associated with pernicious anemia and atrophic gastritis. Growth of ECL cells assumed more significance when identified in the context of the elevated gastrin levels associated with the use of the proton pump inhibitor class of drugs in rats.

1. Gastrin

It is apparent that in addition to stimulating histamine release, gastrin acts as a trophic factor for the ECL cell. Indeed, the hypertrophic and hyperplastic responses of the ECL cell to gastrin became notorious due to the development of ECL cell carcinoids after life long therapy with anti-secretory drugs in rats. While first thought to be a side effect of specific anti-secretory agents, it is now apparent that ECL cell proliferation may occur in any condition resulting in a prolonged elevation of plasma gastrin levels.

The response of the ECL cell to gastrin may be regarded as exhibiting acute, intermediate and chronic phases within which histamine secretion, HDC activation and lastly DNA synthesis occur. Of particular relevance here is the ability of gastrin to stimulate ECL cell hypertrophy, hyperplasia and ultimately neoplasia. The life long administration (2 years) of high doses of acid inhibitory agents in rats is associated with the development of ECL tumors (ECLoma, gastric carcinoids). The changes that the ECL cell undergoes during this time period range from a diffuse hyperplasia through focal aggregation of cells to structures of a more solid appearance culminating in gastric carcinoids. The rat ECL cell exhibits a 4-5 fold increase in numbers compared with a ~30% increase in the oxyntic mucosal thickness in response to gastrin. No other oxyntic endocrine cell increases in number in response to gastrin.

Sequence of Gastrin Effects on ECL Cells

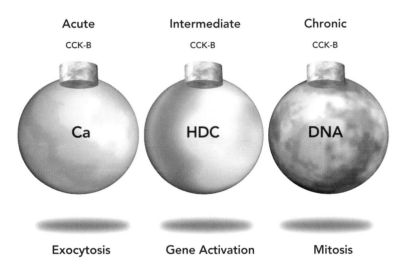

The time of onset of the three major studied effects of gastrin on the ECL cell.

Acute	Intermediate	Chronic
CCK-B	CCK-B	CCK-B
Ca	HDC	DNA
Exocytosis	Gene Activation	Mitosis

In rats treated with the H2 receptor antagonist ranitidine or the long acting H2 receptor antagonist BL-6341 hydrochloride, hypergastrinemia as well as ECL cell hyperplasia and ECL cell carcinoids were produced. Omeprazole dependent hypergastrinemia in rats resulted in an increased proportion of ECL cells which incorporated thymidine in preparation for mitosis, during the first 10-20 weeks of treatment. In addition, ECL cell histidine decarboxylase activity, a marker of ECL cell activation by gastrin, remained elevated for the duration of treatment (1 year). In addition, using isolated ECL cell preparations, the presence of a functional gastrin/CCK-B trophic receptor on the rat ECL cell has been identified. Antrectomy prevented ECL cell changes due to omeprazole administration. Omeprazole and other proton pump inhibitors were without effect on ECL cell growth *in vitro*.

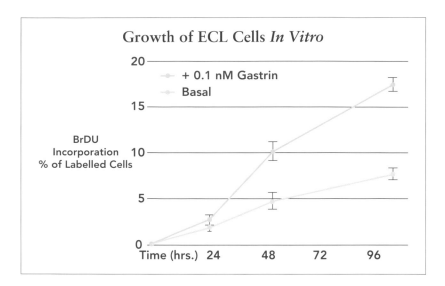

The effect of gastrin on ECL cell DNA replication in *in vitro* culture conditions.

Gastrin stimulates growth of the oxyntic mucosa and lack of gastrin is associated with atrophy of the oxyntic mucosa. Thus the induction of endogenous hypergastrinemia by antral exclusion or by partial removal of the acid reducing part of the stomach (fundectomy or corporectomy) results in increased ECL cell density. Hypogastrinemia induced by antrectomy has the reverse effect. In rats with uremia, hypergastrinemia is associated with increased stomach weight and parietal and ECL cell density. Gastrin immuno-neutralization (gastrin specific monoclonal antibody) significantly inhibited gastric mucosal thickness, parietal and ECL cell density increase but had no effect on gastric weight or the area of the corpus mucosa. Exogenous hypergastrinemia similarly results in ECL cell hyperplasia after 28 days. *In vitro* rodent studies using ^{3}H-thymidine labelled DNA demonstrate that ECL cells display a greater labelling index during the night than during the day which coincides with the time that the rats exhibit a higher circulating gastrin level. Similarly endogenous hypergastrinemia generated by acid inhibitory therapy resulted in an 8-fold increase in the ECL cell labelling index as well as an increase in ECL cell mitotic figures.

Mature ECL cells are capable of dividing but have a relatively low mitotic activity *in vivo* with an estimated cell cycle duration of approximately 60 days in mice. Hypergastrinemia activates self-replication of the ECL cells and there appears to be a direct correlation between the ECL cell proliferation rate and circulating gastrin levels. A recent report suggests that the normal endocrine cells of the human gut have no proliferative capacity and that in this cell lineage, population expansion is preceded by differentiation. If the endocrine (ECL) cell is regarded as terminally differentiated and post mitotic this would suggest that hypergastrinemia acts at the stem cell level rather than on the ECL cells themselves.

ECL cell density thus reflects the circulating gastrin concentration and hypergastrinemia induced by acid inhibition is responsible for the proliferation of ECL cells. In humans, the results of 10 year treatment with omeprazole show no significant change in the ECL cell population, presumably because there is a lack of effect of gastrin on the stem cell population and possibly the mature ECL cell is terminally differentiated in people.

The South African rodent, mastomys, spontaneously develops ECLomas at 12-18 months of age even though it is normo-gastrinemic. Factors other than gastrin are thus required. This situation appears in some ways more analogous to the human multiple endocrine neoplasia type 1 (MEN-1). Hypergastrinemia, despite increased acid secretion, results in development of fundic gastric ECL cell hyperplasia and gastric carcinoids. This process is significantly accelerated by the introduction of acid inhibitory treatment. The generation of hypergastrinemia by any acid inhibiting agent in mastomys results in 2-4 fold elevation of gastrin levels and tumor formation in 3-4 months. The more potent the agent in inhibiting acid and increasing gastrin levels, the more effective its ability to generate ECL cell hyperplasia and neoplasia. The administration of octreotide (a somatostatin analog) results in significant lowering of plasma gastrin levels and decrease of ECL cell hyperplasia and neoplasia.

The incorporation of bromodeoxyuridine (BrdU- a thymidine analogue incorporated into single stranded DNA during the S-phase of cell mitosis) has been predominantly used to study the effects of gastrin on the DNA synthesis of cultured rat or mastomys ECL cells. Under short term culture conditions gastrin stimulated DNA synthesis in ~20% of ECL cells. Isolated ECL cells are not synchronized in their cell cycles. Since mouse ECL cells *in vivo* have a cell cycle of approximately 60 days and hypergastrinemia causes ECL cell proliferation in 4-7 days the increase noted in labelled ECL cells in culture is comparable with *in vivo* data. It has been suggested that ECL cells in short term culture exhibit transit with a time delay from a G0 to a G1 state since the cells are undergoing recovery.

Gastrin directly stimulates DNA synthesis in ECL cells via a gastrin/CCK-B receptor subtype. It has been demonstrated that gastrin receptor activation is associated with protein tyrosine kinase activation. During 48 hours of gastrin stimulation BrdU incorporation increases 2-3 fold. The response of BrdU incorporation was significant at low concentrations between 10^{-12} and 10^{-10} M. These observations correspond to *in vivo* reports of gastrin increasing the ECL cell density 2-4 fold at similar plasma concentrations. Gastrin increased DNA synthesis in ECL cells with an EC_{50} of 1.7×10^{-12} M. This effect was inhibited by L365,260 (IC_{50}, 5×10^{-9} M) and by genistein (10^{-4} M) but was not altered by L364,718 (10^{-8} M). The trophic gastrin effect as well as the acute secretory effect is mediated via a gastrin/CCK-B receptor subtype.

The differential response to gastrin in terms of secretion and DNA synthesis may reflect different intracellular coupling or transduction mechanisms that follow ligand binding. Genistein, a non-selective protein tyrosine kinase inhibitor, inhibits both cytoplasmic and membrane associated tyrosine kinases. At 10^{-4} M genistein failed to inhibit histamine secretion but blocked gastrin stimulated DNA synthesis.

This may reflect differences in the intracellular signal transduction pathways by which gastrin stimulates the ECL cell. In colonic cell lines gastrin has been noted to stimulate DNA synthesis via a tyrosine kinase mediated pathway. It is apparent, however, that the coupling mechanism that stimulates DNA synthesis is not the same as the one regulating histamine secretion. Thus non-sulfated CCK-8 which is equipotent and equally effective in stimulating histamine release and calcium signalling is significantly less effective in inducing DNA synthesis. This may be due to either decreased stability of non-sulfated CCK-8 due to the presence of endopeptidases or reflect different receptor binding to the gastrin receptor. *In vivo* infusion of sulfated CCK-8 which has a similar affinity to the CCK-B receptor as non-sulfated CCK-8 did not induce rat ECL cell hyperplasia at 10-fold plasma concentrations but did increase histamine synthesis.

Acid inhibitory agents such as the proton pump inhibitors omeprazole, lansoprazole and pantoprazole, which are responsible for hypergastrinemia, did not affect BrdU incorporation in isolated ECL cells.

2. Pituitary adenylate cyclase-activating polypeptide (PACAP)

This peptide is widely distributed throughout the fundus and is localized in enteric nerves. In isolated ECL cells it displays a proliferative effect significantly more potent than gastrin which has until recently been regarded as the primary regulator of ECL cell proliferation. The specificity of this effect was confirmed by the identification of a PACAP receptor on the ECL cell using RT-PCR and Southern blot. The inhibition of the proliferative response with the PACAP receptor antagonist, PACAP6-38, further established the functional significance of this peptide. Vasoactive intestinal peptide, a member of the same family, was significantly less potent (as it was for stimulation of histamine release) and use of specific receptor antagonists confirmed the effects to be mediated via the PACAP receptor.

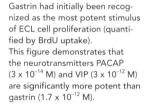

Gastrin had initially been recognized as the most potent stimulus of ECL cell proliferation (quantified by BrdU uptake).
This figure demonstrates that the neurotransmitters PACAP (3×10^{-14} M) and VIP (3×10^{-12} M) are significantly more potent than gastrin (1.7×10^{-12} M).

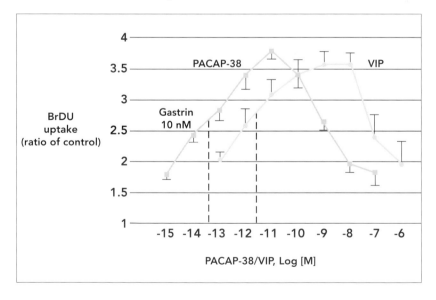

3. Transforming growth factor-α

TGF-α content of ECL cells also increases significantly as measured by radio immunoassay, nuclease protection assay, and Northern blot analysis.

Similarly, EGF receptor expression is correspondingly increased with the duration of hypergastrinemia. Thus, gastrin induced ECL cell proliferation evokes increased ECL cell TGF-α production which may be responsible for a gastrin independent phase of ECL cell proliferation.

4. Histamine

The histamine 1 (H1) receptor agonist (2-[(3- trimethyl)-diphenyl] hista-mine), whilst having no measurable effect alone, reversed the inhibitory effect of the H1 receptor antagonist (terfenadine) on gastrin driven DNA synthesis. The H3 receptor subtype agonist, imetit, stimulated gastrin driven DNA synthesis with an EC_{50} of 10^{-10} M. The H3 receptor antagonist, thioperamide, inhibited gastrin stimulated BrdU uptake (IC_{50} 5×10^{-10} M). These data are consistent with potentiation by histamine of gastrin induced ECL cell prolif-eration via histamine receptor subtypes. Sodium cromoglycate, an inhibitor of histamine release in both the mast and the ECL cell, also inhibits ECL cell proliferation (IC_{50} 10^{-11} M).

5. Somatostatin

Somatostatin has been demonstrated to inhibit ECL cell proliferation (IC_{50} 10^{-10} M) under culture conditions and *in vivo*.

6. General

There are apparently different agents involved in stimulation or inhibition of ECL cell division, depending upon the stage of transformation of the cell. The primary and most potent acute local regulator may be PACAP whilst gastrin may function as an endocrine modulator linking ECL cell and acid secretory activity to cell number. Autocrine regulation may be involved particularly when the cell is moving towards a neoplastic phenotype. In this respect TGF-α appears to exert an important influence. Somatostatin is the predominant inhibitory regu-lator of proliferation acting via a somatostatin 2 receptor subtype.

A cartoon of an isolated ECL cell (EM) demonstrating the variety of peptide agonists which regulate ECL cell DNA synthesis. Somato-statin has been demonstrated to inhibit each of these. TGF-α may in the transformed ECL cell exert an autoregulatory effect.

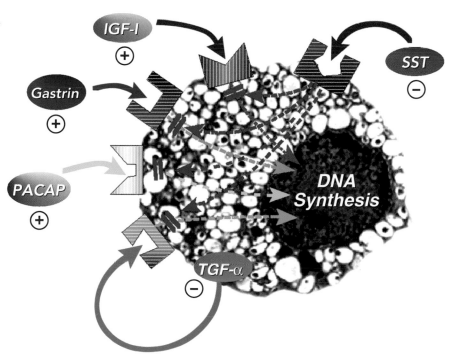

G cell

General

In the adult, gastrin occurs mainly in the G cells of the gastric antrum and duodenum, but small amounts have been identified in the pituitary and some vagal nerve fibers. In early life, the fetal and neonatal pancreas produce gastrin which may be the source of neonatal hypergastrinemia. After birth gastrin production in the periphery is due to the G cell in the antral mucosa. In the circulation the predominant form of gastrin is a heptadecapeptide, G17, although both shorter and longer forms have been identified. Gastrin contains a COOH terminal amide resulting from the post-translational amidation of a glycine extended precursor. Gastrin shares an identical pentapeptide amide with CCK, which results in relatively similar binding to the CCK B receptor. Chole-cystokinin contains a tyrosine residue in the seventh position from the COOH terminal that is always sulfated, whereas gastrin has a tyrosine in the sixth position which may or may not be sulfated. The position and sulfation of the tyrosine residue appears to be critical for recognition by the CCK A subtype receptor. Structural differences in the two peptides result in receptor subtype selectivity and thereby determine selective biological activity.

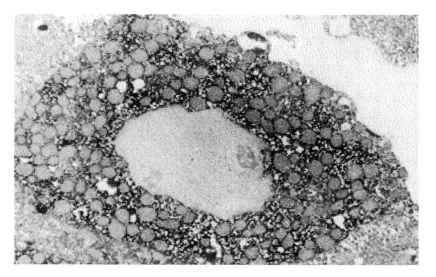

An electron micrograph of a G cell showing the dense granules containing gastrin.

Since the G cells of the gastric antrum are of the "open" type with their apical surfaces reaching the glandular lumen, luminal contents (protons, amino acids), NH_3 may be able to directly modulate G cell activity and the release of gastrin. Intracellular granules containing gastrin are abundant in the basal portion of the cells, and upon stimulation, gastrin is released by an exocytotic process into the extracellular fluid whence it diffuses into the circulation and travels to the gastric fundus. Gastrin thus meets Hardy's archetypal criteria of a true hormone.

Regulation of the G cell

The primary event responsible for the physiological release of gastrin from the antral G cells is the presence of food in the stomach. The mechanism involved in this process comprises at least three stimulatory pathways which include: central neural activation, distension of the antrum, and specific chemical components in the food. At the cellular level, these pathways regulate gastrin release through the actions of ACh, gastrin releasing peptide (GRP), somatostatin, and the direct chemical effects of H^+ and aromatic amino acids. It is likely that other cellular effectors such as adenosine, galanin and epinephrine play a role but their physiological significance is dubious.

Elevation of pH_{in} and Gastrin Release

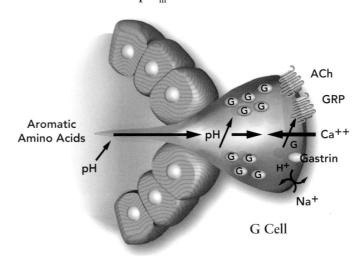

A model of stimulation of gastrin release by aromatic amino acids in the antral lumen, or by pH elevation, and by ACh and GRP on the basal surface. The apical surface has been drawn to emphasize and illustrate the luminal connection.

Vagal influences

Since gastrin is released in response to oro-pharyngeal and central stimuli via the vagus nerve, selective antral vagotomy abolishes both sham feeding and hypoglycemia stimulated release. Given the observation that selective fundic vagotomy leads to an enhanced vagal release of gastrin , it is likely that the vagus also initiates an inhibitory action mediated by the fundus. Since atropine inhibits both the antral release and the fundic inhibitory reflex, it is evident that muscarinic synapses are involved in both pathways. Peripheral mechanisms are primarily stimulatory for gastrin release and the major central influence appears to be inhibition since bilateral truncal vagotomy leads to a sustained elevation of serum gastrin levels. It seems likely that the inhibitory tone exerted by M2 or M4 receptors on the D cell is removed with an increase of somatostatin release.

The presence of food in the stomach activates peripheral pathways which include mechanisms associated both with gastric distension and the chemical composition of the gastric lumen. The study of peripheral mechanisms in the intact animal and *in vitro* often yield conflicting results given the presence or absence of different components of the regulatory system in a specific model. In order to more precisely define these interactions we have opted to focus on the cellular mechanisms participating in the peripheral pathway.

Enhanced release of gastrin follows significant distension of the antral portion of the stomach whereas distension of the fundus alone tends to inhibit gastrin secretion. This phenomenon of distension induced gastrin release is reported to be either inhibited or enhanced by atropine, depending on the dose. Such *in vivo* results suggest that the distension responses are mediated by local neural reflexes. *In vitro* studies that attempt to mimic the local reflex by field stimulation or application of nicotinic agonists, have indicated that ACh stimulates gastrin release from the G cell but also inhibits somatostatin release from antral D cells thus providing a partial explanation for the contradictory actions of atropine. Accordingly, low doses of atropine would suppress somatosatin release, relieving tonic inhibition of the G cell by somatosatin while higher doses would inhibit the G cell directly.

Acid

There are a number of specific chemical components of antral contents that modulate the release of gastrin. The most effective and well studied of these is the pH of the antral lumen, which at values <3 completely suppresses gastrin release. This serves to terminate gastric digestion and if the antral luminal pH remains elevated in the presence of continuing stimulation, hypergastrinemia results.

Amino acids and amines

The presence of aromatic amino acids is responsible for luminal initiation of the release of gastrin. Intact protein fails to increase gastrin secretion whereas the ingestion of peptone, a partially digested protein mix is a powerful stimulant. In this respect the preferential stimulation by aromatic amino acids is consistent with the preferred cleavage sites for the major gastric protease pepsin. The effect of amino acids on gastrin release represents a direct action on the G cell since it can be reproduced *in vitro* and is not blocked by atropine or other inhibitors of neural transmission. Given the fact that the G cell is open to the gastric lumen, chemical effectors can bind to the apical membrane or become internalized by the G cells to influence gastrin secretion.

This is thought to mimic the digestive processes occurring normally and thus to be a physiological mechanism for gastrin release. On the other hand, release of gastrin by amines may be an artifact of high concentration and simply due to the general action of these agents as weak bases.

These would then elevate G cell pH which *per se* can result in the release of gastrin or sensitize the system to GRP or Ach.

GRP

Since a significant component of the neural release of gastrin, whether initiated locally by distension or through the vagus, was known to be atropine resistant, a mediator of this phenomenon was sought. The identification of gastrin releasing peptide (GRP) a neurocrine peptide in the brain, spinal cord, and enteric nerve fibers of the gut prompted examination that it might fulfil this role. GRP was initially defined as the mammalian counterpart to the amphibian peptide bombesin, since the two peptides share 9 of 10 COOH terminal amino acids. Both GRP and receptors for GRP are widely distributed in the body, including fetal and neonatal bronchial epithelium. The last location is of considerable clinical relevance, since GRP acts as an autocrine growth factor for human tumors including small cell lung cancer. Although GRP like peptides are now well documented as mitogens, their initial biological assays measured the release of gastrin and as a result this name has persisted. GRP is localized to enteric gastric nerve fibers, where it is responsible for gastrin release and in the fundus where it may be related to GRP regulation of motility. Administration of GRP does not influence acid secretion in the absence of an intact antrum. Antral GRP is released from enteric nerves, at least in part, through non-muscarinic cholinergic (nicotinic) pathways. Because atropine blocks most of the vagal release of gastrin, it is uncertain which portion of the response is mediated by GRP. Similarly, the role of endogenous GRP in mediating the release of gastrin due to distension or chemical components of food remains uncertain. A substantial role for GRP in gastrin release appears certain.

In studies utilizing isolated G cells, GRP and its analogues effect direct stimulation of gastrin by activation of phospholipase C, leading to liberation of diacyl glycerol and elevation of Ca^{2+}. In addition, the calcium ionophore, A 23187, was found to be a potent stimulus for gastrin release, as were phorbol esters that mimic the action of diacylglycerol in activating protein kinase C. These actions are consistent with the finding that the GRP receptor belongs to the G protein coupled superfamily and appears to be coupled to phospholipase C activation in other cells. Since cAMP analogues and forskolin also stimulate gastrin release, it appears that both cAMP and Ca^{2+} serve as intracellular coupling agents in the G cell. The G cell ligand that activates G_s and hence elevates cAMP is not known.

Somatostatin

An important factor in the regulation of gastrin release is inhibition of the G cell by somatostatin but the infusion of somatostatin at doses sufficient to inhibit acid secretion failed to inhibit gastrin secretion. Presumably the effect of somatostatin on the ECL cell occurs more readily than on the G cell when infused. Immuno-neutralization of somatostatin enhances basal and stimulated gastrin release showing that local release of the peptide is exerting a direct effect on the G cell. Somatostatin therefore acts only as a paracrine agent to suppress gastrin secretion, and any action on antral G cells is not due to circulating somatostatin. There are 5 known subtypes of somatostatin receptor and the receptor subtype on the G cell is probably the type 2.

A model of the G cell is shown in the figure.

Working Model of G Cell Function

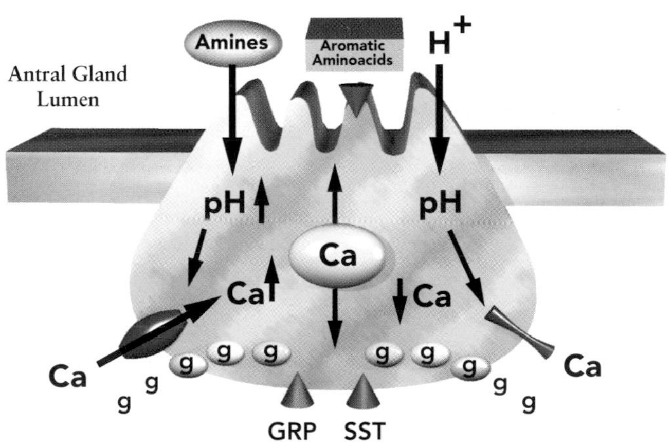

A model of the antral G cell exposed to both serosal and luminal factors for its regulation by modification of cell calcium and pH. Gastrin (g) is depicted as being released into the paracellular spaces from the basolateral domain of the G cell.

D cells

General

D cells are present both in the fundus and antrum and contain somatostatin. The D cells of the antrum exhibit elongated processes that extend to the basal portions of G cells and are more frequent here than in the fundus. These cells also extend processes to the lumen of the antral gland. The fundic D cells are relatively sparse and have no contact with the lumen of the fundic gland.

As for the G cell, the D cells contain a large number of secretory granules and are somewhat larger than the ECL cell and more dense since they do not have hollow vacuoles.

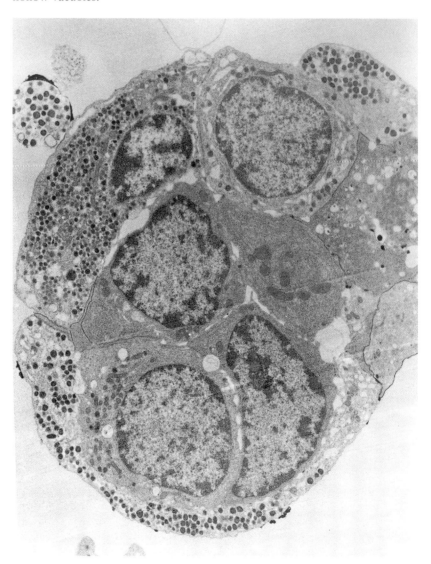

An electron micrograph of antral D cells showing the luminal extension folded onto the surface of the cell (lower part of picture) and the electron dense somatostatin containing granules.

Regulation

Gastrin and CCK

The release of somatostatin from antral D cells, like the release of gastrin from G cells, is regulated by a complex set of mechanisms, not all of which are defined clearly.

Since somatostatin is so widespread in its distribution there is some difficulty in assigning an origin for somatostatin released into the circulation. Gastrin and CCK both stimulate somatostatin release from isolated D cells and this cell type has both CCK-A and CCK-B receptors.

Because CCK stimulates acid secretion *in vitro* through release of histamine from ECL cells but inhibits acid secretion *in vivo*, it is likely that the inhibitory action *in vivo* is due to somatostatin release driven by CCK-A activation.

Gastrin also stimulates the D cell providing a negative feedback mechanism for both G and ECL cell function by the CCK-B receptor.

Secretin/VIP

Peptides of the secretin/VIP family stimulate somatostatin release, and the consequent suppression of gastrin release may account for at least some of the ability of such peptides to inhibit acid secretion *in vivo*. PACAP when injected *in vivo* inhibits gastrin stimulated acid secretion and this is probably due to stimulation of the fundic D cell at a VIP receptor. When somatostatin neutralizing antibody is given along with PACAP, acid secretion ensues due to the effect of PACAP on the ECL cell being revealed.

Acetylcholine

In contrast to the other cells in the gastric mucosa, the D cell has inhibitory muscarinic receptors, of either the M2 or M4 subtype, allowing the conclusion that vagal stimulation of acid secretion inhibits somatostatin release.

Acid

Antral D cells, unlike those of the fundus, project to the gastric lumen and thus are capable of detecting chemical components of food. Of particular interest in this regard is the observation that antral somatostatin is released in response to acidification of the gastric lumen. This may represent a mechanism for suppression of gastrin release at low intraluminal pH, a critical factor in the physiological regulation of gastric acidity. The G and D cells of the antrum both therefore have sensing mechanisms of conditions in the lumen of the antral gland. A simple model would place the amino acid sensor on the G cell and the acid sensor on the D cell. Presumably aromatic amino acids elevate $[Ca]_i$ in the G cell and reduction of pH to < 3.0 elevates the same second messenger in the D cell.

CHAPTER 3
THE PARIETAL CELL

It has been over one hundred years since it was suggested that the secretory canaliculus of the parietal cell was the site of gastric acid secretion. The mechanism of secretion has been known for over 20 years. However, the complexity of the processes that regulate acid secretion by the parietal cell has only been realized since the advent of modern cell and molecular biology and much remains unresolved.

Early work on understanding parietal cell biology was based on data derived from the exteriorized dog flap in a hemi-chamber. More exact physiological data were obtained on isolated amphibian mucosae in Ussing chambers. The major technical breakthrough in defining the stimulatory pathways in the mammalian parietal cell was the development of the rabbit gastric gland preparation with measurement of acid secretion by uptake of the weak base ^{14}C-aminopyrine.

In amphibia and birds, the acid secreting cell is called the oxyntic cell, in

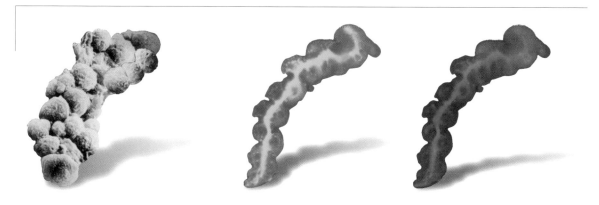

The gastric gland model of acid secretion. In the left figure, a scanning electron micrograph shows the presence of parietal cells and small ECL cells on the surface. The central and right micrographs under fluorescence microscopy show the staining with acridine orange before and after stimulation. The red metachromasia indicates the presence of acid secretion in the parietal cell canaliculus and in the gastric gland lumen.

mammals it is the parietal cell. These are epithelial cells, characterized by a distinction between their mucosal or apical surface and their serosal or basal lateral surface. These two domains are separated by a specialized region of the membrane, the tight junction. The oxyntic cell secretes both acid and pepsin.

The major function of the parietal is the polarized secretion of HCl across its mucosal surface; in some species this cell also secretes intrinsic factor, a protein vital for the absorption of cyanocobalamin. More mature parietal cells perhaps also secrete Cl[-] resulting in water flow by coupling to Na flux across the tight junction. As has been dealt with above, acid secretion is a regulated process and the target for this regulation is the parietal cell, with a variety of receptors on its cell surface. But beyond this cellular target is the proton pump itself, the H,K ATPase. All natural stimuli and inhibitors converge to activate or inhibit this P-type ATPase. The parietal cell has developed extraordinary measures in order to be able to regulate the act of acid secretion. Regulation of acid secretion at the cellular level involves three stages, regulation of receptors on the basal lateral surface, cytoplasmic events consequent to ligand interaction with these receptors and thence regulation of the H,K ATPase itself.

This epithelial cell is derived from stem cells in the isthmus of the gastric

**Development
of the parietal cell**

gland. These cells give rise to progenitor cells which differentiate into parietal cells forming a 3 helical chains spiralling down to the base of the gland. Markers of parietal cell ontogeny are an abundance of mitochondria and the presence of the H,K ATPase. Although the parietal cell itself is a terminally differentiated cell, there appears to be differences between the parietal cells in the neck of the gland and in the lower part of the gland.

For example, stimulation of acid secretion affects the superficial cells more than the deeper cells. Also the deeper cells, although having similar levels of the gastric H,K ATPase also express the $NaKCl_2$ co-transporter (NKCC2), which the more superficial cells do not.

This finding implies that the deeper cells act as Cl^- secreting cells as well as HCl secreting cells. Perhaps there is a need for fluid secretion, independent of acid, for elution of secreted pepsinogen.

Morphology

The morphology of the parietal cell is unique. It is conical, with a small apical and large basal lateral membrane. 34% of cell volume is occupied by mitochondria, dedicated to the synthesis of ATP as an energy source for acid secretion. A large percentage of resting cell volume is also occupied by smooth surfaced membranes called tubulo-vesicles, that when observed by freeze smash electron microscopy are actually elongated tubules. Also there is a small infolding of the apical membrane named the secretory canaliculus.

Upon stimulation, the tubules decrease in number and transform into microvilli decorating the secretory canaliculus which expands in surface area and volume as acid is secreted.

The microvilli contain actin fibres that have moved from the cytoplasm as shown by phallucidin staining.

These morphological events in the parietal cell reflect stimulation-secretion coupling in the parietal cell and much of this chapter will discuss in more depth the mechanisms underlying activation of acid secretion.

The transformation of the tubulovesicles of the parietal cell into the villi of the canaliculus which occurs with stimulation of acid secretion.

Receptors

The parietal cell appears to possess a variety of receptors for both stimulatory and inhibitory ligands. The majority of these have been defined functionally. Since most of the evidence for the action of modulating agents has been obtained in preparations which are heterogeneous with respect to cell type, some caution must be exercised in concluding that the effects are direct rather than indirect. There are few studies reported using specific receptor antibodies or *in situ* probes.

Direct evidence has been obtained for the histamine H2 receptor. An alternative approach, in the case of isolated, dispersed cells or gastric glands, is the use of single cell imaging techniques where direct visualization can provide positive identification of parietal cells and assure that cells are sufficiently well separated to dilute any substances which might be released by potentially intervening cell types. The stimulatory receptors are all of the 7 transmembrane segment trimeric G protein type of receptor as illustrated in the figure. These receptors function by releasing the bound trimeric G protein after ligand binding resulting in a lower affinity state of the receptor. The three subunits, α with GDP bound, β and γ are bound to the receptor or to a member of the RGS protein family.

After ligand binding, the α subunit releases GDP and binds GTP. The GTP liganded trimer dissociates into α monomers and β-γ dimers. The α-GTP monomer then hydrolyses GTP to GDP enabling reassociation of the trimer and termination of the signal. These trimer G proteins are responsible for the effects of ligand binding to the receptor. The nature of the protein constituents of the trimeric G protein determines whether there is activation of adenylate cyclase, or phospholipase C, or inhibition of these enzymes. This determines whether there is an increase of cAMP dependent kinase activity, an elevation of intracellular Ca, or an inhibition of cell responses.

Most receptors are promiscuous in terms of which G proteins are bound. Antagonists of these receptors can be divided into pure antagonists that only displace agonist or inverse agonists that are able to affect the conformation of the receptor in the absence of agonist.

The latter class can therefore affect cell function in the absence of ligand.

The majority of receptors affecting acid secretion belong to the G7 class of receptors (H2, muscarinic, CCK-A or B, somatostatin, prostaglandin). The EGF/TGF-α receptor which also inhibits acid secretion is a tyrosine kinase receptor.

A model of a G7 receptor, showing the membrane topography, with 7 transmembrane segments, the binding of the G trimeric protein mainly to the 3rd intracellular loop and ligand binding in the region of the 3rd and 5th membrane segments. End glycosylation is indicated by *glyc'n* in the diagram. Probably most of the cytoplasmic surface of the receptor is involved in interaction with the G proteins. The illustration shows activation by dissociation of the trimeric G protein, binding of GTP instead of GDP and then dissociation of the trimer into the α and β-γ complex.

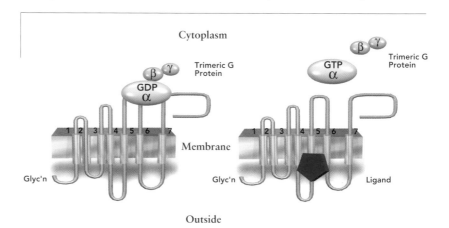

In receptors such as the β adrenergic receptor or others that bind biogenic amines such as histamine, an aspartyl residue in the 3rd transmembrane domain binds the positive charge and two serines in the 5th transmembrane domain (TM5) bind the aromatic residue. A phenylalanine residue in TM6 is also conserved in the biogenic amine responsive G protein coupled receptors. Antagonists may bind in different regions of the receptor such as that close to the 7th transmembrane domain. Peptide agonists have a larger binding domain which includes the 2nd transmembrane segment. Non-peptide antagonists at the peptide receptor bind at the top of TM5 and 6.

Histamine receptor

The stimulatory action of histamine is mediated by the H2 subtype receptor. Histamine stimulation of acid secretion is inhibited competitively by selective H2 receptor antagonists but is not inhibited by agents acting at other receptors indicating that histamine acts directly on the parietal cell. The cellular localization of H2 receptors using both *in situ* hybridization and autoradiographic localization of H2 receptor antagonist binding (^{125}I- aminopotentidine) shows that the H2 receptor is located on the parietal cell.

H2 receptor antagonists inhibit gastrin stimulation fully but not that induced by carbachol (cholinomimetic) showing that the former, but not the latter stimulant depends on histamine release from the ECL cell. Histamine may be permissive for gastrin and removal of this permissive action may account for the inhibition of gastrin stimulation by H2 antagonists. The histamine H2 receptor has been cloned and expressed and the cDNA derived amino acid sequence shows typical features of a G-protein coupled receptor with seven transmembrane segments. The quantitative correlation between stimulation of acid secretion, activation of adenylyl cyclase and accumulation of cAMP shown by a variety of H2 receptor agonists provides strong evidence that the H2 receptor is coupled to activation of adenylate cyclase. The nature of the G_s trimeric proteins coupled to this receptor has not been determined. Addition of histamine also generates Ca signals in the parietal cell. Perhaps both cAMP and Ca pathways must be activated for generation of the morphological transformation essential for acid secretion.

Acetylcholine receptor

Extracts of Belladonna have been used to treat dyspepsia since the Roman Empire and its major component, atropine, was a primary medical treatment for peptic ulcer prior to development of the H2 receptor antagonists. Since atropine is a non-selective muscarinic antagonist it is not possible, based solely on *in vivo* inhibition, to conclude that the parietal cell contains a cholinergic receptor. *In vitro*, particularly in the presence of H2 receptor antagonists, cholinergic stimulation of acid secretion is weak and often transient. That portion of the cholinergic stimulation that is not inhibited by H2 receptor antagonists is blocked by atropine. These results suggest that there is indeed direct action of acetylcholine on the parietal cell in addition to the observed interaction with histamine. Inhibition of acid secretion by atropine indicates that acetylcholine acts through a muscarinic type cholinergic receptor but does not define the specific subtype of muscarinic receptor involved. To date, five muscarinic receptor subtypes have been cloned and sequenced. All are

G-protein coupled and exhibit structural similarities although they couple to different intracellular signaling mechanisms. Pharmacological characterization of cholinergic stimulation of acid secretion *in vitro* indicates that the parietal cell contains an M3 subtype muscarinic receptor. Accordingly, carbachol stimulation of acid formation by isolated gastric glands is found to be inhibited by subtype selective antagonists with a potency order of 4-DAMP > pirenzepine > AF-DX 116. An identical order of potency was found also for displacement of N-methyl scopolamine binding and elevation of intracellular calcium. This is the same order of potency exhibited by the cloned M3 receptor. The presence of an M3 subtype receptor on the parietal cell was further evidenced by detection of mRNA encoding the M3 receptor in parietal cells, whereas no evidence was found for expression of M1 or M2 subtypes. Thus, the direct action of acetylcholine on the parietal cell appears to be mediated by an M3 muscarinic receptor. The M1 antagonist, pirenzepine, is an effective inhibitor of acid secretion. Presumably this occurs at a site in the peripheral regulatory pathway prior to convergence on the parietal cell.

Gastrin receptor

The function of a receptor for gastrin on the parietal cell has been the subject of controversy. The central observation is the total absence or marginal stimulation of acid secretion by gastrin in the presence of H2 receptor antagonists. This has led most investigators to conclude that gastrin acts indirectly on the parietal cell by stimulation of histamine release from ECL cells. Favoring a direct action of gastrin on the parietal cell are reports indicating the presence of gastrin binding sites on gastric mucosal membranes and enriched preparations of parietal cells. These binding sites are characterized as gastrin, or CCK-B type sites in that they show equal affinity for gastrin and sulfated CCK. The presence of gastrin receptors on the parietal cell received further support by the recent cloning and expression of a CCK-B type receptor from a cDNA library derived from purified parietal cell mRNA.

Single cell video imaging has provided direct evidence for a functional CCK-B receptor on the parietal cell. In particular, gastrin has been shown to produce an elevation of intracellular calcium in individual parietal cells which is blocked by the CCK-B antagonist, L365,260. The pattern of intracellular calcium increase, consisting of a biphasic response, indicates a direct action of gastrin on the parietal cell as opposed to mediation by histamine, since histamine is known to induce only small, transient alterations of Ca_{in}. While parallel responses of acid secretion were observed, most of these experiments were not done in the presence of H2 receptor antagonists and therefore one cannot rule out a permissive effect of H2 receptor activity on either the secretory or the cell calcium response. Using confocal imaging it was then shown that H2 receptor antagonists did not block the action of gastrin on ECL cells in rabbit or rat gastric glands but blocked the action of gastrin on parietal cell Ca_{in}. The addition of dbcAMP restored the effect of gastrin on the parietal cell. Isolated hog parietal cells also require the presence of cAMP to demonstrate a Ca response. Thus the linkage of the CCK-B receptor to acid secretion may be complex. The figure shows a confocal image of a gastric gland illustrating the location of the parietal and ECL cells that have been loaded with a calcium sensing dye, calcium orange. This enables dissection of the calcium signaling response to gastrin of the parietal and ECL cell.

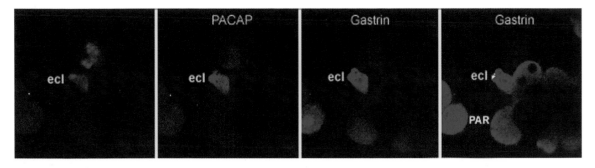

Isolated rabbit gastric glands were loaded with a calcium sensitive dye, mag-fluo-4-AM. The ECL cell was identified by autofluorescence. PACAP was added, and it can be seen that there was a rapid elevation of intracellular calcium. Gastrin was then added and there was a rapid further increase of calcium in the ECL cell. This was followed by an increase of calcium in the parietal cells (PAR).

Miscellaneous receptors

A variety of agents has been reported to stimulate or inhibit acid secretion by a direct action on the parietal cell. Many of these, e.g., cAMP derivatives, forskolin, etc., do not act through cellular receptors while others are suggested to reflect the presence of parietal cell receptors. Although no direct evidence for a parietal cell location exists, the ability of some substances to inhibit histamine stimulation of acid secretion argues for the presence of a parietal cell receptor since the action of histamine is direct. Even in these cases caution is necessary to interpret the inhibition as being direct rather than due to the release of another inhibitor. With this caveat in mind, the parietal cell appears to contain inhibitory receptors for somatostatin, prostaglandins (PG) and epidermal growth factor (EGF). Each of these has been shown to inhibit histamine stimulation of acid formation by isolated cell preparations.

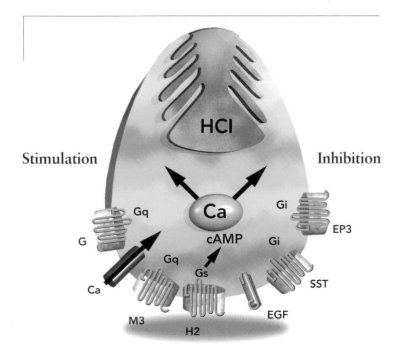

The receptors known to be present on the parietal cell. Illustrated are the 3 major G coupled stimulatory receptors, two G_i coupled inhibitory receptors and the EGF/TGF-α tyrosine kinase coupled receptors.

Somatostatin is thought to act through an inhibitory G-protein to interfere with receptor-mediated second messenger production, explaining the inhibition of histamine stimulation. In the case of EGF, the inhibition appears to occur at a site beyond the H2 receptor since EGF inhibits also dibutyryl cAMP stimulation of acid formation. At relatively high concentrations, PGE2 has been shown to increase production of cAMP, while at lower concentrations prostaglandins inhibit cAMP formation and this is most likely related to the inhibition of acid formation. The conflicting responses of cAMP formation to prostaglandins might be explained by the presence of multiple receptor subtypes. Thus, a low affinity EP_2 receptor acting through a stimulatory G-protein (G_s) would account for the elevation of cAMP while a high affinity EP_3 receptor acting through an inhibitory G-protein (G_i) accounts for the inhibition of adenylyl cyclase and acid formation.

The physiological significance of inhibitory receptors on the parietal cell is not at all clear. A possible role for fundic or circulating somatostatin in controlling gastric acidity is discussed above but this function could be served fully by the action of somatostatin on histamine release from ECL cells. Since the putative direct action of somatostatin on the parietal cell is selective for histamine stimulation, dual inhibition of ECL and parietal cells would seem redundant. In the case of EGF and prostaglandins, it may be speculated that these inhibitors, which are known mediators of wound healing, act only during periods of mucosal injury to reduce acidity and allow more rapid healing.

A model showing these receptors on the parietal cell is shown in the figure.

Intracellular signals

Intracellular messengers

The gastric histamine H2 receptor is coupled to the formation of cAMP whereas activation of the parietal cell M3 cholinergic receptor or the CCK-B receptor leads to an elevation of intracellular calcium. The elevation of cAMP by the H2 receptor appears to result from a direct coupling, via a G-protein, to adenylate cyclase, the elevation of Ca_{in} proceeds by a more complex mechanism. The stimulation of a Gq coupled receptor results in dissociation of the trimeric protein. Thence there is activation of phospholipase C with breakdown of PIP_2 to IP_3 and diacyl glycerol. The former results in release of Ca from intracellular stores, perhaps aided by binding of the β-γ complex. The latter activates protein C kinase. Stimulants of C kinase such as the phorbol esters do not activate acid secretion in gastric glands. Activation of Ca entry accompanies release from intracellular stores perhaps due to the interaction of the IP_3 receptor with a membrane located calcium channel.

Using fluorescent indicators with single cell video imaging, the Ca_{in} responses of individual parietal cells are typically found to be biphasic, consisting of an initial peak elevation which rapidly declines to a sustained steady state elevation. This pattern of Ca_{in} response is seen in many cell types and is interpreted to result from an initial release of calcium from intracellular storage sites followed by a sustained influx of calcium from the extracellular fluid. Similar mechanisms appear to be involved in the agonist induced Ca_{in} of parietal cells. Accordingly removal of extracellular calcium or blockade of influx with La^{3+} abolishes the steady state elevation but not the initial peak response.

In analogy with other cells, it is assumed that the intracellular pool of calcium is stored in specialized regions of the endoplasmic reticulum (ER) where it is released through calcium channels and re-sequestered by a calcium pump in the endoplasmic reticulum. Thapsigargin, an inhibitor of the ER calcium pump binding to the loop between TM3 and TM4, raises Ca_{in} in parietal cells indicating that a typical calcium pump is involved in maintaining the intracellular pool. The release of Ca_i appears to occur via a regulated calcium channel, two types of which have been identified. In muscle, the ER calcium channel binds ryanodine and is regulated by voltage, and possibly by various ligands. In non-excitable cells, presumably including the parietal cell, the predominant ER calcium channel appears to be one regulated by inositol 1,4,5-trisphosphate (IP_3).

The observations that cholinergic agonists elevate IP_3 levels in gastric cells and that IP_3 releases calcium from internal stores in permeabilized parietal cells provide evidence that the initial peak response of Ca_i is due to activation of IP_3 receptor activated Ca^{2+} channels. This is consistent also with the finding that the cloned M3 receptor mediates phosphoinositide hydrolysis. The agonist dependent formation of IP_3 is likely due to activation of phospholipase C. There are various isoforms of this enzyme. The exact mechanism for calcium influx which results in the steady state elevation of Ca_i remains unidentified. The influx pathway is not a voltage-dependent channel since it is not blocked by dihydropyridine type channel blockers.

There is ignorance as to the target of Ca_i as a coupling signal. The initial observation that removal of external calcium blocked the acid secretory response to cholinergic agonists suggested that the calcium influx was necessary for secretion. It was argued however that removal of calcium depleted the intracellular pool which was the true second messenger and acid secretion could be related to the peak Ca_i response. Recent studies in which the peak and steady state phases of the Ca_i response to carbachol could be distinguished by antagonist sensitivity demonstrated that the steady state, but not the peak elevation, is necessary for stimulating acid secretion. Interestingly, elevation of Ca_i, to the same extent as seen in the steady state response to carbachol, with ionomycin or arachidonic acid failed to induce a secretory response. Similarly elevation of Ca_i by thapsigargin mimics steady state calcium response to carbachol but not the secretory response. The acid secretory response to cholinergic stimulation requires the steady state elevation of Ca_i but this alone is not sufficient.

Although the parietal cell CCK-B receptor has not been studied in as much detail as the M3 receptor, it is reasonable to assume that the general mechanisms involved in the Ca_i response apply to both receptor types. However, it is not clear why the CCK-B response requires cAMP and that of the M3 receptor does not.

The long standing observation that cholinergic and gastrin stimulation of acid secretion is potentiated by histamine or agents such as phosphodiesterase inhibitors which elevate cAMP suggests that cAMP and Ca_i interact at some level. Thus histamine, which acts primarily to elevate cAMP, has been shown to produce a small, transient elevation of Ca_i in parietal cells. Further, buffering Ca_i below basal levels inhibits secretory responses to histamine. Accordingly it may be that both cAMP and elevated Ca_i are necessary for an optimal secretory response to the extent that a permissive level of one second messenger is required for a full response to the other.

A summary of the intracellular M3 signaling systems is shown in the figure. Similar coupling mechanisms exist for the other Gq linked receptors.

M3 Receptor Coupling

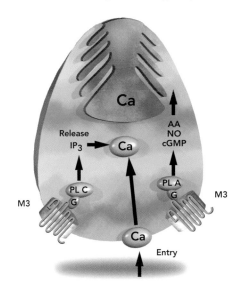

Coupling of the M3 receptor (and other G7 receptors) to various calcium signalling pathways. A similar coupling pathway is present for the CCK-B receptor but requires elevation of cAMP for activity.

Intracellular coupling reactions

The intracellular reactions which ensue from the elevation of Ca_{in} and cAMP are unclear. Indeed, this aspect of stimulus-secretion coupling probably represents the single greatest challenge to our understanding of the mechanisms which regulate gastric acid secretion. Based on their known action in a variety of tissues, it is most probable that the intracellular second messengers, particularly in the case of cAMP, serve to activate protein phosphokinases with subsequent phosphorylation of specific target proteins. With a few notable exceptions, the target proteins for parietal cell protein kinases have not been identified. Two general approaches have been employed in attempting to identify the intermediate reactions of stimulus-secretion coupling in parietal cells. The most popular and seemingly straightforward approach, based on the assumption that activation of protein kinases represents the initial step, has been to attempt identification of stimulation-associated phosphoproteins This approach has been frustrated thus far by technical and conceptual difficulties and has yielded few positive results. A second, recently initiated, approach involves attempts to first identify components associated with the proton pump and then to assess possible modulations related to activation of secretory activity. Perhaps the most significant result from any of these studies is the recognition that the H,K ATPase itself is not the final target for covalent regulatory modification.

The only known action of cAMP is to activate the cAMP-dependent protein kinase (PK-A). In the case of the parietal cell, histamine has been reported to selectively activate a soluble type I PK-A as indicated by the presence of free catalytic subunit. Type II PK-A appears also to be activated but in this case the regulatory subunit and much of the catalytic subunit remain associated with the particulate fraction. This is consistent with the finding that PK-A binding proteins associated with membranes are selective for the type II regulatory subunit. This selectivity may indicate a preferential location of the target proteins for the type II kinase.

Several protein kinases are known to be dependent on or activated by calcium including the isoforms of phospholipid-dependent protein kinase, PK-C, and several calcium-calmodulin dependent protein kinases (CaM kinases). A potential role for PK-C is suggested by the activation of this enzyme by diacylglycerol (DAG). The latter is a product of the cholinergic activation of phospholipase C. However, exogenous activators of PK-C, e.g., phorbol esters, inhibit acid secretion, rather than stimulate it. The presence of a type II CaM kinase has been demonstrated in gastric cells where both parietal and chief cells appear to express the γ and delta subtypes. A potential role for CaM kinase II in cholinergic stimulation of acid secretion has been proposed since the CaM kinase II selective inhibitor, KN-62, inhibits carbachol but not histamine stimulation. An interesting example of a putative direct action of calcium is the activation of the cytoskeletal-associated protease, calpain, which has been proposed to be involved in the cytoskeletal rearrangements associated with activation of the parietal cell.

A variety of experimental approaches have been employed in attempts to identify the specific target proteins of the protein kinases postulated to be activated during stimulation of acid secretion. The general experimental paradigms have included both *in vitro*, i.e., with cell fractions, and *in situ*, i.e., intact cells, phosphorylation followed by isolation and identification of phosphoproteins.

With either approach, the typical result is that a great many proteins appear to undergo protein kinase dependent phosphorylation. The complex patterns of phosphorylation have impeded prohibited identification of specific target proteins. Separation of individual phosphoproteins by 1-dimensional SDS gel electrophoresis has usually been inadequate to allow sequence identification of the protein while 2-dimensional separations have generally yielded insufficient quantities of single proteins to permit sequence analysis. Since many proteins appear to undergo phosphorylation, it is not clear which, if any, of them are true intermediates in stimulation of acid secretion as opposed to parallel events such as metabolic activation or transcriptional regulation.

The single exception to the negative results has been the identification of the cytoskeletal linking protein, ezrin, as a potential intermediate in parietal cell activation. Initially discovered as a stimulation-related phosphoprotein localized to the apical plasma membrane of the parietal cell, this 80 kDa protein was identified as ezrin. Ezrin is a member of a gene family related to the erythrocyte Band 4.1 protein. These proteins, including radixin, moesin and talin act as end-capping actin-modifying proteins which serve to link cytoskeletal elements to the plasma membrane. Although the members of this family of proteins are structurally and functionally homologous, they tend to be preferentially localized in different cells and thus serve distinct cellular functions. Ezrin is thought to be associated with cytoskeletal elements at the apical pole of epithelial cells where it is involved in the organization of microvilli. In cultured cells ezrin is found to insert into membrane ruffles and become phosphorylated on tyrosine and serine residues in response to EGF. A similar role for ezrin has been proposed in the parietal cell although in this cell type ezrin does not appear to change location with stimulation nor is there phosphorylation of tyrosine. It may be that the tyrosine phosphorylation observed in other systems associated with growth factor stimulation may be required for translocation while serine phosphorylation is sufficient for actin interactions. Since the formation of microvilli at the canalicular surface is part of the parietal cell response to stimulation, the phosphorylation of ezrin is considered to be a direct intermediate in the coupling reactions. However, as discussed below, the two critical events in activation of the proton pump are the translocation of H,K ATPase to the canalicular membrane and the association or activation of a KCl permeability pathway. Neither of these events has been related to ezrin as yet. There is also the presence of dynamin associated with the actin microfilaments. Dynamin is a GTPase often involved in endocytosis.

An alternate approach to identifying intermediates in the stimulus secretion coupling events is based on the assumption that cellular components associated with the H,K ATPase undergo regulatory modification with parietal cell stimulation. Accordingly, substantial effort has been made to identify proteins associated with the H,K ATPase containing membranes with a long term view to define which of these may serve a regulatory function.

This approach has yielded limited but promising results. In particular, it has been found that low molecular weight GTP-binding (LMWG) proteins are associated with the cytoplasmic vesicles in parietal cells. The LMWG proteins constitute a large group of monomeric peptides with molecular masses in the range of 20-30 kDa. These peptides share structural homology with the oncogenic peptide, Ras, and appear to function as intermediates in a wide range of regulatory functions including growth and secretion.

The LMWG proteins associated with the parietal cell membranes appear to belong to the Rab (Ras-related rat brain) subgroup. Rab peptides, particularly Rab 3a, have been implicated in synaptic vesicle exocytosis, release of histamine from mast cells and exocytosis in pancreatic acinar and adrenal chromaffin cells. Accordingly it has been suggested that Rab peptides may be involved in the fusion of cytoplasmic membrane tubules with the secretory canaliculus, which is a central event in the activation of the proton pump.

The extent and exact nature of Rab involvement in pump activation is under investigation and holds promise for defining further the events linking second messengers to acid secretion. Whereas Rab 3 proteins are not found in the parietal cell, Rab 11a is present. However it remains associated with membranes in both the resting and stimulated states. Similar data have been observed for Rab 25.

A schematic model of these activation events is shown in the following figure. Two possible models are envisaged, expansion or fusion. The fusion model is the dominant hypothesis in the field. In assessing the evidence, the finding that the ATPase is present in tubules not vesicles suggests that fusion is restricted to the tips of the tubules and does not really resemble exocytosis in the strict sense. Following fusion there must be eversion of the tubules to form the microvilli. Presumably the KCl pathway is at the base of the microvilli to allow effective reabsorption of K.

A model showing eversion of cytoplasmic tubules to form the secretory microvilli along an actin cytoskeleton, with ezrin present in the microvilli and Rab 11 and 25 as well as dynamin associated with the microtubules.

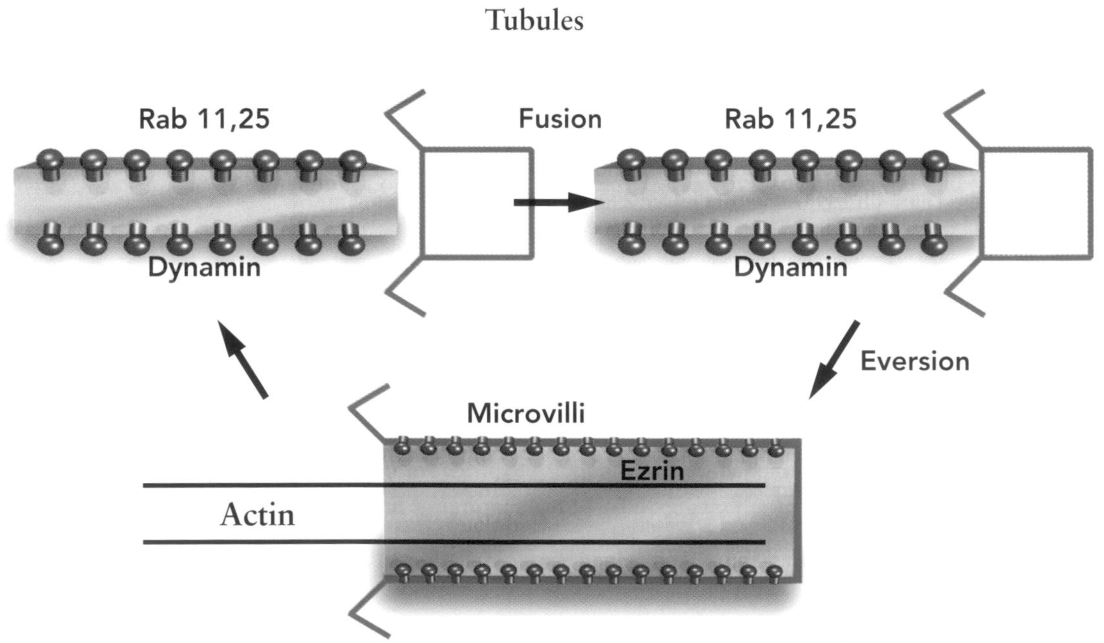

Tubules

Rab 11,25   Fusion   Rab 11,25

Dynamin   Dynamin

Eversion

Microvilli

Ezrin

Actin

Activation of the H,K ATPase

Acid secretion is a discontinuous process, whose rate is determined by its necessity following a meal. Consequently, the eventual result of the complex mechanisms for regulation of secretion described in previous sections is to activate the H,K ATPase. In contrast to the regulation of many other enzymes there is no evidence for any chemical factors which directly influence the activity of the H,K ATPase other than the availability of the necessary substrates MgATP, H^+ and K^+. Since within the parietal cell the availability of protons and MgATP are not likely to be rate limiting, it follows that the major, if not the only, factor which controls proton transport is the availability of K^+ at the extracytosolic surface of the H,K ATPase. Substantial evidence has accumulated to indicate that this is indeed the case and that activation of the proton pump results from association of the H,K ATPase with a K^+ permeability in the membrane of the secretory canaliculus.

When gastric membrane vesicles are isolated from unstimulated tissues essentially all the H,K ATPase requires addition of K^+ ionophore to exhibit enzymatic or transport activity. When isolated from stimulated tissues the H,K ATPase is able to transport protons in the absence of ionophore indicating that the membrane vesicle now contains an endogenous K^+ permeability. Similarly, in permeabilized parietal cells the proportion of ATPase and transport activity which requires ionophore decreases with cell stimulation indicating that more of the H,K ATPase is associated with an endogenous K^+ permeability. When intact cells are incubated with NH_4^+, a membrane permeable K^+ substitute, the H,K ATPase becomes activated. NH_4^+ gains access to the extracytosolic exchange site of the H,K ATPase as the permeable gas NH_3 acquires a proton to form the exchangeable species, NH_4^+, which is recycled back to the cytosolic surface. Accordingly, although NH_4^+ activates the proton pump, no acid actually accumulates under this condition and the enzyme activity is measured as ATP hydrolysis or some index of metabolic turnover. These findings show that association of the H,K ATPase with an endogenous K^+ permeability is necessary and sufficient for activation of the proton pump in the parietal cell.

Activation of H,K ATPase in the parietal cell by either ACh or histamine. Modeled here is translocation of the pump from cytoplasmic to canalicular membrane concomitant with activation of KCl transport across the canalicular membrane. Elevation of cAMP and $[Ca]_i$ are both able to stimulate acid secretion.

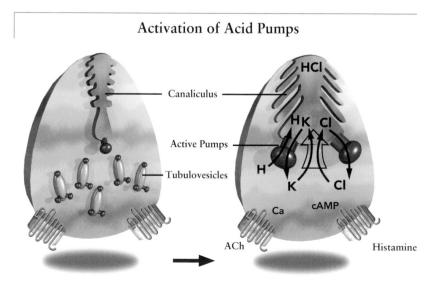

Activation of Acid Pumps

The exact mechanism by which the H,K ATPase associates with a K$^+$ permeability remains controversial. It has been known for some time that stimulation of the parietal cell leads to a change in the morphology of the cell involving a disappearance of cytoplasmic tubules and the development of the secretory canaliculus. This was the basis on which Golgi proposed the parietal cell as the site for acid secretion over 100 years ago. It now is accepted generally that the canaliculus forms as a result of incorporation of cytoplasmic tubules into the apical surface of the parietal cell. Additionally there is a reorganization of the cytoskeleton to form microvilli at the canalicular surface. Likely it is within the events of cytoskeletal reorganization that the membrane cytoskeletal linker, ezrin, contributes to the stimulus-secretion coupling pathway. While there still is controversy concerning the mechanism for incorporation of tubule membrane into the canaliculus, a clear consequence of this event is the translocation of H,K ATPase molecules from the tubules to the canalicular microvilli. When present in the cytoplasmic tubules the H,K ATPase is inactive as a proton pump due to the lack of K$^+$ access to the interior (extracytosolic) of the tubule. It should be noted that if K$^+$ access is provided exogenously, the proton pump can be activated even in the tubules. Translocation of the H,K ATPase from the tubules to the canaliculus results in activation of the proton pump since the canaliculus contains a K$^+$ permeability.

The nature and origin of the K$^+$ permeability which is associated with the H,K ATPase in the canaliculus remain undefined. It has been proposed that the canalicular membrane contains parallel conductances for K$^+$ and Cl$^-$ or alternatively that there is a KCl cotransporter. Attempts to demonstrate a K$^+$ conductance in the apical membrane generally have given a negative result although there is good evidence for a Cl$^-$ conductance. Regardless of the nature of the K$^+$ pathway, it must be argued that most of the K$^+$ permeability is lost from the apical membrane in the unstimulated parietal cell. If this were not the case, the gastric mucosa would continuously secrete KCl in substantial quantities. Thus the molecules representing the K$^+$ permeability must be inactivated, removed from the surface or both during the transition from a secreting to a non-secreting parietal cell.

Assembly and trafficking of the H,K ATPase

The two subunits of the ATPase are synthesized in the endoplasmic reticulum of the parietal cell. The only other location of the pump is in the intercalated cells of the distal tubule of the kidney. Formation of transmembrane segments requires interaction of hydrophobic sequences during translation with the interior surface of the translocon. A sequence that determines membrane insertion with its N-terminal cytoplasmic and C-terminal extracytoplasmic is termed a signal anchor sequence. A sequence that returns the translating protein back to the cytoplasm, hence with its N-terminal extracytoplasmic is named a stop transfer sequence.

The process of assembly of the transmembrane domain of the α subunit involves co-translational insertion of the first 4 transmembrane segments as sequential signal anchor/stop transfer sequences. Insertion of the 5th, 6th, 7th and 8th transmembrane segments appears to occur as a bundle with protein-protein interaction of the 5th and 6th segments more significant than protein-membrane lipid interaction. The 9th and 10th segments then insert as signal anchor and stop transfer sequences respectively. The single transmembrane domain of the β subunit is efficiently inserted as a signal anchor sequence and the remaining 200 amino acids are located extracytoplasmically. All 7 N-glycosylation consensus sequences are utilized and are core glycosylated in the endoplasmic reticulum and then processed in the Golgi to form the mature subunit.

The β subunit is required for stabilization of the a subunit and is sorted to the plasma membrane in transfected cells. The strong interaction between the TM7/TM8 loop of the α subunit and the two regions of the β subunit discussed in the chapter on the structure of the H,K ATPase thus not only stabilizes but sorts the α subunit to the plasma membrane.

In the parietal cell, the Na,K ATPase is sorted to the basal lateral surface and the H,K ATPase to the cytoplasmic tubules destined for insertion into the canalicular membrane with stimulation of secretion. The basis for this selective sorting is not well defined. Part of the sorting signal may be due to the β subunit. Recent work has shown that mutation of tyr 19 in transgenic mice results in retention of the ATPase in the canalicular membrane suggesting that perhaps phosphorylation of this residue is important in the stimulatory cycle of the enzyme. However, this event is subsequent to the cellular sorting of the two pumps.

Synthesis and turnover of the H,K ATPase

Biosynthesis of the two subunits of the ATPase takes place in the endoplasmic reticulum of the parietal cell. It appears that there is a need for co-assembly of the two pump subunits for stabilization of the α subunit and for targeting of the dimer to the post Golgi membrane compartment and the plasma membrane.

Upstream sequences have been identified by gel retardation assay on both the α and β genes that bind gastric nuclear proteins selectively, but the role of these particular proteins has not been identified.

Activation of the H2 receptor by histamine injection or by elevation of histamine release by gastrin results in a transient increase in mRNA for the α subunit. H2 receptor antagonists prevent the gastrin or histamine dependent elevation of mRNA and appear to reduce mRNA to slightly below basal levels. These data were obtained in the rat, and the ATPase genes of this species possess cAMP and Ca responsive elements.

The half life of the α subunit has usually been inferred rather than directly measured. Treatment of rats with cycloheximide resulted in a loss of ATPase activity with a half-life of 72 hrs. Recovery from inhibition with the covalent inhibitor, omeprazole, showed a half-life of 30 hrs in the same series of experiments. Other workers have claimed a half life of recovery as short as 15 hrs. Direct measurement of the half life of the ATPase in the rat gave a value of 54 hrs. Treatment with omeprazole did not change this value, whereas treatment with the H2 receptor antagonist, ranitidine, gave a value of 125 hrs, a statistically significant increase. From these data, it may be that reversal of PPI inhibition is due, not only to *de novo* pump biosynthesis, but also to removal of the bound inhibitor, due either to chemical instability of the S-S (disulfide) bridge or to access of GSH (glutathione) as the pump cycles between canalicular and tubular compartment.

The determinants of pump turnover are not well understood. From the above data, evidently binding of the covalent inhibitor, omeprazole, does not affect turnover, whereas inhibition of cell stimulation slows turnover. An hypothesis that would explain these observations is that pump turnover depends mainly on endocytosis of the pump from the canalicular membrane. Stimulation of acid secretion, which results in more pump being present in that membrane, would increase turnover; inhibition of acid secretion by reducing stimulation which results in less pump being present in the canaliculus will slow turnover. Neutral events such as inhibition of the pump itself, if there is no change in the amount of pump in the canalicular membrane, will result in a rate of turnover similar to that found in untreated individuals.

A model depicting turnover and biosynthesis of the H,K ATPase is shown in the following figure.

The biosynthesis, membrane cycling and turnover of the H,K ATPase in the parietal cell, with the various t½ values of insertion and retrieval.

Life Cycle of Acid Pump

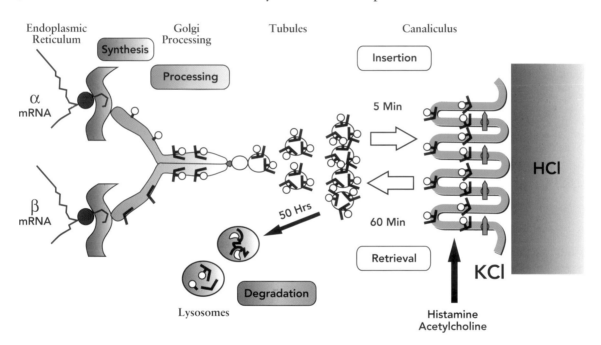

Parietal cell homeostasis

The secretion of 160 mM HCl across the canalicular membrane of the parietal cell represents a significant challenge to the cell's ability to maintain pH and electrolyte balance. In the steady state, transporters located in the basolateral membrane must respond to this challenge by replacing the secreted Cl⁻ and removing the accumulated excess base. A general model depicting the components involved maintaining parietal cell homeostasis is presented.

The existence of the various transporters shown has been demonstrated experimentally, although the quantitative role of each component still is subject to some speculation.

Activity of the H,K ATPase results in a primary secretion of 160 mM HCl into the secretory canaliculus. Since the H,K ATPase is electroneutral, it is necessary that the KCl permeability pathway associated with the canaliculus transfer a minimum of 160 mmoles of KCl for each liter of fluid secreted.

This is true whether the KCl pathway consists of conductive or electroneutral transporters. It is likely, in fact, that the KCl pathway allows transfer of a slight excess of KCl over the minimum required for the production of HCl. This is suggested both by the observation that gastric secretions contain a low but significant concentration of KCl and by the likelihood that the H,K ATPase is not fully efficient at recovering K^+ from the canalicular fluid. In the absence of other mechanisms, the combined activity of the transporters at the apical pole of the parietal cell would lead to alkalinization of the cell and depletion of cellular Cl^- and K^+. The potential disturbances in electrolyte balance are prevented by the activity of transporters at the basolateral membrane. These include an anion exchanger (AE), a sodium, proton exchanger (NHE), and the Na,K ATPase.

Basolateral transporters

The existence of a basolateral AE in the parietal cell was postulated since the conductance of the parietal cell for H^+, OH^-, and HCO_3^- was insufficient to account for the removal of intracellular base. A mechanism in erythrocyte membranes which exchanges HCO_3^- for Cl^- led to the proposal that such a mechanism in the parietal cell could account both for the extrusion of base and for the replacement of secreted Cl^-. Cloning and sequencing of AE proteins indicates that there is a family of Band 3 related proteins which exhibit differential tissue expression. The AE isoforms appear to have conserved C-terminal regions containing the membrane spanning domains and variable N-terminal sequences. The isoform designated AE_2^- appears to be the predominant transporter of the parietal cell.

The presence of an Na/H exchanger (NHE) in parietal cells is demonstrated by the finding that recovery of intracellular pH (pH_i) from an acid load is dependent on sodium in the medium and blocked by high concentrations of amiloride (Na/H exchange inhibitor). As with the AE, the NHE's are known to be a family of proteins. In contrast to the AE isoforms however, the NHE isoforms exhibit a variable C-terminal region and a conserved N-terminal region that contains the membrane spanning domains. It is suggested that isoform NHE-1 is the primary transporter in gastric chief cells and mucous cells while NHE-4 may be the basal lateral transporter of the parietal cell. The significance of differential cellular expression of the isoforms is unclear although it may relate to differential sensitivity of the isoforms to regulatory factors. Most of the consensus sequences for covalent modification by protein kinases are located in the isoform specific C-terminal regions.

The two exchangers, together with the Na,K ATPase, appear to be the primary transporters responsible for maintaining parietal cell homeostasis. An additional transporter, a $NaHCO_3$ cotransporter, has been reported to be present in the parietal cell but its functional significance has not been defined.

The basolateral membrane of the parietal cell also contains conductive channels for both K^+ and Cl^- since these two ions dominate the membrane potential.

The presence of a basolateral K^+ conductance has been confirmed by direct electrophysiological measurements whereas the Cl^- conductance has not as of yet. The contribution of the conductances to the net fluxes of K^+ or Cl^- have not been determined but likely are small relative to those of the Na pump and AE.

In addition it has recently been shown that older parietal cells express the $NaKCl_2$ cotransporter which suggests that these cells secrete Cl ion since Cl is maintained above equilibrium by coupling of basal lateral Na,K and 2Cl entry across the transporter to activity of the basal lateral Na,K ATPase. This Cl secretion model applies to other epithelia such as intestine and kidney.

Homeostatic responses

Under nonsecreting conditions, as with most cells, the parietal cell most likely maintains its electrolyte balance thru activity of the Na pump and nominal responses of the NHE and AE to incidental perturbations of pH_i.

Upon activation of the proton pump it would be anticipated that the parietal cell becomes more alkaline since for each proton secreted an equivalent OH^-, rapidly converted to HCO_3^- by carbonic anhydrase, is accumulated within the cell. However, experimental measurements during stimulation of acid secretion indicate only a small or no change in pH_i as compared to the non-stimulated state.

Only changes of pH_{in} on the order of 0.1 pH units were observed for individual parietal cells. While somewhat larger changes were reported for populations of isolated parietal cells, most of this response was not blocked by inhibition of the H,K ATPase with SCH28080. It is noted that the small responses of pH_i were monophasic with a relatively slow onset indicating that there is no transient alkalinization followed by recovery to a new steady state value.

The minimal responses of pH_i to stimulation initially could reflect intracellular buffering but in the steady state require that the AE, which is primarily responsible for base excretion, be activated coordinately with the H,K ATPase.

The simplest explanation for the increase in AE activity is that the slight increase of intracellular HCO_3^- (indicated as a small rise of pH_{in}) combined with a decrease of intracellular Cl^- is sufficient to increase the rate of anion exchange by the observed 3-5 fold. NHE activity is inhibited during steady state secretion and this also is attributed to the small rise of pH_{in}.

Alternatively, it has been proposed that the second messengers, i.e., cAMP and Ca_{in} which activate the proton pump may modulate the pH_i regulatory transporters directly by altering their pH set-point. Accordingly stimulation of parietal cells was observed to result in an elevated pH_i which occurred before detectable acid secretion and which was blocked by amiloride, suggesting a direct activation of the NHE.

Further, it was suggested that an initial rise of pH_i due to activation of the NHE could result in an anticipatory activation of the AE and thus prevent any significant transient alkalinization of the parietal cell.

While it is reasonable to expect that the NHE and AE interact in so far as both are required for normal pH_i regulation and are inversely affected by changes in pH_i, it is unclear whether such interactions include a cause and effect response to stimulation.

Apart from a role in regulating pH_i in the resting parietal cell the NHE may serve indirectly to supply K⁺ which is lost into the gastric secretions. Although the NHE activity is inhibited during secretion, it is not abolished. The exchange of cellular protons for Na⁺ by the NHE would lead to uptake of K⁺ by the Na,K ATPase and thus replace any net loss of K⁺ across the apical membrane. Perhaps the observed initial activation of the NHE is more critical for K⁺ conservation than it is for AE activation and regulation of pH_{in}. This would be the case if any decrease in intracellular K⁺ due to secretion were insufficient to stimulate Na pump activity directly. Despite the apparent complexity of interactions it appears that the responses of the AE, NHE and Na pump are qualitatively sufficient to account for electrolyte balance in both the resting and the secreting parietal cell. A representation of the homeostatic mechanisms available to the parietal cell is shown in the figure.

The parietal cell is a remarkable example of the product of evolution dedicating an epithelial cell to the production of HCl, by providing ATP via a large number of mitochondria, a specialized ion pump, regulatory receptors and an intrinsic intelligence enabling secretion of 160 mm HCl without damage to itself.

Ion Transport Homeostasis

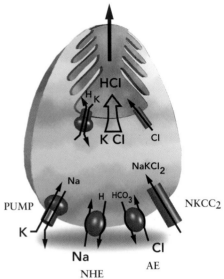

The ion pathways in the parietal cell. On bottom left is the Na,K ATPase, then the Na/H exchanger (NHE), then the anion exchanger (AE) and finally the NaKCl₂ cotransporter (NKCC2).

REFERENCES

Adams, H., Card, W., Riddell, M. et al. *Dose-response curves for effect of histamine on acid secretion in man*. Br. J. Pharmacol. 9, 329-334 (1954).

Altman, R. *Die Elementarorganismen und ihre Beziehung zu den Zellen*. Leipzig: Veit and Co, 1894.

Alvarez, W. *Sixty years of vagotomy: A review of some 200 articles*. Gastroenterol. 10, 413-441 (1948).

Andersson, K., Chen, D., Hakanson, R., Mattson, H., Sundler, F. *Enterochromaffin-like cells in the rat stomach: effect of alpha-fluoromethylhistidine evoked histamine depletion*. Cell Tissue Research. 270, 7-13 (1992).

Ash, A., Schild, H. *Receptors mediating some of the actions of histamine*. Br. J. Pharmacol. 27, 427-439 (1966).

Barger, G., Dale, H. *The presence in ergot and physiological action of B-imidazolylethylamine*. J. Physiol. Lond. 40, 38-40 (1910).

Black, J.W., Duncan, W.A.M., Durant, C.J., Ganellin, C.R., Parsons, M.E. *Definition and antagonism of histamine H2 receptors*. Nature 236, 385 (1972).

Bayliss, W., Starling, E. *Preliminary communication on the causation of the so-called "peripheral reflex secretion" of the pancreas*. Lancet 2, 810-813 (1902).

Bayliss, W. *Principles of general physiology*. London: Longmans, Green, 1915, p. 700-706.

Beaumont, W. *Experiments and observations on the gastric juice and physiology of digestion*. Plattsburgh, New York: A.P. Allen. Facsimile of the original edition of 1833 together with a biographical essay, *A Pioneer American Physiologist*, by Sir William Osler. Cambridge, Massachusetts: Harvard University Press, 1929.

Beaumont, W. *Further experiments on the case of Alexis St. Martin, who was wounded in the stomach by a load of buckshot, detailed in the Recorder for 1825*. Med Recorder 9, 94-97 (1826).

Bertaccini, G., and Coruzzi, G. *Control of gastric acid secretion by histamine H2 receptor antagonists and anticholinergics*. Pharmacol. Res. 21, 339 (1989).

Best C and McHenry E. *The inactivation of histamine*. J. Physiol. Lond. 70, 349-372 (1930).

Brillat-Savarin J.A. *The Physiology of Taste (Meditation on trascendental gastronomy)*. San Francisco, CA: Northpoint Press, 1986.

Brimblecombe, R.W., Duncan, W.A.M., Durant, G.J., Emmett, J.C., Ganellin, C.R., Leslie, G.B., Parsons, M.E. *Characterization and development of cimetidine as a histamine H2-receptor antagonist*. Gastroenterology 74, 339 (1978).

Brodie, B. *Experiments and observations on the influence of the nerves of the eighth pair on the secretion of the stomach*. In: *Abstracts of the Papers Printed in the Philosophical Transactions of the Royal Society of London, 1800-1814*, London: Taylor, Red Lion, Court, Fleet Street, 1832, p. 102-106.

Capella, C., Vassallo, G., Solcia, E. *Light and electron microscopic identification of the histamine-storing agyrophil (ECL) cell in murine stomach and of its equivalent in other mammals*. Zeitschrift Zellforschung 118, 68 (1971).

Card, W., Marks, I. *The relationship between the acid output of the stomach following "maximal" histamine stimulation and the parietal cell mass*. Clin. Sci. 19, 147-163 (1960).

Carter, D.C., Forrest, J., Werner, W., Heading, R.C., Park, J., Shearman, D.J.C. *Effect of histamine H2-receptor blockade on vagally induced gastric acid secretion in man*. Br. Med. J. 3, 554 (1974).

Chew, C.S., Hersey, S.J., Sachs, G., Berglindh, T. *Histamine responsiveness of isolated gastric glands*. Am. J. Physiol. 238, G312 (1980).

Code, C. *Histamine and gastric secretion*. In: *Histamine*, edited by Wolstenholme, G. and O'Connor, C. Boston: Little, Brown & Co., 1956, p. 189-219.

Code, C. *The role of gastric juice in experimental production of peptic ulcer*. Surg. Clin. North Am. 23, 1091-1101 (1943).

Costa, M., Furness, J.B., Llewellyn-Smith, I.J. *Histochemistry of the enteric nervous system*. In: Johnson, L.R. (ed.) *Physiology of the Gastrointestinal Tract*. 2nd ed., Vol. 1, Raven Press, New York, U.S.A., p. 1, 1987.

Dale, H. *Adventures in physiology*. London: Pergamon Press, 1953.

Debas, H.T., Lloyd K.C.K. *Peripheral regulation of gastric acid secretion*. In: Johnson, L.R. (ed.) *Physiology of the Gastrointestinal Tract*. 3rd ed., Vol 2, Raven Press, New York, U.S.A., 1994, p. 1185.

Dohlman, H.G., Thorner, J., Caron, M.G., Lefkowitz, R.J. *G-proteins*. Ann. Rev. Biochem. 60, 653 (1991).

Dolinsky, J. *Etudes sur l'excitabilité sécrétoire spécifique de la muqueuse du canal digestif, l'acide, comme stimulant de la secretion pancreatique*. Arch. Soc. Biol. St. Petersbourg 3, 399-427 (1895).

Dragstedt, L. *Section of the vagus nerves to the stomach in the treatment of peptic ulcer*. Ann. Surg. 126, 687-708 (1947).

Edkins, J. *The chemical mechanism of gastric secretion*. J. Physiol. Lond. 34, 133-144 (1906).

Fujita, T., Kobayashi, S. *Structure and function of gut endocrine cells*. Int. Rev. Cytol. 6, 187 (1977).

Gantz, I., Schaeffer, M., Del Valle, J., Logsdon, C., Campbell, V., Uhler, M., Yamada, T. *Molecular cloning of a gene encoding the histamine H2-receptor*. Proc. Natl. Acad. Sci. U.S.A. 488, 429 (1991).

Gerber, J.G., Payne, N.A. *The role of gastric secretagogues in regulating gastric histamine release in vivo*. Gastroenterology 102, 403 (1992).

Gregory, R., Tracey, H. *The preparation and properties of gastrin*. J. Physiol. Lond. 149, 70-71 (1959).

Hakanson, R., Owman, C.H., Sporong, B., Sundler, F. *Electron microscopic identification of the histamine-storing argyrophil (enterochromaffin-like) cells in the rat stomach.* Z. Zell-forschung Mikroskop. Anatomie 122, 460 (1971).

Hakanson, R., Boettcher, G., Ekblad, F., Panula, P., Simonsson, M., Dohlsten, M., Hallberg, T., Sundler, F. *Histamine in endocrine cells in the stomach.* Histochemistry 86, 5 (1986).

Hanzel, D., Reggio, H., Bretscher, A., Forte, J.G., Mangeat, P. *The secretion-stimulated 80K phosphoprotein of parietal cells is ezrin, and has properties of a membrane cytoskeletal linker in the induced apical microvilli* [published erratum appears in EMBO J 1991 Dec; 10(12): 3978-81]. EMBO J. 10, 2363-2373 (1991).

Heidenhain, R. *Untersuchungen über den Bau der Labdrusen.* Arch. Mikro. Anat. 6, 368-406 (1870).

Hirschowitz, B.: *Neural and hormonal control of gastric secretion.* In: *Handbook of Physiology*, Section 6: *The Gastrointestinal Tract.* Vol. 3, Oxford University Press, New York, 1989, p. 127.

Hoffman, H.H., Schnitzlein, N.N. *The number of vagus fibers in man.* Anat. Rec. 139, 429 (1969).

Home, E. *Hints on the subject of animal secretions.* In: *Abstracts of the Papers Printed in the Philosophical Transactions of the Royal Society of London, 1800-1814*, London: Taylor, Red Lion, Court, Fleet Street, 1832.

Hunter, J. *Essays and Observations on Natural History, Anatomy, Physiology, Psychology and Geology.* Vols. 1 and 2. London: J. Va. Vooret, 1861.

Johnson, R.G., Carty, S.E., Scarpa, A. *Coupling of H^+ gradients to catecholamine transport in chromaffin granules.* Ann. N.Y. Acad. Sci. 456, 254 (1985).

Kahlson, G., Rosengren, E., Svann, D. et al. *Mobilization and formation of histamine in the gastric mucosa as related to acid secretion.* J. Physiol. Lond. 174, 400-416 (1964).

Kajimura, M., Reuben, M., Sachs, G. *The muscarinic receptor gene expressed in rabbit parietal cells is the M3 subtype.* Gastroenterology 103, 870 (1992).

Komarov, S. *Gastrin.* Proc. Soc. Exp. Biol. Med. 38, 514-516 (1938).

Kopin, A.S., Lee, Y.M., McBride, E.W., Miller, L.J., Lu, M., Lin, H.Y., Kolakowski Jr., L. F., Beinborn, M. (1992) *Expression cloning and characterization of the canine parietal cell gastrin receptor.* Proc. Natl. Acad. Sci. U.S.A. 89, 3605-3609 (1992).

Larsson, H., Golterman, N., De Magistris, L., Rehfeld, J.F., Schwartz, T.W. *Somatostatin cell processes as pathways for paracrine secretion.* Science 205, 1393 (1979).

Lewin, M.J.M. *The somatostatin receptor in the GI tract.* Annual Review of Physiology 54, 455 (1992).

Lichtenberger, L.M. *Importance of food in the regulation of gastrin release and formation.* Am. J. Physiol. 243, G429 (1982).

Major, R.H. *Jean Cruveilhier.* In: *Classic description of Disease.* Springfield, IL Charles C. Thomas, 1932, p. 593-596.

Modlin, I.M, Waisbren, S.J. *Pavlov in the U.S.A.* Gastro. Int. 6 (1), 48-53 (1993).

Montegre, A.J. *Expériences sur la digestion dans l'homme. Presentées a la première classe de l'Institut de France, le 8 Septembre 1812.* Paris: Le Normant Colas, 1814.

Müller, E. *Über der Fundusdrusen des Magens.* Z. Wissensch. Zool. 64, 624-647 (1898).

Nwokolo, C.U., Smith J.T., Sawyerr, A.M., Pounder, R.E. *Rebound intragastric hyperacidity after abrupt withdrawal of histamine H2 receptor blockade.* Gut 32, 1455 (1991).

Padfield, P.J., Balch, W.E., Jamieson, J.D. *A synthetic peptide of the Rab3a effector domain stimulates amylase release from permeabilized pancreatic acini.* Proc. Natl. Acad. Sci. U.S.A. 89, 1656-1660 (1992).

Prinz, C., Kajimura, M., Scott, D.R., Mercier, F., Helander, H.F., Sachs, G. *Histamine secretion from rat enterochromaffin-like cells.* Gastroenterology 105, 449 (1993).

Prinz, C., Sachs, G., Walsh, J., Coy, D., Wu, V. *The Somatostatin Receptor Subtype on Rat Enterochromaffin-like Cells.* Gastroenterology, 107, 1067 (1994).

Rangachari, P.K. *Histamine, mercurial messenger in the gut.* Am. J. Physiol. 262, G1 (1992).

Schepp, W., Prinz, C., Hakanson, R., Schusdziarra, V., Classen, M. *Effects of bombesin-like peptides on isolated rat gastric G-cells.* Reg. Peptides 28, 241 (1990).

Schubert, M.L., Makhlouf, G.M. *Regulation of gastrin and somatostatin secretion by intramural neurons: effect of nicotinic receptor stimulation with dimethyl-phenylpiperazinium.* Gastroenterology 83, 626-632 (1982).

Seal, A.M., Yamada, T., Debas, H.T. *Somatostatin 14 and 28, clearance and potency on gastric function in dogs.* Am. J. Physiol. 143, G97 (1982).

Simonsson, M., Eriksson, S., Hakanson, R., Lind, T., Loenroth, L., Lundell, L., O'Connor, D.T., Sundler, F. *Endocrine cells in the human oxyntic mucosa.* Scand. J. Gastroenterol. 23, 1089 (1988).

Tache, Y. *Central nervous system regulation of acid secretion.* In: Johnson, L. R. (ed): *Physiology of the Gastrointestinal Tract.* 2nd ed., Vol. 2, Raven Press, New York, U.S.A., 1987, p. 911.

Thomas, H.A., Machen, T. E. *Regulation of Cl/HCO_3 exchange in gastric parietal cells.* Cell Regul. 2, 727-737 (1991).

Vesalius, A. *De Humani Corporis Fabrica.* Basel, 1543, p. 327-330.

Walsh, J.H. *Gastrointestinal Hormones.* In: Johnson, L. R. (ed): *Physiology of the Gastrointestinal Tract.* 3rd ed., Vol. .1, Raven Press, New York, U.S.A., p. 181-254, 1994.

Wilkes, J.M., Kajimura, M., Scott, D.R., Hersey, S.J., Sachs, G. *Muscarinic responses of gastric parietal cells.* J. Membrane Biol. 122, 97 (1991).

Wood, J.D. *Physiology of the enteric nervous system.* In: Johnson, L. R. (ed): *Physiology of the Gastrointestinal Tract.* 3rd ed., Vol. 1, Raven Press, New York, U.S.A., 1994, p. 423.

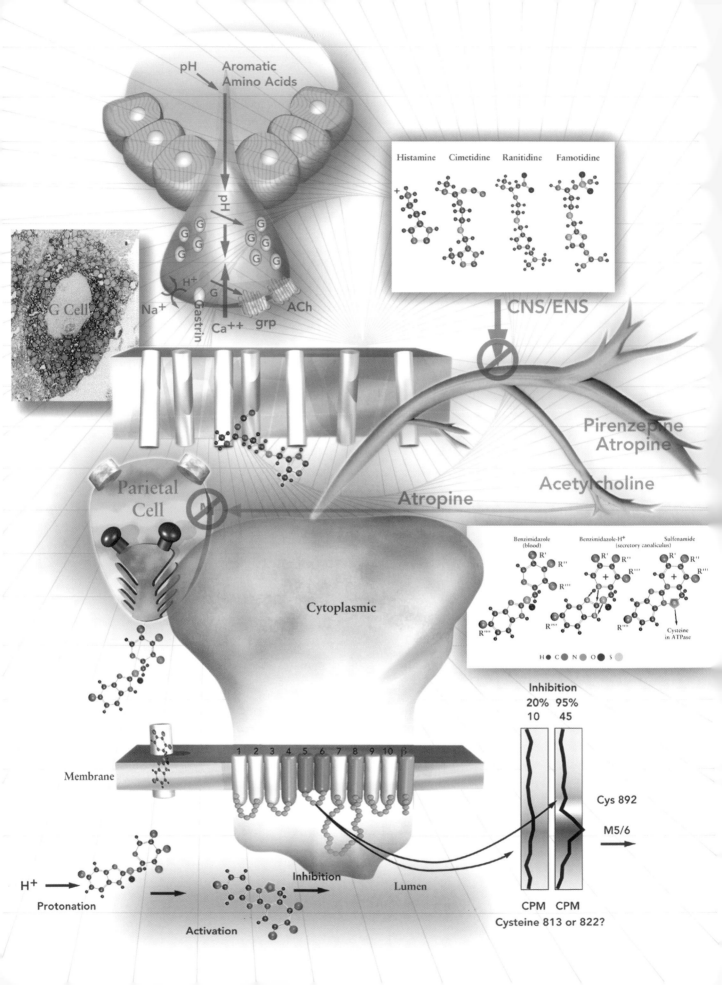

S E C T I O N   3

PHARMACOLOGY
OF
ACID
SECRETION

CHAPTER 1

**History of Therapeutic Approaches
to Acid Related Diseases**

CHAPTER 2

Inhibition of the Histamine 2 Receptor

CHAPTER 3

Inhibition of the Gastric Acid Pump

CHAPTER 1
HISTORY OF THERAPEUTIC APPROACHES TO ACID RELATED DISEASES

The evolution of therapy

Prout initially identified gastric acid as hydrochloric acid in 1823. However, it was only in the late nineteenth century that hyperchlorhydria was recognised as contributing to ulcer generation. For centuries treatment had not changed. Only as pathogenesis and stimulatory pathways became recognized, did surgical and then medical therapy became more focussed and more effective.

Diet

In 1915 Dr. Bertram Sippy advocated hourly feedings of milk, eggs and purees from 7:00 a.m. to 8:00 p.m. Between these hourly feedings and every half hour for two and one half hours after the last feeding, Sippy powder (calcium and sodium bicarbonate) was administered. In addition, to relieve dyspepsia, the patient's stomach was aspirated at regular intervals each night. This regimen provided a challenge both for the patient and the nursing staff.

An alternative dietary therapy developed by Dr. Richard Doll involved the use for up to three weeks of continuous milk drips through a nasogastric tube with or without alkali. While this therapeutic strategy seemed to improve the nutritional status of his patients, the obsessional need for dietary management and regulation of alkali intake so interfered with the lifestyle of patients and so often failed to prevent complications from developing, that even surgery became a reasonable option.

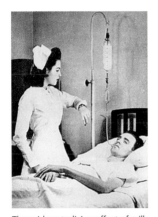

The acid neutralizing effect of milk and alkalis administered by nasogastric tube was proposed by R. Doll to promote ulcer healing and relieve pain. Many felt that the positive effect reflected the result of prolonged bed rest, female care and the Freudian power of maternal milk. The treatment soon fell into disregard.

B. Sippy of Chicago devised a complex dietary regimen of bland food which included alkali administration. Patients and physicians found the meticulous timing of meals and the detailed attention necessary to determine their contents difficult to adhere to on a long-term basis.

Surgery

André Raphael Latarjet (1877-1947). (Courtesy of M. Latarjet). His anatomic work laid the basis for the successful management by vagotomy (1923) of individuals with peptic ulcer disease.

The first dedicated operation was gastrectomy but the high morbidity and mortality engendered a degree of caution in both patient and physician alike. Subsequently vagotomy, which had been initiated in France by Raymond Latarjet and then reactivated in North America by Lester Dragstedt, provided a better alternative for management. Dragstedt's observations that gastric acid output was decreased by vagotomy were widely cited in favour of this operation. Initial post-operative problems due to decreased gastric emptying were subsequently obviated by the construction of a variety of pyloroplasties to facilitate drainage. Recurrence of peptic ulcer disease and the long term side effects of the surgery itself show this therapy option was suboptimal.

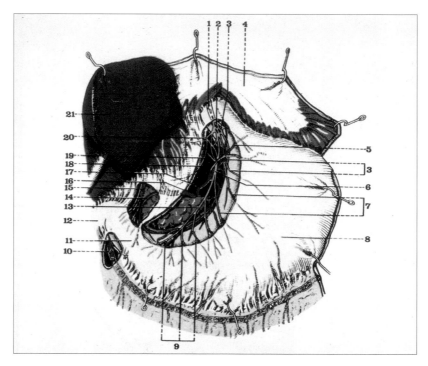

Original hand drawing by Latarjet depicting the vagal nerve distribution along the lesser curvature of the stomach (Nerves of Latarjet). 1925.

Antacids-surfactants

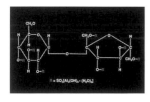

Sucralfate chemical structure. The development of complex surfactant agents to neutralize and protect the ulcerated mucosa resulted in effective healing rates and avoided some side effects of other agents. Of particular interest has been the ability of such compounds to promote ulcer healing by the proposed mechanism of growth factor delivery to the ulcer site itself.

The evolving trend to utilize less invasive methodology in the management of peptic ulcer disease resulted in a significant interest in the use of antacids in association with both diet modification and bed rest.

Numerous preparations with different concentrations of alkali or buffers were developed to remove the pain of peptic ulceration and to facilitate healing. Their widespread availability and relative safety resulted in broad popular acceptance.

Such agents required four to six daily administrations and resulted in a high frequency of side effects which included constipation, diarrhea, and decreased absorption of concomitantly administered medications. Large doses of baking soda even have led to gastric rupture!

Protective agents

The liquorice plant was regarded as an important component of many early herbal remedies.

Glycerrhetinic acid is a constituent of liquorice which had been used in folk remedies for peptic ulcer disease. For some time this compound in the form of carbenoxolone was tried as a means of peptic ulcer treatment but its toxicity prevented its introduction. A sulfated polysaccharide, sucralfate, was introduced to the market as a protective agent and has had some following for treatment of peptic ulcer disease. It is claimed to enhance the gastric barrier.

Gastric receptors

As it became recognized that acid secretion depended on stimulation by a variety of ligands such as acetylcholine, gastrin and histamine, a more logical approach to pharmacotherapy could be taken.

The atropine family

Extract of belladonna began to be used towards the latter half of the nineteenth century for treatment of peptic ulcer disease. The active principle, atropine, is a non-selective muscarinic antagonist able to block transmission in

Atropine-like derivatives of plants including deadly Nightshade (Belladonna) were utilised for their cosmetic influence on woman's eyes as well as their acid inhibiting properties.

the enteric nervous system. This medication was administered one hour before each meal and at bed-time, but in order to ensure effectiveness, the evening dosage had to be sufficiently high to control symptoms throughout the night. The widespread distribution of muscarinic receptors results in unpleasant and often intolerable side effects such as blurred vision, dry mouth and bladder dysfunction. A possible solution was to develop more selective muscarinic antagonists. One such was pirenzepine, a relatively selective muscarinic M1 receptor antagonist. There were still side effects and relatively low efficacy. A higher affinity M1 antagonist, telenzepine arrived too late to make any impact on ulcer treatment.

Prostaglandins

These natural products were discovered in the 1960s. They are derived from arachidonic acid which is released from phospholipids or diacyl glycerol by the action of phospholipase A2. There are two enzyme cascades responsible for prostaglandin generation, based on cyclooxygenase 1 (constitutive) and cyclooxygenase II (regulated).

After the initial conversion of arachidonic acid into the prostaglandin core structure, several modifications generate various prostaglandins with specific affinities to different prostaglandin receptors. Prostaglandins of the E class are potent inhibitors of acid secretion by action at a G_i coupled EP3 receptor. These therefore were natural lead compounds for development of anti-ulcer agents. The natural prostaglandins have a short half-life and before subtypes of the receptors were recognized, the concept driving development of these compounds was prolongation of their half life. The compound that is now on market, misoprostil, is not particularly receptor subtype selective and results in stimulation of intestinal secretion and diarrhea in at least 20% of treated individuals.

It was introduced as therapy for NSAID based gastric damage based on replacement of natural prostaglandins depleted by administration of Cox 1 inhibitors such as aspirin or indomethacin. The impending introduction of selective Cox II inhibitors will likely remove the necessity for prostaglandin replacement therapy in NSAID treatment. They do appear to play a role in stimulation of bicarbonate secretion, especially that stimulated by acid.

The H2 receptor antagonists

The first series of H2 receptor antagonists was synthesized in Welwyn Garden City, at a site of a stately home occupied by Smith, Klein & French (SK&F). This house had been used for development of diving gear during WW II since there was a very deep pond on the property. Cimetidine reformed the treatment of acid-related diseases by introducing effective pharmacotherapy that was free of significant side effects and largely negligible adverse events. Peculiarly James Black, the project leader, Bill Duncan, the site director and Bryce Douglas, the head of research of SK&F (based then in Philadelphia), were all Glaswegian Scots. As Welwyn was working on the receptor antagonist, Philadelphia was working on pump inhibitors.

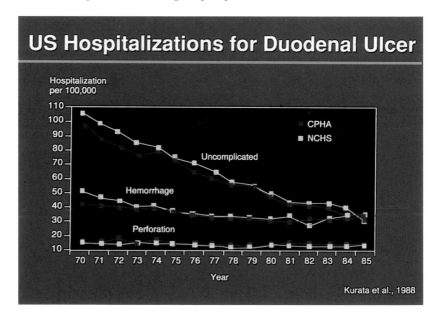

The introduction of H2RA's was associated with an exponential decrease in hospital admissions, although duodenal ulcer patient numbers were already declining.

During the 1980s, the H2 receptor antagonists became first-line therapy in peptic ulcer disease and led to an improvement in quality of life for a large number of patients. It was found to be superior to any other form of medication at the time, giving good inhibition of night time secretion and lesser inhibition of day time acid secretion.

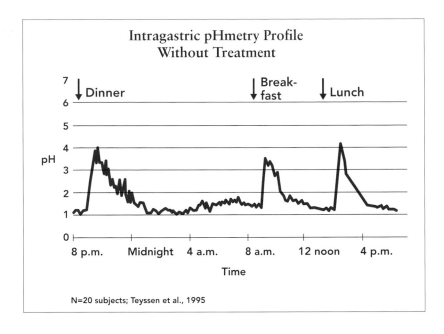

Intragastric pHmetry Profile Without Treatment

N=20 subjects; Teyssen et al., 1995

Typical profile for intragastric pH for untreated healthy individuals.

Whereas the introduction of the H2 receptor antagonists class of agents revolutionized the management of acid peptic related disease and provided a major increase in the quality of life for innumerable patients, it was apparent that further improvement in the regulation of the acid secretory process would yield better clinical results.

This was especially true of erosive esophagitis. The identification of the proton pump as the final step in the pathway of parietal cell acid secretion provided a unique opportunity for better control of parietal cell secretion.

Gastrin antagonists

The central role of gastrin in stimulation of ECL cell release of histamine has resulted in some significant effort being applied to development of gastrin antagonists. For many years after the definition of the structure of gastrin, gastrin antagonists were sought in the form of peptide analogs of pentagastrin, but without success. More recently, non-peptide antagonists of both the CCK-A and CCK-B receptors have been synthesized based on a benzodiazepine core structure. Some of the more recent compounds are potent and highly selective for their receptor subtype and may be introduced clinically, although it would be surprising if proved superior to H2 receptor antagonists

Proton pump inhibitors (PPI's)

The concept that drove the development of alternatives to H2 receptor antagonists was the recognition that these would have limited efficacy. It seemed that inhibition of the pump itself would be a more effective way of control of acid secretion. Work towards this end began at SK & F in Philadelphia, but was terminated with the launch of cimetidine. As will be discussed in the section on inhibition of the H,K ATPase, the synthesis of timoprazole heralded not only a novel therapeutic approach to acid control but also a novel drug design.

The proton pump inhibitors have a unique mechanism of action, being acid activated prodrugs. They covalently inhibit the gastric H,K ATPase based on their accumulation in the acid space generated in the secretory canaliculus of the parietal cell. This accumulation is followed by acid activation. The introduction of this class of drug produced a conflict between companies marketing H2RA's and those marketing PPI's that could form the basis for a course in pharmaceutical company strategies and even ethics. At this time, PPI's have superseded H2 receptor antagonists in most countries as prescriptions for acid related disease.

Acid pump antagonists

Whereas the proton pump inhibitors have a unique mechanism of action based on their chemistry, acid pump antagonists have a structural specificity for their target, the K^+ binding region of the H,K ATPase. Although they have been actively pursued for almost 15 years, thus far none of these compounds has reached the market place. They promise a more rapid onset of inhibition than the proton pump inhibitors and an inherent stability which will allow design of more flexible formulations.

The targets for inhibition of acid secretion are shown below.

Pharmacological Targets for Control of Acid Secretion

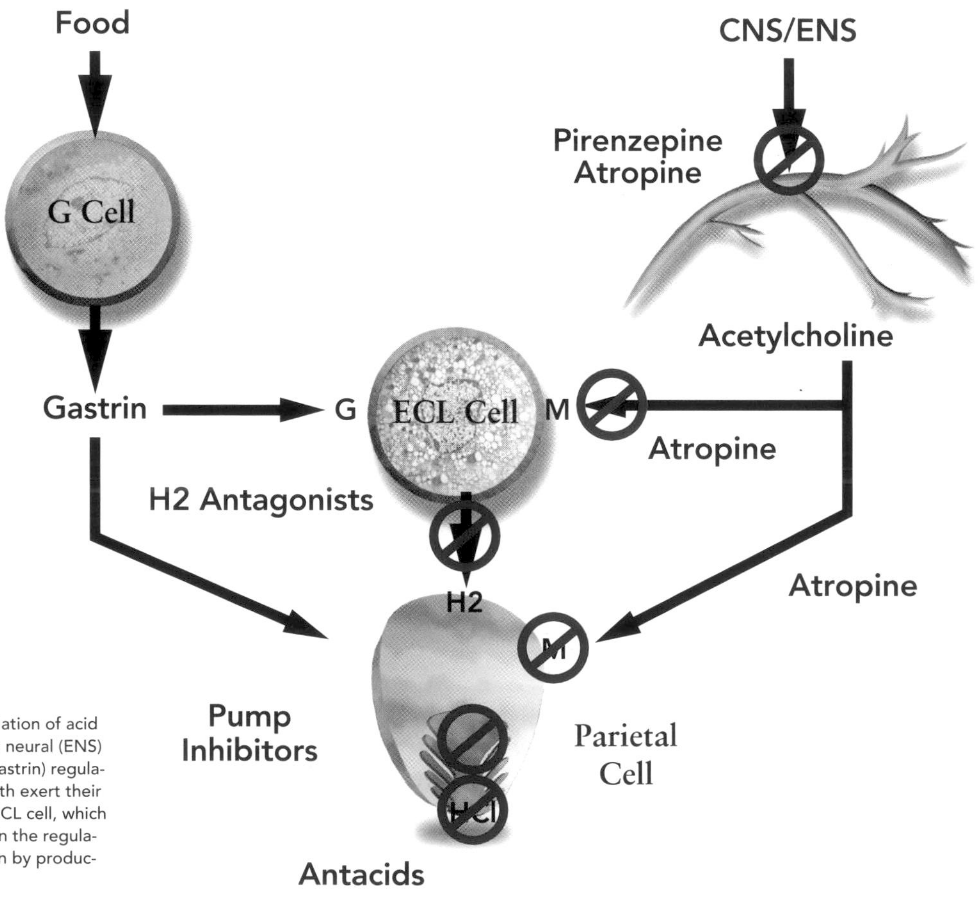

The peripheral regulation of acid secretion has both a neural (ENS) and an endocrine (gastrin) regulatory component. Both exert their effect through the ECL cell, which plays a pivotal role in the regulation of acid secretion by producing histamine.

CHAPTER 2
INHIBITION OF THE HISTAMINE 2 RECEPTOR

Histamine antagonists

Pharmaceutical industry had long recognized the importance of peptic ulcer disease and many companies had intensive programs searching for a treatment. In most cases they used an animal model such as the pylorus ligated rat measuring the change in ulceration given by compounds in their chemical libraries. This approach was unsuccessful because the real target was acid secretion not the number of ulcers found in these rat stomachs.

Histamine 1 receptor antagonists were first synthesized by Boivet in the 1950s. Most of these structures were derived by the modification of the imidazole ring of histamine leaving the ethylamine side chain intact.

These antagonists often penetrate the CNS resulting in drowsiness. The recognition of the presence of a different subtype of a histamine receptor in the stomach by Keir led to an intensive program for the development of an antagonist selective for what became the histamine 2 receptor. At that time, the histamine 3 receptor had not been discovered.

The H2 receptor is found on the parietal cell of the gastric mucosa where it plays a dominant role in stimulation of acid secretion by binding the histamine released from the ECL cell due to gastrin and PACAP. It is also found in the uterus and in the heart, but does not appear to play a medically significant role in these tissues.

Success in treatment with a receptor antagonist depends on several factors. The expression of several subtypes of receptor for the same ligand differently in different tissues allowed the development of receptor selective agonists and antagonists. Selectivity is of course a paramount requirement for therapy free of side effects.

Lack of side effects depends largely on the distribution of the receptor and its role in the different organs where it is found. Lack of toxicity depends on the nature of the molecule, its metabolism and its metabolites. Adverse events are idiosyncratic happenings not predictable from pre-clinical profiles of the compound; side effects result from lack of target uniqueness and structural problems in the drug.

Black and his colleagues, after many attempts to modify the imidazole ring to create a H2 receptor selective antagonist, turned their attention to the side chain and fairly rapidly thereafter generated the first H2 receptor antagonist, burimamide. The screen used by this group was inhibition of histamine induced acid secretion in the perfused rat stomach in the Gosh-Schild preparation, an eminently suitable screen for the discovery of a gastric targeted anti-histaminic! Metiamide and cimetidine followed this first success, and cimetidine was introduced for treatment of acid related diseases in 1977.

The perception of the SK&F research team that imidazole ring was essential for H2 antagonism allowed relatively simple bypass of the SK&F patent by a group of chemists working at Allen and Hanbury led by David Jack, also from Glasgow.

The imidazole ring was exchanged for a furan, a small side chain modification was made and then ranitidine was announced to the world. Ranitidine (Zantac™) became the world's leading medication for many years. Thereafter the most potent of the H2 receptor antagonists was introduced, famotidine with a thiazole ring, and this was followed by nizatidine. Famotidine is the largest selling anti-ulcer medication in Japan. The structures of some of these molecules is shown in the figure.

After the first flush of success with the short acting H2 receptor antagonists, considerable effort was expended on finding compounds which were longer acting, hence relatively irreversible or insurmountable in order to improve the acid inhibitory profile of this class of drug. For reasons still not understood, so far all of these, such as loxtidine, have given toxicities such as generation of adenocarcinomata of the gastric epithelium but have provided excellent acid control in animal models.

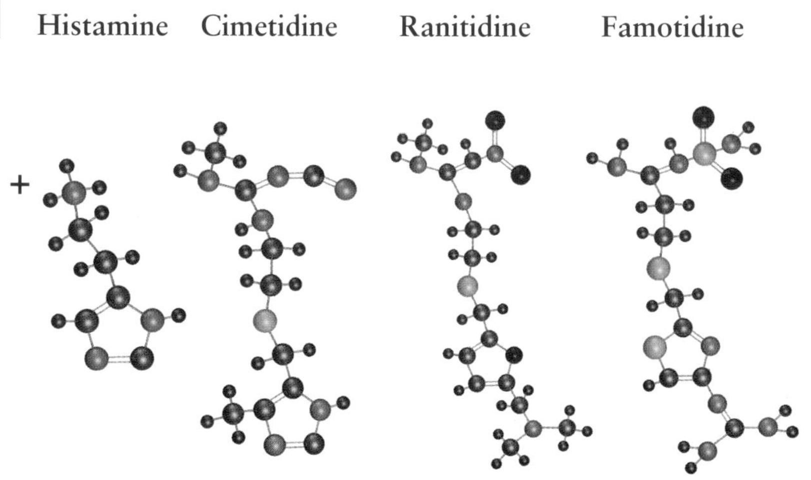

Some examples of histamine receptor antagonists. All of these are positively charged at neutral pH. Introduction of a methyl group in histamine to give N-methyl histamine, gives a chemical with a permanent positive charge, albeit bulkier than a proton. The compound is still effective at the H2 receptor arguing for the requirement of a charge in this region for effective antagonism.

Histamine   Cimetidine   Ranitidine   Famotidine

The Histamine 2 receptor

The histamine 2 receptor is a member of the trimeric G coupled protein receptor family. These have seven transmembrane segments, with the N terminal exposed on the cell surface with one or more N-linked glycosylation sites. There are 3 intracellular loops and a C-terminal cytoplasmic domain. The third loop is thought to be the region mainly responsible for coupling to the alpha subunit of the heterotrimeric G proteins such as G_s, G_q or G_i. However, the C terminal region also determines the relative affinity of coupling to a panoply of G proteins present in almost every mammalian cell. The coupling to the G proteins and some other aspects are also discussed in more depth in the section on parietal cell stimulation.

Cloning and expression of the histamine 2 receptor showed that it was a seven transmembrane segment protein with N-terminal glycosylation and its C terminus in the cytoplasm as shown in the following figure.

Histamine 2 Receptor

The amino acid sequence of the human histamine 2 receptor, with the transmembrane domains illustrated as well as the N linked glycosylation site (CHO).

The understanding of the structure of these receptors did not enable design of the original H2 receptor antagonists, but knowledge of the amino acid sequence and protein-protein interactions should be able to explain many of the idiosyncracies of their effects, such as tolerance.

Binding of histamine and its antagonists is thought to involve the loop between TM 4 and 5 and the surface of the transmembrane segments 3 and 5 similar to concepts evolving for the beta adrenergic receptor. For example the aspartyl group (D) in the middle of TM3 is thought essential for the binding of the $-NH_3^+$ of the ethylamine side chain of histamine and for the positive charge at the end of all the H2 receptor antagonists.

Binding of histamine results in activation of adenylate cyclase by interaction with a G_s trimeric G protein and also a small Ca signal due to weak interaction with a G_q trimeric G protein. The reason for the presence of both signals may be that the cAMP cascade is necessary for pump activation and that elevation of intracellular calcium is necessary for redistribution of the pump to the microvilli of the secretory canaliculus.

Pharmacology of H2 receptor antagonism

The availability of these selective antagonists was instrumental in establishing that histamine was a direct mediator of stimulation of acid secretion. Concomitantly, the role of gastrin was relegated largely to the release of histamine from ECL cells while maintaining its standing as a trophic factor for the gastric fundic epithelium. When initially introduced, cimetidine was prescribed 4 times a day since it was recognised that its duration of action was relatively short. When ranitidine was launched it was slightly more potent and was recommended twice a day. Recently however the prescribing recommendation has fallen to once at night. This is because with general use of these medications in combination with intragastric pHmetry, it was found that there was remarkably little effect on daytime acidity but a large effect on nocturnal acid output. The reason for the failure to control day time pH adequately is still not understood since unsurmountable H2 antagonists such as loxtidine were effective over a 24 hr period. These drugs have been reasonably effective in treatment of duodenal ulcer disease, less effective in gastric ulcer treatment and more or less ineffective in treatment of erosive esophagitis. They still form the mainstay for prescriptions for dyspepsia or other relatively vague upper GI disturbances. Their effect on healing was carefully analyzed in a series of meta analyses of duration and magnitude of elevation of intragastric pH as a predictor of optimization of healing as shown.

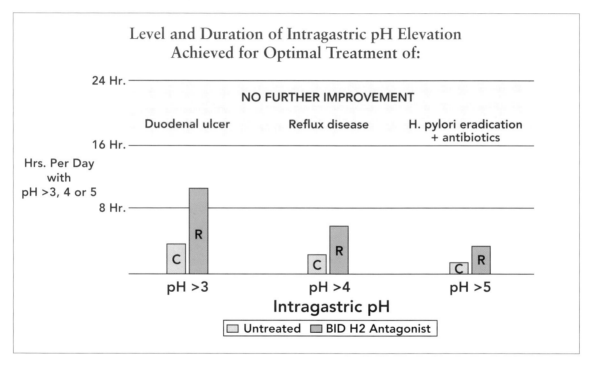

The duration of elevation of intragastric pH above pH 3.0 (DU), 4.0 (GERD) and 5.0 (*H. pylori* eradication) required for optimization of treatment. Mean intragastric pH is 1.4 in healthy untreated individuals.

Treatment of duodenal ulcer requires elevation to a pH >3.0 for 18 hrs per day. It can be seen that whereas the H2 receptor antagonist, ranitidine bid, shows very significant improvement over placebo, the benefits are much less in reflux disease (pH 4.0 18 hrs/day) and eradication therapy. Indeed cimetidine and its followers were found to be relatively ineffective in treatment of erosive esophagitis and later of little use in eradication of *H. pylori*. H2 receptor blockade displays rapid tolerance during therapy. In pHmetric studies with H2 receptor antagonists, an increase in the median intragastric pH relative to the beginning of treatment was evident after 7 days of drug administration and the effect became even more pronounced after 4 weeks of therapy. This tolerance did not depend on up-regulation of the H2 receptor since increasing the dose of H2 antagonist several fold did not reverse the tolerance. No change in gastrin levels was noted either, denying the possibility that changes in gastrin could account for the tolerance. It may be that there is up-regulation of other pathways elevating cAMP in the parietal cell.

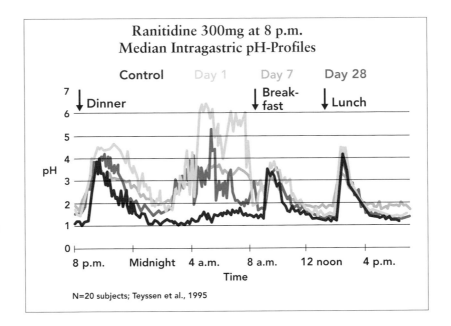

Ranitidine 300mg at 8 p.m.
Median Intragastric pH-Profiles

N=20 subjects; Teyssen et al., 1995

The recognition of tolerance to H2 receptor antagonists.
In pH metry studies with H2 receptor antagonists, a decrease in the median intragastric pH was evident after 7 days of drug administration and the decrease was even more after 4 weeks.

A typical set of intragastric pHmetric curves vividly illustrates the tolerance experienced with H2 receptor antagonists and their lack of effect on pH during the day as compared to their good effect at night.

Up-regulation of the H2 receptor on the parietal cell is thought to account, in part, for the acid rebound found after withdrawal of H2 receptor antagonists. Up-regulation of this receptor would sensitize the parietal cell to the normal levels of histamine released from the ECL cell. Another factor that should be considered is the delay in pump turnover induced by H2 receptor antagonists leading to more pumps per parietal cell. Both factors result in acid hypersecretion after withdrawal of H2 antagonist therapy. These shortcomings have enabled the successful introduction of significantly more effective agents, the proton pump inhibitors.

CHAPTER 3
INHIBITION OF THE GASTRIC ACID PUMP

H^+ transport by the gastric ATPase is the final step in acid secretion. It follows that inhibition of the ATPase would be an effective means of regulating acid secretion. There are various parameters that need to be considered when designing a drug for inhibition of this process by inhibiting the ATPase.

There has to be a large therapeutic index. The acid related diseases are in general not life threatening and although theoretically less effective, there are several H2 receptor antagonists available both as generics and over the counter in most countries in the world. These latter drugs have a large margin of safety and compounds that treat acid related diseases by inhibition of the gastric acid pump have to have at least an equal margin of safety. There are several P type ATPases and a gastric drug needs to be selective for the gastric ATPase. Whereas design of small ligand antagonists is not easy, at least the structure of the natural ligand provides a blueprint for such molecules. In the case of the ATPase, the natural ligands are ATP and the hydronium ion, H_3O^+, on the cytoplasmic side and K^+ on the luminal surface. A compound competing with ATP in cell cytoplasm would obviously be non-specific, inhibiting all other ATP dependent processes. Design of molecules to act as H_3O^+ surrogates would have to take advantage of a special structure in the pump able to bind hydronium ion without affecting other such binding sites. Similar considerations would apply to design of compounds substituting for K^+ on the outside surface.

An advantage accrues in drug design from the specialized location of the functioning ATPase. In the actively secreting parietal cell, the active pumps are present in the microvilli of the secretory canaliculus producing a large pH gradient with therefore by far the most acidic space in the body. In fact it is about 1000 fold more acidic than anywhere else. Protonatable weak bases will accumulate selectively in the canalicular space as a function of their pK_a. This is because the protonated positively charged form is significantly less permeable than the uncharged species. Since this is the only space in the body with a pH of less than 4.0, weak bases with a pK_a of 4.0 or less will accumulate only in the canaliculus of active parietal cells. The unprotonated form will permeate the basal lateral and canalicular membrane of the parietal cell and the protonated form, being relatively membrane impermeable, will concentrate in the canaliculus. In the fully active cell, the pH of the canalicular lumen is about 1.0, therefore a compound of a pK_a of 4.0 will accumulate about 1000 fold in this space and gain a significant therapeutic advantage if presented to the parietal cell in the serosal space. The acidity of the space can also confer a chemical advantage if such weak bases are also acid labile and convert more rapidly in acid to compounds able to inhibit the ATPase. As will be seen, this prodrug concept has played a vital role in the development of the current drugs used to control acid secretion by covalent pump inhibition.

The ATPases as targets for drugs

There are several mammalian P ATPases and each has several isoforms but there are sufficient differences in amino acid sequence to enable specificity of inhibitory agents. For example, the cardio-glycosides such as digoxin have only one known target, the Na,K ATPase. Similarly, thapsigargin targets the endoplasmic reticular but not the sarcoplasmic reticular Ca ATPase. Bafilomycin targets only the V type ATPases and oligomycin largely the F_1F_0 ATPase. There is therefore good reason to expect that drugs targeted against the gastric H,K ATPase will have strict specificity if properly designed.

The target amino acids in the gastric H,K ATPase

The three dimensional structure of the pump is only partially resolved, and therefore cannot provide a template for design of specific inhibitory ligands. However, if an acid activated compound generates a reactive chemical, it is possible to define the amino acids in proteins that are able to react under biological conditions. Whereas relatively harsh conditions are used for chemical reaction with carboxylic acids, histidines, lysines, arginines and tyrosines, the most reactive amino acids under biological conditions are cysteines by virtue of the higher reactivity of the –SH group under biological conditions. Given that an –SH reactive group has to be generated in the canalicular space, it is the cysteines accessible from the luminal space that are potential specific targets for thiol reactive (thiophilic) prodrugs.

It is therefore pertinent to inquire as to which of the 28 cysteines in the catalytic subunit of the pump and which of the 9 cysteines of the beta subunit are available for stable derivatization. From the analysis of the structure of the membrane domain of the catalytic subunit, there are at least 5 possible cysteines that are accessible from the luminal side of the pump to a fairly bulky cationic organic molecule, the cysteines at position 321, 813, 822, 892 and 981 in or between the 3rd, 5th and 6th membrane segments, in the loop between TM7 and TM8 and at the luminal end of TM9 respectively. Since the cysteines in the beta subunit are in disulfide linkage either they are not attacked or reform after reaction.

K^+ competitive ligands such as the imidazo pyridines bind non-covalently and their specific site of attachment is much harder to predict since the region of the protein that binds K^+ or whose conformation prevents K^+ binding is not known.

Digoxin target in the Na,K ATPase

The site of ouabain inhibition of the Na pump has been studied in some detail using site specific and random site mutagenesis. Ouabain binds to the outside surface of the pump in a partially K^+ competitive manner. It was well known that rat Na,K ATPase was relatively resistant to ouabain compared to other species. When various Na pumps were sequenced, it was found that the luminal boundary amino acids of the rat were arg and asp as compared to gln and asn in other species at the end of TM1 and the beginning of TM2 respectively. Mutation of rat enzyme to the more usual amino acids resulted in a ouabain sensitive form of the enzyme. Hence one ouabain binding site is in the region of the loop between TM1 and TM2. This finding enabled a series of studies on Na pump expression by transfecting cell lines expressing ouabain sensitive pumps with rat enzyme. Random mutagenesis also provided evidence for interaction of ouabain with the TM3 and TM4 domain using ouabain binding as a marker. Hence there are at least two binding regions for this inhibitor.

The gastric H,K ATPase is not inhibited by ouabain and chimers of the Na,K and H,K ATPases are ouabain sensitive when the N terminal of the chimer is Na,K ATPase and the C terminal is H,K but ouabain resistant when the N terminal half is the H,K ATPase. This shows that ouabain binds to the N terminal half of the sodium pump but not to the N terminal half of the acid pump.

Target region of the H,K ATPase

A series of inhibitors has been found for the H,K ATPase which are K^+ competitive inhibitors of enzyme activity. The most potent of these are heterocyclic imidazopyridines, but other heterocyclics such as arylquinolines or azaindoles and many other structures are also effective. In general these have much lower affinity for the Na,K ATPase. These are currently in development.

Analysis of their mechanism of action showed that the protonated form of an inhibitor such as SCH28080 was more effective and that their reaction was with the external surface of the enzyme. This conclusion was reached since the quaternary form generated by methylation of the pyridine N of SCH 28080 was ineffective in intact right side out vesicles of the H,K ATPase and also their K_{app} decreased with decreasing pH. Since these inhibitors are non-covalent, the site of binding can be investigated by mutational analysis or by generating photoaffinity derivatives of, for example, SCH 28080 an imidazo-1,2α pyridine. The azido form of the methylated imidazo-pyridine, MeDAZIP$^+$ was shown to be K competitive and after photolysis was covalently bound to the TM1/TM2 domain of the H,K ATPase. Substitution in the loop between TM1 and TM2 did not affect inhibition, resulting in the conclusion that inhibition depends on interaction of the inhibitor with the membrane domain itself rather than with the connecting loop. Construction of a chimer between TM1 and TM2 of the H,K and the fungal H ATPase resulted in a SCH28080 sensitive ATPase, again confirming the site of inhibition by these compounds.

The substituted pyridyl methylsulfinyl benzimidazoles

Discovery

The development of the first of this series of drugs is due to a combination of serendipity, mechanism and conviction that the ATPase was the best target for control of acid secretion. A compound, pyridine-2-acetamide, had been purchased by a company (Hässle in Göteborg, Sweden) for possible use as an antiviral agent. This compound was found ineffective but had some anti-secretory activity. It was modified to pyridine-2-thioacetamide in order to improve its anti-viral efficacy but this did not happen although it retained its anti-secretory activity. In 1973, SK&F announced the development of cimetidine, the world's first H2 receptor antagonist. Based on its structure, a benzimidazole ring was added to the anti-secretory drug with the hope that the mechanism of action of these forerunners was H2 antagonism. Anti-secretory activity was retained. Finally the sulfide was modified for stabilization to a sulfoxide and timoprazole was born.

This compound had rather remarkable anti-secretory properties: it inhibited gastric acid secretion whatever the stimulus; it inhibited secretion in isolated gastric glands whatever the stimulus but was relatively acid unstable and showed inhibition of iodide uptake by the thyroid and was thymotoxic. The first poly-

Chemical Development of Omeprazole

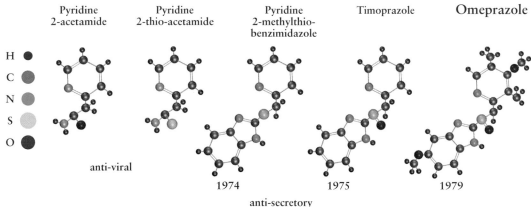

| Pyridine 2-acetamide | Pyridine 2-thio-acetamide | Pyridine 2-methylthio-benzimidazole | Timoprazole | Omeprazole |

H ●
C ●
N ●
S ●
O ●

anti-viral

1974   1975   1979

anti-secretory

The evolution of the structures culminated in the development of omeprazole.

The sites of modification of the core structure, timoprazole, that have been used to develop the PPI class of compound.

Timoprazole (core structure)

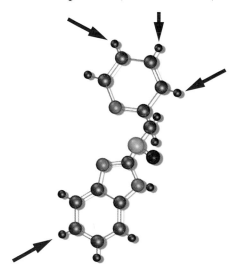

Unstable at Neutral pH

Thyrotoxic   Thymotoxic

Designed PPI's Stable at Neutral pH and with No Organ Toxicity

clonal antibody against the H,K ATPase reacted with stomach of course, but also mysteriously with the thyroid and thymus. This suggested that perhaps the ATPase was the target of timoprazole. By 1977, a compound picoprazole had been made retaining the core structure of timoprazole. It was shown that this compound did inhibit the gastric ATPase only when the ATPase was making acid, and that there was a lag phase of inhibition of transport activity. Since the compound was a weak base, the steps that were thought to result in inhibition of ATPase activity and acid secretion involved accumulation of the compound in the acid space of the isolated gastric vesicle during H⁺ transport (or the parietal cell canaliculus) followed by conversion to an active compound. It was postulated that this class of compound acted as a prodrug that only reacted with the ATPase after acid catalyzed conversion to an active form, perhaps the sulfenic acid. Later, it was proven that this active form in solution was a rearranged planar tetracyclic compound containing a highly reactive sulfenamide group. In order to optimize the acid stability of the parent compound and to generate absolute selectivity for accumulation in the acid space of the parietal cell, omeprazole was synthesized in 1979 and became the compound that was launched in 1988 at the Rome World Congress of Gastroenterology.

The name coined for this class of drug was proton pump inhibitor (PPI). Following publication in 1981 of the first of a series of papers on the mechanism of action of these drugs, a variety of derivatives were synthesized that also led to the introduction of other drugs with generally similar properties to omeprazole.

The core structure of all currently marketed benzimidazoles, with points of substitution is shown in the figure at left.

Mechanism of action

Chemistry

The key steps are (a) acid gradient dependent accumulation of the prodrugs (b) an acid or enzyme surface catalyzed conversion of the prodrugs to a tetra-cyclic, planar sulfenamide. A detailed mechanistic analysis of the chemistry behind the substituted benzimidazoles was published recently. Recent findings may suggest that the pump itself may play a role in its own inhibition.

The structure of 4 examples of these drugs is given in the illustration. It can be seen that they all share the same backbone, a 2-pyridyl methylsulfinyl benz-imidazole with various substitutions on the pyridine or benzimidazole moieties, which are added to modify solution reactivity or to decrease toxicity.

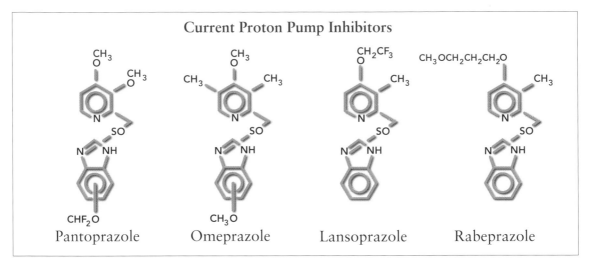

Current Proton Pump Inhibitors

Pantoprazole   Omeprazole   Lansoprazole   Rabeprazole

The current proton pump inhibitors, pantoprazole omeprazole, lanso-prazole and rabeprazole.

Biological accumulation of weakly basic compounds depends on a pH gradient between solution or cytoplasm and a membrane bounded or enclosed compartment of lower pH. The protonated form of the weak base is relatively membrane impermeable and therefore the chemical accumulates in acidic compartments depending on the gradient and the pK_a of the chemical. There are various acidic compartments, such as lysosomes, neurosecretory granules and endosomes that have a pH_i of about 4.5-5.0. The active secretory canaliculus of a fully stimulated parietal cell has a pH_i of close to 0.8. Therefore to target only the acidic compartment of the parietal cell the pK_a of a PPI must be 4.5 or less to avoid accumulation in lysosomes or neurosecretory granules. Since the compound accesses this compartment by crossing both the plasma membrane and the canalicular membrane, it also has to be membrane permeable requiring a log P of 2 or greater. Too high a log P drives the chemical into the hydrophobic domain of the membrane bilayer, perhaps decreasing access to the target or generating inappropriate target site; too low a log P reduced membrane permeability and access to the acid space.

The prodrug forms as shown are ampholytic, with 3 N atoms able to accept or donate protons. The important site of protonation for accumulation of these drugs is the pyridine N, with a pK_a of 4.0 or thereabouts. This pK_a ensures that accumulation of the prodrug will occur only in the secreting parietal cell canaliculus and nowhere else and is high enough to restrict neutral pH conversion to the sulfenamide.

With a pK_a of 4.0, the drugs can accumulate a thousandfold in the secretory canaliculus as compared to plasma levels, an enormous targeting advantage. The pyridine of timoprazole, the core structure, has a pK value of 2.9. Although this would seem appropriate for acid space targeting, the unsubstituted lead compound was unstable at neutral pH due to the higher nucleophilic reactivity of the pyridine N, an undesirable property when considering either biological targeting or formulation stability since the sulfenamide would form spontaneously at neutral pH.

The compounds undergo an acid catalyzed conversion to a relatively acid stable sulfenamide. This is probably the active compound in free solution since methylation of the benzimidazole N inactivates the drugs. The molecular rearrangement depends on the presence of a deprotonated pyridine N and a protonated benzimidazole N. The reaction involves a nucleophilic attack by the unprotonated pyridine N on the 2C of the benzimidazole, therefore an increase of the electrophilicity of this 2C is also required. This is achieved by protonation of the benzimidazole N. The figure illustrates the general chemical mechanism of all current PPI's.

Mechanism of Pump Inhibition

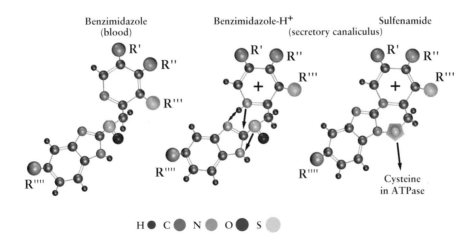

The chemistry behind the efficacy of the PPI's. The drugs accumulate in the secretory canaliculus of the parietal cell due to protonation of the pyridine N. This is followed by an acid catalyzed conversion to a cationic sulfenamide which in turn reacts with a cysteine or cysteines in the H,K ATPase catalytic subunit.

An alkoxy group at the pyridine 4 (green R") position flanked by a substituent at the 3 position is the substitution pattern common to all the PPI drugs giving the best combination of efficacy and selectivity. A decrease of the nucleophilicity of the pyridine N (a higher pK_a) was able to increase neutral pH stability. In the case of omeprazole this was achieved by the addition of a methyl group at the 5 position; in lansoprazole the fluorination of the ethoxy moiety also contributes to this decreased nucleophilicity and in pantoprazole this was performed by the addition of a second methoxy substitution in the 3 position. This substitution also increases the polarity in this region of the molecule which may play a role in the cysteine selectivity of this particular drug (see below). The substitution in rabeprazole results in a pK of 4.9 which may contribute to its neutral pH instability but will increase the accumulation in the parietal cell canaliculus.

The rate limiting step in the formation of the sulfenamide in solution is the formation of the spiro intermediate which requires folding of the prodrug to allow approach of the pyridine N to the benzimidazole N with intramolecular proton transfer. This is followed by attack of the pyridine N on the 2C of the benzimidazole. Access to the transition state is also important. For example the 3 CH$_3$ substitution favors a folding and interaction of the two ring systems whereas a 6 CH$_3$ substitution appears to hinder folding and hence activation. This latter reactivity can be modified by substitution in the benzimidazole moiety, but this is less important than substitution in the pyridine ring. The difluoromethoxy substitution used in pantoprazole reduces the pK$_a$ of the benzimidazole N, explaining the greater neutral pH stability of this compound relative to the other PPI's.

The pH activation curve for the 4 compounds differs significantly. They are all rapidly converted to the sulfenamide below pH 2.0. However the half maximal rate of activation is found at pH 3.0 for pantoprazole, pH 4.0 for omeprazole and lansoprazole and pH 5 for rabeprazole. Protein binding of these drugs may markedly alter the rate of conversion to the sulfenamide resulting in an unexpected efficacy of pH unstable compounds.

The sulfenamide that is formed from all of these drugs is a permanent cation. This is of benefit since the compound retains its membrane impermeability even after acid secretion into the canaliculus has been inhibited. It is unlikely therefore that the active compound can get to the parietal cell cytosol *in vivo* adding to the safety profile of these compounds.

This property also ensures targeting only to those SH groups accessible from the luminal or extracytoplasmic surface of the gastric acid pump. The sulfenamide is stable, in the absence of SH groups, in acidic medium and is very unstable at neutral pH. Again, this adds to the safety profile of the drugs in that, were the sulfenamide to enter the cytoplasm of a cell, it would have a half-life in the millisecond range.

The common reaction path taken by the four currently available PPI's is illustrated below.

The reaction pathway of the 4 PPI's in clinical use showing the commonality of reaction. There is protonation dependent accumulation in the canalicular space of the active parietal cell, followed by an acid catalyzed conversion to the sulfenamide.

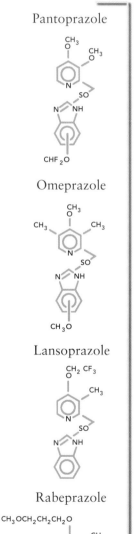

Pantoprazole

Omeprazole

Lansoprazole

Rabeprazole

Reaction Pathway of Proton Pump Inhibitors

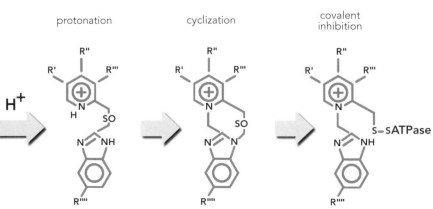

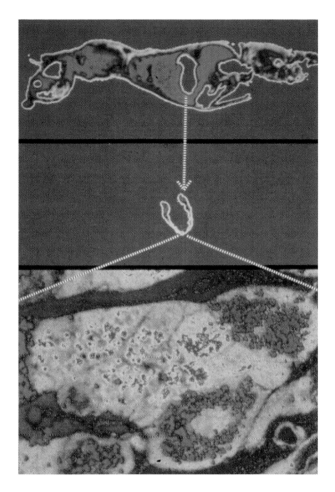

A whole body autoradiogram of an albino mouse injected with labelled omeprazole. At 5 minutes, general distribution of the radioactivity is seen. After some hours, the gastric mucosa is the only organ showing significant labelling. At higher magnification, it can be seen that only the parietal cell is labelled. In a separate experiment below, rabbit gastric glands were stimulated and then labelled omeprazole was added and the glands fixed after 15 minutes of incubation. Black dots show omeprazole labelling.

The reaction of the sulfenamide with SH groups in solution is diffusion limited. However, this does not necessarily extend to the situation *in vivo* where the compact structure of the membrane and extracytosolic domains of the H,K ATPase have to be taken into account. This 3 dimensional structure of the ATPase could, in principle, dictate derivatization of cysteines that are easily reached from acidic solution and those that are not.

Biological mechanism

1. Cellular

The chemistry of the PPI's dictates reaction with electrophilic groups in amino acids after acid catalyzed conversion of the prodrug. The reactive group is the free –SH of cysteine which can then form a disulfide bond with the sulfenamide derivative. In principle, cysteine disulfides can also react but reformation of the native disulfide would eliminate the bound drug.

There are, as discussed above, five potentially reactive cysteines in the catalytic subunit and 3 disulfide bonds in the beta subunit. After development of omeprazole and knowledge of its chemistry it was important to show that the mechanism deduced from its chemistry applied to the biological situation.

Whole body autoradiography of a mouse injected intravenously with tritiated omeprazole showed general labelling after 5 minutes, but after some hours, labelling was found only in the stomach. Higher magnification showed that labelling was present only in the parietal cell.

Reaction of omeprazole with isolated gastric glands results in inhibition of acid secretion. Treatment with thiol reducing agents reversed the inhibition in the parietal cell. Omeprazole therefore depends on formation of disulfide bonds for its inhibitory action on gastric acid secretion as deduced from its chemistry.

Treatment of isolated gastric glands with tritiated omeprazole under non-secreting and acid secreting conditions allowed analysis of the distribution of the drug as a function of time. The drug labelled mainly under acid secreting conditions and initially labelled only the canalicular compartment as illustrated in the figure.

The sites in the parietal cell that bind omeprazole after stimulation of acid secretion in isolated gastric glands. Binding is found only in the canaliculus immediately after stimulation, but subsequently binding is seen in the tubulo-vesicles of the cell due to recycling of the enzyme out of the canaliculus back to the cytoplasmic tubules.

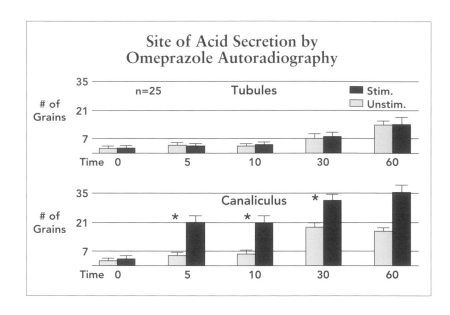

In the unstimulated state there is no labelling of the canaliculus until about 30 min after introduction of omeprazole. This is due to a basal level of acid secretion. With stimulation, there is rapid labelling of the canaliculus with a $t_{1/2}$ of about 10 min. The tubules are not labelled until about 30 min. Hence omeprazole reacts only in the acidic compartment of the canaliculus. Labelling of the cytoplasmic tubules depends on turnover of the canalicular component.

The mechanism of inhibition of the gastric H,K ATPase *in vivo* that results from these experimental data suggests that the drug, provided it is given in a gastric acid protected form, reaches the cytoplasm of the cell via the circulation. It then is accumulated in the canaliculus only if the cell is secreting and then reacts only with the active pumps present in the membrane lining the canaliculus as illustrated.

Benzimidazole Inhibition of Acid Secretion

This illustrates the general mechanism for benzimidazole inhibition of gastric acid secretion. The PPI is absorbed from the duodenum, passes via the blood into the parietal cell. If the cell is secreting acid, the prodrug accumulates in the canaliculus, undergoes acid catalyzed conversion to the sulfenamide whereupon it reacts with cysteines in the active H,K ATPase molecules.

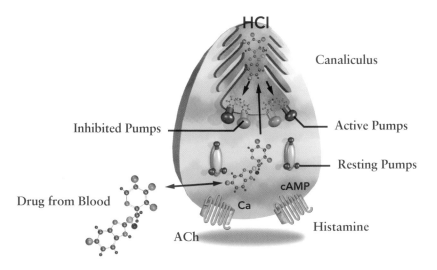

2. Enzymic

Treatment of a rabbit with radioactive omeprazole, isolation of gastric membranes and separation using SDS Page, showed that only the catalytic subunit of the H,K ATPase was labelled. Hence the drug is specific for the alpha subunit of the pump. The general mechanism of pump inhibition by these compounds is illustrated. The drug is accumulated on the luminal face of the pump where it undergoes acid conversion to the sulfenamide which then reacts with one or more exposed cysteines on the luminal surface of the enzyme.

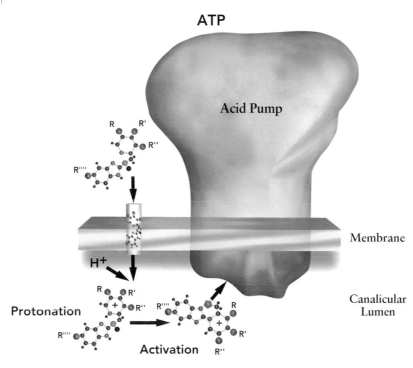

Parietal Cell Cytoplasm
Inhibition of Acid Secretion by PPIs

ATP

Acid Pump

R R' R'' R''''

Membrane

H^+

Protonation R R' $+$ R'' R'''' R'''' R $+$ R'

Activation R''

Canalicular Lumen

General reaction mechanism of the PPI's with the H,K ATPase in the membrane of the parietal cell canaliculus, showing passive diffusion across the canalicular membrane, accumulation of the protonated form, conversion to the sulfenamide and reaction with one or more cysteines in the catalytic subunit of the H,K ATPase.

Reaction of PPI's with the isolated ATPase resulted in inhibition of the ATPase only under acid transporting conditions. This was found for all the PPI's. Inhibition was reversed by mercapto-ethanol or dithiothreitol also showing that disulfide formation was responsible for inhibition of the gastric acid pump.

The PPI's inhibited ATPase activity or acid transport at different rates. The order of reactivity was rabeprazole > omeprazole = lansoprazole > pantoprazole, consistent with the order of acid stability.

The location of the site of binding of the PPI's on the pump identifies the cysteine(s) critical for inhibition of enzyme activity. Radioactive PPI's were used in acid transporting ATPase. Labelling at essentially full inhibition showed that lansoprazole labelled cys 321, 813 or 822 and cys 892. A similar set of cysteines was labelled by rabeprazole. Omeprazole labelled cys 813 or 822 and cys 892, whereas pantoprazole labelled both cys 813 and 822 and no other cysteine. Cys

The Reaction of Omeprazole with the H,K ATPase

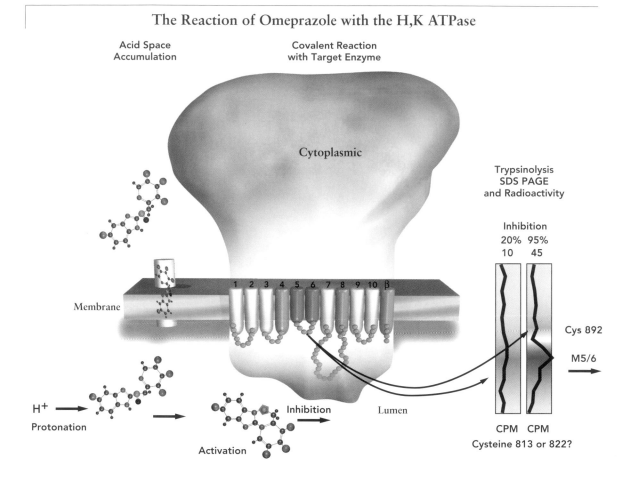

Acid Space
Accumulation

Covalent Reaction
with Target Enzyme

Cytoplasmic

Trypsinolysis
SDS PAGE
and Radioactivity

Inhibition
20% 95%
10   45

Membrane

1 2 3 4 5 6 7 8 9 10 β

Cys 892

M5/6

H⁺ →

Protonation

Inhibition

Lumen

Activation

CPM CPM
Cysteine 813 or 822?

A schematic illustration of identification of the labelled membrane segment pair of the H,K ATPase following incubation with ³H-omeprazole. The experiment incubated acid transporting enzyme with the radioactive compound and the labelled protein is digested with trypsin and the membrane fragments are separated by SDS gel electrophoresis, the labelled fragments identified by autoradiography and peptide N-terminal sequencing. Labelling of M5/M6 correlates with inhibition.

321 is at the end of TM3, cys 813 and 822 are in the M5/M6 domain and cys 892 is in the large outside loop between TM7 and TM8.

When the time course of labelling was compared to the time course of inhibition for all the PPI's, labelling of cys 813 or 822 correlated with inhibition. Definition of which of these two cysteines was labelled was done by using labelled omeprazole under transport conditions, tryptic digestion, isolation of the labelled peak by SDS-tricine gradient PAGE, re-digestion with thermolysin and sequencing of the peak retaining the labell. It was deduced that cys 813 was labelled in the M5/M6 domain. Since the sulfenamide is a bulky cation, this would place cys 813 in the loop between M5 and M6. However, the yield of labelled peptide was very low, and cleavage at various sites by thermolysin which is a relatively non-specific labell could possibly obscure the major site of labelling. A model for the omeprazole site is shown in the figure when cys 813 is placed in the loop between M5 and M6.

An alternative strategy to find the essential cysteine target was to generate mutants of cys 813 or 822 where these were replaced by thr or gly respectively, the amino acids found in these positions in the Na pump respectively. Determination of NH_4^+ stimulated ATPase activity of these expressed pumps showed that it was normal. Further ATPase activity and ^{86}Rb transport were inhibited by SCH28080, a K competitive inhibitor. On the other hand, acid

Inhibition in Transport Region of Acid Pump

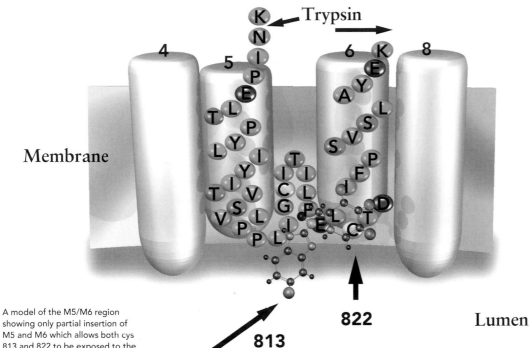

A model of the M5/M6 region showing only partial insertion of M5 and M6 which allows both cys 813 and 822 to be exposed to the protonated PPI's or their sulfenamide derivative. Two common tryptic cleavage sites are shown at the beginning of M5 and at the end of M6.

activated omeprazole and rabeprazole inhibited ^{86}Rb transport as usual in the cys 813thr mutant but was without effect in the cys 822gly mutant. These experiments point to cys 822 as the required amino acid for inhibition by PPI's. It is in the middle of a small hydrophilic sector containing two carboxylic acids. From these data, binding to cys 822 is therefore the key reaction in inhibition of the pump and acid secretion by the parietal cell and this binding is followed by covalent derivatization of cys 813. This suggests that both cysteines are accessible to the bulky cations formed by the PPI's. This is consistent with labelling of both of these cysteines by pantoprazole.

If now this cysteine is placed in the loop between M5 and M6, there is a significant change in the modeling of this region, placing additional hydrophilic amino acids at the cytoplasmic end of M6 as well as placing a tryptic cleavage site within the membrane. A more likely structure is to place cys 822 and 813 as both accessible to the reactive PPI's. This generates a model for this region of the pump which contains the ion transport pathway of the enzyme as shown in the figure, with M5 and M6 as membrane inserted but not transmembrane.

K competitive inhibitors

There are several protonatable tertiary amines that have been synthesized which are capable of inhibiting the ATPase. This class of drug has been called acid pump antagonists (APA's) since they bind reversibly and K competitively to the ATPase. In contrast to the PPI's they are able to inhibit the pump without acid activation, but since they are also weak bases they are accumulated in the parietal cell canaliculus and their potency is increased as a function of their pK_a.

The original lead structure, SCH28080 (3-cyanomethyl-2-methyl-8-(phenylmethoxy) imidazo[1,2α]pyridine) binds to the enzyme largely in its protonated form and to a site accessed from the luminal surface of the pump. As discussed above, a photoaffinity analog, MeDAZIP+, after photolysis binds within the membrane domain in the region of TM1 and TM2. Its K_i, calculating for the protonated form, is in the region of 10 nM. It does not inhibit the Na,K ATPase, as ouabain does not inhibit the H,K ATPase.

Some examples of acid pump antagonists either imidazopyridines (SCH 28080, MeDAZIP+) or arylquinolines (MDPQ).

SCH 28080   McDAZIP+   MDPQ

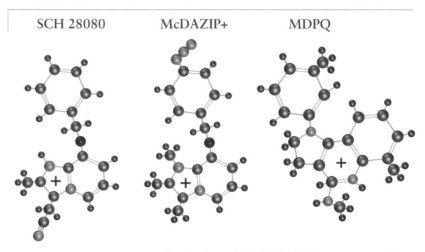

BY 841

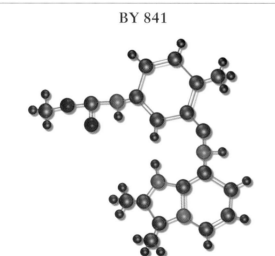

BY 841, a K competitive antagonist of the H,K ATPase that has been used to study effects of acid pump antagonists in man.

Derivatives of the SCH 28080 structure, such as BY 841, are also K competitive, and its effect has been studied in people. This compound produces rapid (within 30 min) full inhibition of acid secretion and in principle could be used as a therapeutic antacid with the speed of symptom relief of an antacid and the healing properties of a proton pump inhibitor. A different series of chemical structures, the arylquinolines have also been developed as therapeutic agents and this type of structure is illustrated also as MDPQ. This particular compound is fluorescent and its fluorescence is enhanced upon binding to the enzyme and with addition of ATP. This latter reaction suggests that the conformation of the ion "out" site changes with phosphorylation such that it is probably deeper within the membrane. Their kinetic mechanism involves binding either to the free enzyme or the phosphoenzyme form as illustrated in the ion "out" or E2 configuration.

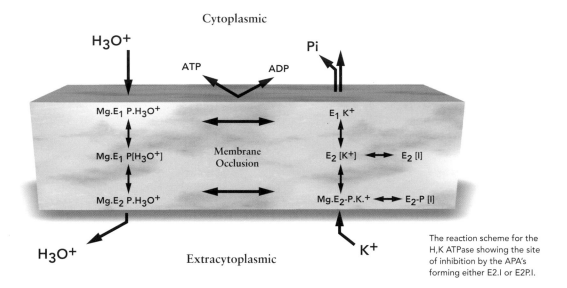

Cytoplasmic

The reaction scheme for the H,K ATPase showing the site of inhibition by the APA's forming either E2.I or E2P.I.

In vivo inhibition by proton pump inhibitors

When these compounds were introduced clinically there was not only some degree of confusion as to the inhibition of acid secretion obtained but also intentional marketing attacks by competitors on what has proven to be the most effective and safe means of controlling acid secretion. It is interesting to analyze the consequences of covalent inhibition of the gastric H,K ATPase that also depends on acid secretion being present for inhibition to occur.

The PPI's, since they are acid labile, must be formulated so as to pass through the stomach without exposure to acid. In the case of omeprazole this was achieved by micro-encapsulation, providing a coating that was acid resistant and dissolved only at pH > 6.1. Since acid secretion should be present, the drug is given 30 minutes after breakfast usually once a day. However, even after a meal, not all parietal cells, let alone all pumps, are active. Therefore the first dose of the drug will inhibit only those pumps present in the canalicular membrane. As inactive pumps are recruited, acid secretion will reappear, albeit at reduced volume.

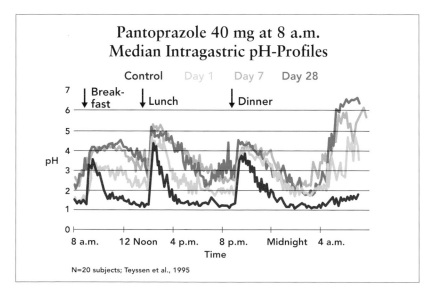

pH metric curves derived under the following conditions: in the absence of treatment, on day 1, 7 and 28 of treatment.
The effect of a PPI such as pantoprazole on intragastric pH showing rapid onset, steady state inhibition by D3, good day-time pH elevation and no tolerance.

On the second dose, more pumps will have been recruited and these will be inhibited; hence, inhibition will be more effective on the second day. On the third day, an additional fraction of pumps have been recruited and further inhibition of acid secretion may be expected.

However, new pumps are also being synthesized. The half-life that was experimentally determined in the rat of pump protein is about 48 hrs. Therefore, if recovery of acid secretion depended solely on pump synthesis, recovery after cessation of PPI administration should also have a half-life of 48 hr. ATPase activity and acid secretion however were restored with a half-life of about 15 hrs in the rat and about 22 hrs in man after lansoprazole administration for 14 days. Recovery therefore also involves reversal of the disulfide linkage of the drug to the pump. Steady state inhibition on once a day dosage is reached at about the third dose. At steady state in man, once a day dosing results in 66% inhibition of maximal acid output after 5 days of drug administration. This is the degree of inhibition expected with a 24 hr half-life of pump recovery and 80% active pumps at the time of drug administration.

The following chart illustrates the % of pumps compared to control available for inhibition immediately prior to drug administration on each day assuming that 80% of the pumps are active during the presence of the drug ($t_{1/2}$ = 90 min in blood), the % of pumps remaining without covalently bound inhibitor after administration and the % time that intragastric pH is greater than 4.0.

It can be seen that the combination of *de novo* biosynthesis and reversal of disulfide linkage results in about 50% of pump capacity inhibited 24 hr after the first dose and about 38% 48 hr after the first dose and 30% 72 hr after the first dose.

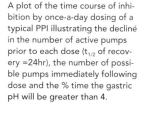

A plot of the time course of inhibition by once-a-day dosing of a typical PPI illustrating the decline in the number of active pumps prior to each dose ($t_{1/2}$ of recovery =24hr), the number of possible pumps immediately following dose and the % time the gastric pH will be greater than 4.

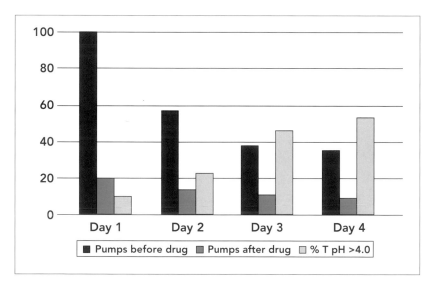

It can be seen that steady state inhibition of stimulated acid output is expected by day 3, as is stabilization of intragastric pH and the degree of inhibition immediately following drug administration. The latter parameter is the most rapidly affected, still providing better acid control than H2 receptor antagonists. To improve the response of acid secretion, since the lag is due to the maximal number of pumps active during the dwell time of the drug in blood, the dose should be divided rather than increased.

The PPI's as a class have a plasma half-life of about 60 to 90 minutes. Their covalent mechanism allows inhibition of secretion to persist long after effective levels of the drug have disappeared from the circulation. The bioavailability of the different PPI's varies, either as a function of their metabolism or the particular formulation developed for their administration. Further if there is some acid instability of the formulation, bio-availability will increase as a function of duration of administration and the degree of acid inhibition achieved.

Because this is covalent inhibition, the efficacy of inhibition is related not to the maximal level of prodrug but to the total exposure of the parietal cell to above threshold levels of the PPI, which is most easily related to the area under the curve of plasma levels. Analysis of pH metric curves shows that steady state is achieved by day 3 and that , in contrast to H2 receptor antagonists, there is effective inhibition of day time acid secretion and no tolerance.

The elevation of intragastric pH achieved by once daily (OD) PPI's as compared to twice daily (BID) ranitidine, showing the superior elevation of pH and resultant improvement in healing of duodenal ulcers and erosive esophagitis. BID PPI's further improve elevation of intragastric pH.

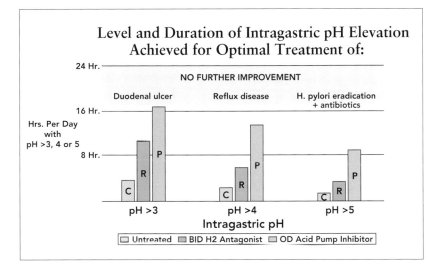

The meta-analysis of efficacy of H2 receptor antagonists presented earlier to analyze pH elevation as a function of once a day dosing with PPI's may be extended to provide the data shown in the figure above. Elevation to pH >3.0 and optimization of healing of duodenal ulcer is indeed achieved by once-a-day doses. Treatment of GERD by elevation of gastric pH to >4.0 is also reached for most patients and the pH is also elevated sufficiently to synergize with amoxicillin and clarithromycin in eradication of *H. pylori*.

In vivo inhibition by acid pump antagonists

In contrast to PPI's, the action of APA's is independent of the secretory status and there is no lag time expected. These are therefore fast acting compounds able to abolish acid secretion during their presence in the blood. Their efficacy will be related more to peak levels than area under the curve, unless time release formulations are developed. If these compounds have a plasma half-life similar to that of the PPI's, a pH > 5.0 will be found for about 4 hrs, but acid secretory capacity will be restored fully after two half-lives, namely within 4 to 6 hrs of administration.

REFERENCES

Bell, N.J., Burget, D., Howden, C.W., Hunt, R.H. *Appropriate acid suppression for the management of gastro-oesophageal reflux disease*. Digestion 51 (Suppl. 1), 59-67 (1992).

Bertaccini, G., Coruzzi, G. *Control of gastric acid secretion by histamine H2 receptor antagonists and anticholinergics.* Pharmacol. Res. 21, 339 (1989).

Besancon, M., Shin, J.M., Mercier, F., Munson, K., Miller, M., Hersey, S., Sachs, G. *Membrane topology and omeprazole labelling of the gastric H+,K+-adenosinetriphosphatase.* Biochemistry 32, 2345-2355 (1993).

Besancon, M., Simon, A., Sachs, G., Shin, J.M. *Sites of Reaction of the Gastric H,K-ATPase with Extracytoplasmic Thiol Reagents.* J. Biol. Chem. 272, 22438-22446 (1997).

Black, J.W., Duncan, W.A.M., Durant, C.J., Ganellin, C.R., Parsons, M.E. *Definition and antagonism of histamine H2 receptors.* Nature 236, 385-390 (1972).

Brimblecombe, R.W., Duncan, W.A.M., Durant, G J., Emmett, J.C., Ganellin, C.R., Leslie, G.B., Parsons, M.E. *Characterization and development of cimetidine as a histamine H2-receptor antagonist.* Gastroenterology 74, 339 (1978).

Brandstrom, A., Lindberg, P., Bergman, N-A., Alminger, T., Ankner, K., Junggren, U., Lamm, B., Nordberg, P., Erickson, M., Grundevik, I., Hagin, I., Hoffmann, K-J., Johansson, S., Larsson, S., Lofberg, I., Ohlson, K., Persson, B., Sk'nberg, I., Tekenbergs-Hjelte, L. *Chemical Reactions of Omeprazole and Omeprazole Analogues. I. A Survey of the Chemical Transformations of Omeprazole and its Analogues.* Acta Chem. Scand. 43, 536-548 (1989).

Brandstrom, A., Bergman, N-A., Lindberg, P., Grundevik, I., Johansson, S., Tekenbergs-Hjelte, L., Ohlson, K. *Chemical Reactions of Omeprazole and Omeprazole Analogues. II. Kinetics of the Reaction of Omeprazole in the Presence of 2-Mercaptoethanol.* Acta Chem. Scand. 43, 559-568 (1989).

Brandstrom, A., Bergman, N-A., Grundevik, I., Johansson, S., Tekenbergs-Hjelte, L., Ohlson, K. *Chemical Reactions of Omeprazole and Omeprazole Analogues. III. Protolytic Behaviour of Compounds in the Omeprazole System.* Acta Chem. Scand. 43, 569-576 (1989).

Brandstrom, A., Lindberg, P., Bergman, N-A., Grundevik, I., Tekenbergs-Hjelte, L., Ohlson, K. *Chemical Reactions of Omeprazole and Omeprazole Analogues. IV. Reactions of Compounds of the Omeprazole System with 2-Mercaptoethanol.* Acta Chem. Scand. 43, 577-586 (1989).

Brandstrom, A., Lindberg, P., Bergman, N-A., Tekenbergs-Hjelte, L., Ohlson, K., Grundevik, I., Nordberg, P., Alminger, T. *Chemical Reactions of Omeprazole and Omeprazole Analogues. V. The Reaction of N-Alkylated Derivatives of Omeprazole Analogues with 2-Mercaptoethanol.* Acta Chem. Scand. 43, 587-595 (1989).

Brandstrom, A., Lindberg, P., Bergman, N-A., Grundevik, I., Tekenbergs-Hjelte, L., Ohlson, K. *Chemical Reactions of Omeprazole and Omeprazole Analogues. VI. The Reaction of Omeprazole in the Absence of 2-Mercaptoethanol.* Acta Chem. Scand. 43, 595-611 (1989).

Burget, D.W., Chiverton, S.G., Hunt, R.H. *Is there an optimal degree of acid suppression for healing of duodenal ulcers? A model of the relationship between ulcer healing and acid suppression.* Gastroenterology 99, 345-351 (1990).

Carter, D.C., Forrest, J., Werner, W., Heading, R.C., Park, J., Shearman, D.J.C. *Effect of histamine H2-receptor blockade on vagally induced gastric acid secretion in man.* Br. Med. J. 3, 554 (1974).

Code, C.F. *Histamine and gastric secretion: a later look, 1955-1965.* Federation Proc. 24, 1311-1321 (1965).

Davenport, H. *A History of Gastric Secretion and Digestion.* New York, NY: Oxford University Press, 1992, p. 320-321.

Feldman, M. *Inhibition of gastric acid secretion by selective and nonselective anticholinergics.* Gastroenterology 86, 361 (1984).

Feldman, M., Burton, M.E. *Histamine H2 receptor antagonists.* N. Engl. J. Med. 323, 1672 (1990).

Feldman, M., Burton, M.E. *Histamine H2 receptor antagonists. Part two.* N. Engl. J. Med. 323, 1749 (1990).

Fellenius, E., Berglindh, T., Sachs, G., Olbe, L., Elander, B., Sjostrand, S.E., Wallmark, B. *Substituted benzimidazoles inhibit gastric acid secretion by blocking (H+ + K+)ATPase.* Nature 290, 159-161 (1981).

Figala, V., Klemm, K., Kohl, B., Rainer, G., Schaefer, H., Senn-Bilfinger, J., Sturm, E. *Acid Activation of H+-K+-ATPase inhibiting 2-(2-Pyridylmethylsulphinyl)benzimidazoles: Isolation and Characterization of the Thiophilic 'Active Principle' and its Reactions.* J. Chem. Soc., Chem. Commun., 125-127 (1986).

Fitton, A., Wiseman, L. *Pantoprazole, a review of its pharmacology and therapeutic use in acid-related disorders.* Drugs 51, 460-82 (1996).

Forte, J.G., Ganser, A., Beesley, R., Forte, T. M. *Unique enzymes of purified microsomes from pig fundic mucosa.* Gastroenterology 69, 175-189 (1975).

Fryklund, J., Gedda, K., Wallmark, B. *Specific labelling of gastric H^+,K^+-ATPase by omeprazole.* Biochemical Pharmacology 37, 2543-2549 (1988).

Gantz, I., Schaffer, M., Del Valle, J., Logsdon, C., Campbell, V., Uhler, M., Yamada, T. *Molecular cloning of a gene encoding the histamine H2 receptor.* Proc. Natl. Acad. Sci. U.S.A. 88, 5937 (1991).

Gedda, K., Scott, D., Besancon, M. et al. *The turnover of the gastric H,K ATPase (subunit and its relationship to inhibition of gastric acid secretion).* Gastroenterology, 109, 1134-1141 (1995).

Havu, N. *Enterochromaffin-like cell carcinoids of the gastric mucosa after life-long inhibition of gastric secretion.* Digestion 35, 42 (1986).

Hawkey, C.J., Long, R.G., Bardhan, K.D., et al. *Improved symptom relief and duodenal ulcer healing with lansoprazole, a new proton pump inhibitor, compared with ranitidine.* Gut 34, 1458-1462 (1993).

Helander, H.F., Ramsay, C.H., Regardh, C.G. *Localization of omeprazole and metabolites in the mouse.* Scand. J. Gastroenterol. 20 (suppl 108), 95-104 (1985).

Herzog, P., Grendahl, T., Linden, J., Schmitt, K.F., Holtermueller, K.H. *Adverse effects of high dose antacid regimen. Results of a randomized, double-blind trial.* Gastroenterology 80, 1173 (1980).

Hollender, L.F., Bahnini, J. *Jules Emile Péan.* In: Nyhus, L.M., Wastrell, C. (eds). *Surgery of the stomach and the duodenum.* Little, Brown and Co., 1986, p. 39-41.

Im, W.B., Blakeman, D.P., Davis, J.P. *Irreversible inactivation of rat gastric (H^+-K^+)-ATPase in vivo by omeprazole.* Biochem. Biophys. Res. Commun. 126, 78-82 (1985).

Im, W.B., Blakeman, D.P., Sachs, G. *Reversal of antisecretory activity of omeprazole by sulfhydryl compounds in isolated rabbit gastric glands.* Biochim. Biophys. Acta 845, 54-59 (1985).

Jaup, B.H., Bloomstrand, C.H. *Cerebro-spinal fluid concentration of pirenzepine after therapeutic dosage.* Scand. J. Gastroenterol. 15, 35 (1980).

Keeling, D.J., Fallowfield, C., Underwood, A.H. *The specificity of omeprazole as an $(H^+ + K^+)$-ATPase inhibitor depends upon the means of its activation.* Biochem. Pharmacol. 36, 339-344 (1987).

Keeling, D.J., Laing, S.M., Senn Bilfinger, J. *SCH 28080 is a lumenally acting, K^+-site inhibitor of the gastric $(H^+ + K^+)$-ATPase.* Biochem. Pharmacol. 37, 2231-2236 (1988).

Koop, H., Schepp, W., Damman, H.G., et al. *Comparative trial of pantoprazole and ranitidine in the treatment of reflux esophagitis: results of a German multicenter study.* J. Clin. Gastroenterol. 20, 192-195 (1995).

Lamberts, R., Creutzfeldt, W., Strueber, H.G., Brunner, G., Solcia, E. *Long-term omeprazole therapy in peptic ulcer disease. Gastrin, endocrine cell growth, and gastritis.* Gastroenterology 104, 1356 (1993).

Lambrecht, N., Corbett, Z., Bayle, D., Karlish, S.J.D., Sachs, G. *Identification of the site of inhibition by omeprazole of a (-(fusion protein of the HK-ATPase using site directed mutagenesis.* J. Biol. Chem. 1998 (in press).

Lanzon Miller, S., Pounder, R.E., Hamilton, M.R. et al. *Twenty four hour intragastric acidity and plasma gastrin concentration before and during treatment with either ranitidine or omeprazole.* Aliment. Pharm. and Therap. 1, 239-251 (1987).

Larsson, H., Carlsson, E., Jinggren, U., Olbe, L., Sjàstrand, S.E., Sk¬nberg, I., Sundell, G. *Inhibition of gastric acid secretion by omeprazole in the dog and rat.* Gastroenterology 85, 900-907 (1983).

Larsson, H., Carlsson, E., Mattsson, H. *Plasma gastrin in gastric enterochromaffin-like cell activation and proliferation: studies with omeprazole and ranitidine in intact and antrectomized rats.* Gastroenterology 90, 391-399 (1986).

Larsson, H., Carlsson, E., Mattson, H., Lundell, L., Sundler, F., Sundell, G., Wallmark, B., Watanabe, T., Hakanson, R. *Plasma gastrin concentrations and gastric enterochromaffin-like cell activation and proliferation.* Gastroenterology 90, 391 (1986).

Latarjet, A. *Preliminaire sur l'innervation et l'enervation de l'estomac.* Lyon Med 130, 160-166 (1921).

Latarjet, A. *Resection des nerfs de l'estomac; technique operatoire; resultats cliniques.* Bull. Acad. Natl. Med. Paris 87, 681-691 (1922).

Levine, R.A., Kohen, K.R., Schwartzel Jr., E.H., Ramsay, C.E. *Prostaglandin E2-histamine in interactions on cAMP, cGMP, and acid production in isolated fundic glands.* Am. J. Physiol. 242, G21-G26 (1982).

Lind, T., Cederberg, C., Ekenved, G., Haglund, U., Olbe, L. *Effect of omeprazole – a gastric proton pump inhibitor – on pentagastrin stimulated acid secretion in man.* Gut 24, 270-276 (1983).

Lind, T., Cederberg, C., Ekenved, G., Olbe, L. *Inhibition of basal and betazole-and sham feeding induced acid secretion by omeprazole in man.* Scand. J. Gastroenterol. 21, 1004-1010 (1986).

Lindberg, P., Nordberg, P., Alminger, T., Brandstrom, A., Wallmark, B. *The mechanism of action of the gastric acid secretion inhibitor omeprazole.* J. Med. Chem. 29, 1327-1329 (1986).

Lindberg, P., Brandstrom, A., Wallmark, B., Mattsson, H., Rikner, L., Hoffmann, K.-J. *Omeprazole: the first proton pump inhibitor.* Medicinal Res Reviews 10, 1-54 (1990).

Lorentzon, P., Jackson, R., Wallmark, B., Sachs, G. *Inhibition of (H⁺ + K⁺)-ATPase by omeprazole in isolated gastric vesicles requires proton transport.* Biochim. Biophys. Acta 897, 41-51 (1987).

Maton, P.N. *Omeprazole.* N. Engl. J. Med. 324, 965 (1991).

Mattson, H., Havu, N., Braeutigam, J, Carlsson, K., Lundell, L., Carlsson, E. *Partial gastric corpectomy results in hypergastrinemia and development of gastric enterochromaffin-like carcinoids in the rat.* Gastroenterology 100, 311 (1991).

McTavish, D., Buckley, M.M.T., Heel, R.C. *Omeprazole. An updated review of its pharmacology and therapeutic use in acid-related disorders.* Drugs 42, 138 (1991).

Modlin, I.M., Waisbren, S.J. Lester R. *Dragstedt and his role in the evolution of therapeutic vagotomy in the United States.* Am. J. Surg. 167, 344-359 (1994).

Morii, M., Takeguchi, N. *Different biochemical modes of action of two irreversible H⁺,K(⁺)-ATPase inhibitors, omeprazole and E3810.* J. Biol. Chem. 268, 21553-21559 (1993).

Munson, K.B., Gutierrez, C., Balaji, V.N., Ramnarayan, K., Sachs, G. *Identification of an extracytoplasmic region of H⁺,K⁺-ATPase labelled by a K⁺-competitive photoaffinity inhibitor.* J. Biol. Chem. 266, 18976-18988 (1991).

Munson, K.B., Sachs, G. *Inactivation of H⁺,K⁺-ATPase by a K⁺-competitive photoaffinity inhibitor.* Biochemistry 27, 3932-3938 (1988).

Naesdal, J., Bodemar, G., Walan, A. *Effect of omeprazole, a substituted benzimidazole on 24 hr intragastric acidity in patients with peptic ulcer disease.* Scan. J. Gastroenterol. 19, 916-922 (1984).

Nwokolo, C.U., Smith, J.T., Gavey, C., Sawyer, A., Pounder, R.E. *Tolerance during 29 days of conventional dosing with cimetidine, nizatidine, famotidine or ranitidine.* Aliment. Pharmacol. Ther. 4 (Suppl. 1) p. 29-45 (1990).

Nwokolo, C.U,. Smith, J.T., Sawyerr, A.M., Pounder, R.E. *Rebound intragastric hyperacidity after abrupt withdrawal of histamine H2 receptor blockade.* Gut 32, 1455 (1991).

Prinz, C., Scott, D.R., Hurwitz, D., Helander, H.F., Sachs, G. *Gastrin effects on isolated rat enterochromaffin-like cells in primary culture.* Amer. J. Physiol. 267, G663 (1994).

Pue, M.A., Laroche, J., Meineke, I., de Mey, C. *Pharmacokinetics of pantoprazole following single intravenous and oral administration to healthy male subjects.* Eur. J. Clin. Pharmacol. 44, 575-578 (1993).

Rabon, E., Sachs, G., Bassilian, S., Leach, C., Keeling, D. *A K⁺-competitive fluorescent inhibitor of the H,K-ATPase.* J. Biol. Chem. 266, 12395-12401 (1991).

Regardh, C.G., Gabrielsson, M., Hoffman, K.J. et al. *Pharmacokinetics and metabolism of omeprazole in animals and man.* Scan. J. Gastroenterology 20, 79-94 (1985).

Ryberg, B., Tielemanns, Y., Axelson, J., Carlsson, E., Hakanson, R., Mattsson, H., Sundler, F., Willems, G. *Gastrin stimulates the self-replication of enterochromaffin-like cells in the rat stomach.* Gastroenterology 99, 935 (1990).

Ryberg, B., Axelson, J., Hakanson, R., Sundler, F., Mattson, H. *Trophic effects of continuous infusion of [Leu15]-gastrin-17 in the rat.* Gastroenterology 98, 33 (1990).

Sachs, G., Shin, J.M., Briving, C., Wallmark, B., Hersey, S. *Pharmacology of gastric H,K ATPase.* Ann. Rev. Pharmacol. Toxicol. 35, 277-305 (1995).

Sachs, G., Carlsson, E., Lindberg, P., Wallmark, B. *Gastric H,K-ATPase as therapeutic target.* Ann. Rev. Pharmacol. Toxicol. 28, 269-284 (1988).

Sachs, G., Shin, J.M., Besancon, M., Prinz, C. *The continuing development of gastric acid pump inhibitors (Lansoprazole)*. Aliment. Pharmacol. Ther. 7 (Suppl. 1), 4-12 (1993).

Schepp, W., Heim, H.K., Ruoff, H.J. *Comparison of the effect of PGE2 and somatostatin on histamine stimulated 14C-aminopyrine uptake and cyclic AMP formation in isolated rat gastric mucosal cells*. Agents Actions 13, 200-206 (1983).

Scott D., Besancon M., Sachs, G., Helander H.F. *The effect of antisecretory drugs on parietal cell structure and H/K ATPase levels in rabbit gastric mucosa in vivo*. Dig. Dis. Sci. 39, 2118 (1994).

Senn-Bilfinger, J., Kruger, U., Sturm, E., Figala, V., Klemm, K., Kohl, B., Rainer, G., Schaefer, H., Blake, T.J., Darkin, D.W., Ife, R.J., Leach, C.A., Mitchell, R.C., Pepper, E.S., Salter, C.J., Viney, N.J., Huttner, G., Zsolnai, L. *(H⁺-K⁺)-ATPase Inhibiting 2-[(2-Pyridylmethyl)sulfinyl]benzimidazoles. 2. The Reaction Cascade Induced by Treatment with Acids. Formation of 5H- Pyrido[1',2':4,5][1,2,4]thiadiazino[2,3-a]benzimidazol-13-ium Salts and Their Reactions with Thiols*. J. Org. Chem. 52, 4582-4592 (1987).

Shin, J.M., Besancon, M., Simon, A., Sachs, G. *The site of action of pantoprazole in the gastric H⁺/K⁺-ATPase*. Biochim. Biophys. Acta 1148, 223-233 (1993).

Simon, B., Muller, P., Marinis, E., Lohmann, R., Huber, R., Hartmann, M., Wurst, W. *Effect of repeated oral administration of BY1023/SK&F96022 – a new substituted benzimidazole derivative – on pentagastrin-stimulated gastric acid secretion and pharmacokinetics in man*. Aliment. Pharmacol. Therap. 4, 373-379 (1990).

Smallwood, R.A., Berlin, R.G., Castagnoli, N. et al. *Safety of acid suppressing drugs*. Dig. Dis. Sci. 40 (suppl), 63-80 (1994).

Sturm, E., Kruger, U., Senn-Bilfinger, J., Figala, V., Klemm, K., Kohl, B., Rainer, G., Schaefer, H., Blake, T.J., Darkin, D.W., Ife, R.J., Leach, C.A., Mitchell, R.C., Pepper, E.S., Salter, C.J., Viney, N.J., Huttner, G., Zsolnai, L. *(H⁺-K⁺)-ATPase Inhibiting 2-[(2-Pyridylmethyl)sulfinyl]benzimidazoles. 1. Their Reaction with Thiols under Acidic Conditions. Disulfide Containing 2-Pyridinio-benzimidazolides as Mimics for the Inhibited Enzyme*. J. Org. Chem. 52, 4573-4581 (1987).

Tielemanns, Y., Hakanson, R., Sundler, F., Willems, G. *Proliferation of enterochromaffin-like cells in omeprazole treated hypergastrinemic rats*. Gastroenterology 96, 723 (1989).

Tielemanns, Y., Axelson, J., Sundler, F., Willems, G., Hakanson, R. *Serum gastrin affects the self-replication rate of enterochromaffin-like cells in the rat stomach*. Gut 31, 274 (1990).

Wallmark, B., Skaenberg, I., Mattson, H., Andersson, K., Sundler, F., Hakanson, R., Carlsson, E. *Effects of 20 weeks ranitidine treatment on plasma gastrin levels and gastric enterochromaffin-like cell density in the rat*. Digestion 45, 181 (1990).

Wallmark, B., Brandstrom, A., Larsson, H. *Evidence for acid-induced transformation of omeprazole into an active inhibitor of (H⁺ + K⁺)-ATPase within the parietal cell*. Biochim. Biophys. Acta 778, 549-558 (1984).

Wallmark, B., Briving, C., Fryklund, J., Munson, K., Jackson, R., Mendlein, J., Rabon, E., Sachs, G. *Inhibition of gastric H⁺,K⁺-ATPase and acid secretion by SCH 28080, a substituted pyridyl(1,2a)imidazole*. J. Biol. Chem. 262, 2077-2084 (1987).

Wallmark, B., Larsson, H., Humble, L. *The relationship between gastric acid secretion and gastric H⁺, K⁺-ATPase activity*. J. Biol. Chem. 260, 13681-13684 (1985).

Wangensteen, O. *The rise of surgery*. Minneapolis, University of Minnesota Press, 1978, p. 154-150.

CHAPTER 1
THE BARRIERS OF THE UPPER GASTRO-INTESTINAL TRACT

Introduction

The common acid related diseases of the upper GI tract can be considered as primarily due to a defect in barrier function either of the esophageal epithelium or primarily the lower esophageal sphincter in the case of GERD or of the gastric mucosal or duodenal epithelium in the case of gastric or duodenal ulcers. The defect may be natural or induced, for example by infection with *H. pylori*. In rarer situations such as Zollinger Ellison syndrome, the extraordinary levels of acid may overwhelm otherwise normal barriers. The lower esophageal sphincter will be discussed in some detail in the section on GERD and this introduction to acid related diseases will focus on the acid resistance properties of the esophageal, gastric and duodenal epithelia.

Historical aspects

Archibald Pitcairn, the noted Iatro-mathematician, questioned why the stomach failed to digest itself.

Once it had become apparent that digestion was an active process involving acid and pepsin which was initiated in the stomach, a further fundamental question arose. Why did the stomach not digest itself? This problem had long been pondered and Archibald Pitcairn, the great Iatromathematician had himself questioned the Iatrochemists rigourously on this issue: "…*Why upon the digestion of food upon the stomach, which is as easily digestible as the food, yet the stomach itself should not be dissolved?*" No reasonable answer was forthcoming and the pundits such as John Hunter could only perseverate upon the existence of a putative vital force which maintained the gastric wall intact under the circumstances of digestion. Issues such as the existence of a "*locus minoris resistentia*" were entertained to explain ulceration and embraced the concept that this was indeed local digestion of the stomach mucosa.

Nevertheless, it seemed difficult to understand why food in the lumen of the stomach would be broken up whilst the wall of the stomach remained intact.

The invocation of "vital spirit" was of little satisfaction and represented a regression to archaic views on the nature of digestion. Further reflection on the matter resulted in the recognition that the stomach wall itself must harbor an intrinsic "force" capable of resisting digestion. Indeed the attractive concept that a breakdown of such an intrinsic mechanism might be responsible for the development of ulcers or even neoplasia became a source of considerable speculation. Nevertheless little evidence existed to delineate the specific nature of the mechanism responsible for the generation of mucosal protection from acid, pepsin and even noxious agents that might be ingested.

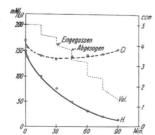

Gastroenterology 9:425-443, 1947

ELECTROLYTE DIFFUSION IN RELATION TO THE ACIDITY REGULATION OF THE GASTRIC JUICE

TORSTEN TEORELL

From the Institute of Physiology, University of Uppsala, Uppsala, Sweden

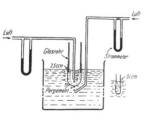

The apparatus and graphic information used by T. Teorell to determine H⁺ back diffusion.

In the early 1930s Torsten Teorell had begun to examine the permeability characteristics of gastric mucosa by suggesting that H⁺ diffused back through

the mucosa in exchange for Na^+. Thus issues had arisen as to whether acid was neutralized within the lumen or after diffusion into the mucosa in the interstitial fluid. An alternative hypothesis had been that the bicarbonate content of gastric secretion might be responsible for some of the acid which was neutralized. Nevertheless, the ability of the stomach to retain the acid it secreted under normal circumstances without digesting itself once again raised the concept of the existence of a "gastric mucosal barrier". Teorell began the delineation of the barrier properties by demonstrating that unionized organic acids but not ionized mineral acids would disappear rapidly from the gastric contents by diffusing into the mucosa. Whilst not fully resolving the issue, his concept of a diffusion process in the mucosa had by 1947 initiated the formal evaluation of the intrinsic mechanisms available to deal with back diffusion of acid into the interstitium of the stomach.

Am J Physiol 183:604, 1955

Barrier offered by gastric mucosa to absorption of sodium. CHARLES F. CODE, JOHN F. SCHOLER*, ALAN L. ORVIS*, AND JOHN A. HIGGINS*. Mayo Clin. and Mayo Fndn., Rochester, Minn.

It has been found that sodium is not absorbed from the stomach of fasted healthy human beings (REITEMEIER, CODE AND ____ers (COPE *et al.* and EISENMAN *et al.*) ____ated, however, that sodium is slowly ____ stomach of fasted animals. The p____ ____dertaken to determine the cause ____ Anesthetized dogs with the antrum ____ion were used. The finding that isot____ ____owly absorbed (12–35%/hr.) from the ____ ____sted dogs anesthetized

Charles Code, who was an initial proponent of the critical role of histamine in acid secretion, also proposed the existence of a gastric mucosal barrier.

In 1955 Davenport and Code published a series of experiments under the title *The Functional Significance of Gastric Mucosal Barrier to Sodium* and thus initiated the first formal usage of the term "barrier". They described the results of the relative rates of disappearance of radiolabelled K^+, Na^+, thiocyanate or ^3H_2O from solutions in contact with oxyntic mucosa. They observed that when the gastric contents were neutral, ^3H_2O disappeared rapidly but $^{42}K^+$ slowly and $^{22}Na^+$ at an intermediate rate. However, when the gastric contents were acid, or gastric secretion was stimulated by histamine, the rates of disappearance of THO and $^{42}K^+$ were unaffected whereas the rates of disappearance of $^{22}Na^+$ fell to zero. In recognition of the significance of this observation, Code commented presciently on this subject in the manuscript entitled *The Barrier Offered by the Gastric Mucosa to Sodium*.

Further experiments in this area were designed to identify the site of this zone and resulted in proposals that it was mucous which construed the barrier function. Proof for this however was difficult to obtain and a reconfiguration of this proposal by others resulted in the hypothesis that bicarbonate secreted by the gastric mucosa neutralized acid and thus created a biochemical barrier. Further elaboration of this line of work generated much discussion about the "unstirred layer" and held that the modest concentration of bicarbonate held in this would produce a barrier of both functional and physical significance to acid. In a fashion reminiscent of the determination of the physical aura produced by plants, the size of this barrier was then measured and its certain presence fixed in the minds of the believers. Davenport in later work further explored the concept of the gastric mucosal barrier by seeking to damage it with various agents including eugenol, fatty acids and alcohol and was able to prove that back diffusion into the mucosa of acid occurred under such conditions. These observations were substantiated by anatomical evidence of increased mucosal permeability by demonstrating damage to the surface epithelial cells and underlying tissues, including vessels. Some support was thus provided for the important associa-

tion of barrier breaking and its relationship to acute mucosal ulceration and stress bleeding.

An immense body of work was then undertaken by diverse investigators to identify the effects of hypoxia, acid, bile salts, aspirin, non-steroidal anti-inflammatory agents, prostaglandins, etc. on the integrity of the barrier. The commutations and permutations of these studies achieved little, except to further document the existence of the mucosal barrier and the ability of a variety of agents to break it. Unfortunately this did little to identify the precise site and mechanism of the phenomenon. The summation of much work established that the barrier represented a generalized function common to a polarized epithelial cell system and that acids, in an unionized state, and fat solubilizing agents were capable of acting as barrier breaking agents. Breaking the barrier in itself was not sufficient but represented an initial step in the process of mucosal injury. A subsequent cascade of physiological events involving back diffusion of acid with liberation of histamine and the activation of pepsinogen was involved.

FUNCTIONAL SIGNIFICANCE OF GASTRIC MUCOSAL BARRIER TO SODIUM

HORACE W. DAVENPORT, M.D.,* HUGH A. WARNER, M.D., AND CHARLES F. CODE, M.D.

*Section of Physiology,
Mayo Clinic and Mayo Foundation.*

Normal gastric mucosa of man, dogs, cats, and rats offers a nearly complete barrier to the passage of sodium ions.[1-5] The ready permeability to sodium of the mucous membranes in the rest of the alimentary canal suggests that the impermeability of the gastric mucosa to this ion has functional significance.

Gastroenterology 47:142-152, 1964

H. Davenport in collaboration with C. Code sought the pathophysiological basis for mucosal permeability to ions.

The exploration of the multiplicity of associated phenomena provided further complex information regarding the fact that the barrier might not be a single entity but represent a multiplicity of physiological protective mechanisms. The more recent usage of sophisticated techniques to investigate cell function has determined the relevance of tight junctions and identified the specific property of the apical membrane of the gastric mucosal cells as being of vital importance in maintaining barrier function.

Davenport and Code thus deserve credit for extending the word "barrier" to include the property of the mucosa governing its permeability to H⁺. In subsequent years, the word would become a term broadly used to designate permeability of the mucosa in general. Fromm, in an evaluation of the entire subject, was to later remark that "barrier" and "barrier breakers" were simply catch phrases which *while novel and clever, reflect our ignorance.* Davenport himself in summarizing his accomplishments in the area, published them in a book whimsically entitled *The Gastric Mucosal Barrier: A Swan Song.*

The esophageal epithelium

Malfunction of the lower esophageal sphincter results in acid reflux into the esophagus. The acid load presented to the esophagus is likely to be the major determinant of heartburn or erosion. Reflux is mainly episodic, so that the esophagus is not often presented with a continuous acid load. Expulsion of the refluxate back into the stomach shortens the time of exposure.

The volume of reflux is also an important parameter for estimation of the acid load on the esophageal epithelium. Finally, the pH of the gastric contents that are refluxed into the esophagus also determines the possible damage. Intra-esophageal pH monitoring provides an approximate measure of the acid load to the lower esophagus in terms of the pH of refluxate and dwell time of the acid solution and is probably the most useful semi-quantitative measure of the

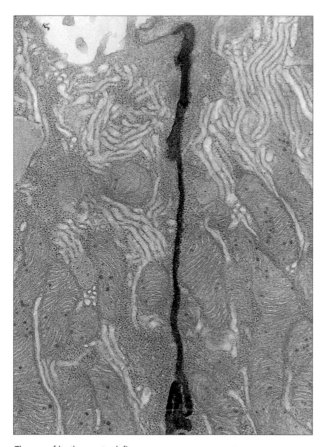

The use of lanthanum to define the tight junctions of the gastric mucosa. The electron dense lanthanum fails to pass the "tight" tight junction at the apex of the mucosal cells.

degree of exposure of the esophageal epithelium. The human esophageal epithelium is a multi-layered, stratified squamous epithelium. Afferent nerves are present reaching into the superficial layers of the epithelium. With incompetence of the lower esophageal sphincter (LES), acid reflux results with consequently the possibility of pain and damage to the epithelium depending on the pH of the refluxate. Rather than being protected by a continuous tight junction, this epithelium has largely regional cell to cell contact via desmosomes. There is some evidence for the presence of tight junctions in the first layer of the epithelium, but the very few strands seen on EM freeze fracture show that these at best are "leaky" tight junctions. This epithelium, being multi-layered, provides a winding path for proton diffusion into the deeper layers of the epithelium. It is significantly more acid sensitive than the gastric epithelium that is provided with "tight" tight junctions. The threshold of acidity for damage and pain may be different. A higher acidity is likely needed for damage to the epithelial cells compared to the acidity required for stimulation of the pain fibres. This is probably because the epithelial cells have acid recovery mechanisms (such as Na^+/H^+ or anion exchange) mostly absent in the pain fibres. Dependent on the location of the pain fibres and access thereto of H^+, individuals will have different sensitivities to luminal acidity. The therapeutic aims of acid control may vary, being elevation of mean diurnal pH for healing of erosions or prevention of acidic excursions for symptom relief or both.

Esophageal handling of acid and pepsin

Given the absence of continuous tight junctions or only leaky tight junctions, the lower esophageal epithelium is an inviting target for acid back diffusion. Mucus is an aqueous gel and is unlikely to provide a significant barrier to acid. In water, protons can move faster than other cations due to their ability to jump from water molecule to water molecule, and there are continuous chains of water in aqueous gels.

Resistance to acid may therefore depend more on the ability of the esophageal epithelium to neutralize an acid load than on restriction of entry of acid between the cells. Neutralization of acid occurs at the surface, due to net HCO_3^- secretion, and also in the paracellular pathway since the epithelial cells can produce buffer or absorb H^+. However, once damage has occurred, this paracellular pathway is shorter or more open and the lesion consequently more sensitive to acid than the normal epithelium. The measured average net flux of bicarbonate is about 78 µmol/30 min/10 cm in the human esophagus. It appears to be subject to regulation by muscarinic receptors, responding to the

vagal stimulation of acid secretion by the stomach. It is possible to approximate the pH of unbuffered refluxate that can be neutralized by esophageal surface secretion. If buffering is present, such as that due to amino acids or weak acids such as citrate, the acid load will be greater in the buffering range of gastric contents and reflect not only pH.

With reflux of unbuffered gastric contents at a pH of 4.0, there is a load of acid equivalent to 100 nmol/ml. If 10 ml of gastric contents at that pH is refluxed each min for 30 min and spreads over a length of 10 cm, 30 μmol of acid is presented to this length of the esophagus in that 30 min time span. This is within the average neutralizing ability of the secreted HCO_3^-. Reflux at pH 4.0 should therefore be largely neutralized at or close to the esophageal surface. This calculation may explain the results of a meta-analysis of the ideal pH elevation for the most rapid healing of esophageal lesions as discussed below.

At pH of 3.0, there is 10-fold more acid and 300 μmol of acid is presented to the lower esophagus with 10 ml refluxing each minute. This is beyond the capacity of net HCO_3^- secretion to neutralize the HCl. Acidification of intercellular spaces is likely, which may result in pain in some individuals. Epithelial cell pH may remain within viable limits given adequate Na^+/H^+ or Cl^-/HCO_3^- exchange.

At pH 2.0, the limits of the HCO_3^- response are greatly exceeded and the intercellular spaces will acidify even more and to a deeper level. At this stage, the ability of the epithelial cells to maintain constant intracellular pH may be overcome due to the high acid load, with resultant erosion. As the more superficial cells are eroded, pepsin may also back diffuse, adding proteolytic insult to acid injury.

These calculations, although fraught with assumptions, do predict that elevation to a mean diurnal pH of > 4.0 will optimize healing of erosions of the lower esophagus. Gastric contents contain pepsin in addition to acid. Proteolytic activity of pepsin requires a pH < 3.0 and probably there is adequate neutralization of intercellular pH if the refluxate does not fall much below 3.0. At a refluxate of pH 2.0, since the esophageal surface cannot neutralize this acid load, peptic activity may begin to contribute to esophageal damage. Peptic activity is less likely to contribute directly to pain.

Rationale for treatment of GERD with PPI's

Treatment of reflux esophagitis can be accomplished by improving the response or structure of the LES or by effective inhibition of acid secretion. Currently available compounds targeted to the LES are relatively non-selective compounds and have lower efficacy than acid inhibition. Ideally, control of GERD, in terms of both healing and symptom relief would not allow gastric pH to fall much below 4.0 at any time.

On once-a-day PPI treatment, the inhibition of maximal acid output is about 70%. Steady state inhibition is found on about the third day on once-a-day dosing since previously resting pumps have to be recruited to respond to the drug. Improvement in effect of PPI's is achieved by divided doses, not by increasing the single dose. On twice a day treatment, inhibition of maximal acid output rises to 80% and steady state is achieved on day two. Even then in many individuals there are still rapid transient periods of relatively high acidity with the possibility of episodic pain.

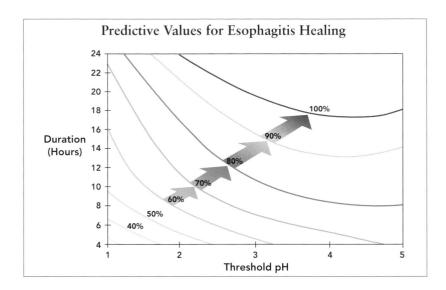

Predictive Values for Esophagitis Healing

Increasing the duration of the elevation of pH values increases the percentage probability of esophagitis healing.

Meta-analysis of the degree of acid inhibition required for optimization of healing rates for erosive esophagitis has shown that elevation of mean diurnal intra-gastric pH to at least 4.0 is required for about 18 hrs per day. This result may reflect the calculated ability of the epithelium and its cells to handle acid reflux. This seems to be achieved in most patients on once-a-day PPI therapy. If eradication of *H. pylori* blunts the effect of PPI's on intragastric acidity, as has been recently suggested, twice-a-day PPI therapy may be required to reach optimal healing pH. Twice a day therapy for H2 receptor antagonists only achieves the required pH for half the time, due mainly to poor day time pH elevation but good night time pH increase. These drugs are therefore more effective for night time pain relief but have rather weaker effects on ambulatory reflux as they are administered at night.

Thus inhibition to pH > 4.0 is sufficient to optimize healing but may be often inadequate for complete symptom control, since intra-gastric acidity may increase to pH < 2.0 especially towards the end of digestion of a meal. Short periods of high acidity which may not result in epithelial damage may be sufficient to stimulate esophageal nerves and the meta-analysis only addresses mean diurnal pH, not periods of high acidity. Rapid symptom control may require more frequent dosing for the first 3 days until steady state inhibition is reached or reformulation of the PPI's. It also may be that there are anatomical variations between patients either in terms of access of acid to the nerves, resulting in a more sensitive esophagus. One is left with the paradox that the severe disease is more easily dealt with than the milder symptoms.

The gastric epithelium

The presence of high concentrations of acid in the normal gastric lumen without damage to the epithelium has always puzzled investigators, given that most cells in the body have an exquisite sensitivity to acidic excursions of pH. This has led to the idea that the gastric mucosa has developed specialized mechanisms to protect itself against acid, under the collective sobriquet, the "gastric barrier", explicitly enunciated by a gastric physiologist, Horace Davenport, as

outlined above. The function of acid itself is not entirely clear. Evidently, acid secretion is not essential for survival, since patients with total gastrectomy or pernicious anemia do not suffer from consequences of the lack of gastric digestion. It is often thought of as providing a barrier to bacterial infection, but several pathogens have developed mechanisms to resist gastric acid and transit the stomach to their site of infection. Some organisms, such as the gastric *Helicobacter sp.*, have even adapted so well to gastric acidity that they are able to colonize the gastric mucosa of animals and humans, implying not only survival but growth in gastric acid. Peculiarly the gastric *Helicobacter* do not survive in the rest of the gut. Mucus secretion is a prominent feature of gastric surface epithelial cells. Gastric mucus as part of the gastric barrier is considered to restrict back diffusion of acid or to expand the unstirred layer on the gastric surface, enabling maintenance of locally high concentrations of HCO_3^- emanating from the mucosa. Mucus is an aqueous gel and is therefore physically unlikely to provide a significant barrier to acid back diffusion.

Experiments on *in vitro* mucosae have shown that K^+ addition to the mucosal side results in rapid changes in transepithelial potential, indicating that mucus is not a significant barrier to this cation and also suggesting that it would not be a significant barrier to H^+.

HCO_3^- secretion was first shown to occur in *in vitro* preparations of amphibian stomachs (both fundus and antrum). The secretion was found to consist of two components, an active secretion and a passive diffusive component. HCO_3^- secretion was then shown to be an important property of the human stomach.

The idea that cells themselves manufacture agents that aid in recovery from or prevention of acid injury came from the area of prostaglandin research. Andre Robert showed that administration of low doses of a prostaglandin, 16,16-dimethyl prostaglandin E2, prevented gross damage to rat stomachs after treatment with high levels of alkali, acid, alcohol or heat.

This cyto-protective mechanism replaced acid inhibition as the target of prostaglandins as anti-ulcer medications.

There are several components of this barrier currently under consideration as contributing to the pathogenesis of acid related disease, the mucus layer, HCO_3^- secretion and cellular factors providing "cytoprotection" such as prosta-glandin biosynthesis or generation of a phospholipid layer similar to lung surfactant. Defects in one or more of these is thought to pre-dispose to ulcer disease where the defensive factors are overcome by normal aggressive elements. Adequate perfusion of the gastric epithelium by the local blood supply is also a factor often ignored in consideration of pathogenesis of mucosal damage.

The luminal membrane of the epithelial cells and the tight junctions connecting the epithelial cells is a major deterrent to acid back diffusion, and agents which damage either must also render the stomach subject to damage.

Both acid and pepsin contribute to aggressive factors enabling peptic ulcer disease or reflux erosions. The recent implication of *H. pylori* in generation of duodenal and gastric ulcer disease has added an additional element for consideration as an aggressive factor that can result in loss of epithelial integrity.

Following damage, several options are open for initiation and completion of the repair process. Restitution, wherein the surface cells migrate to cover the

lesion and release mucus to form a mucoid cap is among the earlier events, and epithelial cell renewal, stimulated by local release of TGF-alpha is a later step in the repair process.

The model summarizes the concepts of the gastric barrier at the level of the surface epithelial cell.

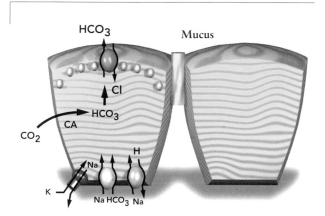

Components of the gastric "barrier" Illustrated is a mucus coat, which acts as an "unstirred layer" inhibiting fast diffusion of secreted HCO_3^- via an apical anion exchanger. The basal lateral surface has pH regulatory mechanisms such as sodium proton exchange or sodium dependent entry of bicarbonate. The necessary Na^+ gradient is driven by the sodium pump and bicarbonate is formed by the action of carbonic anhydrase (CA).

Mucus secretion

The gastric mucosa is divided into acid secreting and non-acid secreting portions. The fundic area contains the acid secreting parietal cells in deep invaginations, the fundic glands, which also contain chief or peptic cells. The latter secrete pepsinogen I. The antral region is devoid of parietal cells but still contains peptic cells as well as G and D cells that make luminal contact. The chief cells of the antrum contain pepsinogen II. This region, in contrast to the acid secretory fundus, is largely absorptive. The transition between fundus and antrum, the transitional zone, contains some parietal cells and a mixed population of chief cells secreting both types of pepsinogen.

Surface cells of the gastro-intestinal epithelium secrete mucus by a process of regulated exocytosis. Mucus secretion by the columnar surface cells of the gastric epithelium is especially abundant. The mucus is composed of a complex set of sulfated polysaccharides with several O or N-linked oligosaccharide cores that create an aqueous gel at the surface of the epithelial cells. In the last several years cloning of the genes encoding the peptide domain has shown the presence of several genes, each with a signal sequence enabling secretion into the secretory organelle. There is both unregulated basal secretion and regulated secretion by muscarinic and β adrenergic agonists, prostaglandins, and perhaps secretin. Both cAMP and Ca signaling pathways are used. As an aqueous gel, although gastric mucus cannot retard back diffusion of hydrogen ions, it can provide an extended unstirred layer with some retardation of HCO_3^- diffusion. Most likely its major function is for lubrication of freshly ingested food.

Secretion of HCO_3^-

This is mainly the product of gastric surface epithelial cells and is stimulated by acetylcholine released by vagal stimulation showing that there is central regulation. Much is energy dependent *in vitro* suggesting active secretion. Probably entry of bicarbonate is via Na^+/HCO_3^- cotransport and efflux by Cl/HCO_3^- exchange. Gastric acid is also a powerful stimulant of HCO_3^- secretion when the pH is less than 2.0. It seems that HCO_3^- secretion is enhanced with stimulation of acid secretion improving the neutralizing capacity of the gastric surface cells. It may be noted that the HCO_3^- content of the interstitial fluid of the secreting fundic mucosa rises sharply due to HCO_3^- production by the activated parietal cells, providing more intracellular HCO_3^- for secretion across the cell membrane. This anion can also diffuse between the cells via a paracellular pathway although this pathway is considered to be a minor contributor to bicarbonate secretion in the stomach.

SECTION 4

THE BIOLOGY OF ACID RELATED DISEASE

CHAPTER 1
The Barriers of the Upper Gastro-Intestinal Tract

CHAPTER 2
Intragastric pH

CHAPTER 3
Pepsin

CHAPTER 4
Intrinsic Factor

CHAPTER 5
Regulation of Growth of Gastric Epithelium

The secretion of HCO_3^- by gastric mucosa is at most 10% of acid output. Assuming that the stomach is secreting 100 mM HCl, 10 mM HCO_3^- can be secreted. Hence this base is not able to neutralize a gastric solution at pH 1.0. However, if the stomach is only secreting 10 mM HCl, this can be neutralized by 10 mM HCO_3^-. Secretion of the base could in principle then neutralize an unbuffered solution at pH 2.0.

Cytoprotection

The production of arachidonic acid in the gastric epithelial cells can result in production of prostaglandins via cyclo-oxygenase and leukotrienes via lipoxygenase. Prostaglandins of the E2 subtype have been shown to reduce gastric mucosal blood flow and hence reduce hemorrhage due to tissue injury. They inhibit acid secretion by binding to an EP3 receptor in the parietal cell which is linked to G_i inhibiting cAMP production. Clearly agents which inhibit the constitutive cycloxygenase I (cox I) are capable of inducing severe gastric damage. Newer agents that inhibit the inducible cox II are less likely to induce gastric damage. It also appears that low doses of misoprostil are able to reduce NSAID induced damage. Depletion of endogenous prostaglandins does appear to have a deleterious effect on gastric mucosal integrity although the mechanism of this remains entirely obscure.

Gastric mucosal perfusion

There is a marked change in the blood flow upon the stimulation of gastric acid secretion, such that blood is now supplied in large quantities to the gastric epithelium by relaxation of the mucosal arterioles. Histamine, prostaglandins and NO are some of the factors increasing epithelial perfusion. Limitation of blood flow, such as in hemorrhagic shock, predisposes to gastric ulceration.

Apical cell membrane

For many years following the development of techniques investigating black lipid membranes, it was thought that natural bilayers had a high proton permeability. This was based on observations in these artificial membranes which however were due to artifacts such as contamination with weak acids and weak bases. More recent findings when these contaminants were removed showed that the permeability of phospholipid bilayers to protons was about the same as that to Na^+ or K^+. Further, the lipid composition of the membrane containing the H,K ATPase is similar to that of other membranes and this enzyme can generate a pH of 0.8 without measurable back leak into the cytoplasm of the parietal cell. For protons to move across membranes, transport proteins must be present that are capable of transporting protons.

Hence since the apical membranes of the gastric epithelial cells do not contain proteins capable of proton transport, they are *per se* acid resistant. In contrast, the basal lateral membranes not only contain specific proton pathways such as Na^+/H^+ or anion exchange but may also contain proteins that allow passive inward leak of protons. Specific experiments demonstrated that monolayers of isolated peptic cells resist a pH of 2.0 on their apical surface.

Cellular disposal of acid

The gastric surface cell is able to deal with limited amounts of intracellular acidity due to acid extrusion by the Na/H exchanger and HCO_3^- entry via Na^+/HCO_3^- co-transport. Given the low permeability of the apical membranes and paracellular pathway, these disposal mechanisms suffice under normal conditions.

A freeze fracture EM of a "tight" tight junction between parietal cells of gastric mucosa showing a belt of about 15 strands of protein.

Tight junctions

In contrast to the leaky tight junctions of intestinal epithelia, the gastric junctions show multiple strands of embedded protein without visible defect in freeze fracture. These are therefore "tight" tight junctions generally resistant to acid back diffusion. The junctions in the fundus are tighter than those in the antrum where there may be less acid exposure.

Surfactant

There have been reports that the gastric surface is coated with a phospholipid, which is in principle similar to the surfactant found in the lung. If present as a continuum, and this is difficult to demonstrate, such phospholipid could prevent access of protons to the gastric surface. In the fundus, under acid secretion, it is unlikely that such a bilayer would persist, but it may do so in the antrum.

Surface pH measurements

Several laboratories have shown the presence of a pH gradient when the surface pH is probed with microelectrodes such that there is measurement of a neutral pH when the luminal pH is 3.0 or greater. These observations have generally been interpreted as showing the "barrier" function of mucus in combination with HCO_3^- secretion. All of these workers also seem to agree that this pH gradient disappears when the pH in the luminal solution is 2.0. Further, it is claimed that acid secretion from fundic pits (the confluence of 5 gastric glands in mammals) streams through channels in the mucus and does not diffuse laterally.

These data may be correct but possible artefacts exist. The pH electrodes used in these studies are usually open tip microelectrodes with a small volume of aqueous solution at the tip. This is followed by an oil layer containing an electrogenic protonophore and then a KCl solution to make electrical contact with the wire leading to the voltmeter. When a pH gradient exists across the oil, the protonophore moves protons across the oil layer thereby generating a potential that measures pH. If inward diffusion into the pipette tip is restricted, such as by compressed mucus, the pH in the aqueous solution in the tip would rise since the protonophore would remove the excess protons. This electrode then would report a higher pH than really existed outside its tip.

One way of eliminating this possible artifact is to calibrate the electrode on the gastric mucosa in strong buffer, e.g. 100-200 mM citrate. There is no way that the gastric HCO_3^- secretion could neutralize this level of buffering, therefore no pH gradient should be measured. However, the pH gradients were the same as those found without buffer. This is suggestive of a tip artefact. Indeed recent measurements using confocal microscopy argue against the presence of a pH gradient on the surface of an exteriorized rat stomach.

H. pylori is an acid tolerant neutralophile with most of its urease being internal. This internal urease is acid activated and easily detected *in vivo*, especially after acid stimulation. The bacteria dwell on the mucosal surface and, if this were neutral, only low urease activity would be detected. Further urease activity is toxic to these bacteria at neutral pH since the enzyme elevates pH to >8.0. If the organism is a pH biosensor, it is then reporting on the presence of an acidic pH in its environment on the gastric surface. Indeed, it is not found in gastric fundic epithelium in an infected rat model showing that this region is too acidic even for its survival (pH < 2.5).

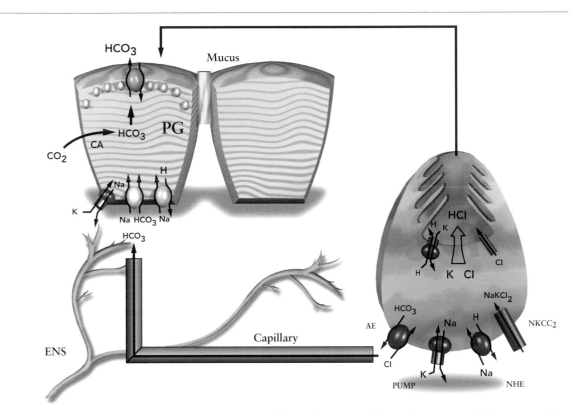

An integrated model of acid resistance of the gastric epithelium, where the surface cell provides neutralization, and a generally proton impermeable barrier. The parietal cell extrudes bicarbonate into the serosal side to supply this anion to the surface cell and acid also appears to stimulate surface cell bicarbonate secretion

In summary, it would seem that most of the acid resistance of the gastric epithelium can be accounted for by the proton impermeability of apical cell membranes and the tight junctions. Bicarbonate secretion may be effective in part in increasing surface pH under low acid secretory conditions, and mucus may retard the diffusion of this anion to make it more effective as a local buffering agent.

Agents such as NSAID's and *H. pylori* decrease the effectiveness of this barrier for gastric ulcers to appear. Whether these agents affect the integrity of the cell membrane or of the tight junctions is not known, although at least one of these is a likely target for initiation of epithelial damage. The figure illustrates some of the integrated protective functions of the gastric epithelium.

Duodenal barrier

The duodenum is composed of a monolayer of cells, divided into villus cells with brush borders and deeper crypt cells. The brush border membranes contain a large variety of proteins and are significantly proton permeable. The duodenal tight junctions are significantly leakier than those of the gastric mucosa. The exact resistance of the mammalian duodenal tight junction is not known but is probably comparable to that of the jejunum since tissue electrical resistance is low. In Necturus, the paracellular pathway here is about 10-fold greater than that of the stomach. In some contrast to the stomach, the duodenum, especially the proximal region, is capable of strong HCO_3^- secretion and is also bathed by the alkaline secretion of the pancreas.

The early duodenum is exposed to gastric acid and therefore must have properties enabling survival in the face of this high luminal acidity. Much of this is attributed to HCO_3^- secretion by this tissue.

Both cellular and paracellular pathways contribute towards duodenal bicarbonate secretion. The paracellular pathway contributes about 40% of net HCO_3^- secretion in this tissue, a much larger fraction than in the gastric mucosa. This is due to the low resistance of the paracellular pathway in this tissue. Cellular secretion is stimulated by various agents but there is abundant species variation. In humans, CCK, prostaglandins and VIP stimulate secretion. Intracellular stimulants such as dbcAMP and forskolin stimulate secretion in animal models.

Both exchange and conductive pathways seem to be present. The villus cells appear to be major contributors. Carbonic anhydrase inhibitors decrease secretion as do NSAID's. Luminal acidity also stimulated HCO_3^- secretion, the threshold however being about pH 3.0 in the duodenum as compared to pH 2.0 in the stomach. It is thought that this response to acid is mediated by prostaglandins and that there are surface pH receptors. Atropine blocks only 30% of duodenal secretion in dogs and is without action in humans. Vagal stimulation of acid secretion in animals seems to be mediated by nicotinic rather than muscarinic receptors in the duodenum, in contrast to the stomach. The figure illustrates the pathways of alkali secretion by the duodenal villus cell.

It has been repeatedly demonstrated that HCO_3^- secretion is impaired in duodenal ulcer patients. It seems that infection with *H. pylori* must play a role in this inhibition, but whether this is a direct effect of local infestation or remote as a function of the organism's pathogenic effects on the gastric mucosa is not clear.

A major contributor to loss of duodenal integrity may be the production of NH_3 at the duodenal surface following neutralization of the acidic NH_4Cl load from the stomach.

Pathways of acid resistance in the duodenum showing apical bicarbonate secretion by anion exchange and bicarbonate conductance, paracellular bicarbonate secretion and generation of intracellular bicarbonate by carbonic anhydrase and entry of the anion by sodium cotransport.

CHAPTER 2
INTRAGASTRIC pH

Profound acid suppression has raised several concerns about the possible consequences of long-term acid inhibition. These have included loss of bactericidal activity of gastric acid with an increase in bacterial overgrowth, with the predisposition either to enteric infection or the increased production of potentially carcinogenic N-nitrosamines and nitrosamides by colonization of the stomach by nitrate reducing bacteria. Elevation of plasma gastrin has been associated with ECL cell hyperplasia and the possibility of the development of gastric carcinoids. Long-term pharmacological suppression of acid secretion has been equated to conditions such as pernicious anemia or to situations analogous to those found after subtotal gastrectomy, where, after 15 to 20 years, an increased risk of gastric cancer has been proposed. In order to evaluate both the benefits of acid suppression and some of the issues related to the subsequent prolonged elevation in pH and gastrin levels, the measurement of actual gastric acid secretion in addition to gastric luminal pH needs to be considered.

Hypochlorhydria and achlorhydria

A confusing terminology has grown up around the inability to adequately quantify low levels of gastric acid secretion.

In 1886, Chan and Von Mehring associated pernicious anemia with anacidity. In 1889, Einhorn first utilized the term achylia gastrica to describe the absence of both enzymes and acid in the stomach. Achlorhydria was utilized to denote the absence of free acid as determined by Topfer's reagent. Despite these different terminologies, there was no good agreement as to what they meant; neither did they identify whether the conditions that caused them were reversible or irreversible. In addition, achlorhydria suggested that no acid at all was being secreted, whereas in fact, the presence of some parietal cells secreting acid might be obscured by bicarbonate secretion and thus absence of gastric secretion could not be detected by pH measurement alone. In 1952, Card and Sircus proposed that a pH of 6 be used to define anacidity. A reasonable definition, therefore, of achlorhydria is the persistent failure of intragastric pH to fall below 6 in the presence of any stimulation of gastric acid secretion.

The terminologies hypochlorhydria and hypoacidity have not achieved wide acceptance since the pH electrode does not distinguish between HCl and other inorganic or organic acids and acid secretion varies widely, depending both on the time of measurement and the methodology utilized.

An arbitrary maximal acid output (MAO) of < 5 mmol/per hour has been used to define this term. Even in such situations, however, the gastric juice pH may fall below 2 and thus provide information difficult to interpret in 24-hour pH measurement techniques.

W. I. Card (above), I.N. Marks and W. Sircus defined the different levels of acid secretion and their chemical relevance.

Quantification of gastric acid secretion

Two approaches have been utilized to measure gastric acid secretion, one quantitative and the other qualitative. The quantitative measurements have included: basal and stimulated acid secretion, nocturnal acid secretion, food stimulated acid secretion using intragastric titration and 24-hour acid secretion. The qualitative measurements utilize 24-hour intragastric acidity. For the most part quantitative measurements are rarely used today except under experimental circumstances to define physiological pathways or to evaluate the effect of therapeutic agents on gastric acid secretion. Stimulants include histamine, pentagastrin, insulin, 2-deoxyglucose, or sham feeding. Currently the use of quantitative acid secretory measurement is rarely applied except in the diagnosis of the Zollinger-Ellison syndrome and even here has mostly been supplanted by plasma gastrin measurements and the secretin provocation test.

pH metric measurement of acid secretion is now the most frequently applied method. This obtains a profile of intragastric acidity and evaluates the state of acid secretion as well as the influence of pharmacological agents on ulcer healing and symptomatology. 24-hour intragastric acidity may be evaluated either by repeated rapid sampling of small volumes of gastric juice by aspiration or, alternatively, by continuous recording of intragastric acidity using intragastric pH electrodes. Whilst the primary agent of interest is acid secretion, the values obtained may also be influenced by bicarbonate secretion, ingested food and fluids, reflux alkaline duodenal juice, and the rate of gastric emptying. Nevertheless in an individual patient, measurement under such circumstances closely defines the events occurring in that particular stomach.

The measurements obtained have some drawbacks in both qualitative and quantitative groups. Thus in the aspiration group, pH is measured at fixed time points and fails to define events that might occur in the intervening time. Continuous recording with a pH electrode provides a better overall picture but the site of the electrode is of critical relevance in determining the pH measurements. Furthermore since the pH profile varies in different parts of the stomach, not only are sites important but also the maintenance of location throughout the measured time period. An advantage of the pH electrode methodology is its ability to establish the pH in the duodenal bulb thus quantifying the effects of hypersecretion and the acid load to which the duodenum or a duodenal ulcer is exposed. A critical difficulty in this type of evaluation, however, is stabilizing the pH electrode in the correct position and maintaining it in position for the duration of the study. It has, however, been established that luminal acidity in the duodenal bulb is no higher in ulcer patients than in controls by day or night and neither fasting nor food produce any difference between these two groups.

In quantitative evaluation of acid secretion, total acid output is the product of the $[H^+]$ (millimoles per liter) and the volume of gastric juice secreted (milliliters per hour). In order to evaluate acid secretion, the measurements that have been most commonly utilized include basal acid output (BAO), peak acid output (PAO), and maximal acid output (MAO). BAO represents acid secretion in the absence of stimulation whereas PAO and MAO are measured in response to stimulation using pentagastrin at a maximal dose and expressed as millimoles per hour (mmol/hr). Alterations in gastric acid secretion may be due either to changes in secretory volume and/or changes in the acid concentration of the gastric juice secreted. There is usually a relationship between the volume of secretion and acid concentration with concentration increasing in parallel with increased volume.

There is some discussion as to what might be the best methodology for expressing the information provided by pH monitoring. pH is a logarithmic expression of $[H^+]$ activity and, therefore, the mean pH is not numerically the same as the mean $[H^+]$ converted to pH units. Thus averages of pH recordings reflect a geometric mean whereas average concentration derived data only provides an arithmetic mean. Since the two means do not provide the same value, they are capable of producing different assessments of acid suppression particularly in the evaluation of acid suppressive agents.

Thus, reporting that gastric pH may be above or below a particular pH value somewhat marginalizes the information since an increase in pH of one unit reflects a suppression of acidity of 90%. Similarly it is difficult to evaluate whether an alteration of pH of 2 to 1 as opposed to 4 to 3 is reasonable since both are equivalent of 90% acid suppression. Similar problems apply to the expression of the information when using the area under the concentration/time or pH/time curve and it seems likely that the best compromise may be the use of median pH or hydrogen ion concentration $[H^+]$. Nevertheless since it is not possible to utilize all data points, analyses are usually conducted using summary values and particular time points compared to specific activities such as meals, sleeping, and drug ingestion.

pH metric curve in a normal, untreated volunteer, showing long periods of high acidity.

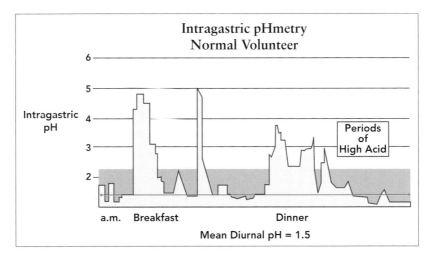

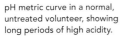

Factors effecting gastric acid secretion

The physiological regulation of acid secretion is complicated, as has been delineated in section 2 of this book. A number of other factors including *H. pylori,* age, smoking, non-steroidal anti-inflammatory drugs, and mental status influence both secretory events and the health of the gastric mucosa. In general, acid secretion has been noted to fall with advancing age. To a large extent this reflects the increasing gastritis in older individuals and is reflected by a decrease in both basal and histamine stimulated acid secretion noted with increasing age. In individuals who do not exhibit the atrophic gastritis often noted in older persons, basal, food stimulated and gastrin-17 stimulated acid secretion may be normal or even higher than in younger subjects, especially women. Overall it appears that whilst age is a critical determinate in the decreasing of acid secretion, to a large extent this represents that state of the gastric mucosa and the presence or absence of gastritis.

The role of *H. pylori* is a complex one with gastric acidity appearing to influence its ability to survive as well as its presence influencing gastric acidity itself. A detailed evaluation of this issue appears in section 7. In brief, however, *H. pylori* is highly susceptible to the pH of its environment and seeks to alkalize its microenvironment as it colonizes the gastric epithelium. Low intragastric acidity is an unwelcome scenario for *H. pylori* as noted in the low prevalence of infection evident in patients with pernicious anemia. Similarly treatment with proton pump inhibitors suppresses *H. pylori* growth. *H. pylori*, by its effect on gastrin and somatostatin cells, similarly alters the gastric acid secretory profile.

The subject of smoking as it relates to peptic ulcer disease has been one of considerable public and medical interest. Overall, smoking increases basal and maximal acid output, and pepsin secretion as well as decreasing bicarbonate output with result that an increased acid load and a decreased buffering capacity in the duodenum are evident. Such effects are most obvious during daytime when cigarette consumption is highest. Overall they serve to prolong the period during which the duodenal bulb pH falls below 3.5 in both normal subjects and acid hypersecretors. Since duodenal ulcer is more common in individuals who smoke than non-smokers and since relapse is more frequent in smokers, it has been accepted that smoking in an as yet ill-defined fashion renders the duodenal bulb more prone to ulceration.

Whilst it is clearly evident that NSAID's are related to mucosal ulceration, their direct effect on the alteration of gastric acid secretion or pH has not been firmly established. Nevertheless whilst there exists clinical evidence to support the fact that acid is of relatively little importance in the development of NSAID associated gastric ulcers, both duodenal and gastric ulceration in patients receiving NSAID's heals with anti-secretory therapy. It is, however, evident that such healing is augmented if the NSAID is discontinued suggesting that a direct mucosal effect of the drug is of relevance.

Traditional concepts of mental status influencing acid secretion and peptic ulceration have indicated that stress may result in punitive effects on the gastroduodenal mucosa. The precise effects of stress on acid secretion have, however, been variable and hypnosis has been demonstrated to either increase or decrease gastric secretion dependent upon the particular mood induced. Given the critical relevance of the brain and regulation of gut function, it is likely that the central nervous system effects on acid secretion are of significance, however, they remain to be defined.

Low acid states

The long term maintenance of a low acid state has raised five general concerns: 1) the loss of the primary bactericidal barrier against the ingestion of enteric pathogens, 2) the alteration of the absorption of important nutrients, 3) the alteration of the gastric mucosal morphology, 4) risks of adverse drug effects, 5) the development of hypergastrinemia and the induction of mucosal hyperplastic changes. These initial theoretical concerns have faded with the widespread long term usage of PPI's (> 300 million treatments) without evidence of any significant sequelae to treatment.

Definition of a low acid state

Achlorhydria can be defined as a luminal pH greater than 6, which cannot be decreased by stimulation with histamine or pentagastrin. Achlorhydria may be present in pernicious anemia, and can be achieved transiently with intravenous PPI's. The existence of a low acid state might be more operationally defined as a luminal pH above 3 or 4, since such levels have been demonstrated to be necessary for optimal benefit for patients with duodenal ulcer disease or GERD. Perhaps such a pH could be defined as hypochlorhydria. It should be remembered that even at this luminal pH, significant acidity exists at the secretory surface of the mucosa. The output is low allowing neutralization.

The duration of an achlorhydric or hypochlorhydric state may be life-long in atrophic gastritis, pernicious anemia, and post-surgical procedures such as vagotomy, with or without antrectomy. In addition, acid suppression may be induced acutely in the management of patients in intensive care units at risk for stress bleeding. Alternatively, acid suppression may be employed for longer periods of time, from 4 weeks to months, or even years, in the management of intractable peptic ulcer disease, gastrinoma (ZES) or GERD.

Areas of potential concern

Enteric pathogens

The acid milieu of the stomach provides a barrier against the promulgation of ingested pathogens into the lower gastrointestinal tract. In the presence of decreased acid, colonization of the stomach with pathogenic bacteria may occur, and these organisms may even transit the stomach, unimpeded by the normal acid barriers. Studies in less developed countries with poor sanitation do show an increased susceptibility to cholera and Shigella in patients with low acid states. In contrast, no such susceptibility data exists in developed countries where the water supply is more highly regulated. Western travellers using acid inhibitory therapy probably do not need to be cautioned before making journeys to poor sanitation areas. The possibility of nosocomial pneumonia developing secondary to gastric bacterial aspiration in ventilator-dependent, intensive care unit patients treated with anti-secretory therapies, has been shown to be virtually non-existent.

Alteration of nutrient absorption

The presence of gastric acid promotes the absorption of important nutrients by release of minerals, particularly calcium, from their complexed organic forms. However, low acid states do not appear to predispose to decreased calcium absorption in man. In contrast, the absorption of ferric iron is decreased in achlorhydric states and in gastrectomized patients. This deficit is related directly to the low solubility of ferric iron at a pH > 5. Nevertheless, the absorption of heme-iron is not compromised, and no evidence exists for a predisposition to iron deficiency anemia. In the case of vitamin B12, neither PPI's or H2RA's have been implicated in significant alterations in absorption of this compound.

Progression of chronic atrophic gastritis

This is a dynamic process which progresses with age and is independent for either the antral or oxyntic mucosa. The long term nature of this process makes it difficult to study the effects of drugs on its development. Nevertheless, concerns have been raised that long term PPI treatment might be associated with progression of chronic active gastritis. In the few studies published, there does appear to be a small (< 1.5%) increase in its incidence in these patients. This is not however associated with alterations in cell lineage, or the development of intestinal metaplasia, apart from the occasional occurrence of type I metaplasia, with no evidence of dysplasia.

Inhibition of cytochrome P450, risk of adverse toxic drug interactions and putative genotoxicity

Metabolism of polycyclic compounds by the hepatic cytochrome P450 systems is a critical step in drug metabolism. Of the various PPI's currently available, pantoprazole appears to have the cleanest profile with no significant effects as regards drug interaction. None of the PPI's have been shown to have clinically significant drug interactions, however. In addition, PPI's induce the P450 1A isozyme which initially raised concerns of compounding tumorigenesis since this P450 may result in carcinogen formation from other compounds. However, no evidence exists for either the induction of the isozyme *in vivo* or an elevated incidence of tumorigenesis by any of the PPI's. Most data indicate that induction (if it occurs) is protective rather than harmful. No genotoxic effects can be ascribed to PPI's.

Hypergastrinemia

The effect of gastrin on the proliferation of the gastric mucosa has been well described. Of particular interest is the more recent appreciation of its ability to stimulate ECL cell proliferation, and its putative influence on the development of gastrointestinal neoplasia. Normal fasting levels vary, but range between 50-100 pg/ml. Short-term treatment courses of anti-secretory therapies seldom result in significant elevations of gastrin levels. Nevertheless, in long-term studies, these therapies raise serum gastrin above normal (usually in the range of 200-300 pg/ml), but do not achieve the levels noted in pernicious anemia (2000 pg/ml), which are an order of magnitude higher and sustained throughout the day.

Chronic active gastritis and pernicious anemia

Whilst both differences in populations and environment certainly modulate the risks of the development of gastric neoplasms, data from a number of studies suggest that patients with pernicious anemia and chronic active gastritis are at a higher risk for specific types of gastric carcinoma. Such patients may require long-term, careful endoscopic follow-up to ensure these diseases do not manifest. Other reports indicate that, in addition to a long-term risk of gastric carcinoma, patients with chronic active gastritis and pernicious anemia may be at risk for developing gastric endocrine cell hyperplasia and carcinoids.

Colonic neoplasia

Apart from the stomach, the trophic effect of gastrin on other GI organs is less well accepted. Overall the experimental data (in cell lines and animal models) is equivocal and is not uniform in supporting a role for gastrin in growth regulation in the colon. Clinical observations also fail to support a direct relationship between gastrin and colonic cancer. No evidence supporting a direct relationship between plasma gastrin levels and the evolution of colonic neoplasia in humans exists.

Gastric adenocarcinoma

Whereas achlorhydria has been linked to an increased incidence of gastric adenocarcinoma, the mechanism for this is probably not related to hypergastrinemia. A number of studies instead have demonstrated associations between gastric tumors and hypo- or normo-gastrinemia, which argues against a role for gastrin. It is probable that the development of neoplasia may be related to alterations initiated by the concomitant presence of *H. pylori* and its effects on T and B cell function. This issue is dealt with in detail in the section on MALT lymphoma in section 7. However, the increasing prevalence of chronic active gastritis and colonic polyps in elderly patients may correlate with hypergastrinemia.

The effect of acid suppression and hypergastrinemia on ECL cell proliferation in rats. Chromagranin staining of gastric fundic ECL cells in rat mucosa. Left: normal; center: mild hyperplasia (6 months); right: severe hyperplasia (12 months).

ECL cell hyperplasia/carcinoids

It has been established that gastrin is a potent proliferative stimulus for the ECL cell system in rats. Initially the ECL cell hyperplasia is modest but over an as yet undefined period of time it may progress and eventually become dysplastic and even exhibit micro-carcinoid formation. The progression to an autonomous carcinoid lesion has not been demonstrated in humans taking PPI's for time periods as long as 10-15 years unless the patient has multiple endocrine neoplasia syndrome. The issue of ECL cell proliferation is dealt with in detail in section 5.

Gastric fundic polyps

These have been described in normal mucosae but may be seen more frequently in association with high dose PPI's taken for two years or more. They seem more frequent in cases with accompanying hepatic cirrhosis. They are outgrowths or extensions of the gastric epithelium with all cell types represented and show no evidence of any cellular transformation. There is some degree of parietal cell hyperplasia. Their etiology is obscure but may come from inhi-

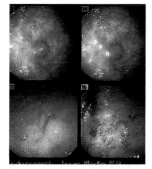

Small, sessile fundic gastric polypi (histologically carcinoid) occurring in a patient with atrophic gastritis.

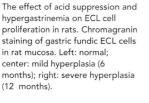

bition of acid secretion without accompanying inhibition of pepsinogen secretion resulting in a hypertonic gland lumen. This in combination with gastric hypertension due to liver cirrhosis may predispose to benign polyp formation. Another possibility is local effects of ECL cell stimulation by gastrin to produce a preponderance of fundic polyps as compared to areas where there are fewer ECL cells. The factor released by ECL cells may be the REG protein.

Clinical relevance of gastrin levels and PPI therapy

Current opinion on hypergastrinemia and its consequences reflects a substantial decrease of concern in this area. Only in cases where long-term therapy is contemplated should there even be a thought about measuring gastrin levels. In long-term therapy, where reflux disease is the therapeutic concern, it is safe to assume that occasional symptoms indicate a level of acidity sufficient to inhibit the G cell appropriately. It is only when the patient responds with achlorhydria that consideration may be given to determining the degree of elevation of gastrin. No data have however been advanced in clinical studies to indicate that even a considerable elevation of gastrin is of concern.

CHAPTER 3
PEPSIN

History
of pepsinogen

Ueber das Wesen des Verdauungsprocesses.
Von Dr. Th. Schwann,
Gehülfen am anatomischen Museum in Berlin.

Durch die glänzende Entdeckung von Eberle haben
wir in den mit verdünnten Säuren behandelten Schleim-
häuten ein Mittel kennen gelernt, die Verdauung auf
künstlichem Wege eben so gut zu bewirken, wie auf na-
türlichem Wege. Durch...

The frontispiece of T. Schwann's original description of pepsin. In a period of less than six months during 1835 Schwann identified pepsin and characterised its properties. In addition, Schwann was responsible for the recognition of the basic cellular composition of organisms. In 1839 Schwann published *Mikroskopische Untersuchungen*. In this he identified the common cellular origin of all living matter. In 1841 he received the Sommering Medal.
In 1847, the Sydenham Society published an English version of *Mikroskopische Untersuchungen*. In the introduction, Smith presented the following judgement: *"The Treatise has now been seven years before the public, has been most acutely investigated by those best competent to test its value, and the first physiologists of our day judge the discovery which it unfolds as worthy to be ranked amongst the most important steps by which the science of physiology has ever been advanced."*

Pepsinogen is a potent digestive enzyme secreted by the chief cell of the gastric gland into the lumen of the stomach. This agent is an active barrier breaker and is likely to play a significant role in the pathogenesis of peptic ulcer disease. Although abnormalities in this protein have been epidemiologically linked to gastric carcinoma and its precursors, no specific pathogenic role exists for this potent and prolific enzyme.

The story of this poorly understood enzyme began in the Berlin laboratory of J. Muller, where in 1836, Theodor Schwann described a water-soluble factor in gastric juice which digested egg-white. He called it "pepsin", after the Greek word for digestion.

Schwann had just obtained his MD degree and was continuing as an assistant in Muller's laboratory. His investigation of gastric glands was initiated by the latter, who had asked him to attempt to subject the physiological properties of either an organ or a tissue to physical measurement. Schwann intially developed a muscle balance, and became the first to establish the basics of the tension-length diagram. Thereafter, whilst successfully measuring secretion from the gastric gland, he stumbled upon a proteolytic enzyme, whose properties he characterized, and soon thereafter published.

Unfortunately for the science of the stomach, this observation became lost in the subsequent spate of diverse investigative work which emanated from the young man. He moved onto fermentation, and was the first to demonstrate the importance of oxygen for both alcoholic fermentation in yeast as well as for putrefaction. His work with yeast led to probably his greatest discovery, which was the assertion of a common cellular basis for all living matter. However, his failure to win a chair at the University of Bonn, appeared to have damaged his impetus for scientific investigation – his last useful digestive observation, which appeared 40 years before his death, was the necessity of bile for digestion (and for survival). He had modified a biliary fistula model for these experiments, which also happened to be the last physiological experiments he would conduct.

Three years after the initial identification of pepsin by Schwann, Wasmann was able to isolate the protein and thereby establish the premise for protein digestion. In 1846, Claude Bernard wrote extensively on the digestive ferments of the pancreas, whilst the possibility of a pro-enzyme, pepsinogen, was formally postulated by Epstein and Grutzner in 1854. The first evaluation of the protein products of gastric digestion was described by Meisner in 1859. Heidenhain, whilst studying the pancreas, was soon thereafter able to describe the secretory mechanisms of proteolytic zymogens. Eight years into his tenure as Professor of Physiology at Breslau, Heidenhain began a systematic study of glands, which would occupy him for almost the next thirty years. During this time, his experimental work suggested to him that all secretory phenomena were intracellular rather than mechanical processes. From these, he was able to draw some important conclusions about gastric physiology. Firstly, he conclud-

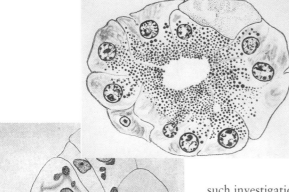

By the late 19th century investigators were able to differentiate Chief cells (*Hauptzellen*: top right), with granules from *Belegzellen* (parietal cells) which possessed canaliculi (bottom left).

Th obituary notice of John Newport Langley (1852-1925): *"The main achievements of Langley's research work are familiar to the readers of the Journal of Physiology and need little here in the way of description or comment. They stand permanently in their place, not merely as additions here and there to knowledge, but as indispensable stepping stones along which at this point, or that, the progress of knowledge has actually made its way. Each gain he made was a step placed securely and finally, and few indeed of them as the road has become more firmly and widely trodden by others following, have been found wrongly placed. All his chief works keep, and must always keep, their place in the significant history of Animal Physiology. The bare titles of his papers and books deployed there along the years give the plainest testimony to me to his unvarying, unhalting service to science. No single year in all that series, extending well nigh for half a century, from youth to age, appears without its contribution of effective work".*
W. M. Fletcher. 1926, J Physiol.

"The fresh gastric glands contain no pepsin; they do however, contain a large quantity of pepsinogen; consequently the granules of the chief cells consist wholly or in part of pepsinogen".

J. Langley, 1879.

ed that the secretion of saliva was an indicator of blood flow, and secondly, that there were two kinds of cells in gastric glands: those that secrete hydrochloric acid which he named "Belegzellen", and those that secrete pepsin, "Hauptzellen". His histological notes also describe a yellow stained small cell, situated adjacent to these cells, which 100 years later would be identified as the endocrine ECL cell. His use of a surgical pouch for investigating acid physiology later became the standard model for such investigations.

Heidenhain's observations were followed by those of Kuhne who theorized that since the stomach itself was not digested by pepsin, the gastric ferments must have inactive protein precursors (e.g. pepsinogen). It was Kuhne who developed the term "zymogen" for these precursors, as well as the term "enzyme". He also identified the proteolytic pancreatic enzyme, trypsin, in 1868, and influenced the work of his later English admirers.

However, it remained for Langley at Cambridge in the 1880s to formalize the study of pepsinogen and the mechanisms of its secretion. Langley's introduction to the gastric gland was driven by chance. His mentor, the great physiologist, Foster, suggested he study the effects of the drug, *jaborandi*, on the heart. These studies in 1874 led him towards studying its effects on secretion. After an intial prelude in the submaxillary gland, Langley dove into the regulation of secretion in the stomach, which he would pursue for the better part of the next twenty years.

He undertook histological studies of the gland structure during activity and rest and checked the interpretation of the appearance of killed and stained cells with that of direct observation of living gland cells. He correlated these findings with the effect of nervous influence on the glands, and linked these observations to chemical estimations of the changes in the quality of secretion under different circumstances. Indeed, his drawings and sketches, although now over a hundred years old, attest to his clear understanding of the nature of zymogen secretion and some of the mechanisms of its stimulation. In addition, Langley was so impressed with Heidenhain's contribution that he was to borrow and translate his terms for the cells in the stomach into English as "border" and "chief" cells respectively. Langley also coined the term "oxyntic" to identify the role of the acid secreting cells. In a series of publications between 1879 and 1882, he established the basic morphology and secretory characteristics of the pepsin-forming glands of the stomach and esophagus. In addition, he was able to correct Heidenhain, by showing that contrary to previous reports, gland cells became

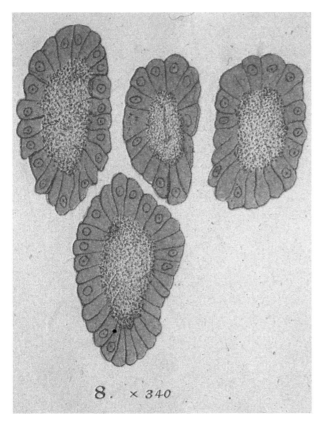

8. × 340

Esophageal gland of *Rana tempo-raria* (September 1879). A drawing by Langley shows the end tubes of the esophageal gland of a frog fed with a sponge for 35 hours before expelled by vomiting. The animal was killed 10 hours thereafter and the tissue placed in absolute alcohol for 24 hours and then dilute carmine for a further 24 hours. These cells show stained non-granular zones and unstained granular zones. This is consistent with contemporary biological understanding of apical exocytosis of pepsinogen granules.

less granular as secretion took place. He demonstrated that granules were stored up during rest and passed out during secretion in not only the pancreas, but also the stomach and salivary glands. To quote:

"The fresh gastric glands contain no pepsin; they do however contain a large quantity of pepsinogen; consequently the granules of the chief cells consist wholly or in part of pepsinogen."

Most of Langley's work was conducted in amphibia, and like present day investigators, he must have struggled with the problem of disappearing peptic granules in the wintertime! Of additional interest is that Langley's pupil Edkins would later discover gastrin in 1905. Langley's colorimetric test of digestion of carmine stained fibrin, was so useful that it would only be improved on fifty years later.

The first photographs of pepsinogen granules, from *Salmo salar*, were published in 1898, but it required another 30 years before chemistry had evolved sufficiently to identify that enzymes were in fact proteins. Northrop, in 1930, was the first to crystallize pepsin, but further research in this area, was initially hindered by the primitive assays for its biological activities. The description of the colorimetric tyrosine assay for digested hemoglobin in 1932 by Anson and Mirsky, allowed for rapid advances thereafter in this field. Indeed, the newly purified pepsin was soon implicated in ulcerogenesis, and Howes, in 1936, reported that although acid alone failed to prevent gastric ulcers in the cat, pepsin and acid together did. Six years later, Schiffrin demonstrated that luminal pepsin was requisite for intestinal ulcer formation in the same animal.

It is of interest that numerous other contributors to this field, after Langley and Schwann, raised many controversial issues, some of which remain unresolved to this day.

Although Brucke in 1861 first proposed that pepsin was reabsorbed from the gut lumen into the blood, and subsequently excreted in the urine, little further understanding of this process has been acquired. Indeed, today there is still controversy as to whether pepsinogen is directly secreted into the blood, or whether it represents an ill understood back-diffusion process. Van Slyke, in 1893, believed that pepsin circulated combined with an inhibitor complex, although alternate ideas ranged from white blood cells to fibrin as carriers. 1912 saw the demonstration of anti-pepsin: pepsin complexes which were theorized to be set free in the kidney, and thus accounting for the existence of urinary pepsinogen. To date, no good explanation for the presence of this proteolytic enzyme in the blood exists and it has been identified in diverse anatomical sites as far afield as spermatozoa. Its complex role in physiology has been proposed to range from that of a digestive enzyme to a luminal initiator of gut neuro-endocrine maturation after weaning. Pepsinogen secretion and pepsin function is still a grey area in the science of gastroenterology. Although its role in pathology has yet to be defined, its relationship to peptic ulcer has received undeservedly scant attention.

Properties of pepsinogen

Pepsinogens are a heterogeneous group of inactive pro-enzymes, each of which gives rise to a unique pepsin. Pepsinogen consists of the active pepsin plus a variable NH_2-terminal sequence of amino acids acting as a signal peptide.

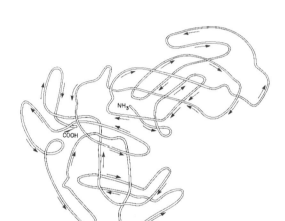

The prolate ellipsoid structure of pepsinogen.

Based on the DNA sequence, pepsinogen is synthesized initially as a pre-pepsinogen containing a 15 amino acid signal sequence at the NH_2-terminus. *In vitro* translation of pepsinogen mRNA from rat gastric mucosa also results in a pre-pepsinogen containing a 16 amino acid signal sequence. The signal sequence is lost during translational processing, since the secreted protein lacks the signal sequence.

Under acidic conditions pepsinogen is converted to pepsin by autocatalytic (i.e., intramolecular) catalysis, which results in loss of an additional NH_2-terminal sequence. This conversion occurs slowly at pH values of 5 to 6, but very rapidly at pH 2. One of the NH_2-terminal peptides released during the conversion possesses anti-pepsin activity. This peptide (MW 3,200) and its analogs complex with pepsin at pH values of 5 to 6 to inhibit catalytic activity. However, at lower pH the inhibitor dissociates and is digested by pepsin. Thus, it seems unlikely that the inhibitor serves any significant physiologic function, at least in the adult stomach.

Following the loss of the NH_2-terminal sequence, pepsin undergoes a further conformational change to expose a binding cleft that can accommodate a substrate with about eight amino acid residues. The active site contains two aspartyl residues, which are found in separate exon coding sequences, suggesting that the pepsinogen gene evolved by duplication of a smaller ancestral gene. Once activated, pepsin may be irreversibly denatured at pH values above 7.2 or temperatures above 65 °C. In contrast, pepsinogen is resistant to denaturation by pH values up to 10 or temperatures up to boiling. The difference in alkali resistance led Langley to postulate the existence of a pro-enzyme and provides an operational definition of pepsinogens, as distinct from other acid proteases.

The catalytic activity of pepsin is described in general as acid-active proteolysis. The pH optimum for hydrolysis of hemoglobin is 1.5 to 2.5, but the pH optimum is quite broad and depends on the isozyme and specific substrate, e.g., milk clotting exhibits an optimum at pH 5.5. Pepsin acts on a wide variety of peptide bonds including acidic residues. Part of the broad specificity range may reflect the existence of several isozymes.

Mammalian gastric pepsinogen can be separated electrophoretically into multiple bands. There are at least seven distinct pepsinogens, designated as Pg 1 to 7 in order of decreasing electronegativity. The seven pepsinogens have been divided into two major groups, pepsinogen I and II (PGI and PGII), based on immunologic reactivity using specific, noncross-reacting antibodies. PGI contains Pg I to 5, and PG II contains Pg 6 and 7. Apart from immunologic reactivity, the two pepsinogen groups display interesting differences. The pH optimum for PGI is 1.5 to 2.0, whereas PGII exhibits an optimum at pH 3.2. PGI is more sensitive to alkali denaturation (pH 7.2 vs 8.0) than PGII, but less sensitive to heat denaturation. The distribution of the two groups also differs. Both groups are found in the body of the stomach, but only PGII is found in the gastric antrum, proximal duodenum, and Brunner's glands. Serum contains both PGI and PGII, but only PGI is found in normal urine (uropepsin) whereas only PGII is found in semen.

In recent years, pepsinogens and pepsins from a number of species have been isolated and characterized. Amino acid sequencing and X-ray crystallographic studies revealed substantial homologies and similar tertiary structures of pepsinogens from different species.

Molecular weight estimates for pepsinogens from various species, including amphibians, fish, and mammals, range from 29 to 65 kD. Some of this heterogeneity arises from differences in the NH_2-terminal activation sequence, but significant differences exist in the catalytic peptide as well. Despite such differences, the catalytic site appears to be similar in all species.

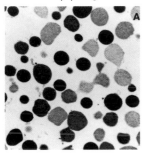

Pepsinogen granules. Electronmicrograph of isolated pepsinogen granules from rabbit gastric glands. The different size and density of granules represent maturation of pepsinogen.

Pepsinogen

Pepsinogen possesses no catalytic activity and therefore can be measured only with an immunoassay. Specific radio-immunoassays for PGI and PGII have been developed and employed for measurements of pepsinogen in tissues, serum, and urine. This method is very sensitive and highly specific. When a less sensitive assay is adequate, the pepsinogen may be converted to pepsin and the resulting acid protease activity used as a measurement. The classic method of Anson and Mirsky using hemoglobin substrate at pH 2.0 and read out of the tyrosine released remains a reliable, inexpensive assay. This assay has been adapted for the autoanalyzer to allow for a large number of samples.

In confirmation of Langley's hypothesis, immuno-cytochemical studies have identified the gastric chief cell as the major source of pepsinogen in mammals. The chief cells are found primarily in the basal portion of the gastric glands of the body and the fundus of the stomach, but the exact distribution of chief cells varies from species to species. Pepsinogen is found also in the mucous neck cells of fundic glands and caution is required when attempting to identify chief cells based solely on the presence of pepsinogen. The fundic glands contain both PGI and PGII. The cardiac glands in the gastric cardia and the pyloric glands of the gastric antrum contain pepsinogen, but only PGII has been found in these regions. Since the cardiac and pyloric glands do not contain chief cells, the pepsinogen is thought to be associated with mucous neck cells. PGII but not PGI is found in the Brunner's glands of the proximal duodenum and is secreted by the prostate gland into seminal fluid.

Vertebrate species other than mammals do not possess chief cells *per se*. Instead, a single cell type, the oxyntic cell, is responsible for gastric secretion of both acid and pepsinogen. As with the mammalian chief cell, the oxyntic cells are confined to the fundus or body of the stomach, being absent from the antrum. In certain amphibia (frog and Necturus), glands located in the lower esophagus contain peptic-like cells that secrete pepsinogen. The esophageal pepsinogen is unusual in having a low molecular weight, but it has immunologic reactivity and a pH optimum characteristic of the PGI group.

Regulation of secretion

General considerations

Secretion of pepsinogen by the gastric chief cells involves a sequence of events leading to the appearance of this proenzyme in the gastric juice. Studies of both intact animals and *in vitro* preparations have identified a wide variety of agents that stimulate pepsinogen secretion. Some of these agents are naturally occurring and are believed to mimic endogenous regulatory mechanisms. Other stimuli, although found endogenously, have not been identified with a normal regulatory process. Still other stimuli are believed to act purely as pharmacologic agents. In order to provide some organization, the stimuli, and agents related to them, are grouped into three categories: neurotransmitters, peptide hormones, and miscellaneous agents.

Both cAMP and intracellular calcium are used as second messengers by this cell. The former mediates adrenergic and histamine induced secretion, the latter CCK and cholinergic (M3) stimulation.

Neurotransmitters

The least controversial of the stimuli for pepsinogen secretion are cholinergic agents. Acetylcholine and its analogs stimulate pepsinogen secretion in intact animals, gastric glands, and monolayer cultures. The stimulation is antagonized by atropine, indicating a muscarinic receptor. The receptor, at least in the dog and the mouse, appears to be of the M-l type, i.e., having a high affinity for pirenzepine. The efficacy of cholinergic agonists differs between species, but responses have been observed in all systems examined, from humans to amphibians. Cholinergic stimulation is believed to reflect an endogenous neural control mechanism mediated either by the internal plexi or by vagal innervation of the gastric mucosa. Atropine inhibits the pepsin secretion elicited by direct stimulation of the vagus or by the vagally mediated hypoglycemic response. However, the results of *in vitro* studies showing a direct cholinergic stimulation of pepsinogen secretion indicate that at least part of the response to vagal stimulation is due to a direct action on the chief cells.

A somewhat novel finding from *in vitro* studies is that the β adrenergic agonist, isoproterenol, stimulates pepsinogen secretion by rabbit isolated gastric glands. The adrenergic stimulation was found to be inhibited by propranolol but not by atropine or cimetidine, indicating a direct action on the chief cell. Moreover, the stimulation appears to be specific for pepsinogen secretion, since isoproterenol does not stimulate acid secretion by the parietal cells.

As with other β-adrenergic systems, stimulation of pepsinogen secretion by isoproterenol is associated with activation of adenylate cyclase and an increase in cellular cyclic AMP.

Histamine stimulates pepsinogen secretion in the human, and several other species, as judged by *in vivo* results. These responses are mediated by an H2-type of histamine receptor. Stimulation of pepsinogen secretion by histamine *in vivo* has been the subject of controversy, because the dose-response curve shows reduced secretion at high doses of histamine. This observation led to the suggestion that histamine leads to pepsin output by stimulating electrolyte, i.e., HCl, and water secretion, which "washes out" pre-secreted pepsinogen, and not by directly stimulating pepsinogen secretion. This argument might hold for experiments employing a cumulative dose-response method, but since a similar pattern is seen with dose-response curves constructed from individual doses, the "washout" explanation seems unlikely. Both actions of histamine are postulated to be mediated by H2 receptors having different affinities. The combined possibilities of "washout", acid activation, and species differences indicate that extreme caution is needed in the interpretation of results concerning the stimulation of chief cells by histamine.

A cartoon depicting the ligands and the transduction mechanisms activating the chief cell to secrete pepsinogen. Under acidic conditions, cleavage of the N-terminal sequence of pepsinogen results in autocatalytic catalysis and activation to pepsin.
N = nucleus;
R = rough endoplasmic reticulum;
CV – condensing vacuoles;
SG = secretory granules.

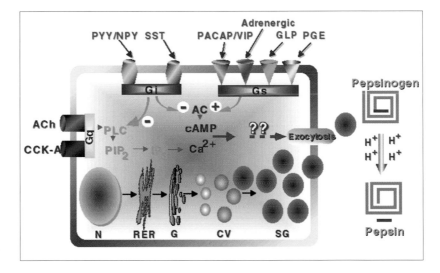

Peptide hormones

Gastrin and pentagastrin stimulate pepsinogen secretion by intact animals. The interpretation of this finding is complicated by the observation that gastrin stimulation is inhibited by atropine or histamine H2-receptor antagonists. Thus, a direct stimulation of the chief cell cannot be demonstrated. In the case of acid secretion by parietal cells, similar observations have led to the recognition that gastrin releases histamine, which is essential for the full response to this peptide. In the case of pepsinogen secretion, the release of histamine by gastrin could lead to an indirect stimulation of the chief cell via histamine in sensitive species or via the consequent increase in acid secretion. Studies using *in vitro* preparations indicate that gastrin does not stimulate pepsinogen secretion by a direct action. Thus, gastric glands isolated from rabbit secrete pepsinogen in response to gastrin, but only at doses well above that required to stimulate acid secretion and pentagastrin does not stimulate pepsinogen secretion by either canine chief cells or frog esophagus. At present, therefore, the evidence does not favor direct activation of chief cells by gastrin as a physiologic mechanism for stimulating pepsinogen secretion.

In contrast to the results with gastrin, *in vitro* studies have shown a potent stimulation of pepsinogen secretion by cholecystokinin-like peptides. Stimulation by the C-terminal octapeptide of cholecystokinin (CCK-8) appears to be a direct action on the chief cell, since it is not inhibited by atropine, propranolol, or cimetidine but is antagonized competitively by dibutyryl cyclic GMP. The latter observation is significant, because stimulation of acid secretion in gastric glands by CCK-8 is not inhibited by dibutyryl cyclic GMP. Monolayer cultures of canine chief cells also respond to CCK-8 but not to pentagastrin. These results indicate that the mammalian chief cell is able to distinguish between gastrin and CCK, despite the structural similarity of the active C-terminal portions of these peptides. Potency sequences for CCK-related peptides indicate that one crucial feature for chief cell activation is sulfation of the tyrosine residue. This does not appear to be the case for parietal cells, since gastrin-I (non-sulfated) and gastrin-II (sulfated) are equipotent for stimulation of acid secretion. The exact position of the sulfated tyrosine also appears to be important for stimulating pepsinogen secretion, since gastrin-II (tyrosine at sixth position from C-terminal) is much less potent than CCK-8 (tyrosine at seventh position from C-terminal) and only slightly more potent than gastrin-I.

The difference in potencies of CCK and gastrin analogs for acid versus pepsinogen secretion suggests that parietal and chief cells may possess different peptide receptors. This concept is supported by the results of radiolabeled ligand-binding studies. The combined results of secretion and ligand-binding studies implicate a CCK-like peptide as a stimulus for pepsinogen secretion. However, CCK is not known as a potent stimulus *in vivo*, and the concentrations of CCK required to stimulate secretion *in vitro* appear to be somewhat higher than normal blood levels. Thus, in order to postulate a physiologic role for a CCK-like peptide, it may be necessary to show that the peptide is released locally, perhaps from nerve terminals or endocrine cells, at high concentration. Whatever future studies on CCK may reveal, it is reasonably clear that gastrin does not act by direct stimulation of the chief cell.

Secretin has been reported to stimulate pepsinogen secretion in the intact animal and human. The dose of secretin required to elevate pepsinogen secretion appears to be within the normal range, indicating that this hormone may play a physiologic role. Since secretin inhibits acid secretion, the stimulation of pepsinogen output is not due to a washout of presecreted pepsinogen or acidification of the gastric lumen. Based on *in vitro* studies, it is likely that vasoactive intestinal peptide (VIP) shares a common receptor mechanism with secretin, but a physiologic role for VIP in regulating pepsinogen secretion has not been demonstrated as yet.

Additional peptide hormones have been implicated as modulators of pepsinogen secretion such as bombesin, glucagon, and somatostatin. Bombesin, or a bombesin-like peptide, stimulates pepsinogen secretion by frog esophageal glands through a direct action, but in mammals this peptide is thought to act indirectly by modulating gastrin release. Glucagon, which is structurally similar to secretin, is reported to inhibit both acid and pepsinogen secretion. The interpretation of these findings is complicated, since glucagon has several actions in the intact animal, including elevation of blood glucose and reduction in gastric volume secretion. Somatostatin, which is found throughout the gastrointestinal tract, has been shown to inhibit pepsinogen secretion elicited by several stimuli in the intact animal.

Miscellaneous agents

A variety of agents have been found to alter pepsinogen secretion *in vitro*. Most of these agents cannot be employed for *in vivo* studies because of solubility or toxicity problems. Many of the compounds do not occur naturally or at least not in the extracellular environment and thus do not represent normal physiologic mechanisms. The best characterized group of agents is the cyclic nucleotides and compounds that alter cyclic nucleotide metabolism. Cyclic AMP and its derivatives stimulate pepsinogen secretion in all of the *in vitro* preparations examined. Thus, the present evidence indicates that intracellular cyclic AMP is an effective mediator of pepsinogen secretion

Several agents have been reported to alter pepsinogen secretion either directly or by influencing responses to other stimuli. In general, the mechanism of action of these agents is unknown. The exact mechanisms by which these factors influence pepsinogen secretion have not been identified. One observation that seems of particular interest is that a variety of weak bases will stimulate pepsinogen secretion or potentiate the action of other stimuli. This is of interest for two reasons. First, identifying the mechanism of action could provide important clues regarding pepsinogen secretion. Second, many agents that are reported to alter pepsinogen secretion are weak bases or weak acids, and caution is urged in distinguishing between a specific action and the possibility that these agents are merely acting as weak acids or bases.

Significance of pepsinogen

Physiologic

The function of pepsin is the initiation of protein digestion. Although this role of pepsin has been recognized for over a century, there is little information available on the quantitative contribution of pepsin versus pancreatic enymes to the overall digestive process. Since pepsin is highly active on collagen, it is more important for digestion of meat than for vegetable protein. In addition, pepsin is likely to be more important in species in which mastication is limited or absent. Although pepsin can release small peptides and free amino acids, relatively large peptides normally enter the intestine before peptic digestion is complete. Apart from a primary role in protein digestion, pepsin also acts as a milk-clotting factor. This action occurs at a higher pH than proteolysis and may be more significant in the neonate than in the adult.

A second major physiologic role of pepsin is its contribution to the overall regulation of the digestive process. This regulatory role has received less attention than the enzymatic activity but is no less important. The digestion of proteins by pepsin leads to the formation of peptides that serve as signals for the release of various hormones, including gastrin and CCK. In turn these hormones serve as the major regulators of the digestive process. Thus, pepsin can initiate a coordinated set of responses that lead to the digestion and absorption of protein.

Clinical

Several studies have shown that instillation into the stomach of HCl alone does not cause ulceration, but inclusion of gastric juice or pepsin with the acid results in ulcer formation. In duodenal ulcer patients both basal and stimulated pepsin secretions, like acid secretion, are greater than in normal controls. This evidence suggests that pepsin may be a necessary, or at least contributing, factor in ulcer formation. A possible specific role for antral or duodenal pepsinogen in ulcer formation also has been considered. Serious efforts to treat or prevent ulcers by inhibiting pepsinogen secretion or pepsin activity have not been made, despite the probable involvement of pepsin in these diseases. The lack of interest in anti-pepsin treatment is due, in part, to the success of antacid therapy, particularly the histamine H2 receptor antagonists. Since acid secretory inhibitors also suppress pepsinogen secretion and maintain a higher luminal pH, their efficacy may be due partly to a reduced pepsin activity. Development of specific anti-pepsin agents could provide an alternative approach, which likely would avoid the hypergastrinemia associated with many antacid treatments.

The demonstration of pepsinogen in plasma and urine suggested the possible use of such measurements for diagnosis or prediction of ulcer disease. This has not proven to be of clinical value. The diagnosis of ulcer disease is performed more easily and more definitively with endoscopy. Although correlations have been obtained between serum pepsinogen and such diseases as pernicious anemia and Zollinger-Ellison syndrome, the plasma values likely reflect changes in gastric mucosal mass that accompany the disease and therefore are of little value in early detection. Attempts have been made to correlate serum pepsinogen with susceptibility to ulcer formation and gastric cancer, but thus far no firm basis for prediction has been established.

CHAPTER 4
INTRINSIC FACTOR

Historical issues

Although pernicious anemia was clearly recognized by Addison in 1855, this fatal anemia did not have any effective treatment until 1926 when Minot and Murphy documented satisfactory management with the ingestion of large amounts of raw liver. A debt of gratitude is owed to Castle who proposed that impaired gastric function was responsible for the disease and successfully proved his hypothesis. Thus neither beef (200 g daily) nor normal human gastric juice (150 ml) administered by stomach tube produced a hematopoietic response. Nevertheless simultaneous administration of both resulted in a positive response as effective as that induced by liver alone. It subsequently became apparent that liver contained high levels of cobalamin and since intrinsic factor was not needed for the non-specific diffusion of the vitamin across the mucosal membranes, cure resulted – albeit in an inefficient fashion. The availability of isotopically labelled cyanocobalamin in 1950 allowed for the full understanding of the role of intrinsic factor in the absorption of cobalamin. Further studies enabled the localization of the site of intrinsic factor production to the parietal cell and identified two distinct functional sites on the intrinsic factor molecule. The further identification of ileal membrane receptors for intrinsic factor bound cobalamin demonstrated a role for the pancreas as well as the stomach in normal cobalamin absorption. In addition to intrinsic factor, it also became apparent that there were other cobalamin binding proteins involved in the normal transport of the vitamin.

J.A.M.A 87:470-476, 1926
Treatment of pernicious anemia by a special diet
Minot GR & Murphy WP

THE
AMERICAN JOURNAL
OF THE MEDICAL SCIENCES
SEPTEMBER, 1930

ORIGINAL ARTICLES.

OBSERVATIONS ON THE ETIOLOGIC RELATIONSHIP OF ACHYLIA GASTRICA TO PERNICIOUS ANEMIA.*

III. THE NATURE OF THE REACTION BETWEEN NORMAL HUMAN GASTRIC JUICE AND BEEF MUSCLE LEADING TO CLINICAL IMPROVEMENT AND INCREASED BLOOD FORMATION SIMILAR TO THE EFFECT OF LIVER FEEDING.†

BY WILLIAM B. CASTLE, M.D.,
ASSISTANT PROFESSOR OF MEDICINE, HARVARD MEDICAL SCHOOL, AND ASSOCIATE PHYSICIAN, THORNDIKE MEMORIAL LABORATORY, BOSTON CITY HOSPITAL,

The original contribution of Minot facilitated the identification by W. Castle of the critical role of the stomach in pernicious anemia.

Cobalamin

Initial confusion in the nomenclature of the cyanocobalamin reflected the fact that the vitamin exists as hydroxycobalamin, methylcobalamin, and adenosylcobalamin. Given the fact that all of the above compounds have the biological activity formally attributed to vitamin B12, the general term cobalamin is now used. The structure of adenosylcobalamin is a single cobalt atom in the nucleus of a molecule coordinated in the center of a planer corrin ring by the nitrogens of four pyroline rings. Cobalamin cannot be synthesized by mammalian tissues but only by microorganisms. Thus a wide variety of bacteria and protozoa are capable of production of cobalamin, and microbial synthesis of the vitamin serves as the ultimate source for the mammalian organism. Mammalian tissues are capable of efficiently converting hydroxycobalamin to the coenzymes methylcobalamin and adenosylcobalamin. It is of considerable importance that the mammalian organism exhibits absolute dependence on the vitamin for normal cellular replication. Despite the fact that the vitamin is crucial for tissue viability, mammalian organisms are not effectively able to assimilate cobalamin by a simple passive process. The relatively large molecule has a radius far in excess of "effective pore size" of intestinal absorptive membranes. By virtue of its structure however, it is highly soluble in water and virtually insoluble in most organic solvents. This bulky, polar, water soluble, lipid insoluble molecule therefore is not easily able to pass the lipid bi-layer of biologic membranes and requires a highly specialized membrane transport system for assimilation and utilization. Since only 10-15 micrograms per day of cobalamin are available in a diet, the membrane transport process requires precise identification of the molecule and an effective extraction process. Similarly transport needs to be specific to avoid absorption of cobalamin-like molecules which are either inactive or possibly harmful.

Cobalamin binding transport proteins

There exist three distinct transport proteins for high affinity binding of the cobalamin molecule: R proteins, transcobalamin II and intrinsic factor. The latter is secreted by the stomach whereas transcobalamin II is present in the plasma and the R proteins are a family of glycoproteins found in plasma, granulocytes and several glandular secretions. All three binding proteins bind cobalamin in a macromolecular complex that involves a single cobalamin binding site per protein molecule. The affinity of cobalamin for its transport proteins is extremely high and the association constants are in the picomolar range. Of the three binding proteins, intrinsic factor is by far the most selective. Transcobalamin II is somewhat less specific and the R proteins are non-specific binding a wide variety of cobamides. Each cobalamin binding transport protein has highly specific membrane receptors present on the surface of functionally relevant cells. Thus receptors for intrinsic factor are present on microvillous membranes of ileal absorptive cells whereas a wide variety of dividing cells contain receptors for transcobalamine II. Hepatocytes are the only cells which possess receptors specific for R proteins.

Intrinsic factor

The oxyntic mucosa of the body and fundus of the human stomach are the site of intrinsic factor secretion. Total gastrectomy is associated with cobalamin malabsorption and unless the vitamin is administered, cobalamin deficiency will occur within 3-5 years. The gastric parietal cell is the source of intrinsic factor in almost all species including humans. The protein is present on the membranes of the peri-nuclear envelope, rough endoplasmic reticulum, Golgi apparatus and the tubulo-vesicular membrane system of the parietal cell. It is of interest that intrinsic factor is found in the chief cell of the mouse and the rat whereas in the pig, intrinsic factor is located in the mucous cells of the duodenum and pyloric area of the stomach.

Far more intrinsic factor is secreted than is needed to bind and assimilate dietary cobalamin. Thus in a 60 minute period, the stimulated human stomach secretes enough intrinsic factor to bind all cobalamin ingested in a 24-hour period. Intrinsic factor secretion appears to be stimulated by all agents which stimulate acid secretion. It is thus secreted under stimulation by histamine, pentagastrin, and cholinergic agents and is similarly inhibited by cimetidine.

The pattern of intrinsic factor secretion, however, differs from that of acid secretion. Exposure to an agonist results in a rapid stimulation with peak levels of intrinsic factor within 15-30 minutes while acid increases over a far slower period. When acid secretion is at a maximum level, intrinsic factor secretion has returned to control levels.

This phenomenon was initially attributed to a wash-out of pre-formed intrinsic factor, but repetition of the stimulus results in secretion of additional intrinsic factor and a continuous infusion of an agonist results in steady state intrinsic factor secretion for prolonged periods. The cellular mechanism of intrinsic factor secretion appears to be related to cyclic AMP. Morphologic observations of human gastric mucosa suggest that the parietal cell secretes intrinsic factor by membrane translocation. In those species where intrinsic factor is in chief cells, the protein is secreted in parallel with pepsinogen.

Intrinsic factor is a globular glycoprotein that contains about 15% carbohydrate. It has a molecular weight of 44,000 Daltons and consists of a single polypeptide chain. Intrinsic factor binds cobalamin at a ratio of 30 µg per milligram of intrinsic factor protein suggesting that each molecule of intrinsic factor binds one molecule of cobalamin. The macromolecular complex exhibits tight binding with a high affinity for the protein and occurs virtually instantly upon exposure of the two substances to each other. Although the bond that is formed between intrinsic factor and cobalamin is extremely strong under physiological conditions, it is readily disrupted above a pH of 12.6, and below a pH of 3 the affinity is markedly reduced. In an acid environment the binding of cobalamin to R protein is greatly favored over binding to intrinsic factor. Once the intrinsic factor molecule binds to cobalamin, it becomes more compact with a 10-15% decrease in its calculated Stokes radius and apparent molecular weight. The cobalamin bound intrinsic factor complex is resistant to destruction by protease to a far greater degree than free extrinsic factor itself.

A schematic representation of the physiological events necessary to enable absorption of Vit B12.

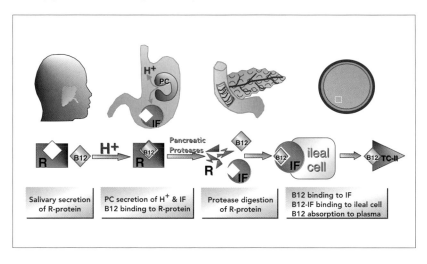

Cobalamin absorption

Only 1-2 micrograms daily of cobalamin are required to maintain normal stores. Almost all sources of animal protein such as liver, kidney, fish, milk and eggs contain substantial quantities of cobalamin and the average dietary intake is usually 10-20 micrograms per day. Vegetarian diets lack adequate cobalamin to avoid deficiency disease. In the case of herbivores who do not have access to meat, they depend on either rumen bacteria or regular access to microbial products by coprophagy to obtain adequate cobalamin. Under normal circumstances, healthy subjects absorb 30-60% of an oral dose of one microgram of cyanocobalamin. Assimilation of the vitamin occurs by two almost completely different processes. Thus in small quantities, absorption is quite efficient whereas in the ingestion of large quantities of cobalamin, much is lost. Although the process is efficient, the absorption of physiological amounts of the vitamin is extremely slow and occurs almost entirely from the ileum. In the face of large quantities of cobalamin, absorption is by non-specific diffusion across the entire alimentary canal. The distal half of the ileum is the major site of cobalamin absorption and resection of this area leads to malabsorption. The colon is not able to assimilate the bound vitamin.

Efficient absorption of cobalamin requires that the vitamin form a macromolecular complex with the glycoprotein secreted by the stomach. In patients with pancreatic insufficiency, cobalamin absorption is poor, suggesting that pancreatic proteases are necessary for this process although the mechanism responsible has not yet been identified. For efficient absorption the distal small bowel must be intact and in its absence, the absorption of cobalamin is limited. Within the ileal mucosa the assimilation process is extremely slow which presumably reflects a series of molecular processing events which have not yet been fully delineated.

Absorption sequence

Upon the ingestion of a physiologic quantity of cobalamin, a series of specific events occur in a sequential fashion to ensure appropriate and adequate absorption. Firstly cobalamin is released from dietary proteins whereupon the salivary R proteins ensure intragastric binding of the substance. Thereafter intraduodenal digestion of the R protein cobalamin complexes occur particularly by pancreatic proteases which are responsible for the release of cobalamin. Once cobalamin is free within the duodenum or upper small bowel, binding of the vitamin by intrinsic factor occurs prior to its transport to the lower ileum. At this point, the intrinsic factor-bound cobalamin is attached to the apical membrane of the ileum cells and absorption via specific receptor mediated pathways occurs. The transcellular transport of cobalamin in the ileal mucosa is a slow process and presumably involves endocytosis. The vitamin is thereafter released into the portal circulation and passes to the liver for processing.

The stomach and duodenum are of considerable importance in the absorption of cobalamin. Since the dietary proteins that bind cobalamin are largely apoenzymes, an acidic environment in the stomach is necessary to ensure rapid release of cobalamin from such proteins. This step does not require pepsin and is not a rate limiting step for absorption. It is, however, evident that individuals with achlorhydria do not effectively extract and absorb dietary vitamin even though they may secrete adequate amounts of intrinsic factor and are capable of normal absorption of cobalamin. The free cobalamin within the stomach binds almost exclusively to R proteins which have been secreted by the salivary glands. The cobalamin bound to such R protein is released immediately upon entering the proximal small intestine by the action of pancreatic proteases which are responsible for a rapid degradation of the R proteins. Once the cobalamin is released from the R protein it rapidly combines with intrinsic factor to generate the stable macromolecular complex previously described. This complex of cobalamin and intrinsic factor is extremely stable and not digestible by proteolytic enzymes of the pancreas or upper bowel. In addition, the binding to intrinsic factor protects the vitamin from bacterial utilization within the small bowel whilst the macromolecular complex is being transported to the ileum.

Whilst much attention has been focused on the regulation of acid secretion and pepsinogen, the mechanisms responsible for the secretion of intrinsic factor and its subsequent role in the absorption of cobalamin are vital to the organism. Indeed it might be said that without adequate intrinsic factor secretion or cobalamin ingestion, all other secretory processes of the stomach would be defunct within a 3-5 year period as the organism perished.

CHAPTER 5
REGULATION OF GROWTH
OF GASTRIC EPITHELIUM

Introduction

Disease occurs because of disruption or malfunction of the different barriers of the upper GI tract. Recovery from damage depends on the properties of the epithelial cells and their ability to repair injury.

The gastric mucosa contains several cell types, each programmed to undergo cell division at a specific rate and to equal this rate of cell division by an equal rate of apoptosis. Increased apoptosis without change in cell division results in atrophy; increased cell division without change in apoptosis results in hyperplasia. It is an exquisitely modeled epithelium with distinct regions containing specific cell types. Clearly maintenance of differentiation in order to generate the normal epithelium is quite specific and requires a precise programming of growth, differentiation and apoptotic factors.

The cells of the gastric fundic epithelium that appear clinically relevant are the surface epithelial cells, the neck cells, the parietal and chief cells and the endocrine cells, mainly the ECL and D cells. In the antrum there are the surface cells, the neck and gland cells, the D and G cells and a chief cell that secretes a different isoform of pepsinogen. The neck region of the glands contains the progenitor cells for the surface, parietal and peptic cells.

Rather little attention was paid to growth regulation of many of these cell types until the development of modern knowledge of gastrin. Gastrin was originally considered only of relevance in terms of stimulation of acid secretion, but Rusty Johnson showed in the early seventies that gastrin was trophic for the fundic but not the antral epithelium. Since then much effort has been expended into a better definition of the mechanism of action of gastrin, at first on the ECL cell and later on the parietal/peptic cells. Several other trophic factors have now been shown to be present or induced following epithelial damage, but it is far too early to even begin to define the program that allows expression of the mature gastric epithelium with its multiple cell types in the right place at the right time.

Cell growth in the stomach

The rat stomach has formed the primary *in vivo* model for studies of the growth regulation of the epithelium, usually by measurement of DNA synthesis (^{3}H thymidine or BrdU incorporation).

Starvation for 24 or 48 hrs results first in a degree of fundic atrophy. Re-feeding then produces a large increase in DNA synthesis in the neck cells of the fundic glands which contain the progenitor cells for the surface and the glandular structures. There is also incorporation of these markers into ECL cells scattered throughout the fundus. Re-feeding is several fold more effective than gastrin, showing that gastrin is overshadowed by other factors in this particular model.

The transit time of surface epithelial cells is about 72 hrs, whilst that of parietal and chief cells is about 90 to 120 days.

There is detailed knowledge of cell lineage and growth in the intestinal mucosa not matched by knowledge of these properties of the gastric mucosa.

There are stem cells very few in number that divide slowly to provide daughter cells. One of these two is destined to remain a stem cell, the other divides to form pre-progenitor cells which in turn divide to form progenitor cells which then form cell type precursors and finally the mature cell type. This program is held within the cells and outside the cells by external factors generated by other cell types. The stem cells of the gastric mucosa are pluripotent.

The generation of parietal cells is in the neck region and it is possible to recognize pre-parietal or progenitor cells which then differentiate to form a triple helix chain of cells down the length of the gastric gland. Parietal cells are recognizable by their large mitochondrial content (34% cell volume), expression of the gastric acid pump and of the histamine 2 and CCK-B receptors. They are end cells and have not been shown capable of cell division.

Chief cells are found generally deeper in the fundic gland, mostly in the bottom third. They are recognizable because of their high content of pepsinogen and expression of the CCK-A receptor subtype. They appear to have some residual capacity for division. There is currently no explanation for their anatomic localization. A slower generation time than the parietal cells would enable deeper localization of these cells.

ECL cells are the major endocrine cell of the fundic mucosa and are found towards the lower third of the gastric fundic gland. In animals these cells are clearly capable of cell division.

Some claim that the ECL cell in the human mucosa is also an end cell like the parietal cell, but it is unusual to find a wide gap between man and other mammals in something as fundamental as capacity for cell division.

In recent years the ECL cell has achieved prominence as the target for gastrin's hyperplastic effect on the endocrine cell population in the stomach. They are easily identified due their histamine, acidic vacuole and histidine decarboxylase content.

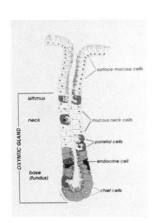

A cartoon of the gastric gland demonstrating the location and relationship of the different cell types.

Growth receptors in gastric mucosa

A large number of factors have been shown to stimulate gastric cell replication *in vivo* and in gastric cell lines *in vitro*. Surely a well conducted orchestra of these factors is necessary for the generation and regeneration of a normal gastric epithelium. How the integration of all these factors enables replacement of the mature epithelium remains a challenge for the future as it does in all organ biology.

Gastrin

This is the best studied of the various factors influencing growth in the fundus of the stomach. Recent investigations using CCK-B receptor knock out mice have confirmed the critical role of gastrin/CCK in mucosal growth. Although capable of stimulating ECL cell replication, it is less effective than many other factors in driving gastric cell replication. On the other hand, the hypergastrinemia induced by treatment with PPI's can result in animals and in some patients in parietal and chief cell hyperplasia as well as ECL cell hyperplasia.

It has however been repeatedly demonstrated that these are without clinical consequence in the 15 years that maintenance omeprazole studies have been present. An even longer period of surveillance of selective or highly selective vagotomy patients, where hypergastrinemia results with about the same elevation found in maintenance PPI therapy, has shown no unexpected changes in gastric mucosal cells. The apparent affinity for the growth receptor on the ECL cell appears to be about 50-fold higher than the affinity for the receptor activating histamine release from the same cell type. Neutralizing antibodies to gastrin result in at least 50% inhibition of the feeding response on gastric DNA synthesis, arguing for a continuing important role of this hormone in gastric growth regulation.

Why there is not a trophic action of gastrin on the antrum is completely unknown. As discussed elsewhere gastrin also regulates histamine decarboxylase expression in ECL cells.

Epidermal growth factor/ Tissue growth factor EGF/TGF-α

These peptide hormones are potent stimuli for cell division in the gastric mucosa and also potent inhibitors of gastric acid secretion. The former action is undoubtedly due to a tyrosine kinase action, the latter due to extracellular signal-regulated kinases (ERKs) 1 and 2 activation. The inhibition of acid secretion that occurs at the same time as stimulation of growth suggests that the presence of acid secretion is inimical to growth. TGF-α is upregulated in the vicinity of gastric ulcers, suggesting a real physiological role for this peptide and its receptor in ulcer healing.

Hepatocyte growth factor (HGF)

This is also a potent mitogen, acting at a c-met receptor. It stimulates expression of VEGF receptor for endothelial cell growth and permeability. It is implicated as one of the mediators in mucosal repair

Keratinocyte growth factor (KGF)

This peptide also significantly stimulates division of gastric cells *in vivo* and *in vitro*, although its site of production in the gastric mucosal vicinity has not been established.

TGF β 1, 2 and 3

These in general inhibit cell division in the gastric mucosa and show differential regulation among the different cell types. TGF β1 is localized exclusively to the parietal cells, β 2 is found in chief cells and β 3 in parietal, chief and mucus cells. Their role in ulcerogenesis is unclear.

Cytokines

Increased expression of a variety of interleukins have been found in gastric mucosa subsequent to infection by *H. pylori*, such as IL-1β and IL8. The former has clearly been shown to inhibit cell growth in the stomach. Which of these plays a role in the ulcerating damage caused by the organism is not entirely clear.

Ammonia (NH₃)

H. pylori produces large quantities of NH_3 from urea especially during periods of acid secretion. *In vitro*, NH_3 has been shown to inibit cell growth, induce alkalinisation of the cell interior and increase intracellular Ca. This product of infection may exert pleiotropic negative effects on the gastric mucosa. The action of NH_3 entry into cells is alkalinization of the cell interior. This leads to unloading of calcium stores that are IP_3 sensitive but also leads to partial unloading of other stores such as those in mitochondria. This latter event may be pro-apoptotic.

Epithelial restitution

This term describes the finding that surface epithelial cells migrate over the surface of a gastric wound without undergoing cell division. HGF is a stimulant of restitution, which is the result of the changed expression of a variety of integrins. The targeting scaffold upon which restitution rests is an important, but as yet unexplored area of gastric biology.

An *in situ* hybridisation preparation of an experimental gastric ulcer demonstrating the expression of the "growth factor" pS_2 in the advancing surface epithelium as well as glands.

Mucosal healing and trefoil peptides

The mucosal lining of the stomach, and the epithelial cells in particular, undergo constant renewal. Thus new cells are created from precursors in the proliferative zone and under the influence of "growth factors" undergo maturation and differentiation over the course of a five to seven day period whilst they move toward the luminal surface. At this site they perish, not necessarily by passive shedding into the lumen, but by an active process of cell death termed apoptosis. Indeed this may be considered the ultimate terminal differentiation event. In the gastric mucosa, cells also move downwards (at a much slower rate) from the proliferative zone at the base of the gastric crypts, into the glands. This constant and rapid turnover of the stomach mucosa is well suited to the prompt restoration of mucosal integrity following damage that may occur during acid peptic disease.

After the establishment of a mucosal breach or ulcer, three main healing events have been defined. The first is a rapid phase of epithelial restitution during which existing viable epithelial cells at the ulcer edge migrate inward to close the gap. Secondly, over the next few days new cells are formed by proliferation to repopulate the mucosal gap. Thirdly, new matrix is laid down, as non-epithelial cells in the lamina propria replace inflammatory cells. This remodeling is accompanied by angiogenesis. The migrating epithelial cells are not merely undifferentiated and immature but instead have a specialized and polarized phenotype uniquely adapted to movement. The precise differentiation of this migratory phenotype is influenced by a number of factors, including at least the extra cellular matrix, peptides, and the more classical growth factors. It has been established that a chronic and repetitive mucosal insult as opposed to an acute event significantly influences epithelial restitution. Thus an acceleration of restitution may occur as an adaptive response, as compared to that found in "*unconditioned*" mucosa, and is associated with a widening of the proliferative zone.

This process also appears to involve a decrease in parietal and gastrin secreting cells and a tendency to increase somatostatin secreting cell numbers. A further change is the generation of a new population of "*vesiculated*" cells, some of which have features of immature mucus neck cells. These are present in the lower third of the gastric gland in an area previously populated by parietal cells. Such vesiculated cells may represent a distinct lineage of cells ideally located to promote proliferation and healing through the local secretion of mucosal repair proteins. The relationship between this observation and the reports of an ulcer associated cell lineage (UACL) by Wright and his colleagues may be an important issue in the elucidation of mucosal repair in the upper gastrointestinal tract.

Of considerable importance is the identification of the molecules, which are critical to the regulation of mucosal repair. In more recent times a number of key mucosal repair peptides have been identified and classified according to their function. Epidermal growth factor (EGF) is capable of performing many of the functions essentially for good repair and is considered an example of a luminal surveillance peptide. Although continually secreted into the lumen, it is only able to bind to its receptor located on the basal lateral surface of the epithelial cell when mucosal integrity is breached. On the other hand, pancreatic secretory trypsin inhibitor and transforming growth factor alpha are considered mucosal integrity peptides, ensuring normal barrier function.

The third group, the trefoil factors, appears to act as rapid response molecules up regulated at times of injury. Of particular relevance to the healing process is a distinct glandular constituent – the *ulcer associated cell lineage* – which produces several repair peptides including trefoil peptides and epidermal growth factor, as well as mucus. It has, therefore, been suggested that these cells act as a "*first aid kit*", pouring healing agents onto the ulcer base. The ulcer-associated lineage is present only at the site of chronic mucosal injury and probably arises from the duct region of metaplastic epithelium such as intestinal metaplasia in the stomach.

The trefoil peptides are a highly conserved group of molecules that are wide-

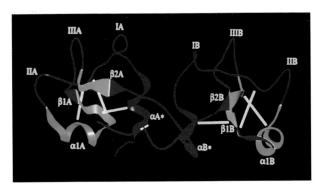

3-D magnetic resonance imaging of a trefoil peptide motif growth factor. Evaluation of peptides with growth factor activity has been of value in understanding the regulation of ulcer healing.

ly distributed in the gastrointestinal tissues, although they have been demonstrated elsewhere in sites as disparate as the breast and lung. It is likely that their primary role, however, is in the gastrointestinal tract. The group takes it title from the characteristic *trefoil motif*, a three-loop structure secured by disulfide bonds based on cysteine residues. The super secondary structure of the trefoil motif has been examined by 3D nuclear magnetic resonance, confirming its presence and demonstrating that it consists of a seven residue length of alpha helix followed by a short anti-parallel β sheet formed from two strands of four amino acids each. This novel structure clearly identifies the trefoil motif as a new class of module distinct from other types of highly disulfide cross linked domains such as those found in epidermal growth factor and insulin like growth factor-1.

pS$_2$ was the first molecule characterized and consists of a 60 amino acid peptide with a 24 amino acid signal peptide and is homologous with pancreatic spasmolytic polypeptide (PSP). Although found in abundance in human breast cancers, the predominant pS$_2$ gene expression is most evident in the

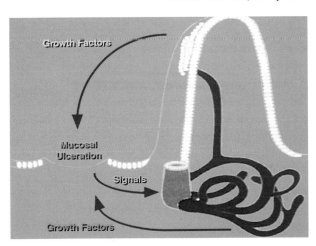

A schematic representation (above) of the development of the "ulcer associated cell lineage" evident in the photomicrograph (right).

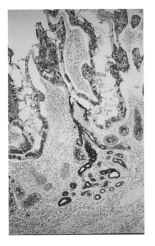

surface and foveolar cells of the stomach. pS$_2$ is found in normal gastric juice and is secreted by the surface and foveolar cells. Human SP is co-expressed with pS$_2$ in gastric foveolar cells and is also expressed abundantly by the basal antral glands. Both these peptides have been demonstrated to be widely expressed in gastrointestinal tissues during disease states, particularly those related to chronic ulcerative conditions. More recently, studies have demonstrated that what was previously regarded as pyloric metaplasia in chronic gastrointestinal ulceration is in fact a differentiating cell lineage.

This buds initially from the bases of intestinal crypts adjacent the ulcer and its tubules ramify in the lamina propria before emerging from the mucosal surface through a newly formed duct which in the small intestine grows upward through the core of an adjacent villus to emerge through a pore in its side. The newly formed gland thus passes its secretion to the surface, and cells from the lineage pass out through the pore to displace the indigenous cell lineage and then close the villus surface. As the cells migrate through the tubular system they acquire differentiation antigens and also develop a proliferative zone within the duct itself.

The glandular portion of this ulcer associated cell lineage secretes immuno reactive EGF/URO that is then available to combine with its receptors and to stimulate mucosal healing. It is likely that this process or variations of it represent a basic template whereby mucosal healing of the gastrointestinal tract mucosa occurs.

Presumably, site specific variations take place particularly at the junctional zones of the gastroesophageal area and the pyloro-duodenal area. Since the majority of gastric ulcers occur close to the junctional zone between the fundus and the antrum, the zones of junctional instability presumably possesses mechanisms important for determination of cell lineage and phenotype.

The exact role of the individual trefoils in ulcer healing is unclear. Experimentally the use of human spasmolytic peptide has been shown to result in a moderate reduction in gastric damage induced by indomethacin. EGF has similar effects but appears to be more potent. It seems likely that each region of the gut may have a particular trefoil peptide as has been demonstrated for the mucin genes. Indeed trefoil expression and mucin genes are linked geographically and in some lower animals are even encoded by the same gene providing an explanation for their co-expression in mammals. It is probable that under normal circumstances the secretion of trefoils and mucin are probably coordinately regulated. During disease states they may become uncoupled or produced at a site remote from where they are usually evident, providing a state of *"molecular metaplasia"* in the terminology originally proposed by Podolsky.

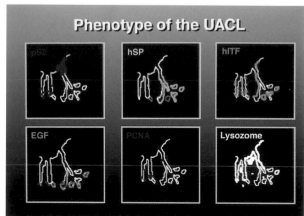

A cartoon depicting the location in the UACL of cells producing specific growth regulators.

The ulcer associated cell lineage expresses both the hSP and pS_2 genes in a site-specific manner. Thus the surface cells and the upper duct cells of the ulcer associated cell lineage express abundant pS_2 whereas hSP is found only in the lower duct and glandular area. Thus the ulcer associated cell lineage secretes pS_2 and hSP, together with EGF/URO into the local micro environment around the ulcer, indicating that trefoil peptides may be of considerable importance in mucosal healing and possibly even cytoprotection. Thus as cells migrate through the ulcer associated cell lineage they also sequentially change the pattern of peptide gene expression with EGF/URO being found in the basal acini, hSP in the acini and ducts and pS_2 in the upper duct and surface cells. Of interest is the fact that adjacent mucosal cells express EGF receptor and that the normal cell lineage in the mucosa adjacent to the ulcer associated cell lineage also expresses pS_2. Local mucin secreting cells express pS_2 which is co-packaged by the Golgi apparatus into the mucous granules and secreted into the visco-elastic layer covering the mucosa. Of particular interest is the fact that pS_2 is also co-packaged into neurosecretory granules of neuroendocrine cells bordering the ulcer associated cell lineage.

The situation is unusual in that the same peptide is co-packaged into secretory granules that are released in different ways – the mucous granules in an apocrine manner from the apical surface into the lumen and the neuro-

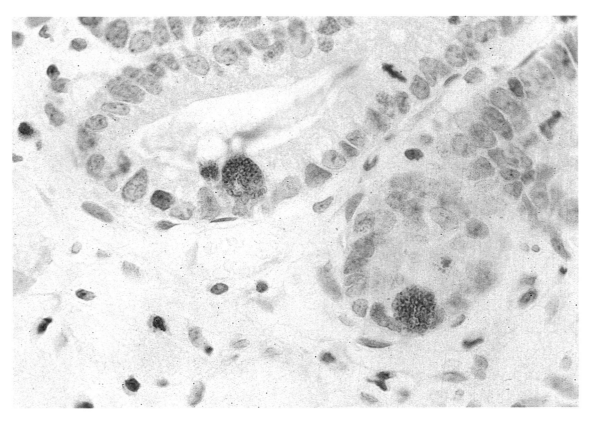

An immunohistochemical preparation demonstrating the co-localisation of chromogranin staining material in goblet cells co-producing trefoil peptides in healing mucosa. This provides evidence that phenotype alterations may be of considerable relevance in the healing mucosa. Growth factors and neuro-endocrine regulatory agents are critical.

endocrine granules through the baso-lateral surface – where the contained peptides can act in a paracrine fashion on other local cells. Whether this represents a common denominator factor whereby neuro-endocrine cells regulate not only physiological responses but are also important in the modulation of repair of damaged mucosa is not known. Of particular interest is the observation that, in damaged mucosa, goblet cells can be demonstrated not only to produce trefoil peptides but also neuro-endocrine products. Indeed the novel concept must now be considered whereby enterocytes, mucous cells, and neuro-endocrine cells are linked in a common system to regulate the repair of damaged mucosa.

Thus the focus of the management of acid peptic induced mucosal disease by targeting the noxious agents of acid and pepsin may well one day be supported by agents capable of up-regulating the healing response. In this respect a further understanding of the goblet cell and its products may be of considerable scientific relevance. Rat intestinal goblet cells have been reported to produce mucin, intestinal trefoil factor as well as the trefoil peptide, spasmolysin. The mucin genes are encoded by a gene family of several members, and MUC 1 is expressed in breast, stomach, salivary gland, and the ulcer associated cell line tissues, where pS_2 has also been detected. Thus pS_2 and possibly other trefoil peptides may follow MUC 1 expression. It is thus possible that each mucin type may be co-secreted with its own trefoil peptide and that trefoil peptides themselves play an important part in the function of mucus which itself may be an as yet unrecognized significant modulator of mucosal healing.

What little knowledge of the healing process exists has been mostly directed at the role of epithelial cells in mucosal repair. Nevertheless the role of non-epithelial cells, particularly in the lamina propria, may be of considerable relevance in areas more complex than simply *"filling the gap"*. In this respect they may be responsible for producing some of the repair molecules necessary for providing the matrix upon which healing can take place. Thus hepatocyte growth factor has been demonstrated to be produced by gastric fibroblasts in culture and appears to be an extremely potent mitogen as well as a mitogen for epithelial cells. Cell migration is typically accompanied by a reduction in cell-cell interactions and mucosal repair must also involve alterations in the interaction of cells with the extracellular matrix, which are typically mediated by integrin molecules. In addition, mucosal repair is likely to be dependent upon the regulation of matrix protein synthesis as well as its degradation by collagenases and metallo-proteinases.

A further important component of the repair process is angiogenesis. The development of a number of agents capable of modulating new vessel formation and thus facilitating mucosal repair is a source of potential considerable scientific and clinical relevance. Basic fibroblast growth factor which is potently angiogenic as well as being mitogenic to a variety of cell types accelerates epithelial restitution and has been studied in therapeutic trials. It is possible that agents such as sucralfate, which had always been thought to function as surface protectants, may actually provide some more sophisticated effects by binding agents such as fibroblastic growth factor to breaches in the mucosa.

The fact that mucosal repair occurs after *H. pylori* eradication alone and without acid inhibition suggests that the organism itself must inhibit mucosal repair. Separating the effect of *H. pylori* from the effect of the accompanying inflammatory process is difficult, but it is apparent that epithelial cell function can be modulated by cytokines in many different ways. Since *in vivo*, chronic *H. pylori* infection appears to increase epithelial proliferation, the effect of *H. pylori* on restitution, matrix deposition, and angiogenesis remain areas that require evaluation. Similarly the proteolytic action of pepsin on matrix proteins will delay healing if matrix deposition is involved in mucosal repair. Indeed one of the most powerful effects of acid suppression may well be to move the median pH outside of the optimum required for activation of pepsinogen.

Interference with gastric healing

Many factors influence the rate of gastric healing both by interfering with restitution and with cell growth and differentiation. NSAID's, by inhibiting the constitutive enzyme cox 1 as one of their targets, deplete cells of prostaglandins. Aspirin can also transport protons into cells as an additional damaging factor. *H. pylori* lyses in the gastric mucus or on its surface and in so doing releases its 1,200 cytoplasmic proteins such as Vac and Cag that have been associated with pathogenicity. Inflammatory cells themselves release a host of cytokines that variously, and often adversely, affect cell homeostasis.

REFERENCES

Allen, A., Newton, J., Oliver, L., et al. *Mucus and H. pylori.* J. Physiol. & Pharmacol. 48, 297-305 (1997).

Atherton, J.C., Cockayne, A., Balsitis, M., Kirk, G.E., Hawkey, C.J., Spiller, R.C. *Detection of the intragastric sites at which Helicobacter pylori evades treatment with amoxycillin and cimetidine.* Gut 36, 670-674 (1995).

Baumgartner, A., Koelz, H.R., Halter, F. *Indomethacin and turnover of gastric mucosal cells in the rat.* American Journal of Physiology. 250 (6 Pt. 1), G830-5 (June 1986).

Carmel, R. *Cobalamin, the stomach and ageing.* Am. J. Clin. Nutr. 66, 750-9 (1997).

Castle, W.B., Townsend, W.C., Heath, C.W. *The nature of the reaction between normal gastric juice and beef muscle leading to improvement and increased blood formation similar to the effect of liver feeding.* Am. J. Med. Sci. 180, 305-335 (1930).

Cavill, I. *Diagnosis of cobalamin deficiency: the old and the new.* Brit. J. Haematol. 99, 238-9 (1997).

Code, C.F., Scholer, J.F., Orvis, A.L. et al. *Barrier offered by gastric mucosa to absorption of sodium (abstract).* Am. J. Phsyiol. 183, 604 (1955).

Davenport, H.W., Warner, H.A., Code, C.F. *Functional significance of gastric mucosal barrier to sodium.* Gastroenterology 47, 142-152 (1964).

Denker, B.M., Nigam, S.K. *Molecular structure and assembly of the tight junction.* Am. J. Physiol. 274 (1 Pt. 2), F1-9 (Jan. 1998).

De Vault, K.R. *Current management of GERD.* Gastroenterologist 4, 24-32 (1996).

Engel, E., Garth, P.H., Nishizaki, Y. et al. *Barrier function of the gastric mucus gel.* Am. J. Physiol. 269, G994-9 (1995).

Engel, E., Peskoff, A., Kauffman, G.L. Jr., Grossman, M.I. *Analysis of hydrogen ion concentration in the gastric gel mucus layer.* Am. J. Physiol. 247, G321-38 (1984).

Flemstrom, G. *Gastric and duodenal mucosal bicarbonate secretion. In: Physiology of the gastrointestinal tract.* 2nd ed., edited by L.R. Johnson, J. Christensen, M.J. Jackson, E.D. Jacobson and J.H. Walsh. New York, Raven, 1987, p. 1011-1029.

Goodlad, R.A. *Acid suppression and claims of genotoxicity. What have we learned?* Drug Safety 10 (6), 413-9 (June 1994).

Heidenhain, R. *Ueber die Pepsinbildung in den Pylorusdrüsen.* Pflugers Archiv fur die Gesämte Phsyiologie 18, 169-171 (1878).

Heidenhain, R. *Ueber die Absonderung der Fundusdrüsen des Magens.* Pflugers Archiv fur die Gesämte Phsyiologie 19, 148-166 (1879).

Hein, H.K., Piller, M., Schwede, J. et al. *Pepsinogen synthesis during long term culture of porcine gastric chief cells.* Biochem. Biophys. Acta 1359, 35-47 (1997).

Hunter, J. *Essays and observations on Natural History, Anatomy, Physiology, Psychology and Geology.* Vols 1 and 2, London, J. Va. Vooret, 1861.

Johnson, L.R. *Gastrointestinal hormones and their functions.* Ann. Rev. Physiol. 39, 135-58 (1977).

Kimura, Y, Shiozaki, H., Hirao, M., Maeno, Y., Doki, Y., Inoue, M., Monden, T., Ando-Akatsuka, Y., Furuse, M., Tsukita, S., Monden, M. *Expression of occludin, tight-junction-associated protein, in human digestive tract.* American Journal of Pathology 151 (1), 45-54 (July 1997).

Laboisse, C., Jarry, A., Branka, J.E. et al. *Recent aspects of the regulation of intestinal mucus secretion.* Proc. Nutr. Soc. 55, 259-64 (1996).

Langley, J.N., Sewall. *On the changes in pepsin-forming glands during secretion.* Proc. Royal. Soc. XXIX, 383-388 (1879).

Langley, J.N., Edkins, J.S. *Pepsinogen and Pepsin.* J. Physiol. VII, 371-415 (1886).

Lehy, T, Accary, J.P., Dubrasquet, M., Lewin, M.J. *Growth hormone-releasing factor (somatocrinin) stimulates epithelial cell proliferation in the rat digestive tract.* Gastroenterology 90 (3), 646-53 (March 1986).

Logan, R.P.H., Walker, M.M., Misiewicz, J.J., Kirk, G.E., Hawkey, C.J., Spiller R.C. *Changes in the intragastric distribution of Helicobacter pylori during treatment with omeprazole.* Gut 36, 12-16 (1995).

Lozniewski, A., de Korwin, J.D., Muhale, F., et al. *Gastric diffusion of antibodies used against H. pylori.* Int. J. Antimicrobial Agents 9, 181-93 (1997).

Ludwig, M.L., Matthews, R.G. *Structure-based perspectives on B12 dependent enzymes.* Ann. Rev. Biochem. 66, 269-313 (1997).

Modlin, I.M. *To repair the fault or end the acid reign.* Scand. J. Gastr. 30 (Suppl. 210), 1-5 (1995).

Modlin, I.M., Hunt, R.H. *Critical reappraisal of mucosal repair mechanisms.* Scand. J. Gastro. 30 (Suppl. 210), 28-31 (1995).

Modlin, I.M., Kidd, M., Sandor, A. *Perspectives on stem cells and gut growth: tales of a crypt - from the walrus to Wittgenstein. In: The gut as a model in cell and molecular biology,* Kluwer Academic Publishers, Boston, 1997, p. 121-136.

Modlin, I.M., Poulsom, R. *Trefoil peptides: mitogens, motogens or mirages?* J. Clin. Gastroenterol. 25 (Suppl. 1), S94-100 (1997).

Modlin, I.M., Zhu, Z., Tang, L.H., Kidd, M., Lawton, G.P., Miu, K., Powers, R.E., Goldenring, J.R., Pasikhov, D., Soroka, C.J. *Evidence for a regulatory role for histamine in gastric enterochromaffin-like cell proliferation induced by hypergastrinemia.* Digestion 57 (5), 310-21 (1996).

Myers, C.P., Hogan, D., Yao, B., Koss, M., Isenberg, J.I., Barrett, K.E. *Inhibition of rabbit duodenal bicarbonate secretion by ulcerogenic agents: histamine-dependent and -independent effects.* Gastroenterology 114, 527-35 (1998).

Orlando, R.C. *The pathogenesis of gastroesophageal reflux disease: the relationship between epithelial defense, dysmotility and acid exposure.* Am. J. Gastroenterology 92, 35-55 (1997).

Patel, K., Hanby, A.M., Ahnen, D.J. et al. *The kinetic organisation of the ulcer-associated cell lineage (UACL): delineation of a novel putative stem cell.* Epith. Cell. Biol. 3, 156-60 (1994).

Pitcairn, A. *A dissertation upon the motion which reduces the aliment in the stomach to a form proper for the supply of blood.* In: *The Whole Works.* Translated by G. Sewell and J.T. Desaguliers. London, J. Pemberton, 1727, p 106-138.

Plebani, M. *Pepsinogens in health and disease.* Curr. Rev. Clin. Lab. Sci. 30, 273-328 (1993).

Quigley, E.M., Turnberg, L.A. *pH of the microclimate lining human gastric duodenal mucosa in vivo. Studies in control subjects and in duodenal ulcer patients.* Gastroenterology 92, 1876 (1987).

Raufmann, J.P. *Gastric chief cells: receptors and signal transduction mechanisms.* Gastroenterology 102, 699-710 (1992).

Rondon, M.R., Trzebiatowski, J.R., Escalante-Semerena, J.G. *Biochemistry and molecular genetics of cobalamin biosynthesis.* Prog. Nuc. Acid Res. & Mol. Bio. 56, 347-84 (1997).

Sanders, M.J., Ayalon, A., Roll, M., Soll, A.H. *The apical surface of canine chief cell monolayers resists H^+ back-diffusion.* Nature 313, 52 (1985).

Schade, C., Flemstrom, G., Holm, L. *Hydrogen ion concentration in the mucus layer on top of acid-stimulated and -inhibited rat gastric mucosa.* Gastroenterology 107, 180-188 (1994).

Schwann, T. *Ueber das Wesen des Verdauungsprocess.* Arch. Anat. Physiolwiss. Med., 90-138 (1836).

Shao, J.S., Schepp, W., Alpers, D.H. *Expression of intrinsic factor and pepsinogen in the rat stomach identifies a subset of parietal cells.* Am. J. Physiol. 274, G62-70 (1998).

Sharp, R., Babyatsky, M.W., Takagi, H., Tagerud, S., Wang, T.C., Bockman, D.E., Brand, S.J., Merlino, G. *Transforming growth factor alpha disrupts the normal program of cellular differentiation in the gastric mucosa of transgenic mice.* Development 121 (1), 149-61 (Jan. 1995).

Shimizu, N., Kaminishi, M., Tatematsu, M. et al. *Helicobacter pylori promotes development of pepsinogen-altered pyloric glands, a pre-neoplastic lesion of glandular stomach of BALB/c mice pretreated with N-methyl-N-nitroso urea.* Cancer Letters 123, 63-9 (1998).

Silen, W. *Gastric mucosal defense and repair.* In: Johnson, L.R, ed. *Physiology of the gastrointestinal tract.* 2nd. edition, Vol 2, p.1055. Raven Press, New York U.S.A., 1987.

Smout, A.J., Geus, W.P., Mulder, P.G. et al. *GERD in the Netherlands. Results of a multicenter pH study.* Scand. J. Gastro. Suppl 218, 10-15 (1996).

Surraf, C.E., Alsion, M.R., Ansari, T.W. et al. *Subcellular distribution of peptides associated with gastric mucosal healing and neoplasia.* Microsop. Rev. and Tech. 31, 234-41 (1995).

Teorell, T. *On the permeability of the stomach mucosa for acids and some other substances.* J. Gen. Physiol. 23, 263-274 (1939).

Teorell, T. *Electrolyte difussion in relation to the acidity regulation of the gastric juice.* Gastroenterology 9, 425-443 (1947).

Tsukita, S., Furuse, M., Itoh, M. *Molecular architecture of tight junctions: occludin and ZO-1.* Society of General Physiologists Series. 52, 69-76 (1997).

Verdu, E.F., Armstrong, D., Idstrom, J.P. et al. *Intragastric pH during treatment with omeprazole: role of H. pylori and H. pylori associated gastritis.* Scan. J. Gastro. 31, 1151-56 (1996).

Wallace, J.L., Granger, D.N. *The cellular and molecular basis of gastric mucosal defense.* FASEB J. 10, 731-40 (1996).

Wetscher, G.J., Hinder, R.A., Perdikis, G. et al. *Three dimensional imaging of the lower esophageal sphincter in healthy subjects and gastroesophageal reflux.* Dig. Dis. Sci. 41, 2377-82 (1992).

Williams, G.R., Wright, N.A. *Trefoil factor family domain peptides.* Virchows Archiv 431, 299-304 (1997).

Yasugi, S. *Regulation of pepsinogen gene expression in epithelial cells of vertebrate stomach during development.* Int. J. Develop. Biol. 38, 273-9 (1994).

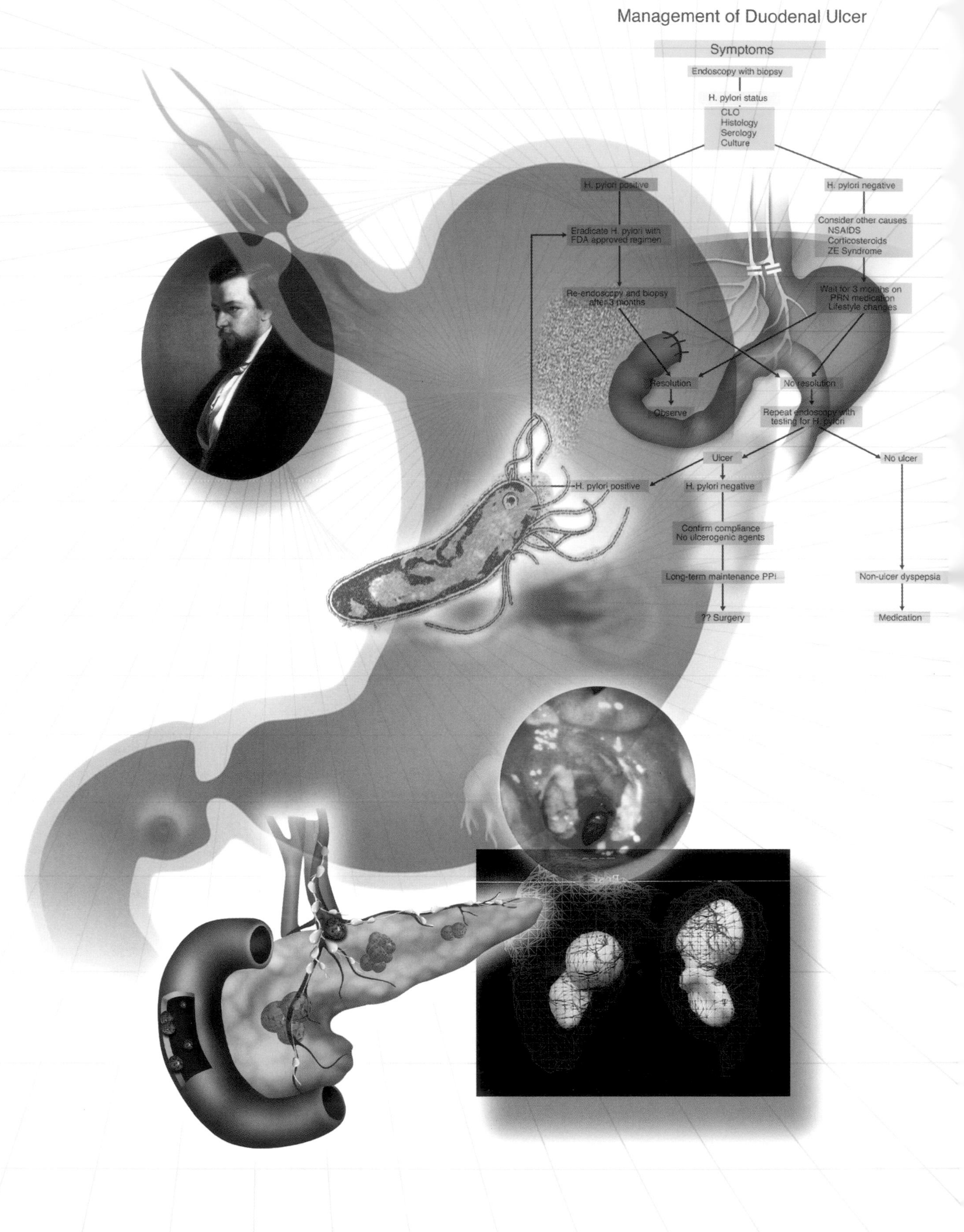

Management of Duodenal Ulcer

Symptoms

Endoscopy with biopsy

H. pylori status
CLO
Histology
Serology
Culture

H. pylori positive

H. pylori negative

Eradicate H. pylori with
FDA approved regimen

Consider other causes
NSAIDS
Corticosteroids
ZE Syndrome

Re-endoscopy and biopsy
after 3 months

Wait for 3 months on
PRN medication
Lifestyle changes

Resolution

No resolution

Observe

Repeat endoscopy with
testing for H. pylori

Ulcer

No ulcer

H. pylori positive

H. pylori negative

Confirm compliance
No ulcerogenic agents

Non-ulcer dyspepsia

Long-term maintenance PPI

Medication

?? Surgery

SECTION 5

GASTRIC AND DUODENAL ULCER DISEASE

CHAPTER 1
History

CHAPTER 2
Peptic Ulcer Disease

CHAPTER 3
Gastrin Carcinoid

CHAPTER 4
Dyspepsia

CHAPTER 5
Intravenous Use
of Acid Suppressants

CHAPTER 1
HISTORY

Introduction

The elucidation of the pathobiology of acid peptic related disease of the stomach and duodenum has accelerated dramatically in the last 20 years with the advent of scientific techniques which have facilitated the study of the cell biology of the gastric mucosa. The identification of cellular mechanisms has facilitated the development of therapeutic strategies capable of not only ameliorating the mucosal ulceration but eradicating or abrogating the putative causes. Whilst acid and pepsin have long been recognized as pathogenic as regards the mucosa it is only relatively recently that an infective component has been established as of critical relevance to the etiology of gastric and duodenal ulcer disease.

Early management strategies thus focused briefly on the avoidance of acid-containing foods or substances containing capsaicin related compounds. The use of bland diets was then augmented with the addition of neutralizing compounds and antacids. Unfortunately such regimes lead to a significant decline in the quality of life and in addition to side effects (diarrhea, milk/alkali syndrome) associated with the use of excessive alkali and cation-containing agents. The development of histamine 2 receptor antagonists and proton pump inhibitors dramatically altered the efficacy of treatment whilst the recognition of a bacterial component of the disease and its antibiotic eradication have more recently further amplified therapeutic gains. Within the context of the advance of the knowledge of regulatory mechanisms, various therapeutic strategies have evolved leading to a substantial change in different types of intervention. In this respect surgery has for the most part become obsolete as methods of decreasing acid secretion have evolved into more targeted and precise pharmacological options. Nevertheless the early surgical remedies were to a certain extent based upon a reasonable grasp of the pathophysiology and the recognition of the need to effect relief of the problem of ulceration and its sequelae of pain, bleeding, perforation and stenosis. The recognition that the ulcer was the crux of the issue led initially to the development of techniques to simply resect the area. Unfortunately the rapid recurrence of the lesion obviated the use of this technique and alternative strategies were evaluated to decrease the secretion of acid. The subsequent identification of the regulatory role of the vagus nerves to the stomach inspired a multiplicity of procedures to ensure their severance as well as the development of innumerable methods to overcome the subsequent negative alterations in gastric emptying. Further recognition that the fundus of the stomach contained the acid secreting cells and the antrum a major component of the regulatory mechanism led to the development of an extraordinary variety of permutations and combinations of antral and fundic resection. Such operations were devised with the view to variously removing the ulcer, decreasing gastrin stimulation, ablating neural stimulation and decreasing the parietal cell mass.

Benjamin Sippy, an early advocate of bland diets and antacids.

T. Billroth, the first report of a successful gastrectomy.

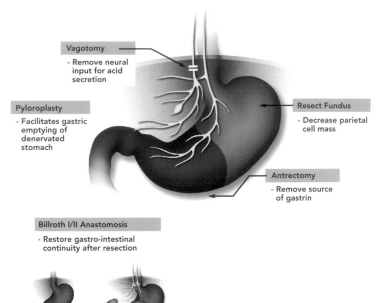

Historical Surgical Concepts of Acid Inhibition

Vagotomy
- Remove neural input for acid secretion

Pyloroplasty
- Facilitates gastric emptying of denervated stomach

Resect Fundus
- Decrease parietal cell mass

Antrectomy
- Remove source of gastrin

Billroth I/II Anastomosis
- Restore gastro-intestinal continuity after resection

The principles of gastric surgery for peptic ulcer disease involved vagal nerve severance as well as varying degrees of gastric resection. If vagotomy alone was undertaken, a pyloroplasty was necessary. Gastric resection required construction of a Billroth I or II anastomosis to re-establish continuity of the stomach and intestine.

Sadly, they were plagued not only by operative morbidity and even mortality but in addition generated a panoply of symptomatology broadly designated as "post gastrectomy syndromes" as the gut failed to accomodate to the loss of neural innervation, pyloric function and the severe neuro endocrine aberrations consequent upon resective intervention.

At this juncture it is rare to consider surgical intervention in acid peptic disease for anything less than a major complication, the evolution of the surgical strategies is worthy of consideration, if only to indicate the relative advantages of pharmacological intervention as opposed to invasive modalities.

The advent of H2RA's and PPI's has virtually abolished the need for peptic ulcer surgery except to deal with complications. For the most part, gastric resections are associated with a morbidity and are therefore avoided unless circumstances absolutely dictate surgical intervention. Gastric resections may be of some benefit in very early neoplastic disease of the stomach.

Surgical Stategies

Diagnosis	Procedure	Advantage	Disadvantage
Uncomplicated DU, GU	Highly selective vagotomy	Laparoscopic Only denervate fundus	High recurrence rate (up to 15%) Lesser curve necrosis
	Vagotomy and pyloroplasty	Rapid	Duodeno-gastric reflux possible Post vagotomy syndrome
Recurrent DU, GU	Vagotomy and antrectomy BI reconstruction BII reconstruction	Relatively physiological Lower recurrence rate	BI: stricture 2-5% leakage 3-5% (mortality) BII: Dumping syndrome Duodenal stump blowout Afferent-loop syndromes
Perforated duodenal ulcer	Omental patch	Rapid and safe/laparoscopic	Etiology untreated
Perforated gastric ulcer	Ulcer excision, plication, patch	Rapid, technically easy, safe	Malignancy needs to be excluded Recurrence
MALT lymphoma	Partial/total gastrectomy	70-90% cure	Recurrence if high grade lymphoma
Early gastric carcinoma	Subtotal gastrectomy BII reconstruction	High cure rate (up to 90%)	Aff. Eff. loop syndrome
Extensive gastric carcinoma	Extended/radical or total gastrectomy	Decreases chance of perforation, bleeding, obstruction	Cure uncommon Anastomotic leakage Post gastrectomy syndromes Morbidity 12%, mortality <2%
Zollinger-Ellison syndrome - Pancreatic gastrinoma - Duodenal gastrinoma	? Total gastrectomy ? Pancreatic resection ? Whipple procedure	Effective ulcer prevention	Nutrient sequelae Tumor recurrence common Altered glucose homeostasis

Early management of peptic ulcer disease

Jean Cruveilhier (1791-1873). A brilliant pupil of Dupuytren and the first incumbent of the chair of pathology in the Paris Faculty. He abjured the use of microscopy but nevertheless produced extraordinarily well illustrated pathology texts.

The earliest of human text addresses issues of the cosmos and the meanings of life, endlessly examining the nature of divinity, pantheism, and the fate of the soul. Throughout these erudite texts run a common and fundamental issue, speculated upon both in metaphor and fact. The commonality of food, the stomach, and digestion can be noted in writings as divergent as the Sufi Mystics, the Sephardic Sages, Philosophers of the Tang Dynasty, or the Odes of the Mantuan Bard. Food and its digestion represent the theme of universal interest surpassed only by pre-occupation with the ephemeral concept of love. *Homo est quod est* – Man is what he eats. It is therefore no wonder that the subject of digestion has been a matter of concern to doctors and their patients for as long as records exist. Unfortunately little rational therapeutic intervention was available for the treatment of gastric disorders. Indeed, up until the later 19th century, the stomach was often not clearly recognized as a source of symptoms. From the earliest times chalk, charcoal and slop diets had been noted to provide symptomatic relief from dyspepsia.

In the 17th century chalk and pearl juleps were utilized for infant gastric disorders but little comment was made about adult problems except for Sydenham who wrote about gout and dysentery. Jan Heurne, the first proponent of bedside teaching, left a posthumous pamphlet on the diseases of the stomach in 1610. Similarly, Martin Harmes and Ferriol in 1684 and 1668 respectively produced books on diseases of the stomach and intestines. In 1664 Swalbe published a long satire on *"the quarrels and opprobria of the stomach"* (*prosopopoia*). The favorite theme of the 17th century physicians was the dyspepsia due to gastric atony implicit in the title *De imbecilitate ventriculi*. This term was continued into the 18th century when it was equated with the "hectic stomach" (Arnold 1743) and later with the term of *"embarras gastrique"* utilized by the French physicians.

Throughout the 18th century there were various descriptions of gastric and intestinal diseases but no specific and logical remedies were recorded. The doctrine of acidity was widespread and prevalent and the general literature of dyspepsia was large. Thus in 1754, Joseph Black writing on the subject of carbon dioxide commented on *De humore acido a cibo orto*. In 1835 in Paris, Cruveilhier had written extensively on the pathology of peptic ulcer and the condition was referred to as Cruveilhier's disease. Yet in all these tomes little specific therapy apart from dietary adjustments or homeopathic remedies are apparent.

The issue of surgery of the stomach had been confounded for years by the problems related to sepsis and lack of adequate anesthesia. As late as the end of the 19th century, Naunyn felt obligated to describe it as "an autopsy *in vivo*". Nevertheless, by 1881 Billroth, Péan and Rydiger had resected the

Ludwig Rydiger of Chelmo on November 16, 1880 performed the second documented gastrectomy. It was unsuccessful!

VIII.

Ueber penetrierende Magen- und Jejunalgeschwüre.

Von

Dr. Karl Schwarz,

Primararzt am Spital der barmherzigen Brüder in Agram.

I.

Penetrierende Magengeschwüre.

Die den Magen durchbrechenden und sich in die Nachbar-
organe, namentlich Bauchwand, Leber, Pankreas, hineinfressenden,
mit mächtiger entzündlicher Bindegewebswucherung einhergehenden,
förmliche Pseudotumoren bildenden peptischen Geschwüre verdienen
wohl, daß ihnen in dem großen Kapitel der Magengeschwüre eine
Sonderstellung eingeräumt werde. Sie waren schon seit langem den
pathologischen Anatomen bekannt, aber auch manchen Chirurgen
nicht entgangen, ich erinnere an die grundlegende Arbeit Hof-
meister's[1].

"Ohne saueren Magensaft keinpeptisches Geschwur"

Karl Schwarz in his discussion of penetrating ulcers of the stomach and intestine was amongst the first to note that "without acid there is no ulcer" ("Ohne saueren Magensaft keinpeptisches Geschwur").

stomach and Wölfler had successfully developed the procedure of gastroenterostomy. By the turn of this century, Moynihan had transformed the treatment of peptic ulcer disease into a unique surgical discipline.

Unfortunately the consequences of gastric and vagal surgery produced a generation of patients with either significant post vagotomy problems or post gastrectomy syndrome. The recognition in the first part of the century that the mucosal damage was caused by acid ("*no acid-no ulcer*") and that this acid could be decreased by luminal neutralization resulted in a wave of enthusiasm for antacid preparations, bland diets and milk infusion as therapeutic options. The subsequent identification of the histamine 2 receptor subtype and the development of agents specifically capable of blocking acid secretion by antagonism at this receptor revolutionized the management of the disease process and virtually obliterated surgery as a therapeutic option for peptic ulcer except in cases of emergency.

The more recent identification of the molecular mechanism of acid secretion – the proton pump – resulted in the development of a new class of therapeutic agents, the proton pump inhibitors.

By defining the pump as the therapeutic target an almost complete inhibition of acid secretion with consequent therapeutic efficacy hitherto as yet undreamed of, can be achieved.

Although there is much debate about the initial observations of ulceration of the gastroduodenal mucosa some of the best original descriptions originated in the work of Jean Cruveilhier (1791-1873). Born in Limoges in France, he subsequently studied with the great surgeon of Paris, Dupuytren, and having attained the Chair of Pathology in Paris in 1836, subsequently became one of the foremost authorities on stomach ulcers in France. Cruveilhier's interest in the subject of gastric ulcers was substantial and his knowledge and experience in this area was widely recognized. In France, at this time, the management of stomach ulcers became so closely linked with his contributions that the lesions were referred to as Cruveilhier's disease. His comments thoughtfully addressed issues as to why an ulcer of the stomach might occur in a single place when the rest of the stomach

"Le Maladie de Cruveilhier" The first autopsy that he witnessed so upset Cruveilhier that he returned to his original desire to become a priest and entered the Seminary Sulpice of St. Sulpice. Cruveilhier pondered as to why an ulcer of the stomach might occur in a single place when the rest of the stomach was "in a state of perfect integrity". Details of the case notes of the management of haematemesis and the autopsy findings are of interest in regard to current therapeutic strategies. In the case of the unfortunate carpenter on autopsy he noted a deep ulceration "6 lines in dimension". A stylet introduced into the coronary artery of the stomach pushes a clot out of the center of the ulcer and enters the stomach.

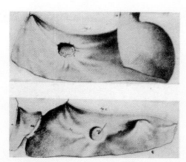

A carpenter, aged 29

April 15, 1830	RECURRENCE OF EPIGASTRIC PAIN
April 3	HAEMATEMESIS: carried to Charite Rx: bleeding produced by gross anaemia Mustard plasters to feet
May 1	SMALL HAEMATEMESIS ONLY Rx: 20 leeches to epigastrium Mustard plasters in calves Rice with eau de Kabel & syrup of quinces Diet
May 2	ISQ Rx: 20 leeches to anus Mustard plasters same drink HAEMATEMESIS - DEATH

AUTOPSY: LESSER GASTRIC ULCER
OPENING OF BRANCH OF CORONARY ARTERY

Lord Berkeley Moynihan (1865-1936), wrote extensively on the surgical management of duodenal ulcer disease. His contributions to the scientific foundation of gastric surgery were internationally recognized. As President of the Royal College of Surgeons of England, he was the prime mover in the introduction of science into surgical training programs.

was "*in the state of perfect integrity*". Cruveilhier carefully documented case histories and autopsies, and defined in detail the pathology and sequelae of chronic gastric and duodenal ulceration.

Similarly contributions to the understanding of the management of peptic ulcer disease were provided by Berkley Moynihan of Leeds in England, and so powerful was his effect on prevailing thoughts in this area that British physicians referred to duodenal ulcer as Moynihan's disease.

Cruveilhier's great contributions lay mostly in the pathological description of stomach ulcers. However, the therapy of his time was modest and revolved chiefly around the application of leeches, mustard plasters, bleeding, and various alcoholic concoctions which presumably allayed anxiety and relieved pain. Moynihan, on the other hand, defined many of the early surgical therapeutic strategies for peptic ulcer and became widely known for his contributions to gastric surgery. Despite his exaggerated enthusiasm for the surgical management of duodenal ulcer disease, Moynihan is noteworthy for his contribution to the scientific foundation of gastric surgery and as the President of the Royal College of Surgeons of England, he became the prime mover for the first introduction of science into surgical training programs.

The recognition of the association of ulceration of the duodenum with specific circumstances such as burns was first attributed to Curling in 1841, who called attention to the connection between cases of burn and acute ulceration of the duodenum. Although it is likely that Dupuytren observed this relationship more than a decade prior to Curling, the former published little of his work and his observations were not initially widely known. In 1836 Dupuytren had noted the congestion of the various mucous membranes of the alimentary canal in the early stages of burns.

He described in detail the ulceration and bleeding in the stomach and duodenum consequent upon severe burns some five years before Curling provided the definitive description of duodenal ulceration association with cutaneous burning. Confusion regarding the primacy of this observation was further clouded by the fact that Moynihan claimed that in 1834 James Long of Liverpool had first described duodenal ulcer in two patients with burns.

To date, the precise pathophysiology of the relationship between severe cutaneous burns and the development of peptic ulceration still remains unclear although the association is important.

A further association of duodenal ulceration with surgery of the posterior cranial fossa was noted by Harvey Cushing and initially attributed to alteration in neural pathways regulating gastric physiology. Current investigation is still focused upon the central nervous regulation of gastro-duodenal physiology but clear answers in this area are still lacking.

Further correlations between gastroduodenal ulceration and other related conditions noted the association of pancreatic tumors with peptic ulceration. The further elucidation of the neuroendocrine tumor source of gastrin and the consequences of acid hypersecretion led to the resolution of this relationship by

Cushing and Pavlov, 1929. Harvey Cushing had defined neurosurgery as a unique discipline following an "*Arbeid*" with Kocher in Berne in 1901. Pavlov's interest in surgery prompted Cushing to let him use the surgical cautery device recently devised by Bovie. He signed his name on a piece of steak still preserved in the Cushing Surgical Collection at Yale. Cushing was the first to recognize that after posterior cranial fossa surgery duodenal ulcers often occurred.

Zollinger and Ellison. They identified the existence of a syndrome of pancreatic neuroendocrine tumors associated with a peptic ulcer diathesis. Similar observations in conditions such as basophil leukemia and mastocytosis noted the excessive production of histamine with consequent acid hypersecretion and peptic ulcer disease in such patients.

Associations between the intake of salicylate containing compounds and peptic ulceration were followed by similar observations in individuals using non-steroidal anti-inflammatory drugs (NSAIDS) for the management of joint and muscle disease.

Nevertheless, despite the identification of a number of such associations with gastroduodenal ulceration, the etiology of the disease process was for the most part unrecognized until the identification of *H. pylori* and the elucidation of its relationship to peptic ulcer disease.

Gastric surgery

Until the mid 19th century the techniques of surgery were mostly confined to the extremities and usually related to the management of trauma. No surgeon would reasonably consider the violation of a body cavity prior to the introduction of anesthesia and antisepsis. Even under the latter conditions both the morbidity and mortality were such that incursions into the peritoneal cavity were undertaken with considerable trepidation.

For the most part, the early reports of stomach surgery reflected the consequences of either military action with war wounds or incidental trauma. A therapeutic gastrostomy was reported in 1819 to remove a silver fork which had been "inadvertently" swallowed by a 26 year old female servant. Jacques-Mathieu Delpech (1777-1832) of Montpellier confirmed the diagnosis of a penetrating fork upon noting a red inflamed mass on the anterior abdominal wall five months after the fork had been ingested. He was a shrewd enough clinician to persuade a colleague, Cayroche of Mende, to remove this foreign body (May 1, 1819) via an anterior abdominal incision. Delpech was subsequently assassinated by a former patient who felt that a varicocele operation had rendered him impotent. Sedillot subsequently reported the first successful construction of a gastrostomy (November 13, 1849) using a technique not much different from that developed originally by Blondlot to study gastric secretion in dogs. Nevertheless the principal contributions in surgery at that time emanated from the work of Dupuytren. Few surgeons have evoked more controversy and divergent opinions. He was variously known as "*the first of surgeons and the least of men*" or a "*genius but of unprecedented unkindness and coldness*". Born on October 5, 1777 to a family of modest means, his extraordinary intelligence was apparent from an early age.

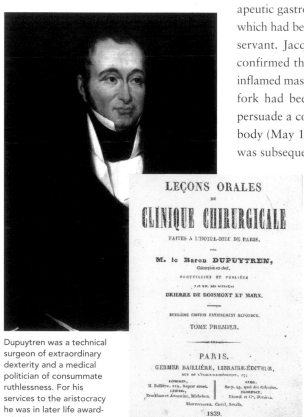

Dupuytren was a technical surgeon of extraordinary dexterity and a medical politician of consummate ruthlessness. For his services to the aristocracy he was in later life awarded a baronetcy.

In 1802, at the age of 25, he was appointed to the Hôtel-Dieu, and by 1815 he was chief surgeon, a post he held until his death some 20 years later. Despite the fact that he dressed with appalling taste and that his personal habits left much to be desired, he was highly regarded not only as a teacher but also as a surgeon of extraordinary intellectual and technical proficiency. His workload was extraordinary and it is reported that at the apogee of his career, he would see some 10,000 private patients a year.

Although Dupuytren's fame as a surgeon and teacher was prodigious, he wrote little and most of his work is recollected by renditions of his lectures in notebook form. The majority of his teachings were collated in a book entitled *Leçons Orales* and published by his students. His teachings cover a diverse range of conditions ranging from ano-rectal problems to chronic bleeding, arterial aneurysms, urinary calculi, and cataract management. Amongst his notable contributions are the following: he classified burns, was the first to remove the mandible, drained brain abscesses, treated torticollis by surgery and performed cervical excision for uterine cancer. His comments on duodenal ulceration were of critical relevance. Although Curling, in 1841, had called attention to the connection between cases of burn and acute ulceration of the duodenum, it was Dupuytren who had first made this observation. In 1836, he drew attention to the congestion of various mucous membranes in the alimentary canal in the early stages of burns. He described in detail the ulceration and bleeding of the stomach and duodenum consequent upon such an event, some five years before Curling provided the definitive description of duodenal ulceration associated with cutaneous burning.

Dupuytren's contributions as a leader, surgeon and teacher to surgery in Paris provided the foundations of the great surgical tradition which would initiate the performance of the first gastrectomy by Jules Emile Péan. Born in 1830 to the family of a miller in 1855, Péan attended medical school in Paris, and in 1868, after training with Denon Villiers and Nelaton, was awarded a doctor of medicine degree in surgery. Péan's reputation as a clinician and a surgeon was prestigious. His day began early at the Augustine's and Frères-St.-Jean de Dieu surgical clinics followed by surgery at the St. Louis Hospital, and would continue until well after dinner at night. Although his initial contributions to abdominal surgery were in the area of ovarian cystectomy, in 1867 he undertook the first successful splenectomy during a laparotomy for an ovarian cyst in which incidental damage to the spleen had occurred. A further major contribution in 1868 was the development of a special hemostatic clip made by Gueride which he successfully utilized for hemostasis.

On April 8, 1879, Péan undertook what was to be his most epic contribution to surgery by resecting a pyloric gastric cancer. The operation lasted 2 1/2 hours and the patient initially recovered successfully. Unfortunately, over the subsequent three days, the patient received two blood transfusions of 50 and 80 ml, and died on the fifth postoperative day prior to a further transfusion. Although the cause of death is unknown, the recognition of blood groups did not occur for some 40 years later and it seems likely that either sepsis or transfusion incompatibility may have contributed to this fatality. Nevertheless, to Péan goes the credit for having undertaken the first (albeit unsuccessful) gastrectomy.

On November 16,1880, Ludwig Rydiger of Chelmo performed the second

ON
ACUTE ULCERATION
OF
THE DUODENUM,
IN CASES OF BURN.

BY T. B. CURLING,
LECTURER ON SURGERY AND ASSISTANT SURGEON, LONDON HOSPITAL, ETC.

READ JUNE 29TH, 1842.

Moynihan stated that it was neither Curling nor Dupuytren but James Long of Liverpool who first described duodenal ulcer in two patients with burns in 1834. More than 150 years later, the nature of the relationship between burns and duodenal ulceration is still unresolved.

Doctor Péan operating. Painting by Henri Toulouse Lautrec (1891-1892). In 1891 Lautrec shared an apartment with his friend Dr. Henri Bourges and became friendly with other physicians. Gabriel Tapié de Celeyran was a cousin of Lautrec and had trained with Péan. It is likely that Lautrec had thus been invited to observe an operation and recorded it (oil on cardboard). Péan is operating on an oral lesion. Presumably a fore-runner of his epic contribution to gastric surgery. (Sterling and Francine Clark Institute, Williamstown, MA). Lautrec's medical interest was not confined to surgery. He utilized pharmaco-logical compounds (thujones) contained in high concentration in absinthe to amplify his creativity and color perception.

After his training with Billroth, Anton von Eiselberg achieved considerable recognition as a surgical leader and contributed extensively to the technical modifications of gastrectomy.

documented but also unsuccessful gastrectomy. Like Péan, he undertook a partial resection of the pre-pyloric portion of the stomach in a patient with gastric cancer. Some two months later in Vienna, Billroth became the first surgeon to successfully undertake a gastrectomy. The third reported gastrectomy was also for a pyloric tumor but in this instance the patient, Theresa Heller, survived to be discharged home 3 weeks postoperatively. The cumulative operative survival from gastrectomy in the two decades following Péan's initial operation rarely exceeded 50%.

As a result of the substantial mortality involved in gastrectomy in the pre-antiseptic era, lesser procedures were usually contemplated in an attempt to deal with diseases of the stomach thought to require surgical intervention.

The most popular operation was the gastroenterostomy pioneered by Mathieu Jaboulay. Born on July 5, 1860, and educated in the Lyon area, he achieved wide renown as a surgeon of considerable intellectual and technical skill. One of his initial accomplishments had been to remove the vagi, coeliac ganglion

Theodor Billroth in the auditorium of the Allgemeine Krankenhaus in Vienna by A.F. Seligman, 1889. In 1890, the painting was exhibited at the Society of Artists in Vienna where it was severely criticized by A. Ilg. In Munich the work was highly regarded. At the World's Fair in Chicago and Madrid it received a bronze medal and in Berlin and London a gold medal. In 1904 it was purchased by the Ministry of Education and presented to Hochenegg, Chief of the Billroth clinic. Unfortunately the painting was lost until Karel B. Absolon was able to locate it during a visit to Vienna. Dr. Böttcher hands Billroth the scalpel. Dr. Josef Winter holds the anesthetized patient's head. To Dr. Winter's left is Dr. Anton Eiselberg, the anesthetist. Dr. Leo Dittel is next to him and finally Dr. Salzer. The assistant, with the scissors, is Dr. Heidenthaller. Sitting is Dr. Beck. Left in the lowest row is Karl Theodor, the Duke of Bavaria, who commonly attended Billroth's lectures. The painter, A.F. Seligman, is in the first row on the right. The medical student standing in the first row is Alphons Rosthorn, the gynecologist. The patient is an old man, suffering from trigeminal neuralgia, who has a neurotomy performed.

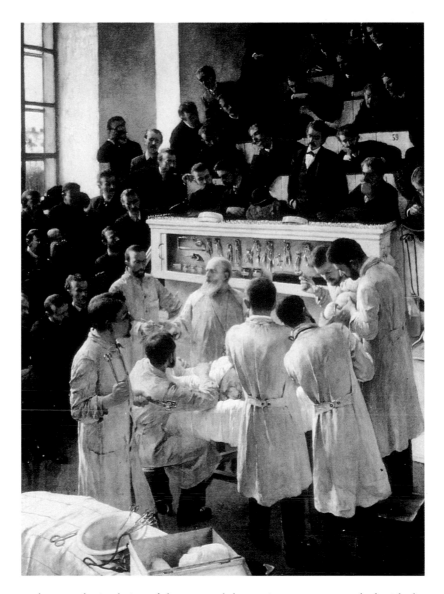

The pathological specimens of the stomach and tumor of Theresa Heller on display at the Josephinum, in Vienna. The left bottle is the resection specimen containing the obstructed pyloric antrum that was successfully resected. The right specimen is of the stomach recovered at autopsy three and a half months later when the patient died of hepatic metastases. The patent gastroduodenal anastomosis is evident.

and sympathetic chains of the upper abdomen in an attempt to deal with the discomfort induced by the lightning pains of *tabes dorsalis*. Jaboulay's later development of the gastroenterostomy procedure to obviate problems generated by the gastric outlet obstruction consequent upon vagotomy achieved widespread popularity in Europe.

Indeed gastroenterostomy remained the standard of choice for the first two to three decades of the twentieth century as the preferred surgical treatment of either peptic ulcer or gastric neoplasia.

Thereafter, better techniques developed to ensure the safety of the anastomosis after gastric resection and with the advent of Listererian antisepsis the era of the gastrectomist supervened. The early use of gastrectomy in peptic ulcer disease focussed on the management of complications such as obstruction and bleeding. Initial problems related to the leakage of the anastomosis between the duodenum and the gastric remnant led to the widespread acceptance of the gastro jejunal anastomosis known as the Billroth II.

Modifications of Gastrectomy

Classic Billroth I
1881

Standard Billroth I

Kocher 1891

Shoemaker 1911

Von Haberer 1922
Finney 1923

Kutscha-Lissberg 1925

Winkelbauer 1927

Leriche 1927

Von Haberer 1933

Some examples of the numerous varieties of gastric resection devised to facilitate safety and ameliorate post-operative symptoms.

The significant disturbances in physiology consequent upon this procedure (dumping syndromes, afferent and efferent loop syndromes) were thought tolerable as compared to the invariable mortality associated with a leak from a Billroth I type anastomosis.

In order to obviate the development of such symptomatology a great number of modifications of the procedure involving the construction of valves or different bowel loop lengths were introduced almost to no avail. Similarly the recognition of the high rates of ulcer recurrence with vagotomy alone led to the amplification of the magnitude of gastric resection in an attempt to decrease the acid secreting area.

The further addition of antrectomy to remove the source of gastrin accentuated the diminution of gastric reservoir size and augmented the difficulties experienced by the patient.

A loss of gastric receptive relaxation engendered by the vagotomy added to the problem of early satiety and compounded with a variety of post gastrectomy syndromes served to establish a patient group with an entirely new disease complex initiated by the sequelae of surgical intervention.

Billroth II Gastrectomy

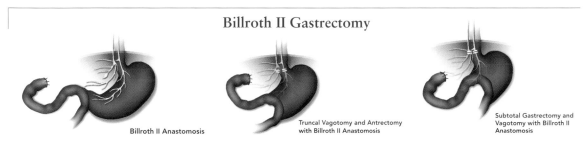

Billroth II Anastomosis

Truncal Vagotomy and Antrectomy
with Billroth II Anastomosis

Subtotal Gastrectomy and
Vagotomy with Billroth II
Anastomosis

The Billroth II anastomosis was utilized since it was a safer technical procedure than the Billroth I anastomosis. Unless acid suppressive medication is unavailable, vagotomy is rarely utilized even if gastric resection is required.

Surgery of the vagus

Although investigations of the vagus nerve began as long ago as two thousand years, it has only been within the last century that its role in the regulation of acid secretion became apparent. Armed with this knowledge, a handful of surgeons appreciated the therapeutic possibilities of interfering with vagal innervation of the stomach. To a large extent the consideration of such surgery reflected the recent introduction of anesthesia and antisepsis, which enabled body cavities to be entered with some degree of safety. Brodie had early in the 19th century identified that the vagus played a role in gastric secretion and by the turn of the century Pavlov had delineated the neural regulation of gastric secretion.

At almost the same time that Pavlov was experimenting with vagotomy in dogs, other intrepid surgeons were attempting this operation upon humans. It seems probable that, in the late 19th century, Jaboulay of France performed the first vagotomy upon a human patient. Jaboulay excised the celiac plexus of a man suffering from the lightning pains of tabes dorsalis. A few years later, Exner similarly divided the vagi in a number of patients afflicted with tabes, but presciently observed that a percentage of these individuals subsequently suffered from the effects of gastric atony.

Below, a portrait of Mathieu Jaboulay, 1895. Although Anton Wölfler (1850-1917) had introduced gastroenterostomy in 1881, the technique devised by Jaboulay was subsequently most widely utilized.
On the right, Jaboulay (1901) demonstrating his surgical skills in a picture taken by Harvey Cushing during his tour of French surgical clinics *en route* to work with T. Kocher in Berne. Tha lack of masks, gloves and the formal suit of the principal surgeon (M.J.) reflect the current state of surgical antiseptic technique.

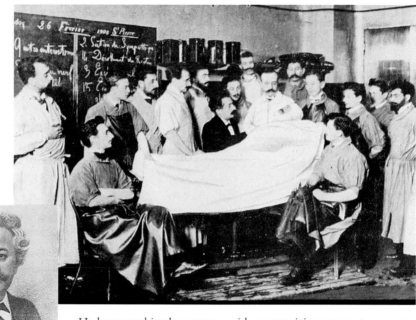

He later combined vagotomy with a gastrojejunostomy to promote gastric emptying. In time, other surgeons, including Kuttner, Borchers and Podkaminsky, attempted vagotomies on patients. By 1920, the results of 20 sub-diaphragmatic vagotomies for treatment of gastric ptosis were reported by Bircher. He observed decreased acidity and, curiously, improved tonus in 75 per cent of his patients. Alvarez reviewed the work of Bircher and concluded: *"His vagotomies were probably incomplete because, aside from some lowering of acidity, he did not seem to obtain the usual effects of a complete nerve resection."*

The outcome of these early clinical vagotomies inspired M. A. Latarjet of Lyons to further evaluate the procedure. Latarjet made the most detailed investigations into the anatomy of the vagi to date and applied his findings to the surgical patients he treated. The eponymous attribution of the anterior and posterior vagal nerves of the gastric lesser curve attest to his profound influence and excellent work in this area.

Latarjet was born on August 20, 1877 in Dijon and studied medicine in Lyons. Because of financial pressures, Latarjet was forced to choose between a primary career in surgery or anatomy. The pathway to a practice in surgery was difficult in the hospitals of Lyons, and Latarjet was not financially able to support himself in private practice. He therefore chose a career based principally in anatomy. As an anatomist, he never relinquished his initial dedication to surgery, and together with Raymond Gregoire in Paris, became one of

Bulletin de l'Académie de Medecine, 1922
RÉSECTION DES NERFS DE L'ESTOMAC 681

Résection des nerfs de l'estomac. Technique opératoire. Résultats cliniques,

par M. A. LATARJET, correspondant national.

...e rendre plus clair l'exposé de la technique opératoire ...section des nerfs de l'estomac et des résultats obtenus, ...erai les observations anatomiques et les recherches expé-...ales que j'ai entreprises depuis 1818, d'abord seul, puis en ...oration pendant ces deux dernières années, avec M. Wert-...mer, prosecteur, dont la thèse inaugurale prochaine déve-...oppera le sujet qui fait l'objet de cette communication.

M. A. Latarjet of Lyons in 1922 first described vagotomy for the management of peptic ulcer disease and confirmed that it caused amelioration of symptoms as well as a decrease in acid secretion.

Wertheimer's thesis, *De L'Enervation Gastrique*, 1921, provided the anatomic information necessary to enable M. Latarjet to successfully undertake vagotomy.

the champions in the field of what was later to become known as applied anatomy. His research was directed broadly towards the innervation of the abdominal organs. Thus, over a period of twenty years, he wrote extensively on nerves of the colon, biliary tract and the pelvis in both men and women. The detailed study of the hypogastric and sacral plexuses in females resulted in the development of a surgical treatment for dysmenorrhea (*operation de cotte*).

Probably his most important contribution relates to the work undertaken with his colleague, Pierre Wertheimer.

In 1921, Wertheimer completed his thesis *De l'Enervation Gastrique*. This study documents both anatomical and experimental work in regard to the vagal innervation of the stomach. Of particular note is the observation that cutting the vagi significantly impaired gastric motility and emptying and resulted in a substantial inhibition of acid secretion. The subsequent publication, in 1923, of the surgical studies in which vagotomy and a drainage procedure were utilized resulted in the international recognition of Latarjet's contributions and his eponymous attribution to the gastric vagi. Some two decades later, on January 14, 1943, in Chicago at the Merrit Billings hospital, Lester Dragstedt undertook the first truncal vagotomy in North America.

The subsequent enthusiasm for vagotomy as a method of managing duodenal ulcer disease brought further recognition to the contributions of Latarjet in defining the physiological and therapeutic possibilities of the vagus.

The principal difference between the work of Latarjet and his predecessors was his decision to perform vagotomy in a systematic manner for patients with dyspepsia. His operation, first reported in 1921, entailed denervation of the greater and lesser curvatures and the suprapyloric region, with partial circumcision of the serosa and muscularis down to the level of the submucosa. He designed this operation to sever all the extrinsic nerves to the stomach and pylorus leaving intact the large branch of the right gastric nerve that accompanies the left gastric artery to the celiac plexus.

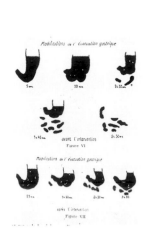

Latarjet's studies of gastric emptying undertaken in 1922. As a consequence of vagotomy, gastric stasis was noted and then quantified by use of radio opaque material and serial radiographic pictures. These investigations documented the need for a surgical drainage procedure of the stomach to be a component of the operation of vagotomy.

In 1922, Latarjet reported his results on 24 patients to the French Academy of Surgery. Like Exner before him, he found delayed gastric emptying in many of these vagotomized patients and later added a gastro-jejunostomy to this operation. He explained: "*Indeed, in all of our cases, gastroentero-anastomosis was done at the same time as denervation, either for reasons of promoting mechanical order or to avoid the possibility of an aggravated ulcer evolution as a consequence of the prolonged journey of food in a stomach which has been rendered hypotonic by denervation*". Almost 30 years later, Lester Dragstedt would come to a virtually identical conclusion.

As early as 1927, Charles Mayo was aware that operations not based on sound physiologic principles have no place in the surgical repertoire. "*If anyone should consider removing half of my good stomach to cure a small ulcer in my duodenum, I would run faster than he."* (C. H. Mayo, 1927)

Similarly, surgeons who wish to introduce new procedures must first determine, in the surgical laboratory, the anatomic and physiologic sequelae of their proposed operations. Only when an experimental operation has been shown to be physiologically sound may it be applied for use on patients. The development of the operative procedure known as a vagotomy initially followed such a course.

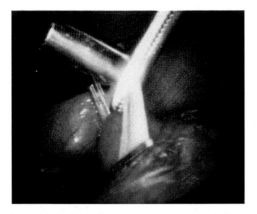

Laparoscopic vagotomy. In recent times it has been proposed that the advantages of minimally invasive surgery would facilitate the undertaking of acid inhibitory operations such as vagotomy. The minimal physiological consequences of surgery without laparotomy combined with the ability to clearly define vagal anatomy have been proposed as providing significant advantages for this mode of vagal section. The widespread availability and safety of PPI's have rendered vagotomy for the most part an archaic procedure irrespective of the technology utilized to sever the nerves.

Unfortunately, Latarjet never formally confirmed that vagotomy was a successful therapy for peptic ulcer disease. One theory of ulcerogenesis popular during the 1920s was that ulcers were caused by gastric stasis. Thus, some of his contemporaries proposed that the fine results of his procedure might be attributed to the concomitant gastroenterostomy – not the vagotomy. Indeed, for this reason and possibly because of the provincial location of Lyons, his pioneering work was received with little enthusiasm by his colleagues. Fewer than 100 of these operations were performed before 1940 and Latarjet published nothing further related to his operative procedure after 1923.

At about the same time that Latarjet was conducting his studies, E. D'Arcy McCrea of Manchester, England, published an extensive and often-cited review of anatomy, physiology and surgical treatment of the vagi. McCrea argued that *"operative interference with the nerves of the stomach is both feasible and in certain instances justifiable"*. He recognized, however, that physiology of vagal function was, in many instances, not clear.

McCrea claimed that the vagi were either "augmentors" or "inhibitors" of gastric function. In his studies he noted that the *"vagi regulate both tonus and movement, and moreover, that these may be independent of one another"*. In the resting stomach, the vagi served as augmentors, he argued, but in the actively digesting organ their work was that of an inhibitor. The theories of McCrea were novel since he was the first to recognize the vagi as a potential cause of disease: *"A lesion of the gastric or duodenal wall, the result of infection or injury is more likely to become chronic if an irritation of the nerves is set up"*. He further speculated that *"local spasm with resultant anemia is a probable cause of the chronicity of ulcer aided by factors such as retention and infection set up by reflex spasm"*. A lesion in any part of the nerve path, he contended, caused the ulcer to develop.

McCrea, however, was ambiguous. He contradicted himself in relating these nerve lesions and their therapy to acid secretion and its clinical sequelae and his inconsistencies negated, to a certain extent, his recommendation of a Latarjet operation for peptic ulcer disease. Thus, although the review by McCrea was widely read and generally accepted, it appears to have done little to promote the therapeutic use of vagotomy. In fact, very little was written about and very few operations were performed upon the vagus nerves during the next two decades. Indeed the standard anti-ulcer operation in the first half of the 20th century was either a partial gastrectomy or gastro-enterostomy.

On 18 January 1943, Dragstedt performed a sub-diaphragmatic vagal resec-

The nerves of Latarjet. The branches of the vagus nerve passing down the lesser curvature supply both the fundus and antrum. Based upon the results of denervation at surgery and under experimental conditions, it seems likely that the vagal branches to the fundus are responsible for the regulation of acid secretion and motility while those to the antrum are of importance in regulating gastrin release and gastric emptying. Of more relevance at this time is the role of the central neural mechanisms of secretory regulation in the modulation of mucosal cellular function. It is more likely that the development of specific pharmacological probes designed to target local neurotransmitters or their receptors will be more effective than neural ablation and its consequent indiscriminate physiological sequelae.

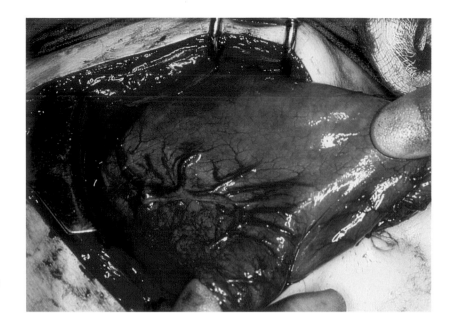

tion on a patient with an active duodenal ulcer and so ushered in the modern era of vagotomy. Dragstedt concentrated his research on the pathogenesis of peptic ulcer disease. He was fascinated by the work of Hunter and Bernard which showed that normal stomachs do not digest themselves. He recognized that "*pure gastric juice as it is secreted by the fundus of the stomach, has the capacity to destroy and digest various living tissues, including the wall of the jejunum, duodenum, and even the stomach itself. It does not do this under normal conditions because the usual and appropriate stimulus to gastric secretion is ingestion of food. This dilutes and neutralizes the gastric juice and decreases its corrosive powers*". He did not recognize the high acidity that often occurs.

Dragstedt further postulated that mucosal damage takes place at night when people do not eat and that this acid secretion was of nervous origin. He disagreed with his colleagues who speculated that ulcers were caused by diminished mucosal resistance to injury. The key to understanding ulcerogenesis, he reiterated, was acid secretion and, in support of his theory, presented two stimuli of acid hypersecretion: neural and hormonal. In citation of his own experiments, he demonstrated clear evidence that neural stimulation caused increased output of gastric acid. Results of studies from his laboratories of nocturnal output of acid in patients with duodenal ulcers clearly demonstrated levels to be three to 20 times that of normal patients. He termed this phenomenon "fasting hypersecretion". He also noted the clinical success of vagotomy as further evidence of the importance of neural input to acid secretion. Dragstedt recognized that hormonal stimulation could also account for acid hypersecretion. First, he cited the work of Pavlov in which acid secretion had been elicited in response to food introduced into denervated gastric pouches. Next, he somewhat ungenerously credited Edkins, who had postulated the existence of gastrin, with "*one of the most remarkable guesses in the history of gastrointestinal physiology*". Gastrin, Edkins had said, was secreted into the blood stream by the mucous membrane in the antrum in response to contact with

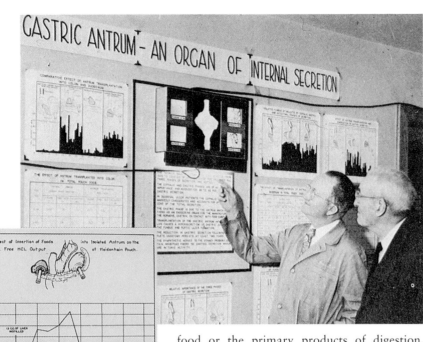

L. Dragstedt and A. Carlson c. 1950. As a young man Dragstedt, who came from a small copper mining town, Anaconda, Montana, had been influenced by Carlson, then Chairman of Physiology at the University of Chicago. Both their families had immigrated from the Götheborg area of Sweden and this close personal and professional relationship lasted throughout their lives. Carlson was a brilliant and rigorous investigator who had begun his life in America by training as a religious minister. No doubt this background provided grist for his famous comment to all his pupils and at meetings *"What is the evidence?"*.

Apart from his contribution to the neural regulation of acid secretion, Dragstedt confirmed Edkins' original proposal of the existence of an antral regulator (gastrin).

The graphic insert demonstrates the effect of food in an antral pouch on HCl output of a Heidenhain pouch. With exquisite surgical technique, Dragstedt designed models to test his physiological hypotheses. In this study, he confirmed the original hypothesis (50 years previously) of Edkins that antral gastrin would function as a hormone to drive fundic acid secretion.

Carl Rokitansky (1804-1878) dissected over 30,000 cadavers in his lifetime. Although he is best remembered for his studies of defects in the septum of the heart, he was the first to describe acute dilatation of the stomach. In addition, he was of the opinion that ulcer disease was due to abnormal function of the vagus nerve. Apart from his brilliance he was a man of wit. Thus of his four sons, two of whom were physicians and two singers, he said *"Die Einen heilen, die Anderen heulen"*.

food or the primary products of digestion. Dragstedt admitted the validity of the theory of Edkins only after he conducted his own experiments. In these studies, Dragstedt excised and transplanted the antrum from a denervated stomach of a dog to its abdominal wall and found markedly reduced gastric secretion. When the antrum was re-implanted with the duodenum, normal gastric secretion resumed. With these studies, he not only confirmed the findings of Edkins, but also established a fundamental observation – that gastrin secretion did not take place in an acid environment. Thus, Dragstedt recognized and described the existence of a feedback mechanism dependent on mucosal pH for the control of secretion of gastrin. In so doing he produced physiological proof of the antral regulation of acid secretion which could be utilized to support the rationale for the introduction of the surgical application of antrectomy.

After delineating aspects of the regulation of gastric secretion, Dragstedt sought the mechanism of ulcer formation. He claimed that duodenal ulcers were of nervous origin (a proposal originally made by Rokitansky of Vienna in 1860) and postulated that the pathologic nervous stimuli that resulted in duodenal ulcers were transmitted by the vagi.

Gastric ulcers, he claimed, were caused by abnormal hormonal stimuli. They resulted from gastric stasis, which caused prolonged antral contact with food and, hence, hypersecretion of gastrin.

From this generous theoretic background, Dragstedt set out to provide a surgical cure for patients with peptic ulcer disease. The operation he proposed was a total vagotomy. The first patient to receive a Dragstedt vagotomy was a 35 year old man who had a bleeding ulcer necessitating multiple blood transfusions despite medical therapy. The young man underwent a bilateral vagotomy by way of a left thoracotomy approach and his abdominal pain immediately subsided. Dragstedt, always the physiologist, instilled 0.1 normal hydrochloric acid into the stomach of the patient for the next couple of weeks. For the first eight days, he was able to reproduce the abdominal pain of the patient. On the ninth day, however, acid infusion no longer caused discomfort. Dragstedt took this to indicate that the ulcer had healed.

Dragstedt went on to perform more than 200 vagotomies during the next four years because of its physiologic basis and clinical success. About one-third of these patients had gastric stasis developeed that was severe enough to necessitate a gastro-enterostomy as a secondary procedure.

To perform these operations simultaneously, an abdominal approach to the vagi was developed. Initially, the drainage procedure of choice was a gastro-enterostomy. During the next decade, however, the technique of pyloroplasty was perfected and became the drainage method of choice. Later, as the role of the antrum in the physiology of gastric secretion became better understood, vagotomy combined with antrectomy was the procedure used to reduce the secretion of gastric acid maximally.

Despite the clinical success of Dragstedt and his physiologic arguments favoring vagotomy for peptic ulcer disease, his medical and surgical colleagues in general resisted his methods. Nonetheless, a number of pioneering surgeons dared to try his techniques on patients with difficult ulcers. Such surgeons as Grimson and Ruffin from Duke University, Walters from Rochester, Minnesota, and Moore from Massachusetts General Hospital performed about 200 vagotomies. Their findings were presented at the Central Surgical Association meeting in Chicago in February 1947.

Surgical Procedures for "Maximal" Acid Suppression

At least four procedures were proposed as necessary to optimise and maximise acid suppressive operations for peptic ulcer disease: 1) selective vagotomy; 2) partial fundectomy; 3) antrectomy; 4) Billroth I anastomosis.

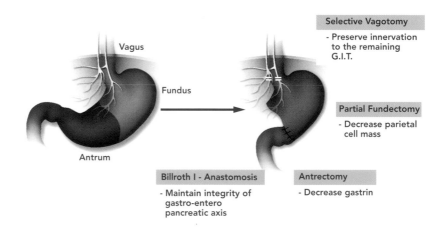

By this time, surgeons from the Mayo Clinic, a relatively conservative institution, had performed about 80 of these operations. They termed the Dragstedt procedure a "gastric neurectomy" and observed that *the results are inconstant, variable and in most cases unpredictable* (Waltman et al., 1947). The most serious complication they encountered was gastric stasis.

Their conclusions were in contrast with that of Francis Moore of Boston, who reported in the same volume of *Archives of Surgery*. Moore found an 87% success rate and claimed that the complication of gastrostasis was only temporary. But the surgeons from Duke disagreed. "*Complete satisfaction occurred more frequently among the patients with combined vagotomy and gastroenterostomy than among patients with vagotomy alone. Transthoracic vagotomy alone should not be used as a standard treatment of duodenal or gastric ulcer*" (Grimson et al., 1947). In the next year, clinical investigators from around the United States reported conflicting conclusions. Jackson from Ann Arbor detailed his abdominal approach to vagotomy and suggested that the operation was feasible for residents to perform.

Francis Moore reiterated this positive view and concluded that "*vague resection is not a cure for duodenal ulcer; it is a physiologic procedure which, by removing the majority of the parasympathetic nerves to the upper gastrointestinal tract renders the management of patients with duodenal ulcer a simple rather than a complicated problem*".

Thus, the practicing surgeons of 1948 had no definite recommendation from their peers in academia. In an attempt to establish a reasonable answer, the American Gastroenterological Association formed the National Committee on Peptic Ulcer in 1952. In a 200 page report, the committee concluded that gastro-enterostomy was the operation of choice for peptic ulcer disease and emphasized: "*It should not be concluded from this study that gastro-enterostomy plus vagotomy is superior to gastro-enterostomy alone*". Fortunately, not all surgeons were persuaded and the usefulness of vagotomy continued to be investigated.

Gradually, more favorable reports appeared. In 1952, Farmer and Smithwick from Boston University recommended that vagotomy be combined with hemi-gastrectomy for treatment of duodenal ulcer disease. They observed that more than 80% of the patients they treated who had this operation suffered no serious side effects and that 93% of these patients had a gastric pH of 3.5 or greater after acid stimulation with either broth or injection with insulin. Refinements in operative technique also yielded better results. By 1956, Weinberg and his colleagues from the Veterans Hospital in Long Beach, California, described an improved single layer pyloroplasty. The single layer method contrasted with the double layer closure of the Heinecke-Mikulicz procedure, which the authors contended could "*cause an infolding of the tissues which constricts the lumen and thus jeopardizes the patency of the canal*". They reported their results using a single layer pyloroplasty on more than 500 patients and found a 5% recurrence rate and a 5% rate of side effects. They attributed these fine results to the elimination of the retrograde movement of food seen with gastro-jejunal anastomoses.

Vagotomy, particularly of the truncal variety, often resulted in antral and pyloric motor dysfunction and gastric stasis. A wide variety of *drainage procedures* were developed to obviate this problem.

Gastric Drainage Procedures

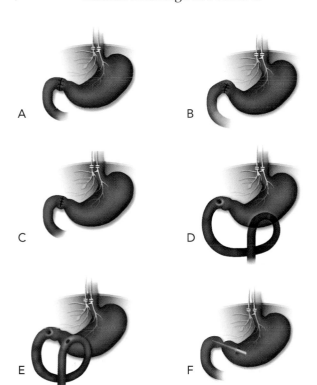

A. Heinecke-Mikulicz pyloroplasty, B. Finney pyloroplasty,
C. Excision pyloroplasty D. Posterior gastroenterostomy,
E. Anterior juxtapyloric gastroenterostomy,
F. Pyloric dilation by gastrotomy

The Surgical Evolution of Vagotomy

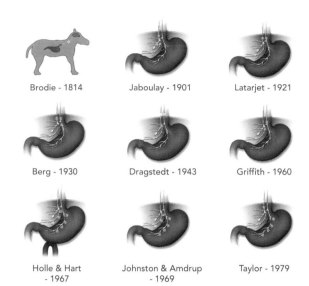

Brodie - 1814

Jaboulay - 1901

Latarjet - 1921

Berg - 1930

Dragstedt - 1943

Griffith - 1960

Holle & Hart - 1967

Johnston & Amdrup - 1969

Taylor - 1979

In an attempt to minimise the extent of vagal resection, numerous procedures designed to improve selectivity were devised. The objective was to only denervate the parietal cell mass without interfering with the innervation of the antrum, pylorus and extra gastric organs.

Nevertheless it was apparent that better methods of preventing gastric stasis were necessary to obviate the side effects of truncal vagotomy. Griffith and Harkins published the theoretic basis for a more selective vagotomy in 1957. They further defined the gastric vagal anatomy and performed a partial vagotomy in ten dogs. They incised the branches of the nerves of Latarjet, which were thought to "supply clusters of parietal cells". As a result, they concluded that the cephalic phase of gastric secretion was eliminated and these dogs experienced minimal to no gastric stasis. Even though they proposed that "*clinical application appears feasible*", ten years elapsed before the first selective vagotomy was performed upon a human.

Holle and Hart performed the first highly selective vagotomy in 1967. Their procedure was combined with a pyloroplasty. By 1969, it became apparent that a drainage procedure was unnecessary. The technique was further developed to selectively denervate the fundus whilst retaining antral innervation to facilitate gastric emptying. The term "parietal cell vagotomy" was utilized to describe operative procedure. Experience from Britain, Scandinavia and the United States demonstrated only 17 deaths after 5,539 highly successful vagotomies. These reports also documented decreased dumping, gastritis and duodenal reflux as compared with the more traditional operations. The ulcer recurrence rate after this operation was reported at about 5%, a result similar to that after truncal vagotomy and drainage. Subsequent authors, however, reported substantial increases in recurrence rates over time, even after the learning curve for this procedure had been overcome.

These observations and the technical tedium of the microvagal dissection led to the search for alternative procedures. Taylor of Edinburgh developed a lesser curve superficial seromyotomy. Initial results from 32 patients revealed no recurrence of ulcer with a short follow-up period. Subsequently, Lygidakis modified the technique of Taylor by performing a posterior truncal vagotomy combined with an anterior superficial seromyotomy. This modification left intact the anterior motor component of the nerve of Latarjet, all that was needed to ensure normal gastric motility. A further putative advantage of the superficial sero-myotomy was the fact that it was a far more rapid procedure than the relatively tedious highly selective vagotomy.

The therapeutic relevance of vagal section has for the most part been overshadowed by the utility of acid inhibitory agents. Indeed except in conditions of dire emergency, surgery vagotomy should no longer be considered as a means of inhibiting acid secretion.

CHAPTER 2
PEPTIC ULCER DISEASE

General

Although the incidence of peptic ulcer disease has steadily declined in the United States since the turn of the century, approximately 500,000 new cases and 4 million recurrences annually are reported. In 1990 it was estimated that the annual direct cost related to diagnosis and treatment of peptic ulcer disease in the United States were between 3 and 4 billion dollars as compared to the 2.5 million estimated in 1975.

Duodenal ulcer is the major lesion in Western populations, whereas gastric ulcers are more frequent in oriental countries, particularly Japan. Japanese-Americans develop duodenal ulcer showing that the frequency of gastric ulcers in Japan is due to environmental factors not genetic constitution.

Although less prevalent than duodenal ulcer, gastric ulcer (0.1% of the population in developed countries) has a higher associated mortality and a greater morbidity resulting from hemorrhage, perforation and obstruction. Frequent recurrence after healing has been a major component of the natural history of gastric ulcer and, without therapy, ulcers recur in 35 to 80% of the patients within 6 to 12 months of healing.

Causes of Duodenal Ulcer

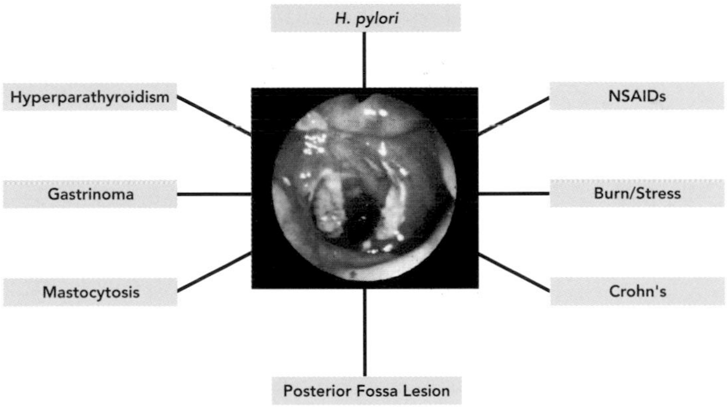

H. pylori

Hyperparathyroidism

NSAIDs

Gastrinoma

Burn/Stress

Mastocytosis

Crohn's

Posterior Fossa Lesion

Despite the fact that *H. pylori* was unrecognized until 1983, it has in the last decade become regarded as the most common cause (85-95%) of all duodenal ulcers.

The advent of *H. pylori* eradication and appropriate acid suppressive therapy in recent times has considerably narrowed the gap in therapeutic outcome between gastric and duodenal ulcer. The recognition that two of the major factors in defining gastric ulcer, namely *H. pylori* and NSAID's can be therapeutically addressed, is mostly responsible for this advance. Therapy, therefore, for gastric ulcers has exhibited a remarkable transition as proton pump inhibitor therapy combined with *H. pylori* eradication produced healing and recurrence rates quite similar to those obtained with duodenal ulceration. Similarly the recognition of NSAID involvement and the use of prophylaxis with acid suppressants or prostaglandins or withdrawal of the NSAID has further amplified healing rates. The introduction of curative therapy, whereby *H. pylori* may be eradicated has been a further significant advance in eliminating the cause of gastric ulceration. The important caveat is that in all patients with gastric ulceration an underlying neoplastic process should be considered and eliminated as a possibility. Multiple biopsies of the ulcer margin and rigorous histological evaluation are critical to ensure that there is no delay in identifying an ulcer of malignant origin. Indeed the failure of a gastric ulcer to heal in the face of a compliance with a curative regime (proton pump inhibitor therapy and *H. pylori* eradication) should be regarded as an alarm symptom or sign suggestive of gastric neoplasia.

In this context, the consideration of mucosal associated lymphoid tumors (MALT) should not be overlooked. Epidemiological studies have concluded that *H. pylori* infection is the major cause of gastric cancer worldwide. The infection increases the risk of gastric adenocarcinoma by 3 to 6 times probably by promoting the development of chronic atrophic gastritis. In addition, *H. pylori* increases the likelihood of the development of the primary non-Hodgkin's lymphoma MALT by approximately 6 fold. In the majority of circumstances, however, the eradication of *H. pylori* is associated with complete remission of this disease process.

The early introduction of appropriate therapeutic measures once a gastric ulcer has been diagnosed will likely lead to a cure rate in at least 90% of individuals. Ensuring that NSAID therapy is withdrawn and *H. pylori* are eradicated is mandatory in individuals who exhibit recurrence of ulceration. Under such circumstances, however, rigorous endoscopic re-assessment by biopsy for the presence of neoplasia should be undertaken. In those individuals who experience a complication such as hemorrhage, perforation, or obstruction, appropriate surgical intervention is necessary. Whilst bleeding gastric ulcers may be underrun with a suture, more often than not they are better managed by appropriate tailored surgical resection. Perforation, which in the past used to mandate resection for management, is currently more often managed by repair of the defect followed by appropriate acid suppressive and *H. pylori* eradication therapy. In some circumstances anatomic considerations may mandate resection, particularly in ulcers close to the G-E junction on the lesser curve.

Chronic gastric obstruction usually in the juxta-pyloric region usually mandates gastric resection with establishment of a Billroth II anastomosis. Overall, however, the picture of gastric ulcer disease as a difficult problem with a high level of complications often necessitating surgical intervention has declined significantly and has more and more begun to resemble duodenal ulcer as a pathological process amenable to conservative medical therapy except in complicated circumstances.

Meta-analysis for predicting the degree of acid inhibition (elevation of pH for a given period of the day) showed that a mean intra-gastric pH of 3.0 for 18 hr per day provided an optimal healing for duodenal ulcer, indicating that the duodenum was able to handle a significant pH load, due to its ability to secrete HCO_3^-. Results of meta-analysis to predict healing of gastric ulcers as a function of pH have not been published. Still, current PPI therapy requires longer administration for healing of gastric as compared to duodenal ulcers, presumably because there is still wall acidity in the stomach impeding healing.

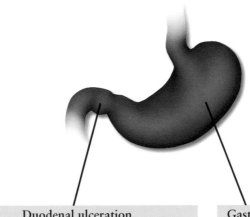

Atypical Causes of Ulceration

Duodenal ulceration		Gastric ulceration
Non HP DU	Penetrating pancreatic cancer	Foreign body
Zollinger-Ellison syndrome	Systemic mastocytosis	Diabetes
Crohn's disease	Amyloidosis Type IV	Crohn's
Coeliac disease	Renal failure	Lymphoma
Ulcerative jejunitis	Stiff skin syndrome	Adenocarcinoma
Lymphoma	Pachydermoperiostosis	Carcinoid
Hypercalcaemia	Cirrhosis	Penetrating neoplasm
Gastrospirillium hominis	Polycythaemia rubra vera	Sarcoma
Duodenal carcinoma	HIV	Leiomyoma
		HIV

Pathogenesis

In the past considerable attention had been directed at the role of acid in the generation of damage to the mucosa. Innumerable studies have correlated levels of acid secretion with ulceration. Pepsin had been noted as a co-factor in such pathology but its precise role in the pathogenesis had been largely ignored in favor of a pre-occupation with neutralizing or inhibiting acid secretion. Confounding factors such as cigarette smoking, alcohol ingestion and spicy foods had been identified, but their precise involvement in mucosal damage remains controversial. The biology of the mucosa itself was not well understood. Cytoprotection had been proposed as a generic entity embracing the concept of gastric mucosal defensive mechanisms. In broad terms, these were regarded as pre-epithelial, epithelial, and sub-epithelial. Each level was proposed to exhibit specialized properties which allowed the gastric epithelium to protect itself against the many noxious agents it was exposed to. A further philosophic entity entitled the mucosal barrier was conceived and variously considered to embrace the mucous bicarbonate barrier, specialized apical ion transport systems and tight junctions which provided an anatomic barrier for acid and pepsin diffusion.

The pathogenesis of peptic ulcer may best be viewed as representing a complex scenario involving an imbalance between defensive and aggressive factors of which the most notable now appears to be *Helicobactor pylori*. Whilst mucosal restitution and the re-establishment of epithelial cell continuity independent of cell proliferation is an important issue closely linked to the expression growth factors and mucosal integrity. The elucidation of its precise role still remains to be defined. Nevertheless mucosal integrity as constituted by a variety of mucosal defense mechanisms is an important issue and will be dealt with separately in the chapter on the gastric mucosal barrier.

Although the subject of *Helicobacter pylori* is separately dealt with further on, in section 7, it is worthy of brief comment at this point in the context of noxious agents effecting the gastric mucosa. Its identification in 90 to 95% of patients with duodenal ulcer and 60 to 80% of patients with gastric ulcer as compared to 25 to 30% incidences in symptomatic control subjects confirms its relevance in the genesis of mucosal ulceration. The prevalence of infection increases with age and infection is more common in those with deprived socioeconomic circumstances. It is apparent that in some countries infection is not always involved with peptic ulceration. Such observations have raised the issue as to whether all types of *H. pylori* are of equal pathogenicity. Nevertheless given the fact that lifetime prevalence for duodenal ulcer is approximately 10% for men and 5% for women, the importance of *H. pylori* as a component of the disease process is substantial. The recognition that there exists a critical association between gastric metaplasia in the duodenal cap and *H. pylori* which appears to confer a predisposition to ulcer disease has been clearly identified. Similarly, strong evidence has accumulated to demonstrate an association between the eradication of *H. pylori* infection and the cure of peptic ulcer disease.

The production of NH_3 by the urease of the organism may also explain part of the role of *H. pylori* in generation of duodenal ulcer. It has been established that the majority of the urease activity of the organism is internal and acid activated. Activity reaches maximum at pH 6.0 and remains steady until pH 2.5. The toxicity of the NH_4^+ depends on entry of NH_3 with consequent increase of intracellular pH and release of calcium from stores in the endoplasmic reticulum and mitochondria. At gastric pH the ratio of NH_3/NH_4^+ is low, but when at the neutral pH of the duodenum, the ratio rapidly rises providing more NH_3 for entry into duodenal cells. Thus the load of NH_3 to the duodenal cell may be a contributing factor to the generation of duodenal ulcers. This is discussed in more detail in the section on *H. pylori*.

pH and disease

There is considerable overlap between 24-hour intragastric pH measurements in normal individuals and in those with duodenal ulcer. Nevertheless there appears to be greater gastric acid secretion in duodenal ulcer patients than normals particularly at night. Overall, however, the 24-hour pH profile is not predictive of the duodenal ulcer in an individual patient. The suppression of nocturnal acid secretion by H2 receptor antagonists proved effective in down regulating increased nocturnal acid secretion but is not essential to promote healing of a duodenal ulcer. Other factors particularly duodenal bicarbonate secretion have been proposed to be implicated in the genesis of duodenal ulceration. For the most part, however, duodenal mucosal bicarbonate effects on luminal pH in the duodenal bulb may only be minor since the overall secretory rate is in the range of one mmol/hr. Given the intermittent release of gastric chyme into the duodenum a steep pH gradient exists between the terminal part of the pyloric antrum and the first part of the duodenum. When gastric pH values are below 4, the correlation between duodenal and gastric pH is linear but this relationship disappears when the gastric pH is above 4 and it is not possible to predict

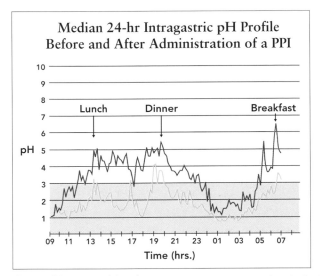

Median 24-hr Intragastric pH Profile Before and After Administration of a PPI

The critical therapeutic ability of the PPI's to increase intragastric pH above 3 for a considerable percentage of a 24-hr. period is translated into a significant increase in ulcer healing for this class of drug.

intraduodenal pH from intragastric pH during anti-secretory therapy. Nevertheless a series of meta-analytic evaluations of clinical trials which evaluated duodenal ulcer healing and pharmaco-dynamic studies of anti-secretory drugs and acid suppression have revealed healing rates for duodenal ulcer to correlate with the suppression of gastric secretion. An evaluation of the pH profiles of individuals with ulcers in whom acid suppressive therapy induced healing revealed three critical determinates predictive of duodenal ulcer healing. These were the degree of acid suppression; the duration of acid suppression within a 24-hour period; and the length of treatment. Thus the healing rates for duodenal ulcer were demonstrated to be highly correlatable with the degree of acid suppression and a daily intragastric pH of 3 for greater than 18 to 20 hours provided conditions that would achieve maximal healing rates for duodenal ulcers at four weeks. It was of interest that increasing acid suppression to intragastric pH greater than 3 did not significantly improve healing. However, increasing the total duration of acid suppression by either lengthening treatment or during the individual 24-hour period itself resulted in higher healing rates. It was also evident that the therapeutic effect of H2 receptor antagonists reflected their ability to suppress nocturnal acidity better than daytime acidity.

Diagnosis

The widespread recognition of symptomatology involving epigastric discomfort related to the ingestion of food and broadly grouped under the nomenclature of dyspepsia is well accepted as synonymous with evidence of acid peptic disease. Although considerable emphasis has in the past been placed upon precise delineation of the symptomatology to determine whether the site of the ulceration is gastric or duodenal, currently the identification of dyspepsia rapidly leads to upper GI endoscopy and the determination of the precise location of the lesion. Of particularly relevance in the history should be the determination of alarm symptoms or signs such as weight loss, vomiting, the development of back pain, or failure to relieve symptomatology with acid inhibitory therapy. Broadly speaking, the presence of such features would suggest the development of either a complicated ulcer (bleeding, penetration, perforation, stenosis, or neoplasia) or that the ulcer may be due to other causes such as aspirin, NSAID's intake, or a gastrinoma. These entities will be discussed separately in further detail.

The establishment of the diagnosis of acid peptic disease requires not only the identification and characterization of the site of the lesion but the determination of the presence of H. pylori. This can be undertaken by a number of techniques, including: histological staining, urease identification in the biopsy material, serology or breath or stool testing. The sensitivity and specificity of such tests are important criteria, although costs will probably be the dominant issue in determining how the organism should be identified.

Medical management

Duodenal ulcer

Ulcer healing and acid suppression

There is a direct correlation between the healing rate of duodenal ulcers and the degree of suppression of 24-hour intragastric acidity associated with the use of anti-secretory agents. Hunt and his colleagues were the first to point out that a primary determinant of duodenal ulcer healing is represented by the fraction of the day for which intragastric pH is maintained above 3 as well as the duration of treatment itself. Using meta analysis, they predicted that all duodenal ulcers could be healed within four weeks if intragastric pH were to be maintained above 3.0 for between 18 to 20 hours per day. In this respect the PPI class of drugs have proved to be superior since they inactivate the H,K ATPase enzyme and produce inhibition of both peripherally and centrally mediated gastric acid secretion. On the contrary the histamine 2-receptor antagonists act via competitive antagonism at the histamine 2 receptor on the baso-lateral membrane of the parietal cell to inhibit histamine mediated acid secretion. Such agents are therefore somewhat less effective in controlling food stimulated gastric acid secretion since cholinergic mediated stimulation is not inhibited. Almost every clinical trial has demonstrated the superiority of PPI's over H2 receptor antagonists in the treatment of both gastric and duodenal ulceration. PPI's thus produce healing in a greater proportion of ulcers than H2 receptor antagonists as well as faster healing and more rapid relief of symptoms. Apart from the personal advantages to the patient of the more rapid amelioration of the disease process both the duration and cost of medical therapy can thus be decreased. A number of comparative studies have demonstrated that omeprazole heals duodenal ulcers faster and more effectively than H2 receptor antagonists. Similarly, other studies have demonstrated that pantoprazole (40 mg daily) produces significantly higher rates of duodenal ulcer healing than ranitidine when compared at both two and four weeks. In a separate series of studies lansoprazole (30 mg daily) produced more rapid and effective healing of duodenal ulcers than 300 mg of ranitidine administered at night. Other data have demonstrated that omeprazole (20 mg daily) resulted in significantly less daytime pain than experienced by patients receiving 300 mg of ranitidine at bedtime. Studies comparing pantoprazole (40 mg daily) with ranitidine (300 mg daily) demonstrated that improvement of pain relief after two weeks was greater in patients receiving pantoprazole than in those receiving ranitidine. Similarly, lansoprazole has been shown to decrease ulcer pain more effectively than raniti-

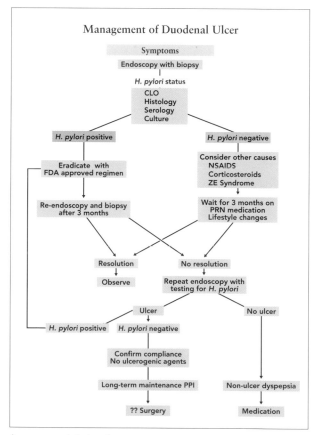

A management strategy for duodenal ulcer disease.

dine with a significantly greater percentage of patients free of symptoms after two weeks using the proton pump inhibitor as opposed to the histamine 2-receptor antagonist.

Comparable observations for the utility of acid suppression in gastric ulcer patients have been found. Omeprazole (20 mg daily) produced consistently higher rates of healing than H2 receptor antagonists. Pantoprazole (40 mg daily) resulted in significantly higher healing rates of gastric ulcers than ranitidine (300 mg daily) at both four and eight weeks. Lansoprazole (30 mg daily) healed significantly more ulcers than famotidine (20 mg twice daily). In addition, pantoprazole, omeprazole and lansoprazole produced more rapid relief of symptoms in patients with gastric ulceration than H2 receptor antagonists. In those individuals with peptic ulcers refractory to long-term treatment with H2 receptor antagonists, a number of clinical trials have demonstrated that pantoprazole, lansoprazole, and omeprazole are capable of generating effective healing.

H. pylori eradication

Upon determination of clinical symptomatology consistent with a putative diagnosis of peptic ulcer disease the site and nature of the lesion should be identified. Thus at endoscopy the presence and site of the ulcer as well as the presence or absence of H. pylori should be determined and documented. The diagnosis of H. pylori can be undertaken by the use of non-invasive or invasive tests. Invasive methodology involves endoscopy with gastric mucosal biopsy and either histology culture or rapid urease testing. The rapid urease test is probably the most useful in routine practice since, in addition to being highly sensitive (85-95%) and specific (98%), it is easy to perform, relatively cheap, and provides a rapid result. Although the histological demonstration of the organism has a high sensitivity (85-90%) and specificity (93-100%), its routine use is limited by its high cost.

Culture of the organism is probably the ideal diagnostic technique but is difficult and has a high failure rate compared to other diagnostic strategies. It is probably, however, that in the future H. pylori culture may be of considerable use in checking bacterial sensitivity particularly in individuals where eradication has failed or macrolide antibiotics or nitro-imidazoles are under consideration as future therapy.

The non-invasive methodologies available for the diagnosis of H. pylori include radio labelled urea breath tests and enzyme linked immunosorbent serological assays (ELISAs).

The drawbacks of the serological studies are related to the relative lack of sensitivity, although, they are easy to perform and relatively cheap. A particular problem is the fact that serological tests are not useful in monitoring the success of eradication therapy since IgG and IgA titers may only drop by 20 to 50% within the month of the cessation of therapy. The currently available labelled urea breath tests are the non-radioactive ^{13}C test and the radioactive ^{14}C test. Current studies suggest that both are equally specific (99%) and sensitive (90-98%). The ^{14}C test is less costly and has recently met with FDA approval. The ^{13}C test is expensive and the equipment expensive and not widely available.

In the presence of peptic ulcer disease it is important to identify the presence of *H. pylori* prior to the institution of therapy in order that eradication of the organism can be confirmed four to six weeks after treatment. In this respect, successful eradication can be documented in duodenal ulcer patients by use of the non-invasive urea breath test. In individuals with gastric ulceration, endoscopy is necessary not only to confirm adequate healing but also to ensure that any neoplasia has been identified.

Under these circumstances a biopsy sample should be utilized to test for *H. pylori* preferably by means of the rapid urease test. It is important that at least two biopsy samples be evaluated (fundic and antral) since if eradication therapy has not been completely successful the organism may be present only in small numbers and may have migrated (a consequence of acid suppressive therapy and the alteration of its ideal pH milieu) from its original site. In those patients who exhibit relapse or recurrence of symptomatology the presence of *H. pylori* should be meticulously assessed.

Bismuth-based anti-microbial therapy

H. pylori has been demonstrated to be sensitive to a wide variety of anti-microbial agents including macrolides, beta lactams, ketoconazoles, tetracyclines, gentamycin, rifampicin, nitrofuran, and some quinolones. Nevertheless the use of any of these agents alone (monotherapy) has generally proved to render sub-optimal results, with eradication rates of approximately 20%. Clarithromycin, a macrolide antibiotic, is more acid stable than its counterpart, erythromycin and is well tolerated, more effective, and has an eradication rate alone of greater than 50%. It is however clearly apparent that the use of more than one antibiotic has resulted in improved cure rates. The most commonly administered combinations include the classic bismuth triple therapy of bismuth, subsalicylate, or subcitrate and metronidazole in combination with amoxicillin or tetracycline (standard bismuth triple therapy). The use of this classic triple therapy mode has limitations.

Evaluation of the two different combinations has demonstrated that triple therapy incorporating amoxicillin is significantly less effective than triple therapy that includes tetracycline since amoxicillin is significantly less effective in eradicating *H. pylori*. A further important clinical issue is the relatively high rate of pre-treatment resistance to metronidazole in some parts of the world. Patients taking less than 60% of their prescribed medication fail to achieve eradication rates greater than 70%. Alternatively if greater than 60% of the prescribed medications are taken, eradication rates up to 95% may be expected. Since the bismuth triple therapy regime requires the ingestion of up to 18

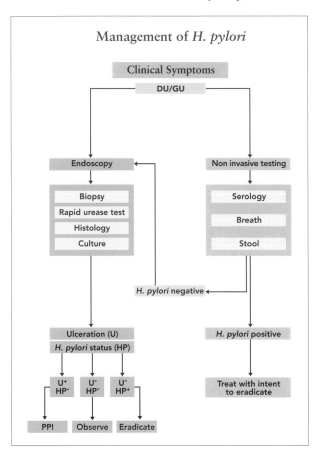

A management strategy for *H. pylori* related acid peptic disease.

tablets daily, such compliance may become a serious issue. Adverse events may be predicted in between 25 and 30% of patients.

Eradication and acid suppressive combination therapy with PPI's

Since gastric acidity is an important component in the genesis of peptic ulcer disease, anti-secretory therapy is of critical relevance in disease management. Thus combinations of anti-secretory agents with antibiotics such as clarithromycin, tetracycline, amoxicillin, and metronidazole are of considerable utility. Given the fact that proton pump inhibitors are more efficacious than other classes of acid suppressing agents in the management of peptic ulcer disease as well as achieving more rapid symptom relief and ulcer healing, their combination with a variety of antibiotics has proved to be of considerable benefit. The rationale for these use is discussed in the section on *H. pylori*.

A number of studies have unequivocally demonstrated that anti-secretory/antibiotic drug combinations including a proton pump inhibitor rather than H2 receptor antagonist provide better eradication of *H. pylori*. Furthermore, the combination of a proton pump inhibitor and one or two antibiotic agent achieves *H. pylori* eradication rates indistinguishable to those found using bismuth triple therapy. Such studies have also noted an acceleration in rapid ulcer healing, less anti-microbial resistance, higher patient compliance and fewer adverse effects compared to those identified in patients utilizing bismuth triple therapy.

Thus combinations of various proton pump inhibitors such as pantoprazole, lansoprazole or omeprazole utilized with either clarithromycin and metronidazole, and/or amoxicillin have all been reported to produce eradication rates and ulcer healing in excess of 90% and as high as 96%. An issue is the duration of therapy. It seems that seven days of b.i.d. combination therapy is required for effective eradication. Continued therapy with the PPI for 4 weeks is still suggested for ulcer healing, but some studies indicate that eradication is sufficient for ulcer healing without the need for acid suppression. However, it is necessary to show a negative breath test within 1 week of therapy to enable this strategy.

Summated information from a large number of studies indicates that the optimal management strategies for either gastric or duodenal ulceration are the use of a PPI and two antibacterial agents. Under such circumstances, eradication rates at about 90% have been reported by a large number of investigators in many different countries.

In those patients whom prior eradication therapy has been unsuccessful or in individuals who exhibit anti-microbial resistance quadruple therapy may be contemplated. Specific diagnosis of clarithromycin resistance can be done by sequencing the specific region of the 23S RNA where a point mutation results in prevention of binding.

Diagnosis of metronidazole resistance requires *in vitro* culture. Under such circumstances, a PPI along with a standard classical triple therapy regime such as colloidal bismuth subcitrate or bismuth subsalicylate with a nitro-imidazole and either tetracycline or amoxicillin may be considered.

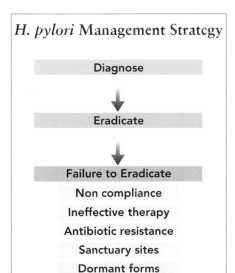

H. pylori Management Strategy

Diagnose

Eradicate

Failure to Eradicate
Non compliance
Ineffective therapy
Antibiotic resistance
Sanctuary sites
Dormant forms

Eradication and acid suppressive combination therapy with RBC

A newer combination of ranitidine and bismuth subcitrate with two antibiotics has also been introduced and approved for eradication. It is claimed that this form of bismuth is more soluble and more available for bactericidal action. However, significant blood levels of bismuth have been detected in some patients and this cation is neurotoxic and nephrotoxic. Most of the data reported have not used intention-to-treat criteria and the general impression is that eradication is less effective. Another issue is that after eradication therapy treatment with ranitidine is continued for the routine period of 8 weeks, rather than the 4 weeks for a PPI.

The treatment paradigm that is most frequently used is triple therapy with PPI's in combination with amoxicillin and clarithromycin. Usually this is b.i.d. treatment with omeprazole/lansoprazole/pantoprazole at standard dose with 1 gm amoxicillin and 500 mg clarithromycin taken simultaneously which in trials have given 90% eradication. Metronidazole may be used in substitution for either antibiotic.

Treatment failure

Although there are a number of reasons for an ulcer to recur, including failure of compliance, inadequate acid suppression, and gastrinoma, by far the most common is the failure to eradicate *H. pylori*. Thus 70% of patients who remain *H. pylori* positive after eradication therapy were reported to have developed ulcer recurrence within one year as compared to only 3% in those whom the organism had been eradicated. Conversely, studies that have examined one-year ulcer recurrence rates in patients in whom *H. pylori* had been successfully eradicated noted a 1.1% rate as compared to a 67.9% rate prior to the introduction of eradication therapy. In this context, studies using a proton pump inhibitor with antibiotic regimes produced similar results whereas monotherapy with a PPI alone is associated with *H. pylori* eradication rates of only 0 to 10%. Although it has been suggested the failure to eradicate may actually represent re-infection, studies that have evaluated this possibility indicate that the true rate of re-infection in developed countries is probably less than 1-2%. The percentage may be higher in developing countries but recurrence of *H. pylori* infection within one year on balance probably represents recrudescence of an original infection that was suppressed rather than eradicated and is less likely to represent a true re-infection.

Nevertheless, there does appear to be a group of patients in whom ulcers recur even after successful eradication of *H. pylori*. In such instances, once other causes of therapeutic failure (non-compliance, salicylate abuse, NSAIDS, gastrinoma) have been eliminated, maintenance anti-secretory therapy should be considered. Long-term anti-secretory agents should thus be reserved for individuals in whom at least two attempts at *H. pylori* eradication have failed or those who have *H. pylori* negative peptic disease and possibly in individuals with complicated ulcers particularly those prone to recurrent bleeding.

Whereas surgery had previously been the mainstay of the management of chronic peptic ulceration and particularly its complications, the advent of H2 receptor antagonists and more recently proton pump inhibitors has virtually abolished elective surgery in the consideration of the management of peptic ulcer disease. Nevertheless, in a small group of patients with chronic or recurrent peptic ulcer disease, surgery may eventually become a consideration. Rarely a patient with a chronic gastric ulcer, which is unresponsive to therapy, may be identified as a covert presentation of a gastric neoplasm. More usually, however, surgery becomes a consideration with the evolution of a chronic peptic ulcer into an acute complication of which bleeding, perforation, and stenosis are the usual events. Thus, for practical purposes apart from the issue of gastrinoma surgery of peptic ulcer disease may be considered primarily as a strategy in the management of complications.

Gastric ulcer

Although previously gastric ulcer had posed a pernicious problem in terms of healing, the identification of *H. pylori* and its role in this disease process has greatly facilitated cure. Although gastric ulcer patients have overall exhibited lower levels of gastric acid secretion than healthy controls healing is reflective of similar critical determinates as identified in duodenal ulcer patients. In the gastric ulcer patients, it is more likely that *H. pylori* infection is present, their older age and defects in mucosal defense factors function in combination to render the disease more difficult to cure. Also the intramural presence of acid and pepsin in higher quantities than in the duodenum may play a role. In meta-analytic studies of gastric ulcer healing the duration of treatment appeared to be the most important single determinate in predicting healing. All treatments show an increase in healing rates from 2 to 4 and from 4 to 8 weeks of treatment. Nevertheless the degree of acid suppression is also important since the greater suppression of 24-hour intragastric acidity produces the highest healing rates. Of relevance is the fact that suppression of 24-hour acidity appears to be more important than suppression of either nighttime or daytime acidity. Thus maintenance of the gastric pH above 3 for 18 hours daily predicts healing in approximately 100% of gastric ulcers by 8 weeks. Whereas, a similar degree of acid suppression might be predicted to heal 100% of duodenal ulcers in 4 weeks. Clearly such data can only be attained with concomitant eradication of *H. pylori*, if present.

At this time there is little doubt that eradication of *H. pylori* is mandatory to ensure successful treatment of gastric and duodenal ulceration. Acid suppression therapy alone is associated with relatively high levels of recurrence. Thus the combination of bacterial eradication, and elevation of pH appears to provide the optimal treat-

A management strategy for gastric ulcer.

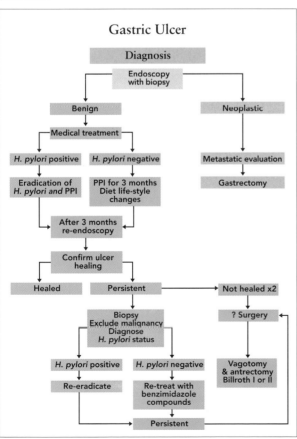

ment not only for ensuring ulcer cure, but abrogating the likelihood of the development of complications such as bleeding. The therapeutic regimes available for management of uncomplicated gastric and duodenal ulceration can be evaluated under the headings of anti-microbial therapy, acid suppressive therapy, and a combination of both entities. For practical purposes the surgery of uncomplicated duodenal and gastric ulceration may be regarded as unwarranted except in instances of perforation, failed conservative management of bleeding, gastric outlet obstruction, and the development of neoplasia. In those patients in whom peptic ulceration may be due to a gastrinoma, surgery directed at removal of the neoplasm and/or its metastases should be considered.

NSAID – Mucosal ulcers

As early as 1875 reports of "dyspeptic indigestion" followed the introduction of sodium salicylate for the management of patients with dramatic disease. This class of drugs achieved widespread usage and the further development of acetyl salicylic acid (aspirin) amplified the problem. The more recent introduction and widespread use of non-steroidal anti-inflammatory drugs (NSAIDS) has been associated with significant morbidity and mortality given their association with gastro-duodenal ulceration. Despite the fact that NSAID's are extremely valuable and effective drugs for the treatment of musculo-skeletal and arthritic disorders, they exhibit a common association with acute and chronic gastro-duodenal injury. It has been calculated that the relative risk of upper GI bleeding and ulcer perforation in individuals using non-aspirin NSAID's increases approximately three-fold and six-fold respectively. In such situations the patient and the physician find themselves in a dilemma since the utility of treatment with NSAID's may nevertheless outweigh the possible adverse effects of potential damage to the mucosa and the consequent ulcer related complications. It is of interest that many patients who develop peptic ulceration on NSAID therapy are asymptomatic and under such circumstances both patient and physician may be unaware of the existence of any lesions until the advent of bleeding or perforation. Nevertheless most individuals receiving NSAID's therapy exhibit endoscopic evidence of gastric erosions of which the majority are gastric as compared to duodenal (2:1 ratio). In rheumatology patients receiving NSAID's between 11 and 22 percent have ulcers although many may be minute and only evident on rigorous endoscopic scrutiny.

NSAID -Ulcers	
Occur in 10-20% of users	
May unmask Silent Peptic Ulcer Disease	
Usually gastric (2:1)	
Presenting symptoms	- Dyspepsia - Bleeding - Occasionally perforated
Aetiology - prostaglandin related	
Treatment	- Withdraw agent - Mysoprostil (side effects) - PPI/H$_2$RA

An outline of information relevant to the diagnosis and management of NSAID ulcers.

Etiology

A number of putative mechanisms have been proposed to explain the relationship of NSAID's and mucosal ulceration. The inhibition of the constitutive cyclo-oxygenase I isoform (Cox I) and the consequent failure to produce endogenous eicosanoids that protect the mucosa is the most widely accepted mechanism at this time. Other factors that have been implicated include associations with bile reflux and a potential direct damaging effect on the mucosa. The latter possibility is not widely accepted and although there is substantial evidence that aspirin exerts a direct effect on the mucosa as well as inhibiting cyclo-oxygenase it is felt that NSAID's do not cause direct topical injury.

Of interest is the fact that depletion of circulating neutrophils in animal models has been shown to decrease the severity of NSAID's induced injury. The question of whether *H. pylori* infection plays a part in the development of NSAID ulceration has been studied in considerable detail. The current body of opinion supports a conclusion that *H. pylori* infection and NSAID use are independent and not synergistic risk factors for gastric ulceration. Thus the prevalence of *H. pylori* infection in NSAID users and non-users with gastric ulceration is similar and NSAID use does not predispose to *H. pylori* infection. Evidence does exist to support the fact that NSAID's have a potentially additive effect in promoting ulcer bleeding, possibly because of their anti-platelet effect but there is insufficient data to support an added role for *H. pylori* in NSAID induced ulceration. Patients at a high risk of developing NSAID ulcers require NSAID ulcer prophylaxis regardless of *H. pylori* status. It is not known whether individuals treated in the past for *H. pylori* gastric ulcers are at an increased risk for ulcers if they receive NSAID's. It would however seem prudent to accept that NSAID ulcer prophylaxis is required in ulcer patients in whom *H. pylori* was successfully treated in the past if the patient requires NSAID therapy.

Risk factors for mucosal damage

The relative risk of developing mucosal damage on NSAID therapy is increased approximately four-fold. A further important factor is the duration of NSAID therapy. Paradoxically, an inverse relationship between the relative risk of complications and the duration of NSAID therapy exists. Thus the risk of bleeding decreases by one-third when the duration of NSAID therapy is extended from 30 days to 90 days. The phenomenon of adaptation has been proposed as an explanation for this surprising observation. It is however, evident that the risk of an NSAID associated ulcer complication is higher in the first weeks of therapy, thus individuals who are less susceptible to the drugs exhibit less problems as therapy persists. An alternative explanation is the fact that NSAID therapy may actually unmask a pre-existing silent ulcer that then exhibits an acute complication early in therapy or on initiation thereof. An alternative explanation is that individuals who are particularly sensitive to NSAID ulcers may be progressively removed from the population taking NSAID's by a process of elimination and that long-term therapy essentially selects out patients not susceptible to the adverse pharmacological effects of NSAID's. Overall, however the potential seriousness of this widely used drug should not be underestimated. A summation of large studies of NSAID treated patients suggests not only an annual 2% rate of ulcer complications but an increased ulcer mortality of three to ten-fold in individuals undergoing NSAID therapy.

Newer classes of NSAID's are being developed which inhibit the inducible form of cyclo-oxygenase, Cox II, that appear to have a lesser predilection for gastric damage and when introduced may render NSAID related gastric ulcers obsolete.

Treatment

Since the likelihood of an NSAID related complication is high, the consideration of ulcer prophylaxis should be regarded as an important component of therapy. An idiosyncratic sensitivity to a particular NSAID may be evaluated by altering the medication since some drugs have been suggested to be associated with more gastro-duodenal problems than others.

Ulcer prophylaxis is particularly relevant in the presence of the risk factors that have been identified for NSAID induced ulceration. These include: patients over the age of 65, a past history of peptic ulceration, simultaneous use of corticosteroids and previous problems during the administration of NSAID's. Individuals who fall into any of the above categories should be considered for prophylactic therapy. Given the efficacy and safety profile of the PPI's, it is clear that these should be the prophylactic drugs of choice. Other less attractive alternatives however are offered.

The use of 200 mg misoprostol, 4 times daily for 3 months, provides significant protection against gastric and duodenal ulceration in patients taking NSAID's. The levels of protection under such circumstances range from between 75% - 90% and the frequency of significant gastrointestinal complications is reduced by 40%. The widespread use of misoprostol, however, is somewhat limited by its tendency to cause diarrhea and abdominal pain in a significant proportion of patients. Such side effects however need to be weighed against the consequences of a complication of mucosal ulceration. Ranitidine therapy has also been demonstrated to be effective in healing NSAID induced ulcers and is particularly effective if the NSAID is withdrawn.

Proton pump inhibitors have been demonstrated to be of superior efficacy in the management of NSAID induced ulceration in several well controlled clinical trials. The dose of the PPI and time of administration should be tailored to the NSAID protocol employed by a particular patient for optimal prophylaxis.

The issue of whether prophylaxis should be routinely used or not in the management of patients taking NSAID's raises the question of cost-effectiveness. It seems likely that in the presence of one or more risk factors (advanced age, previous peptic ulceration, and concomitant steroid administration) prophylaxis is warranted given the adverse economic and clinical impact of an NSAID induced ulcer complication.

Complications of peptic ulcer disease

The complications of acid peptic disease usually represent the sequelae of long standing or chronic ulceration. Occasionally such events may occur in an acute setting but in such circumstances the acute presentation often represents administration of a drug such as an NSAID, aspirin, alcohol or the exposure to the stress of trauma or major surgery. For the most part bleeding and perforation are the most dramatic and the commonest with penetration and obstruction being less frequent and far less acute in their presentation.

Bleeding

Although there exists no good evidence to support the contention that bleeding ulcers are any different to non-bleeding ulcers, a different management

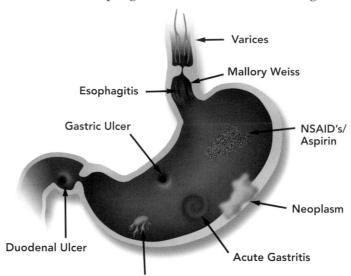

Causes of Esophago-Gastro-Duodenal Bleeding

Varices

Mallory Weiss

Esophagitis

NSAID's/
Aspirin

Gastric Ulcer

Neoplasm

Duodenal Ulcer

Acute Gastritis

Arterio-Venous
Malformation

Although a wide variety of causes for bleeding are recognized, the majority can be identified at endoscopy and the specific therapeutic regime instituted.

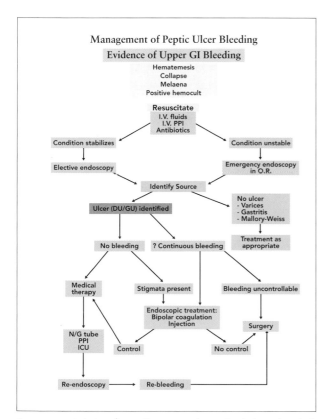

Management of Peptic Ulcer Bleeding

Evidence of Upper GI Bleeding

Hematemesis
Collapse
Melaena
Positive hemocult

Resuscitate
I.V. fluids
I.V. PPI
Antibiotics

Condition stabilizes — Condition unstable

Elective endoscopy — Emergency endoscopy in O.R.

Identify Source

Ulcer (DU/GU) identified — No ulcer - Varices - Gastritis - Mallory-Weiss

No bleeding — ? Continuous bleeding — Treatment as appropriate

Medical therapy — Stigmata present — Bleeding uncontrollable

Endoscopic treatment: Bipolar coagulation Injection — Surgery

N/G tube PPI ICU — Control — No control

Re-endoscopy — Re-bleeding

A management strategy for peptic ulcer associated bleeding.

strategy is required for this complication. Although bleeding is a relatively common complication of peptic ulcer disease, in 70-80% of patients once appropriate resuscitation has been instituted cessation is spontaneous and no further specific intervention is required. A smaller group of such patients, however, exhibit severe persistent or recurrent bleeding and in such instances a mortality of between 6 and 10% may be predicted. Factors which adversely effect survival include active bleeding or the identification of a visible vensulate endoscopy, age over 65 years, re-bleeding in hospital, and major intercurrent medical problems including cardiac and renal disease.

Initial strategies for the management of bleeding were mostly conservative and involved saline lavage and peri-ulcer injection of vasoconstrictors or sclerosants. More sophisticated methodology is now available. Thus in most endoscopy units the use of bi-polar coagulation, laser therapy, or application of topical homeostatic agents or glue is available. The considerable success of such methodology has led to a significant decline in the need for open surgical intervention. In circumstances where surgery may be necessary, but the patient's condition mitigate against general anesthesia and abdominal exploration, selective immobilization may be an option. Failure to specifically obliterate the appropriate arterial vessel in the stomach or duodenum however may result in severe sequelae particularly in the duodenum where mural infraction or pancreatitis may supervene.

In the event of endoscopic strategies failing to halt the bleeding, surgery should be rapidly directed at identifying the bleeding vessels that should then be under run and over-sewn. In the past ligation of the bleeding vessel was usually followed by a vagotomy and pyloroplasty. More recently the recognition that adequate acid suppression and eradication of *H. pylori* will obviate recurrent bleeding has led to a diminution of the necessity to undertake surgical procedures associated with a decrease in acid secretion.

The availability and use of intravenous H2 receptor antagonist or PPI therapy has thus to a large extent obviated the need for emergency gastrectomy and similarly decreased the incidence of recurrent bleeding from either the ulcer site or anastomotic margins.

In patients whose duodenal ulcers have healed after severe hemorrhage without surgical intervention, long-term maintenance therapy with ranitidine (150 mg at night) has been reported to significantly reduce the risk of recurrent bleeding. In a similar fashion it has been noted that the eradication of *H. pylori* infection by changing the natural history of peptic ulcer disease has been effective in the prevention of recurrent bleeding in patients who initially present with bleeding.

Thus in one study of patients in whom *H. pylori* infection had persisted a regime of amoxicillin plus omeprazole which cured the *H. pylori* infection in 60% of the patients reduced the rate of ulcer recurrence from 50 to 3.8% and the rate of recurrent bleeding from 33 to 0%.

Pharmacological therapies evaluating the ability of acid suppression to prevent acute ulcer bleeding have met with limited success. On an intuitive basis one might presume that increasing gastric luminal pH by the inhibition of acid secretion would decrease activation of pepsinogen, prevent fibrinolysis, and support the function of homeostatic mechanisms. Unfortunately, H2 receptor antagonists produce only a relatively modest increase of intragastric pH and thus studies of their utility have failed to document a decrease in the rate of re-bleeding, surgical intervention, or mortality. Surprisingly, a study which utilized intravenous famotidine to maintain intragastric pH at a level above 6 in fasting patients with duodenal ulceration failed to decrease re-bleeding rates or the need for surgery in a group of patients with bleeding peptic ulcers.

It might be that proton pump inhibitors would be more efficacious given their ability to produce a prolonged and profound inhibition of gastric acid secretion

An early report by Krauss documenting perforation as a complication of acid peptic disease.

as compared to H2 receptor antagonist. Current information using intravenous omeprazole indicated a decrease in endoscopic stigmata of re-bleeding of a modest nature but no alteration in the incidence of re-bleeding, surgery, or death. Nevertheless the development of more effective intravenous proton pump inhibitors with a better pharmacokinetic profile suggests that the pharmacological management of acute peptic ulcer bleeding may be worthy of serious further consideration. Thus the ability of intravenous pantoprazole to generate a luminal pH of greater than 6 within 30 minutes of administration and lasting for the duration of the infusion may be predicted to demonstrate clinical benefit.

Perforation

Although the first documented case of perforated peptic ulcer disease dates back more than 2000 years ago to the western Han Dynasty, the problem still continues to confound physicians. In many instances the first indication of a peptic ulcer may be the perforation itself, whilst in others previous vague symptomatology suddenly culminates in acute perforation with peritonitis. The pathogenesis of the situation whereby an indolent or even chronic disease suddenly converts into a dramatic acute event has not been established. It is possible that this represents a locally vascular phenomenon whereby vessels supplying the base of an ulcer are acutely obliterated and a local infraction occurs. Certainly the fact that most perforations occur on the anterior lateral border of the duodenum provided some support for the suggestion. Perforations had been previously clearly described as clinical entities by Bailey and Benjamin Travers prior to 1843, when Edward Crisp reported 50 cases of perforated peptic ulcer and accurately summarized the clinical aspects of the condition. Crisp expressed considerable pessimism about the outcome, stating: "*once the perforation has occurred the case must be considered hopeless. In surgery's present state, the idea of cutting open the abdomen and closing the opening is simply too quixotic to consider*".

In 1884 Mikulicz-Radecki clearly defined the condition and provided the solution, but failed to successfully treat the patient. His observations, however, were most prescient: "*every doctor faced with a perforated ulcer of the stomach or intestine, must consider opening the abdomen, sewing up the hole, and adverting a possible or actual inflammation by careful cleansing of the abdominal cavity*". Nevertheless the first successful operation was undertaken on May 19, 1892 in Barman, currently a part of Wupperthal. Ludwig Heusner was summoned to the home of a 41-year-old man with a classical history of stomach ulcer including pain and nausea for 20 years with four episodes of bleeding who had suddenly acute peritonitis and shock. In a seemingly difficult operation, Heusner repaired the perforation and the patient survived. This successful repair was reported by Heusner's superior, Kriege, and anticipated by one month by a similar successful operation performed by Hastings Guilford in Redding, England.

Mikulicz-Radecki had by 1884 given considerable thought to the management of both stenosis and perforation as complications of duodenal ulcer disease.

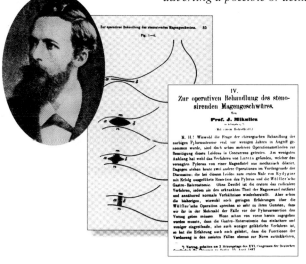

Initial therapy for perforated duodenal ulcers involved laparotomy with omental patch repair. Occasional intrepid surgeons undertook definitive procedures such as vagotomy with pyloroplasty simultaneously, but for the most part the need to perform surgery expeditiously and the fear of peritonitis and subphrenic abscess supported the use of patch repair alone. Modifications to decrease acid secretion included the use of highly selective vagotomy, but for the most part surgeons were content to simply repair the perforation. Whilst early mortality rates in the pre-antibiotic era were close to 25%, most centers now report mortality rates of less than 5 to 10%, with figures as low as 3%. For the most part mortality reflects either delay in arrival at the hospital or the presence of significant co-morbid conditions consequent upon age, prolonged sepsis and cardiac or renal failure.

Despite the fact that the mortality of surgical procedures has declined exponentially, the advent of intravenous histamine 2 receptor antagonists and profound acid suppression by proton pump inhibitors has for the most part precluded the need for consideration of definitive ulcer surgery. Thus older data in the pre-proton pump inhibitor era suggested that after simple closure, ulcer recurrence might occur in 52% of patients, of whom 28% percent would bleed, 15% would exhibit pyloric obstruction, and 9% re-perforation. Further recognition that profound suppression of acid secretion when combined with eradication of *H. pylori* virtually obviated further ulcer activity or complications has led to the growing acceptance that simple ulcer closure and appropriate medical therapy thereafter is perfectly adequate.

Interesting developments in laparoscopic surgery have led to modifications of the acute management of the perforation itself. Thus the use of a laparoscope to identify the perforation, lavage of the abdomen and suture or glue-in omental plugs into the defect has met with good success. A combination of laparoscopic and endoscopic technique whereby the laparoscopic presentation of the omentum into the duodenum is followed by the endoscopic of the omental plug into the duodenal lumen and suture or gluing of the omentum in place can manage even large perforations.

The management of perforated gastric ulcers has similarly undergone an evolution in much the same fashion as perforated duodenal ulcers. Prior to the availability of histamine 2 receptor antagonists and proton pump inhibitor therapy, the majority of perforated gastric ulcers would be managed by partial gastrectomy.

Furthermore it was felt that gastric ulcers in the pre-pyloric area should be managed not only by gastrectomy, but include a vagotomy. More recently, with a recognition of the potency of

An algorithm for the management of perforation.

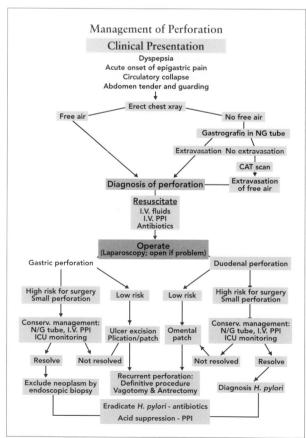

acid suppressive medication and the critical role of *H. pylori* in perforated gastric ulcer, placation of the perforation and omental patch have become the standard of treatment in most centers.

A formal course of proton pump inhibitor therapy with antibiotics to eradicate *H. pylori* has led to successful management in the vast majority of patients.

A particular consideration in the management of a perforated gastric ulcer is the need to reliably confirm the absence of neoplasia. Even if the biopsies at the repair of the acute perforation are negative, endoscopic surveillance should be undertaken at eight weeks with four-quadrant biopsy to confirm absence of neoplasia and eradication of *H. pylori*.

Stenosis

In situations where duodenal ulceration has either been untreated or inadequately treated over a relatively prolonged period time, cicatrisation may occur. Under such circumstances the gastric outlet is narrowed and pyloric function disturbed with a result that gastric emptying is initially slowed and then impeded. Clinically the patient's symptoms of dyspepsia and duodenal ulcer such as epigastric pain relieved by food change in character. Characteristically a sensation of early sitity and bloating are described, followed by progression to a sensation of distension. Symptoms of reflux may also supervene as the stomach becomes filled with food and fluid and disorder peristalsis drives food into the esophagus. The presence of undigested food in the stomach and its colonization with bacteria is associated with eructation of a classically foul smelling nature and the patients' partners or the patients themselves may be aware of severe halitosis. The critical point is reached when gastric emptying is interfered with to the extent that projectile vomiting ensues.

In the latter stages of the disease, vomiting of a projectile nature occurs and is characterized both by the presence of undigested food eaten days before, as well as its foul-smelling nature. The examination of the patient usually provides evidence of weight loss, and a distended stomach with a sucussion splash may be demonstrable. In most circumstances surgery will be required to manage gastric outlet obstruction due to progression of a chronic duodenal ulcer. It is important to determine that the underlying cause is not a pre-pyloric neoplasm of the scirrhous variety. Management should be initiated by passage of a large bore nasogastric tube with lavage of the gastric contents over a period of 3-4 days. Drainage should be maintained for at least 5 days both to allow complete emptying of stomach and enable it to regain tone prior to consideration of surgery. To facilitate surgery the stomach should be decompressed for a reasonable period of time to decrease mucosal edema and allow the size of the organ to approach its normal proportions. The use of non-absorbable antibiotics and anti-fungal agents given orally is of benefit in decreasing gastric colonization and obviating postoperative sepsis. Endoscopic balloon dilatation has been utilized in this situation and in some circumstances may be of benefit in allowing egress of gastric contents. In the vast majority of patients, re-stenosis occurs quite rapidly and surgery is subsequently required. Balloon dilatation should be undertaken with caution since perforation of the duodenal bulb under such circumstances may occur and convert a relatively benign problem into one with a serious morbidity and mortal-

Duodenal Ulcer
Sites and Types of Complications

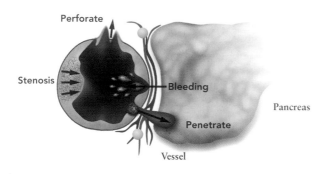

The complications of duodenal ulcer are to a certain extent site dependent. Perforations are usually antero-lateral; penetration is postero-medial; bleeding is postero-medial and stenosis can occur circumferentially.

ity. The surgical procedure is directed at resection of the stenotic area of the duodenum and usually involves antrectomy as a component of a partial gastrectomy. The need to resect the stenosed component of the duodenum usually prevents the construction of a Billroth I gastroduodenal anastomosis, since inadequate length may result in excessive anastomotic tension. In most circumstances a Billroth II gastrojejunal anastomosis is constructed and particular care taken with the closure of the duodenal stump since a leak is a catastrophic event given both its high volume and the presence of bile, pancratic juice, gastric acid and pepsin. In the past a significant proportion of the stomach including the antrum was removed and a vagotomy was undertaken to ensure an adequate enough decrease in acid secretion to prevent the recurrence of a peptic ulcer. The wide-spread availability and efficacy of proton pump inhibitor therapy has obviated the need for vagotomy and the degree of gastric resection should be as small as possible necessary to resect the strictured area and facilitate a safe and patent anastomosis.

Penetration

This complication of chronic duodenal ulcer disease was relatively common in times when acid suppressive therapy was not available and a prolonged clinical course of recurrent disease evident. Clinically, such patients present usually with a long history of untreated or inadequately treated peptic duodenal ulcer disease classically characterized by a change in symptomatology. The customary picture of epigastric discomfort and nocturnal pain now fails to be relieved by the ingestion of food or antacids. In addition, the site of the pain shifts from the epigastrium to the back and attains a constant, boring characteristic which is often worst at night. In most instances the consideration of pancreatic neoplasia is raised and even at endoscopy the duodenal appearance may suggest a neoplasm. The constant back pain, often accentuated by food, and the failure of its relief with acid suppressive medication usually mandate surgery. Under such circumstances resection of the part of the duodenum containing the ulcer with a partial gastrectomy and Billroth II anastomosis is usually the operation of choice. Such operations may be particularly difficult given the chronic nature of the lesion, the surrounding fibrosis and distortion of anatomy. Particular care should be undertaken to avoid damage to the common bile duct or the head of the pancreas.

Hypergastrinemia

Background

Normal fasting gastrin levels are usually in the range of 50 pg/ml and may increase 2-3 fold after a standard meal. Elevated levels of gastrin range from modest increases with H2RA therapy (3-4 fold) to levels that may be 2-3 hundred fold above normal in patients with gastrinomas. For the most part hypergastrinemia is associated with either atrophic gastritis or the use of acid suppressive therapy, particularly the PPI class of drugs. Less common causes include patients with renal failure or individuals who have undergone vagotomy especially those in whom the antrum has not been resected.

The presence of a retained excluded antrum caused by poor surgical technique is rarely evident nowadays given the awareness of the need to resect it entirely at surgery and the virtual disappearance of gastric surgery for peptic ulcer disease. Despite its important biological role in the stimulation of acid secretion and trophic regulation of the gastric mucosa the effects of either acute or chronic hypergastrinemia appear to be minimal, especially if parietal cell function is inhibited (acid suppressive drugs) or absent (diminished) as in atrophic gastritis or pernicious anemia. Indeed prolonged, albeit modest hypergastrinemia as evident after vagotomy has not been associated with adverse effects in numerous patients followed for as long as 30-40 years.

Similarly the rigorous evaluation of patients on PPIs for up to 15 years has not revealed any significant problems. Under certain circumstances elevated gastrin levels are associated with adverse effects which reflect the biological actions of gastrin particularly on gastric ECL cells. The generalized trophic effect of gastrin on mucosal stem cells may be associated with gastric mucosal thickening and occasionally polyp formation. Little evidence has emerged to support the role of elevated gastrin levels in the genesis of colonic carcinoma and its effects are for the most part only relevant to the stomach. Long standing, excessive gastrin drive culminates in ECL cell proliferation, increased histamine secretion and consequently acid hypersecretion. The consequences of the former are varying degrees of ECL cell hyperplasia but rarely neoplasia. On the other hand unregulated acid hypersecretion culminates in aggressive peptic ulcer disease and dramatic complications. The pathological conditions associated with hypergastrinemia will be dealt with in the following section.

Gastrinoma

The original observations of multiple, intractable and aggressive ulcers of the duodenum and the small bowel in association with a pancreatic tumor have evolved into a well-defined pathophysiological understanding of this entity. Previously eponymously recognized as the Zollinger-Ellison Syndrome (ZES), the biological elucidation of a gastrin secreting neoplasm facilitated the development of rational therapy. Early reports of catastrophic multiple gastro-duodeno-jejunal ulcerations associated with dramatic bleeding or perforation episodes have for the most part been supplanted by the identification of the condition in individuals whose peptic ulcer disease fails to respond to adequate acid suppressive therapy.

Pathologically the condition consists of a neuroendocrine tumor(s) arising in either the pancreas or the duodenum which produce excessive amounts of gastrin driving the parietal cell

Gastrin producing cells are not evident in the adult pancreas, yet gastrinomas were previously considered to be predominantly pancreatic endocrine tumors. Currently it is apparent that at least 50% of the lesions occur in the duodenum. In much the same fashion as carcinoid tumors, the majority of lesions are metastatic or multiple at diagnosis.

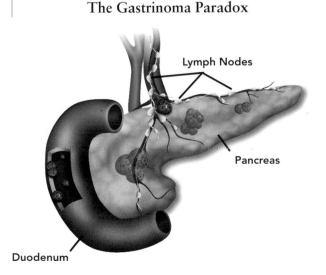

The Gastrinoma Paradox

Lymph Nodes

Pancreas

Duodenum

1) A gastrinoma of the head of the pancreas demonstrated by angiography.

2) Duodenal wall gastrinoma demonstrated by intra operative ultrasound.

3) Duodenal wall gastrinoma at endoscopy.

4) Electron microscopy of a gastrin secreting endocrine tumor of the pancreas. The different density and size of the granules suggest the production of more than one peptide by the lesion.

5) Immunofluorescent identification of gastrin cells. The use of immunofluorescent labelled antibodies to a specific peptide allowed a more precise identification of the secretory granules of a particular endocrine cell.

6) An immunohistochemical photomicrograph of a gastrinoma demonstrating a high level of SST$_2$ receptor expression.

mass to the secretion of hydrochloric acid in quantities which overcome the mucosal barrier of the stomach, duodenum, and upper small bowel. The ensuing ulceration which may occur in multiple sites is aggressive, associated with bleeding and perforation as well as difficulty in maintaining healing. The duodenal or pancreatic lesions may in rare circumstances be part of the multiple endocrine neoplasia type 1 syndrome (MEN I) and under such circumstances consideration should be given to the prior surgical management of the parathyroid or pituitary problems.

Whilst in the past diagnosis was heralded by the identification of aggressive ulceration, failure to heal, and dramatic complications for the most part individuals are now identified early either due to the presence of an ulcer in an

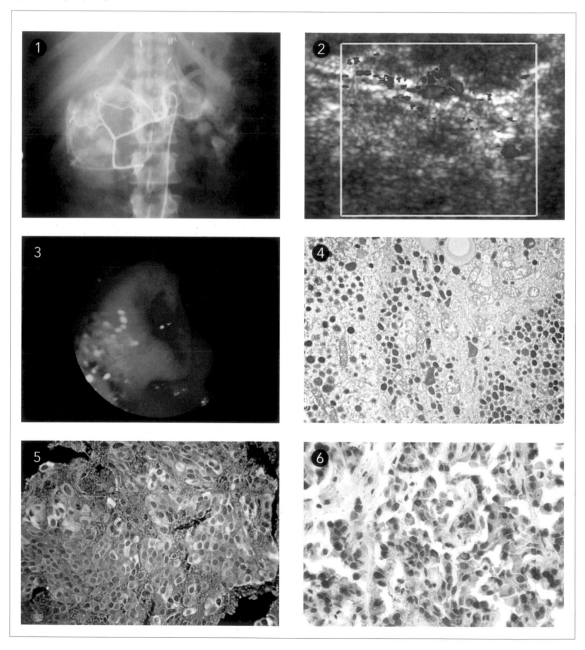

atypical site (post bulbar) or the failure to heal on adequate therapy, particularly if *H. pylori* has been eradicated. Indeed recurrent ulcer disease after demonstration of *H. pylori* eradication and appropriate compliance with proton pump inhibitor therapy should lead to a high index of suspicion with early measurement of fasting gastrin levels. An important clinical clue is the presence of diarrhea in a patient with the diagnosis of peptic ulcer disease, especially if there is no evidence of intake of antacids containing magnesium or other agents known to provoke increased gut motility or secretion. Hypergastrinemia should be defined as of tumor origin by performance of a secretin provocation test and the site of the gastrinoma then identified. The most effective topographic study is the Somatostatin Receptor Scintigram (SRS) (Octreoscan) which utilizes an isotopically labelled somatostatin receptor-2 subtype analogue to detect tumors and their metastases. This study has a high sensitivity and specificity (85-90%) for both primary and secondary lesions and is particularly effective in the detection of lymph node and hepatic metastases. CT scan and MRI are of some utility and may provide further information than available from the SRS scan. It has proved particularly difficult to identify minute and often multiple duodenal gastrinomas. Endoscopic ultrasound has proved to be of use in this area though oftentimes such lesions may only be detectable at surgery itself by transillumination of the duodenal wall, intraoperative ultrasound or formal duodenotomy and palpation.

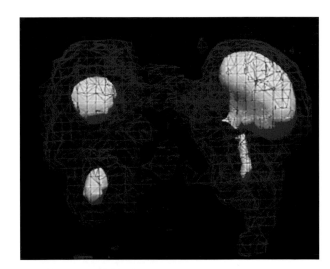

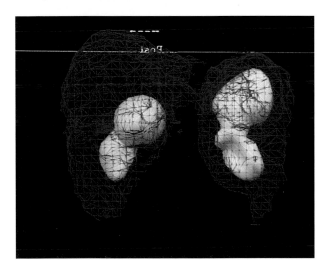

Somatostatin receptor scintigraphy has proved to be of considerable value in identifying gastrinomas and their secondaries. Top: gastrinoma of the head of the pancreas and a hepatic metastasis. Bottom: gastrinoma of the head of the pancreas.

The management of gastrinomas has evolved considerably in the last decade particularly with the advent of proton pump inhibitory therapy. In the past the inability to adequately suppress acid secretion and thus obviate the drastic complications of aggressive peptic ulcer disease led to the wide spread use of total gastrectomy to remove the target organ for gastrin. Whilst this therapy was reasonably successful, it did not address the underlying cause and exposed the patient to all the risks of a major operative procedure as well as the metabolic sequelae of a total gastrectomy. The early mortality of the procedure reflected technical inadequacy as well as the failure to recognize the trophic effects of gastrin and the proliferation of fundic mucosa beyond the gastroesophageal function. As a result gastro-esophageal anastomoses were often exposed to considerable acid secretion from areas of parietal cell bearing mucosa which remained in the esophageal remnant. The subsequent anastomotic leaks and strictures marred the early results of surgery and led to the recognition that at least the lower three centimeters of the esophagus should be removed and frozen sections performed at surgery to confirm the absence of parietal cells at the margins of the anastomosis.

The introduction of histamine 2 receptor antagonists (H2RA) led to a significant diminution in the need for gastric surgery but the high doses of H2RA required to suppress acid adequately were often associated with considerable adverse effects. In addition, the tachyphylaxis associated with competitive receptor antagonism led to a diminution of efficacy and an increase of complications such as bleeding and perforation with time. The introduction of proton pump inhibitory therapy has for the most part obviated such problems and the potency and relative lack of side effects, even at high dosage of this class of drugs, has rendered them the primary therapeutic choice in the management of gastrinomas. Those individuals whose gastrinoma is part of the MEN I syndrome are likely to develop gastric carcinoids within two to three years of proton pump inhibitory therapy. This reflects the relationship between hypergastrinemia and an as yet uncharacterized genomic abnormality since gastrinomas unassociated with the syndrome do not develop such lesions. Gastric carcinoid tumors should be identified and carefully monitored. If they are multiple, rapidly growing, or greater than 2 cm in size consideration should be given to fundic resection to obviate the possibility of perforation, bleeding or the development of metastases. The issue of surgery for the management of gastrinoma remains a controversial question. In those rare instances where the lesion is solitary and/or benign (<10-15%) it should be resected. Gastrinoma tumors of the pancreas appear to be of a more malignant variety and are usually multi-centric and metastatic at diagnosis. The gastrinomas which arise in the duodenum whilst often small, multicentric and difficult to detect, appear to be of a more benign variety and should probably be addressed more actively. In some centers consideration has even been given to pancreaticoduodenectomy. Such operations should be carefully evaluated against the background of the local surgical expertise, the patient's overall condition, and the question of projected life expectancy. Removal of hepatic metastases has been suggested to increase survival but should be carefully considered given the effectiveness of proton pump inhibitor therapy for management of the disease process and the potential risk of abdominal surgery and hepatic resection.

In gastrinoma patients who present with a major complication such as perforation or bleeding, the availability of safe intravenous proton pump inhibitors such as pantoprazole has provided a considerable advantage in the surgical

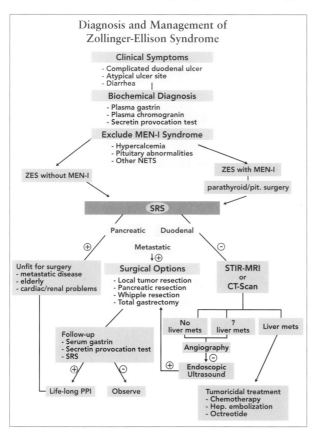

A management algorithm for gastrinoma.

management. The ability to consistently elevate the pH of the stomach to greater than 6 confers a great degree of safety on anastomotic margins and minimizes the post operative complications associated with mucosal ulceration and re-bleeding. Overall long-term maintenance therapy on proton pump inhibitory therapy appears to be the mainstay for the vast majority of gastrinoma patients with surgical resection of tumor being a consideration only in minor proportion of highly selected individuals in institutions where special expertise for such management is available. The use of vagotomy, partial gastrectomy, and other indeterminate surgical procedures is to be abjured since they do not decrease acid secretion adequately and confer on the patient all the risks of surgery as well as the sequelae of gastrectomy without protecting against the underlying disease process. The possibility that gastrinoma tumor growth itself may be addressed by the use of high dosage somatostatin analogs or the introduction of high energy isotopically labelled somatostatin analogs is under evaluation and the preliminary results suggest that such therapy may be of some utility in the future.

Idiopathic hypersecretion

Some individuals secrete high quantities of acid without elevation in serum gastrin. Their secretion is difficult to control with H2 receptor antagonists and sometimes even with PPI's. The basis of this hypersecretion is obscure but may involve cAMP signaling in the parietal cell independent of activation of the H2 receptor.

CHAPTER 3
GASTRIC CARCINOID

It is apparent that during proliferation of the ECL cells, a definable morphological pattern evolves in the course of the transformation from the normal cell to the neoplastic mode. In 1988, Solcia and others delineated a system of classification for the spectrum of proliferative changes of endocrine cells of the gastric fundus.

Histology

Their classification defines histopathological appearances ranging from hyperplasia to dysplasia to neoplasia.

The term pseudohyperplasia has been utilized to describe cell clustering unassociated with cell proliferation.

The successive stages of hyperplasia are termed simple, linear or chainforming, micronodular, and adenomatoid. Dysplasia is characterized by relatively atypical cells with features of enlarging or fusing micronodules, microinvasion, or newly formed stroma. When the nodules increase further in size to greater than 5 mm or invade into the submucosa, the lesion is classified as a neoplasm. This stage is divided into intramucosal and invasive forms.

The entire spectrum of endocrine cell proliferation, from hyperplasia to dysplasia and neoplasia has been observed in MEN 1-ZES and diffuse type A chronic atrophic gastritis. Both hyperplastic and pseudohyperplastic changes occur with low frequency in the *H. pylori* related chronic gastritis associated with ulcer disease or dyspepsia.

However, because no progression to dysplastic or neoplastic lesions have thus far been documented in these latter conditions, their role in gastric endocrine tumorigenesis appears unlikely. Carcinoid tumor is thus characterized morphologically by the criteria of size and invasion.

Biologically, however, the state of neoplasia is recognized by autonomy from the trophic effects of gastrin. A lesion which fails to regress once gastrin levels have been normalized is therefore regarded as a carcinoid tumor.

A histological grading system for the evaluation of ECL cell proliferation.

Classification of ECL Cell Proliferation	
Hyperplasia	Simple (diffuse) Linear Micronodular Adenomatoid
Dysplasia **(Pre-Neoplastic stage)**	Enlarging micronodule Fusing micronodule Microinvasive lesion Nodule with newly formed strata
Carcinoid	Intramucosal carcinoid Invasive carcinoid

A) Gastric body mucosa of a patient with gastric carcinoidosis showing typical features of gastric atrophy: the mucosa is thinned, parietal and chief cells are absent, and there is intestinal metaplasia (note the Paneth cells and goblet cells in the gland on the left) and a lymphoplasmacytic infiltrate (hematoxylin and eosin, X200).
B) Chromogranin expression in mucosa adjacent to that shown in A. Simple hyperplasia of ECL cells is seen in the gland on the extreme right; that in the middle of the field shows linear hyperplasia of the ECL cells (*i.e.*, they form chains without intervening cells), whereas that on the bottom left has developed into a micronodule (immunoperoxidase, X400).
C) In this field there is adenomatoid hyperplasia of the ECL cells, defined as a cluster of five or more micronodules (immunoperoxidase for chromogranin A, X200).
D) Intramucosal ECL cell neoplasm (immunoperoxidase for chromogranin A, X200).

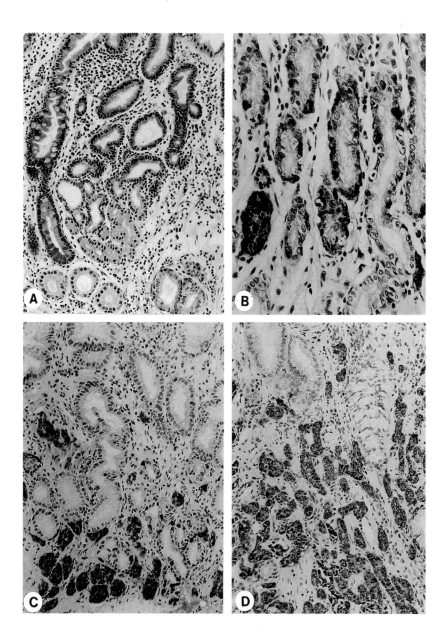

Development

In rats and *Mastomys* it appears that a threshold value of plasma gastrin is necessary not only for ECL cell hyperplasia to occur but for conversion to gastric carcinoid. This value reflects not only gastrin levels but length of exposure and other factors of which the female gender and in humans and *Mastomys* genomic events (MEN-1) are involved. In fact in humans the ECL cell density does not exhibit a relation to plasma gastrin levels in normo-gastrinemic individuals nor reveal any significant differences in duodenal ulcer patients with mild hypergastrinemia. In patients on PPI's for 6 months, no significant changes in ECL cells were noted.

Furthermore, in peptic ulcer patients receiving omeprazole for more than a decade, ECL cells were not significantly affected. If plasma gastrin levels of greater than 400 pg/ml are present, significant proliferation not progressing to dysplasia has been noted. It has, therefore, been suggested that in patients with plasma gastrin levels of >400 pg/ml, gastric biopsy should be undertaken to evaluate endocrine cell status or decrease in the dosage of the PPI's considered. In patients with sustained hypergastrinemia associated with surgical vagotomy alterations in ECL status are not significant. Although duration of exposure appears important it has been noted that ECL cell hyperplasia may be stable with time, provided that gastrin levels do not increase significantly. With hypergastrinemia alone (e.g. sporadic ZES) ECL cell proliferation is usually limited to hyperplastic lesions of the simple or linear type. However, in patients with MEN-1-ZES or type-A chronic atrophic gastritis, ECL cell lesions are usually dysplastic or overtly carcinoid in nature. Factors other than hypergastrinemia must therefore be involved in ECL cell transformation. In the MEN-1 syndrome the loss of a suppressor oncogene on chromosome 11q13 may be related.

Similarly in atrophic gastritis either achlorhydria or the alterations in the biology of the associated mucosa, which have also been suggested to be implicated in the pathogenesis of gastric adenocarcinoma, may be involved. It has been suggested that detection of dysplastic changes or ECL cell carcinoids in a ZES patient warrant screening of both the patient and the family for a covert MEN-1 syndrome.

The hyperplastic effect of hypergastrinemia on gastric mucosal epithelial cells appears not to be restricted to the ECL cells. Foveolar cells and surface mucus cells also undergo hyperplasia in the human stomach under the influence of excessive gastrin drive, often to a considerable degree. This process may be patchy, and not infrequently results in the development of endoscopically detectable polyps which are classified histologically as foveolar hyperplasia. Thus, to add to the confusion surrounding gastric carcinoid tumors, in patients with these lesions arising in a setting of hypergastrinemia at least two types of mucosal polyps can be expected: those due to ECL cell proliferations, and simple foveolar hyperplasias. Whether these foveolar cell hyperplasias represent an early stage on the pathway to gastric adenocarcinoma of the type that occurs with increased frequency in patients with chronic atrophic gastritis type A and pernicious anemia is not known.

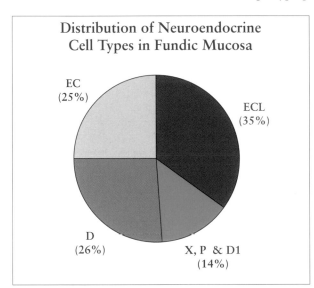

Distribution of Neuroendocrine Cell Types in Fundic Mucosa

EC (25%)

ECL (35%)

D (26%)

X, P & D1 (14%)

The ECL cells are the dominant fundic neuroendocrine cell type, followed by the D cells, which secrete somatostatin. The function of the other types and their biological function have not been clearly characterised.

In a morphometric ultrastructural investigation of sporadic ZES patients, a 168% increase in the volume density of the total oxyntic endocrine cell population was noted. This increase was exclusively due to ECL cells with other types showing a relatively decreased volume. However, in patients with *H. pylori*, the P and D1 cells have been reported to exhibit hyperplasia. This may reflect the metaplastic background in which endocrine cells proliferate.

The oncoprotein, BCL2, enhances cell survival by blocking programmed cell death (apoptosis) due to inhibition of mitochondrial export of cytochrome c. Immunohistochemical expression of BCL2 in endocrine cells of the human oxyntic mucosa has been investigated in patients with normal gastric mucosa, sporadic Zollinger-Ellison syndrome, MEN 1 - ZES, patients with hypergastrinemic atrophic gastritis (HAG) and patients with ECL cell carcinoids. In all patients, BCL2 immunoreactivity was exclusively located in endocrine cells located in the middle layer of the oxyntic mucosa.

The ratio of BCL2 to Chromogranin A reacting cells was low in sporadic ZES (no risk of carcinoid). It was, however, maintained in MEN 1 - ZES and increased in chronic atrophic gastritis A (conditions with intermediate or high risk of carcinoid respectively). BCL2 expression by gastric carcinoid markedly varied from one tumor to another even in the same patient, but was low or absent in most cases. Thus, BCL2 is expressed by normal fundic endocrine cells whose intraglandular location suggests a role for the protein during migration from the neck stem zone to fully differentiated cells at the gland bottom.

| **Experimental model *Mastomys natalensis*** | A novel rodent model available for study of the ECL cell and particularly its neoplastic transformation is the *Mastomys natalensis*. This is a sub-Saharan rodent which was initially utilized in the study of African plague vectors. During these studies it was noted that a substantial percentage of the animals died of a gastric neoplasm. Initially this lesion was identified as a gastric adenocarcinoma. It subsequently became apparent that the cell type was more compatible with a carcinoid lesion. Further investigation identified this neoplasm as a histamine producing ECL cell tumor (ECLoma). |

The tumor is histamine secreting and does not metastasize, which renders it closely comparable to the human type I gastric carcinoid tumor. If untreated, animals develop duodenal ulcers which either bleed or perforate, resulting in demise of the tumor carrier on an acute basis. The tumor could be successfully transplanted to either the subcutaneous or intraocular sites. The *Mastomys* has a genetic propensity to spontaneously develop ECLomas with the incidence depending upon the particular breeding strain. The specific genomic aberration has not been identified. The rates of tumor development vary from 20-70% within the life span of the animal. Of particular interest, however, is the observation that the use of acid inhibitory agents in this animal result in the rapid production of hypergastrinemia with a transformation from a normal ECL cell population to a hyperplastic state by two months and neoplastic lesions are evident in up to 80% of animals by four months. The hyperplastic ECL state is reversible at 8 weeks but by 16 weeks withdrawal of the gastrin stimulus fails to result in tumor regression. The use of the *Mastomys* species has therefore been of considerable utility in studying gastrin induced ECL cell proliferation and has enabled characterization of the ECL cell tumor.

Tumor classification and management

Neuroendocrine tumors of the stomach previously were felt to be responsible for about 0.3% of all gastric tumors and 3-5% of all gastrointestinal carcinoids. More recently, however, these estimates have variously risen to 11-41% of all gastrointestinal neuroendocrine lesions. This increase most likely represents an increase in awareness as well as an association with specific disease entities such as atrophic gastritis.

Distribution of the 8,305 carcinoid tumors contained by the ERG, TNCS and the SEER file (1950-1991) by organ site. The dominant site for carcinoid development is the gastrointestinal system. Gastric carcinoids constitute 3.19% of all carcinoid tumors.

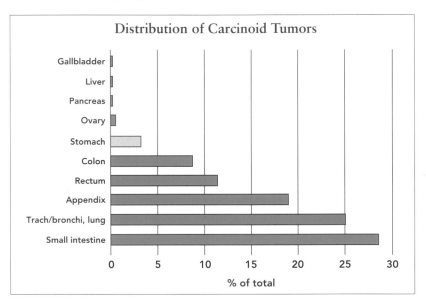

An overall classification of such lesions (carcinoids) was developed in Munich in 1994. Essentially it evaluates lesions on the basis of their histologic behavior and compromises four groups: 1) benign behavior: nonfunctioning, well differentiated tumor of small-size (up to 1 cm) limited to the mucosa-submucosa and without angioinvasion – usually ECL cell tumors of the fundic mucosa associated with chronic atrophic gastritis and hypergastrinemia. 2) Benign or low grade malignant behavior: nonfunctioning, well differentiated tumor within the mucosa-submucosa of small size (>1 up to 2 cm) without angioinvasion or of small to intermediate size (up to 2 cm) with angio-invasion – usually ECL cell tumor of the fundic mucosa associated with chronic atrophic gastritis and hypergastrinemia. Rarely MEN-1 associated or sporadic ECL cell tumors. 3) Low grade malignant behavior (low grade neuroendocrine carcinoma): nonfunctioning, well differentiated tumor of large size (>2 cm) or extending beyond the submucosa; usually sporadic ECL cell tumors; rarely serotonin-producing tumors or others; rarely MEN-1 or chronic atrophic gastritis-associated ECL cell tumors; functioning well differentiated tumor of any size and extension – sporadic gastrinoma, serotonin-producing tumor (EC) or others. 4) Malignant behavior: functioning or nonfunctioning poorly differentiated intermediate or small-cell carcinoma.

In a recent series of gastric neuroendocrine tumor, 46 of 55 tumors (83%) were well differentiated. Only one was a G cell tumor of the antrum - the remaining 45 were well differentiated ECL cell tumors. In reviewing the histology and pathobiology of gastric carcinoids, it is of significance to distinguish

Pathological diagnosis of type-I gastric carcinoids.
A) Surgical resection specimen of fundic mucosa with numerous carcinoid tumor nodules (indicated by arrows).
B) Gastroscopic identification of multiple carcinoid tumors in a patient with pernicious anemia.
C) Histological evaluation using hematoxylin and eosin staining of the fundic mucosa with evidence of ECL neoplasia (indicated by the arrow).
D) Demonstration of a microcarcinoid tumor by chromogranin immunoreactivity (brown staining) in the fundic mucosa.

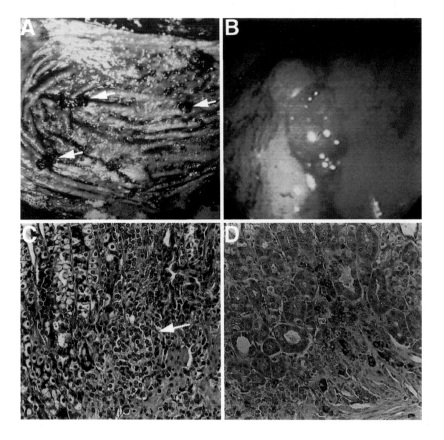

between different types of gastric carcinoids. The presence of hypergastrinemia in particular appears to connote a far more benign situation than lesions occurring under normogastrinemic conditions. Furthermore, solitary sporadic lesions are of considerably worse prognosis compared to multiple or diffuse microcarcinoid lesions. The latter occur relatively frequently in association with hypergastrinemic states in contrast to the more rare sporadic gastric tumors.

Three patterns of gastric carcinoid (ECL cell) tumor have been proposed: (1) argyrophilic carcinoids arising in type A chronic atrophic gastritis (chronic atrophic gastritis/A), (2) argyrophilic ECL cell carcinoids in Multiple Endocrine Neoplasia 1 - Zollinger-Ellison Syndrome (MEN 1- ZES), and (3) sporadic argyrophil carcinoids.

The characteristic features of the different types of gastric carcinoid tumors.

The Three Types of Gastric Carcinoid Tumor

Nomenclature	Tumor Characteristics	Histology	Hyper-gastrinemia	Biological Behavior
Type I	Generally small (< 1 cm) and multiple; often nodular/polypoid	ECL cell lesion. Stages of ECL cell hyperplasia, displasia, and neoplasia present in adjacent mucosa	Present	Slow growth, very rare regional or distant metastases
Type II	Generally small (< 1 cm) and multiple	ECL cell lesion. Stages of ECL cell hyperplasia, displasia, and neoplasia present in adjacent mucosa	Present	Slow growth, may metastasize more often than CAG-associated lesions
Type III	Solitary, often large (> 1 cm)	ECL, EC, or X cells. Tumor formation w/o evidence of hyperplasia or precarcinoid dysplasia in adjacent mucosa	Absent	Relatively aggressive growth, frequent metastases to regional nodes (55%) and liver (24%)

This classification does not include neuroendocrine carcinomas (non-ECL cell), previously known as atypical carcinoids. These represent an aggressive neuroendocrine neoplasm which bears greater resemblance to sporadic carcinoids than to hypergastrinemia associated tumors. They are generally large solitary tumors which frequently display central necrosis. Histopathologically, they feature small to intermediate sized poorly differentiated "protoendocrine" cells, a high mitotic index, and invasive growth. They metastasize with great frequency and progress rapidly.

Carcinoids arising in type A chronic atrophic gastritis (Type I)

Gastric carcinoid tumors arising in the presence of type A chronic atrophic gastritis (chronic atrophic gastritis/A) constitute the most common type of gastric carcinoid (62-83%). Chronic atrophic gastritis/A is characterized by chronic inflammation of the oxyntic mucosa, often associated with autoimmune diseases such as pernicious anemia, and results in atrophy of the oxyntic glands and achlorhydria. Carcinoid tumors related to chronic atrophic gastritis/A are usually small, are often multicentric, and tend to behave less aggressively than sporadic gastric carcinoids.

In a series of 23 patients with gastric carcinoids, 19 of 23 (83%) had concurrent chronic atrophic gastritis/A. Tumors in these patients were single or multiple, were associated with hypergastrinemia and had not spread beyond the mucosa or submucosa. Solcia reported 80 cases of chronic atrophic gastritis with hypergastrinemia and found focal or diffuse endocrine cell hyperplasia in all of them. In addition, he identified 20 individuals (25%) with dysplastic (precarcinoid) lesions, and 24 patients (30%) with carcinoids and concluded that dysplastic, but not hyperplastic, changes are linked to the development of multiple gastric carcinoids. Stolte studied 55 patients with gastric carcinoids of whom 46 (83.6%) had chronic atrophic gastritis and reported that in 27 non-operated patients followed up by endoscopy and biopsy for an average of 3.6 years, there were no alteration in their original findings. They proposed that for patients with small (<1 cm) gastric carcinoids, expectant therapy with endoscopic follow-up may be advisable. In a series examined by Rindi 28 of 45 (62%) patients with gastric carcinoids also had chronic atrophic gastritis/A and 64% patients had multiple tumors. Of the 12 patients in whom gastrin was measured, all were hypergastrinemic. The tumors were small, with a median size of 0.7 cm and none metastasized. Of 25 patients who were followed for an average of 6 years, 20 (80%) were alive, including 6 (24%) who did not undergo surgery. None died from causes related to their tumors. On the basis of this experience, it has been argued that expectant therapy or endoscopic removal of accessible tumors may be appropriate for gastric carcinoids associated with hypergastrinemia. This conservative form of management would reflect the relatively benign behavior of the majority of such tumors.

Others have observed that antrectomy has resulted in regression of tumors, presumably because the source of gastrin, the proposed principle promoter of tumor growth, has been removed. Hirschowitz et al. reported three patients with pernicious anemia, hypergastrinemia, and multicentric gastric carcinoids. After antrectomy, gastrin levels returned to normal in all three patients. Follow-up gastroscopy with biopsy 12-18 months post-operatively revealed foci of micro-carcinoid in all three patients, but biopsies at 21-30 months revealed complete regression of both carcinoids and ECL cell hyperplasia. Richards and colleagues performed an antrectomy on one patient with hypergastrinemia and multiple tumors. After the operation, gastrin levels were normalized and total regression of the tumor was reported. Eckhauser reported two cases of multicentric carcinoids, atrophic gastritis and hypergastrinemia. One patient had tumor involving one regional lymph node and the other had a single liver metastasis. After antrectomy (and removal of the liver nodule in the patient with hepatic metastasis), gastrin levels returned to normal in both patients. Upon gastroscopy with biopsy four to six months post-operatively, the patient with nodal metastasis had residual neoplasm in the stomach and the other patient's tumor had completely regressed. Whether these lesions were ECLomas or neuroendocrine carcinomas is not clear. Caruso et al. reported one patient with atrophic gastritis and multiple gastric carcinoids. Initial management involved gastric resection with antrectomy at which time it was noted that the largest of the tumors present was a composite carcinoid-adenocarcinoma. One month later, a complete gastrectomy was therefore undertaken and regressive changes in the ECL cell proliferations in the gastric remnant were reported. Kern et al. described a patient with pernicious anemia, hypergastrinemia, and ECL cell hyperplasia. The patient underwent antrectomy, which resulted in resolution of his hypergastrinemia. Nine months later, the remainder of the stomach was resected and morphometric evaluation revealed a marked reduction in the number and size of endocrine cells in the gastric mucosa. Wangberg and colleagues performed an antrectomy on a patient with atrophic gastritis, pernicious anemia, hypergastrinemia and multiple gastric carcinoids. Although the patient's gastrin levels returned to normal, multiple fundic carcinoids developed 23 months after surgery. They proposed that antrectomy may be appropriate in the treatment of early lesions, but that large primary lesions in combination with nodular hyperplasia should be treated with total or subtotal gastrectomy. In a small number of patients, spontaneous regression of chronic atrophic gastritis/A associated tumors has been reported.

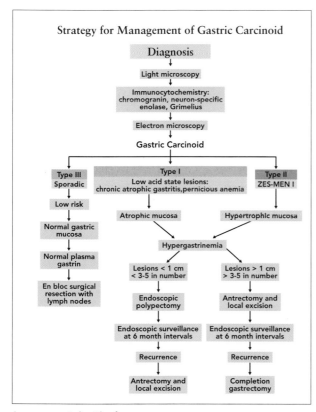

A management algorithm for gastric carcinoids.

Nevertheless, special attention is necessary for the management of patients with large (1.6-2.0 cm) and deeply invasive type I well differentiated ECL tumors that tend to have a low grade malignant behavior. This clinical profile closely matches that of the 197 chronic atrophic gastritis associated gastric neuroendocrine tumors previously published and of the 27 similar tumors included in the series of 104 gastric carcinoids recently reported.

ZES-MEN-1 associated gastric carcinoids (Type II)

Individuals with ZES-MEN-1 have a well recognized propensity to develop gastric carcinoids. In a group of 48 ZES patients, Lehy et al. reported 17 with ZES and MEN-1, of whom 5 developed gastric carcinoid tumors (29.5%). None of 31 patients with sporadic ZES exhibited gastric carcinoids. Despite a substantial level of hypergastrinemia, patients with sporadic ZES have very rarely been reported to develop gastric carcinoids. Hypergastrinemia is, however, associated with proliferation of ECL cells in these patients. In individuals with MEN-1, a genetic predisposition presumably exists which facilitates the development of carcinoid tumors.

More recently, Cadiot and colleagues reported the identification of loss of heterozygosity near the MEN-1 locus on chromosome 11q13 in a gastric carcinoid tumor of a ZES-MEN-1 patient. They argued that this observation suggested that the MEN-1 gene was a tumor suppressor gene for fundic argyrophil tumors in ZES. Proliferating ECL cells of hypergastrinemic patients express β-FGF 37 which is known to exhibit potent mitogenic properties for a wide variety of mesoderm derived cell types. These cells may therefore be the source of abnormally high circulating levels of the β FGF-like mitogen factor that has been identified in MEN-1 patients. ECLoma producing β-FGF may thus be responsible for the unusual proliferation of smooth muscle cells, presumably originating from the muscularis mucosa that is often associated with ECL cell carcinoids, particularly in areas of submucosal invasion.

Rindi et al. described seven cases of gastric carcinoid occurring against a background of hypertrophic gastropathy. Of the 7 patients, 6 had ZES-MEN-1. All 7 of the patients displayed hypergastrinemia as well as hyperplasia and dysplasia of argyrophil cells in non-tumor mucosa. The tumors in these patients were small, with a median size of 0.5 cm.

Two of the 6 ZES-MEN-1 patients had local lymph node metastases, but none had distant metastases. None of the ZES-MEN-1 patients died from tumor related disease during a mean follow-up of 79 months. These tumors are composed predominantly of ECL cells, although some lesions contain a heterogeneous population of cell types. The behavior of gastric carcinoids associated with ZES-MEN-1 appears to occupy a middle ground between that of the relatively more aggressive sporadic lesions and the more benign tumors seen in conjunction with chronic atrophic gastritis.

Sporadic argyrophil carcinoids (Type III)

Sporadic argyrophil carcinoids are isolated tumors which arise against a background of normal gastric mucosa. They tend to be larger (2-3 times) than the other types of gastric carcinoids, and to behave more aggressively, exhibiting deep mucosal invasion. Rindi et al. reported their experience with 10 sporadic tumors which ranged in size from 0.5 to 5 cm (median 2 cm). At the time of diagnosis, 6 of the 10 sporadic tumors had metastasized, 2 locally and 4 to the liver. In addition, 8 of 10 displayed lymphatic invasion. Other series have demonstrated a correlation between tumor size and metastasis for gastric carcinoids of all types. Nevertheless, minute tumors which have spread have been reported. Other factors which predict aggressive behavior by sporadic tumors include moderate cellular atypia, 2 or more mitoses per 10 high powered fields, angio-invasion, and deep invasion of the gastric wall. Sporadic gastric carcinoids display a fairly uniform histopathological appearance. The cells have uniform round nuclei. Their growth pattern may be trabecular or gyriform, medullary or solid, glandular or rosette-like, or a combination of these types. The lesions are argyrophilic but not argentaffin and display immunoreactivity for numerous markers including chromogranin A, neuron-specific enolase, synaptophysin and S-100. In addition, they may contain small numbers of serotonin, somatostatin, or even gastrin positive cells. Ultrastructurally, the lesions appear to contain a mixture of cell types. Generally, some of the cells are identifiable as ECL cells whereas others resemble EC or X cells. Overall, lesions of this type may be regarded as bearing greater similarity to neuroendocrine carcinomas rather than carcinoids *per se*. Indeed, their biological behavior is far more aggressive with invasive growth and metastasis as predictable features in their evolution.

Lifetable analysis of gastric carcinoids in the SEER (1973-1991) file. The overall observed 5-yr survival rate is 48.6%. This grouping may, however, reflect the outcome of a variety of different types of gastric neuroendocrine tumors. Many of the tumors were probably of the sporadic type (Type III), whose prognosis is very much worse than the lesions associated with hypergastrinemia (Type I and II).

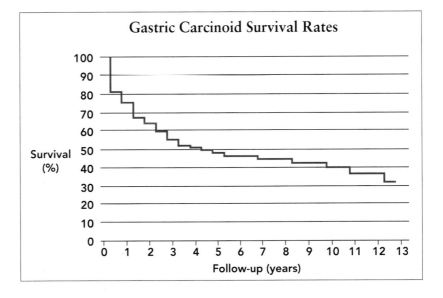

Complete or partial gastrectomy with local lymph node resection is recommended therapy in surgical candidates with solitary, large (>1 cm) or invasive tumors. For patients with metastatic disease involving the liver, surgical resection of tumor foci may reduce symptoms and improve survival. Similarly, selective hepatic artery ligation or embolization has a beneficial effect. Chemotherapy alone has been reported to produce a 20-40% tumor response rate in patients with disseminated disease. Commonly used chemotherapeutic agents include streptozocin, 5-fluorouracil, cyclophosphamide, and doxorubicin. The somatostatin analogue octreotide has proven effective in reducing symptoms of the carcinoid syndrome as has leukocyte interferon in some instances.

In a series of 265 cases Modlin reported a 52%, overall 5 year survival rate for patients with gastric carcinoids of all stages, 48.6% for patients with local lesions, 39.5% for patients with regional metastases, and 10% for patients with distant metastases. This study, however, did not distinguish between different types of gastric carcinoid and therefore represents a summation of outcome information. More recent series have produced similar results for sporadic tumors. The outcome for the sporadic tumors may be regarded as poor compared to lesions which are purely of ECL cell origin and/or associated with hypergastrinemia.

Distribution of gastric carcinoid tumors by stage in the ERG (1950-1969) and the SEER (1973-1991) files. Although the percentage of localized disease increased from 45.2% to 52.9%, it decreased from 28.6% to 10.3% for lesions with regional metastasis and from 23.8% to 20.6% for lesions with distant metastasis. At least 50% of gastric carcinoids are nonlocalized at diagnosis. Unstaged carcinoid tumors constituted 2.4% of the ERG and 16.2% of the SEER database.

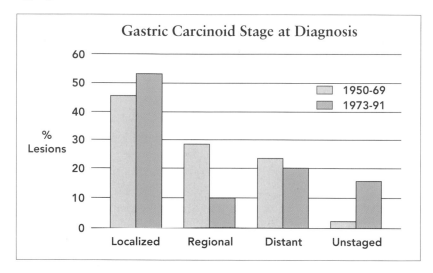

CHAPTER 4
DYSPEPSIA

Non-ulcer dyspepsia

One of the major limitations of medical practice in the management of dyspepsia is the inability to identify a mucosal lesion. To a large extent this may actually reflect the limitations of current endoscopic technology or the macular acuity of either the endoscopist or his pathologist. As the discriminant index for the identification of lesions has decreased with the advent of more sophisticated technology, the group or individuals in which a diagnosis cannot be established has similarly decreased. Nevertheless a conundrum is provided by a situation where a patient complains vigorously of a group of symptoms which have been generically accepted by the physician as synonymous with dyspepsia if no lesion can be identified. In some circumstances the skill of the practitioner and the affect of the patient will allow for consideration of functional overlay. In other instances, the symptoms are not diagnostic of dyspepsia and indeed may wax and wane in severity as well as altering somewhat in nature as time passes.

The critical difficulty in patients of this type relates to the actually definition and meaning of the word of dyspepsia. Whilst this has been broadly defined as *"pain or discomfort centered in the upper abdomen"*, this definition does not include co-existing symptoms which may occur at other sites. In order to override the limitations that subjective descriptions of symptomatology proffered by a patient might generate a more cohesive definition of functional dyspepsia may be utilized. In brief, this embraces the dyspepsia complex of symptoms using three broad categories: a) ulcer-like dyspepsia, b) dysmotility-like dyspepsia, and c) unspecified (non-specific) dyspepsia. In the ulcer-like dyspepsia group, upper abdominal pain should be a predominant complaint usually located in the epigastrium relieved by foods and antacids and occurring before meals or when hungry. Occasionally this pain may awaken the patient from sleep and be associated with a timing pattern characteristic of periodicity with remissions and relapses. It is likely that this group actually contains patients who may have acid peptic disease but in whom no overt (macroscopic) ulceration can be detected by conventional technology. In many of these patients relief will occur with the use of H2 receptor antagonists as well as proton pump inhibitors.

In a second group of dysmotility-like dyspeptic patients, pain is not the dominant symptom, although upper abdominal discomfort is present. Usually the discomfort is chronic and character-

A depiction of the complex interplay between the different types of symptomatology broadly grouped together as "dyspepsia".

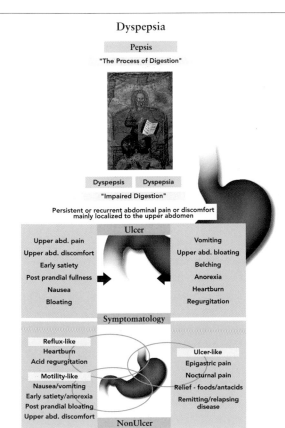

Dyspepsia

Pepsis
"The Process of Digestion"

Dyspepsis | Dyspepsia
"Impaired Digestion"
Persistent or recurrent abdominal pain or discomfort mainly localized to the upper abdomen

Ulcer

Upper abd. pain | Vomiting
Upper abd. discomfort | Upper abd. bloating
Early satiety | Belching
Post prandial fullness | Anorexia
Nausea | Heartburn
Bloating | Regurgitation

Symptomatology

Reflux-like
Heartburn
Acid regurgitation

Motility-like
Nausea/vomiting
Early satiety/anorexia
Post prandial bloating
Upper abd. discomfort

Ulcer-like
Epigastric pain
Nocturnal pain
Relief - foods/antacids
Remitting/relapsing disease

NonUlcer

ized by early satiety, postprandial fullness, nausea, retching, and even vomiting. Although the patient may describe a bloating sensation in the upper abdomen, no visible distension is evident, although it and all the above the symptoms are aggravated usually by food. The symptomatology of this group of patients is not at all well understood and overall reflects the generallly poor clinical understanding of motility disorders. Some of these patients, however, may not only represent abnormalities of gastric emptying but also disturbances of either gall bladder function or colonic motility.

The last group of patients who are categorized as exhibiting unspecified or non-specific dyspepsia are a heterogeneous group, which may include individuals with definable neurosis and demonstrable functional disorders, if evaluated by a psychiatrist. Part of this group, however, may fall into the poorly understood and heterogenous syndromic collaquation of "irritable bowel syndrome". When carefully questioned they may also allude to pain in the lower abdomen with or without constipation, diarrhea, and mucus. It should, however, be born in mind that the symptom repertoire of the gastrointestinal tract is relatively limited given the fact that the neural connections are mostly of a visceral nature rendering somatic interpretation of gastro intestinal sensation both difficult and often imprecise. Careful consideration should especially be given to patients whose complaints are not only repetitive but accurately and consistently reproducible over a period of time. In some instances, a thorough investigation will reveal evidence of covert gall bladder disease, chronic pancreatitis, or even a carcinoid tumor of the small bowel.

A term, which is almost as confusing as dyspepsia, is the widely used "heartburn". This is generally described as a symptom of "a burning sensation under the lower part of the center of the chest that rises towards or into the neck". It is frequently aggravated by consumption of food or by changes in posture such as lying or stooping. In comparison to dyspepsia, there is considerable agreement as to the usage of this term and individuals who exhibit both heartburn and dyspepsia are considered to have symptomatic gastroesophageal reflux disease, if the heartburn is the dominant complaint.

It should, however, be recognized that there are other causes of thoracic and esophageal pathology which may produce similar symptomatology, at least in the early stages of the disease. Individuals who have heartburn for at least three months and have no endoscopic esophagitis as well as a normal 24-hour esophageal acid exposure have been classified as suffering from "functional heartburn". Discussions have arisen as to the precise use of the terminology functional whether applied to dyspepsia or heartburn.

One proposal that has no rigorous data to support its validity is that such individuals are acid sensitive and physiological amounts of acid, either in the duodenum, stomach, or esophagus, generate sensations that are centrally interpreted as pain (dyspepsia or heartburn). In some such individuals the use of acid suppressive therapy may be of benefit.

A strategy for the evaluation and management of dyspepsia.

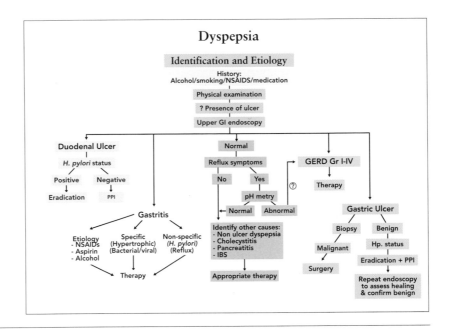

Dyspepsia
and heartburn

Approximately 25% of the general population in any western country may have recurrent dyspepsia over a 12-month period. There appears to be no significant difference between Europe and the United States nor between men and women, although prevalence does decline significantly as age increases. Epidemiological studies have reported that 15% of individuals suffer heartburn at least once a week, whilst 7% have heartburn daily. This number is likely to increase in pregnant women and individuals that are either overweight or whose occupation involves frequent stooping or bending. In those whose heartburn and reflux symptoms are significant enough to seek medical advice and endoscopy, 30-60% may exhibit evidence of esophagitits. Nevertheless the overall prevalence of erosive esophagitis in the general population is approximately 2%, which is 15 times less than the prevalence of reflux symptoms. Nevertheless in individuals who are referred for endoscopic evaluation, reflux esophagitis can be documented in up to 15%. It is evident that more than 75% of patients whose symptoms may be classified as dyspepsia or heartburn never seek medical advice and self medicate. The reasons for this are complex but include the fear of the detection of serious disease or anxiety that the physician may either suggest alterations in lifestyle, prescribe medication, or initiate investigations prompting further conflict and concern.

The long-term outcome of individuals with dyspepsia whose cause cannot be identified is difficult to be certain about. Between 10 and 15% of such individuals become asymptomatic on an annual basis and overall symptoms tend to decrease with age. Alternatively, it has been noted that in control population groups approximately 12 to 15% on an annual basis develop symptoms of dyspepsia and heartburn for which no cause can be identified.

Despite the fact that a specific disease process in the upper gastrointestinal may not be definable even after serious investigation of symptoms, the disease entity *per se* represents a considerable socioeconomic problem. Since dyspepsia accounts for between 20 and 70% of all gastrointestinal consultation with general practitioners, a significant amount of physician time is spent evaluating the problem. Up to a third of such individuals may be referred to a gastroenterologist for further evaluation. The majority of these are treated, even if no objective evidence of mucosal ulceration is detectable. Thus (80%) receiving H2 receptor antagonists include 30% prescribed for heartburn and 40% for functional dyspepsia. No studies are available to determine whether the use of such medication improves the long-term outcome of the disease process.

In Sweden, in 1994, it was calculated that the costs of functional dyspepsia were greater than 55,000 USD per 1,000 citizens. Such costs are significantly higher in the United States and will continue to increase as the cost of healthcare grows. Patients with the diagnosis of functional dyspepsia have been reported to have a 2 to 3 fold increase in the number of days of reported sickness from their work. When studied utilising quality of life scales, they attain scores significantly lower than their cohorts.

Thus functional dyspepsia, whether subdivided into functional heartburn or dyspepsia with motility related disturbances, remains an area of therapeutic and diagnostic difficulty. Clearly some of these patients have centrally mediated problems that are outside the care of the gastroenterologist but others likely have organic pathology which has as yet not been identified. In terms of the practical management of such individuals it is important to exclude gastro-esophageal reflux disease (GERD), gastro-duodenal ulceration, and the presence of *H. pylori*. In the absence of any obvious pathology, a therapeutic trial of acid suppressive therapy is warranted in those patients whose dyspepsia or heartburn falls within the ulcer-like dyspepsia classification. In individuals whose symptoms are more likely to refer to the dysmotility-like dyspepsia group, acid suppressive therapy may be combined with a prokinetic agent. If symptomatic relief is obtained in either of the two groups it should be assumed that mucosal disease is present and careful follow up should be undertaken to ensure symptom relief and no recurrence of the disease process.

To ensure that *H. pylori* is not overlooked serology should probably be repeated. In patients in whom no relief is obtained a complex series of patient doctor interactions is likely to occur. Firstly, consideration should be given to ruling out the presence of any other covert disease process, particularly in the gall bladder, pancreas, or colon. Failing this symptomatic support should be provided with by counseling or the use of appropriate drugs which may decrease symptoms and allay anxiety. It is important that such individuals be carefully monitored lest their symptoms are early harbingers of some more serious medical problem.

As discussed above, specific treatment for this non-specific disease is not available. Probably one's reflex is to first give H2 receptor antagonists, followed by prescription of proton pump inhibitors.

Their failure is often diagnostic of non ulcer dyspepsia (NUD). If *Helicobacter* is found, eradication is undertaken, but this has no effect on symptoms. If one takes the view that this is neurogenic in origin, what are the gastric afferent nerve receptors that mediate the symptoms, where do they connect, what stimulates them? Perhaps the most effective agents are PPI's. If they are given to levels where acid is ablated, would the history of NUD change?

CHAPTER 5
INTRAVENOUS USE
OF ACID SUPPRESSANTS

H2 receptor antagonists and proton pump inhibitors

A variety of H2 receptor antagonists are available for intravenous use. These antagonists have a short half-life, hence their effect is no longer evident within 3-4 hrs. Nevertheless, they are widely used in a variety of acute indications and also pre-operatively in situations where it is felt that the gastro-duodenal mucosa may be at risk. Proton pump inhibitors are not only more effective, but they have long lasting action due to the fact that they bind covalently to the acid pump. In man, even in the absence of stimulation of acid secretion by food, there is basal acid secretion . In this situation there is still cycling of the pump into the active state with a half-life of 1-2hrs. With sufficient plasma levels of a PPI such as pantoprazole or omeprazole from a single bolus injection, acid suppression is more effective and has a longer duration of action than an H2 receptor antagonist.

Acute medical indications for intravenous use of acid suppressants

Hemorrhage

Of the various complications of peptic ulcer disease, hemorrhage and perforation are the most serious acute emergency situations. Bleeding occurs due to acid/peptic erosion of blood vessel walls at the site of ulceration. Spontaneous arrest of bleeding may often not occur, and large amounts of blood may be lost prior to the formation of a stable clot. The clinical consequences of continued bleeding are life threatening and can require different forms of interventional therapy which in themselves may carry a risk. Acidity is thought to prevent clotting either by interfering with the coagulation cascade itself or at least by destabilizing the clot by activating pepsinogen.

Treatment of bleeding therefore involves direct intervention in terms of stopping the bleeding with electrocautery or laser cautery and at the same time suppression of acid secretion by intravenous administration of either a H2 receptor antagonist or a proton pump inhibitor. The latter type of drug is significantly more effective than the H2 receptor class of antagonists. Such effects may be of particular benefit in variceal bleeding where the failure to adequately elevate the pH may accentuate the erosive effect of refluxate on bleeding esophageal varices.

A single injection of 80 mg omeprazole or pantoprazole abolishes acid secretion within 30 minutes. The effect of pantoprazole lasts for a mean of 16 hours. In order to ensure the maintainance of an achlorhydric state, additional injections are required. Alternatively, intra venous infusion of these compounds at a rate of 8mg/hr has been shown to prevent recurrence of acidification. The neutral pH instability of the PPI's requires a

A dose response curve measuring intragastric pH following i.v. administration of various doses of pantoprazole showing full suppression of intragastric acidity with a dose of 80 mg i.v.

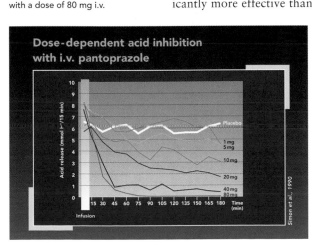

Dose-dependent acid inhibition with i.v. pantoprazole

Simon et al., 1990

formulation that has to be reconstituted at the time of use into a relatively alkaline buffer. Even with this formulation, some degree of H^+ dependent conversion to first the sulfenamide and then other products such as the sulfide can be anticipated. This is particularly likely to occur with the more unstable compounds. Hence it is usual practice to use these intravenous preparations relatively acutely.

Some years ago, it was reported that bolus administration of omeprazole to a number of critically ill patients in intensive care units was associated with visual side effects. A careful analysis of these claims demonstrated that they were without foundation.

In particular, the more serious cases could all be ascribed to anterior ischemic optic nerve neuropathy (AION) due to the primary underlying pathology such as severe hemorrhage or massive fluid loss associated with extensive burns, for example. Since these observations were also claimed to be associated with i.v. bolus administration of omeprazole, in Germany, intravenous omeprazole is now routinely administered over a 10-20 min period.

Subsequent rigorous evaluation of the effects of very high dose omeprazole in rabbits using computerized visual field analysis or clectro-rctinography failed to demonstrate any effect on vision.

Control of hyper-hyperacidity

A small number of individuals suffer from Zollinger-Ellison syndrome which is characterized by high levels of gastric acid secretion due to the hypergastrinemia resulting from the gastrinoma(s) lesion(s) of the duodenum, pancreas or their metastases. These patients rapidly develop aggressive ulcers with potential complications even in the absence of infection by *H. pylori*. Sometimes it is difficult to control the gastric hypersecretion initially with oral therapy even if PPI's are utilized. In such instances intravenous injections are utilized in order to reduce acid secretion to non-injurious levels prior to dose ranging the oral formulation. In some circumstances acute complications in gastrinoma patients

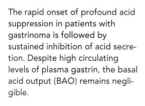
The rapid onset of profound acid suppression in patients with gastrinoma is followed by sustained inhibition of acid secretion. Despite high circulating levels of plasma gastrin, the basal acid output (BAO) remains negligible.

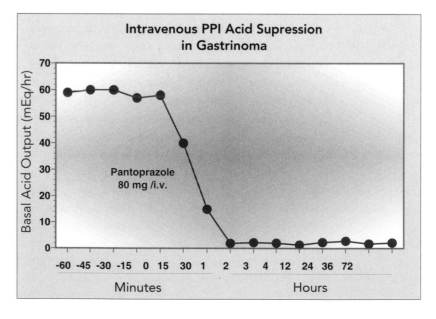

may result in the need for surgery. In such an event the intra and postoperative suppression of acid secretion may be a major problem and is best managed with i.v. PPI administration.

There are also individuals who are hypersecretors without elevation of gastrin levels (idiopathic gastric acid hypersecretors) and present with acid/pepsin induced ulceration as an emergency situation. Here again, intravenous use of PPI's may be an important agent in the initiation of appropriate therapy.

Intensive care patients

Individuals in intensive care units are often unable to tolerate oral medication and aspiration of acidic gastric juice is to be avoided given the disastrous pulmonary consequences of such an event. Furthermore the suceptibility of such patients to acute mucosal ischemic damage renders them vulnerable to acute bleeding. Again, acid control can be obtained by intravenous administration of acid suppressants. The undoubted superiority of PPI's make them the drugs of choice.

Surgical indications for intravenous use of acid suppressants	**Perforation**

Perforation

This complication of peptic ulcer disease requires surgical intervention. Clearly full inhibition of acid secretion is required. In certain circumstances such as extreme delay before presentation or major operative risk due to associated co-morbid factors conservative therapy may even be indicated. The greater efficacy of proton pump inhibitors is a major determinant supporting their usage. Since the use of oral medication is precluded given the underlying condition, intravenous injection of 80 mg of a PPI is required.

Pre-operative medication

Aspiration of acidic gastric contents is a potential complication of general anesthesia. This is a particular problem in emergency situations and also in pregnant women undergoing Caesarian section. Many anesthetists and surgeons routinely administer intravenous H2 receptor antagonists with a view to preventing gastric acidification. These antagonists are able to inhibit basal acid output but are much less effective in inhibition of vagally stimulated acid secretion. Further since they have a short duration of action, they may only adequately cover the patient during surgery if this does not last for more than 2-4 hrs. Their effect will not be evident during the post operative recovery phase or in the case of longer operations. Similarly, the use of acid suppression to protect vulnerable and often elderly patients undergoing prolonged and major surgery such as cardiac procedures, extensive multiple trauma surgery, hip replacements or major bowel resections may provide a valuable measure of added protection in the postoperative phase.

Intravenous proton pump inhibitors are effective whatever the stimulus for gastric acid secretion and have a prolonged action. These drugs should be able to provide profound anti-secretory activity generally from a single bolus injection during surgery and exhibit a sustained effect that will persist during the recovery period.

REFERENCES

Agreus, L., Talley, N.J. *Dyspepsia: current understanding and management.* Annu. Rev. Med. 49, 475-93 (1998).

Akerstrom, G. *Management of carcinoid tumors of the stomach, duodenum, and pancreas.* World Journal of Surgery 20 (2), 173-82 (Feb. 1996).

Aronson, B. *Update on peptic ulcer drugs.* American Journal of Nursing 98 (1), 41-6 (1998).

Azzoni, C., Doglioni, C., Viale, G., Delle Fave, G., De Boni, M., Caruana, P., Ferraro, G., Bordi, C. *Involvement of BCL-2 oncoprotein in the development of enterochromaffin-like cell gastric carcinoids.* American Journal of Surgical Pathology 20 (4), 433-41 (Apr. 1996).

Baldwin, G.S. *The role of gastrin and cholecystokinin in normal and neoplastic gastrointestinal growth.* Journal of Gastroenterology & Hepatology 10 (2), 215-32 (Mar.-Apr. 1995).

Bobrzynski, A. *Hormonal, secretory and morphological alterations in gastric mucosa in the course of Helicobacter pylori eradication in patients with duodenal ulcer and non-ulcer dyspepsia.* Journal of Physiology & Pharmacology 48, Suppl 3, 1-56 (Junc 1997).

Bordi, C., Falchetti, A., Azzoni, C., D'Adda, T., Canavese, G., Guariglia, A., Santini, D., Tomassetti, P., Brandi, M.L. *Aggressive forms of gastric neuroendocrine tumors in multiple endocrine neoplasia type I.* American Journal of Surgical Pathology 21 (9), 1075-82 (1997).

Bordi, C., D'Adda, T., Azzoni, C., Pilato, F.P., Caruana, P. *Hypergastrinemia and gastric enterochromaffin-like cells.* American Journal of Surgical Pathology 19, Suppl 1, S8-19 (1995).

Borin, J.F., Tang, L.H., Kidd, M., Miu, K., Bortecen, K.H., Sandor, A., Modlin, I.M. *Somatostatin receptor regulation of gastric enterochromaffin-like cell transformation to gastric carcinoid.* Surgery 120 (6), 1026-32 (Dec. 1996).

Borum, M.L. *Gastrointestinal diseases in women.* Medical Clinics of North America 82 (1), 21-50 (Jan. 1998).

Brenner, H., Rothenbacher, D., Bode, G., Adler, G. *The individual and joint contributions of Helicobacter pylori infection and family history to the risk for peptic ulcer disease.* Journal of Infectious Diseases 177 (4), 1124-7 (Apr. 1998).

Brenner, H., Rothenbacher, D., Bode, G., Adler, G. *The individual and joint contributions of Helicobacter pylori infection and family history to the risk for peptic ulcer disease.* Journal of Infectious Diseases 177 (4), 1124-7 (Apr. 1998).

Brunner, G., Luna, P., Hartmann, M., Wurst, W. *Optimizing the intragastric pH as a supportive therapy in upper GI bleeding.* Yale J. Biol. Med. 69, 225-31 (1996).

Cornell, S. *New treatments for peptic ulcer disease.* Advance for Nurse Practitioners 5 (3), 57-9 (Mar. 1997).

De Boer, W.A. *Helicobacter pylori and non-ulcer dyspepsia.* Scandinavian Journal of Gastroenterology 32 (11), 1183-4 (Nov. 1997).

Debelenko, L.V., Emmert-Buck, M.R., Zhuang, Z., Epshteyn, E., Moskaluk, C.A., Jensen, R.T., Liotta, L.A., Lubensky, I.A. *The multiple endocrine neoplasia type I gene locus is involved in the pathogenesis of type II gastric carcinoids.* Gastroenterology 113 (3), 773-81 (Sept. 1997).

Dupuytren, G. *Leçons Orales.* Brussels, 1836.

Eastwood, G.L. *Is smoking still important in the pathogenesis of peptic ulcer disease?* Journal of Clinical Gastroenterology 25, Suppl. 1, S1-7 (1997).

el-Nujumi, A., Williams, C., Ardill, J.E., Oien, K., McColl, K.E. *Eradicating Helicobacter pylori reduces hypergastrinaemia during long-term omeprazole treatment.* Gut 42 (2), 159-65 (Feb. 1998).

Ephgrave, K.S., Kleiman-Wexler, R., Pfaller, M., Booth, BM., Reed, D., Werkmeister, L., Young, S. *Effects of sucralfate vs antacids on gastric pathogens: results of a double-blind clinical trial.* Archives of Surgery 133 (3), 251-7 (Mar. 1998).

Fass, R., Fullerton, S., Naliboff, B., Hirsh, T., Mayer, E.A. *Sexual dysfunction in patients with irritable bowel syndrome and non-ulcer dyspepsia.* Digestion 59 (1), 79-85 (1998).

Figura, N. *Are Helicobacter pylori differences important in the development of Helicobacter pylori-related diseases?* Italian Journal of Gastroenterology and Hepatology 29 (4), 367-74 (Aug. 1997).

Figura, N. *Helicobacter pylori factors involved in the development of gastroduodenal mucosal damage and ulceration.* Journal of Clinical Gastroenterology 25 (Suppl 1), S149-63 (1997).

Fitton, A., Wiseman, L. *Pantoprazole, a review of its pharmacology and therapeutic use in acid-related disorders.* Drugs 51 (1996).

Freston, J.W. *Long-term acid control and proton pump inhibitors: interactions and safety issues in perspective.* American Journal of Gastroenterology 92 (Suppl. 4), 51S-55S, discussion 55S-57S (Apr. 1997).

Froehlich, F., Gonvers, J.J., Beglinger, C. *Has the time now arrived to eradicate Helicobacter pylori routinely in non-ulcer dyspepsia?* European Journal of Gastroenterology & Hepatology 9 (9), 917 (Sept. 1997).

Gambassi, G., Festa, V., Bernabei, R. *Could there be an aspirin good to your stomach?* American Journal of Gastroenterology 92 (11), 2135 (Nov. 1997).

Gilvarry, J., Buckley, M.J., Beattie, S., Hamilton, H., O'Morain, C.A. *Eradication of Helicobacter pylori affects symptoms in non-ulcer dyspepsia.* Scandinavian Journal of Gastroenterology 32 (6), 535-40 (June 1997).

Graham, D.Y. *Nonsteroidal anti-inflammatory drugs, Helicobacter pylori, and ulcers: where we stand.* American Journal of Gastroenterology 91 (10), 2080-6 (Oct. 1996).

Gullotta, R., Ferraris, L., Cortelezzi, C., Minoli, G., Prada, A., Comin, U., Rocca, F., Ferrara, A., Curzio, M. *Are we correctly using the inhibitors of gastric acid secretion and cytoprotective drugs? Results of a multicentre study.* Italian Journal of Gastroenterology and Hepatology 29 (4), 325-9 (Aug. 1997).

Haga, Y., Nakatsura, T., Shibata, Y., Sameshima, H., Nakamura, Y., Tanimura, M., Ogawa, M. *Human gastric carcinoid detected during long-term antiulcer therapy of H2 receptor antagonist and proton pump inhibitor.* Digestive Diseases & Sciences 43 (2), 253-7 (Feb. 1998).

Hawkey, C.J., Yeomans, N.D., Gillon, K. *Helicobacter pylori, NSAIDs, and peptic ulcers.* Lancet 351 (9095), 61, discussion 61-2 (Jan. 3, 1998).

Higham, A.D., Dimaline, R., Varro, A., Attwood, S., Armstrong, G., Dockray, G.J., Thompson, D.G. *Octreotide suppression test predicts beneficial outcome from antrectomy in a patient with gastric carcinoid tumor*. Gastroenterology 114 (4), 817-22 (Apr. 1998).

Hippocrates. *The Geniune Works of Hippocrates*. Translated by F. Adams. London, Sydenham Soc., 1899, p. 155-161.

Hunt, R.H., Cederberg, C., Dent, J. et al. *Optimizing acid suppression for treatment of acid-related diseases*. Dig. Dis. Sci. 40, 24S-49S (1995).

Jolobe, O.M. *Helicobacter pylori, NSAIDs, and peptic ulcers*. Lancet 351 (9095), 61 (1998).

Judmaier, G., Koelz, H.R. *Comparison of pantoprazole and ranitidine in the treatment of acute duodenal ulcer*. Aliment. Pharmacol. Therap. 8, 81-86 (1994).

Kojima, K., Miyake, M., Nakagawa, H., Yunoki, Y., Ogurusu, K., Saino, S., Wani, T., Kawaguchi, Y. *Multiple gastric carcinoids and pituitary adenoma in type A gastritis*. Internal Medicine 36 (11), 787-9 (Nov. 1997).

Kokkola, A., Sjoblom, S.M., Haapiainen, R., Sipponen, P, Puolakkainen, P., Jarvinen, H. *The risk of gastric carcinoma and carcinoid tumours in patients with pernicious anaemia. A prospective follow-up study*. Scandinavian Journal of Gastroenterology 33 (1), 88-92 (Jan. 1998).

Kolby, L., Wangberg, B., Ahlman, H., Modlin, I.M., Granerus, G., Theodorsson, E., Nilsson, O. *Histidine decarboxylase expression and histamine metabolism in gastric oxyntic mucosa during hypergastrinemia and carcinoid tumor formation*. Endocrinology 137 (10), 4435-42 (Oct. 1996).

Levenstein, S. *Stress and peptic ulcer: life beyond Helicobacter*. BMJ. 316 (7130), 538-41 (Feb. 1998).

Metz, D.C. *Eradicate the bug before you start the drug?* American Journal of Gastroenterology 93 (2), 279-80 (Feb. 1998).

Mittal, B.R., Dhiman, R.K., Maini, A., Sewatkar, A.B., Das, B.K. *Gastric emptying in patients with non ulcer dyspepsia (dysmotility type)*. Tropical Gastroenterology 18 (2), 67-9 (April-June 1997).

Modlin, I.M. *From Prout to the Proton Pump - A history of the Science of Gastric Acid Secretion and the Surgery of Peptic Ulcer*. SG&O 170, 81-96 (1990).

Modlin, I.M., Gilligan, C.J., Lawton, G.P., Tang, L.H., West, A.B., Darr, U. *Gastric carcinoids. The Yale Experience*. Archives of Surgery 130 (3), 250-5, discussion 255-6 (Mar. 1995).

Modlin, I.M., Gilligan, C.J., Lawton, G.P., Tang, L.H., West, A.B., Lindenberg, R. *Observations on relationship between hypergastrinemia, multiple gastric carcinoids, and pancreatic mass*. Digestive Diseases & Sciences 41 (1), 105-14 (Jan. 1996).

Modlin, I.M., Goldenring, J.R., Lawton, G.P. et al. *Aspects of the theoretical basis and clinical relevance of low acid states*. Am. J. Gastroenterol. 89, 308-318 (1994).

Modlin, I.M., Sandor, A. *Analysis of 8305 cases of carcinoid tumors*. Cancer 79, 813-829 (1997).

Modlin, I.M., Sandor, A., Tang, L.H., Kidd, M., Zelterman, D. *A 40-year analysis of 265 gastric carcinoids*. American Journal of Gastroenterology 92 (4), 633-8 (Apr. 1997).

Modlin, I.M., Tang, L.H. *The Enterochromaffin-like cell - an enigmatic cellular lesion (ECL)*. Gastro. 111, 738-810 (1996).

Modlin, I.M., Waisbren, S.J. *Pavlov in the U.S.A.* Gastro. Int. 6, 48-53 (1993).

Nakajima, N., Kuwayama, H., Ito, Y., Iwasaki, A., Arakawa, Y. *Helicobacter pylori, neutrophils, interleukins, and gastric epithelial proliferation*. Journal of Clinical Gastroenterology 25 (Suppl. 1), S198-202 (1997).

Parsonnet, J. *Helicobacter pylori*. Infectious Disease Clinics of North America 12 (1), 185-97 (Mar. 1998).

Perng, C.L., Kim, J.G., El-Zimaity, H.M., Osato, M.S., Graham, D.Y. *One-week triple therapy with lansoprazole, clarithromycin, and metronidazole to cure Helicobacter pylori infection in peptic ulcer disease in Korea*. Digestive Diseases & Sciences 43 (3), 464-7 (Mar. 1998).

Raiha, I., Kemppainen, H., Kaprio, J., Koskenvuo, M., Sourander, L. *Lifestyle, stress, and genes in peptic ulcer disease: a nationwide twin cohort study*. Archives of Internal Medicine 158 (7), 698-704 (Apr. 13, 1998).

Rindi, G., Bordi, C., Rappel, S., La Rosa, S., Stolte, M., Solcia, E. *Gastric carcinoids and neuroendocrine carcinomas: pathogenesis, pathology, and behavior*. World Journal of Surgery 20 (2), 168-72 (Feb. 1996).

Ryberg, B., Tielemanns, Y., Axelson, J., Carlsson, E., Hakanson, R. et al. *Gastrin stimulates the self-replication rate of enterochromaffinlike cells in the rat stomach. Effects of omeprazole, ranitidine, and gastrin-17 in antrectomized rats*. Gastroenterology 99, 935-942 (1990).

Sippy, B.W. *Relative value of medical treatment and surgical treatment of gastric and duodenal ulcer*. JAMA 26 (July 1, 1922).

Sprung, D.J., Apter, M.N. *What is the role of Helicobacter pylori in peptic ulcer and gastric cancer outside the big cities?* Journal of Clinical Gastroenterology 26 (1), 60-3 (Jan. 1998).

Sundler, F., Willems, G. *Gastrin stimulates the self-replication of enterochromaffinlike cells in the rat stomach*. Gastroenterology 99, 935-942 (1990).

Tang, L.H., Modlin, I.M. *Somatostatin receptor regulation of gastric carcinoid tumours*. Digestion 57 (Suppl. 1), 11-4 (1996).

Tang, L.H., Modlin, I.M., Lawton, G.P., Kidd, M., Chinery, R. *The role of transforming growth factor alpha in the enterochromaffin-like cell tumor autonomy in an African rodent Mastomys*. Gastroenterology 111 (5), 1212-23 (Nov. 1996).

Tielemanns, Y., Willems, G., Sundler, F., Hakanson, R. *Self replication of enterochromaffinlike cells in the mouse stomach*. Digestion 35, 23-41 (1986).

Veldhuyzen van Zanten, S.J. *The role of Helicobacter pylori infection in non-ulcer dyspepsia*. Alimentary Pharmacology & Therapeutics 11 (Suppl. 1), 63-9 (Apr. 1997).

Wangberg, B., Nilsson, O., Theodorsson, E., Modlin, I.M., Dahlstrom, A., Ahlman, H. *Are enterochromaffinlike cell tumours reversible? An experimental study on gastric carcinoids induced in Mastomys by histamine2-receptor blockade*. Regulatory Peptides 56 (1), 19-33 (Mar. 7, 1995).

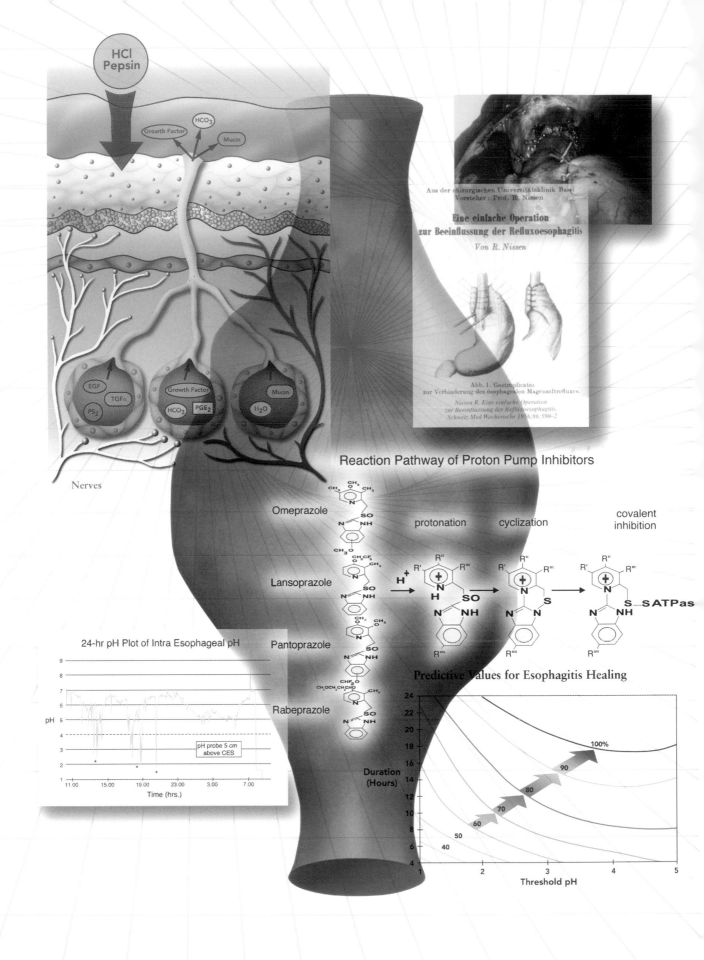

HCl
Pepsin

Growth Factor

HCO₃

Mucin

EGF

TGFα

PS₂

Growth Factor

HCO₃

PGE₂

Mucin

H₂O

Nerves

Aus der chirurgischen Universitätsklinik Basel
Vorsteher : Prof. R. Nissen

Eine einfache Operation
zur Beeinflussung der Refluxoesophagitis

Von R. Nissen

Abb. 1. Gastroplicatio
zur Verhinderung des ösophagealen Magensaftrefluxes.

Nissen R. Eine einfache Operation
zur Beeinflussung der Refluxoesophagitis.
Schweiz Med Wochenschr 1956;86:590–2

Reaction Pathway of Proton Pump Inhibitors

Omeprazole

Lansoprazole

Pantoprazole

Rabeprazole

protonation   cyclization   covalent
inhibition

H⁺

S—S ATPas

24-hr pH Plot of Intra Esophageal pH

pH

9
8
7
6
5
4
3
2
1

11.00   15.00   19.00   23.00   3.00   7.00

pH probe 5 cm
above CES

Time (hrs.)

Predictive Values for Esophagitis Healing

Duration
(Hours)

24
22
20
18
16
14
12
10
8
6
4

100%

90

80

70

60

50

40

1   2   3   4   5

Threshold pH

GASTRO-ESOPHAGEAL REFLUX DISEASE

THE PROBLEM OF THE NEXT MILLENNIUM

CHAPTER 1

Evolution of the Disease

CHAPTER 2

Biology

CHAPTER 3

Physiology and Functional Studies

CHAPTER 4

Management

CHAPTER 5

Barrett's

CHAPTER 6

Consensus

CHAPTER 1
EVOLUTION OF THE DISEASE

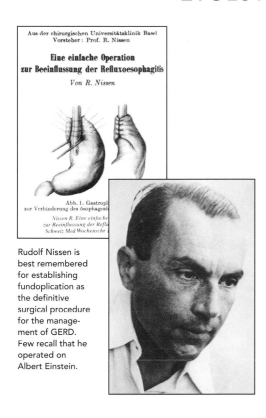

Rudolf Nissen is best remembered for establishing fundoplication as the definitive surgical procedure for the management of GERD. Few recall that he operated on Albert Einstein.

In recent years there has been an increased awareness among both patients and doctors of the increasing prevalence of gastroesophageal reflux disease (GERD). It has been estimated that as much as 20% of the population of the USA experience symptoms associated with the disease. Of interest is the observation that the incidence of diagnosis appears to be increasing in a linear fashion in countries which are generally regarded as of the first world, whilst in less developed areas the disease is still relatively rare. Indeed in the early part of the century the disease was virtually unknown and as late as 1930 the literature contained information on less than 100 patients. Current information suggests that the disease has reached almost epidemic proportions in some areas and has raised the specter of a similar increase in the identification of Barrett's esophagus. This increase in diagnosis and awareness has been associated with recent changes in the availability of effective pharmacological and surgical treatments for the condition, and an increasing knowledge of some of the basic mechanisms underlying gastroesophageal reflux.

Peptic ulcer of the esophagus was first reported by Albert in 1839 and its histology described in 1879 by Quinke. However by 1906 Tilestone could report a mere 8 patients. The disease was regarded as so rare and obscure that in 1926 Von Hacker and Lothiesicu could only collect 91 cases although few were verified by autopsy. In 1929 Friedenwald and his colleagues reported 13 cases and their experimental results in animals documented that esophageal ulcer healed rapidly if hydrochloric acid was withheld from the lesion. Stewart noted one esophageal ulcer in 10,000 autopsies in 1929 and in the same year Sir Arthur F. Hurst, the doyen of British Gastroenterology could only document 11 patients. In Philadelphia Chevalier Jackson in 1929 in reviewing 4,000 consecutive esophagoscopies identified 88 cases (21 active and 67 healed). The alteration in incidence and recognition of this disease process in the remainder of the century has been remarkable and is worthy of consideration.

The prevalence of GERD varies considerably from country to country and reflects not only the level to which subjective symptomatology is investigated but the psyche of the population and its physicians. Overall it may range from less than 1% in Senegal to almost 23% in the United Kingdom. Gastroesophageal reflux is now the most common upper gastrointestinal disorder in the Western world. Thus 7 to 10% of the adult population

The increased prevalence of GERD appears to be reflected in the economic and social development of countries.

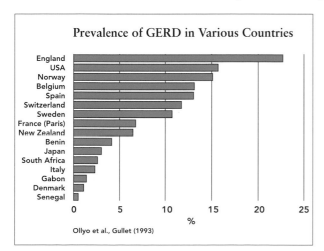

Prevalence of GERD in Various Countries

Ollyo et al., Gullet (1993)

may report daily heartburn, while up to 30 - 40% of patients complain of symptoms compatible with the disease on a monthly basis. The spectrum of complaints ranges from only occasional heartburn to a far more severe course. This may include increasing degrees of esophageal injury with associated progressive sphincter dysfunction culminating in the development of Barrett's metaplasia and even adenocarcinoma. This disease currently represents one of the fastest growing categories of cancer in the United States with a threefold increase during the time period 1983-1987 as compared to 1973-1977. Although up to 40% of adults complain of heartburn, only 2% of this group show erosive esophagitis to an extent that warrants pharmacological therapeutic intervention. Complications have been variously reported to develop in up to 21.6% of such patients. These may include either ulcer (2-7%), hemorrhage (< 2%), stricture (4-20%) or Barrett's esophagus (10-15%). Symptomatic GERD is a chronic disease requiring long-term management in most patients. Although the treatment initially exhibited a bias toward surgical management, it has become pharmacologically orientated during the past two decades. The introduction of two classes of gastric acid inhibitory agents: the H2RA's and PPI's resulted in a massive amplification of the utility of medical therapy. Two pivotal issues have required consideration in management. The first is the recognition that relapse continue to be a significant event in the pharmacological management of such patients. More than 80% of the patients relapse within 6 months after the cessation of therapy. Long-term drug therapy is usually necessary. The second is the recent availability of minimally invasive surgery and the suggestion that the nature and consequences of surgical intervention now require re-evaluation. The enthusiasm for laparoscopically undertaken anti-reflux procedures has mounted exponentially since the initial experience reported by Dallemagne in 1991. It is a widely held belief amongst surgeons that a laparoscopic procedure combines the potential of excellent long-term results with low morbidity/mortality and significant cost-effective advantages. Whether such claims can be substantiated in the long-term remains to be resolved.

The concept of GERD progressing into a series of potential complications is linked to the uncontrolled reflux of acid and pepsin into the lower esophagus.

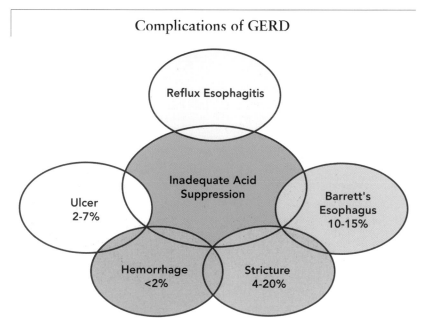

Complications of GERD

Reflux Esophagitis

Inadequate Acid Suppression

Ulcer 2-7%

Barrett's Esophagus 10-15%

Hemorrhage <2%

Stricture 4-20%

The recognition in the first part of this century that mucosal damage was caused by acid ("*no acid - no ulcer*") and that this acid could be decreased by luminal neutralization resulted in application of antacid preparations, bland diets and milk infusion as therapeutic options. The subsequent categorizing of the H2RA and the development of agents specifically capable of blocking this receptor revolutionized the management of acid related diseases and virtually abrogated surgery as a therapeutic option for peptic ulcer except in cases of emergency. However, the relatively large relapse rates for GERD even on high dose H2RA therapy still engendered considerable enthusiasm for surgical intervention in the management of reflux disease. The more recent identification of the specific molecular mechanism of acid secretion – the proton pump (H,K ATPase) – resulted in the development of a new class of therapeutic agents, the proton pump inhibitor (PPI) class of drugs. These are significantly more effective in the treatment of GERD given their improved efficacy as acid secretory inhibitors. Generalized concepts of loss of sphincter tone, inability of clearance of the lower esophagus of refluxed acid peptic material and the insidious effects of a variety of ill defined noxious agents are all tenable etiologic factors in these diseases. Nevertheless, the principle of decreasing gastric acid secretion and increasing the pH in the lower esophagus has been clearly demonstrated to be therapeutically effective. Arguments regarding which compound, which dosage and which schedule of administration appear to be reasonably specious at this time based on the obvious recognition that the longer the time period for which the pH is elevated, the greater the degree of symptom relief and healing. Similarly the higher the level of pH achieved, the better the results. This observation reflects the well defined enzyme kinetics and pH optima for pepsin which probably plays a major catalytic role in the genesis of mucosal damage and in addition obviates optimal healing.

Utilizing such criteria, the PPI class of drugs clearly are today the primary therapeutic agents. A secondary pharmacological option which may well be of considerable clinical relevance once appropriate agents are developed is the use of motility directed or pro-kinetic substances to facilitate clearance of acid-peptic material from the lower esophagus. Similarly, the introduction of agents to increase the lower esophageal sphincter (LES) tone thus further inhibiting the ability of gastric contents to regularly enter the lower esophageal area would confer an obvious advantage. The current failure to identify a specific agent capable of targeting the lower esophageal sphincter has to date hindered the widespread clinical use of this type of strategy.

Unfortunately, whilst drugs can be delivered via existing anatomic routes, the surgical option required a significant degree of trauma to obtain its quotient. For this reason, the introduction of laparoscopic surgery has engendered extraordinary enthusiasm based upon the swelling chorus of acclamation relating to its minimally invasive nature. A further significant consideration is that surgery in a definable fashion increases (albeit unpredictably) lower esophageal sphincter pressure, thus ameliorating reflux. Such surgery appears to have advantages as regards reduced hospital stay and faster return to activity thus supporting a notion that is cost-effective. Additionally both surgeons and patients purport to express a high degree of satisfaction with this procedure.

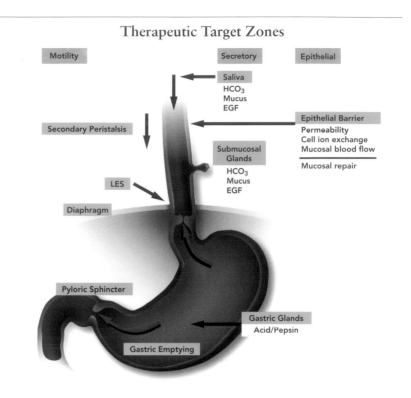

The possible sites of therapeutic intervention in GERD are related to the areas of pathophysiology involved in the genesis of the disease process.

Etiology

The esophagus, stomach, and duodenum should be a one-way system for the transit of food into the rest of the gastrointestinal tract. The stomach functions both as a reservoir and as a pump. Gastric peristalsis results in an increase in pressure whereby the valve constituted by the pylorus opens at a lower pressure than the lower esophageal sphincter. The gastric pacemaker initiates pressure waves directed toward the pyloric valve further ensuring that food mixed with acid and pepsin exits from the gastric pump/reservoir in an aboral fashion. The reflux of gastric contents into the esophagus is an abnormal situation and generally has been accepted as reflective of failure of the esophageal component of the system. It is, however, worthy of consideration that the failure of the pylorus to relax appropriately or the gastric peristaltic wave to be coordinated with the function of both sphincters may also play a part in the genesis of the reflux scenario. Under such circumstances the lower esophageal sphincter, which normally opens intermittently to permit food to enter the stomach, exhibits an inability to remain closed as gastric pressure increases to force food toward the pylorus, through it and into the duodenum. In mechanical terms reflux, therefore, simply represents leakage of the proximal (lower esophageal sphincter) valve system of a one-way cycling pump (the stomach). As a result of failure of either motility coordination and/or valve competency, noxious agents are delivered into the lower esophagus for varying periods of time.

The ability of the esophagus to withstand the presence of barrier breaking agents such as acid, pepsin, and occasionally bile, is in general maintained by the stratified squamous epithelial barrier. In addition, protection is afforded by the secretion of glands in the lower third as well as the presence of esophageal "stripping" waves, whereby refluxate is readily and efficiently cleared from the esophagus back into the stomach. Under circumstances where a number of different factors may function suboptimally (decreased pressure of the lower esophageal sphincter, decreased clearance of lower esophageal contents, decrease of the barrier function), inflammatory sequelae are initiated in the lower esophagus. Since the stratified squamous epithelium of the lower esophagus does not have either the tight junctions or the apical barrier properties of the gastric mucosa, damage to it results in inflammation which may be difficult to heal. Indeed meta analysis data indicate that the pH of the lower esophagus needs to be significantly greater than that in the duodenum to ensure healing.

Repeated episodes of inflammation with incomplete healing presumably reflect an ongoing pathological process which culminates both in the loss of esophageal glands and the development of scar tissue. A further progression of the ongoing healing /damage cycle is the alteration in the phenotype of the mucosa towards a columnar epithelium predominance and ultimately intestinal metaplasia. Presumably the interface between the squamous epithelium of the esophagus and the columnar of the stomach represents a junctional zone with a degree of instability and even susceptibility to damage. Once injury has failed to heal or been initiated on a number of occasions, the area presumably becomes more vulnerable and esophagitis remains in place with constant susceptibility to further reflux and damage. Under such circumstances the chronic nature and relapsing course of GERD are understandable.

Reflux Etiology

Current concepts in the etiology of GERD.

The clinical problem is best characterized by the loss of an efficient reflux barrier which results in a retrograde passage of gastric contents in the esophagus. Whilst the mean basal pressure of the lower esophageal sphincter is significantly lower in patients with GERD, especially in those with severe esophagitis, there is significant overlap between normal and GERD patients. Whether this is a *post hoc* phenomenon or reflects the primary etiology of the disease has not been adequately established. Nevertheless it seems apparent that transient lower esophageal sphincter relaxation, not associated with swallowing, may be responsible for GERD in some patients with mild to moderate disease. The spectrum of alterations in lower esophageal sphincter pressure, however, is wide. Thus in some circumstances basal lower esophageal sphincter pressure may be normal but the number of transient inappropriate lower esophageal sphincter relaxations abnormally high. Alternatively in some individuals a persistent, but as yet uncharacterized, defect of lower esophageal sphincter control is associated with permanent low resting sphincter pressure and almost constant reflux. It is unknown at present what regulates the transient spontaneous relaxation of the lower esophageal sphincter but it is apparent that in up to 80% of GERD patients reflux episodes are associated with transient lower esophageal sphincter relaxation. The modulation of lower esophageal sphincter function has been determined to include at least: vagal pathways, hormones such as gastrin and cholecystokinin, nitric oxide, and a number of other regulators including VIP, acetyl choline and serotonin.

Botulinum toxin has been demonstrated to result in profound lower esophageal sphincter relaxation and proposed to be of some putative efficacy in the management of achalasia. Although its current application by endoscopic injection is somewhat impractical it may provide a viable avenue for further exploration of the function of smooth muscle system at the gastroesophageal junction. Presumably the delineation of the function of the gastric pacemaker and its efferent regulatory mechanism will be needed to further define the regulation of the pumping action of the stomach and its associated valves.

Once reflux has occurred the degree of mucosal damage reflects a number of variables. Firstly, the ability of the esophagus to clear the reflux material. Secondly, the precise nature of the refluxate and lastly, the degree of mucosal resistance. It is clearly apparent that there exists a direct correlation between the exposure of the esophagus to acid and the severity of GERD. Thus individuals with severe disease suffer from longer reflux periods and demonstrate more frequent reflux episodes. Moreover their esophageal pH remains below 4 for significantly longer periods of time than those patients with milder forms of the disease.

The stomach itself is an important variable in determining GERD. Indeed it has even been proposed that the entire disease process may be a consequence of disordered gastric motility. Abnormalities in antral motor motility either due to disordered pacemaker cycling or in-coordinate peristalsis may result in gastric contents being inappropriately moved in a retrograde fashion towards the oral valve (lower esophageal sphincter). Under such circumstances alterations in the rate of gastric emptying, duodeno-gastric reflux, and the volume of gastric contents as determined by the degree of gastric accommodation and distension may be critical variables in the establishment and maintenance of gastric esophageal reflux disease. In many individuals delayed gastric emptying is demonstrable and in fact the gastric emptying rate can be related to the degree of esophageal damage.

Of further importance is the fact that patients with GERD who are resistant to medical therapy have been demonstrated to display delayed gastric emptying of solids more often than those who respond well to treatment. Thus it becomes more apparent that the mechanical issues relating to reflux may be the primary determinant of the disease process whilst the inflammatory responses simply reflect the sequelae of the refluxate itself. Under such circumstances treatment directed towards the diminution of damage to the lower esophagus should be recognized as addressing the aftermath of the problem rather than dealing with the problem itself. In this respect the motor function of the corpus fundus region of the stomach is little understood. This area which is directly adjacent to the lower esophageal sphincter is primarily responsible for the regulation of intragastric pressure whereby the physiological function of accommodation is utilized to increase the gastric capacitance without a concomitant increase in pressure. Although a complex interrelationship between the smooth muscle fibers of the lower esophageal sphincter and the gastric wall of this region has been anatomically defined little knowledge is available regarding the physiological interface between the lower esophagus and the gastric fundus as a functional unit. A loss of regulatory interaction between the gastric fundus and the lower esophageal area which involves alteration in the function of the lower esophageal sphincter might easily therefore be a critical component of the initiating pathogenesis of this disease process. It has been demonstrated that in patients with GERD, fundic distension results in a lower esophageal sphincter pressure response when compared to healthy controls. Under such circumstances it might be predicted that delayed gastric emptying of either liquids or solids would facilitate gastroesophageal reflux.

In summary, esophagitis should be regarded as a mucosal inflammatory disease secondary to mechanical events which infringe upon the function of the lower esophageal sphincter. The high relapse and recurrence rate of GERD may be predicted based on the fact that the majority of current therapy is directed at dealing with the consequences of the pathology (inflammation) and its healing rather than the primary etiology which is an as yet inadequately characterized mechanical or electrical phenomenon, probably of gastric origin. Under such circumstances it may be predicted that once a certain degree of damage has been inflicted upon the lower esophageal mucosa, acid suppressive therapy is only able to ameliorate symptomatology and maintain or stabilize the damage and scar already present. In this respect, medical therapy while successful in facilitating healing, can do little more than maintain a steady state whilst the motor abnormalities of the stomach, pyloric valve and lower esophageal sphincter persist.

CHAPTER 2
BIOLOGY

The esophageal epithelium

The junctions between the squamous epithelial cells lining the esophagus are quite different from the junctions between epithelial cells in other regions of the gastrointestinal tract, where tight junctions link the luminal ends of columnar epithelial cells by a functional "belt" comprising specialized membrane and intra-cellular proteins such as occludin and Zoo 1. Such tight junctions can be classi-fied based on the number of strands into "tight" and "leaky" tight junctions. The gastric epithelium has "tight" tight junctions with as many as 15 adhesive strands of protein. At best the tight junctions visualized in the first layer of the esophageal epithelium contain 2 or so strands and must be extremely leaky. In the stratified squamous epithelium of the esophagus, adjacent epithelial cells are joined more loosely by desmosomes (gap junctions), connected by intracellular intermediate filaments. The barrier function of the cells lining the esophagus is therefore normally dependent not upon tight junctions but by the multiplicity of cell layers comprising the stratified epithelium and the intercellular spaces between these

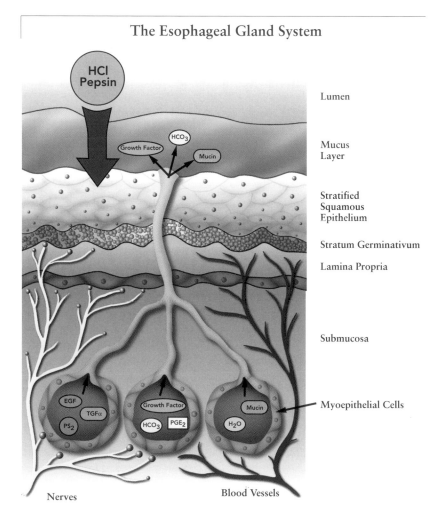

The Esophageal Gland System

Lumen

Mucus Layer

Stratified Squamous Epithelium

Stratum Germinativum

Lamina Propria

Submucosa

Myoepithelial Cells

Nerves

Blood Vessels

The lower end of the esophagus has a limited supply of glands. These are of importance as a component of the defense mech-anism to reflux and may be of relevance in healing.

cell layers. The esophagus may be considered as analogous to "wet skin" and in this respect even behave in a similar fashion when damaged.

In GERD the spaces between squamous epithelial cells enlarge, thereby perhaps allowing luminal contents more access to the submucosa. Whether enlargement of the intercellular space is the primary event or secondary to cell shrinkage is not entirely clear and requires to be determined.

Esophageal anatomy and physiology

The esophagus is normally a collapsed empty tube. During swallowing, transient phrenic ampulla form as a consequence of physiologic herniation associated with longitudinal muscle contraction during peristalsis. The process of esophageal emptying slows significantly with formation of the phrenic ampulla from about 3 cm/sec characteristic of peristalsis to about 1 cm/sec. The ampulla appears to form as a result of longitudinal shortening of the esophagus thus forming a closed chamber, bound above by the distal esophagus, and below by crural diaphragm. Since the lower esophageal sphincter moves about 2 cm with each swallow, an important part of its anatomic stabilisation is the elastic recoil provided by the phreno-esophageal ligament. Emptying of the ampulla occurs in conjunction with relengthening of the esophagus. These mechanistic descriptions have anatomic implications.

There appears to be a sequential activation of esophageal longitudinal muscle with progression of the peristaltic contraction. It is possible that each longitudinal section is subsequently re-elongated by contraction of the adjacent distal segment. The distal end of the esophagus is anchored to the diaphragm by the phrenoesophageal (PE) membrane, formed by the fused endothoracic and endoabdominal fascia. The PE membrane has elastic properties and inserts circumferentially into the esophageal musculature close to the squamocolumnar junction, normally residing within the esophageal hiatus. Thus the PE ligament is stretched with each swallow and its elastic recoil is responsible for pulling the squamocolumnar junction back to its normal position after shortening. This repetitive stress subjects the PE ligament to substantial wear and tear, making it a plausible target of age-related degeneration.

Gastroesophageal junction

The gastroesophageal junction is a complex sphincter composed of both a diaphragmatic element and the smooth muscle lower esophageal sphincter (LES). This anatomically and physiologically complex organ is vulnerable to dysfunction by several mechanisms. Mechanically, the gastroesophageal junction must protect against reflux in both static and dynamic conditions. Failure to adequately prevent reflux is associated with both the initiation of GERD as well as relapse and chronicity of the disease.

A prerequisite for the development of GERD is movement of acid and pepsin from the stomach into the esophagus. Under normal circumstances, gastroesophageal reflux is prevented by a competent gastroesophageal junction.

This antireflux barrier is an anatomically complex zone whose functional integrity has been variably attributed to intrinsic lower esophageal sphincter pressure, extrinsic compression of the lower esophageal sphincter by the crural diaphragm, intra-abdominal location of the lower esophageal sphincter, integrity of the PE ligament, and maintenance of the angle of entry of esophagus into the stomach (His).

It is most probable that competence of this barrier is attributable to more than one of these factors, and incompetence becomes increasingly severe as more mechanisms are compromised.

However, evidence for functional integrity is most compelling in the cases of the lower esophageal sphincter and the crural diaphragm.

Gastroesophageal Junction Pressure Zone

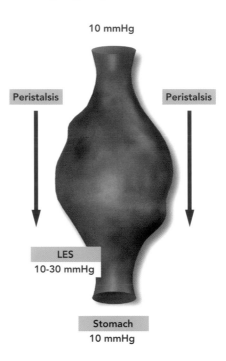

The lower 5-7 cm of the esophagus function as a dynamic peristaltic mechanism or ampulla serving both to empty swallowed material into the stomach and dispose of gastric refluxate.

The lower esophageal sphincter

Over the last three decades considerable attention has focused on those factors which are normally responsible for maintaining the lower esophageal sphincter (LES) contracted, yet allowing for transient relaxation during a swallow. It is known from animal models that electrical stimulation of the lower esophageal sphincter leads to relaxation. Early research on the control of sphincter tone led to the cholinergic hypothesis, in which it was felt that the tone of the lower esophageal sphincter was controlled by cholinergic nerves. However, not all of the experimental evidence fitted neatly. For example, in humans, vagotomy does not in general reduce this tone. Also, in the 1970s, gastrin was demonstrated to be a modulator, but since none of the classical neurotransmitters or peptide hormones then identified accounted for all lower esophageal sphincter tone, an inherent myogenic tone was also proposed as a component of the system.

Most recently, studies have shown that at least 50% of the neurons innervating the lower esophageal sphincter possess nitric oxide synthase, thus implicating nitric oxide as a possible mediator in relaxation of the lower esophageal sphincter. In an animal model, the lower esophageal sphincter can be induced to contract or relax when exposed to arachidonic acid and its metabolites. Since arachidonic acid is produced by the action of phospholipase A2, and is a precursor of prostaglandins and leukotrienes, these pro-inflammatory substances may also be implicated in lower esophageal sphincter pathology.

The lower esophageal sphincter is a 3-4 cm long segment of tonically contracted smooth muscle at the distal end of the esophagus. Resting tone varies between 10-30 mmHg in normal individuals and is least in the postcibal period and greatest at night. Intra-abdominal pressure, gastric distension, peptides, hormones, various foods, and many drugs affect this pressure. Lower esophageal sphincter tonic contraction itself is a property of both the surrounding muscle and the extrinsic innervation. Anatomically, the proximal margin of the lower esophageal sphincter is effectively about 1.5 cm above the Z line, which is in close proximity to the PE ligament. In contrast, the distal margin is about 2cm distal to the Z line, bounded inferiorly by the angle of His. The resultant is a segment whose distal portion herniates through the hiatus as a consequence of esophageal shortening, with the formation of the phrenic ampulla.

The crural diaphragm encircling the lower esophageal sphincter serves a sphincteric function. The diaphragm appears to augment the lower esophageal sphincter during transient periods of increased intra-abdominal pressure (e.g. inspiration, coughing). Electrical and mechanical inhibition of the crural diaphragm have been demonstrated during transient lower esophageal sphincter relaxations. The concept of the intrinsic pressure zone augmented by an extrinsic system has enabled consideration of a dual mechanism known as the two sphincter hypothesis of gastroesophageal junction competence.

CHAPTER 3
PHYSIOLOGY AND FUNCTIONAL STUDIES

Esophageal function testing

Motility

The detection of reflux and abnormal motility as well as disturbances in gastric emptying is easily visualized using fluoroscopy. Although fluoroscopy displays patterns of transit secondary to motor events with excellent resolution, manometry is usually required to define the underlying patterns which may be radiologically revealed. Imaging is useful in demonstrating obstruction and even reflux but is not particularly effective in identifying "underpowered" peristalsis, which is best delineated using manometric techniques. The identification of reflux events on fluoroscopy can be misleading in the short time period of such an examination and require esophageal pH monitoring and even manometric studies to fully define and confirm the clinical relevance of such events.

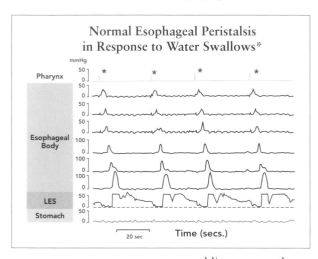

Normal Esophageal Peristalsis in Response to Water Swallows*

Esophageal peristalsis in a complex electro-myometric series of descending sequenced contractions culminating in a terminal sphincter (LES) relaxation.

Intraluminal pressures in the esophagus may be measured by either water perfused manometric assemblies connected to external pressure transfusers or recording assemblies utilizing intraluminal transfusers. The latter technique does not require water perfusion which is an advantage but is expensive, fragile and costly to repair. The perfused manometric assemblies are, therefore, most widely used given their relative low cost, easy maintenance and reliable function. They consist of an extrusion with multiple fine channels each of which open sideways at the esophageal lumen at different levels thus enabling recordings of pressure simultaneously at multiple levels. Using a low compliance manometric pump, each hole and its associated channel transmits pressure to an external transducer enabling a pressure profile of the sphincteric zone and the area of interest to be developed. Since the lower esophageal sphincter has a maximal pressure zone, which is only a few millimeters, positioning is of critical importance, especially given the fact that the lower esophageal sphincter moves approximately 10 cm each time a swallow occurs. The pull-through technique was previously utilized to precisely identify the pressure zones but is uncomfortable for the patient and involves repeated manipulation of the manometric assembly. For the most part, swallow-induced esophageal peristalsis is utilized to define the site of the lower esophageal sphincter and measure its function. A perfused sleeve of 6 cm in length provides reliable monitoring of both basal and swallow induced changes of sphincteric pressure, since this length is adequate to accommodate the predictable movement of the lower esophageal sphincter relative to the manometric assembly. Primary peristalsis can be evaluated using 5 mL water boluses and provides information, which enables the termination of appropriate esophageal clearing. A peak threshold pressure of 33 mmHg/ml is reached in the distal esophagus for reliable fluid transport by primary peristalsis. Esophageal transport of solids depends in a large part on secondary peristalsis since the primary peristaltic wave moves too rapidly to propel solids in the esophageal body thus passing over them and moving them only a small part of the esophageal length. Secondary peristalsis is the event, which follows the primary peristaltic wave and initiates a powerful initially static contraction, which occurs directly around the boluses. Abnormalities in primary and secondary peristalsis need to be defined in patients with GERD, particularly in those whom a surgical remedy may be sought.

The best methodology for evaluating secondary peristalsis is to abruptly insufflate 10 ml of air into the mid-esophageal body via the wide core lumen of a manometric extrusion system. The motor response of the esophagus to this distension can then be evaluated.

The measurement of lower esophageal sphincter relaxation is of particular importance not only in the early diagnosis of achalasia and the assessment of dysphagia following anti-reflux surgery but to determine the appropriateness of lower esophageal sphincter contraction and relaxation. Water-swallow induced lower esophageal sphincter relaxation has a duration of 4.1 (3.0-5.4 range) seconds with a mean nadir pressure of relaxation of 1.0 (0.2 range) mmHg. Some conditions such as achalasia or diffuse esophageal spasm can be easily defined, but in some instances only a non-specific motor defect is evident. This somewhat vague term embraces individuals with "underpowered" peristalsis and results in the failure of development of an adequate propulsive force to clear the esophagus.

The identification of a manometric abnormality is important in helping define the cause of GERD or the failure of acid suppressive medication to provide adequate relief and healing. In addition, it provides information necessary to confirm the need for a prokinetic agent. Under circumstances where defined motor abnormality is evident, the use of surgery should be carefully considered since wrap procedures performed under such circumstances may not function adequately. In individuals who meet the criteria for elective surgery based upon demonstration of abnormal lower esophageal sphincter function, manometric evaluation is useful as a quantitative tool to evaluate efficacy of the surgery or alternatively define causes for its failure.

Esophageal pH monitoring

Esophageal pH monitoring is an important adjunct to clinical assessment and endoscopy in the diagnosis of gastroesophageal reflux disease (GERD). Methods of esophageal pH monitoring have advanced substantially in the last decade. Better and more versatile recording equipment has been developed and is now widely marketed. Computers and purpose designed software have extended the scope of interpretation of the recordings and made this process more time dependent.

In contrast to endoscopy or the Bernstein test, ambulatory esophageal pH monitoring records spontaneous reflux events and measures directly the degree of esophageal acid exposure, fundamental factors in the pathogenesis of this disease. Not surprising therefore is the regard by many that this is the gold standard for the diagnosis of reflux disease. However, as in any medical test, it is not without limitations. There are both methodological and inappropriate approaches to analysis and interpretations of the results.

Equipment

The major components are the pH electrode, data recorder and software. There are three main types of pH electrode: glass, mono-crystalline antimony and ion-selective field effect transistor (ISFET) electrodes. The first two are the most widely used. Glass electrodes are distinguished by having a linear response over a pH range from 1 to 12 and are relatively drift free, particularly when used with an internal reference in the form of a combination electrode. They are also the most durable of electrodes (can be chemically sterilized) and have a service life of approximately 100 studies. Their main disadvantages are their expense, fragility and relative bulkiness. The resultant is that they are often difficult to pass and require extra care with handling. Indeed, nasal passage, particularly with combination electrodes can often be difficult and uncomfortable. Antimony electrodes are cheaper than their glass counterparts, are smaller in size and are more resistant to mechanical shock. The caveats are that they are less sensitive than glass electrodes, and exhibit non-linear responses even over the physiologic pH range from 1 to 7. In addition, they exhibit some drift, and temperature sensitivity. They also have a limited lifespan because of corrosion and oxidation, and are not chemically resistant, making them easily damaged by glutaraldehyde. Nevertheless, studies directly comparing glass and antimony electrodes demonstrate both the accuracy of the latter as well as similar results in clinical studies. A reference electrode is a prerequisite for accurate results. Both intraluminal and external (skin) references are used; the former providing the more accurate recordings (skin-enteric potential differences introduces errors up to 0.6 pH units). The pH signal is digitized and stored in a portable data storage device or data recorder which may have up to four channels. For clinical purposes, a single channel (recording pH in the distal esophagus) is usually sufficient. Most data recorders sample the pH signal at eight samples per minute (0.13 Hz), which provides sufficient information for the calculation of mean or median values. However, accurate determination of individual pH fluctuations or reflux episodes requires a sample rate of at least 1 Hz (1 sample/min.). Software should be able to display both a numerical summary as well as a time course of esophageal pH onto which can be added indicators for specific time periods (e.g. supine, postprandial and symptom events). Most programs can calculate reflux indices, circadian plots and frequency curves.

Technique

It is not unusual for pH monitoring to be performed without the patient taking any antireflux therapy.

Before the study, histamine 2 receptor antagonists and pro-kinetics should be stopped for 24-72 hrs. pH monitoring however is flexible enough to assess the efficacy of anti-reflux treatment on esophageal physiology. Prior to beginning a study, the electrode should be calibrated in a neutral and acid buffer (pH < 2), and again at the end to check for electrode drift. Glass electrodes should not exceed 0.2 pH units in drift. Antimony electrodes require special buffers, because they

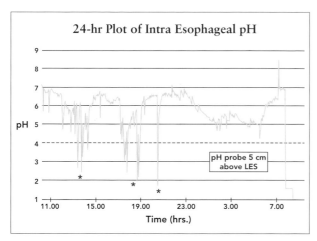

24-hr Plot of Intra Esophageal pH

pH probe 5 cm above LES

Episodic reflux events are documented by a sudden drop in esophageal pH (*).

can be irreversibly damaged by many of the standard buffers. For standard pH monitoring, the electrode is positioned 5 cm above the proximal margin of the lower esophageal sphincter (lower esophageal sphincter). Variation from this position can significantly influence the recorded value for esophageal acid exposure; the closer to the lower esophageal sphincter, the greater the level of acid exposure. Location of the electrode relative to the lower esophageal sphincter is best done by reference to manometric definition of lower esophageal sphincter position. Less adequate alternatives include using both the step up in pH that occurs as the electrode is withdrawn from the stomach and endoscopic measurements. Patients are encouraged to continue normal physical activity as much as possible, with the exclusion of acidic foods and drinks and antacids. Maintenance of an accurate diary is essential, with the recording of minimum information (meals, snacks, sleep). Traditionally, ambulatory pH monitoring is performed over a 24 hr. period.

Analysis

There are two major considerations in the analysis of pH recordings: measurement of the amount of reflux and the relationship between the patient's symptoms and reflux. Interestingly, these two issues are not necessarily related, and rather appear often to be complementary aspects of the analysis and interpretation of pH recordings. Traditionally, reflux is thought to occur when esophageal pH falls below 4. This threshold is clinically relevant because heartburn occurs at pH < 4, and peptic activity diminishes rapidly above this level. Interestingly, it is common for buffering of gastric contents early in the postprandial period to lead to reflux of gastric contents with a pH > 4. In addition, falls in pH that do not reach pH 4 can also be symptomatic, and in some circumstances (e.g. gastric resection), it may be appropriate to set the threshold above pH 4 or 5. The end of the reflux period is defined as the point at which esophageal pH rises above 4 (or 5); it is recommended that a minimum time (18 seconds) should elapse before a new reflux period is scored. Reflux events occuring at pH < 4 are not currently identifiable but do not have an adverse impact on the clinical importance of pH monitoring. Shifts in esophageal pH >7 (alkaline pH events) have been interpreted as reflux of alkaline duodenal contents. However, more recent analysis has suggested that these may be as a result of swallowed saliva. Inclusion of such events in the final analysis is therefore potentially inappropriate. The duration of pH < 4, usually expressed as a percentage of the recording time, is the variable most often used in the analysis of esophageal pH recordings. It is a measure of the degree of esophageal exposure to acid and correlates with the severity of esophagitis. The overall 24-hr. esophageal acid exposure however appears to be the best single determinant to discriminate between normal subjects and patients with esophagitis.

The upper level for normal for total duration of esophageal acid exposure ranges between 5 and 7%. Reasonable intrasubject reproducibility (75-86%)

has been recorded in patients with esophagitis. However, actual values may differ as much as three-fold. Unfortunately, reproducibility is lowest in endoscopy negative patients or those with atypical symptoms, as well as in studies of less than 24 hours. Although much emphasis has been placed on the measurement of esophageal acid exposure to classify patients as either normal or having reflux disease, this approach has its limitations. Levels of exposure to acid do not indicate whether the symptoms are related to reflux. This suggests the necessity therefore of a symptom analysis. Minor increases in the level of exposure above normal, therefore should be interpreted with caution. Assessment of the relationship between reflux and the patient's symptoms has proven to be a significantly greater challenge than quantification of acid exposure. The problem lies in the potential independent relationship of these two variables. Despite the many attempts to express the relationship objectively (symptom specificity index, symptom sensitivity index, symptom associated probability, and binomial symptom index), an ideal approach has yet to be devised.

Applications

Esophageal pH monitoring is not essential in all patients with suspected GERD. Endoscopy is the investigation of first choice because it is the most sensitive means of diagnosing reflux esophagitis and assessing its severity, which then is the major factor influencing initial therapy. Esophageal pH monitoring is most applicable in those patients with troublesome symptoms but without endoscopic signs of esophagitis in whom a trial therapy has failed, in patients with atypical symptoms which cannot be clearly related to reflux, and in patients considered for antireflux surgery. It is also useful in assessing the adequacy of acid suppression in patients who fail to respond to what would appear to be adequate levels of acid suppressant therapy. In summation, esophageal pH monitoring is an important adjunct to clinical assessment and endoscopy in the diagnosis of reflux disease. Although it is the gold standard for the measurement of esophageal exposure to acid and assessment of relationships of symptoms to reflux, the weaknesses in both these functions should be understood when applying this test for the diagnosis of reflux disease.

The greater the period of time the esophagus is exposed to a pH < 4.0, the greater both the likelihood and extent of damage.

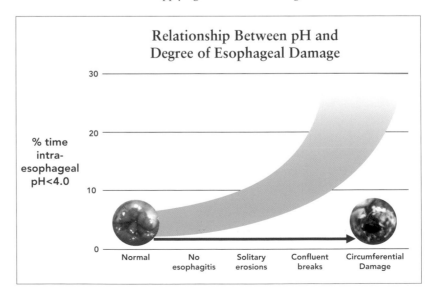

Relationship Between pH and Degree of Esophageal Damage

% time intra-esophageal pH<4.0

30

20

10

0

Normal | No esophagitis | Solitary erosions | Confluent breaks | Circumferential Damage

Pathophysiology

It is well recognized that whereas the etiology of GERD is due to impaired function of the lower esophageal sphincter, the pathological effects of this are mostly or entirely mediated by acid and pepsin reflux.

The esophageal epithelium appears more susceptible to acid damage than either the gastric or duodenal epithelium and the explanation for this is found in the structural and secretory properties of the squamous lining of the esophagus adjacent to the stomach.

Malfunction of the lower esophageal sphincter results in acid reflux into the esophagus. Reflux is mostly episodic, so that the esophagus is not often presented with a continuous acid load.

Prediction of esophageal disease related to reflux takes into account the pH of the refluxate and the duration of reflux. Expulsion of the refluxate back into the stomach shortens the time of exposure. The volume of reflux is also an important parameter for estimation of the acid load on the esophageal epithelium. It is the magnitude of this acid load that determines the presence or absence of pathology or symptoms. Intra-esophageal pH monitoring provides an approximate measure of the acid load to the lower esophagus.

The human esophageal epithelium is a multi-layered, stratified squamous epithelium. Afferent nerves are present reaching into the superficial layers of the mucosa. With incompetence of the lower esophageal sphincter (lower esophageal sphincter), acid reflux results with pain and damage to the epithelium depending on the pH of the refluxate.

Rather than being protected by a continuous tight junction, this epithelium has largely regional cell-to-cell contact via desmosomes, but, being multi-layered, provides a winding path for proton diffusion into the epithelium. It is nevertheless significantly more acid sensitive than the gastric epithelium that is provided with "tight" tight junctions.

The threshold of acidity for damage and pain may be different. A higher acidity is likely needed for damage to the epithelial cells compared to the acidity required for stimulation of the pain fibres. This is probably because the epithelial cells have acid recovery mechanisms (such as Na/H or anion exchange) mostly absent in the pain fibres. Dependent on the location of the pain fibres and access thereto of H^+, different individuals will have different sensitivities to luminal acidity. The therapeutic aims of acid control may vary, being elevation of mean diurnal pH for healing of erosions or prevention of acidic excursions for symptom relief or both.

The central hypothesis regarding the pathogenesis of esophagitis is dependent upon the extent of esophageal injury which itself is a reflection of the mucosal acidification time. Overall motility disorder as a basis for esophagitis can therefore be considered as due either to a markedly increased propensity to incur reflux events (lower esophageal sphincter abnormality) or a markedly impaired acid clearance (peristaltic dysfunction).

The dominant abnormality leading to the development of esophagitis and GERD can vary from patient to patient and may even evolve with time as scarring and damage progresses.

At this time there are three theories which consider gastroesophageal junction incompetence or variations thereof as the critical issue in the genesis of

GERD: 1) excessive transient lower esophageal sphincter relaxations (lower esophageal sphincters); 2) a hypotensive lower esophageal sphincter without any accompanying anatomic abnormality, or 3) an anatomic disruption of the junction by hiatal hernia. It has been proposed that the dominant mechanism may vary as a function of disease severity or possibly even be a determinant. Thus lower esophageal sphincter may predominate in mild disease, whilst mechanisms associated with a hiatal hernia or weak sphincter be more prevalent in individuals with more severe disease.

It seems likely that lower esophageal sphincters account for the majority of reflux events in normal individuals and in patients with normal lower esophageal sphincter pressure at the time of reflux. Transient lower esophageal relaxations probably represent a physiologic response to gastric distension by food or gas, and are the primary mechanisms responsible for gastric gas venting. Acid reflux (at the same time) would therefore appear to be an associated phenomenon. Investigations suggest that the functional lower esophageal sphincter consists of integrated motor responses involving not only lower esophageal sphincter relaxation, but also crural diaphragmatic inhibition, and contraction of the costal diaphragm. They appear to occur without an associated pharyngeal contraction, are unaccompanied by esophageal peristalsis, and persist for longer periods (> 10 secs.) than do swallow-induced lower esophageal sphincter relaxations. However, not all lower esophageal sphincters are accompanied by reflux.

GERD may take place during episodes of diminished lower esophageal sphincter pressure associated by either stress reflux or free reflux. Stress reflux (which is an unusual mechanism of reflux) appears to occur when a hypotensive lower esophageal sphincter is transiently overcome by an abrupt increase in intra-abdominal pressure and the lower esophageal sphincter is overcome. Observations of the anti-reflux mechanism during stress maneuvers such as leg raising and abdominal compression suggest a pinching effect of crural contraction (the second sphincter) that augments the antireflux barrier. Vulnerability to reflux under abrupt increases in intra-abdominal pressure (e.g. bending, coughing) depends on both the susceptibility of the lower esophageal sphincter and the diaphragmatic sphincter to dramatic pressure change.

Patients with hiatal hernia exhibit progressive disruption of the diaphragmatic sphincter which is proportional to the extent of axial herniation. Although neither hiatal hernia nor hypotensive lower esophageal sphincter alone results in severe gastroesophageal junction incompetence, the effects of the two on this complex are probably synergistic.

Free reflux on the other hand is characterized by a fall in the intra-esophageal pH without either an identifiable change in either intragastric or lower esophageal sphincter pressure.

Instances of free reflux only occur when the resting lower esophageal sphincter pressures is within 0-4 mmHg of intra gastric pressure. Nevertheless it is likely that a substantial number of individuals with mild or moderate GERD are susceptible to stress reflux when their lower esophageal sphincter pressure has been temporarily diminished by specific foods (chocolate, onion, coffee), drugs or personal habits.

Reflux in the Presence of a Hiatus Hernia

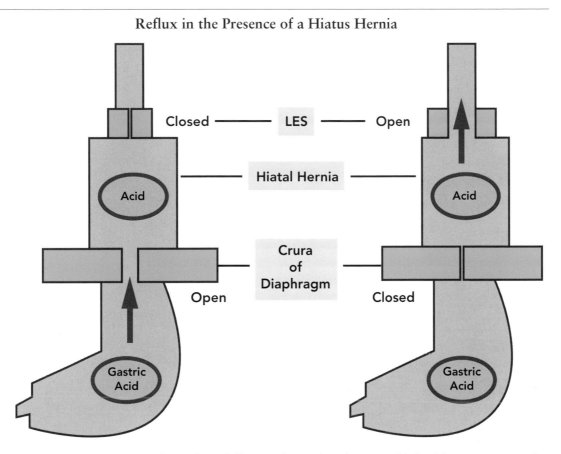

In the presence of a hiatus hernia, the diaphragmatic crura play a role in producing an "acid space" above the diaphragm and increasing the likelihood of reflux. Hiatus hernia was initially thought to be "*the*" cause of GERD. Subsequent revisionist consideration declared it to be nothing more than a correlate epiphenomenon. More recent evidence (P. Kahrilas) has been advanced to support its role in the genesis of GERD.

A number of discrete observations have provided evidence to suggest that hiatal hernias may play a significant pathogenetic role in up to 50% of instances of GERD. It would appear that hiatal hernias constitute only an abberation from normal anatomy, based on the concept of the well documented physiological herniation observed during swallowing. It has been proposed that the phrenoesophageal (PE) membrane, which is stretched during each peristaltic contraction, gradually loses its elasticity with the passage of years. As the PE membrane weakens, the extent of herniation during swallowing gradually increases, with the resultant sequelae. Under such circumstances it is plausible that large hernias may impair the normal process of esophageal emptying, thereby prolonging the clearance time of acid and increasing the mucosal acidification exposure time of the esophagus, particularly in the supine position. Therefore hiatal hernias, whilst not an initiating factor in GERD, may be considered as providing a significant contribution to the chronicity of the disease. A critical issue however is the need to think in more precise terms in regard to the identification of the hiatus hernia itself. Thus axial length both at rest and during distention need to be evaluated as well as the competence of the diaphragmatic hiatus.

The pathogenesis of GERD probably does not lend itself to reductionist thinking. Integration of both anatomical and physiological studies of the gastroesophageal junction suggest the multifactorial nature of the anatomic disruption of the diaphragmatic hiatus, the physiologicaal dysfunction of the lower esophageal sphincter and the resulting disease, esophagitis and GERD.

CHAPTER 4
MANAGEMENT

Lower esophageal sphincter function in GERD

When placed in the esophagus, over 90% of acid is cleared into the stomach by a rapid peristalsis, but the other 10% is cleared more slowly, by saliva and other host defenses. Most diseases of the esophagus, including GERD, do not cause a loss of peristalsis, but do reduce the amplitude of the contractions of the fast peristaltic phase. A hiatus hernia may thus interfere with normal peristaltic waves, and therefore prevent complete acid clearance, because acid can become trapped in the hiatal pouch. Experimentally, cisapride, a 5-HT$_4$ agonist, has effects not only on the sphincter but also on increasing salivary volume which have been proposed to be of benefit in facilitating the esophageal clearance of acid.

GERD may be due to an extremely hypotensive sphincter, and this was the rationale for the use of metoclopramide in the past. But it is now appreciated that this abnormality is rare and that most GERD is probably due to spontaneous but excessively prolonged (30-60 seconds) relaxation of the lower esophageal sphincter.

The stimulus for these prolonged relaxations may be distention of the fundus, for example by large meals, and perhaps by signals from the pharynx. Chronic reflux patients may have numerous episodes of these prolonged relaxations, even up to 12 per hour. It is also apparent that transient lower esophageal sphincter incompetence is more common with age. In this respect the role of hiatus hernia which had been out of vogue has once again enjoyed an etiological renaissance as a component of the causation of GERD. Thus, the age-related increase in prevalence of hiatal hernias, which are capable of interfering with normal gastric mechano-reception in the fundus, may lead to delayed gastric emptying of solids and over-distention of the stomach. The debate concerning the association of a hiatus hernia and gastroesophageal reflux disease has gone back and forth for many decades. However, current beliefs are that a hiatus hernia is indeed contributory to GERD and sophisticated analyses examining the effect of a hiatus hernia on the mechanics of gastroesophageal reflux and sphincter tone support this view.

The wide variety of surgical options available to improve the tone of an incompetent sphincter, both laparoscopic and open, suggest that none is perfect. Even different surgeons performing what they believe to be the same operation may not agree on the precise details, so it is often difficult to compare surgical results between centers and between individuals. Generally, the more the surgeon does, the more likely is the patient to be cured of reflux but also to develop dysphagia and the disabling symptoms of an inability to belch. Clearly, an experienced surgeon is the most important determinant of surgical success, and because of the potential problems of the surgery, a careful preoperative assessment of peristaltic function by a motility study is mandatory. The identification of individuals with poor motor function who will not do well with surgery is critical to avoid iatrogenically induced accentuation of the GERD. It is also necessary to make a positive diagnosis of GERD prior to surgery; either by endoscopy or 24-hour pH measurement. A trial of a proton pump inhibitor is a useful predictor of likely surgical success - if the patient's symptoms are markedly improved by this drug, then they will probably also be helped by surgery.

Therapeutic targets

The lower esophageal sphincter

Whilst considerable attention has been directed to acid pepsin refluxate in the genesis of GERD, it is the lower esophageal sphincter which remains one of the critical variables in the disease process. Unfortunately, current knowledge of sphincter physiology is limited and in the case of the lower esophagus this is particularly apparent. In most situations the diagnosis of GERD is undertaken on a clinical basis, although, endoscopy is utilized if alarm symptoms are present or a particular patient demands endoscopic confirmation of the diagnosis prior to institutional therapy. For the most part, however, study of the lower esophageal sphincter itself and the esophageal peristalsis is usually reserved for patients who fail acid suppressive therapy, exhibit obvious symptoms consistent with motility problems, or are being contemplated for surgery. Documentation of the function of the lower esophageal sphincter and the motility status of the esophagus are important in the management of such individuals.

The lower esophageal sphincter in GERD appears to malfunction either by exerting a pressure zone, which is too low to prevent reflux from the stomach, or alternatively to produce transient episodes of relaxation which are either too frequent or prolonged. In the 1950s surgical techniques were developed to wrap a mobilized portion of gastric fundus around the lower esophageal sphincter (Nissen, Belsey) in an attempt to increase lower esophageal sphincter pressure and obviate reflux. Innumerable modifications of this procedure failed to provide a reliable high pressure barrier zone to reflux and the morbidity of the operation as an open procedure was substantial (12-18% complications). Furthermore, the inability to precisely calibrate the increase in lower esophageal pressure generated by the wrap led to failures either due to excessive wrapping or inadequate pressure increase. The subsequent development of prokinetic agents such as metoclopramide designed to pharmacologically ameliorate motility disturbances associated with GERD met with limited success. This reflected the relative non-selectivity of the agent and a high incidence of adverse effects. It is, however, apparent that in certain circumstances the mechanical defects associated with GERD, which are principally located in the area of esophageal peristalsis and particularly lower esophageal sphincter pressure, need to be addressed.

The Principles of Fundoplication (Wrap)

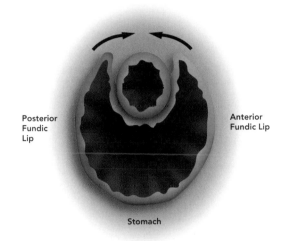

Posterior Fundic Lip

Anterior Fundic Lip

Stomach

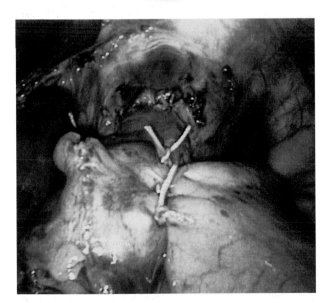

The principle of the wrap technique is diagrammatically depicted above. Below is a laparoscopic view of the completed wrap.

285

Fundoplication

In circumstances where the patient is young, requires maintenance acid suppression therapy, is fit for surgery and desires an operation, manometric testing should be undertaken to confirm the absence of esophageal peristalic abnormalities and define the function of the lower esophageal sphincter. If all the criteria for surgery are met, the most appropriate operation at this time appears to be a Nissen fundoplication undertaken by laparoscopic technique. In brief, this consists of the introduction of a number of ports into the upper abdomen whereby dissection and mobilization of the fundus and esophagus of the stomach can be undertaken. A gastric wrap is performed having mobilized the lower 4 to 5 cm of the esophagus and moved the stomach behind it prior to suturing it anteriorly in front of the esophagus through the residual portion of the gastric fundus which has been mobilized but not moved behind the esophagus. Criti-

The most common antireflux procedure is the Nissen fundoplication. The procedure can be performed through the abdomen or the chest either open or through a laparoscope. Nissen described the procedure as a 360° fundoplication around the lower esophagus for a distance of 4 to 5 cm. Although this provided good control of reflux, it was associated with a number of side effects, which have encouraged modifications of the procedure. These include taking care to use only the gastric fundus to envelop the esophagus in performing the fundoplication, sizing the fundoplication with a 60-French bougie, and limiting the length of the fundoplication to 1 to 2 cm. The essential elements necessary for the performance of a transabdominal fundoplication are common to both the laparoscopic and the open procedure.

The surgical steps are illustrated in the pictures.

1) Crural dissection and identification and preservation of both vagi and the anterior hepatic branch.

2) Circumferential dissection of the esophagus.

3) Crural closure.

4) Fundic mobilization by division of short gastric vessels.

5) Traction of the fundus behind the esophagus.

6) Creation of a short, loose fundoplication by enveloping the anterior and posterior wall of the fundus around the lower esophagus, over a 60-French bougie in the esophagus.

7) Suture to each other and anterior wall of stomach.

8) Completed wrap.

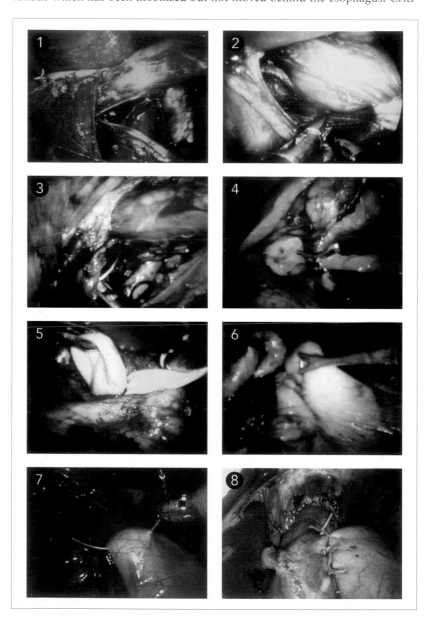

cal areas involve the need to avoid damage to the stomach and esophagus as well as the vagus nerves.

The diameter of the esophagus embraced by the wrap is determined by insertion of a large bougee through the gastroesophageal junction from the mouth. Results using this technique have been reported as successful in up to 85% of patients with a morbidity level varying between 10 and 15%. The precise details of surgery and its advantages and disadvantages have been dealt with in the surgical section. Under some circumstances, however, both physicians and patients would prefer to avoid surgery and in such cases the use of prokinetic drugs in addition to antisecretory agents should be strongly considered.

Prokinetic agents

Prokinetic agents are those that are intended to restore, normalize, and facilitate motility in the gastrointestinal tract. The development of this group of pharmacological agents is historically traceable to the appreciation of the role of dopaminergic receptors in gut smooth muscle. The recognition of their presence stimulated an investigation of agents, which would even neutralize or antagonize the inhibitory effects of dopamine on gut motility. The first agent of this class was metoclopramide, which was useful in that it improved gastric emptying, accelerated transit through the small bowel, and provided for the first time an agent capable of modulating gut motility. Unfortunately metoclopramide cross the blood brain barrier, resulting in central nervous system antidopaminergic effects and up to 20% of individuals suffered from experimental side-effects of varying degrees of intensity. Further problems related to the generation of hyperprolactinemia including breast enlargement, nipple tenderness, galactorrhea, and menstrual irregularities.

To a certain extent these disadvantages were overcome by the development of domperidone which, although it had minimal experimental side-effects, still caused hyperprolactinemia and its related symptomatology. Its effect on enhancing motility of the esophagus, stomach, and small bowel was useful but its primary therapeutic utility was its anti-emetic properties at the chemoreceptor trigger site.

The subsequent development of cisapride, an agonist of the serotonin receptor 5-HT$_4$, was a significant improvement over both previous agents. This prokinetic agent facilitates the release of acetylcholine from post ganglionic cholinergic fibers within the myenteric plexus. The overall result of this biochemical effect has been to improve propulsive motor activity of the esophagus, stomach, small bowel and large bowel. In addition to its motor effects, cisapride has been documented to enhance salivary secretion by stimulation of the esophagosalivary reflex with the result that increased saliva flow as well as the protective agent within it (bicarbonate, glycoconjugate, EGF, and PGE2) are all delivered in larger quantities to the lower esophageal sphincter area and are postulated to accentuate healing. Cisapride is a substituted piperidinyl benzamide which is chemically related to metroclopramide but did not exhibit the major central nervous system effects. Nevertheless somnolence and fatigue have been reported as well as some experimental effects.

The particular problem with cisapride has been its relative non-selectivity in terms of a target of smooth muscle function. In some individuals serious diarrhea and abdominal pain have proved to be major drawbacks in its usage. Nevertheless, cisapride has been demonstrated to significantly increase lower esophageal pressure as well as promote gastric emptying. Given its positive effects on promoting esophageal peristalsis, the quotient of these pharmacological events has been to produce a prokinetic agent of therapeutic benefit in patients suffering from GERD. Indeed, in individuals in whom acid suppression may not adequately obviate relapse, the use of cisapride as a adjuvant agent has met with some reasonable success.

A number of studies have demonstrated that cisapride alone is more effective than placebo in symptom relief and healing in patients with heartburn of the esophagitis grade 0 to 3 range. Similarly it has been reported that episodes of gastroesophageal reflux are decreased in patients taking cisapride and that in individuals using acid suppression in combination with cisapride, efficacy of symptom relief and healing are greater than when acid suppression alone is used.

Gastric acidity

Gastric juice is harmful to esophageal squamous mucosa. In general, the secretion of acid, pepsin and bile as measured by classical secretory studies using naso-gastric tubes, is no different in patients with or without GERD, suggesting that hypersecretion is not the cause of the disease. Indeed, most experimental models suggest that it is not acid alone which is injurious. The damage is due to the presence of other contents of the refluxate, including at least pepsin, bile, ingested material, and lysolecithin.

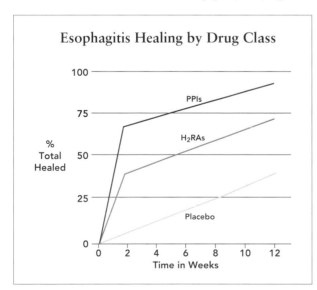

Esophagitis Healing by Drug Class

The proton pump inhibitor class of drugs are significantly more effective than H2RA's in healing esophagitis. This reflects their ability to provide a far greater sustained level of acid suppression.

Although acid may have direct effects on the esophageal mucosa including widening intercellular spaces and altering the esophageal potential difference, its main function may be to facilitate the damage initiated by pepsin and bile and as well as activating pepsinogen to pepsin. Although acid may not be the only cause of the damage in GERD, acid suppression is a very effective treatment. In the evaluation of data acquired by meta-analysis, it is apparent that the greater the acid suppression, the better the healing of esophagitis, and the more rapidly the symptoms are relieved. It is interesting that certain regulatory agencies have failed to accept this concept, and still require head-to-head clinical studies between individual acid suppression medications to prove efficacy. In general, the most effective acid suppression is achieved with proton pump inhibitors, and there are currently several of these available including pantoprazole, lansoprazole and omeprazole. The latter agent was the initial pump inhibitor shown to be far more effective than H2RA's in the healing of GERD but subsequently many compounds of the proton pump inhibitor class of drugs have been shown to exhibit equivalent superiority.

There is little difference in the one month healing rates between any of these agents. Lansoprazole at a dose of 30 mg daily is claimed to be more effective than omeprazole 20 mg daily for symptom relief, perhaps just reflecting the higher dose or superior bio-availability of lansoprazole. There is also some person to person variability in the secretory response to omeprazole, and to a lesser degree to lansoprazole. Pantoprazole appears to have the most advantageous pharmacokinetic profile and is negligible in its effects on the hepatic P450 cytochrome system. This latter factor may be of relevance in the context that the vast majority of older patients take other medications as well as PPI's.

Despite the efficacy of these medications, at least 10% of all patients will continue to have symptoms after two months of proton pump inhibitor therapy. This reflects the fact that many patients present for treatment at a point well into the evolution of the disease process and exhibit an esophagus which is either scarred or so damaged that the healing process cannot maintain mucosal integrity in the presence of anything other than the presence of the most limited amounts of acid or pepsin. This further emphasises the need to not only tailor treatment for GERD to the individual patient but to ensure early institution of therapy with proton pump inhibitors rather than observation of repeated recurrence of symptomatology and accentuation of damage during a trial of inadequate acid inhibitory therapy.

Gastroesophageal reflux disease and esophageal pH

There is a clear predictive relationship between intragastric pH and intra-esophageal pH as both correlate with healing of esophagitis. The greater the severity of the esophagitis, the greater the requirement for acid suppression. The conventional pH threshold for aggressive vs. non-aggressive reflux is regarded as pH 4 and this has been supported by pH measurements in patients with defined severities of GERD. Overall, it is apparent that the severity of mucosal injury in GERD is dependent on the pH of the reflux material and its dwell time in the esophagus. In this respect, 24-hour esophageal pH monitoring has proved to be the most effective measurement of gastroesophageal reflux since it records both the pH of the reflux and the duration of the exposure. It is evident that the daily duration of time for which the intragastric pH is elevated to 4 or higher correlates closely with the healing of erosive reflux esophagitis. Nevertheless, esophageal pH monitoring studies reveal in some patients the presence of GERD despite normal or near normal acidic exposure values.

This paradox probably reflects alterations in reflux patterns that vary from day to day as well as variations in pH between different regions of the esophagus. Esophageal pH rises as the distance from the lower esophageal sphincter increases and, in addition, pH appears to be lower at the peaks of the esophageal folds which are exposed to acid as opposed to the tufts where there is a greater degree of protection afforded by bicarbonate and mucus. This variation in esophageal pH is presumably responsible for the linear distribution of erosive esophagitis evident at endoscopy in some patients. Overall, it does not appear that patients with GERD are acid hypersecretors. Nevertheless repeated measurements of 24-hour intragastric acidity in individual patients reveal considerable variations.

The percentage of patients with esophagitis that heal over time is dependent upon the class of agent used for acid suppression.

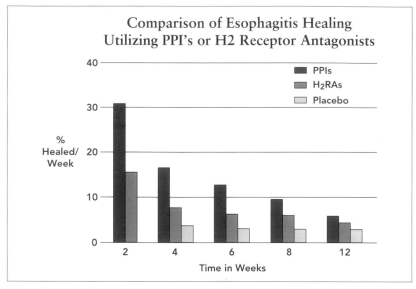

Comparison of Esophagitis Healing Utilizing PPI's or H2 Receptor Antagonists

In some patients abnormal duodenal gastric reflux may make gastric juice especially aggressive to esophageal mucosa. In this respect, delayed gastric emptying may contribute significantly to pathological gastroesophageal reflux. Similarly abnormally frequent transient lower esophageal sphincter relaxation as well as inappropriate esophageal clearance and the presence of a hiatal hernia may contribute to the development of GERD. 24-hour esophageal pH monitoring in endoscopically-negative or mild reflux disease has shown that most acid exposure occurs during the day in the post-prandial. Furthermore, several esophageal-monitoring studies have demonstrated that individuals with Barrett's esophagus exhibit high levels of esophageal exposure to gastric reflux. Nevertheless rigorous data supporting that Barrett's esophagus is linearly related to the level of acid reflux are not available.

The key role of acids in the development of GERD is best exemplified in patients with gastrinoma disease where peptic esophagitis is directly related to the level of acid suppression achievable. It is likely that the marginal efficacy of H2 receptor antagonists in the management of GERD is related to their failure to control esophageal acid exposure. Other factors involved in the development of GERD which are pH related include the ability of the esophagus to clear acid and to deal with activated pepsinogen. In up to 50% of patients with GERD, it has been demonstrated that the higher the acid concentration in the refluxate the longer it requires for clearance. The reasons for the diminished rate of clearance are at this time unclear but may represent either abnormally low swallowing rates or ineffective primary or secondary peristalsis. Whilst salivary bicarbonate is of importance in determining esophageal acid clearance, little information is available on salivary gland function in GERD patients. The pH necessary to activate pepsinogen is an important variable in the sensitivity of the esophageal epithelium through acid peptic insult. The higher the pH the further outside the optimum pH profile for pepsinogen activation and hence the less the likelihood of damage. A similar pathogenesis is probably involved in damage caused by bile acids but this usually reflects a smaller sub-group of patients who have had previous gastric surgery or exhibit major motility disorders.

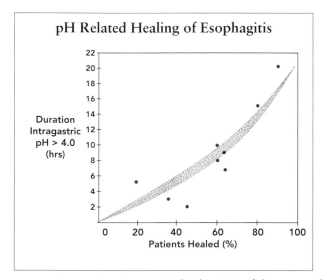

pH Related Healing of Esophagitis

Duration Intragastric pH > 4.0 (hrs)

Patients Healed (%)

The more sustained the duration of pH > 4.0, the greater the percentage of esophagitis healing.

Given the fact that the degree of esophageal acid exposure correlates almost linearly with the severity of esophagitis, the primary aim of acid suppression therapy is to raise the pH of the refluxate. In this respect, H2 receptor antagonists are not effective in anything other than the mildest of GERD situations due to their inability to maintain a pH above 4 for a sustained period of time. A number of meta-analytic studies have indicated that a threshold of pH 4 appears to be the critical determinate for ensuring esophageal healing. Thus the longer the esophageal acid exposure to a pH greater than 4 the more likely it is that healing will occur. The rapid relapse of esophagitis upon withdrawal of acid suppressive therapy indicates that the duration of therapy is of critical relevance in determining complete healing. In this respect agents such as the proton pump inhibitor class of drugs are clearly superior given their ability to not only provide a higher degree of acid suppression but maintain pH levels elevated both during the daytime and the night-time regardless of stimulation by meals. It may well be that the efficacy of the prokinetic agents is to a certain extent provided by their effect on acid clearance. Relatively poor responses to prokinetic agents suggest that abnormally delayed gastric emptying may be a relatively minor factor in the pathogenesis of GERD. Since they do not result in a major decrease in the frequency of reflux episodes, it seems likely that at this time the suppression of gastric acid secretion will remain the primary goal of GERD therapy.

Helicobacter pylori

It is interesting to note that the increase in the reported prevalence of GERD has coincided over the last 50 years or so with a natural decline in *H. pylori* infection in the West. This has led to some speculation that the two may be causally related, and that *H. pylori* may have been of some symbiotic benefit to humans. One possible mechanism by which *H. pylori* may influence GERD is through engendering an alteration in acid secretion.

Although *H. pylori* increases acid secretion in patients with duodenal ulcer disease, it may be responsible for decreasing acid secretion in those individuals infected early in life who develop gastritis of the gastric corpus. Several lines of evidence support this view. Thus, in Japan the gastric cancer and *H. pylori* incidence rates have fallen dramatically over the last 20 years, and there has been an associated increase in gastric acid secretion in the population, as well as an increasing recognition of GERD. It has been reported that the eradication of *H. pylori* in a series of people with duodenal ulcer disease led to some of them developing GERD for the first time. Although this finding remains controversial, it raises interesting questions and cannot be ignored. The issue of whether harboring *H. pylori* in the stomach is associated with an unexpected beneficial effect of the bacterium by the protection afforded from GERD may be quixotic but requires examination.

Eradication of *H. pylori* alters the acid secretory response of the stomach to GRP (gastrin releasing peptide) stimulation and omeprazole inhibition. The precise mechanism by which the effects of H. pylori on acid secretion occur have not been defined. They include both a direct effect of the organism on parietal cells and effects on the neuroendocrine cells responsible for the regulation of acid secretion.

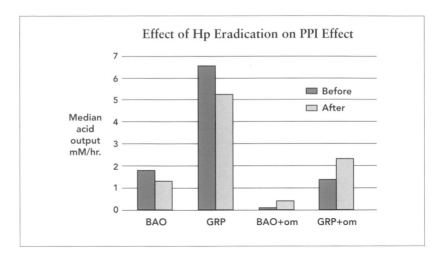

Another observation of relevance is that lower dose of anti-secretory medications appear effective in the management of GERD when *H. pylori* is present. The explanation for the latter phenomenon is currently lacking and the potential benefit to the individual of retaining their *H. pylori* to lower the proton pump inhibitor dose when treating GERD, is offset by the reports suggesting that the development of gastric atrophy, a pre-neoplastic change, is accelerated by the presence of *H. pylori* in patients taking omeprazole. This controversial finding initially provoked considerable scepticism, but has more recently acquired further support in studies which addressed the same question. Given the considerable support for the use of maintenance PPI treatment in the management of GERD, this issue is of critical relevance and requires definitive resolution. At this time, the safest approach is eradication of Hp positive GERD patients taking PPI's on a chronic basis.

Determination of GERD and management

In general practice, dyspepsia occurs in around half of the population, and even patients who have reflux symptoms often also have ulcer-like symptoms. The endoscopic evaluation of esophagitis remains an area of both controversy and difficulty. There is no completely satisfactory classification and many schemes vie for widespread acceptance. Even within individual classifications, agreement between the classifiers is not uniform. Although agreement between observers is good for severe changes of esophagitis - stricture and erosions, there is often extremely poor agreement between observers for minor changes. Since the prevalence of endoscopynegative reflux disease far outweighs those who have positive endoscopic findings, the precise role of endoscopy in diagnosis needs serious consideration. Given its expense, invasiveness and relative insensitivity as a diagnostic tool, initial enthusiasm has been replaced by a healthy degree of scepticism. A once-in-a-lifetime endoscopy, towards the beginning of treatment rather than later, is probably a useful maneuver, if only to rule out other unexpected lesions. However, repeat endoscopy in a patient with uncomplicated GERD is probably not indicated unless Barrett's esophagus has been identified and verified. In such individuals, cost-effectiveness analyses have suggested that surveillance should be performed every five years, although given the current reduction in endoscopy costs in the United States, the financial equation may change in favor of more frequent evaluation.

MUSE Classification

The MUSE classification of esophagitis allows for objective evaluation of the precise extent of the disease process.

	Metaplasia	Ulcer	Stricture	Erosion
Absent	M_0 ☐ Absent	U_0 ☐ Absent	S_0 ☐ Absent	E_0 ☐ Absent
Mild	M_1 ☐ "fingers" +/- "islands	U_1 ☐ 1 discrete ulcer	S_1 ☐ >9mm (standard endoscope passes)	E_1 ☐ only on peaks of folds
Severe	M_2 ☐ circumferential	U_2 ☐ > discrete or confluent ulcers	S_2 ☐ >9mm (standard endoscope does not pass)	E_2 ☐ confluent: on & between folds

Hiatus Hernia Yes ☐ No ☐

Medical strategies

A number of algorithms have been developed for the management of erosive esophagitis. These tend to be somewhat different from country to country or between different health systems. Once the diagnosis of GERD has been established, an attempt at lifestyle modification with or without antacids, mucosal protectant agents or alginic acid is usually undertaken as an initial step. If unsuccessful, an acid inhibitory agent is then introduced into the therapeutic regimen. In patients with mild disease (grade 1 - 2) an H2RA is often utilized. If this fails (failure to relieve symptoms or relapse on cessation of therapy), a PPI is usually utilized. Since a significant number of patients fail to heal with the H2RA therapy, or alternatively relapse, PPI's have increasingly been rightly considered as a first line of therapy. Within broad parameters the general algorithm employed includes: initial evaluation by endoscopic examination with biopsy followed by 24-hour pH monitoring, measurement of lower esophageal sphincter pressure followed by an 8-week course of a PPI. If symptom relief and healing do not occur under these circumstances, a second course of PPI therapy is usually undertaken (often at a higher or divided dosage). Depending upon the age of the patient, severity of symptomatology and the physician level of concern, a number of relapses may lead either to the introduction of a prokinetic agent or alternatively the considera-

Initial Medical Therapy for GERD

Drug	Dose (mg)	Patients (n)	(%) Cumulative Healing Rate
Pantoprazole	40	1561	92.4
Omeprazole	40	1138	84.8
Omeprazole	20	305	81.4
Lansoprazole	30	347	87.8
Ranitidine	300	306	55.4
Famotidine	40	874	54.1
Famotidine	80	363	72.5
Cimetidine	1,600	202	38.6
Nizatidine	300	248	42.5
Nizatidine	600	252	44.5
Cisapride	20	300	67
Cisapride	40	285	63.5

n=51 studies (1989-1996)

Cumulative healing rates after initial therapy with different drugs.

tion of surgery. For the most part, the latter option now entails laparoscopic surgery. In those individuals who at initial diagnosis exhibit evidence of a complication of GERD, the use of short-term medical therapy prior to surgical intervention is usual. Utilizing this general management strategy or reasonable variations thereof, it appears that between 85-95% of all patients can be adequately managed medically and some 5-15% of patients either exhibit complications or are non-amenable to long-term acid inhibitory therapy and thus require consideration for surgery.

In a review of 31 randomized studies performed between 1986 and 1995, initial medical therapy over 8-12 weeks resulted in an overall healing rate with PPI's of 87.1% (n = 1725 patients), H2 receptor antagonists of 57.2% (n = 2262), prokinetic agents of 66.0% (n = 209) and placebo of 23.7% (n = 719). The prokinetic data are probably too small to enable reasonable comparison. In a further evaluation of 36 studies undertaken between 1989 and 1995, the relapse rate for H2 receptor antagonists was 77.3% compared to an overall relapse rate of 26% for the PPI group of drugs. When analyzed individually on an agent specific basis, the relapse rate after short-term treatment was 39.2% for omeprazole, 22.3% for lansoprazole and 17.5% for pantoprazole. In regard to the long-term outcome after maintenance therapy with omeprazole or lansoprazole a remission rate of 79-90% can be achieved over 12 months period. The issue of adverse events using medical therapy was evaluated in 16,816 patients comprising 9 studies performed between 1989 and 1995. The majority of these events were minor and rarely required cessation of the therapy. They included headache, diarrhea, abdominal pain, skin rash and drowsiness. When summated, treatment related incidents occurred in the H2RA group in about 23% whilst use of the proton pump inhibitor class of agent was associated with reportable events in approximately 18%. This difference was not statistically significant. Individually adverse effects were reported with pantoprazole in 13%, lansoprazole in 18% and omeprazole in 22.3% of patients. These are no different from placebo events.

Relapse rates after maintenance therapy.

Maintenance Therapy for GERD

Drug	Dose (mg)	Patients (n)	Mean Follow-up* (months)	Relapse (%)
Pantoprazole	40	197	27	17.5
Omeprazole	20	1246	13.6	39.2
Omeprazole	20 (wknd)	201	9.6	67.2
Lansoprazole	30	52	12	15.4
Lansoprazole	15	48	12	29.2
Ranitidine	300	99	12	79
Ranitidine	150	47	12	90
Cimetidine	1,600	52	12	63
Cimetidine	3,200	45	12	57
Cisapride	10	37	6	20

n=36 studies (1989-1996) *Range: 6 mos.- 48 mos.

Surgical strategies

The majority of surgeons concur that clearly defined requirements for an anti-reflux procedure have to be fulfilled prior to consideration of a patient for surgery. These include: (1) pathological esophageal acid exposure on 24-hour pH monitoring, (2) significantly decreased lower esophageal sphincter pressure, (3) normal parameters of esophageal contractility and (4) normal esophageal length. In the published literature, surgical intervention is for the most part regarded as a laparoscopic Nissen fundoplication, although other procedures including the Toupet have been utilized with considerable success. The difficulty with the evaluation of surgical techniques is that few of the studies have been performed in a prospective randomized fashion and even fewer have been evaluated by blinded observers. Similarly, whilst most patients undertaking medical therapy at centers are included in cumulative reports, few surgeons rush to press to report their failures or to amplify in the public domain the complications of surgical intervention. This difference is further reflected in that prior to the introduction of a new therapeutic agent not only are levels of evaluation (Phase I, II, III) required but, in addition, Federal Government approval is necessary. In contrast the introduction and acceptance of a novel surgical procedure is usually as a result of informal generalized approval by peers.

Thus surgical data may err quite significantly on the side of optimistic evaluation. In evaluating all published series which embraced the management of anti-reflux surgery over the last 5 years, it was apparent that there had been a substantial shift to the use of laparoscopic anti-reflux procedures. Although follow-up is somewhat limited, it is apparent from these reports that between 85-95% of all patients can be predicted to improve after surgery, irrespective of the technique utilized. The complications for laparoscopic surgery appear to be about half of those reported for open surgery, although this may reflect the fact that only experts are undertaking laparoscopic anti-reflux surgery whereas open anti-reflux surgery is still regarded as the province of almost all general surgeons. The mortality for laparoscopic surgery was 0.4% whereas that reported for open surgery was 0.5% (review of 11 non randomised studies from 1991 to 1994 comprising 1237 patients). This significant difference may again reflect selection bias of patients and the comparison of expert surgeons functioning under extremely rigorous conditions as compared to summated information from many different levels of hospitals.

It is worth noting that in a comparison of randomized vs. non-randomized studies of anti-reflux surgery the symptomatic improvement remains the same whereas the complications reported for individual patients of the randomized group were higher. Nevertheless, few of these complications were of any major significance and no deaths were reported. The postoperative problems most often reported include dysphagia, gas bloat and flatulence. Those individuals

Laparoscopic Antireflux Surgery

Author	yr	n	Improve (%)	Complications (%) surgical intraop	Complications (%) surgical postop	Complications (%) non surg.	Mortality (%)
Cuschieri A	1993	116	91	14	13	?	0
Goossen HG	1993	62	73	8	?	3.2	0
Gotgen T	1994	59	100		min. morb.		0
Jamieson GG	1994	155	99	1.9	1.9	5.8	.6
Hallerback B	1994	60	90	6.7	0	1.7	0
Hinder R	1994	198	97	3.5	2.5	3.0	.5
Pitcher DE	1994	70	100	8.6	4.3	7.1	0
Anvari M	1995	168	100	1.2	2.4	5.4	0
Cadiere GB	1995	162	98	2.5	1.8	1.2	0
Coster DD	1995	52	90	11.5	5.8	9.2	0
Dallemagne B	1995	368	90	4		?	0
Mc Kernan JB	1995	283	100	3.5			0
Patti MG	1995	68	98	2.9	1.5	?	0
Watson DI	1995	230	98	3.0	2.6	3.0	.4
Bell RCW	1996	102	excellent	3.9	2.9	2.0	0
DePaula AL	1996	110	94	2.7	2.7	0.9	0
Galloway GQ	1996	207	96	4			0
Samana G	1996	79	92	2.5	2.5	?	0

A summary of published data on the results of laparoscopic anti-reflux surgery (1997).

Complications of Laparoscopic Antireflux Surgery

Surgical	Range (%)	Mean (%)
esophageal or gastric perforation	0 - 5.1	1.5
hepatic lesion	0 - 1.0	0.6
splenic lesion	0 - 6.9	2.5
splenectomy	0 - 1.7	0.7
inadvertent vagotomy	0 - 6.3	0.6
wound infection	0 - 4.4	2.2
incisional hernia	0 - 1.9	0.3
intraperitoneal, mediastinal abscess	0 - 1.9	0.6
herniation into chest	0 - 1.0	0.2
severe stricture	0 - 1.0	0.2
postoperative bleeding	0 - 3.4	0.6
Non Surgical	1.2 - 11.4	4.0

n=2066 patients (23 studies)

A summation of the reported complications of laparoscopic anti-reflux surgery (1997).

who fail to benefit from anti-reflux surgery may under certain circumstances return for further surgical intervention. Although accurate data are difficult to collect in this group, it is evident that the reoperative (for the most part by open procedure) complication rates in such patients are significantly higher and the mortality substantially increased. Thus surgical therapy carries an initial morbidity and mortality and re-operative surgical intervention substantially amplifies this problem. This should be contrasted with failure of medical therapy which is not associated with such grave consequences.

Symptoms and healing

It has been established that elevation of the pH in the esophagus leads to healing of the esophagitis and that this healing is almost linearly related to the level of pH reached and the duration of the elevated pH. The relationship to symptomatology is an additional feature which requires clarification. Numerous clinical studies have defined the relative efficacy of the various treatment choices by comparison of healing of rates at specific but arbitrary time intervals. In these studies the results of healing did not reflect a true rate but rather represented a proportion of those healed as compared to those treated at any given time point. The two medications which might both heal esophagitis completely and achieve the same healing proportion of 100% whilst one medication might heal in 4 weeks and the other take 12 weeks or longer. Thus the true rate or speed at which healing occurs is considerably different. It is evident that the greater the severity of the esophagitis the less effective are H2 receptor antagonists. Meta-analytic studies of acid suppression data support the statement that healing of erosive GERD and the healing proportions are directly related to the degree and duration of acid suppression. Nevertheless, to the patient, the proportions of individuals who are healed are less important than the speed at which healing takes place. The healing rate may be determined by the slope of a healing time curve and can be assessed as the percentage of erosive esophagitis healed per unit of time. By comparison of such information the speed of healing and the speed of symptom relief may be deduced thus providing information relevant to both patient and physician. Overall, the PPI's provide the highest healing proportion (83.6 ± 11.4%) irrespective of drug dose and duration of therapy. Other drug classes especially sucralfate showed inconsistent healing. The H2RA's provided an overall healing proportion of 51.9 ± 17.1%. There appeared to be little therapeutic gain obtained with using higher dosages of H2 receptor antagonists even if the higher dose levels were given for as long as 12 weeks. Indeed in comparison with PPI's, H2 receptors antagonists healing rates were still significantly lower than those observed with PPI's even after shorter 6 weeks duration. Nevertheless, it was evident that the efficacy of H2 receptor antagonists can be improved up to a point; however, this requires four times daily dosing, significant compliance, and substantial increases in costs. In this respect the great efficacy and once daily dosage of the PPI therapy appeared more satisfactory.

As regard to speed of healing, it is apparent that PPI's heal at a rate approximately twice as fast as H2 receptor antagonists at all time points and the largest gain in efficacy is evident early in the treatment period. As the duration of therapy becomes prolonged the larger proportion of esophagitis patients are healed and the speed of healing decreases since there are fewer patients left to be healed. Nevertheless even at this component of the time sequence PPI's maintain a significant advantage. It is estimated that PPI patients healed at an average rate of $11.7 \pm 0.5\%$ per week which is almost twice as fast as H2RA's which heal at $5.9 \pm 0.2\%$ per week and is four times faster than placebo healing rates of $2.9 \pm 0.2\%$ per week. It is likely that the more prolonged and greater degree of acid suppression established by PPI's is responsible for the greatest speed of healing.

Of importance is the observation that H2RA's are less effective than PPI's in the management of grade II disease than has been previously proposed. Thus the concept of H2RA's being more useful in lower grade levels of esophagitis remains unsubstantiated. Also of note is the fact that the patients studied with peptic strictures the necessity for repeat dilatation and reports of greater relief of dysphagia further support the use of PPI's as compared to H2 receptor antagonists even at the higher grades of esophagitis. Thus, in terms of acute healing of esophagitis therapeutic targeting of a greater and more sustained pH elevation is clearly achieved by the PPI's class of drugs and is clearly more effective than H2 receptor antagonists. Since in a substantial proportion of patients, especially those with erosive esophagitis, recurrence is common, the issue of maintenance therapy is of considerable relevance. In this respect a number of studies using different PPI's have demonstrated that maintenance of esophagitis healing is consistently superior when compared to H2 receptor antagonists.

From the patients' point of view, however, the issue of symptom relief may in the short term be more critical than the issue of healing. In this respect studies of PPI treated patients demonstrate a significantly greater overall proportion of patients free of heartburn, at the end of the study, and nearly twice as many as noted with individuals receiving H2 receptor antagonists. It is apparent that the correlation between the speed of healing and the rate of symptom relief is closely correlated. Thus in PPI treated patients the speed of heartburn relief was $30.7 \pm 7.5\%$ patients per week becoming asymptomatic by week two. This was approximately twice as fast as identified in patients treated with H2RA's. The rate of symptom relief declined for both classes of drugs with longer duration of treatment, as the increments of patients who were still symptomatic became smaller. Thus by week two $58 \pm 16.9\%$ of PPI treated patients were heartburn free and $63.4 \pm 6\%$ of such patients were healed. It is thus apparent that healing rates correlate almost directly with symptom relief. Analysis of symptom relief studies

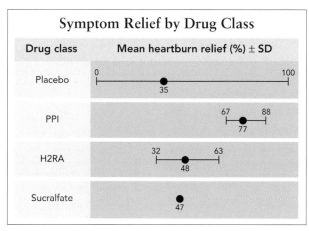

Symptom Relief by Drug Class

Drug class	Mean heartburn relief (%) ± SD
Placebo	0 — 35 — 100
PPI	67 — 77 — 88
H2RA	32 — 48 — 63
Sucralfate	47

A meta-analysis of the rate of symptom relief in esophagitis compared to the class of drug used for therapy.

utilizing linear regression analysis has demonstrated that PPI's provide the fastest overall rate of symptom relief ($11.5 \pm 0.8\%$ per week) which is almost twice as fast as that detected with H2RA's. Of relevance, however, is the fact that the slopes of symptom relief-time curves are comparable to the slopes of the healing time curves for both PPI's and H2RA's indicating that symptom relief and healing occur in parallel. In studies which use scoring systems to grade symptoms, it was evident that more complete heartburn relief occurred with PPI's as compared to H2RA's. Thus at the termination of such studies more than 50% of the patients who had received H2RA's persisted with mild to moderate heartburn even after eight weeks of treatment whereas after four weeks only 18.4% of patients still had residual mild to moderate heartburn if treated with PPI's. The PPI class of drugs, therefore, appears to provide patients with not only more complete heartburn relief but to facilitate its occurrence in a more rapid fashion.

Atypical GERD manifestations

Despite the fact that the majority of patients with GERD present with heartburn and its constellation of related symptoms, an ever-increasing percentage exhibit an atypical symptom complex. The initial group that were recognized were those with atypical or non cardiac chest pain. A second group of ever increasing prevalence are individuals, often children, who exhibit asthma-like symptoms. A third group comprises individuals with a diversity of ear, nose and throat complaints of which laryngitis may be the most common and often misinterpreted presenting complaint.

A variety of conditions have been associated with esophagitis. In not all of the circumstances is the nature of the relationship clear.

Conditions Associated with GERD	
Disease	Putative Mechanism
Hiatal Hernia	LES function disorganized
Obesity	Increased intra-abdominal pressure
Laryngitis, hoarseness	Acid reflux material; vagal reflex
Chronic obstructive pulmonary disease	Aspiration of reflux contents; smoking delays gastric emptying; decreased LES pressure
Coronary artery disease	Treatment with nitrates and calcium antagonists, which decrease the LES pressure; detection bias with chest pain evaluation
Diabetes	Delayed gastric emptying (autonomic neuropathy)
Duodenal ulcer	Detection bias of upper gastrointestinal endoscopy
Pregnancy	Increased intra-abdominal pressure; decreased LES tone by estrogens
Rheumatoid arthritis	Treatment with NSAIDs resulting in erosive esophagitis and stricture; possibly also impaired peristalsis
Degenerative joint disease	NSAIDs
Sicca syndrome	Impaired salivation; diminished clearance of reflux contents; secretion of epidermal growth factor diminished
Systemic sclerosis, CRST syndrome	Impaired peristalsis and decreased clearance of reflux material
Mental retardation	Unknown; neural regulation of LES impaired or incoordinate peristalsis and decreased clearance of reflux
Achalasia (postmyotomy)	Myotomy or dilation; disruption of LES barrier to reflux
Zollinger-Ellison syndrome	Increased acid output; increased LE acid load

Non-cardiac chest pain

It has been estimated that between 20-30% of individuals undergoing coronary angiography for chest pain have normal studies. This group of individuals have been designated as suffering from chest pain of non-cardiac origin. In 40-45% of this group acid reflux has been identified and episodes of chest pain can be correlated with reflux episodes. In some circumstances, albeit rarely, both coronary artery disease and reflux may occur in the same individual and require both Holter as well as pHmetry monitoring for identification. In the past, the acid infusion or Bernstein test was utilised to confirm the diagnosis, but for the most part this has proven to be relatively insensitive and has been superceded by the use of esophageal pH monitoring. Once the diagnosis has been confirmed treatment with PPI's has been shown to be effective in up to 85% of patients. In some centers individuals have undergone fundoplication with comparable resolution of symptomatology.

Asthma

Although the association between asthma and a distended stomach was first remarked upon more than a hundred years ago by Sir William Osler, it is only recently that the relationship between GERD and asthma has become well defined. Asthmatics have an increased frequency of GERD with a prevalence that varies between 34-89%. Since as many as 20% of adults may experience intermittent bronchospasm the potential benefits of identifying a subgroup of patients whose disease is initiated by GERD is of considerable clinical relevance.

It is likely that at least 2 mechanisms are operative in the interface between GERD and asthma.

The most commonly accepted cause is micro-aspiration of gastric contents. Alternatively it has been suggested that a vagally-mediated reflex exists whereby acid reflux into the lower esophagus initiates bronchoconstriction via a shared autonomic innervation between the esophagus and the bronchi based upon their common embryonic origin. Support for the latter proposal is based upon two lines of evidence. Firstly, acid infusion of the esophagus in asthmatic children results in increased airway resistance which can be reversed with antacids. Secondly the infusion of antacids into the distal esophagus of asthmatic children during sleep induces bronchoconstriction suggesting the presence of a protective mechanism.

The possible relationship between acid reflux and GERD can be established by the use of a barium esophagogram, upper GI endoscopy and esophageal manometry. By far the most useful, however, is pH monitoring since increased acid reflux can be identified in more than 50% of asthmatics and may occur in 70-80%. In about 50% of wheezing episodes no relationship to reflux can be established indicating that many other factors are involved in the genesis of asthma even if acid reflux is involved.

The best management of asthma-related GERD involves aggressive acid suppression with PPI's which not only significantly reduce the asthmatic episodes but considerably improve pulmonary function in almost 80% of patients. In those individuals who underwent a fundoplication procedure as many as 75% were cured or improved significantly.

Ear, nose and throat

This recently recognized association is now recognized to be common. Patients may present with hoarseness, chronic cough, throat clearing, chronic laryngitis, globus, vocal cord granulomas, laryngeal or tracheal stenosis and even carcinoma of the larynx. Only 40% of such individuals may exhibit the typical signs and symptoms of GERD itself. Indeed, in some circumstances ENT complaints may be the sole manifestation of GERD. Thus,10% of persistent coughers, 5-10% of patients with hoarseness, 25-50% of individuals with a globus sensation and a small number of patients with laryngeal neoplasia exhibit GERD as a primary etiological factor. The relationship is based upon at least four possible mechanisms. Firstly, the presence of a vagally-mediated reflex in which acid in the lower esophagus mediates a response which involves chronic repetitive throat clearing and coughing which culminates in laryngeal symptoms and finally lesions. The second involves the deposition of refluxate by aspiration directly onto the laryngeal structures themselves with ensuing inflammation and damage. A further factor that has been defined is the identification of lower levels of upper esophageal sphincter (UES) pressure in patients with reflux into the pharynx. Thirdly it is evident that in individuals with esophagopharyngeal reflux, UES pressure decreases significantly at night potentially leaving the pharynx unprotected to nocturnal esophageal reflux. Fourthly it has been noted that in up to 60% of individuals with persistent ENT symptoms esophageal motility disorders were evident with almost 80% exhibiting abnormal acid clearance from the lower esophagus.

Once the ENT diagnosis has been established the existence of GERD needs to be validated. Prolonged esophageal pH monitoring with a dual pH probe system (one in the hypopharynx or just below the UES and a second probe at the lower esophageal sphincter) is the most sensitive and specific method for diagnosing GERD-related ENT disease. Proximal pH monitoring is difficult howeve, since the probes may dry out or in the large space reflux may actually be missed. If the diagnosis is satisfactorily established, long-term administration of PPI's have proven to be the most efficacious method of treating ENT symptoms. Under unusual circumstances consideration may be given to anti reflux surgery.

Economics

We utilized costs in place at Yale New Haven Hospital as of 1996. The standard management profile includes a clinical consultation, then diagnostic endoscopy with biopsies followed by the decision to treat. The failure of initial therapy is usually followed by evaluation utilizing 24 hour pH monitoring and esophageal manometry. Assuming that all of the above are undertaken in an individual patient, a cost of $3,243 is incurred. We have calculated at our institution that the cost of formal medical therapy with one relapse is $4,773, with two relapses $6,304 and with three relapses $7,835. This assumes one endoscopy with biopsy per year and utilizes costs currently available at our pharmacy. If maintenance therapy is continued with omeprazole 20 mg daily, the cost is $1,324 on an annual basis. If this is included with endoscopy and biopsy on an annual basis, the cost is $2,448. However, as generic omeprazole becomes available, the drug related cost may fall by more than half.

The surgical costs can be calculated using (at least) the first year of medical therapy as an inclusion since it is highly unlikely that any patient will be operated upon without first undergoing endoscopic evaluation and a course of therapy. The costs for the laparoscopic Nissen procedure are $16,251 as compared to the open Nissen which is $21,601. The major difference between these two procedures is reflected in the slightly longer operating room time for the open Nissen and the increased length of hospitalization after open surgery as compared to minimally invasive laparoscopic surgery.

Factors that are not entered into the equation are the costs of either major or minor complications of each procedure.

Thus, a wound infection or pneumonia which would increase hospital stay, require further investigation (radiology, bacterial culture), and appropriate antibiotic therapy might be predicted to increase the costs by approximately $5,000. More significant complications requiring further surgical intervention could be predicted to attain at least the same costs as the original procedure. A further issue is the decrease in the costs of the laparoscopic Nissen procedure generated by a shortened hospital stay. Much of this cost is simply transferred out of the hospital to the home situation where visiting nurse organizations, family members and primary care physicians contribute to impact on a different cost center not used in these calculations.

Thus surgical costs as currently presented may well be somewhat artificially less than those actually encountered.

Given the constraints of the numerous variables and the different permutations and commutations of individual therapies, variations of management strategy and individual patient requirements, one may derive a generalized financial assessment.

These calculations have excluded the considerable financial costs generated by loss of earnings and decreased productivity during episodes of relapse.

A simplified analysis of the potential costs involved in GERD management. The diagonal lines above each operation represent the potential increase in cost generated by a complication. Although laparoscopic procedures are claimed to be more cost-effective, their cost is underestimated. Some hospital costs are transferred to home services and often are not included in calculations. In a complex evolving economic environment, it is likely that drug costs will fall with the passage of time.

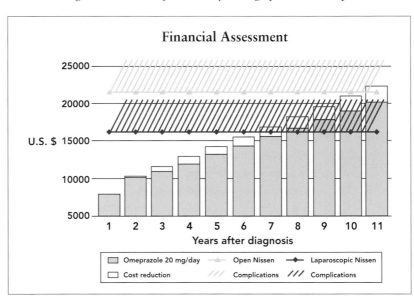

Using the clinical management scenarios previously described, it is apparent that at the seven year point after surgery the cost effectiveness of a laparoscopic Nissen procedure will intersect with that of GERD managed by omeprazole therapy. Similar analysis indicates that it will take at least a decade before the cost analysis construct for maintenance medical therapy attains the costs of an open procedure. These calculations are in general valid for the USA.

In other countries with differently structured healthcare systems the costs can vary and an operation may attain cost-effective status earlier.

CHAPTER 5
BARRETT'S

Malignant transformation of the esophageal epithelium

As with neoplasia elsewhere, the transformation from normal to a malignant mucosa occurs through a series of morphological changes accompanied by specific molecular genetic events. The histological changes in the squamous mucosa exposed to gastroesophageal reflux include an increase in the height of the rete pegs and an increase in the number of cycling epithelial cells. Whether the latter phenomenon is a direct effect of exposure of the gastric contents to the esophageal squamous epithelium or whether it is indirect is not known. Similarly, whether direct damage including erosions is necessarily the stimulus for transformation from squamous to columnar epithelium, as in Barrett's esophagus, is not clear. Currently it is felt that the development of a Barrett's-type mucosa containing gastric and/or small intestinal and/or colonic-type cells, often together in the same metaplastic esophageal gland, is due to an altered process of differentiation from the pluripotent epithelial stem cell. The presence of abundant growth factors in the esophageal gland system suggests that a process analogous to that described for the ulcer associated cell lineage sytem may be implicated in the local repair process. As in many other cancers, p53 mutations and aneuploidy are common in esophageal dysplasia and cancer, and alterations of other molecules such as cyclins and rab proteins have been described. The precise relevance of such diverse molecular events to the pathobiology of the system is at this stage unclear. Indeed, the sequence of genetic events occurring in esophageal cancer is not as well established as in the colon, although the potential utilization of these markers for screening purposes and possibly prognostic information is an area of considerable clinical and scientific interest.

Barrett's esophagus

History

Although Norman Barrett initially proposed that the columnar lined lower end of the esophagus was stomach, he subsequently revised his view recognizing that the structure was esophagus that now possessed a columnar lining.

Norman Barrett, in 1950, published a report in the British Journal of Surgery in which he defined the esophagus as *"that part of the foregut, distal to the cricopharyngeal sphincter, which is lined by squamous epithelium"*. He went on in this article to describe a number of patients who had ulcerations in a tubular, inter-thoracic organ that appeared to be to the esophagus except that its distal portion was lined extensively by a gastric type of columnar epithelium. Since the esophagus was by definition a squamous-lined structure, Barrett believed that the columnar lined organ was a tubular segment of stomach generated by traction induced by a congenitally short (squamous-lined) esophagus and tethered within the chest. In this report Barrett did not identify intestinal features (goblet cells) in the columnar lining of the tubular organ, nor did he raise the question of intestinal metaplasia. This issue was first noted in 1951 by Bosher and Taylor, who commented upon the appearance of heterotopic

SURGERY

VOL. 41   JUNE, 1957   No. 6

Original Communications

THE LOWER ESOPHAGUS LINED BY COLUMNAR EPITHELIUM
N. R. BARRETT, LONDON, ENGLAND

DEFINITIONS

gastric mucosa in the esophagus with ulceration and stricture formation. They noted that *"the gastric mucosa was composed of glands which contained goblet cells but not parietal cells"*.

A year later Basil Morson together with Belcher commented upon the relationship of adenocarcinoma of the esophagus and ectopic gastric mucosa. They noted that in an individual with adenocarcinoma the esophageal mucosa exhibited *"atrophic changes with changes towards an intestinal type containing many goblet cells"*. In 1953 Allison and Johnstone proposed that Barrett had misidentified the columnar lined intrathoracic structure as stomach and that in reality it was the esophagus lined with gastric mucus membrane. They noted that in contrast to the stomach the structure lack a peritoneal covering, often harbored islands of squamous epithelium, and possessed some mucosal glands and a *muscularis propria* characteristic of the esophagus. Thus, seven years after his original report, Barrett reversed himself and concurred that the columnar lined organ that he had previously believed to be the stomach was in fact the esophagus and suggested that the condition now be called *"lower esophagus lined by columnar epithelium"*. Despite this *volte face* the condition to this time remains known as Barrett's esophagus and continues to evoke as much confusion as when initially described.

In the first decade of its recognition, most believed that the esophageal columnar lining was congenital in origin but noted a common association with hiatal hernia and severe reflux esophagitis. It remained until 1959 for Moersch and his colleagues to propose that the columnar epithelium was not congenital in origin but acquired as a sequela of reflux esophagitis. Hayward, in 1961, commented upon the vulnerability of the squamous epithelium at the site where it joined the gastric epithelium. He felt that it would be liable to digestion at this junctional zone and proposed *"a buffer zone of junctional epithelium which does not secrete acid or pepsin but is resistant to them and has to be interposed"*. For the subsequent two decades the histology of the columnar lined epithelium remained a controversial issue. Various investigators described an esophagus lined by junctional epithelium, some noted the presence of acid and acid secreting fundic type of epithelium and others described an intestinal type of epithelium with goblet cells. In 1976, Paull clarified the situation in patients with Barrett's esophagus by obtaining biopsy specimens at specified levels throughout the esophagus using manometric guidance.

Using this technique, the distal esophagus was noted to possess a combination of 1 to 3 types of columnar epithelium, a) junctional type of epithelium; b) a gastric fundic type of epithelium; and c) a distinctive type of intestinal metaplasia that was termed "specialized columnar epithelium". The former two epithelial types were noted to be indistinguishable from the columnar epithelium normally identified in the stomach. However, the specialized intestinal metaplasia with its prominent goblet cells could readily be distinguished from normal mucosa. In addition, the three epithelial types were noted to occupy different zones in the esophagus with a specialized intestinal metaplasia adjacent to squamous epithelium in the most proximal segment of the columnar lining. The junctional type epithelium was noted to be present in the most distal esophageal segment and the gastric fundic type epithelium was directly adjacent to the columnar mucosa of the stomach which it joined.

The Histological Evolution of Barrett's Esophagus

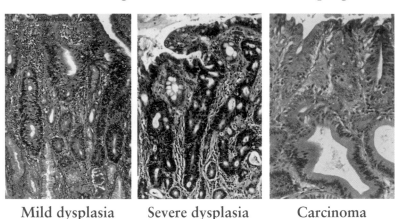

Mild dysplasia   Severe dysplasia   Carcinoma

Continued damage to the lower esophagus over a varying period of time results in transformation of the cell type and may culminate in neoplasia.

By the 1970s it was firmly established that the columnar lined esophagus was often associated with severe GERD. It was controversial as to whether normal esophagus could be lined by columnar epithelium.

Since the association of large hiatal hernias with extensive esophageal inflammation often obscured the endoscopic landmarks of the junction between the esophagus and the stomach, false positive diagnoses of Barrett's esophagus abounded.

This became a source of considerable concern with the widespread recognition of the relationship between adenocarcinoma and Barrett's esophagus. In the latter instances the columnar epithelium surrounding the tumor invariably contained specialized intestinal metaplasia that often exhibited dysplasia. The recognition that specialized intestinal metaplasia was the epithelial type that pre-disposed to dysplasia and cancer development generated a major interest in the biology of this lesion and its early identification.

Current status

The last decade has led to disagreement as to the diagnosis and management of Barrett's esophagus particularly as it relates to the possible evolution of malignant disease. To a large extent the issue has been fueled by the extraordinary rise in incidence of adenocarcinoma of the esophagogastric junction and the gastric cardia in particular.

The critical questions, which have arisen, have not as yet been adequately resolved. Thus the precise definition of Barrett's esophagus by the identification of the extent of esophageal columnar lining has not been confirmed. Furthermore problems in defining Barrett's esophagus by the presence of intestinal metaplasia require certainty as regards to biopsy sampling sites and histological identification.

Lastly, there exists a considerable degree of confusion in regard to the relationship between the extent of the esophageal columnar lining, specialized intestinal metaplasia, and gastroesophageal reflux disease.

It is, however, apparent that the greater the length or extent of the esophageal columnar lining of the esophagus, the greater the frequency of the finding of intestinal metaplasia. Indeed the frequency of specialized intestinal metaplasia at the squamo-columnar junction may be said to vary linearly with the extent of columnar epithelium lining the esophagus.

Given the degree of confusion that exists regarding the term "Barrett's esophagus", an alternative classification, which does not rely on arbitrary and imprecise endoscopic measurements, has been proposed by Spechler. Thus when columnar epithelium is detected in the esophagus regardless of its extent, the condition should be called columnar lined esophagus as originally proposed by Barrett. Once biopsy samples have been obtained from this esophageal columnar lining, the use of histological criteria can then be used to classify the condition as either columnar lined esophagus with specialized intestinal metaplasia or columnar lined esophagus without specialized intestinal metaplasia.

This proposal provides considerable improvement in clarity for both physicians and pathologists in regard to the entity under consideration in a particular patient.

Whilst both conditions may be associated with GERD, the association is variable and appears to be related to the extent of the columnar lining. Thus individuals with long segments of esophageal columnar lining often exhibit both severe GERD and specialized intestinal metaplasia. Signs and symptoms of GERD, however, may be absent in patients with short segments of columnar lining in the distal esophagus, even when biopsy specimens reveal specialized intestinal metaplasia.

Complications of Barrett's Esophagus

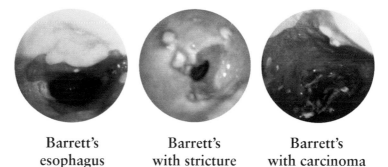

Barrett's esophagus   **Barrett's with stricture**   **Barrett's with carcinoma**

The histological changes in the lining of the lower esophagus are associated with topographic alterations of considerable biological and clinical relevance.

Thus endoscopic surveillance for adenocarcinoma may be recommended in individuals who have columnar lined esophagus with intestinal metaplasia irrespective of the extent, whereas columnar lined esophagus without specialized intestinal metaplasia does not require endoscopic surveillance.

In the situation where the distal esophagus appears normal and specialized intestinal metaplasia is identified at the squamo-columnar junction, which does not extend appreciably above the anatomic junction of the esophagus and the stomach, the condition should be called specialized intestinal metaplasia at the esophagogastric junction. It has not been established whether this condition is related to GERD nor is it evident that the risk of cancer applies to patients with this condition.

Clinical Relevance of Barrett's Esophagus			
Classification	Association with Gerd	Association with Adenocarcinoma	Endoscopic Surveillance Recommended
Columnar-line esophagus with specialized intestinal metaplasia	Variable	Yes	Yes
Columnar-lined esophagus without specialized intestinal metaplasia	Variable	Unlikely	Probably not
Specialized intestinal metaplasia at the esophagogastric junction	Unclear	Probable	Unclear

A re-evalutaion of the approach to Barrett's esophagus has been proposed by S. Spechler and R. Goyal. Intestinal metaplasia may represent the critical variable of most pathological significance.

Barrett's esophagus had been identified primarily in patients with the signs and symptoms of GERD and in whom endoscopic examination revealed a long segment of columnar epithelium extending well up into the esophagus. Biopsy specimens taken from the columnar lining usually reveal an unusual form of intestinal metaplasia called specialized intestinal metaplasia, and the intestinal lining is invariably evident in the columnar epithelium surrounding Barrett's adenocarcinomas. As a result of such observations, Barrett's esophagus with specialized intestinal metaplasia became recognized as a major risk factor for adenocarcinoma at the gastroesophageal junction. The similar recognition that adenocarcinoma of the gastroesophageal junction was increasing at a dramatic rate in the USA and western Europe led to the development of a high level of interest in the pathology, early identification and treatment of the condition. Of note is the observation that individuals who undergo esophagectomy for adenocarcinoma at the gastroesophageal junction often do not exhibit endoscopically apparent Barrett's esophagus, but more often have short inconspicuous segments of specialized intestinal metaplasia only evident at histological examination of the specimen. This observation accords well with reports that in 18% of elective endoscopy patients with no evidence of Barrett's esophagus (columnar lined epithelium < 3 cm of the distal esophagus) biopsies of the Z line (squamo-columnar junction) revealed specialized intestinal metaplasia. It is evident from this and other similar studies that short inconspicuous segments of specialized intestinal metaplasia can be frequently found at the Z line in predominantly Caucasian populations.

The precise relevance of the metaplasia is however not certain. In particular the question of whether columnar metaplasia develops as a sequela of GERD has not been resolved. Thus different studies have variously reported: a) an association with GERD symptoms; b) no association with GERD; c) no association with endoscopic esophagitis; d) an occasional association with histologic esophagitis. Given these inconsistent observations, the traditional concept that intestinal metaplasia develops as a consequence of GERD requires further scrutiny. Similarly, the cancer risk for individuals with short segments of intestinal metaplasia is unknown. Indeed given the relatively high prevalence rates reported for intestinal metaplasia at the Z line and the infrequency of cancers at this location (irrespective of the rise in incidence) it seems likely that the risk associated with the short segments of specialized intestinal metaplasia is quite small.

Nevertheless, the concerns in regard to neoplasia in relation to GERD and Barrett's esophagus remain a source of concern. In 1990, Cameron and colleagues showed that for every case of Barrett's esophagus in patient with esophageal cancer, many more are unrecognized.

Similarly, in at least 5 separate studies it has been demonstrated that of all individuals undergoing endoscopy, up to one in five individuals will have specialized intestinal metaplasia at the gastroesophageal junction, whether or not abnormalities are evident at the time of endoscopy.

Despite the screening recommendations for Barrett's esophagus mentioned above, a recent study in the UK has suggested that the yield of a Barrett's surveillance program may be too low to justify economically.

Interesting issues have been raised in regard to the relationship between *H. pylori* and GERD and in particular between these two disease entities and the possible relationship to adenocarcinoma at the gastroesophageal junction. Similarly claims that acid inhibitory therapy may be implicated in the genesis of gastroesophageal junction intestinal metaplasia and neoplasia are not supported by data. At this time any such pathogenic linkage is speculative and rigorous studies are required before such relationships can be substantiated.

At present given the advances in endoscopic detection and a better understanding of metaplasia the definition and pathogenesis of Barrett's esophagus seem less clear than previously envisaged. Thus, the definition of Barrett's solely by the presence of specialized intestinal metaplasia regardless of its extent may serve to significantly overestimate the disease process (by this definition, one in every five endoscoped patients has Barrett's esophagus). It is probably more realistic to restate the observation in terms of the identification of a condition known as "*columnar epithelium lined esophagus with specialized intestinal metaplasia*". Upon identification of such an entity a specific focus can then be developed to identify cellular or molecular markers consistent with the development of dysplastic and neoplastic transformation. The wide usage of the term "Barrett's esophagus" and its associated emotive and artificially numinous connotations of GERD and neoplasia should be avoided lest it engender overly emotional therapeutic responses.

If the principal issue is to impact upon the incidence of adenocarcinoma of the esophagus, which is currently the most rapidly increasing cancer in the United States, and amplify therapeutic gain a different strategy is required.

Thus better tests to identify at-risk patients than the use of endoscopy in patients with known Barrett's esophagus are needed. In particular the identification of molecular markers of cell transformation in the esophagus are mandatory to facilitate the identification of individuals whose metaplasia is of pathological significance.

CHAPTER 6
CONSENSUS

Management consensus

GERD presents as a complex set of clinical variables which require interpolation into a cohesive management strategy. PPI's are the most effective therapy, although surgery may have a role in a very small proportion of patients if rigorous and specific criteria are met. The utility of prokinetic agents remains ill-defined.

Most patients with GERD present to and are managed by general practitioners, some of the care for patients with GERD will require referral to a gastroenterologist and a surgeon. The management of GERD is a continuum, with management based upon not only symptoms, but referral patterns and, more increasingly, financial constraints. The first step in the management of the patient with suspected gastroesophageal reflux disease is a history and physical examination. A history of retro-sternal burning-type chest pain radiating up from the epigastrium towards the throat is characteristic of GERD, and such symptoms have a high specificity for the diagnosis. If the patient has either atypical symptoms, or any alarm symptoms such as dysphagia, anemia, weight loss, predominantly abdominal pain, or pain that does not respond to antacids, or first develops symptoms after the age of 50, then prompt referral for endoscopy is necessary.

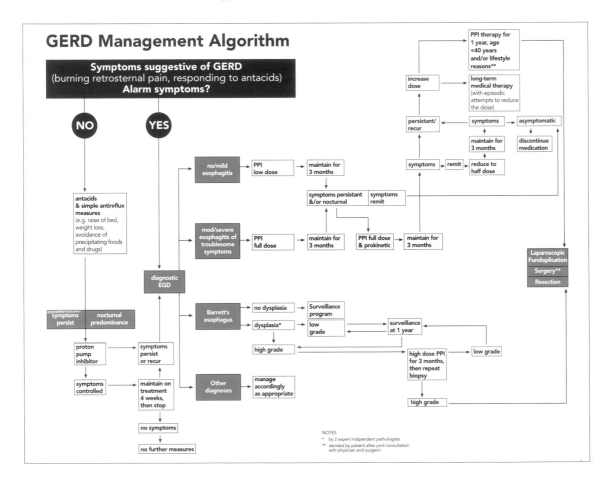

The majority of patients probably do not require endoscopy initially and such patients should be counselled in regard to more simple anti-reflux measures, which may include: elevation of the head of the bed, weight loss, and the avoidance of precipitating foods and drugs. It is of note, however, that there exists little rigorous data to support the concept that such measures are either of proven or long term benefit in the management of GERD. The patient should also be advised to take antacids at the time of symptoms, and to avoid heavy meals late at night or within 3 hours of retiring to bed. If symptoms persist after 2-4 weeks of these simple measures or if antacids are needed often if not daily then formal therapy should be instituted. In the past the first line of treatment was considered to be the use of an H2-receptor antagonist but the current almost uniform positive clinical experience with the use of proton pump inhibitors at the standard (low dose) as initial therapy suggests that this strategy is more acceptable to both clinicians and patients. In circumstances where the pain is a consistent component of the symptomatology and particularly if there is a nocturnal component the use of a proton pump inhibitor should be given unequivocal consideration.

If the symptoms are more suggestive of a motility problem or it is felt that evidence of a motility component to the presentation is evident, a pro-kinetic drug such as the $5-HT_4$-receptor agonist cisapride may be considered. Such agents (motility) are, however, non-specific in their site of gastro-intestinal action and often display considerable adverse effects. These drugs should be given initially as a one month trial, and then discontinued. If symptoms recur after this 4-week trial or if they are not relieved during this treatment period, then the patient should be referred for endoscopy. Although the decision to undertake endoscopy at this time is somewhat arbitrary, it is consistent with the widely accepted position that a "once in a life time endoscopy" in reflux disease is acceptable. Thus an endoscopic evaluation can be included in the data base of the patient before major (and possibly) long-term therapeutic decisions are undertaken.

At the time of endoscopy, particular attention should be paid to the presence of erythema, erosions, and other signs of esophagitis and, the gastroesophageal junction should be examined carefully. If there is any suspicion of Barrett's esophagus, then four-quadrant biopsies should be taken at the gastroesophageal junction, but a gastroesophageal junction of normal appearance should not be biopsied routinely. Antrum and corpus biopsies should be taken for the diagnosis of *H. pylori* even in the absence of peptic ulceration given the recent reports of accelerated gastric atrophy in patients with *H. pylori* taking long-term proton pump inhibitors. Thus, prophylactic eradication of *H. pylori* in this group would be mandatory. There still exists a minority opinion which believes that since *H. pylori* infection is common, and in most circumstances does not lead to harm, establishing whether or not *H. pylori* was present may be irrelevant and potentially confusing.

It is uniformly accepted that a critical issue in the management of GERD is the need to ensure appropriate effective therapy to minimize the risk of the development of Barrett's esophagus and to identify it accurately. Patients found to have Barrett's esophagus at biopsy but with no dysplasia, should be placed in a surveillance program with approximately 5-year intervals between surveillance endoscopies. This opinion is to a large extent based upon cost effectiveness analysis data and may need to be modified with the significant alterations in endoscopic charges. If the pathologist diagnoses Barrett's esophagus and identifies the presence of dysplasia, then the material should be reviewed by two expert independent pathologists to confirm the diagnosis and to establish whether the changes conform to a pattern consistent with low or high grade dysplasia. The identification of low grade dysplasia mandates repeat biopsy at one year to determine whether there is progression to high grade dysplasia. If at the one year time point multiple biopsies fail to identify evidence of dysplasia, the patient should return to the normal surveillance program; if low grade dysplasia persists, then endoscopy and biopsy should again be repeated in one year. If there is a diagnosis of high grade dysplasia at the initial or any follow-up biopsy, then the patient should be treated with a high dose proton pump inhibitor for three months, e.g. pantoprazole 40 mg b.i.d, omeprazole 20-40 mg b.i.d. or lansoprazole 30 mg b.i.d. for three months, to rule out the possibility of inflammatory pseudodysplasia. If the repeat biopsy after three months confirms high-grade dysplasia then the patient should be referred for consideration of surgery. Some experts have expressed the opinion that very carefully repeated endoscopic surveillance of high-grade dysplasia can be performed to monitor for and biopsy any visible mucosal abnormality. Under such circumstances surgery might be obviated until a carcinoma is discovered. However the majority of authorities in this field are uncomfortable with this approach and express a preference for prophylactic surgery once the presence of a high grade lesion had been reliably identified. Ablation therapy by laser, bicap, heater probe or photo-dynamic therapy for Barrett's esophagus and/or dysplasia should be currently regarded as experimental.

In the absence of Barrett's esophagus or for Barrett's esophagus without high grade dysplasia, the primary goal of treatment of GERD should be to relieve symptoms. Thus, with the identification of minimal or modest esophagitis at endoscopy and mild symptoms, a proton pump inhibitor should be the initial agent of choice. There is no longer much support for initial treatment with either an H2 receptor antagonist or prokinetic agents given their modest efficacy and the adverse effects noted particularly at the high dosage levels needed to attain a consistently elevated pH. The cost to the patient in terms of life style and work loss generated by initial failed therapy using such agents is no longer acceptable.

There is uniform agreement that in the event of moderate or severe esophagitis or particularly troublesome symptoms, all patients should be treated with a proton pump inhibitor immediately. If a patient had been placed on H2 receptor antagonist or prokinetic therapy and failed to resolve their symptomatology or relapsed, a proton pump inhibitor should be prescribed. Under such circumstances it was accepted that proton pump inhibitors such as omeprazole (20 mg daily), pantoprazole (40 mg daily) or lansoprazole (30 mg) should initially be given at these standard doses. In rare instances, when these fail to provide symptom relief for all patients, they may need to be increased to b.i.d. dosing or even more, to achieve full symptom relief. Based upon currently available information, it is felt that the addition of a pro-kinetic agent to therapy in conjunction with a proton pump inhibitor is likely to be of only marginal benefit for GERD. Once a dose of either H2 receptor antagonist, prokinetic agent, and/or proton pump inhibitor which relieves symptoms is identified, this dose should be maintained for a period of three months. After this time, an attempt should be made to reduce the dose, with the aim of maintaining a stable clinical status (asymptomatic) on half dose PPI's or alternatively on alternative day therapy. If symptoms recur, then the patient should go back to the full dose of proton pump inhibitor and a plan formulated for long-term treatment.

The long-term treatment options are either medical therapy, with attempts to reduce the dose of medication occasionally, or consideration for surgery. With regards to patients who might enter long-term therapy, it should be noted that many, particularly those in the older age group, may be taking several medications. Thus, careful attention should be directed to the drug interaction profile of the various types of proton pump inhibitors.

Surgery is an attractive option for younger patients (age <40 years) and for patients who do not want to take chronic medication for lifestyle reasons. Thus individuals who require proton pump inhibitor therapy continually for a year, are unlikely to be able to manage without these medications. Prior to surgery, patients should have the opportunity of a full and frank discussion with both their gastroenterologist and the surgeon, preferably together, regarding all the risks and benefits of long-term medical versus surgical therapy. Although there are as yet no long-term data available, laparoscopic fundoplication generally appears to be safe, and preferable to open surgery. Preoperative motility studies are essential both to precisely delineate the state of the sphincter as well as to facilitate follow up if there is any post surgical relapse. The critical determinant of successful surgery is the choice of surgeon. The practice of surgery for the treatment of gastroesophageal reflux should be confined to those surgeons both experienced and expert in surgery for this condition. Current information supports the use of a "wrap" type procedure and no data exist to suggest that the addition of any form of vagotomy confers further benefit. (Indeed given the cumulative experience of almost half a century of post vagotomy patients it is probably malpractice to undertake such a procedure electively.) However, above the age of 60, the risks from surgery probably outweigh the benefits and under such circumstances the use of an appropriate PPI is probably safer than general anesthesia and violation of the peritoneal cavity. For patients with Barrett's esophagus as a component of intractable GERD symptomatology, it is essential to continue the surveillance program even if the patient is asymptomatic after surgery, since progression of Barrett's esophagus after successful GERD surgery is well recognized.

A defective fundic wrap not only increases the costs for the surgical procedure, but significantly complicates further treatment and evidently increases risk if reoperation is undertaken. Published data indicate an incidence of defective fundic wrap of 7% after 7 months, of 23% after 77 months and of 29% after 20 years. Thus, the reoperation rate may ultimately be as high as 5-10% for individuals who have previously undergone a Nissen procedure. While questions have been raised about long-term medical therapy the issue of the long-term viability of a fundic wrap may also require some consideration. Another problem with the surgical procedure is the postoperative dysphagia, which may require clinical treatment and occasionally even endoscopic management with dilation. The negative influence on the cost and outcome analysis of these events have yet to be precisely determined.

Given the rate of scientific and medical advance at this time, it is not unreasonable to propose that more specific pharmacotherapeutic probes targeting the lower esophageal sphincter are likely to become available within the foreseeable future. In addition, the area of mucosal healing is a subject which is under extensive investigation and the possibility of the development of agents capable of amplifying the healing process or altering the quality of the healed mucosa is significant (i.e. less likely to recur). Certainly, if one reviews medical advances made in the management of acid inhibition and the control of gastric mucosal inflammatory disease in the last five years, one might predict significant pharmacological advances in the medical management of GERD in the upcoming time. In those patients who have indications which warrant surgery but are reluctant to undergo anesthesia and invasive procedures, a cautiously optimistic but conservative posture should be adopted by their physicians.

REFERENCES

Allen, M.L., Di Marino, A.J, Jr. *Swallowing and LES relaxation with reflux: not by chance*. Gastroenterology 114 (2), 422 (Feb.1998).

Anonymous. *Guidelines for surgical treatment of gastroesophageal reflux disease (GERD)*. Society of American Gastrointestinal Endoscopic Surgeons (SAGES). Surgical Endoscopy 12 (2), 186-8 (Feb. 1998).

Anvari, M., Allen, C. *Laparoscopic Nissen fundoplication: two-year comprehensive follow-up of a technique of minimal paraesophageal dissection*. Annals of Surgery 227 (1), 25-32 (Jan. 1998).

Armstrong, D., Bennett, J.R., Blum, A.L. et al. *The endoscopic assessment of esophagitis: a progress report on observer agreement*. Gastroenterology 11, 85-92 (1996).

Cameron, A.J., Zinmeister, A.R., Ballard, D.J. et al. *Prevalence of columnar lined (Barrett's) esophagus. Comparison of population-based clinical and autopsy findings*. Gastroenterology 99, 918-22 (1990).

Castell, D.O., Katz, P.O. *Acid control and regression of Barrett's esophagus: is the glass half full or half empty?* American Journal of Gastroenterology 92 (12), 2329-30 (Dec. 1997).

Crawford, J.M. *Membrane trafficking and the pathologist: esophageal dysplasia*. Laboratory Investigation 77 (5), 407-8 (Nov. 1997).

Crookes, P.F. *Gastroesophageal reflux after partial gastrectomy*. American Journal of Gastroenterology 93 (1), 3-4 (Jan. 1998).

De Caestecker, J.S. *Measuring duodenogastro-oesophageal reflux (DGOR)*. European Journal of Gastroenterology & Hepatology 9 (12), 1141-3 (Dec. 1997).

De Meester, T.R., Ireland, A.P. *Gastric pathology as an initiator and potentiator of gastroesophageal reflux disease*. Diseases of the Esophagus 10 (1), 1-8 (Jan. 1997).

Dent, J. *Australian clinical trials of omeprazole in the management of reflux esophagitis*. Digestion 47, 69 (1990).

Dent, J. *Patterns of lower esophageal sphincter function associated with gastroesophageal reflux*. American Journal of Medicine 103 (5A), 29S-32S (Nov. 24, 1997).

Dent, J. *Roles of gastric acid and pH in the pathogenesis of gastro-esophageal reflux disease*. Scand. J. Gastroenterol. Suppl. 201, 55-61 (1994).

Dent, J., Talley, N. *Heartburn and dyspepsia: diagnostic challenge, health care dilemma*. Aliment. Pharmacol. and Therapy, Suppl 2, 11 (1997).

Donahue, P.E. *Basic considerations in gastroesophageal reflux disease*. Surgical Clinics of North America 77 (5), 1017-40 (Oct. 1997).

Donahue, D., Navab, F. *Significance of short-segment Barrett's esophagus*. Journal of Clinical Gastroenterology 25 (2), 480-4 (Sept. 1997).

Eggleston, A., Wigerinck, A., Huijghebaert, S., Dubois, D., Haycox, A. *Cost effectiveness of treatment for gastro-oesophageal reflux disease in clinical practice: a clinical database analysis*. Gut 42 (1), 13-6 (Jan. 1998).

Galmiche, J.P., Janssens, J. *The pathophysiology of gastro-esophageal reflux disease: an overview*. Scand. J. Gastroenterol. Suppl. 211, 7-18 (1995).

Giaretti, W. *Aneuploidy mechanisms in human colorectal preneoplastic lesions and Barrett's esophagus. Is there a role for K-ras and p53 mutations?*. Analytical Cellular Pathology 15 (2), 99-117 (1997).

Hatlebakk, J.G., Johnsson, F., Vilien, M., Carling, L., Wetterhus, S., Thogersen, T. *The effect of cisapride in maintaining symptomatic remission in patients with gastro-oesophageal reflux disease*. Scandinavian Journal of Gastroenterology 32 (11), 1100-6 (Nov. 1997).

Hunt, R.H., Cederberg, C., Dent, J. et al. *Optimizing acid suppression for treatment of acid-related diseases*. Dig. Dis. Sci. 40, 24S-49S (1995).

Jaup, B. *Gastroesophageal reflux after cure of H. pylori infection*. Gastroenterology 113 (6), 2019 (Dec. 1997).

Johnsson, F., Weywadt, L., Solhaug, J.H., Hernqvist, H., Bengtsson, L. *One-week omeprazole treatment in the diagnosis of gastro-oesophageal reflux disease*. Scandinavian Journal of Gastroenterology 33 (1), 15-20 (Jan. 1998).

Kahrilas, P.J. *Anatomy and physiology of the gastro-esophageal junction*. Gastroenterology Clinics of North America 26 (3), 467-86 (Sept. 1997).

Katz, P. *The ambulatory pH study is normal, but the patient is not – the importance of the symptoms index*. American Journal of Gastroenterology 93 (1), 129-31 (Jan. 1998).

Kim, S.L., Wo, J.M., Hunter, J.G., Davis, L.P., Waring, J.P. *The prevalence of intestinal metaplasia in patients with and without peptic strictures*. American Journal of Gastroenterology 93 (1), 53-5 (Jan. 1998).

Kuipers, E.J., Lundell, L., Klinkenberg-Knol, E.C. et al. *Atrophic gastritis and Helicobacter pylori infection in patients with reflux esophagitis treated with omeprazole for fundoplication*. New Engl. J. Med. 334, 1018-22 (1996).

Labenz, J., Blum, A.L., Bayerdorffer, E. et al. *Curing Helicobacter pylori infection in patients with duodenal ulcer may provoke reflux esophagitis*. Gastroenterology 112, 1442-7 (1997).

Labenz, J., Tillenburg, B., Peitz, U. et al. *Helicobacter pylori augments the pH increasing effect of omeprazole in patients with duodenal ulcer*. Gastroenterology 110, 725-32 (1996).

Laine, L. *H. pylori eradication in gastroesophageal reflux disease*. Gastroenterology 113 (6), 2019-20 (Dec. 1997).

Ledson, M.J., Tran, J., Walshaw, M.J. *Prevalence and mechanisms of gastro-oesophageal reflux in adult cystic fibrosis patients*. Journal of the Royal Society of Medicine 91 (1), 7-9 (1998).

Leggett, P.L., Churchman-Winn, R., Ahn, C. *Resolving gastroesophageal reflux with laparoscopic fundoplication. Findings in 138 cases*. Surgical Endoscopy 12 (2), 142-7 (1998).

Maziak, D.E., Todd, T.R., Pearson, F.G. *Massive hiatus hernia: evaluation and surgical management*. Journal of Thoracic & Cardiovascular Surgery 115 (1), 53-60, discussion 61-2 (Jan. 1998).

McDougall, N.I., Johnston, B.T., Collins, J.S., McFarland, R.J., Love, A.H. *Disease progression in gastro-oesophageal reflux disease as determined by repeat oesophageal pH monitoring and endoscopy 3 to 4.5 years after diagnosis*. European Journal of Gastroenterology & Hepatology 9 (12), 1161-7 (Dec. 1997).

Mittal R.K., Balaban, D.H. *The esophagogastric junction*. New England Journal of Medicine 336 (13), 924-32 (Mar. 27, 1997).

Modlin, I.M., Goldenring, J.R., Lawton, G.P. et al. *Aspects of the theoretical basis and clinical relevance of low acid states*. Am. J. Gastroenterol. 89, 308-318 (1994).

Moss, S.F., Arnold, R., Tytgat, G., Spechler, S., Delle Fave, G., Rosin, D., Jensen, R., Modlin, I.M. *Consensus Statement for Management of Gastro Esophageal Reflux Disease*. J. Clin. Gastro, 27 (1), 1998.

Nissen, R. *Operation zur Beeinflussung der Refluxoesophagitis*. Schweiz Med. Wochenschr. 86, 590-592 (1956).

Parkman, H.P., Urbain, J.L., Knight, L.C., Brown, K.L., Trate, D.M., Miller, M.A., Maurer, A.H., Fisher, R.S. *Effect of gastric acid suppressants on human gastric motility*. Gut 42 (2), 243-50 (Feb. 1998).

Patti, M.G., Gantert, W., Way, L.W. *Surgery of the esophagus. Anatomy and physiology*. Surgical Clinics of North America 77 (5), 959-70 (Oct. 1997).

Penagini, R., Hebbard, G., Horowitz, M., Dent, J., Bermingham, H., Jones, K., Holloway, R.H. *Motor function of the proximal stomach and visceral perception in gastro-oesophageal reflux disease*. Gut 42 (2), 251-7 (Feb. 1998).

Provencale, D., Kemp, J.A., Arora, S. et al. *A guide for surveillance of patients with Barrett's esophagus*. Am. J. Gastroenterol. 89, 670-680 (1994).

Richter, J.E. *Extraesophageal presentations of gastroesophageal reflux disease*. Seminars in Gastrointestinal Disease 8 (2), 75-89 (Apr. 1997) [published erratum appears in Semin. Gastrointest. Dis. 8 (4), 210, Oct. 1997].

Saslow, S.B., Thumshirn, M., Camilleri, M., Locke, G.R. 3rd., Thomforde, G.M., Burton, D.D., Hanson, R.B. *Influence of H. pylori infection on gastric motor and sensory function in asymptomatic volunteers*. Digestive Diseases & Sciences 43 (2), 258-64 (Feb. 1998).

Smit, C.F., Tan, J., Devriese, P.P., Mathus-Vliegen, L.M., Brandsen, M., Schouwenburg, P.F. *Ambulatory pH measurements at the upper esophageal sphincter*. Laryngoscope 108 (2), 299-302 (Feb. 1998).

Smythe, A., Bird, N.C., Troy, G.P., Globe, J., Johnson, A.G. *Effect of cisapride on oesophageal motility and duodenogastro-oesophageal reflux in patients with Barrett's oesophagus*. European Journal of Gastroenterology & Hepatology 9 (12), 1149-53 (Dec. 1997).

Spechler, S.J. *Epidemiology and natural history of gastroesophageal reflux disease*. Digestion 51 (Suppl. 1), 24-29 (1992).

Stein, H.J., Balint, A. *Surgery for gastro-oesophageal reflux disease: laparoscopic versus traditional approach*. Italian Journal of Gastroenterology and Hepatology 29 (5), 391-4 (1997).

Stein, H.J., Crookes, P.F., DeMeester, T.R. *Three-dimensional manometric imaging of the lower esophageal sphincter*. Surgery Annual 27, 199-214 (1995).

Stewart, M.J., Hurst, A.F. *Gastric and duodenal ulcer*. London, Oxford University Press, 1929, p. 498.

Straathof, J.W., Lamers, C.B., Masclee, A.A. *Effect of gastrin-17 on lower esophageal sphincter characteristics in man*. Digestive Diseases & Sciences. 42(12):2547-51, 1997 Dec.

Thogersen, C., Rasmussen, C., Rutz, K., Jakobsen, E., Kruse-Andersen, S. *Non-parametric classification of esophagus motility by means of neural networks*. Methods of Information in Medicine 36 (4-5), 352-5 (Dec. 1997).

Trus, T.L., Laycock, W.S., Wo, J.M., Waring, J.P., Branum, G.D., Mauren, S.J., Katz, E.M., Hunter, J.G. *Laparoscopic antireflux surgery in the elderly*. American Journal of Gastroenterology 93 (3), 351-3 (Mar. 1998).

Vandenplas, Y. *Commentary: oesophageal pH monitoring: how gold is the gold standard?* Italian Journal of Gastroenterology and Hepatology 29 (4), 302-4 (Aug. 1997).

Washington, N., Steele, R.J., Wright, J.W., Bush, D., McIntosh, S.L., Wilkinson, S., Washington, C. *An investigation of lower oesophageal redox potentials in gastro-oesophageal reflux patients and healthy volunteers*. Physiological Measurement 18 (4), 363-71 (Nov. 1997).

Wilmer, A., Van Cutsem, E., Andrioli, A., Tack, J., Coremans, G., Janssens, J. *Ambulatory gastrojejunal manometry in severe motility-like dyspepsia: lack of correlation between dysmotility, symptoms, and gastric emptying*. Gut 42 (2), 235-42 (Feb. 1998).

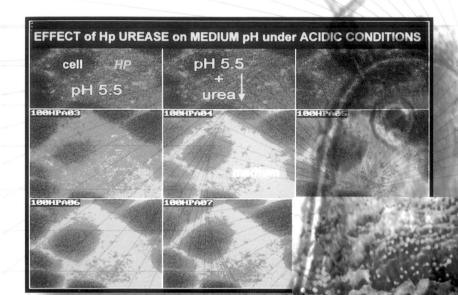

EFFECT of Hp UREASE on MEDIUM pH under ACIDIC CONDITIONS

cell *HP* pH 5.5	pH 5.5 + urea ↓	
100HPA03	100HPA04	100HPA05
100HPA06	100HPA07	

H. pylori Urease Activates at lower Medium pH

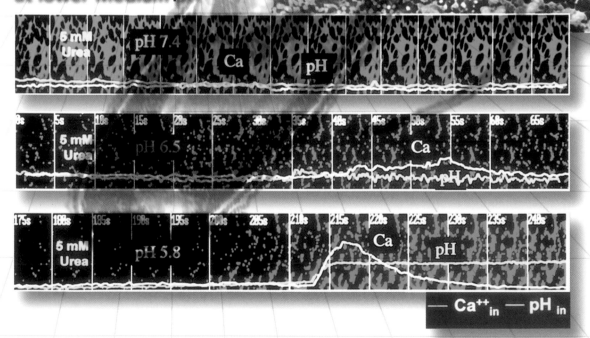

— Ca^{++} in — pH in

SECTION 7

HELICOBACTER PYLORI

CHAPTER 1
History

CHAPTER 2
**Biological Basis of
Gastric Colonization by *Helicobacter***

CHAPTER 3
Pathogenicity

CHAPTER 4
Infection and its Consequences

CHAPTER 1
HISTORY

Introduction

Although the association between *Campylobacter (Helicobacter) pylori* and ulcers was discovered by Robin Warren in 1979 and the organism was cultured by Barry Marshall in 1982, resulting in their seminal publications in Lancet in 1983, the historical origins of its discovery are rooted in the latter half of the nineteenth century. It was during this period, that the eminent German bacteriologist Robert Koch, proved scientifically that bacteria were the cause of certain diseases. Almost simultaneously, the Frenchman Louis Pasteur, having been galvanized by Koch's contributions, was in the process of developing vaccines against the microbes causing cholera and rabies. In Sicily, in a small home-made laboratory in Messina, an émigré Russian, Elie Metchnikoff, had discovered phagocytosis thus initiating an entirely new vista of biological investigation: host defense mechanisms.

Early bacteriology

Although Leeuwenhoek was probably the first to see both gastrointestinal and oral bacteria, it was O.F. Muller (1730-1784) of Copenhagen who provided the first definitive observations and descriptions of microorganisms; he also coined the terms "bacillus" and "spirillum". Ferdinand Cohn (1828-1898) from Breslau, the botanist now regarded as one of the founders of bacteriology classified microorganisms into several groups: bacterial (short, cylindrical cells), bacilli (longer cells), spirilla (wavy or spiral forms) and coccoid (spherical) and noted the fixity of bacterial species. Thus, even under varying conditions he was never able to obtain cocci from bacilli and vice versa. In 1870, Cohn established his own journal, "*Beitrage zur Biologie der Pflanzen*" and in this communication hosted most of the original, classical bacteriology papers, authored by both himself and his young protégé, Robert Koch. The classic postulates of the latter would subsequently form the logical basis for the inves-

A historical timeline of the individual contributions which led to the identification of *H. pylori*.

Observations on Gastric Infection

Year	Individual	Observations
1875	G. Bottcher/M. Letulle	demonstrated bacteria in ulcer margins
1881	C. Klebs	bacterial colonization and 'interglandular small cell infiltration'
1888	M. Letulle	experimental induction of acute gastric lesions in guinea pigs (*S. aureus*)
1889	W. Jaworski	spiral organisms (*Vibro rugula*) in gastric washings
1893	G. Bizzozero	identified spirochetes in gastric mucosa of dogs
1896	H. Salomon	spirochetes noted in gastric mucosa and experimentally transfered to mice
1906	W. Krienitz	spirochetes in gastric contents of patient with gastric carcinoma
1908	F.B. Turck	induced gastric ulcers in dogs by *Bacillus (Eschericea) coli*
1916	E.C. Rosenow	described streptococcus induced gastric ulcers
1917	L.R. Dragstedt	identified bacteria in experimental ulcers, no significant role identified
1921	J.S. Edkins	experimental physiology of *S. regaudi* (*H. felis*)
1924	J.M. Luck	discovered gastric mucosal urease
1925	B. Hoffman	described *B. hoffmani* - putative ulcerous agent
1930	B. Berg	partial vagotomy inhibits secondary infections in ulcers
1938	J.L. Doenges	spirochetes/inflammation in *Macacus* monkey and man
1940	A.S. Freedberg/L. Barron	identified spirochetes in man - no etiologic role
1940	F.D. Gorham	postulated gastric acidophilic bacteria as an etiologic agent in ulcer disease
1954	E.D. Palmer	no spirochetes detected using HE in 1,180 suction biopsies
1975	H.W. Steer	polymorphonuclear migration in ulcers - isolated *Pseudomonas aeruginosa*
1983	J.R. Warren	identified *Campylobacter (Heliobactor) pylori* in human gastritis
1983	B. Marshall	isolated and cultured *H. pylori*
1985-1987	B. Marshall/A. Morris	ingested and proved the infectivity of *H. pylori* (Koch's 3rd postulate)

From left to right: Leeuwenhoek, Cohn, Koch.

A. Leeuwenhoek (1632-1723), the enthusiastic pioneer of the biological microcosmos, was the first to see gastrointestinal bacteria (mouth, colon), but due to his lack of medical training ascribed no pathologic importance to this new world. Once microscopes had sufficiently evolved, order was brought to the vague Linaèan genus of 'Chaos' by the morphological classification of bacteria by F. Cohn (1828-1898). Cohn's protégé, R. Koch (1843-1910), one of the founders of modern bacteriology, was also first to develop the correct theory of species specific infectious diseases.

tigation and identification of the disease-causing potential of bacteria. In 1872, Cohn published his mature exposition on bacteriology entitled *Untersuchungen über Bakteria*, wherein he further expanded the classification of bacteria into genera and species. He suggested an expanded classification into four groups: sphacrobacteria (cocci), microbacteria, desmobacteria (bacillus and vibrio) and spirobacteria (spirillum and spirochete). This work was well received and became so popular that it was reprinted in 1875 and again in 1876.

In 1878, the term "microbe" was introduced by C.E. Sedillot (1804-1883), a French surgeon who was responsible for undertaking the first gastrostomy and may have unwittingly happened upon the organism. He proposed this term, derived from the Greek for "small life", with the caveat that such "small lives" must have the especial ability to cause fermentation, putrefaction or a disease process. This was a proposal much favored by T. Schwann (1810-1882), who had himself not only discovered pepsin in 1834, but written extensively on the role of fermentation, as well as the single cell theory of disease.

Early data on gastric bacteriology

Careful analysis of gastric contents revealed that under fasting conditions the normal stomach contained mucus, a few bacilli and some yeast cells, whilst in stagnant gastric contents, obtained from patients with gastric disease, bacilli, micrococci, yeast and fungus could readily be seen. Such early observations supported speculations regarding a putative causative role of these "foreign bodies" in gastric pathology. It was however unclear to these early, eager, gastric bacteriologists whether a specific organism was the cause of a gastric disease entity or whether it was simply an abnormal accumulation of organisms in the stomach itself which culminated in gastric disturbances.

One of these first gastric bacteriologists was G. Bottcher, a German who, along with his French collaborator M. Letulle (1853-1929), could demonstrate bacterial colonies in the ulcer floor and in its mucosal margins. His convictions in regard to the disease-causing potential of ingested organisms, were so ardent that by 1875 he had attributed the causation of ulcers to the bacteria which they could demonstrate. However, this was not a popular point of view and in spite of an 1881 report by the pathologist C. Klebs, of a bacillus-like organism evident both free in the lumen of gastric glands and between the cells of the glands and the tunica propria with corresponding "interglandular small round cell infiltration", the "bacterial hypothesis" fell into disuse. Bottcher was, however, probably the first to report the presence of spiral organisms in the gastrointestinal tract of animals, although spiral organisms were already well known and had been described as early as 1838 by Ehrenburg. The pathogenic properties of these particular organisms had similarly been recognized by Obermeier of Berlin, who in 1872, could demonstrate their presence in the blood of patients with relapsing fever. An examination of the report of Klebs indicates that he had noted the presence of an inflammatory infiltration,

In 1889 W. Jaworski discovered and postulated a pathogenic role for the spiral organisms (*Vibrio rugula*) he found in gastric contents.

ALLGEMEINE

DIAGNOSTIK UND THERAPIE

DER

MAGENKRANKHEITEN

NACH DEM HEUTIGEN STANDE DER WISSENSCHAFT

BEARBEITET

VON

Dr. I. BOAS,
SPECIALARZT FÜR MAGEN- UND DARMKRANKHEITEN IN BERLIN.

MIT 23 HOLZSCHNITTEN.

LEIPZIG.
VERLAG VON GEORG THIEME.
1890.

Since Boas could generate similar morphological forms chemically he suggested that Jaworski's cells were the result of the inter-reaction of gastric mucus and acid. Boas was responsible for the co-discovery of the Oppler-Boas bacterium, which he thought was implicated in the etiology of gastric carcinoma.

although he made no specific comments in regards to its significance. However, could this have been the first notation of, if not *H. pylori* infectious gastritis, then at least lymphoid tissue in the gastric mucosa?

In 1889, Walery Jaworski, professor of Medicine at the Jagiellonian University, Cracow, Poland, was the first to describe in detail spiral organisms in the sediment of washings obtained from humans. Amongst other things, he noted a bacterium with a characteristic spiral appearance which he named *Vibrio rugula*. He suggested that it might play a possible pathogenic role in gastric disease. Jaworski supposed that these "snail" or "spiral" cells were only to be found in rare cases. However, Ismar Boas (Berlin), already a luminary for his gastrointestinal contributions and for the discovery of the "Oppler-Boas" *lactobacillus*, found these cells quite constantly in all "fasting" gastric contents containing hydrochloric acid. Further detailed analysis by Boas' assistant, P. Cohnheim, indicated that such "cells" could be induced by the reaction of bronchial or pharyngeal mucus and hydrochloric acid. This led to the suggestion that Jaworski had consistently observed acid altered myelin and that similar secondary structures, threads and small masses could also be induced by these simple chemical reactions. Cohnheim and Boas therefore inferred from their experiments that Jaworski's "cells" were most probably the product of gastric mucus and acid chyme.

The observations of Bottcher and Letulle had suggested a causative bacterial agent in ulcer disease and by 1888, Letulle was actively searching for this postulated entity. A few years earlier in 1881, the Scottish surgeon and bacteriologist, Alexander Ogston (1844-1929) had identified *Staphylococcus pyrogenes aureus* both in acute and chronic abscesses. Noting the similarity of this bacterium to their postulated entity, Letulle, in the time honored tradition of his day, undertook a classical experiment. He used two modes of administration to guinea pigs: intramuscular injection of Ogston's pure, cultured *Staphylococcus* or oral intake of the agent. Not surprisingly, this resulted in the formation of acute gastric lesions perfectly consistent, at least to him, with the predictable mode of generation of gastric ulcers. Matters were, however, somewhat complicated by the fact that he obtained similar results with dysentery organisms and with pyrogenic *Streptococci*. Letulle was never able to experimentally discriminate between these different agents and was therefore not able to conclusively prove a role for bacteria in ulcer disease. Nevertheless, the experimental work of Letulle inspired a number of other scientists to follow his lead and similar results were attained with *Lactobacillus*, diphtheria toxin, and *Pneumococcus*.

In a time frame contiguous to these sophisticated experiments, the Italian anatomist G. Bizzozero (1846-1901), was busy engaged in the extensive study of the comparative anatomy of vertebrate gastrointestinal glands with his adept

G. Bizzozero, A. von Kolliker and G. Golgi in Pavia, 1887. Bizzozero had a profound interest in the gut and inspired Golgi to study the canalicular apparatus of the resting and stimulated gastric gland. Although Bizzozero's main contribution was the identification of the platelets of the blood it is clear that he noted the presence of spiral organisms in the gastric mucosa although he unfortunately ascribed no particular significance to them. Von Kolliker was later instrumental in securing the Nobel for Golgi and Y. Cajal.

and capable pupil, the future Nobel prize winner, Camillo Golgi. In the specimens of the gastric mucosa of six dogs, Bizzozero noted the presence of a spirochete organism in the gastric glands and both in the cytoplasm and vacuoles of parietal cells. He commented that this organism affected both pyloric and fundic mucosa, and its distribution extended from the base of the gland to the surface mucosa. Although he neglected to ascribe any clinical relevance to these observations, he did however remark upon their close association with the parietal cells.

Three years later, in 1896, in a paper entitled *"Spirillum of the mammalian stomach and its behavior with respect to the parietal cells"*, H. Salomon reported spirochetes in the gastric mucosa of dogs, cats and rats, although he was unable to identify them in other animals, including man. In this early paper, Salomon undertook a series of somewhat bizarre experiments in which he tried to transmit the bacterium to a range of other animal species by using gastric scrapings from dogs. He failed to transmit it to owls, rabbits, pigeons and frogs; however the feeding of gastric mucus to white mice resulted in a spectacular colonization within a week, as evidenced by the series of drawings of infected gastric mucosa reproduced in the original paper. The lumen of the gastric pits of the mice were packed with the spiral-shaped bacteria and invasion of the parietal cells was also noted. Almost two decades later, in 1920, Kasai and Kobayashi successfully repeated these experiments, and using spirochetes isolated from cats, demonstrated pathogenic results in rabbits. Histological examination indicated both hemorrhagic erosion and ulceration of the mucosa in the presence of masses of the spirochetes.

H. Salomon extensively studied *H. felis* in domestic animals. In this article, published in 1896, he described his unsuccessful attempts both at culturing the bacteria *in vitro*, and at establishing the mode of transmission of the organism. Nonetheless, after failing in frogs, rabbits and pigeons, he succeeded in infecting white mice with the bacterium. He also noted the invasion of the glands as well as the close association with parietal cells. His studies refuted the then current hypothesis that parietal cells were guards at the entrance of the stomach, and acted to limit the entrance of microorganisms into the gastrointestinal tract.

Twentieth century

J. Cohnheim (1839-1884) postulated that chemical factors played the critical role in the etiology of ulcers.

The foundations for the role of acid in the genesis of ulcer disease were laid by A. Kussmaul (1822-1902), who developed a method for intubating patients and who also advocated the use of bismuth subcitrate for the treatment of this disease.

By the beginning of the twentieth century physicians involved in the treatment of gastrointestinal disease were generally familiar with some infective processes of the digestive tract: the ulcerative processes of typhoid fever, a variety of dysenteric conditions and tuberculosis. Kiyoshi Shiga had discovered a bacterium, erroneously recognized as *Shigella dysenteriae* in 1898, and an unspecified type of upper gastrointestinal (gastric) bacterial infection, not accompanied by signs of active inflammation, and designated as "bacterial necrosis" had also been annotated and was described in detail in Hemmeter's text of 1902. This pathology was characterized by the invasion of bacteria, usually into the lower depths of the mucous membrane, followed by bacterial growth and subsequent tissue necrosis.

J. Cohnheim (1839-1884), professor of Pathology at Kiel, who as early as 1880, had prophesised that the young Koch would surpass all others in the field of medical bacteriology, had suggested that the formation of ulcers depended on chemical factors. Shortly thereafter, F. Reigel attributed hyperchlorhydria as the cause of chronic ulcers. The scientific foundations for the recognition of the role of gastric juice (acid) in the genesis of ulcer disease were laid firstly by A. Kussmaul (1822-1902), who had in 1869 developed a method of intubation of the stomach and secondly by the creation of the experimental gastric pouch preparation by I.P. Pavlov.

In 1906, Krienitz identified spirochetes in the gastric contents of a patient with a carcinoma of the lesser curvature of the stomach and commented that upon microscopic examination, three types of spirochetes, including *Spirochete pallidum*, could be identified. He did not address the question of etiology. Spirochetal dysentery, as well as the presence of spirochetes in the stool of healthy individuals were known, and Muhlens and, independently, Luger and Neuberger, had all reported these organisms to be evident in the stomach contents of patients with ulcerating carcinomas of the stomach. The latter authors also noted the rarity of these organisms in the gastric mucosa and gastric juice of healthy individuals. Experimental biology, however, dominated gastric research and in the same year, Turcke had undertaken an experiment in which he fed broth cultures of *Bacillus coli* to dogs for a number of months. This resulted in the development of chronic gastric ulceration. In an attempt to establish cause and effect, he thereafter cultured *B. coli* from the feces of ulcer patients, which were then injected intravenously into dogs, without effect. However, when the animals ingested the micro-organism, every single dog reacted with a spectrum of non-specific gastric and duodenal alterations, which Turcke loosely called "ulcers". When Gibelli attempted to repeat this work, he could not confirm the results obtained by Turcke.

In Cincinnati, Ohio, the American bacteriologist, E.C. Rosenow, over a decade from 1913 to 1923, vehemently maintained that ulceration of the stomach could be reproduced in laboratory animals by *Streptococcus*. He isolated this bacterium from foci of infection in humans with ulcer disease and injected the culture into a wide range of animals including rabbits, dogs, monkeys, guinea pigs, cats and mice. A higher incidence of experimental lesions were identified using this particular inoculum than from cultures isolated from foci in other patients. Of additional interest was that *Streptococci* isolated from jeju-

L.R. Dragstedt (1893-1975) initially investigated the role of bacteria in experimental ulcer disease in 1917, but thereafter turned to the vagus and its resection as a means to physiologically understand and treat the disease. His preoccupation with surgical acid suppression sadly led him to ignore the infectious pathogenesis of acid peptic disease.

J.S. Edkins (1863-1940) is best known for his controversial (at the time) discovery of gastrin in 1905. What is less appreciated is his work on a spiral organism, most probably *H. felis*, in the stomach of cats. Apart from his critical contributions to the field of croquet, Edkins deserves credit for these two seminal observation in the field of gastroenterology.

296

SPIRELLA REGAUDI IN THE CAT[1].

By J. S. EDKINS.

(From the Physiological Laboratory, Bedford College.)

(With Plates VIII—X including Figs. 1–23.)

THE spiral organism found in the stomach of various carnivora has been investigated by several observers (see the references at the end of this paper). Such studies have been mainly directed to the morphology of the organism, its infectivity and the part it plays in producing a pathological condition. In the present paper I have been concerned rather with the physiological condition of its host as influencing the prevalence and location of the organism in different regions of the stomach. I was anxious further to ascertain if the organism affected the normal processes of digestion in the stomach either to the advantage or the disadvantage of the animal entertaining it.

nal ulcers in Mann-Williamson operated dogs, also caused acute gastritis and duodenal ulcers which were limited to the upper gastrointestinal tract in experimental animals. Based upon these observations, Rosenow postulated that "gastric ulcer producing *Streptococci*" had a selective affinity for the gastric mucosa and produced a local destruction of the glandular tissue. He further proposed that consequent upon such damage ulcers would thereafter form given the autolytic capacity of gastric acid. Rosenow thought that the reservoir for these bacteria were carious teeth, and advanced the idea that a hematogenous bacterial invasion would result in the formation of an ulcer. These experiments were continued by Hardt in dogs, and later by McGown in guinea pigs, with analogous results.

One of the early scientific interests of L.R. Dragstedt was the causation of gastro-duodenal ulceration, although he would subsequently (1943) achieve renown as the surgeon who established the "physiological" rationale for vagotomy as a treatment for duodenal ulcer disease.

As early as 1917, as a young physiologist, he had attempted to define the different mechanisms by which gastric juice could affect healing of acute gastric and duodenal ulcers. Aware of Rosenow's work, and the question of the importance of the virulence of different bacterial strains in determining the chronicity of ulcers, he attempted to isolate and culture any bacteria he could find in the silver nitrate induced ulcers of five experimental Pavlov pouch dogs.

Bacteriologic examination revealed *Streptococcus*, *Staphylococcus* and *Bacillus species*, which were similar to those types of bacteria isolated from clinical ulcers in man.

Dragstedt concluded that these bacteria colonized the damaged mucosa following ulcer formation and proposed that they had migrated up from the alimentary tract. He did not believe that they played a substantial role in the etiology of the disease, and did not pursue these studies further, choosing to rather focus on the role of vagal innervation in acid induced ulceration.

Fifteen years later, at the Mount Sinai Hospital, B. Berg, utilized partial vagotomy to reduce "secondary" infections in ulcer margins. Soon thereafter, however, he turned his attention to the colon and along with his collaborator Crohn became more famous for his role in the discovery of the etiology of this disease.

J.S. Edkins (1863-1940), of London, made a significant contribution to the elucidation of gastric physiology by the discovery of gastrin.

Motivated by his previous disappointment incurred in the investigation of gastrin, Edkins still maintained his enthusiasm for the exploration of gastric patho-physiology. In contrast to the inoculation mode of experimental studies, he proceeded to investigate how the host itself might affect the prevalence and location of the spirochete organisms in different parts of the stomach. The organisms were named *Spirochete regaudi*, after Regaudi who considered that the

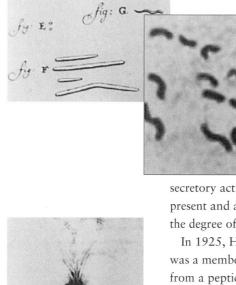

organisms of the gastric mucus layer of cats was morphologically analogous to the syphilis spirochete. Using the Giemsa stain to identify the organisms in stomach sections, Edkins identified them in both the fundus and the antrum, and noted specific invasion of the epithelial cells of the fundic glands. It was also evident that the organism appeared to have a preference for the surface epithelium, or for thick mucus of the feline experimental model. Of note was the demonstration of organisms not only in the sub-epithelial lymphoid tissue, but even located within the phagocytic cells.

He also described a "beaded form" of the organism in fasting cats, an observation consistent with the discovery of sporulation bodies. Gastric secretory activity did not appear to be compromised when the organisms were present and abundant, and indeed, there appeared to be a parallelism between the degree of acid and the abundance of the organisms.

In 1925, Hoffman investigated whether the causative agent of ulcer disease was a member of the bacillus family by the injection of 5 cc of gastric contents from a peptic ulcer patient into Guinea pigs. He successfully produced gastric ulcers from which he recovered gram-negative, fine slender rods which when inoculated into another guinea pig once again produced the same lesions. He modestly named his organism *Bacillus Hoffmani*, but it was evident after further study that the lesion producing capabilities of this bacterium were nonspecific. In 1930, Saunders demonstrated that the *Streptococcus* organism isolated from peptic ulcers in humans was of the alpha variety, and identified specific antibodies against this agent in serum from patients. However, he was not able to produce ulcers in animals by injecting the inoculum and proposed that laboratory animals do not spontaneously form gastric ulcers, since they exhibited an innate resistance to this organism.

Based to a certain extent on the recognition of the widespread scourge of luetic disease, at around the beginning of the Second World War, spirochetes returned to gastric prominence.

J.L. Doenges observed the organisms to invade the gastric glands of every single one of the *Macacus rhesus* monkeys he studied and to be present in 43% of human gastric autopsy specimens. In contrast to the monkey, the organisms appeared to be difficult to identify in human gastric mucosa and only 11 of the 103 specimens showed appreciable numbers.

Doenges' specimens however were autolytic which precluded the attachment of any major significance to his observations. Of especial note, however, was his observation that the organism was restricted to the gastric mucosa and not evident in the intestinal mucosa.

These reports prompted Freedberg and Barron in 1941 to investigate the presence of spirochetes in the gastric tissue of patients who had undergone

Evolution of the depiction of bacterial spiral forms from Leeuwenhoek to the present day. Leeuwenhoek's drawings of an *Oral spirillum* in 1683 (top left, fig. G), Salomon's drawings of *H. felis* in domestic animals in 1896 (top right), an electron micrograph of a negatively stained preparation of the same organism showing the characteristics tufts of polar flagellae (bottom left) and a confocal section (bottom right) of *H. pylori* expressing green fluorescent protein (GFP) co-cultured with AGS cells in the background, stained with a mitochondrial dye.

partial resection surgery. Both authors were familiar with the methods of identifying the organism, and used the silver staining method of DaFano, which they had previously successfully used (but not published) to identify spirochetes in dogs. In spite of such expertise, they were not able to identify the organisms, although they could demonstrate that spirochetes were more frequently present in ulcerating stomachs as compared to non-ulcerated stomachs (53% vs 14%). Based upon their own difficulties with adequate identification, and the apparent histological differences noted in Doenges' observations in the *Macacus* mucosa, they concluded that no absolute etiopathologic role for these organisms could be defined. It is with almost tragic irony that one reads that, in the report of the discussion of this paper, Frank D. Gorham, of St. Louis, Missouri, noted:

> *"I believe that a further search should be made for an organism thriving in hydrochloric acid medium (and variations of hydrochloric acid are normal in all stomachs) as a possible factor of chronicity, if not an etiologic factor, in peptic ulcer."*

Of interest is that Gorham also wrote that he had, over the previous ten years, successfully treated patients who had refractory ulcer disease with intramuscular injections of bismuth! Although Gorham may have seemed to be ahead of his time, as early as 1868, A. Kussmaul had advocated the use of bismuth subnitrate for the treatment of gastric ulcer. In fact, the oral use of bismuth for gastrointestinal symptoms was well accepted, and as early as the late 18th century, reports of the therapy had begun to appear in the English literature. The antibacterial properties of bismuth, which may or may not have been known to Gorham, had already been successfully exploited by R. Sazerac and C. Levaditit in 1921, who used it to cure experimental syphilis in rabbits. Gastric syphilis had also been described, the ulcers associated with this disease were well known, and the infective agent, *Spirochete pallida*, had been successfully isolated and cultured from syphilitic abscesses.

The negative results of Freedberg and Barron and the ambivalent results of Doenges subsequently prompted E.D. Palmer, in the early fifties, to investigate spirochetes in human gastric samples. He obtained gastric mucosal biopsies from 1180 subjects using a vacuum tube technique, but using standard histological techniques failed to demonstrate either spirochetes or any structures resembling them. Although Palmer did not attempt to identify the organisms with the more reliable silver stain, he concluded (confidently) that the results of all previous authors could be best explained as a *post mortem* colonization of the gastric mucosa with oral cavity organisms. He also postulated that spirochetes were normally occurring commensals of the mouth. Palmer's work may thus be credited with the envious distinction of setting back gastric bacterial research by a further 30 years.

Ammonia and gastric urease

Whilst ammonia was noted in gastric juice as early as 1852, it was not until 1924 that Luck discovered gastric mucosal urease. His subsequent work and the work of others, especially the Dublin biochemist, E.J. Conway, who specialized in investigations of the redox mechanism of acid secretion, confirmed the presence of gastric urease in a number of mammals. Histochemical studies demonstrated that enzyme activity appeared to be concentrated in the surface layers of the mucosa, in close conjunction with oxyntic cells. In addition, tissues surrounding gastric ulcers were found to be particularly rich in urease, whilst cancerous or achlorhydric stomachs were devoid of urease activity. These observations, as well as the longstanding observation of ammonia in gastric juice, prompted the proposal that urease activity was somehow coupled to hydrochloric acid secretion.

This hypothesis was however swiftly refuted upon the demonstration that the mucosa could secrete acid in the complete absence of urea. Nevertheless, a clinical role for urea in gastric physiology was postulated by O. Fitzgerald (Conway's medical colleague), who postulated that gastric urease functioned as a mucosal protective agent by providing ions to neutralize acid. This led to a number of studies (usually on medical students) in which the ingestion of urea containing solutions was utilized to alter histamine-stimulated gastric acid secretion. Notwithstanding the unpleasant side effects of this administration (diarrhea, headache, polyuria, painful urethritis), Fitzgerald further applied his hypothesis by treating ulcer patients with this regimen in 1949. Although he charitably summarized his results as "in general, satisfactory", no further therapeutic studies were undertaken with this particular agent.

Within five years, investigators of gastric urease-containing tissue suspensions were also able to demonstrate the presence (contamination) of urea-splitting organisms. This led to the suggestion that gastric urease might actually be of bacterial origin. Preliminary feeding of antibiotics (penicillin and terramycin) to animals resulted both in reduced expiration of $^{14}CO_2$ from intra-peritoneally injected ^{14}C-urea, as well as the abolition of urease activity in mucosal homogenates. Similar studies with analogous results were also performed in controls and subjects with uremia.

These observations, whilst establishing that gastric urease was of bacterial origin, failed to initiate an investigation of the relationship between urease-containing bacteria and ulcer disease. Indeed the prevailing notion by the end of 1955 was that neither the bacterial gastric urease nor the bacteria played any essential role in gastric pathology. Interestingly, at the time however, the clinical information derived suggested to some that antibacterial therapy could be utilized in patients with liver disease and elevated gastric ammonia levels. Antibiotic therapy was noted to reduce gastric urea and ameliorate the associated encephalopathy.

In 1975, Steer, while studying polymorphonuclear leukocyte migration in the gastric mucosa in a series of biopsy material obtained from patients with gastric ulceration, identified bacteria in close contact with the epithelium and suggested that white cells migrated in response to these bacteria.

In this seminal contribution, he not only clearly demonstrated bacterial phagocytosis, but provided electron microscopic images consistent with ingestion of a *Helicobacter*. Steer also attempted to isolate and culture the organism, but being unfamiliar with micro-aerophilic techniques, succeeded only in growing and identifying *Pseudomonas aeruginosa*.

Discovery of *H. pylori* and its etiological role in peptic ulcer

By 1980, reports concerning an "epidemic gastritis associated with hypochorhydria" had been published. These observations coupled with Steer's findings of an apparent association between "active gastritis" and a Gram-negative bacterium suggested that the simultaneous occurrence of bacteria in the stomach and peptic ulceration might represent more than a correlatable epiphenomenon. Robin Warren, a pathologist at the Royal Perth Hospital, had for many years observed bacteria in the stomach of people with gastritis. Although he was convinced that they somehow played a role in gastric disease, in the light of the prevailing dogma of acid induced ulceration and the scepticism of his colleagues, he had been reluctant to discuss this controversial observation in the wider gastroenterological community.

THE LANCET, JUNE 4, 1983

UNIDENTIFIED CURVED BACILLI ON GASTRIC EPITHELIUM IN ACTIVE CHRONIC GASTRITIS

UNIDENTIFIED CURVED BACILLI IN THE STOMACH OF PATIENTS WITH GASTRITIS AND PEPTIC ULCERATION*

BARRY J. MARSHALL   J. ROBIN WARREN

Departments of Gastroenterology and Pathology, Royal Perth Hospital, Perth, Western Australia

J.R. Warren (top left) observed the presence of a proliferating bacterium on the gastric mucosa from mucosal biopsies and established a close relationship to active chronic gastritis. B.J. Marshall (bottom right) successfully collaborated with Warren, resulting in the culture and classification of this new (old) gastric pathogen.

In 1982, a young gastroenterology fellow, Barry Marshall, was looking for a project to complete his fellowship. The iconoclastic hypothesis of Warren attracted Marshall, who persuaded Warren to allow him to investigate this further in the appropriate clinical setting. Later in the year, Marshall submitted an abstract detailing their initial investigations to the Australian Gastroenterology Association. It was flatly rejected, along with a handful of other abstracts. Young, unfazed, and seeking an alternative audience for the work, Marshall submitted the same abstract to the International Workshop of *Campylobacter* Infections, where it was accepted. Although the audience was sceptical of Marshall and Warren's results, some members became interested enough to attempt to repeat some of their observations. Soon after the meeting, both Warren and Marshall published their initial results as two short letters in the Lancet. In the introduction to his seminal article on an S-shaped *Campylobacter*-like organism, Warren noted both the constancy of bacterial infection, as well as the consistency of the associated histological changes, which he had identified in 135 gastric biopsy specimens studied over a three year period. He commented that these microorganisms were difficult to see with hematoxylin and eosin, but stained well in the presence of silver. Furthermore, he observed the bacteria to be most numerous in an "active chronic gastritis", where they were closely associated with granulocyte infiltration. It is a mystery, he wrote, that bacteria in numbers sufficient to be seen by light microscopy were almost unknown to clinicians and pathologists alike! He presciently concluded: "*These organisms should be recognized and their significance investigated*".

Koch's second postulate states that "*the germ should be obtained from the diseased animal and grown outside the body*". In the same issue of the Lancet, Marshall described the conditions necessary to fulfil this requirement. Utilizing the knowledge that these bacteria resemble the species of campylobacters rather than spirochetes, he used campylobacter isolation techniques (microaerophilic conditions) to successfully grow isolates on moist chocolate agar. It is interesting to note that no organism growth was detected after two days culture in the first 34 endoscopic biopsies Marshall tried to grow. The 35th plate however was left to culture over the long (6 days) Easter weekend.

In order to substantiate that the micro-organism was actually a disease causing agent, it was necessary to demonstrate that it could colonize normal mucosa and induce gastritis (Koch's third and fourth postulates). To prove pathogenicity, Marshall looking back in time for guidance, decided to be his own guinea pig. Marshall who had a histologically normal gastric mucosa and was a light smoker and social drinker, received, per mouth, a test isolate from a 66-year-old non-ulcer dyspeptic man. Over the next fourteen days a mild illness developed, characteristic of an acute episode of gastritis, and was accompanied by headaches, vomiting, abdominal discomfort, irritability and "putrid" breath. The infectivity of the agent was then successfully confirmed, when after ten days, histologically proven gastritis was endoscopically documented. The disease process later resolved on its own accord by the fifteenth day. A fellow Australian, Morris, later followed Marshall's lead, and in a similar experiment ingested the same inoculum of *H. pylori*. Although, this did not establish, a repeat challenge of the mucosa with a different, local (New Zealand) inoculum was more successful. In fact so successful, that a 2 month treatment of an antibacterial agent and bismuth was required to "eradicate" the organism. Morris and Nicholson established a direct effect of infection on acid secretion, but unfortunately for Morris, who had residual gastritis, a relapse was inevitable. Five years after the initial experiment Morris was finally cured. There has been no recorded third experiment. Marshall went on to describe the urease of the organism and recognized its role in enabling survival of the organism in acidic media. Subsequent work showed that eradication of the organism reduced recurrence of duodenal ulcer to the level found with maintenance therapy with histamine 2 receptor antagonists, and acceptance of this organism as causative in association with acid is now universal.

The importance of these findings is enormous and must rank among the great iconoclasms in medicine. Some 15 years after the start of the modern *Helicobacter* era, many of the important issues remain unresolved. There is still a lack of knowledge about many aspects of the organism itself, its mode of transmission, how it causes disease and why only a select few develop ulcers, and what the correct clinical management of this infection should be, both in practice and as a public health issue. The following text highlights the areas of both knowledge and uncertainty which represent the current information available on this ubiquitous and enigmatic organism and its effects on the human stomach.

CHAPTER 2
BIOLOGICAL BASIS OF GASTRIC COLONIZATION BY *HELICOBACTER*

Introduction

The eradication of *H. pylori* for treatment of peptic ulcer disease not associated with NSAID's, steroids or severe stress is now accepted as part of medical treatment of this set of illnesses. Currently therapy with proton pump inhibitors and two antibiotics is the most frequently prescribed medication, with perhaps bismuth along with ranitidine and also two antibiotics as other possible therapy. The rationale for the need for the former combination is becoming clearer but monotherapy would be more desirable, simplifying treatment and avoiding the use of antibiotics necessary for treatment of other infections. In order to understand the biological basis of this infection and pave the way for better treatment, the biology of *H. pylori* is being investigated on many fronts.

It has been mysterious as to how an organism came to inhabit the mammalian stomach, an environment often of high acidity and certainly in the case of carnivores of also persistent neutrality. It is also generally an aerobic environment therefore aerobes or micro-aerophile bacteria had to adapt to this pH variable situation. The bacteria had to adapt by being able to maintain their bioenergetic capacity (i.e. a sufficient electrochemical gradient of H^+ for ATP synthesis, nutrient uptake and cation homeostasis) over an unusual pH range for organisms growing optimally at neutral pH. This also implies that their overall metabolism had to adapt so as to be maintained over a wide range of environmental acidity. Although a variety of factors are undoubtedly involved, a major factor was in the acquisition of a high level of constitutive urease activity coupled with a means of regulation of their urease responsive to their occasionally acidic environment.

Bacterial bioenergetics

The inhabitation of the gastric mucosa by *Helicobacter* species, such as *H. pylori*, requires specialization of properties of this micro-aerophilic bacterial species to enable survival and growth on the gastric surface and within antral glands. It should be noted that there are also *Helicobacter* that do not inhabit the stomach, although why some of them have gastric adapted and some not is as yet unknown.

Bacteria have adapted remarkably to a variety of environments, acidic, neutral or alkaline. Bacteria surviving and growing in acidic media are classified as acidophiles, either obligatory or facultative, those able to survive and grow in neutral media are neutralophiles and those able to survive and grow in alkaline media are classified as alkalophiles.

The work to be described shows that *H. pylori* is uniquely an acid tolerant neutralophile.

Aerobic bacteria (including microaerophilic bacteria) synthesize ATP by coupling metabolic generation and oxidation of substrates to the formation of a electrochemical proton gradient across their cytoplasmic membrane and dissipation of this proton gradient through the cytoplasmic membrane's ATP synthase. The proton gradient is composed of two components, an actual pH gradient and a potential difference across the membrane. A balance of these two constituents of the proton energy charge of the membrane enables bacterial survival over a range of pH 2.0 to 11.0 depending on whether they are acidophiles, neutralophiles or alkalophiles.

The outer membrane contains porins which usually allow passage of protons. An acid dwelling organism can either accept high acidity in the periplasmic space and regulate H$^+$ entry by changing the transmembrane potential or it can choose to regulate the pH of the periplasmic space thus changing the pH component.

The circulation of protons across the cytoplasmic membrane is electrogenic, that is to say that export of protons by the redox pumps oxidizing substrate generates current and voltage cytoplasmic side negative. Uptake of protons through the F$_1$F$_0$ ATPase driven by the pH and electrical gradient tends to dissipate the potential.

The gradient of hydrogen ions should be expressed as a function of the chemical and electrical potential where the electrochemical gradient of hydrogen ions is the driving force for ATP generation by the chemi-osmotic mechanism first recognized by Peter Mitchell in 1961. The thermodynamic equation describing the electrochemical gradient for H$^+$:

$$p.\,m.\,f\ (in\ mV) = \Delta\,\bar{\mu}_H^+ = -RT/nF\ ln[H^+_{out}]/[H^+_{in}] + \Delta\psi = -61\Delta pH + PD$$

[where $\Delta\,\bar{\mu}_H^+$ is the electrochemical gradient for protons, R is the gas constant, T the temperature in degrees Kelvin, F is the Faraday constant, n is the valence of the ion, and $\Delta\psi$ is the transmembrane potential, referred to in text as PD].

ATP Synthesis by Electrochemical H$^+$ Gradient in *Helicobacter*

The chemi-osmotic mechanism for ATP synthesis by a neutralophile. The electrochemical gradient of H$^+$, the proton motive force, is generated by redox pumps (oxido-reductase) across the cytoplasmic membrane. This drives H$^+$ across the F$_1$F$_0$ ATP synthase resulting in 1 mol of ATP synthesis for every 3H$^+$ transported inward.

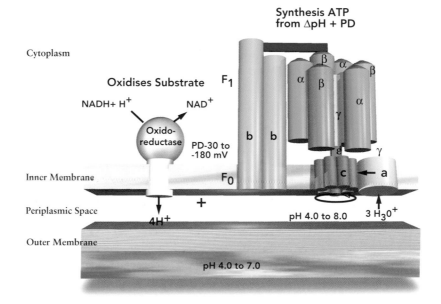

329

predicts that there is a reciprocal relationship between the pH gradient and the potential difference i.e. as the inward pH gradient increases, the PD decreases and vice versa in order to maintain a relatively constant proton motive force. The chemi-osmotic mechanism for ATP generation by a neutralophile is illustrated in the figure.

Since mean intragastric pH in people is 1.4, the issue arises as to the bioenergetic nature of *H. pylori*: is it an acidophile that has learnt to colonize human stomach? Or is it a neutralophile that has developed adaptive mechanisms to combat the variable acidity of its environment?

Structure of *H. pylori*

H. pylori is a motile, Gram-negative organism that can be cultured in microaerophilic (low O_2) conditions, although it adapts to high O_2 at higher culture densities. As such it has an outer membrane, the outer leaflet of which is lipopolysaccharide, a cell wall and periplasmic space, an inner membrane and cytoplasm. The bioenergetic survival of the organism depends on the maintenance of an adequate proton motive force between the periplasmic space and the cytoplasm across its inner or cytoplasmic membrane.

The organism is helical or spiral in shape, and possesses 6 to 8 flagella at one end. Flagellar function depends on the activity of a flagellar motor, also driven by the proton motive force generated across the cytoplasmic membrane of the organism. Given the structure of the organism, it is control of periplasmic pH that is vital for survival and growth of the organism.

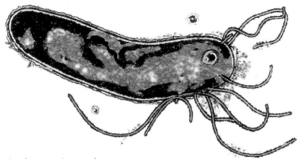

An electron micrograph of *H. pylori* showing its inner and outer membrane and the polar flagellae.

Some of the transporter genes that have been identified in the genome of *H. pylori*.

Transporters of *Helicobacter pylori*

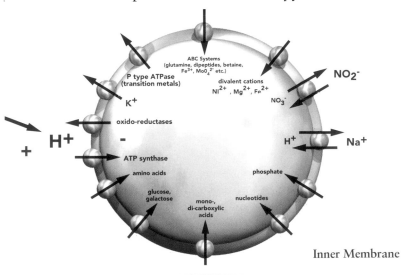

The bacterial genome

Modern molecular biological methods for defining the genome have been applied to the genetic structure of *H. pylori*. The genome contains about 1500 genes, 300 of which encode membrane proteins, many of as yet unknown functions. The genome contains sequences encoding for membrane proteins such as the F_1F_0 ATP synthase complex and various oxido-reductases such as cytochrome o, several transporters and a variety of two component signaling systems (the equivalent of eukaryotic receptors). Some of the recognized transporters are illustrated in the figure on the previous page.

The organism contains enzymes for glucose metabolism, lacks β galactosidase (hence is unable to metabolize lactose), some of the enzymes of the Krebs cycle (no isocitrate dehydrogenase), and most importantly, the urease operon encoding UreA and UreB (urease) and Ure E,F,G,H and I. Synthesis of urease is constitutive, accounting for as much as 15% of the organism's protein. The genome also encodes for several outer membrane proteins (OMP's) some of which are porins, able to transport a variety of molecules into or out of the periplasmic space. Some of these have a higher iso-electric point than those of neutralophiles such as *E. coli* or *B. subtilis*.

One method of generating specific therapeutic agents is to eliminate one gene at a time and to determine whether it is essential for the viability of the bacterium either *in vitro* or *in vivo*. This is followed by development of assay methods for function of the protein encoded by the essential gene in order to discover chemicals as specific inhibitors of protein function.

Survival and growth characteristics of *H. pylori*

The survival and growth of organisms as a function of medium pH is diagnostic of their bioenergetic profile. For example, neutralophiles such as *E. coli* characteristically are able to survive between pH 4.0 to 8.0 and grow well between pH 6.0 and 8.0. When these properties of *H. pylori* are measured as shown in the figure it seems that this organism shares survival and growth characteristics with *E. coli*.

The survival (green) and growth (yellow) of *H. pylori* as a function of fixed medium pH in the absence of urea.

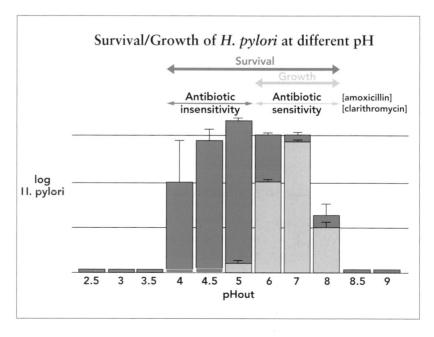

Survival/Growth of *H. pylori* at different pH

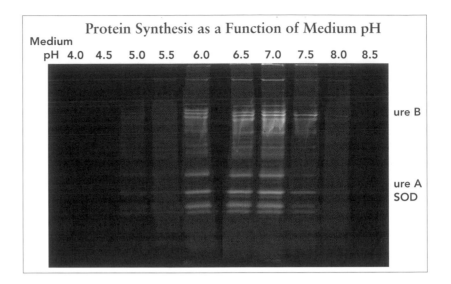

Protein Synthesis as a Function of Medium pH

Medium pH 4.0 4.5 5.0 5.5 6.0 6.5 7.0 7.5 8.0 8.5

ure B

ure A
SOD

The synthesis of protein by *H. pylori* as a function of fixed medium pH. This was done by measuring the incorporation of ^{35}S methionine at the different indicated pH values. Synthesis of protein corresponds to growth, mainly between pH 6.0 and 8.0.

From the measurement of survival which is found at a medium pH of only greater than 4.0 it is obvious that without specialized acid adaptive mechanisms *H. pylori* would not be found in the stomach. It is also clear that any colonization without adaptive mechanisms would be impossible given the pH characteristics of growth. A similar conclusion can be derived from measurements of protein synthesis *in vitro*, where a correlation is found between protein synthesis and growth as illustrated. The organism must have mechanisms preventing the collapse of the proton motive force in acid to survive and even mechanisms for enabling elevation of periplasmic pH in acid to grow. If the mechanism involves alkalinization by urease, it also must restrict activity at neutral pH to prevent over zealous production of base which is also lethal.

Bioenergetic profile of *H. pylori*

Knowledge of the potential difference and pH gradient across the cytoplasmic membrane of *H. pylori* as a function of medium pH would also enable conclusions as to the nature of the membrane homeostatic machinery necessary for gastric habitation by this organism. The organism is too small for microelectrode measurements of pH or potential difference, and less direct methods using dye probes of these parameters have proved successful.

Cytoplasmic pH

A dye, bis-carboxyethylcarboxyfluorescein acetomethoxy ester, BCECF-AM, is loaded into the microorganisms and becomes fluorescent as shown.

When this dye is used to measure internal pH at a medium pH of 7.0, using what is called a null point method (i.e. comparing change of fluorescence with all other gradients equal when intracellular pH is made equal to medium pH with the addition of an equilibrating ionophore), internal pH is found to be 8.4 at a medium pH of 7.0.

This is equal to a potential difference of about −90 mV. A similar measurement of internal pH in *E. coli* is about 7.8, somewhat lower than that found in *H. pylori*.

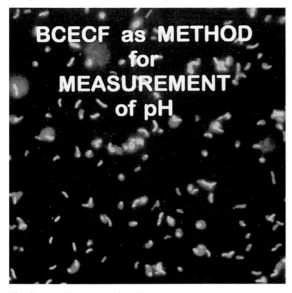

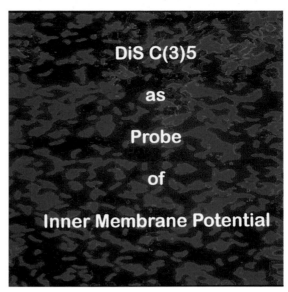

The dyes used to measure the pH of *H. pylori* (green dye) or the transmembrane potential (red dye).

Membrane potential

As for cytoplasmic pH, fluorescent dyes have been used to measure trans-membrane potential. Illustrated in the figure is staining of the organism with a lipophilic fluorescent cation, di-S-C$_3$ (5). This dye is taken up and its fluores-cence quenched as a function of an internal negative potential.

The membrane potential is also calibrated by a null point method, where the K selective ionophore, valinomycin, is added to set the membrane potential equal to that due entirely to the transmembrane K gradient. Then K is added until there is no fluorescence quench (i.e. PD = 0) and thence the internal K is known ($K_{in} = K_{out}$). From this $[K]_{in}$ the membrane potential with the addition of valinomycin and then before addition of valinomycin is calculated. At pH 7.0 it is −131 mV (a value also found by studies of distribution of a lipophilic cation). The proton motive force across the inner membrane of this gastric denizen is therefore −220 mV.

The cytoplasmic membrane potential of *H. pylori* as measured using a dye probe and a null point method with valinomycin and variable K$^+$. The measurable potential extends between pH 4.0 and 8.0.

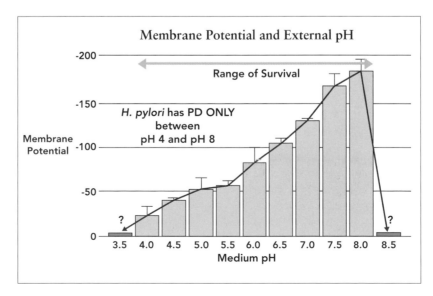

Membrane Potential and External pH

Range of Survival

H. pylori has PD ONLY between pH 4 and pH 8

Membrane Potential

Medium pH

When membrane potential was measured as a function of medium pH, the change in PD calibrated by the valinomycin method was found to extend between pH 4.0 and pH 8.0, exactly the pH range over which the organism survives as shown in the earlier illustration. Again, for gastric survival and growth, the pH range over which a membrane potential can be generated must be extended.

Effects of acute changes of medium pH

From the above, there is an absence of membrane potential and survival at pH < 4.0 and > 8.0. Gastric acidity undergoes rapid changes as a function of the rate of acid secretion and buffering of gastric contents. The duration of survival of the organism at the extremes of pH is therefore highly relevant in terms of the rate at which it has to adapt to acid. An experiment in which this was tested is shown in the illustration below.

Here the bacteria were added to an acidic medium at pH 3.5 and their membrane potential measured by the dye uptake method outlined earlier. No membrane potential was found at that pH. After 5 minutes buffer was added to elevate medium pH to 6.2 and no restoration of the potential was found, indicating death of the organism. On the other hand, when buffer was added almost immediately to bring the pH back to 6.2, there was a slow recovery of membrane potential to the control value expected for a medium pH of 6.2. Hence *H. pylori* is able to survive only short exposure to acid and its acid adaptive response must happen relatively quickly.

Metabolism as a function of medium pH

Bacterial metabolism should also correlate with survival and therefore the pH range of the proton motive force. There are various ways of measuring metabolism, such as oxygen consumption, CO_2 production from labelled glucose or incorporation of radioactivity into protein. A particularly convenient means, that is also adaptable to monitoring of survival, is the measurement of pH changes induced by a bacterial suspension.

H. pylori were added to a medium of pH 3.5 containing the dye for measurement of membrane potential. No transmembrane potential is seen, as expected. If buffer is added within 1 minute to bring medium pH instantly to 6.2, there is gradual recovery of membrane potential to about –65 mV by 5 minutes. If, however, 5 minutes elapse before the addition of buffer, no restoration of the potential is found. Tetrachlorsalicylanilide, an electrogenic protonophore, is added to collapse the membrane potential so as to confirm that membrane potential is being measured.

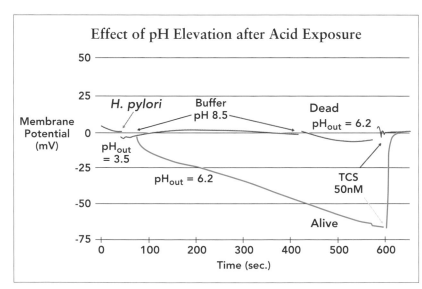

A microphysiometer is an instrument capable of very sensitive measurement of pH changes in a flow-through system, which avoids the use of strong buffers to maintain a constant pH environment. Basically, a light addressable pH sensor is computer controlled to measure the pH within 8 chambers simultaneously that contain about 10^5 immobilized bacteria through which solution is pumped. The pH change is read out in μV/sec as the pump is stopped for 16 sec in a 40 sec pump cycle.

The bacteria are able to acidify the medium at neutral pH between pH 6.0 and 8.5, due to the production of metabolic acid, and alkalinize the medium below pH 6.0 down to pH 4.0 due to reabsorption of H for ATP synthesis as shown. The range of metabolism displayed here again corresponds to what is found using standard survival measurements and measurement of the range over which the organism maintains a PD across its inner membrane. Metabolism is immediately blocked when the H electrochemical gradient is collapsed by a protonophore such as tetrachlorsalicylanilide (TCS).

H. pylori behaves as a neutralophile based on growth/survival-maintenance of a proton motive force and metabolism. The organism displays no evidence for acidophilic mechanisms that would enable survival at the highly acidic pH that gastric contents must reach severally during the day. It is regulation of the periplasmic environment that is important for the organism rather than that of environmental pH.

The metabolism of *H. pylori* as a function of perfusion pH using 1 mM phosphate buffer in glucose or glucose plus glutamine solutions, detected as acidification above pH 6.0 and alkalinization below pH 5.5.

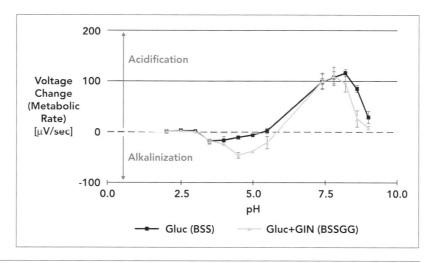

Acid adaptation by *H. pylori* by activation of urease

The action of urease is the hydrolysis of urea to ammonia and carbamic acid followed by spontaneous breakdown of carbamate to ammonia and CO_2:

$$CO(NH_2)_2 + H_2O \longrightarrow NH_3 + HCO_2NH_2 \longrightarrow NH_3 + CO_2$$

thus resulting in strong alkalinization of the medium. In the absence of strong buffering the pH of the medium will reach the pK_a of the NH_4^+/NH_3 couple, namely 9.5. Urease is composed of two subunits, ureA and ureB, and contains Ni^{2+} as an essential ion. It is the major protein synthesized by *H. pylori*.

The urease activity was recognized as an important parameter enabling acid survival early on in research on the gastric mechanisms of *H. pylori*. The enzyme is found both in the cytoplasm and loosely associated with the cell surface, presumably binding to the lipo-polysaccharide of the outer leaflet of the outer membrane.

It has been thought that this external urease is responsible for elevating the microenvironment outside the organism to a level compatible not only with life but with growth. This is probably an oversimplification, given the measurement of the pH activity curve of the external enzyme as compared to the activity of the cytoplasmic enzyme as displayed in the figure.

The pH activity curve of urease found external to the organism (right hand curve) and in the intact organism (left hand curve) showing acid pH-dependent activation of cytoplasmic urease.

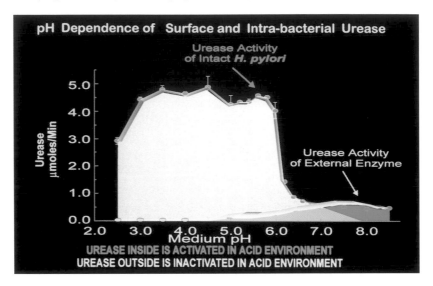

This figure illustrates a vital point in understanding the role of urease in enabling the organism to live in the gastric niche. Free urease or surface bound urease has a pH optimum of between 7 and 8, and activity declines until the pH reaches 4.5, and below that there is no detectable urease activity. Hence unless the pH of the bacterial environment is greater than 4.0, surface urease activity will have no effect on acid survival of the organism.

The situation is quite different when urease activity is measured in the intact organism. There is little measured activity until pH 6.5 is reached and then there is a greater than 15-fold increase in urease activity with a steady state of urease activity being held down to a pH of 2.5. The maintained internal urease activity in acid accounts for much of the acid adaptation of *H. pylori*. It is predicted therefore that internal urease activity will be able to neutralize periplasmic pH in gastric acid.

A similar activation of urease is seen when pH measurements are made in the cytosensor and the rate of alkalinization correlated with urease activity as shown in the figure. There is about a 20-fold activation of urease activity as the pH falls to below 4.0. At higher pH in the small volume of the chamber urease activity is able to elevate chamber pH very rapidly, hence urease activity is only transient. At pH of 3.0, the level of acid is sufficient to require significant levels of urease activity in order to attempt to elevate pH. These data also show that internal urease is activated by acidification of the medium, but stays relatively inactive at neutral pH. Of the various genes of the urease operon, ureI, which has homology with components of amidase operons of other organisms, is likely to represent a urea

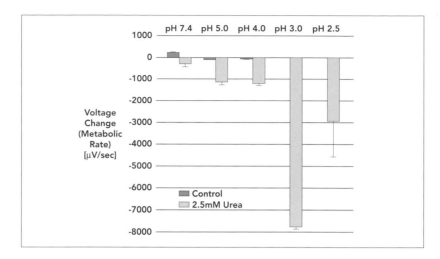

Measurement of urease activity by alkalinization of perfusing medium in the microphysiometer, showing large activation at acidic pH.

transporter that is activated as the pH falls to about 6.5. In the absence of activity of this urea transporter, urea has slow access to the urease and there is low activity of the urease above pH 6.5. Expression of this gene may enable gastric habitation of *Helicobacter* species. Lack of this gene may prevent gastric colonization and result in colonization of other *Helicobacter* species elsewhere, such as in the bile duct or in the intestine.

The rate of activation of urease by pH < 6.2 is sufficiently rapid to enable the organism to survive acidic excursions as shown by the data where the effect of urea addition on periplasmic pH and cytoplasmic membrane potential is measured.

Here, the bacteria are added to media at fixed pH and rapidly thereafter 5 mM urea is added. There is a rapid increase of periplasmic pH to 6.2, whether the medium pH is fixed at 3.0, 4.0 or 5.0. At higher pH there is no effect since internal urease is inactive.

The set point of pH 6.2 is where activation of internal urease is expected to occur. Along with elevation of periplasmic pH, the addition of urea results in rapid elevation of membrane potential.

The effect of urea addition on the periplasmic pH after the organism has been exposed to pH 4.0 or 5.0, showing a rapid elevation of the pH to a set point of 6.2.

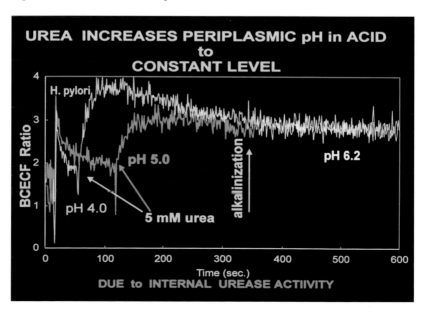

For measurement of potential difference effects of urea, bacteria are added to strongly buffered media at pH 4.0, 5.0 and 6.0 and with the addition of urea there is a rapid increase in transmembrane potential to a relatively constant value of about −100 mV.

The organisms are added to media of pH 4.0, 5.0 and 6.0 and when the dye signal has stabilized, urea is added. A constant potential is reached, independent of starting pH.

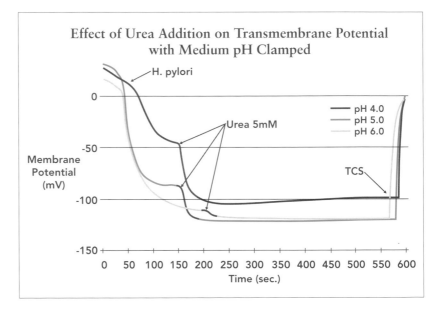

These data show that the presence of urea and activation of urease by acidic medium pH enable acid survival of *H. pylori*. A model for the activation of internal urease by activation of a urea transport system is shown in the following figure.

According to this model, at a medium pH > 6.2, the urea transporter is inactive and mainly surface urease modifies pH. Below pH 6.2, the transporter is

A model showing that at pH < 6.2 a urea transporter is activated, allowing urea access to cytoplasmic urease. Activity of this urease results in NH₃ exit into the periplasmic space enabling a pH of 6.2 over a range of medium acidity between pH 2.5 and 6.0. At higher pH, the internal urease is inactive due to restricted entry of urea.

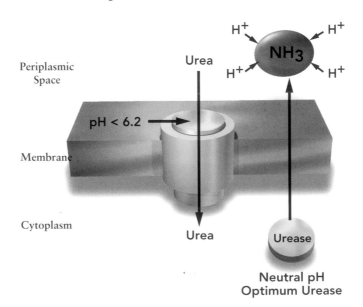

Adaptation of *Helicobacter Urease*

activated and urea accesses internal urease. Internal urease activity results in the outward diffusion of NH_3 and elevation of periplasmic pH to 6.2.

Above this periplasmic pH, the transporter and therefore internal urease is inactivated, below this pH the transporter and therefore internal urease is activated, enabling the set point of pH 6.2 to be reached down to a pH of 2.5 at mM levels of urea.

The model of survival of the organism in acidic media that results from these experiments is shown in the illustration.

Acid Protection by Internal Urease

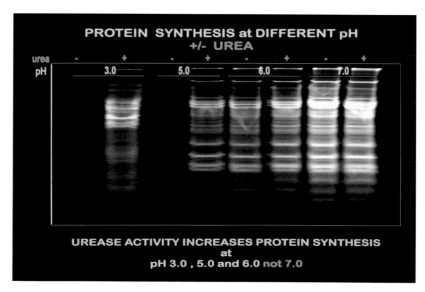

Acidity activates urea transport and internal urease activity is able to elevate periplasmic pH to 6.2 even in gastric acid.

Urease activation and growth

Earlier it was shown that protein synthesis was seen between pH 6.0 and 8.0. Growth is essential for bacterial colonization. The ability of internal urease activity to elevate periplasmic pH to 6.2 in the face of gastric acidity ensures that the organism can also grow in the gastric environment, not only survive.

The stimulation of protein synthesis at various fixed medium pH values with and without urea addition is shown in the figure.

The effect of urea addition at pH 3.0, 5.0, 6.0 and 7.0 on protein synthesis by the organism.

PROTEIN SYNTHESIS at DIFFERENT pH +/- UREA

urea	-	+	-	+	-	+	-	+
pH	3.0		5.0		6.0		7.0	

UREASE ACTIVITY INCREASES PROTEIN SYNTHESIS at pH 3.0 , 5.0 and 6.0 not 7.0

For example, to the left of the figure it can be seen that there is virtually no protein synthesis at pH 3.0 or 5.0 unless urea is added. There is also some stimulation at pH 6.0 and then none at pH 7.0. The presence of urea will allow growth of the organism in the gastric acidity present at the gastric surface.

Surface urease activity

As mentioned above, urease is found in the cytoplasm and also bound to the outer membrane. It appears that this surface urease is due to binding of urease released after lysis of the organism and is not due to specific export of the enzyme. One of the prevailing concepts has been that this urease activity is able to elevate the pH of the microenvironment of *H. pylori* and thereby enable survival. The data already discussed show that this urease would not be effective at a pH < 5.0. However, it is able to function at a pH > 5.0.

The pH activity curve of this surface urease shows that activity is expected above pH 5.0 and optimal activity is between pH 7 and 8. Urease activity at neutral pH is able to elevate medium pH quite rapidly, and membrane potential measurements have shown that the organism dies above pH 8.0 or so. The figure shows what happens to membrane potential when urea is added in lightly buffered medium at pH 7.0 as compared to pH 3.5

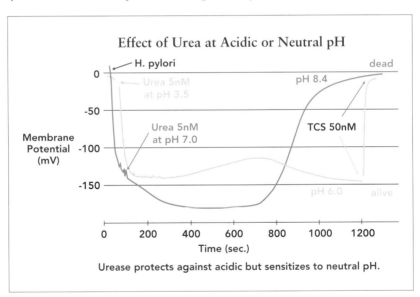

Effect of Urea at Acidic or Neutral pH

Urease protects against acidic but sensitizes to neutral pH.

The effect of urea addition at acidic or neutral pH on the membrane potential of the bacterium.

When urea is added at pH 3.5, there is a rapid rise of potential to that expected for a periplasmic pH between 6 and 7. However, when urea is added at pH 7.0, there is an increase to about −180 mV and then a decline to zero over the next 15 minutes. At that point medium pH has risen to 8.4, which is lethal for the organism.

Using the microphysiometer it is also possible to measure urease activity by the alkaline shift of the pH sensor and to determine survival of the bacteria by showing that acidification is restored when the perfusing medium is returned to neutrality in the absence of urea. These experiments show that alkalinization occurs due to surface urease activity in the flowing medium at a urea concentration of 2.5 mM values, but that at 10 mM urea the degree of alkalinization

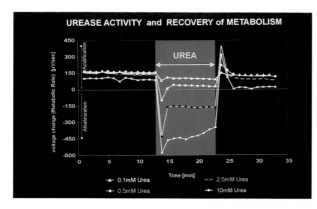

The metabolism and urease activity of *H. pylori* at neutral pH following the addition of various concentrations of urea. It can be seen that normally the bacteria acidify the medium but urease activity results in alkalinization at 2.5 or 10 mM urea. When 0.5 or 2.5 mM urea are removed, acidification returns, but when 10 mM urea is removed, the organisms are no longer able to metabolize.

is sufficient to prevent restoration of metabolism at neutral pH when urea is removed.

Evidence that urease activity at neutral pH is lethal has been obtained by determining survival of *H. pylori* in media of different pH in the absence and presence of urea. The effect of urea is biphasic, enabling survival in acid, preventing survival when the initial pH is neutral.

This role of urease in preventing survival of the organism at neutral pH may explain why *H. pylori* is found only in the stomach and not in regions where there is urea but no acid.

The effect of bacterial urease activation on medium pH is illustrated by the experiment shown in the figure below. When BCECF fluorescence is used to monitor medium pH at 5.8 the only regions of higher pH are the bacteria themselves fluorescing bright green. When urea is added, there is an initial increase in bacterial periplasmic pH followed by a rapid elevation of medium pH. This figure illustrates the potent effect of urease on the pH of the environment when it is mildly acidic. This could account in part for the higher intragastric pH found in *H. pylori* positive patients under chronic PPI therapy and for the positive effects of acid ingestion on the urea breath test. If no further acid is secreted, the pH elevation will be toxic to the organism and could account for the decrease in antral bacteria with PPI therapy.

An experiment showing the effect of bacterial urease activity on medium pH where bacteria are co-cultured with AGS cells and urea added at pH 5.8 using BCECF to monitor medium pH. Each square represents 5 sec.

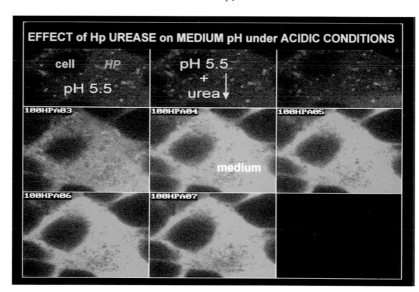

Urease is essential for *H. pylori*

The elimination of urease activity by either growth selection for urease negative mutants or intentional removal of one of the urease enzyme genes results in strains that are unable to infect animal models. It is possible to obtain some infection with these urease negative mutants if acid is severely inhibited by omeprazole, but the infection does not persist after removal of the drug. In summary, all current data suggest that *H. pylori* is an acid tolerant neutralophile rather than being a facultative acidophile.

CHAPTER 3
PATHOGENICITY

With the recognition that gastric infection was associated with ulcer disease also came the realization that infection was more frequent than ulcers. Much effort has been expended in attempts to identify the culprit genes responsible for the pathogenic consequences of infection.

The first unique gene identified was CagA, producing proteins of about 120-140 kDa. Its function is unknown, but it is part of what has been called a pathogenicity island. As for other bacteria, this region, which contains about 40 genes, appears to affect virulence. Another product that is co-expressed with CagA is VacA. There are several variants in this region showing that this gene is a mosaic. Another gene more recently identified with virulence is IceA. There appears to be a relatively clear relationship between expression of those genes and clinical outcome.

Within the pathogenicity island, there are a number of membrane-inserted proteins, many thought to be involved in export of proteins. The most frequently used protein secretory pathway is that involving the sec mechanisms which relates to co-translational insertion of a cleavable signal sequence into the translocon. After insertion of this sequence, the rest of the protein is externalized and the signal sequence is cleaved outside the inner membrane resulting in export of the protein. For externalization of the flagella a different system is used, the type III secretory systems. The flagellar motor proteins are part of this and a specialized protein is also present in the outer membrane which allows extrusion of the flagellar protein in proper orientation through both membranes. Type IV secretion has been suggested.

Protein secretion by *H. pylori* may be a minor player in pathogenicity, however. With the discovery of urease and association of external urease with the bacterial surface, the concept arose that urease was a secreted product of the organism enabling acid protection.

Two sets of experiments showed that if secretion of urease occurred, it was only a minor contributor to the outside urease. A comparison of the protein composition of the organism with the medium in which it was grown showed a remarkable similarity indicating that the medium proteins had arisen by lysis of the organism. This was confirmed further by showing that the pattern of *de novo* synthesized proteins in the presence of ^{35}S methionine was essentially identical in the organism and in the medium and further that external protein radioactivity did not appear for about 16 hrs. This experiment, illustrated in the following figure, shows that none of the major proteins appear to be secreted. Rather whole cell lysis is the major mechanism for release of intracellular proteins. There is, however, a class of secreted proteins that may play an important role in pathogenesis.

A possibility not addressed by this experiments is direct injection of protein into cells to which the organisms adhere. It is going to be a difficult task to prove that such a direct pathway exists, but given that the pathogenicity island contains protein export genes, it may be that such a mechanism does exist.

The inevitable gastritis that results from infection may well relate to the

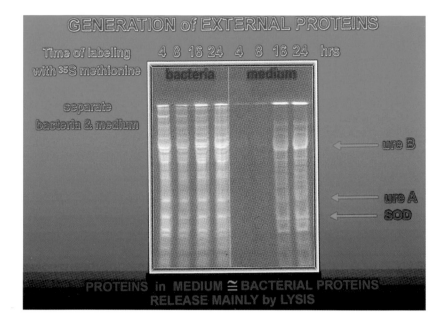

PROTEINS in MEDIUM ≅ BACTERIAL PROTEINS
RELEASE MAINLY by LYSIS

An experiment illustrating the absence of significant secretion of either UreA or UreB, the constituents of urease, by *H. pylori*. It is of note that the patterns of internal and external protein are very similar.

generation of NH_3 by bacterial urease. The finding that the vast majority of urease activity results from acid activation of internal urease promotes the idea of synergism between the organism and acid in causing initial damage. An increase of NH_3 on the surface of gastric cells results in an increase of intracellular pH. In turn this results in an increase of intracellular calcium and initiation of calcium signal dependent phenomena. These could be the harbingers for arrival of inflammatory cells that in turn produce the cytotoxic effects observed.

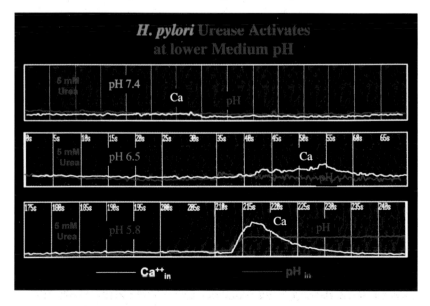

The effect of medium pH on urea effects with *H. pylori* co-cultured with AGS cells. Every rectangle represents 5 sec.

An experiment is shown where *H. pylori* are co-cultured with AGS cells and urea added at different medium pH and effects observed with confocal and video microscopy. BCECF is used to monitor medium pH in confocal mode, and BCECF-AM and Fura-2-AM are used for pH_i and $[Ca]_i$ in video mode. It can be seen that urea has no effect at pH 7.4, a slight effect at pH 6.5 but at pH

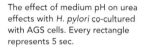

5.8, where bacterial urease is activated, there is a large change in medium pH (green fluorescence) accompanied by a rise in cell pH and cell calcium. If this type of effect is found *in vivo*, the activation of urease by acid will result in high urease activity. If the quantity of NH_3 is sufficient, especially when gastric juice is neutralized, elevation of duodenal or transitional surface cell pH would result in calcium signals and perhaps cell damage, especially if exacerbated by the vacuolating effect of Vac A.

Adhesion

For *H. pylori* to establish and cause gastritis, it is likely that specific adhesion must occur to the surface membrane of gastric cells. The organisms tend to bind at regions of contact between cells *in vivo* and *in vitro*. These regions may

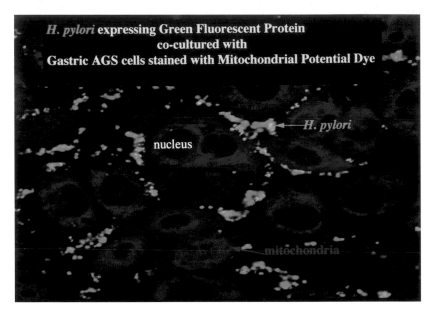

Green fluorescent protein expressing *H. pylori* co-cultured with human AGS cells, showing, by confocal microscopy, adhesion at contact regions of this region of confluence.
Mitochondria are stained with $diSC_3(5)$.

contain specific receptor proteins for the organism, such as cadherins, integrins or Lewis' type antigens. Such points of contact can result in pedicle formation and changes in intracellular distribution of cytoskeletal elements, perhaps aiding initiation of cell pathology.

Immunogenic effects

Many patients with *H. pylori* infection and atrophic gastritis have antibodies against the beta and often also the alpha subunit of the gastric H,K ATPase. The mechanism whereby these antibodies arise is not known, but may result from improper membrane trafficking in the pre-parietal cell due to the gastric epithelial disturbance caused by the inflammation resulting from the fundic habitation of the organism.

CHAPTER 4
INFECTION AND ITS CONSEQUENCES

Gastric acid secretion after infection

Acute phase

In early infection, acid secretion decreases, and at least two acid inhibitory substances have been purified from *H. pylori*, with one partially sequenced. It appears to represent a metabolic gene. There is inevitably an acute gastritis observed in animal models, with ingress of a variety of inflammatory cells into the submucosa. The reason for the gastritis is obscure, but it is found after infection by any strain of *H. pylori*. It seems possible that NH_3 production is the explanation, since all strains that are infective produce large quantities of NH_3 that would tend to alkalinize the interior of gastric epithelial cells.

The addition and removal of NH_4Cl has large effects on cell pH. With addition, NH_3 is rapidly permeant across cell membranes relative to NH_4^+ and upon entering a cell, is protonated to NH_4^+, hence alkalinizing the cell. When the salt is removed, NH_3 leaves the cell and acidification results. Alkalinization of the cells increases intracellular Ca^{2+}, which in turn could result in the production and secretion of cytokines such as IL-8 and others, resulting in the inflammation. From the urease properties defined above, NH_3 production would be much larger and constant between pH 6.2 and 2.5. However, at acidic pH the NH_3/NH_4^+ ratio would decline, resulting in lower concentrations of the permeant NH_3. But if there were periods of elevated pH or regions where gastric acid containing NH_3 were rapidly neutralized, then the concentration of NH_3 would rise, permeate cells, and elevate internal pH and thence intracellular calcium. This hypothesis suggests that ammonia production in parallel with varying acidity could account for many of the sequelae of infection.

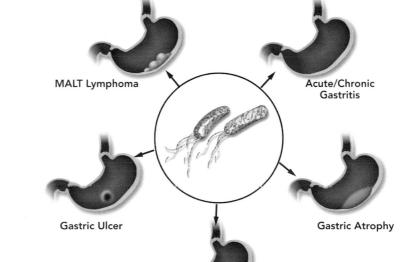

H. pylori Disease Profile

MALT Lymphoma

Acute/Chronic Gastritis

Gastric Ulcer

Gastric Atrophy

Duodenal Ulcer

The different clinical and pathological manifestations of *H. pylori* in the gastro-duodenal area.

Chronic phase

It has been known for many years that duodenal ulcer patients have, on the average, higher acid output than patients without duodenal ulcer. Gastric ulcer patients tend to have lower than normal acidity. Counting the number of parietal cells has shown that duodenal ulcer patients have more parietal cells, thus explaining the acid output data.

The gastric effects of *H. pylori* depends in part on the site of infection, be it antral or fundic. Infection therefore results in either antral or fundic gastritis. In the case of antral infection, there is a decrease of somatostatin or the D cell population accompanied by hypergastrinemia. The latter is thought to be trophic for parietal cells, thus accounting for the higher acid output in duodenal ulcer patients. In the case of infection of the gastric corpus, there is often gastric atrophy with loss of acid secreting cells. This would result in a reduced level of acid secretion in those patients with gastric atrophy.

Pathogenic strains

As discussed above, all strains result in gastritis at the site of colonization, but only about 20% of infected individuals acquire peptic ulcer disease. This may be due to variation in organism or in host, or due to other factors.

The finding that eradication appears to increase acid reflux, that in turn may associate with Barrett's esophagus, suggests to some that there may be a benefit to gastric infection. It is true that some frequent human genetic abnormalities may confer protection, such as sickle cell hemoglobin A mutation providing anti-malarial properties or cystic fibrosis transport regulator (CFTR) against typhoid. It does appear unlikely that gastric inflammation is of real benefit to the host.

H. pylori and ulcer site

The duodenal ulceration site is in the first part of the duodenum, usually at a site where it might be supposed the highest acidity is found. Even now, it has not been established that *H. pylori* is actually present at the site of ulceration, or whether gastric metaplasia and ectopic parietal cells are associated with the presence of *H. pylori* at that locale.

The site of gastric ulceration is usually in the transition zone between fundus and antrum. In this region there are still parietal cells and chief cells that may mainly secrete type II pepsinogen. The organism is clearly found in association with gastric ulcers and it may be that this region of the stomach is more susceptible to the consequences of infection than the more hardy fundus and the non-acid secreting antrum.

The presence of acid is as important as that of the organism in the generation of peptic ulcers, and given that the apical membranes of gastric cells are relatively acid impermeable, it is likely that the first site of damage is the tight junction between the epithelial cells. This effect may well be due to inflammation. Once the tight junction is damaged allowing acid back diffusion, further damage can result in the back diffusion of pepsin.

The combination of infection, inflammation and acid and pepsin back diffusion result in ulcer development.

H. pylori and its gastric environment

The organism is found at the gastric surface and within the gastric mucus. There is a degree of controversy about the most frequent site of habitation and as to what the conditions are at the site of habitation. Many believe that the gastric surface is close to neutrality, thus allowing colonization. However, direct measurement has shown that at a luminal pH of 2.0 or less, no pH gradient can be detected at the gastric surface. Since mean diurnal pH is 1.4 in normal people, it is likely that at times during the day the environment of the organism is genuinely acidic and its acid adaptive mechanisms must come into play.

H. pylori, Acid and Gastritis

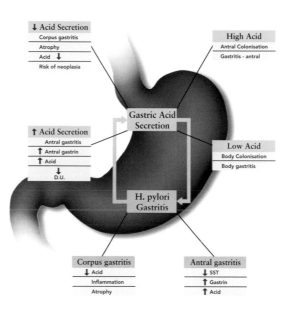

The spectrum of alterations in the level of acid secretion and different stages of mucosal inflammation that may occur during *H. pylori* infection.

It is not known where the first site of colonization is found after infection. It seems that infection often occurs in childhood, perhaps before acid secretion reaches adult levels and therefore either antral or fundic infection could occur. It also seems that infection *per se* transiently reduces acid secretion by the human stomach, thereby enabling better colonization.

The organisms are found with mainly antral colonization when antral gastritis arises (the more frequent manifestation) or with fundic colonization (when fundic gastritis arises, perhaps a later stage of the disease). They are also often associated with the tight junction regions, perhaps because of the higher urea concentration. Organisms are attached to cells by a pedicle with morphological alterations at the cellular side of the pedicle. Whether there are specialized outer membrane proteins then associated with the pedicle enabling more direct entry of NH_3 or perhaps even proteins by type III secretion is not known.

Several papers have claimed that treatment with proton pump inhibitors reduces the number of organisms in the antrum and increases their level in the fundus. Inhibition of acid secretion to the level expected from PPI treatment in principle could reduce acidity on the antral surface to a level where urease activity could be toxic to the organism. An increase of pH on the fundic surface improving the habitat there for the bacteria could increase bacterial frequency

Gastric Cellular Effect of *H. pylori*

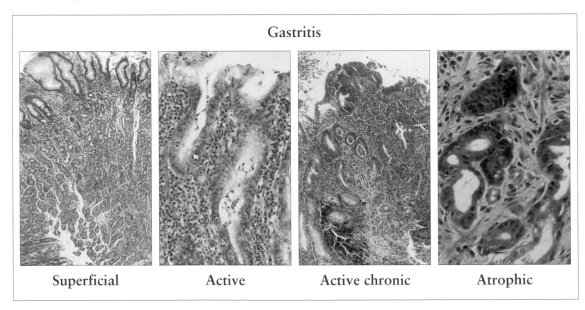

IL8
+

M

- TNF?
ICI6

Fundus

-
+

ECL

Antrum

+
Acid -

-

G

+
TNE?
IL8
INFg

IL8+   M

H. pylori affects a number of cell types of both the fundus and the antrum. These include at least neuroendocrine cells (G, D, ECL), parietal cells, chief cells and immune cells mediating the inflammatory response. The cascade of bioactive peptides and cytokines released results in a variety of different acid/pepsin secretory and trophic responses in the gastric mucosa.

The different histological types of gastritis that are indentifiable during various stages of *H. pylori* infection of the gastric mucosa.

in this region of the stomach. Since there is variation in the response to PPI's, there may also be variation in the effect of PPI's on localization of *H. pylori* in the stomach.

Most agree that fundic infection is able to lead to atrophy, metaplasia and perhaps cancer. If indeed PPI treatment results in relocation of infection to the fundus, there is a strong case to be made for eradication in those patients undergoing chronic therapy with PPI's for GERD.

Serial biopsies taken over many years from patients infected with *H. pylori* indicate that the long-term consequence of infection may include gastric atrophy and intestinal metaplasia and, by implication from earlier studies, these may lead to dysplasia and gastric cancer. Although controversial, the concept that decreased acid secretion and gastric atrophy are intimately related is an old one. While it was previously held that acid inhibition was the result and not the cause of atrophic gastritis, recent data have suggested that if infection with *H. pylori* is present, acid inhibition may result in accelerated atrophy. The mechanism of this effect remains obscure, but pharmacological or surgical reduction of gastric acid secretion are both associated with a more severe inflammatory response to *H. pylori*, which may lead to more severe epithelial cell damage. Interpretation of the data remains difficult, in part because of the problems in defining gastric atrophy, in part because of age mismatch in the cohorts studied.

The recent publication of the updated Sydney system for the classification and grading of gastritis may be helpful in future studies of atrophy. However, whether this scheme will be more clinically useful than its predecessors remains to be evaluated. Nevertheless, the attempt to objectively define gastritis using

Gastritis

Superficial   **Active**   **Active chronic**   **Atrophic**

visual analog scales is a significant advance and may add considerably to the objectivity of the assessment. However, there is still considerable debate concerning the reversibility of atrophy, whether functional or morphological – most would argue that atrophy is not reversible. Unfortunately, due to potential sampling errors in follow-up biopsy studies, convincing data are still lacking and therefore debate on this issue will still continue.

Many studies have established that infection with *H. pylori* and the secondary mucosal inflammatory response increase gastric epithelial cell prolif-

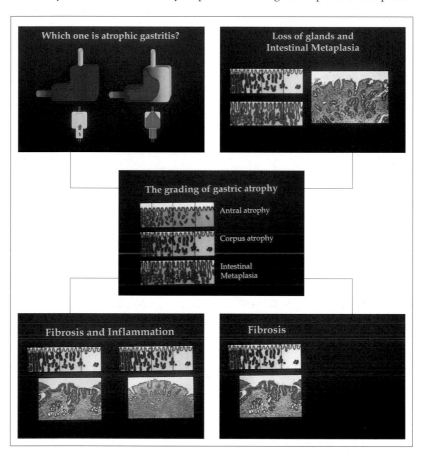

The precise histological criteria for the identification of atrophic gastritis are widely debated between histopathologists. In addition, since biopsy sites in the stomach may vary and individual observer agreement is modest, a precise diagnosis may be difficult. It has therefore been proposed that an analog system be devised to facilitate reporting and allow for appropriate comparison of information.

eration. This may be a necessary step in the process of gastric carcinogenesis, as for many other malignancies. *H. pylori* probably does not increase proliferation directly; increased cell proliferation is more likely a response to apoptosis (programmed cell death) induced by the organism or the inflammatory response. After a compensatory hyperproliferative response, the balance between apoptosis and proliferation may determine whether ulcers and atrophy develop, or conversely, whether mucosal mass grows in an unrestrained fashion. Some information is available from animal models. For example, *H. felis* infection in mice increases cell proliferation, particularly of mucous neck cells, but decreases the number of parietal cells. The hyperproliferative response is more extreme in animals which are homozygous for p53, suggesting that *H. pylori* may act in concert with other oncogenes and tumor suppressor genes to produce neoplasia. Although little is known about the effect of *H. pylori* on the normal gastric cell cycle, it has been demonstrated that the lipopolysaccharide (LPS) of *Helicobacter* displays synergism in gastrin-mediated increased DNA synthesis in ECL cells.

Since the ECL cell is a crucial link between gastrin and acid in the normal stomach, the interaction of *H. pylori* with this cell may throw light upon some of the discrepant information regarding the effects of *H. pylori* on gastrin and acid secretion. Whether the ECL cells are exposed to *H. pylori* lipopolysaccharide directly is unclear, since the ECL cells are not thought to be in communication with the gastric lumen. Nevertheless LPS is present in measurable quantities in the blood stream and may impinge upon the ECL cell in the same fashion that gastrin does. It is possible that mucosal damage induced by *H. pylori* and disruption of tight junctions may also facilitate access. Either way it may be that the population of ECL cells does increase in *H. pylori* infection and, in combination with proton pump inhibitors especially, micronodular carcinoids may develop.

A cartoon of the possible mechanisms by which *H. pylori* LPS may result in the stimulation of ECL cell secretion and proliferation. It has been suggested that *H. pylori* LPS functions by activation of the CD14 receptor. Since the receptor is present on both the ECL cell and monocytes a direct and indirect effect may be possible. Activation of monocytes has been proposed to release cytokines which themselves are capable of stimulating ECL cell proliferation.

H. pylori Lipopolysaccharide Mediated ECL Cell Proliferation

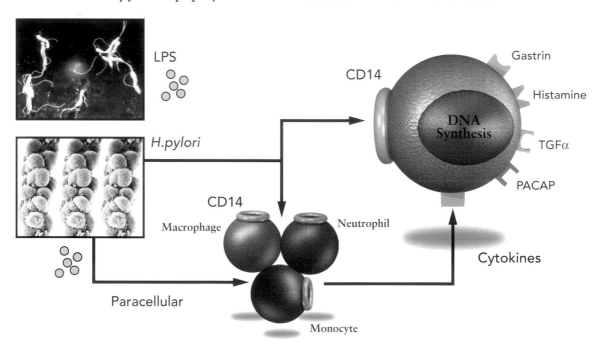

The role of urease and NH₃ in ulcer etiology

Acid activation of urease in the stomach will result in the production of NH_3 which will rapidly convert to NH_4^+. At pH 4.0 for example, with a pK_a of 9.0, there will be a 10^5-fold excess of NH_4^+.

The quantity of NH_3 available to diffuse into the gastric cells with a pH of 4.0 in their environment, given a 10 mM concentration of NH_4Cl, will be small. However, if acid secretion slows or 10 mM NH_4Cl solution is emptied into the duodenum at pH 7.0, there will be a 1,000-fold increase in NH_3 concentration. This would be sufficient to alkalinize the cell and elevate intracellular calcium, perhaps to levels where cytotoxic effects could be observed as shown in the following figure.

H. pylori Urease and Toxicity

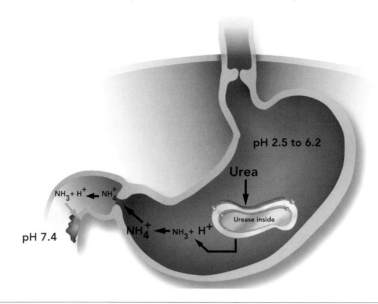

A model showing on the right production of NH₄Cl under acidic conditions due to high internal urease activity, but the pH results in a low concentration of the diffusible NH₃. If this empties into the duodenum with consequent neutralization, free NH₃ rises and with entry into cells and elevation of pH_i and $[Ca^{2+}]_i$ cell damage can arise at a site distal to infection.

pH 2.5 to 6.2

Urea

Urease inside

$NH_3 + H^+ \leftarrow NH_4^+$

$NH_4^+ \leftarrow NH_3 + H^+$

pH 7.4

Mucosa Associated Lymphoid Tissue (MALT) lymphoma

H. pylori vaulted into a position of considerable clinical relevance with the recognition of its critical association with gastroduodenal ulceration. The further observation that the resolution of the genesis of mucosal ulceration might lie with its eradication almost paled in significance when it became evident that the organism was the probable cause of a form of gastric neoplasm. Indeed the link between H. pylori infection and gastric MALT lymphoma is similar to that between the putative small intestinal infection and IPSID (immuno proliferative small intestinal disease). Since the normal stomach possesses no mucosa associated lymphoid tissue the origin of gastric lymphoma is enigmatic. Nevertheless it is apparent that as a sequel of H. pylori infection, MALT, comprised of lymphoid follicles and a lympho-epithelium, accumulates in the gastric mucosa. The organism has been identified in gastric lymphoma and the presence of H. pylori in the stomach is directly associated with MALT lymphoma. Furthermore in areas where there is a high prevalence of H. pylori infection the likelihood of individuals to develop gastric lymphoma is significantly increased. Since the stomach normally possesses no lymphoid tissue in the gastric mucosa, the accumulation of MALT is almost pathognomonic of H. pylori infection. The proposed role of H. pylori presented antigens in driving the lymphoid tissue hyperplasia and its transformation into a neoplasm is consistent with current clinical observations. Thus early antibiotic therapy has been associated with eradication not only of the H. pylori but the lymphomatous disease. Alternatively if the lymphoma has reached a H. pylori independent phase or has transformed from its low-grade status to a high-grade MALT lymphoma, eradication therapy is not effective.

The gastrointestinal tract is the most common site of primary extra nodal lymphoma and gastric lymphoma accounts for the majority of cases. It is of importance to differentiate primary gastric lymphoma from secondary involvement of the stomach by nodal lymphoma, which occurs relatively commonly.

The precise incidence of primary gastric lymphoma is difficult to ascertain given the widely different diagnostic criteria that have been utilized as well as the considerable geographic variation in incidences. Overall there is evidence to support the fact that gastric lymphoma may be increasing in incidence although the incidence of *H. pylori* is decreasing. It is, however, necessary to define primary gastric lymphoma as lymphoma occurring in the stomach with or without the presence of regional lymph nodes with the stomach being the site of the majority of the disease, if not the only site.

Hodgkin's disease rarely occurs in the stomach and the great majority of primary gastric lymphomas are B-cell tumors. Nevertheless, T-cell lymphomas do occur although they are extremely rare. For the most part the histopathological features of low-grade primary gastric lymphoma – MALT (mucosa associated lymphoid tissue) – recapitulate the structure of Peyer's patches rather than lymph nodes. In certain instances low-grade MALT lymphomas may transform to high-grade disease and it is likely that most instances of this entity represent evolution since the tumors are derived from the same B-cell lineage. What is apparent, however, is that gastric MALT lymphomas do not share any of the features common to nodal lymphomas but instead exhibit a marked increase in the frequency of trisomy 3. Similarly the gastric MALT lymphomas differ from their nodal counterparts in that their behavior is usually quite favorable.

The low-grade gastric lymphomas, which have been characterized as MALT, usually occur in individuals over the age of 50 with a peak in the seventh decade. Nevertheless instances of such disease have been described at almost all ages. There appears to be a slight male predominance (1.5:1). More often than not, the symptoms are of a non-specific nature with a central dyspeptic component rather than any specific signs as might occur with a gastric adenocarcinoma. At endoscopy the findings are usually those of a non-specific gastritis with erosions or ulceration, although a mass lesion is occasionally identifiable. It is unusual to be able to detect extra abdominal dissemination, although such events have been recorded. In contrast to the low-grade MALT lymphomas, patients presenting with the high-grade B-cell gastric lymphomas usually do so at a slightly older age (64 vs. 55). In these patients the clinical presentation more commonly represents that of a gastric adenocarcinoma with pain, weight loss, and anemia being the commonest presentations, although rarely perforation may occur as the initial clinical event. At endoscopy an obvious tumor mass is usually evident with ulceration in many instances. For

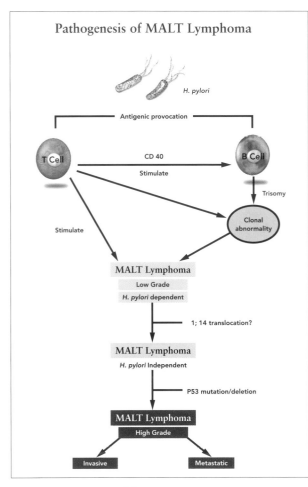

Pathogenesis of MALT Lymphoma

A schematic representation of the pathogenesis of MALT Lymphoma. It has been proposed that *H. pylori* or one of its cellular products functions as a primary antigenic stimulant for the B and T cell lymphocytes resulting in a cascade of immunological events culminating in cell transformation to a neoplastic phenotype.

the most part gastric lymphomas involve the antrum but they may occur at any site in the stomach. The low-grade MALT lymphomas usually are flat infiltrative lesions which are often difficult to diagnose and often require multiple or double level biopsies. The high-grade gastric lymphomas are more commonly large and bulky tumors with considerable infiltration.

The low-grade MALT lymphomas produce a histological appearance closely simulating that of a Peyer's patch. Thus the lymphoma infiltrates around and between reactive follicles in the region corresponding to the marginal zone of a Peyer's patch and spreads diffusely into the surrounding mucosa. Tumor cells are usually small to medium size with moderately abundant cytoplasm with a nuclei that have an irregular outline closely resembling the nuclei of centrocytes. An important histological feature of low-grade MALT lymphomas is the presence of lymphoepithelial lesions formed by the invasion of individual gastric glands by aggregates of tumor cells. At a later stage this is associated with disintegration of the glandular epithelium and eosinophilic degeneration. Occasionally areas of a low-grade lymphoma may be replaced by a high-grade lymphoma suggesting transformation from one form to the other. The presence of confluent clusters or sheets of transformed cells is strongly indicative of transformation to a high-grade lymphoma lesion.

The proposed histological sequence of events initiated by *H. pylori* which has been incriminated in the development of gastric adenocarcinoma.

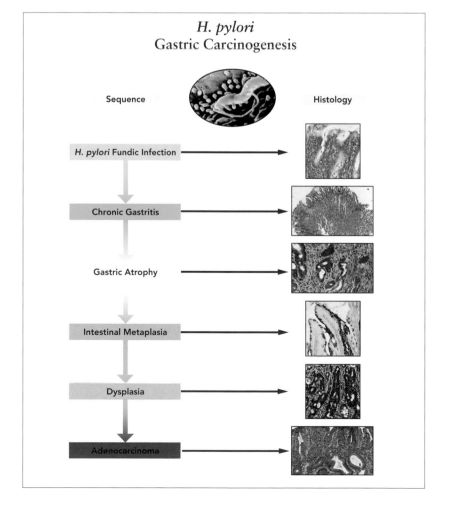

Low-grade MALT lymphomas are seldom disseminated at the time of diagnosis and rarely involve lymph nodes or bone marrow. As a result prolonged survival is common with figures reaching as high 91% at 5 five years and 75% at 10 years if surgical resection is utilized. Nodal low-grade B-cell lymphomas are usually widely disseminated at diagnosis with the majority of patients having bone marrow involvement. Treatment is usually ineffective and most patients perish within 7 to 10 years, often as a result of high-grade transformation. There is controversy as to whether high-grade MALT lymphomas have as favorable a prognosis. On balance it appears that the higher the grade of lymphoma the less favorable is the outcome likely to be.

Low-grade MALT lymphomas commonly involve the local draining lymph nodes, if peripheral spreading occurs it is a late event. This results in a favorable prognosis quite unlike that of the indolent yet progressive disease pattern associated with disease disseminated low-grade B cell lymphomas of lymph nodes. In fact low-grade MALT lymphomas tend to remain localized to their site of origin for prolonged periods, although the reason for this is not clearly defined. It has been proposed that this type of lesion may not even be a malignant lymphoma but represents either a hyperplasia or a "pseudo lymphoma". One suggestion is that the proliferation of the MALT represents the presence of a local antigen presented by *H. pylori* and the process may be a lymphocyte homing phenomenon. Nevertheless, MALT possesses many of the criteria that are used to define a malignant tumor. It is monoclonal, demonstrates the presence of a clonal genetic abnormality, and displays various degrees of invasiveness and dissemination. The low grade of the MALT lymphomas, and especially the gastric lymphoma, suggest some form of immunological control which may be influenced by a local antigen – in this case *H. pylori*. This might well explain the tendencies of such lymphomas to remain localized since lymphoma cells disseminating to peripheral locations would then fail to proliferate in the absence of a specific antigen. Indeed low-grade gastric lymphomas exhibit variable numbers of transformed tumor cells and show plasma cell differentiation, which tends to be maximal beneath surface epithelium. This characteristic would be consistent with a luminal or epithelial antigen causing such effects. Similarly the phenomenon of "follicular colonization" in which lymphoma cells migrating to centers of reactive B cell follicles is also evident and consistent with a manifestation of an antigen effect.

Antibiotics would presumably sterilize the gastric lumen removing the bacterial antigen, which is responsible for driving the proliferation of lymphoma cells. In this context the success noted in treating gastric MALT lymphomas with antibiotics would be consistent with removing the *H. pylori* antigen or product responsible for driving the proliferation of lymphoma cells. Support for this hypothesis reflects not only clinical material but also experimental studies in which cells from individual cases of low-grade gastric lymphoma were stimulated to divide and secrete tumor-specific immunogloblin by specific strains of *H. pylori*. The response of the lymphomatous B cells is mediated via contact with *H. pylori*-specific T cells and considerable practical support has been provided for the organism-driven proliferative theory in studies where patients with MALT gastric lymphoma treated with antibiotics exhibit regression of the lesion as well as eradication of the organism. Nevertheless it is apparent that in more aggressive forms of gastric MALT lymphoma, particularly in those which exhibit more deeply invasive lesions, the lymphoma does not completely regress on eradication therapy. Whether this represents transformation of the neoplastic phenotype into a different mode or failure to completely eradicate the organism is not certain. It has been suggested that the phenotype of gastric lymphomas that have disseminated beyond the stomach and local lymph nodes may have altered, such that their growth would be independent of *H. pylori* stimulated T-cells.

There are still a considerable number of unanswered questions relating to the issue of MALT lymphoma. A number of studies have concluded that in up to 80% of patients with low-grade gastric MALT lymphoma remission may be predicted after cure of *H. pylori* infection using a treatment regime consisting of a proton pump inhibitor, a nitro-imidazole and an antibiotic. It is not yet certain as to whether such high remission numbers are reproducible or whether the histologic and endoscopic remission will remain stable in the long term. In the majority of patients in whom antibiotic and proton pump inhibitor therapy fails, a high-grade lymphoma (autonomous) is often detectable at surgery. In this respect it may be important to use endoscopic ultrasonography to determine the extent of lymphoma. In those lesions, which have invaded the deeper parts of the gastric wall, the likelihood of high-grade lymphoma is higher and the possibility of therapeutic failure should be considered early in the disease course to obviate delay. Overall patients with MALT lymphomas in stage E1 appear curable whereas those in stage E11 do not benefit and may require alternative treatment strategies including surgery.

Difficulties exist with the distinction between induction of remission and cure in patients with low-grade MALT lymphomas. The use of polymerase chain reaction assay to determine the presence of rearranged immunoglobulin heavy changing indicative of B cell lymphoma often remains positive even when clinical appearance of complete remission has been attained. Adequate predictive data from long-term follow-up studies to determine whether the ongoing presence of monoclonal bands in the PCR assay are indicative of a high risk of developing a relapse of the disease are not available.

Diagnosis

Endoscopy cannot be justified merely to diagnose *H. pylori* infection. As a non-invasive test, the urea breath test is extremely useful, particularly in establishing whether active infection exists or if eradication therapy has been successful. The breath test is the only accurate non-endoscopic way to check for successful eradication. While current practice guidelines may recommend the use of confirmatory breath testing for individuals with complicated ulcer disease, the issue of whether confirmatory testing should be performed in uncomplicated cases with continued symptoms is controversial.

Testing to confirm eradication in these patient groups as well as individuals who are asymptomatic after eradication therapy will be driven by cost, accessibility, accuracy and patient demand for diagnostic certainty. The major drawback of the ^{13}C urea breath test is its high cost. It is currently being purposive-

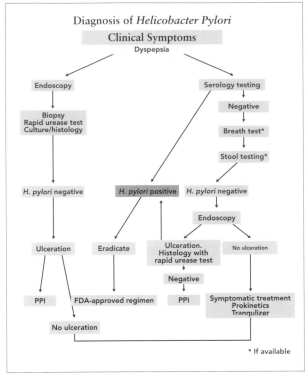

Diagnosis of *Helicobacter Pylori*

Clinical Symptoms
Dyspepsia

Endoscopy

Serology testing

Biopsy
Rapid urease test
Culture/histology

Negative

Breath test*

Stool testing*

H. pylori negative

H. pylori positive

H. pylori negative

Endoscopy

Ulceration

Eradicate

Ulceration.
Histology with
rapid urease test

No ulceration

Negative

PPI

FDA-approved regimen

PPI

Symptomatic treatment
Prokinetics
Tranqulizer

No ulceration

* If available

A flow diagram for the establishment of the diagnosis of *H. pylori*.

ly marketed at a price only slightly below endoscopy, and is significantly more expensive in the USA than elsewhere in the world. However, the newly FDA-approved ^{14}C urea breath test is under $100, thus indicating that market forces may play a critical role in further decreasing the costs of breath tests. Nevertheless, if either breath test is to be used as the initial non-invasive diagnostic test, they must surpass the convenience and accuracy of office-based serological or stool antigen tests which, even if not quite as sensitive or specific as laboratory based serology, are inexpensive, quick and easy to use but only for diagnosis, not for eradication.

Since there is no gold standard for the diagnosis of *H. pylori*, the choice of diagnostic test depends more upon local resources, experience and cost-effectiveness rather than small differences in sensitivity and specificity. Probably serology will be used to establish infection and breath test for efficacy of eradication. However, the accuracy of many of the current serology tests could be improved. False positives lead to needless expense; false negatives to inappropriate security on the part of either patient or physician.

Antibody based tests should be specific and respond rapidly to eradication. Perhaps novel antigens could be used to both improve specificity and analysis of loss of organism. It should be remembered that only a few organisms in a special niche in the stomach could result in false analysis of eradication since these could regrow after some considerable period of time. Hence at least one month should be left in between therapy and eradication testing.

Given that urease activity is largely dependent on acid, breath tests should not be administered immediately following a PPI. In fact, it is probably best to administer the urea in conjunction with citric acid to activate intracellular urease so as to obtain maximal sensitivity of the breath test.

Relevance as a disease entity

In 1994 the NIH consensus statement declared that all patients with peptic ulcers associated with *H. pylori* should have the organism eradicated. In addition, it was stated that more work was needed to evaluate the link between *H. pylori* and non-ulcer dyspepsia before treatment be recommended for these patients. In 1997 the scientific message is basically unchanged, but clinical practice has altered appreciably. Thus, three years ago only die-hard *H. pylori* afficionados would commonly use eradication therapy, even for patients with documented ulcer disease. Currently primary care physicians are comfortable to utilize eradication therapy for a wide variety of indications, while some practitioners choose not to even test for the organism that is to be killed.

It is of interest to reflect on how such a confusing situation has evolved. Of particular concern is whether it will ever be possible to perform the studies necessary to establish cause and effect for non-ulcer dyspepsia? Practicing evidence-based medicine while adopting cost-effective approaches to this potential public health problem, may even be mutually exclusive. For example, some models suggest that the simplest way to manage a patient with ulcer-like dyspepsia, and perhaps even the asymptomatic patient with *H. pylori*, is by *H. pylori*-eradication treatment. Thus, while there is still no hard evidence that *H. pylori* is associated with non-ulcer dyspepsia, it is unlikely that current practice modes will ever allow us to revert to a time where a symptom could be evaluated carefully in the context of the patient's general health. Indeed it is apparent that a new world of marketing and public domain information has led to a situation that *H. pylori* eradication has so permeated the mind of both physicians and public that neither is probably prepared to contemplate living with this potential carcinogen in their stomach.

In retrospect, it seems probable that the 1994 announcement by the International Agency for Research on Cancer of the WHO, that *H. pylori* is a definite carcinogen, may have been somewhat premature. While accepting the epidemiological association between *H. pylori* and gastric cancer, a recent reappraisal of a much wider data base have emphasized the need to keep an open mind on this critical question. Indeed skeptics have raised the philosophical question as to whether it may be possible that not all *H. pylori* are bad. It has been noted that the recent increase in the diagnosis of reflux esophagitis and adenocarcinoma of the lower esophagus and gastric cardia has accompanied the natural decline in *H. pylori* infection in the West over the last 50 years. Thoughtful individuals have questioned whether such observations and phenomena may be related. In general, esophagitis and fundic gastric cancer are not associated with *H. pylori* infection, and in fact, a negative association may exist. Labenz and coworkers have reported that eradicating *H. pylori* from duodenal ulcer patients may even precipitate reflux disease.

H. pylori and NSAIDs are independent risk factors in the etiology of ulcers. This may, however, be an over-simplistic interpretation of studies which have excluded some patients most at risk for NSAID ulcers. In addition, some of these reports have relied on relatively insensitive serological assays, whose performance may be altered by NSAID use, to identify the presence of *H. pylori*. A consequence would be an underestimate of the contribution of *H. pylori* in patients taking NSAIDs who develop ulcers in many studies where serology is the sole criterion for the diagnosis of *H. pylori* infection. It has been reported that in patients anticipating treatment with naproxen, prophylactic *H. pylori* eradication decreased the risk of ulcers, suggesting that the bacterium and NSAIDs may be synergistic.

Epidemiology

The epidemiology of *H. pylori* has been extensively studied and the risk factors for the acquisition of infection determined. It is clear that most infection occurs in childhood and that infection or reinfection is not a clinical problem for most adults, in developed countries at least. How *H. pylori* is transmitted, however, remains unclear and it remains possible that more than one route exists. The evidence for fecal-oral transmission is based mainly on a small group of children in Africa, on contaminated water supplies and by analogy with hepatitis A. Although the organism has been cultured from feces in the developed world, most researchers have only found *H. pylori* in the stool by PCR. Alternative methods of transmission include the oral-oral route, perhaps lurking in dental plaque or by regurgitation of gastric contents, or waterborne. *H. pylori* has been identified by PCR in the water supply occasionally – not only in Peru, but also in Scandinavia. Apart from some early attempts by enthusiastic investigators to fulfil Koch's postulates by drinking *H. pylori*, or occasional episodes of epidemic achlorhydria related to sharing common inadequately sterilized endoscopes or gastric tubes, documented transmission from person to person has been largely elusive. It appears that the routine use of high-level disinfection for endoscopes and reusable biopsy forceps should eliminate iatrogenic transmission of *H. pylori* by physicians.

Perhaps the use of animal models, of which there are many, may clarify the issue of transmission. The earliest animal models required the use of gnotobiotic pigs, but more recently many other animals (cats, ferrets, gerbils, hamsters, rats and mice) have been infected with a variety of *Helicobacter* species – both non-human *Helicobacter* and *H. pylori*. Some of these animals have developed pathology similar to that found in human disease. For example, *H. mustelae* in ferrets produces a multifocal atrophic gastritis. Gastric ulcers can be produced by infection with *H. Heilmanii* (formerly *Gastrospirillum hominis*) in mice, or by *H. pylori* in gnotobiotic pigs. It is of considerable interest that some animals even develop MALT lymphoma and cancer. The outcome of infection in certain animal models has been shown to be dependent not only upon the bacterium inoculated, but also the animal's genotype. Ultimately, animal models may be useful not only for the development of vaccines, but also to determine the natural history of *Helicobacter* infection. They may be of utility in the evaluation of the bacterial and host factors which determine clinical outcome and in the elucidation of the mechanism of the association between *H. pylori* and gastric malignancy.

Treatment

Whom to treat

The identification of the individual who should be treated is probably the most controversial aspect of *H. pylori* at this time. Since most are agreed that a diagnosis of *H. pylori* infection should not be sought unless treatment is to be undertaken, a more pertinent question may be the decision of who should be tested. To date the only proven benefit in eradicating *H. pylori* is for patients with ulcers. Nevertheless there are number of arguments, economic and emotional, not purely scientific, which in practice dictate that many more patients than only those with ulcers should receive treatment. In view of the fact that health policy and management recommendations continue to evolve at a rapid rate, it may never be possible to complete the necessary studies to determine whether *H. pylori* eradication would benefit certain categories of non-ulcer patients. For example, the European Consensus Meeting held in the fall of 1996 at Maastricht suggested considerably extending the 1994 NIH consen-

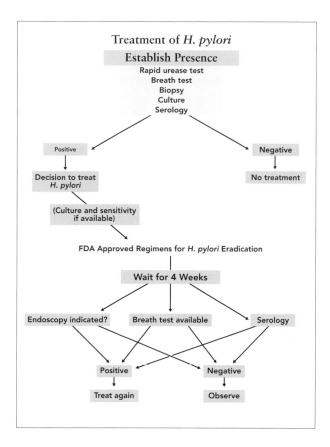

Treatment of *H. pylori*

Establish Presence
Rapid urease test
Breath test
Biopsy
Culture
Serology

Positive → Negative

Decision to treat *H. pylori* → No treatment

(Culture and sensitivity if available)

FDA Approved Regimens for *H. pylori* Eradication

Wait for 4 Weeks

Endoscopy indicated? — Breath test available — Serology

Positive → Negative

Treat again — Observe

A flow diagram outlining the principles of the management of *H. pylori*.

sus indications for treatment. In addition to all ulcer patients, *H. pylori* eradication was recommended, not surprisingly, for early MALT lymphomas (preferably in expert centers, in the context of clinical trials) and also for all patients who had undergone gastrectomy, whether for cancer or ulcers. The argument for treating cancer patients was the persuasive study of a relatively limited number of Japanese patients who had an early gastric cancer resected. In those who thereafter had *H. pylori* eradicated, a reduced chance of a second cancer was noted.

The question of whether treatment can be recommended based on a single report or alternatively whether it is acceptable to delay responding to such information pursuant upon the availability of more extensive information which might take years to assemble, raises both moral and ethical issues. In addition to these indefinite indications for treatment, the European experts also considered other types of patients in whom *H. pylori* eradication therapy might be deemed to be desirable. These included patients with non-ulcer dyspepsia, those with severe (defined macro or microscopically) gastritis, with intestinal metaplasia type II and III, dysplasia and even atrophy (although there exists no definitive evidence that any of these early precancerous lesions will regress). Furthermore, the European consensus concluded that there was probably a need to treat patients who were receiving maintenance proton pump inhibitors (at variance with the recent conclusions by the FDA), patients with a family history of gastric cancer, patients taking or about to take NSAIDs and finally, all patients who desire treatment. It was not discussed which patient, if any, would not choose to eradicate the organism which has been so vilified in the popular press. Indeed the media educated carefully by corporate marketers has virtually empowered patients to determine their therapeutic preferences. Thus complex deliberations in regard to which particular groups of patients ought to have their *Helicobacter* eradicated may be a purely academic exercise, since the desires of patients may be the prime consideration as to whether they are treated. This scenario may however not be the final one, since in the age of managed care, the ultimate and perhaps definitive arguments about who receives therapy may not come from clinicians or patients, but from those who hold the purse strings.

Economics and data analysis

In recent time, an increasing number of analyses have been performed aimed at determining the cost and benefit of a variety of different management strategies for the *H. pylori*-infected patient. Almost all have used modeled best available estimates to a theoretical population, few have closed the loop by reapplying the recommended approach to a real population. All agree that for peptic ulcers associated with *H. pylori*, eradication therapy is not only the most clinically efficacious, but also the most cost-effective long-term treatment. It is however, still unclear what to do with patients with dyspepsia in whom a definitive diagnosis is not available. Should they be screened for *H. pylori* and treated according to the *H. pylori* result (either with or without an endoscopy) or be treated blindly with anti-*H. pylori* medications and/or antisecretory therapy? Alternatively, would it be cost-effective to test and simply eradicate *H. pylori* from all, including the asymptomatic? Even as algorithms are being developed and used (for example suggesting referring to gastroenterologists for endoscopy only those patients who may have a malignancy or who fail conventional treatment), the pressure is on primary care physicians to test and treat all. For example, one recent analysis concluded that the "treat and see" approach will always be less expensive than doing endoscopy in *H. pylori*-positive patients, unless endoscopy costs can be reduced by 90% or more. However, these models are only as good as the data upon which they are based. It is uncertain that someone who has had *H. pylori* eradicated for ulcer disease will never have ulcers or ulcer-like symptoms again. *H. pylori*-negative duodenal ulcers do exist and rather than being a great rarity, they may comprise as much as a quarter of all duodenal ulcers in the USA. Further unknowns complicate the model systems. For example, is it really of no consequence to miss the occasional gastric cancer? How predictable and how expensive to society will be the emergence of non-*Helicobacter* bacterial resistance, secondary to the indiscriminate use of antibiotics?

There are persuasive arguments that the eradication of *H. pylori* should be viewed as a public health measure to prevent future gastric cancer. Again, computer derived evidence suggests that screening for *H. pylori* in the middle aged population and eradicating *H. pylori* from those who test positive, could be relatively cost-effective; certainly no more expensive than other cancer prevention strategies, if eradication reduces the gastric cancer risk by more than 20%. However, it may be unrealistic to expect that eradicating *H. pylori* from middle-aged people will reduce the gastric cancer risk at all – there is no good evidence that gastric pre-neoplasia is reversible. Thus prospective randomized trials of large numbers of patients followed for many years will be necessary to answer this important question. It may be that intervening in children is the only way to prevent the long-term impact of infection.

Finally, it should be noted that we should beware of falling into the trap whereby we blame *H. pylori* for all our ills. The idea of an alien invading and living in our stomachs and causing disease may be popular for those who would like to blame unhappiness and pain on an external agent. In scapegoating this bacterium and closing our minds to other possibilities, we may be deluding both ourselves and our patients. It should be remembered that our previous long-term obsession with acid soured our judgment in the past and we should be cognizant of the potential relevance of pepsin and the possibility of both inherent mucosal defects and other putative infective agents in the genesis of esophago-gastro-duodenal mucosal disease.

Methods of treatment

With the gradual establishment of the role of *H. pylori* in peptic ulcer disease, there were initially trials on a small number of infected individuals with a variety of protocols claiming various degrees of success. At the time of writing this chapter, it has become accepted that the best controlled clinical trials, where intention-to-treat was the analytic criteria, involving an adequate number of patients showed that a 7-day treatment with a combination of a proton pump inhibitor, omeprazole, and two antibiotics, such as amoxicillin and metronidazole and clarithromycin, reached between 85 to 90 eradication efficacy. This triple therapy is given twice-a-day. Trials using other proton pump inhibitors such as lansoprazole or pantoprazole, gave essentially the same results. Another protocol that has received approval is a combination of ranitidine and bismuth subcitrate with two of the above antibiotics. Ulcer disease is then treated with continuation of the secretory inhibitor for the approved length of time, although some studies suggest that eradication on its own is all that is required.

Although earlier approval was granted to a combination of a PPI and a single antibiotic, current thinking is that this regimen is relatively ineffective.

The results of some large studies analyzing a variety of combinations is summarized in the bar graph.

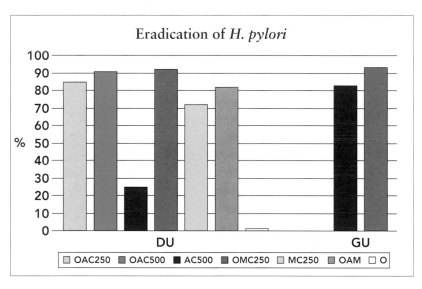

A summary of the results of a series of double-blind multi-center studies using a large number of patients comparing a number of bid regimens, showing the essentiality of triple therapy for good eradication.

In trials so far performed with pantoprazole, equivalent efficacy has been shown.

It can be seen that any two of the three antibiotics in combination with omeprazole reach the 80th percentile eradication. However, only those containing clarithromycin reach the 90th percentile. It is also clear that two antibiotics are ineffective as is omeprazole alone. There is now increasing evidence that resistance to clarithromycin is increasing and some instances of resistance to amoxicillin have been found. Metronidazole resistance is found rather frequently in those populations where treatment with the nitro-imidazoles for other diseases was prevalent.

Newer therapeutic approaches are being sought. In particular, it is felt that if eradication is to be pursued in the general population, only vaccination is a viable option and several vaccine based approaches are being investigated.

Rationale for PPI's in combination therapy

The two antibiotics with which PPI's synergize are amoxicillin and clarithromycin. The former antibiotic inhibits cell wall biosynthesis by inhibiting peptidyl transferase and by binding to other proteins in the cell wall biosynthesis pathways. Cell division is therefore required for the bactericidal action of this class of antibiotic. Clarithromycin binds to the 23S RNA and thereby inhibits protein synthesis. Hence protein synthesis is required for the action of this antibiotic. Metronidazole is reduced to the hydroxylamine derivative which then binds to DNA, hence not requiring cell division or protein synthesis for its efficacy. PPI's do not synergize with this antibiotic. Resistance to metronidazole develops by decrease of the level of reducing enzyme and therefore may be relative or absolute. Resistance to clarithromycin occurs by a base mutation at the binding site on the RNA and is usually absolute.

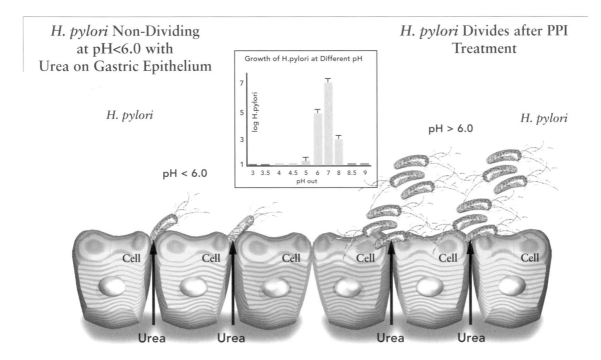

H. pylori Non-Dividing at pH<6.0 with Urea on Gastric Epithelium

H. pylori Divides after PPI Treatment

Growth of H.pylori at Different pH

A model illustrating the rationale for combination with PPI therapy. Insert shows the growth curve of the organism. On the left under normal secretion many organisms are present with their periplasmic pH below 6.0, in spite of the presence of urea and are non-dividing. With PPI treatment, environmental pH is elevated and division occurs, sensitizing the organism to amoxicillin and/or clarithromycin.

Any maneuver which increases the population of *H. pylori* undergoing division will make the bacteria relatively more susceptible to either amoxicillin or clarithromycin or both (since they have biochemically distinct targets). Remembering the survival and growth data previously shown, the organism survives over a much wider pH range than that found for growth. So if antibiotic is given where many of the organisms are non-dividing, poor eradication will be found. If however PPI's are co-administered to decrease the fraction of the population in the non-dividing state, synergism will be observed. Some consider that PPI's increase the gastric bio-availability of these antibiotics but evidence for this is scanty. These considerations are modeled in the illustration.

In the future, alternative therapies will become available, such as monotherapy targeted at a unique gene or unique feature or vaccination may be successful. Both approaches are the focus of active research.

REFERENCES

Andrutis, K.A., Fox, J.G., Schauer, D.B., Marini, R.P., Murphy, J.C., Yan, L., Solnick, J.V. *Inability of an isogenic urease-negative mutant strain of Helicobacter mustelae to colonize the ferret stomach*. Infect. Immun. 63, 3722-3725 (1994).

Atherton, J.C. *The clinical relevance of strain types of Helicobacter pylori*. Gut 40, 701-3 (1997).

Axon, A.T.R. *Eradication of Helicobacter pylori*. Scan. J. Gastroenterol. 31, 47-53 (1996).

Blaser, M.J. *Helicobacter pylori and gastric diseases*. Brit. Med. J. 316, 1507-1510 (1998).

Blaser M.J. *Hypothesis on the pathogenesis and natural history of Helicobacter pylori induced inflammation*. Gastroenterology 102, 720 (1992).

Bode, G., Malfertheiner, P., Lenhardt, G., Nilius, M., Dischuneit, H. *Ultrastructural localization of urease of Helicobacter pylori*. Med Microbiol. Immun. 182, 223-242 (1993).

Chalk, P.A., Roberts, A.D., Blows, W.M. *Metabolism of pyruvate and glucose by intact cells of Helicobacter pylori studied by C-13 NMR spectroscopy*. Microbiol UK 140, 2085-2092 (1994).

Chan, F.K.L., Sung, J.Y., Chung, S.C.S., To, K.F., Yung, M.Y., Leung, V.K.S., Lee, Y.T., Li, E.K.M., Woo, J. *Randomised trial of eradication of Helicobacter pylori before non-steroidal anti-inflammatory drug therapy to prevent peptic ulcers*. Lancet 350, 975-79 (1997).

Chey, W.D., Fey, D., Scheirman, J.M., Nostrant, T., Delvalle, J. *Role of acid suppression in the effects of lansoprazole and ranitidine on the ^{14}C urea breath test*. In: *Developments in Helicobacter research*. Graham, D.Y. and Blazer M.J., ed. 1997, 17-18 (abstract)

Clyne, M., Labigne, A., Drumm, B. *Helicobacter pylori requires an acidic environment to survive in the presence of urea*. Infect. Immun. 63, 1669-1673 (1995).

Current European concepts in the management of Helicobacter pylori infection. The Maastricht Consensus Report. Gut 41, 8-13 (1997).

Dixon, M.F., Genta, R., Yardley, J.H., Correa, P. *Classification and grading of gastritis: the upgraded Sydney system*. Am. J. Surg. Pathology, 20, 1161-1181 (1996).

Dominguez-Munoz, J.E., Leodolter, A., Sauerbruch,T., Malfertheimer, P. *A citric acid solution is an optimal test drink in the ^{13}C urea breath test for diagnosis of Helicobacter pylori infection*. Gut 40, 459-462 (1997).

Dunn, B.E., Cohen, H., Blaser, M.J. *Helicobacter pylori*. Clin. Microbiol. Rev. 10, 720-41 (1997).

Eaton, K.A., Krakowka, S. *Effect of gastric pH on urease-dependent colonization of gnotobiotic piglets by Helicobacter pylori*. Infect. Immun. 62, 3604-3607 (1994).

Eissele, R., Brunner, G., Simon, B., Solcia, E., Arnold, R. *Gastric mucosa during treatment with lansoprazole: Helicobacter pylori is a risk factor for argyrophil cell hyperplasia*. Gastroenterology 112, 707-717 (1997).

European Helicobacter Study Group Current European concepts in the management of Helicobacter pylori infection. The Maastricht Consensus Report. Gut 41, 8-13, 1997

Faraci, W.S., Yang, B.V., O'Rourke, D., Spencer, D.W. *Inhibition of Helicobacter pylori urease by phenyl phosphoramidates: mechanism of action*. Bioorgan. Med. Chem. 3, 605-610 (1995).

Feljou, J.F., Bahame, P., Smith, A.C., Stockbrugger, R.W., Rode, J., Price, A.B. *Pernicious anemia and Campylobacter like organisms; is the antrum resistant to colonisation?* Gut 30, 60-64 (1989).

Fendrick, A.M., Chernew, M.E., Hirth, R.A., Bloom, B.S. *Alternative management strategies for patients with suspected peptic ulcer disease*. Ann. Intern. Med. 123, 260-268 (1995).

Ferrero, R.L., Lee, A. *The importance of urease in acid protection for the gastric colonizing bacteria, Helicobacter pylori and Helicobacter felis*. Microbial Ecology in Health and Disease 4, 121-134 (1996).

Ferrero, R.L., Labigne, A. *Organization and expression of the Helicobacter pylori urease gene cluster in Helicobacter pylori: biology and clinical practice*. Goodwin C.S. and Worley B.W., ed., pp. 171-195 CRC Press, Fla., 1993.

Goodwin, C.S., Carrick, J. *Peptic ulcer disease and Helicobacter pylori infection*. Current Opinion in Gastroenterology 7, 108-1115 (1991).

Graham, D.Y. *Campylobacter pylori and peptic ulcer disease*. Gastroenterology 96, 615-625 (1989).

Graham, D.Y. *Helicobacter: its epidemiology and its role in duodenal ulcer disesase*. J. Gastroenterol. and Hepatol. 6, 105-113 (1991).

Hawtin, P.R., Stacey, A.R., Newell, D.G. *Investigation of the structure and localization of the urease of Helicobacter pylori using monoclonal antibodies*. J. Gen. Microbiol. 136, 1995-2000 (1990).

Kidd, M., Miu, K., Tang, L.H. et al. *H. pylori lipo-polysaccharide stimulates histamine release and DNA synthesis in rat ECL cells*. Gastroenterology 113, 1110-7 (1997).

Koop, H., Stumpf, M., Eissele, R., Lamberts, R., Stockmann, F., Creutzfeldt, W., Arnold, R. *Antral Helicobacter pylori-like organisms in different states of gastric acid secretion*. Digestion 48, 230-236 (1991).

Kuhler, T.C., Fryklund, J., Bergman, N.A., Weilitz, J., Lee, A., Larsson, H. *Structure-activity relationship of omeprazole and analogues as Helicobacter pylori urease inhibitors*. J. Med. Chem. 38, 4906-16 (1995).

Kuipers, E.J., Lundell, L., Klinkenberg-Knol, E.C., Havu, N., Festen, H.P., Liedman, B.,Lamers, C.B., Jansen, J.B., Dalenback, J., Snel, P., Nelis, G.F., Meuwissen, S.G. *Atrophic gastritis and Helicobacter pylori infection in patients with reflux esophagitis treated with omeprazole or fundoplication*. N. Engl. J. Med. 334, 1018-1022 (1996).

Kuipers, E.J., Klinkenberg-Knol, E.C., Vandenbroucke-Grauls, C.M., Appelmelk, B.J., Schenk, B.E., Meuwissen, S.G. *Role of Helicobacter pylori in the pathogenesis of atrophic gastritis*. Scand. J. Gastro., Suppl. 223, 28-34 (1997).

Labenz, J., Tillenburg, B., Peitz, U., Idstrom, J.-P., Verdu, E., Stolte, M., Borsch, G., Blum, A. *Helicobacter pylori augments the pH-increasing effect of omeprazole in patients with duodenal ulcer*. Gastroenterology 110, 725-32 (1996).

Labenz, J., Blum, A., Bayerdorffer, E., Meining, A., Stolte, M., Borsch, G. *Curing Helicobacter pylori infection in patients with duodenal ulcer may provoke reflux esophagitis*. Gastroenterology 112, 1442-7 (1997).

Labigne, A., Cussac, V. , Courcoux, P. *Shuttle cloning and nucleotide sequences of Helicobacter pylori genes responsible for urease activity*. J. Bacteriol. 173, 1920-1931 (1991).

Lee, A., Dixon, M.F., Danon, S.J., Kuipers, E., Megraud, F., Larsson, H., Mellgard, B. *Local acid production and Helicobacter pylori: a unifying hypothesis of gastroduodenal disease*. Europ. J. Gastroenterology and Hepatology 7, 461-465 (1995).

Li, H., Andersson, E.M., Helander, H.F. *Helicobacter pylori infected rats; a study on infection, inflammation, immunology, apoptosis, cell proliferation and gastric ulcer healing*. Gastroenterology 112, A198 (1997).

Lind, T. Bardhan, K.D., Bayerdorffer, E. et al. *Mach 2 Study: optimal Helicobacter pylori therapy needs omeprazole and can be assessed by UBT*. Gastroenterology 112, A200 (1997).

Lind,T., Veldhuyzen van Zanten, S.J.O., Unge, P. et al. *The MACH 1 study: optimal 1 week treatment for H. pylori defined?* Gut, Suppl 1, A4 (1995).

Lind, T., Veldhuyzen van Zanten, S., Unge, P. et al. *Eradication of Helicobacter pulori using one-week triple therapies combining omeprazole with two antimicrobials the MACH I Study.* Helicobacter 1, 138-44 (1996).

Malfertheimer P., Ditschuneit et al. *Helicobacter pylori, gastritis, and peptic ulcer.* Springer Verlag, Berlin, Germany, 1990.

Marshall, B.J., Barett, L.J., Parkesh, C., Mc Callum, R.W., Guerrant, R.L. *Protection of Campylobacter pyloridis but not Campylobacter jejuni against acid susceptibility by urea.* In: B. Kaijser and E. Falson (ed.). *Campylobacter IV.* University of Goteborg, Goteborg, Sweden, 1988, p.402-403.

Marshall, B.J., Barrett, L.J., Prakash, C., McCallum, R.W., Guerrant, R.L. *Urea protects Helicobacter (Campylobacter) pylori from the bactericidal effect of acid.* Gastroenterology 99, 697-702 (1990).

Masubuchi, N., Takahashi, S., Utsunomiya, K., Igarashi, H., Hoshiya, S., Ninomiya, H., Saito,S., Itoh,T., Hirata, I., Arai, T. *Effects of ecabete sodium and benzohydroxamic acid on Helicobacter pylori infection in the cynomologous monkey.* Gastroenterology 106, A2513 (1994).

McGowan, C.C., Cover, TL., Blaser, M.J. *Helicobacter pylori and gastric acid: biological and therapeutic implications.* Gastroenterology 110, 926-38 (1996).

Megraud. *Transmission of Helicobacter pylori: fecal-oral versus oral-oral route.* Aliment. Pharmacol. Ther. 9 (suppl 2), 85-89 (1995).

Mendz, G.L., Hazell, S.L., Burns, B.P. *Glucose utilization and lactate production by Helicobacter pylori.* J. Gen. Microbiol. 139, 3023-3028 (1993).

Mendz, G.L., Hazell, S.L., Vangorkom, L. *Pyruvate metabolism in Helicobacter pylori.* Arch. Microbiol. 162, 187-192 (1994).

Meyer-Rosberg, K., Scott, D.R., Rex, D., Melchers, K., Sachs, G. *The effect of the environmental pH on the proton motive force of Helicobacter pylori.* Gastroenterology 111, 886-900 (1996).

Miederer, S.E., Grubel, P.G. *Profound increase of Helicobacter pylori urease activity in gastric antral mucosa at low pH.* Dig. Dis. Sci. 41, 944-949 (1996).

Misiewicz, J.J., Harris, A.W., Bardhan, K.D. et al. *One week triple therapy for Helicobacter pylori: a multicentre comparative study.* Lansoprazole Helicobacter Study Group. Gut 41, 735-9 (1997).

Mitchell, P. *Chemiosmotic coupling in oxidative and photosynthetic phosphorylation.* Biol. Rev. 41, 445-502 (1966).

Mobley, H.L.T., Island, M.D., Hausinger, R.P. *Molecular biology of microbial ureases.* Microbiol. Rev. 59,451-480 (1995).

Moss, S.F., Calam, J., Agarwal, B., Wang, S., Holt, P.R. *Induction of gastric epithelial apoptosis by Helicobacter pylori.* Gut 38, 498-501 (1996).

Neithercut, W.D., Greig, M.A., Hossack, M., McColl, K.E.L. *Suicidal destruction of Helicobacter pylori: metabolic consequence of intracellular accumulation of ammonia.* J. Clin. Pathol. 44, 380-384 (1991).

Olso, E.R. *Influence of pH on bacterial gene expression.* Molecular Microbiology 8, 5-14 (1993).

Parsonnet, J., Friedman, G.D., Vandersteed, D.P. et al. *H. pylori infection and the risk of gastric cancer.* New. Eng. J. Med. 325, 1131 (1991).

Parsonnet, J., Harris, R.A., Hack, H.M., Owens, D.K. *Modelling cost-effectiveness of Helicobacter pylori screening to prevent gastric cancer: a mandate for clinical trials.* Lancet 348, 150-154 (1996).

Pei, Z.H., Ellison, R.T. 3d., Blaser, M.J. *Identification, purification, and characterization of major antigenic proteins of Campylobacter jejuni.* J. Biol. Chem.266, 16363-16369 (1991).

Peterson, W.L. *Helicobacter pylori and peptic ulcer disease.* New Eng. J. Med. 324, 1043 (1990).

Phadnis, S.H., Parlow, M.H., Levy M., Ilver, D., Caulkins, C.M., Connors, J.B., Dunn, B.E. *Surface localization of Helicobacter pylori urease and a heat shock protein homog requires bacterial autolysis.* Infect. Immun. 64, 905-912 (1995).

Rauws, E.A., Tytgat, G.N. *Cure of duodenal ulcer associated with eradication of Helicobacter pylori.* Eur. J. Gastroenterol. Hepatol. 6, 773-777 (1990).

Report of the Digestive Health Initiative International Update Conference on Helicobacter pylori, February 1997. Presented at Digestive Disease Week, Washington DC, May 1997.

Sachs, G. *Gastritis, Helicobacter pylori and proton pump inhibitors.* Gastroenterology 112, 1033-6 (1997).

Scott, D.R., Weeks, D., Hong, C., Postius, S., Melchers, K., Sachs, G. *The role of internal urease in acid resistance of Helicobacter pylori.* Gastroenterology 114, 58-70 (1998).

Talley, N.J. *A critique of therapeutic trials in Helicobacter pylori-positive functional dyspepsia.* Gastroenterology 106, 1174-83 (1994).

Tomb, J.-F., White, O., Kerlavage, A.R., Clayton, R.A., Sutton, G.G., Fleischmann, R.D. et al. *The complete genome sequence of the gastric pathogen Helicobacter pylori.* Nature 388, 539-47 (1997).

Tsuda, M., Karita, M., Morshed, M.G., Okita, K., Nakazawa, T.A. *A urease-negative mutant of Helicobacter pylori constructed by allelic exchange mutagenesis lacks the ability to colonize the nude mouse stomach.* Infect. Immun. 62, 3586-3589 (1994).

Tytgat, G.N.J. *Endoscopic transmission of Helicobacter pylori.* Aliment. Pharmacol. Ther. 9 (suppl 2), 105-110 (1995).

Tytgat, G.N.J., Lee, A., Graham, D.Y., Dixon, M.F., Rokkas, T. *The role of infectious agents in peptic ulcer disease.* Gastroenterol. Intern. 6, 76 (1993).

Uemura, N., Mukai, T., Okamoto, S., Yamaguchi, S., Mashiba, H., Taniyama, K., Sasaki, N., Haruma, K., Sumii, K., Kajiyama, G. *Effect of Helicobacter pylori eradication on subsequent development of cancer after endoscopic resection of early gastric cancer.* Cancer Epidemiol. Biomakers Prev. 6, 639-642 (1997).

Verdu, E.F., Armstrong, D., Idstrom, J.P., Labenz, J., Stolte, M., Dorta, G., Borsch, G., Blum, A.L. *Effect of curing Helicobacter pylori infection on intragastric pH during treatment with omeprazole.* Gut 37, 743-8 (1995).

Walsh, J.H., Peterson, W.L. *The treatment of Helicobacter pylori infection in the management of peptic ulcer disease.* N. Engl. J. Med. 333, 984-91 (1995).

Warren, J.R., Marshall, B. *Unidentified curved bacilli on gastric epithelium in active chronic gastritis.* Lancet 1, 1273 - 1275 (1983).

Yeomans, N.D., Brimblecombe, R.W., Elder, J., Heatley, R.V., Misiewicz, J.J., Northfield, T.C., Pottage, A. *Effects of acid suppression on microbial flora of upper gut.* Dig. Dis. Sci. 40, 81S-95S (1995).

Yousfi, M.M., El-Zimaity, H.M.T., Cole, R.A., Genta, R.M., Graham D.Y. *Metronidazole, omeprazole and clarithromycin: an effective combination therapy for Helicobacter pylori infection.* Aliment. Pharmacol. Ther. 9, 209-212 (1995).

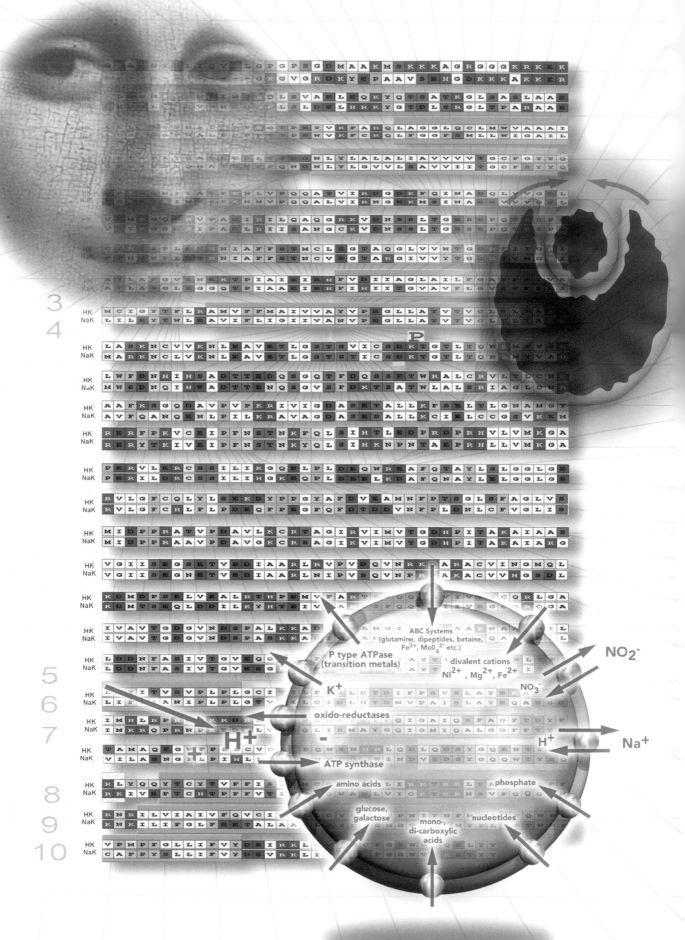

THE 21ST CENTURY

It is foolish to imagine that we, as mere mortals viewing the impending millenium, may be able to predict either the logical or serendipitous progress of science. Imagine the turn of the last century. Certainly, Darwin and Mendel had made their epochal discoveries, but physics was Newtonian, subatomic structure undreamed of, the periodic table of the elements unspecified, biochemistry almost non-existent, and the radio undreamed of. Although the introduction of the telephone, electricity and the automobile had revolutionized man's concept of communication and transport, civilization was still a brittle affair governed by power as much as if not more than understanding. Who might have even dreamed of the contributions of the first 20 years of this century, let alone have predicted the advances of the last 20 years? Whilst contemporary evaluation of progress always suggests that a lesser challenge has been surmounted, the recent advances in the pharmacotherapeutic targeting of disease processes may be measured amongst the most salutary accomplishments of mankind.

In this context there has been a major revolution in the understanding and treatment of gastro-intestinal ulcer disease in the last quarter of this century. The progenitors of this late breaking revolution reflected both individual perspicuity and the evolution and application of sophisticated technology. This reflected advances in the understanding of the physiological regulation of acid secretion and its cellular mechanisms, improved visualization of the lesions using flexible endoscopes, more precise surgical approaches, and the burgeoning arena of sophisticated pharmaceutical research. The discovery of *H. pylori* and its implication in ulcer disease provided a further insight into an expanding biological world of contemporary clinical relevance, whereby bacteria and acid were recognized to have synergistic roles in the pathogenesis of mucosal disease. And this bears witness to only a paucity of the progress that has been made...

We are still arguing about the personality of *H. pylori*. Is it always a pathogen? Is it merely a commensal on occasion, hindering rather helping to initiate disease? The early part of the next century should provide an answer to this conundrum. Whether it will resolve some of our other dilemmas is not as certain. Thus, while treatment of acid related disease has been particularly successful, the treatment of gastric or esophageal malignancies has failed to progress with similar accomplishment. A causative factor in this tardiness has been the relative lack of success in the elucidation of the basic biological processes governing cell transformation. Robotic surgery coupled with imaging technology may amplify the level of precision associated with excision and facilitate levels of curative extirpation impossible at this time. Nevertheless, the cell as a target for anti neoplastic therapy is likely to be more viable from the therapeutic point of view than organ ablation, irrespective of the technology used to accomplish this process.

We await the complete human genome, with its more than 100,000 genes. From this we will learn about, perhaps more rapidly than we can understand, the changes in gene expression in different cell types that orchestrate growth and differentiation. Such information may enable us to diagnose the presence of, or to predict one or more of life's many ills. Such information will almost certainly provide a crowd, if not a host of novel therapeutic targets. At this time, however, the number and variety of oncogenes that have been described, the various cell growth and multiplication cascades still confuse and obfuscate as much as they illuminate. But it is predictable and assured that with genomics, proteomics and their offshoots, better and more detailed descriptions of tumor generation will emerge. From such knowledge one can be assured that more rational and targeted therapy of malignancies will evolve.

Eternal youth, dying old while young, eternal life? Dare we anticipate these? Whose names, whose pictures will illustrate the historical part of this book a hundread years from now? In the immortal words of Pontius Pilate: *Quod scripsi, scripsi!*